AF623806

INTERNATIONAL MARKETING

B. S. RATHOR
M.B.A. (Bradley, U.S.A.), Ph.D. (Punjab)
Reader,
Dept. of Commerce & Business Management,
Punjab University,
Chandigarh.

B. M. JANI
M.A., Ph.D.,
Reader,
Saurashtra University,
Rajkot.

J. S. RATHOR
M.A., M.Com.,
Junior Research Fellow (UGC)

Himalaya Publishing House

MUMBAI • NEW DELHI • NAGPUR • BENGALURU • HYDERABAD • CHENNAI • PUNE
LUCKNOW • AHMEDABAD • ERNAKULAM • BHUBANESWAR • INDORE • KOLKATA

© No part of this book shall be reproduced, reprinted or translated for any purpose whatsoever without prior permission of the publisher in writing.

First Edition : 1994
Reprint : 1996
Third Revised Edition : 1997
Fourth Revised & Enlarged Edition : 2001
Reprint : 2003
Reprint : 2005
Reprint : 2006
Reprint : 2007
Reprint : 2009
Reprint : 2010
Reprint : 2011

Published by : Mrs. Meena Pandey
for **HIMALAYA PUBLISHING HOUSE PVT. LTD.,**
"Ramdoot", Dr. Bhalerao Marg, Girgaon, **Mumbai - 400 004.**
Phones: 2386 01 70/2386 38 63, Fax: 022-2387 71 78
Email: himpub@vsnl.com
Website: www.himpub.com

Branch Offices:

New Delhi : "Pooja Apartments", 4-B, Murari Lal Street, Ansari Road, Darya Ganj, **New Delhi - 110 002.** Phone: 23270392, 23278631 Fax: 011-23256286

Nagpur : Kundanlal Chandak Industrial Estate, Ghat Road, **Nagpur - 440 018.** Phone: 2738731, 3296733 Telefax : 0712-2721215

Bengaluru : No. 16/1 (Old 12/1), 1st Floor, Next to Hotel Highlands, Madhava Nagar, Race Course Road, **Bengaluru - 560 001.** Phone : 22281541, 22385461, Telefax: 080-22286611

Hyderabad : No. 3-4-184, Lingampally, Besides Raghavendra Swamy Matham, Kachiguda, **Hyderabad - 500 027.** Phone: 040-27560041, 27550139, Mobile:- 09848130433 Telefax: 040-27560041

Chennai : No. 85/50, Bazullah Road, T. Nagar, **Chennai - 600 017.** Phone: 044-28344020, 32463737, 42124860

Pune : No. 527, "Laksha" Apartment, First Floor, Mehunpura, Shaniwarpeth, (Near Prabhat Theatre), **Pune - 411 030.** Phone: 020-24496323/24496333/32326733

Lucknow : Jai Baba Bhawan, Near Manas Complex, Church Road, Aliganj, **Lucknow - 226 024.** Phone: 0522-2339329, 9305302158, 9415349385

Ahmedabad : No. 114, "SHAIL", 1st Floor, Opp. Madhu Sudan House, C.G.Road, Navrang Pura, **Ahmedabad – 380 009.** Phone: 079-26560126, Mobiles: 09327324149, 09314679413

Ernakulam : No. 39/104 A, Lakshmi Apartment, Karikkamuri Cross Rd., Ernakulam, **Cochin – 682011**, Kerala. Phone: 0484-2378012, 2378016, Mob.: 09344199799

Bhubaneswar : 5 Station Square, **Bhubaneswar (Orissa) - 751 001.** Mobile: 9861046007, E-mail:- orissa@himpub.com

Indore : Kesardeep Avenue Extension, 73, Narayan Bagh.Flat No. 302, IIIrd Floor, Near Humpty Dumpty School, Narayan Bagh, **Indore (M.P.) 452 007** Mobile: 09301386468

Kolkata : 108/4, Beliaghata, Main Road, Near ID Hospital, Opp. SBI Bank **Kolkata - 700 010.** Mobile: 09910440956, E-mail:- nkmitra@himpub.com

Printed by : A to Z Printers, New Delhi

PREFACE

International Marketing presents a lively picture in the field of International Marketing — a dynamic, competitive, and creative activity that is becoming a part of each Indian businessman's life. With the cry of globalisation, World Trade Organisation has been set-up since January 1, 1995. The world is getting smaller and every country will have the access to businessmen from all over the world. Competition would be keener and only the fittest would survive, particularly privatisation which is taking place all around the world.

This revised edition (2000) contains major revision in chapters on operational part of International Marketing and trade regimes. Export-Import policy for IX five-year plan, W.T.O., FEMA, Euro currency, Multinational joint ventures and currency crisis of Asian countries to boost foreign trade are included in the new edition of this book. Latest data are also added in statistical presentation of International Marketing. Topic like e-commerce is also added as internet-marketing has tried to capture markets of emerging economies as well as of the developed nations. For practical knowledge of international marketing a new chapter of case studies is added to know commodity, currency or country specific issues involved for better marketing practices.

This is a book about International Marketing in the simplest and most direct form. Our goal was to write a book that explains the academic subject of International Marketing in a way that is readable, practical and timely. We want students to appreciate how valuable International Marketing activities are to organisational success.

We hope the readers would find the writing style in International Marketing carefully blends International Marketing concepts and practical examples to help students grasp the essence of International Marketing. The book tries to put many of the different concepts, which are scattered throughout the literature, into one concise framework. In a sense, it constitutes a tool kit for the student of International Marketing without which he might find it difficult to comprehend much of the literature in the area.

In conclusion we wish to thank all those who helped us in the preparation of this book. It is difficult to mention all of them by names, for those whose help we sought were many.

Chandigarh,
January, 2001

— AUTHORS

CONTENTS

SECTION - I

1.	The Nature and Scope of International Marketing	1 - 12
2.	Features of International Marketing	13 - 24
3.	Need for International Trade	25 - 35
4.	Imports and Exports of India	36 - 86
5.	Past-Liberalisation Export-Import Policy	87 - 119
6.	Government Regulations — Exchange Control, FERA 1973, Customs Law, FEMA (1998)	120 - 196
7.	Agencies Helping International Marketing and Measures Taken for Export Promotion	197 - 219
8.	Marine Insurance	220 - 253
9.	Clearing and Forwarding of Cargo	254 - 283

SECTION - II

10.	Trade Practices: A Base for International Marketing	284 - 287
11.	International Trade Agreements and Agencies for Promoting International Co-operation	288 - 307
12.	Trade Blocks	308 - 320
13.	Overseas Marketing Communication	321 - 349
14.	International Marketing in Service Sector Industry (E-marketing)	350 - 361
15.	Methods of Payment for Settlement	362 - 387
16.	South-East Asian Financial Crisis and Marketing	388 - 398
17.	International Marketing Research	399 - 430
18.	Product Development for Overseas Market	431 - 453
19.	Multinationals Marketing and Joint Ventures	454 - 498
20.	Case Studies on International Marketing	499 - 524
21.	Documents Used in Shipment of Goods	525 - 572
	Appendices	
1.	Select Bibliography	573 - 579
2.	Review Questions	580 - 588

SECTION - I

1

THE NATURE AND SCOPE OF INTERNATIONAL MARKETING

The world is passing through a transition period in the order of its economy that promises by far to be the most crucial in its entire history. As a result of the new conditions with which we are confronted and the ever broader front upon which the lines of economic struggle are deployed, we are rapidly becoming world-minded whether willingly or not. The lackadaisical and uninformed days and daze, under which trade was conducted in a world of static repose, no longer exists.

The world trader finds that the more clearly and completely he is able to analyse and interpret world conditions of economic, political, and social import, the more successful he is in developing the world market along profitably enduring lines. Today, more than ever before in the world's history, intelligent analysis of world trends as reflected by current events is indispensable to the successful conduct of all enterprise. No one engaged in any form of commercial activity today, whether he is concerned with selling in markets outside of the domestic field or not, can afford to be other than thoroughly informed on the affairs of the world and their influence on its economy in general, and on our own domestic economy in particular. This is a realistic assessment of the situation facing many marketers in India today. Many Indian marketers have not made much progress in international marketing. One of the reasons for this lack of progress is a failure on the part of many to adopt an international perspective. For many Indian companies, the size and growth of Indian market have been such that a domestic orientation has been sufficient. Many consumers are aware of the kind of impact international trade has on their daily lives.

You may drive a Toyota, Renault, or Mercedes automobile. You may fill your tank at an Indian Oil service station with petrol refined from crude oil from Saudi Arabia. Each of these products comes from a non-Indian company and is made available in India as a result of international marketing. Today, we live in a global village. It is difficult to speak of matters that do not influence or are not themselves influenced by other areas of the world. Jet age transportation, satellite television, computers, and other electronic technologies are reshaping and restructuring the patterns of business. The world is getting smaller. Interaction between the people and governments of various nations is increasing rapidly. Multinational companies based in Japan, the United States, and other developed nations feel completely at ease offering their products in foreign markets. An organisation that sells its products beyond its home nation's boundaries is a *multinational marketer* engaged in *international marketing.*

Multinational or International Marketing involves the adoption of a marketing strategy that emphasises a geographic market segmentation that distinguishes between domestic and foreign markets. Not all Indian based firms choose to market their products outside India. Sher-e-Punjab Restaurant may limit its marketing to Bombay. The organisation's resources or market demand justifies this strategy. However, many firms find that it is advantageous to spend considerable time and effort marketing beyond their national boundaries. Indeed, international markets may promise higher market potential than domestic markets as shown by the following population estimates for the year 2000: USA 300 million; Mexico, 126 million; Brazil, 205 million; Indonesia, 223 million; Pakistan, 138 million; Nigeria, 154 million; and Bangladesh, 146 million. For Indian producers of grain and livestock, these statistics reflect both a tremendous market potential, and a challenge for feeding the world. Population cannot be considered in and of itself. The population's ability and willingness to purchase are additional considerations. Procter & Gamble's Pampers disposable diapers, which has a 6 per cent share of the disposable diaper market in Italy, could not be expected to do as well in Bangladesh, where per capita income is very low.

The same fundamental, marketing concepts that apply in domestic marketing apply in international marketing. Target markets must be determined; marketing mix strategies must be planned and executed to appeal to these target markets; uncontrollable and environmental factors must be analysed.

Although the basic marketing process is the same on a conceptual level, there are several strategic and tactical differences resulting from differences in cultural, economic, political, or legal factors. Language barriers are the most obvious. Effective marketing in South America, for example, requires a knowledge of Spanish and Portuguese as well as English and French. In addition, different cultural values, political instability, and many other problems compound the complexity of the marketing task.

Consider some of these environmental complexities. If we compare India to Western Europe, we can easily see many major differences. Europe consists of many different countries with many different languages, cultures, currencies, and laws. India, by comparison appears to consist of a rather large, fairly homogeneous market. Although the cultural values that affect business may vary slightly within each state, the differences are minor.

Although countries in Europe are quite similar in size to states in India, there are far more barriers between countries. Free trade exists among the states and they share a common set of laws, language, and cultural values. This certainly simplifies matters. Europe and parts of the rest of the world are moving increasingly in this direction.

Multi-disciplinary Approach

International Marketing touches academic branches like, international trade, international economics, foreign exchange management and linking of marketing process to all these branches. Even global trade management also involve trade block wise organisation of marketing. Apart from individual expensive, international marketing is linked with trade organised by UNCTAD, W.T.O. type global level organisations. International Marketing of and marketing for developed and developing nation trade practices and policies are involved. The subject matter of international marketing is concerned with marketing organised by private corporate sector, public sector projects, co-operative organisation to participate in global trade. Apart from trade theories, marketing theories are clubbed with international marketing process. As such organisation-wise objectives of international marketing are differing but ultimate goal is to boost marketing of a product of country in an era of global competition to attract global clients through marketing practices. Thus, subject international marketing is concerned with branches of management like managerial economics, production/distribution management, information technology science, statistical techniques to measure marketed, marketable products in order to expand global level trade.

The Importance of International Marketing

Many Indian companies are heavily involved in international marketing. The Indian government encourages Indian companies to enlarge their international marketing efforts. Yet other measures indicate that our degree of commitment to international marketing is relatively low. India's share in the global trade is 85% only. American exports amount to slightly less than 7 per cent of our gross natural product (GNP) compared to trading nations such as Japan (13 per cent), West Germany (27 per cent), the United Kingdom (20.5 per cent), and Canada (29 per cent).

The explanation for this small percentage is, in part, the result of the large and developed nature of the domestic market in India itself. No other country has such an extensive, well-developed domestic marketplace. Therefore, other nations have had to become involved in international marketing activities. For many, it is an absolute necessity.

There is also a major impact on the domestic economy of any nation as the volume of multinational marketing activity increases. Foreign products are imported into that country to fill needs not being satisfied by domestic manufacturers or producers. Because India cannot supply all of its oil-based needs, it must import oil from other nations. In this sense, imported products are necessary to a way of life. World trade does help some countries meet certain needs. With continued growth, world trade can be expected to raise the standard of living in many parts of the world.

In addition, world trade can stimulate and help improve domestic competition. Consumers have complained that Indian automotive manufacturers are unconcerned about quality and inattentive to market needs. Partly because Japanese and European cars have gained such a large share of the world auto market, Indian producers have recently begun to remedy these deficiencies. Such improvements in domestic competition spur improvements in living standards as well as general economic well-being.

By encouraging domestic companies to increase their involvement in world trade, a nation can develop its own economy. Capital investments in domestic production and the inflow of revenues from the sale of products to other nations certainly can trigger domestic economic growth.

For some countries, however, the costs of involvement in world trade are high. As trade between developed and less-developed nations occurs, cultural differences emerge. A "culture shock" may occur as the ideas, products, and lifestyles of one culture begin to influence those of the other culture. Grumblings have been heard in more traditional societies about the decadent influences of Western products and lifestyles. Certainly, the possibility for unwanted cultural change exists when world trade increases.

Another cost is more directly measurable. Some nations experience trade deficits when the monies for imported goods and government payments made outside the country exceed revenues received for goods exported by that nation. When payments going out exceed the monies coming in, there are difficulties. Such a deficit in the balance of payments of any country often leads to domestic inflation as the government manipulates its money supply, domestic spending, and taxes to help solve the deficit problem. India is one nation whose balance of payments annually shows a deficit. Clearly, international marketing is important to many nations for many reasons.

Definitions

Marketing is the process by which the demand structure for products and services is anticipated or enlarged and satisfied. This process involves analysing whether a marketing opportunity exists for the firm, developing suitable products and services to meet this opportunity, securing distribution of the product, designing promotional strategy to persuade potential consumers of the desirability of the offering, and transferring control over the use of the product from vendor to user so that the user may enjoy the benefits.

International Marketing

International or *multinational marketing* refers to the marketing of products and services in more than one nation. It may consist of exporting goods from one country to another, or it may refer to a firm that both produces and markets in more than one country.

The terms international and multinational apply to situations in which companies have a predominantly domestic focus as well as to those in which firms have substantial investments in so many countries that it is difficult to determine the home country of each firm except by reference to the location of the headquarters office. Most international marketers represent firms which reside somewhere between these extremes.

International Trade

International or world trade refers to the movement of goods across national borders and relates exclusively to exporting and importing. Students of international trade analyse exports and import and conditions under which such transfers take place. The academic study of international trade is concerned with trade flows, commercial policies, resource allocations and adjustments, capital movements, balance of payments analyses, and international monetary arrangements.[1]

---

1. See Franklin Root, *International Trade and Investment* (4th ed., Cincinnati: South Western Publishing Company, 1978) or Charles P. Kindleberger and Peter H. Lindert, *International Economics* (6th ed., Homewood, Ill: Richard D. Irwin, Inc., 1978).

Comparative Marketing

The comparative approach to the study of international marketing, or comparative marketing, focuses on the similarities and differences existing among the marketing systems of various countries. It seeks to identify, classify, and interpret the similarities and differences among the systems used to anticipate demand and market products.[2] Analysis may compare national or sectoral systems either at a particular point in time or over a given period of time. Comparative analysis may be used by management to evaluate the effectiveness of its marketing in several countries. By noting the degree of similarity among countries, executives can determine the relative market potentials and establish more effective controls over the marketing effort. Comparative analysis can be used to estimate the acceptance of the product concept in a developing nation by reference to conditions associated with its acceptance by other nations. Grouping countries on a basis other than physical proximity may lead to more appropriate standards for comparison of marketing strategy and efficiency than the comparison of operations in neighbouring countries. For example, comparative analysis may indicate more similarity in marketing between Australia and Canada than between Australia and Singapore. Management may find that Canadian standards of performance provide a better base for judging marketing efficiency in Australia than Singapore and Indonesia.

Marketing Implications of the Nation-State

The most distinguishable feature between international and interregional marketing is the existence of the national state. Every export marketer must be cognizant of the nation-state, for its laws vitally affect marketing opportunities and operations. Each nation is sovereign with respect to its own internal policies and the manner in which it will deal with other sovereignties. It can impose taxes and regulations on imported merchandise, bank deposits, investments, or any other activities that citizens of other nations seek to perform within its jurisdiction. It may even refuse to give a company or individual the privilege of doing business. No marketer can ignore the state's sovereign rights, nor can it be assumed that the rights and privileges obtained in the homeland are available overseas. Even large firms or the firms of powerful nations cannot act with impunity, although they may attempt to influence policy.

The sovereign nation not only regulates trade within its borders but also facilitates it by trade promotion. A country can also prohibit its firms from trading with specific nations or prohibit the sale of certain strategic

2. J. Boddewyn (ed.), "The Comparative Approach", *Comparative Management and Marketing* (Glenview, Ill: Scott, Foresman and Co., 1969).

goods to specific countries. Furthermore, a citizen or firm can legally deal with citizens or firms of other nations only to the extent permitted by the respective countries. For many years, India did not permit trade with East Pakistan (now Bangladesh). As events since 1971 show, however, such restrictions can be readily changed. An Indian citizen can legally travel abroad only if the Indian government issues a passport; but even with a passport, denial of a visa by a foreign host country precludes legal entry into that country, and the inability to secure a work permit from a host country may not allow the transaction of business by personal contact. Let's look at some other ways in which the existence of the nation-state impacts on marketing activities.

Variations in Laws and Policies

The laws and policies relating to the markets of the world are determined by sovereign governments, and the rights that any corporation or person possesses depend upon a country's laws and the agreements that it has made with other nations. The various treaties of friendship and commerce negotiated between India and a number of foreign nations set out the basic treatments that each will afford to firms of other nations in the conduct of business affairs.

Monetary Systems

Sovereignty lays the foundation for several other factors that add complexity to export marketing. One of these is the right of a nation to establish its own monetary system. Nearly every nation has its own monetary system, thereby creating problems in pricing, fund allocation, profit remission, etc. When international trade occurs, it is often necessary to deal in two or more currencies in completing the transaction. The trading operation that involves the purchase and sale of the currency of one state with the currency of another is called foreign exchange. For example, the number of U.S. dollars that will be exchanged for one Indian rupee is expressed by a foreign exchange rate such as $1 = Rs. 45.

Economic Policies

Today many governments are committed to policies of full employment and improved standards of living for their people. In such situations, more than cold, immediate economic facts may be involved in guiding their commercial and investment policy. Emotion and pride spawn industries not justified by the country's resources or by the local and external markets available under the proposed cost structure (*e.g.,* steel plants). The desire to build a cadre of experienced administrators and to exercise control over the industrial base within its borders leads states to establish work laws requiring the use of nationals in executive positions or laws which restrict the investment of foreigners to that of minority ownership. Nations also vary in their reliance on economic planning and the degree of government control exercised over individual business units.

Economic policies include, foreign exchange reserves, stability in exchange rate, timely external payment by following code of conduct given by global level agencies like UNCTAD, EEC, EMU, WTO. It is equally necessary to know periodic changes in exim policy, industrial policy, tariff policy for better international marketing practices in an era of globalisation and competition. Economic upheaval even like South-East Asian crisis or Dunkel proposals or WTO can reshape global marketing for developing country like India.

National Security Policies

In the case of the more advanced nations, the need to survive in the face of external threats forces them to adopt a national security policy. While often necessary and appropriate, national security also is a banner under which many otherwise unjustified trade restrictions are imposed. Such restrictive policies are used not only by nations desiring a closed trade policy but also by nations formally committed to the development of freer world trade. The contemporary scene demands that political, as well as economic, factors be closely assessed in order to determine the real status of the marketing environment.

Language and Customs

Export marketing is generally identified with people whose language and customs are different. One of the requirements of export to recognize these differences and adapt to them. Communication is essential to the marketing process and language differences pose a potential barrier. Frequently, more than one language is in use within a country. Thus, the marketer is faced with a difficult choice to use the official language. The choice may depend on with whom the firm is communicating. Governmental correspondence may be in the official language, but workers and the majority of consumers may respond better to communication in a local language.

Language, however, is only one aspect of culture affecting the marketing process. Other cultural variables that effect the marketing process include religion, values and attitudes, family, social organisation, and technology. To ignore cultural variables that affect the marketing process include religion, values and attitudes, family, social organisation, and technology. To ignore cultural differences can be disastrous in a world characterised by strong strains of nationalism.

Nationalism and Business Policy

Somewhat less obvious is the impact the state has on the outlook of its business people in their relationships with nationals of other countries. Also important, but not readily apparent, is the manner in which nationalism affects business decisions regarding personnel, management practices, business systems, product lines, and executive development. Business people may be reluctant to conform to the unfamiliar codes of ethics or business practices that they find abroad, even when it is in their best interests to do so. In order to maintain control, it is common to resist the delegation of authority to foreign employees. However, in today's environment, foreign employees are increasingly being appointed to executive positions.

Evolution of the Multinational Firm

The varying orientation of firms towards foreign peoples, ideas, and resources has led to the development of a classification system whereby firms may be designated as ethnocentric (home country oriented), polycentric (host-country oriented), or geocentric (world oriented). This classification system is useful in analysing the basic strategy, operations, and evolution of multinational firm. The inter-relationship of the firm's underlying attitudes towards foreigners and its marketing policy is evident, as shown by the following quote.[3]

> [The ethocentric approach] is concerned with the exploitation of a domestic production base and marketing focus. It is essentially an incremental approach to foreign markets, an attempt to gain marginal business often on an intermittent basis, through the exportation of standard products.
>
> [Polycentricity] emphasizes differences and similarities between markets, resulting from variations in such factors as income level, socio-cultural systems, and legal framework... More often than not, the view is taken that each market is indeed unique; that few, if any, outsiders can truly understand local conditions; and that local marketing managers should largely be left alone.
>
> [Geocentricity] adds the dimensions of coordination and control to a corporation's global marketing effort. In effect, a multinational (geocentric) marketing manager says, "yes, there are differences, but we can understand and manage them." Marketing programmes are

---

3. Howard Perlmutter "The Tortuous Evolution of the Multinational Corporation," *Columbia Journal of World Business* (Jan.-Feb., 1969).

adapted to meet specific marketing needs within the context of an overall corporate strategy.

A firm's early efforts in the international market may bear strong strains of ethnocentricity and are usually characterised by a dominance of home-country personnel, ideas, and strategy. An export policy based on existing products is likely to dominate the marketing approach to foreign markets. Later, if the firm establishes overseas branches or production facilities, a polycentric approach emerges wherein local managers are given a high degree of autonomy. The home-country management is impressed by the uniqueness of the individual markets and therefore does not believe it can effectively control the foreign operation except through financial devices and general policy. Of all the business functions, marketing is especially likely to be decentralized because of the difficulty of interpreting the local market and adapting to the local marketing system and institutions; therefore, the local manager is assumed to be best qualified to determine the appropriate marketing strategy in an area.

At some point, however, it becomes apparent that the polycentric system does not allow the firm to maximise the synergistic benefits of the total company's resources; therefore, management seeks ways in which the various sub-units can be more effectively meshed. The geocentric view provides the necessary worldwide orientation, and management seeks to apply a total system approach. The intent is to find the best solution, regardless of the location and nationality of the units and people. Marketing is also integrated into the overall policy. The geocentric approach is not frequently associated with the larger multinational enterprises and with their more sophisticated control mechanisms.

The *principle of comparative advantage* is the basis of export marketing. Each nation specialises in the production of goods in which it is relatively more efficient, exporting them, and importing in turn those products in which it is the least efficient.

Comparative advantage changes over a period of time. India was a groundnut exporting country till a few years ago. Now it is an importing country. Shifts in markets also continue in developing poor nations. Middle eastern countries are now markets for almost every item because of rising incomes and standard of living in those places.

Nature of International Marketing

International marketing management is generally faced with the following four decisions:

(i) firstly, whether to engage in international marketing activities at all,

(ii) secondly, if a company decides that it wants to enter in the international marketing, then a specific decision has to be made concerning what specific individual markets abroad are to be served,

(iii) thirdly, decision has to be taken on the mode of entry, *i.e.,* whether through direct or indirect exporting, licensing, joint-ventures or direct investment.

(iv) finally, the company must decide on the marketing programme. *i.e.,* must determine how it is going to serve these markets through its marketing mix.

Scope of International Marketing

International marketing involves the managements of marketing not only to but also to some extent in foreign countries. To a great extent repeat sales in international marketing are dependent upon how best the marketing is managed in foreign countries. Thus, other related areas of international marketing include:

(a) *Exporting* — Selling to foreign markets.

(b) *Importing* — Buying from abroad.

(c) *Re-exporting:* Importing semi-finished goods and exporting final goods. In short re-engineering for commodities for export.

(d) Management of International Operations:

(i) Operating marketing and sales facilities abroad.

(ii) Establishing production or assembly facilities in foreign countries.

(iii) Organisation and formation of trade block and settlement of external payment.

(iv) Creating licensing and joint venture arrangements.

(v) Offering management contract (consultancy) and undertaking turnkey projects abroad.

(vi) Foreign Exchange Arrangement and Management.

(vii) Understanding country-wise and commodity-wise tones of marketing - by case to case.

(viii) Monitoring operation of marketing practices of multinationals and other agencies. development of e-marketing.

(ix) Promotional and development role of agencies engaged in marketing practices.

(x) National global policies for international marketing.

Thus, the scope of international marketing is not static but fully dynamic, it depends upon global level changes, national level changes, policy level changes and organisational level changes. International marketing dynamism differs from country to country trade block to block and company to company. Ultimate goal of international marketing is to increase percentage share of individual country or company in global trade and to reach goods and services to the ultimate consumers.

2

FEATURES OF INTERNATIONAL MARKETING

International marketing drive is not confined to India. Every country in the world is trying to get its business firms to internationalise, or at least to start exporting. West Germany, the United Kingdom, and the Benelux and Scandinavian countries are now subsidising marketing programmes in their firms. Denmark pays more than half the salary of marketing consultants to help small and medium size companies get into international trade. Many countries go further and subsidise their companies by granting preferential land and energy costs, and they even supply outright cash so that they can charge lower prices than their competitors.

Nowadays developed countries are establishing their plants in developing countries largely due to low labour cost and to save their home countries from pollution. International marketing process has become complex in its characteristics. Local production may not be possible for local people for their use but companies are trying to hunt overseas market where they seek comparative advantage.

MAJOR PROBLEMS AND DIFFICULTIES WHEN A FIRM WANTS TO GO FOR INTERNATIONAL MARKETING

1. *Huge foreign indebtedness.* Many countries of the world that would otherwise be attractive markets have accumulated such high foreign indebtedness that they cannot even pay the interest

on their foreign debt. Among these countries are Mexico, Brazil, Poland and Romania. India's present balance of payment position was real bad, though now it is looking up.

2. *Unstable governments.* High indebtedness, high inflation, and high unemployment in countries have resulted in highly unstable governments that expose foreign firms to the risks of expropriation, nationalisation, limits to profit repatriation, and so on.
3. *Exchange instability.* High indebtedness and political instability force a country's currency to depreciate, or at least add a lot of volatility to the currency's value. The result is that foreign investors hesitate to hold much of the foreign currency, and this limits trade.
4. *Foreign government entry requirements.* Governments are placing more regulations on foreign firms, such as requiring joint ownership with the majority share going to the domestic partner, a high level of nationals hired for management; technological transfer of trade secrets; and limits on profit repatriation.
5. *Tariffs and other trade barriers.* Governments often impose unreasonably high tariffs against imports in order to "subsidise" or protect their own industries. They also resort to invisible trade barriers such as withholding or slowing down import approval and requiring adjustments in imported products to meet their standards.
6. *Corruption.* Officials in several countries require bribes in order to co-operate. They often award business to the highest briber rather than the best bidder. Kickbacks received by parties in Indian governments' gun deal again is an example.
7. *Technological pirating.* A company locating its plant abroad worries about foreign managers learning how to make its product and breaking away to compete openly. This has happened in such diverse areas as machinery, electronics, chemicals, pharmaceuticals.
8. *High cost of product and communication adaptation.* A company going abroad must study each foreign market carefully, become sensitive to its economics, politics, and culture and make some adaptations in its products and communications to suit foreign tastes otherwise it might make some serious blunders.
9. *International code of conduct* for product to be traded or marketed in a particular country by UNCTAD and World Trade Organisation as per Dunkel proposals.

A rapid increase in foreign exchange earnings through exports is vital for the success of our government's programmes. To intensify the drive for export development, it is not sufficient to explore new markets for non-traditional products alone. Just as the export potential of primary commodities is limited, so is the growth potential of "non-traditional" items marketed in the traditional manner. A major breakthrough resulting in sizable additions to foreign exchange earnings is possible only if we:

(a) Identify new non-traditional products/services for export;

(b) Develop new ways of marketing them in new markets; and

(c) Explore new marketing strategies for securing a fairly consistent and long term foothold in these areas.

India has already started moving in this direction. Construction contracts, turnkey contracts, joint ventures in middle eastern Arab countries and African countries are indicators of this trend. The capital investment made by our country, especially during the last 40 years, in building a sophisticated industrial base and in training a very large number of people in the development and application of modern technology is likely to pay rich dividends in the near future. We should link our future efforts in this direction to a well defined international marketing programme for export development. It, therefore, becomes necessary to focus attention on some of the more important emerging opportunities for international marketing development in the non-traditional sector so that we may gain insights into the types of integrated action needed at the corporate and national levels to convert these opportunities into viable business propositions.

International marketing is of growing importance to Indian business. It is the duty of an international marketer to support the economic development of our country. One should try to sell a portion of one's output abroad. Benefits are gained in the obtaining of quotas for imported materials in exchange of proof of the export of finished goods.

Benefits to International Marketers

There are many benefits which accrue to an international marketer. These are listed below:

(i) A much bigger geographical area of market, so that the exporter may be less dependent upon the tastes and preferences of one particular country;

(ii) With a global market, the exporter is much less likely to be affected by the business cycles and political instability of a particular country — if one country has a recession and sales are

difficult, the exporter may export to other markets which are relatively prosperous;

(iii) A good network of market implies that if a competitor captures one market, only a portion of his sales are likely to be affected;

(iv) Due to bulk selling because of bulk orders, economical manufacturing is possible for the manufacturer-exporter;

(v) If international marketing is properly handled, the payment is guaranteed and quick;

(vi) Exports help in developing domestic trade. Domestic consumers are inclined to have more faith in products which they know are selling abroad. International marketing create a "goodwill" in the eyes of the consumers.

The potential international marketer must learn how to make a start and how to find customers abroad. He must also understand the terms used in international business, the procedure for collecting payment from customers abroad, and have some knowledge of shipping, marine insurance and packing. International marketing brings large orders and they must therefore assure themselves that their production capacity is sufficient to cope with those orders.

The markets abroad are expanding due to the growing economy of various nations and, in particular, of the oil rich countries of the Middle East. Expectations have gone up everywhere. This is a global phenomenon. A strong desire for higher standards of living on the part of the citizens of the world has again given a boost to international markets. A worldwide approach to international marketing management is therefore essential. International marketing is a part of the broad marketing system and *all the principles of internal marketing apply equally to international marketing; but some additional skills are also required.*

(a) Managing International Marketing Plans. This require the capacity to comprehend the economic, political, and commercial connections of the various nations and to design an effective export marketing strategy.

(b) Adapt to International Markets Tastes and Preferences. Certain responsibilities which India as a nation must accept are listed below:

(i) To demonstrate to the world how well the economy can be managed by a democratic country;

(ii) To produce the highest quality merchandise at the lowest possible production cost;

(iii) To sell products everywhere in competition with other countries; and

(iv) To assist in the development of natural resources and the national industries of other countries which desire such help.

(c) International Market Opportunities. International marketing opportunities for Indian businessmen stem from certain fundamental conditions listed below:

(i) We have built up a physical manufacturing machinery capable of supplying merchandise in larger quantities than before;

(ii) We have the financial structure and resources with which to finance the export trade;

(iii) We have a sizable merchant fleet;

(iv) We have developed the system of standardised mass production in various items to a point where it is cheaper for us in spite of our increasing labour costs;

(v) We have a skilled and intelligent labour force which is available at a comparatively cheaper price; and

(vi) We have the requisite infrastructure for international marketing.

India's Weaknesses

(i) Business and industry have not decided to make international business a "must";

(ii) Inflation, high prices, and black markets are staring us in the face. If this situation persists, it may put our price level beyond the means of our customers abroad, no matter how badly they may need our products;

(iii) If our internal economy continues to be as badly managed as it has been in recent years, we may find ourselves impoverished to the point where we cannot supply our own essential needs, let alone have enough with which to supply other nations;

(iv) The economy of standardised mass production rests upon high per capita output. Any attempt by selfish and ignorant groups to promote their own interests by limiting output may completely destroy the gains we have made in the export markets;

(v) The impoverishment of our national leadership may be a fatal bar to the future extension of our economy and to raising the real standard of living in India; and

(vii) Poor business ethics.

(vii) Indian rupee as a currency is not an independently strong currency in international market but has to depend upon hard

currencies like U.S. $ and U.K. £. Relative movement of value of hard currency affects export or import value of commodities in international market in global terms.

(i) DECIDING WHETHER TO ENGAGE IN INTERNATIONAL MARKETING AT ALL

Not all companies need to venture into foreign markets in order to survive. Many companies are local businesses and they simply must market well in the local marketplace. Other companies, however may be export oriented industries. Such industries must organise globally if it is to gain purchasing, manufacturing, logistical and marketing advantages. Firms in export business must compete on a worldwide, coordinated basis if they are to succeed.

Companies become involved in international marketing in one of two ways. *(a)* Some one — a domestic exporter, a foreign importer, a foreign government — solicits the company to sell abroad. Or *(b)* the company starts to think on its own about going abroad. It might face overcapacity or see better marketing opportunities in other countries than at home.

Before going abroad, the company should try to define its international marketing objectives and policies. *First* it should decide what proportion of foreign to total sales it will seek. Most companies start small when they venture abroad. Some plan to stay small seeing foreign operations as a small part of their business. Other companies will have more grandiose plans, seeing foreign business as ultimately equal to, or even more important than their domestic business.

Second, the company must choose between marketing in a few countries or many countries. Generally speaking, it makes sense to operate in fewer countries with a deeper commitment and penetration in each.

A company should enter fewer countries when:

(a) Market entry and market control costs are high,

(b) Product and communication adaptation costs are high,

(c) Population and income size and growth are high in the initial countries chosen,

(d) Dominant foreign firms can establish high barriers to entry.

Third, the company must decide on the types of countries to consider. Country attractiveness is influenced by the product, geographical factors, income and population, political climate, and other factors. The seller may have a predilection for certain group of countries or parts of the world.

(ii) DECIDING WHICH MARKETS ARE TO BE SERVED

Suppose a company has assembled a list of potential international markets, how does it choose among them? Many companies opt for selling to neighbouring countries because they understand them better and they present lower distribution and control costs.

At other times, psychic proximity rather than geographical proximity determines choices. The compatibility of its language and culture is a great consideration.

All the prospective countries should be initially rated on three major criteria, namely:

(i) Market attractiveness,

(ii) Competitive advantage, and

(iii) Risk.

Five steps are involved in estimating the probable rate of return on investment of the candidate countries for international marketing.

1. *Estimate of current market potential.* The first step is to estimate total industry sales in each market. This task calls for using published data and primary data collected through company surveys.
2. *Forecast of future market potential and risk.* The firm also needs to forecast future industry sales, a difficult task. It requires predicting economic and political developments and their impact on industry sales.
3. *Forecast of sales potential.* Estimating the company's sales requires forecasting in probable market share based on its competitive advantage, another difficult task.
4. *Forecast of costs and profits.* Costs will depend on the company's contemplated entry strategy. If it exports or licences, its costs will be spelled out in the contracts. If it locates manufacturing facilities in the country, its cost estimation will require understanding local labour conditions, taxes, trade practices, and so on. The company subtracts estimated costs from estimated sales, to derive company profits for each year of the planning horizon.
5. *Estimate of rate of return on investment:* The forecasted income stream should be related to the investment stream to derive the implicit rate of return. This should be high enough to cover *(a)* the company's normal target return on its investment and *(b)* the risk of marketing in that country.

(iii) DECIDING ON THE BEST MODE OF ENTRY

Once a company decides to target a particular country, it has to determine the best mode of entry. Its broad choices are indirect exporting, direct exporting, licensing, joint ventures and direct investment. Each succeeding strategy involves more commitments, risk, control and profit potential.

(iv) DECIDING ON THE EXPORT MARKETING MIX

Finally, the company must determine how it is going to serve these markets *i.e.* what method or system should be used to get needed products into the hands of the consumers in foreign countries. The basic international marketing mix decision will include planning and strategy with regard to products, promotion, channels of distribution and price.

Companies that operate in one or more foreign markets must decide how much to adapt their marketing mix to local conditions. At one extreme are companies that use standardised marketing mix worldwide. Standardisation of the product, advertising, distribution channels and other elements of the marketing mix promises the lowest costs because no major changes have been introduced. At the other extreme is the idea of a customised marketing mix, where the producer adjusts the marketing-mix elements to each target markets — more costs, but hoping for a larger market share and return. Between these two extremes many possibilities exist.

All the above stated four decisions are inter-related. The apparent practical alternative methods of serving foreign markets that are available to a particular business firm may have an influence on the initial decision to become an international marketer, and most certain will be one of the criteria used in determining what specific markets to do business with.

Similarly, the nature of the specific markets chosen influence how these markets are served in that alternative methods may be limited by such factors as the existing structure of distribution, facilitating institutions, and government policy.

Finally, the underlying philosophy of a company's executives in making the initial decision to enter foreign markets will influence — marketing — planning and strategy formulation in that the degree of seriousness or performance attached to the initial decision by these decision makers will make certain alternative methods impracticable.

Similarities and Differences Between Domestic and Export Marketing

(a) Similarities

(i) The basic management task in broad outline is the same for export marketing as it is for domestic marketing. The broad categories of environmental factors are the same *i.e.*, social, economic and political.

(ii) The broad approach to the solution of marketing problems is identical, namely, the consideration of alternative methods, in light of the firm's environment, to achieve the goal of the firm.

(iii) The basic concepts, activities and processes of marketing apply as fully to export marketing as they do to domestic marketing.

(b) Dissimilarities

The differences between domestic and international marketing arise entirely from differences in national environments within which export marketing is conducted, and the differences in the organisation and programmes of a company operating simultaneously in different national markets.

Although both domestic and international marketing activities are conducted in a legal environment, the components of legal environment differ. Certain types of regulations and laws which are found in domestic countries are missing or are different in export markets. Taxes and tariffs vary wiuely amongst domestic and export markets.

Restrictions such as trade quotas and exchange control are much different in international markets than in domestic markets. There are differences in the type and characteristics of domestic and international currencies in which the export trade takes place and the exchange rates imposed by different countries. Government institutions and banking system vary widely from country-to-country and often have significant influence on marketing activities.

The other commonly recognised environmental differences arise from language, customs, traditions and other cultural differences, geographic distances and climatic variations between domestic and international markets.

The financial condition relating to the conduct of international marketing are quite different in most respects from those employed in financing domestic trade. The method of credit extension and method of financing are extremely different.

There is the entire field of governmental control and restriction exercised by every sovereignty. Competition is generally not open and free. Laws, restrictions, taxes, tariffs and controls are all part of the expressed sovereignty of all foreign countries. Moreover, these devices are constantly changing and they must be followed closely in an export marketing venture, statistical data for many export markets is either non-existent or inaccurate. Language is a major obstacle for export markets. The fundamental problem is the lack of common background and experience which any domestic marketer shares with his consumer.

Thus, the analysis and solution of international marketing problems requires skills, background, and insights in addition to those required to solve strictly domestic marketing problems.

Differences Between Domestic and International Marketing

Domestic Marketing	*International Marketing*
1. One nation, same language and culture.	1. Many nations, many languages and cultures.
2. Transport cost is a major marketing expense.	2. Transport cost influences only to some extent.
3. One currency	3. Different currencies in different countries.
4. Political environment and factors are the same.	4. Different political environments and factors in different countries are vital.
5. Market is relatively homogeneous	5. Markets are diverse and highly heterogeneous.
6. No problems of exchange control and tariffs.	6. There are problems of exchange controls and tariffs and they act as obstacles.
7. Data available, usually accurate and relatively easily collected at less cost.	7. Data collection a formidable task, requiring significantly higher budgets.
8. Relative freedom from government interference.	8. Government. influences business decisions.
9. Individual company has little effect on environment.	9. "Gravitational" distortion by large companies.
10. Chauvinism helps.	10. Chauvinism hinders.
11. Relatively stable business environment.	11. Multiple environments, many of which are highly unstable.
12. Uniform financial climate.	12. Variety of financial climates ranging from overconservative to wildly inflationary.
13. Business "rules of the game" mature and understood.	13. Rules diverse, changeable and unclear.

Major Government Intervention in the Trade Process are Caused by

Import Restrictions

(i) Tariffs;

(ii) Particular restrictions — imports by quota system;

(iii) Buy home-made products;

(iv) Encourage national exports; and

(v) Management of exchange rates.

How to Solve International Marketing Problems?

(i) Have an international outlook.

(ii) International business targets must be realistically assessed and the segment of the world market to be focused on should be selected.

(iii) Relevant environmental factors in the international markets must be analysed.

(iv) An international marketing strategy must be designed with regard to the following factors:

(a) Size and extent of international market must be decided;

(b) Buyer behaviour must be analysed;

(c) Foreign competition must be evaluated;

(d) Legal, political and business factors must be examined; and

(e) Costs must be calculated to arrive at the final price and terms of sale.

In international marketing, service is the most important thing. The products exported should be acceptable to the consumers abroad; and this calls for a constant study of consumers abroad and the adaptation of products, packaging and presentation. The exporter should have respect for all nationalities.

Basic Principle of Successful International Marketing

International marketing is an orderly, methodical and a somewhat technical process of adapting Indian merchandising and marketing methods to conditions in countries outside India.

Salient Features of International Marketing

(i) The process of international marketing must be orderly;

(ii) The process of international marketing must be methodical;

(iii) It must be somewhat technical; and

(iv) The process must be one of adaptation.

Basic Functions of International Marketing

These functions include:

(i) The direction and supervision of international business, including the development of an export import policy;

(ii) The adaptation of the product for international markets, including packing;

(iii) Selling, including such related functions as advertising, sales promotion, sales training, translation, service and the like;

(iv) Transportation of the product, including documentation for shipment, railways, ocean shipping, marine insurance, export credit and guarantee and other related matters;

(v) Credit and terms of payment;

(vi) Financing, including exchange, invoicing and collection; and

(vii) After sales service.

To sum up we may say that there is a necessity in India to develop international marketing; and this calls for a knowledge of sources of information and how to evaluate and use them. In the ultimate analysis, India's international marketing capacity will be determined by a variety of factors, namely:

(i) International division of labour;

(ii) Comparative costs;

(iii) Surplus production;

(iv) Balance of international payments;

(v) Purchasing power of the importing country; and

(vi) Trade promotion.

One of the requirements of international marketing is knowledge of languages and customs of different people and how to deal with them. Every company's management cannot overrule them because they have no power; at the same time, their neglect would amount to a loss of business. Competent management for international marketing in India is required; this calls for a combination of skills, including comprehension, imagination and courage.

3

NEED FOR INTERNATIONAL TRADE

Why do Nations Trade?

Fundamentally, in a market system individuals trade because they expect to profit from the exchange. That is they expect to be better off as a result of the trading. In this respect, trade occurs for the same reasons among nations as it does among regions within a given country.

Historical Perspective

According to Wasserman and Haltman, "International trade consists of transactions between residents of different countries." Thus domestic trade occurs within the political boundaries of a nation whereas international trade occurs across the political boundaries of different nations. The main reason behind both the types of trade is division of labour and specialisation. Each nation or region specialises in that field in which it enjoys maximum comparative advantage.

It can be made clear with the help of an example. India enjoys the comparative advantage in the production of cotton, tea, etc., but West Asian countries have comparative advantage in producing petrol and petroleum products. International trade is the result of geographical specialisation. Thus we find the main similarities between the two types of trade.

Now the question arises: Why does international trade take place?

Firstly, in different nations the entrepreneurial and labour skills differ.

Secondly, in different countries the factor endowments are not the same.

Thirdly, human wants are multiple and varied. No single country satisfies all of them. Thus any nation has to depend on other countries and in return it has to pay back in the shape of exports of those items which can be produced at a lower rates as compared to other nations.

Fourthly, the level of technology is different in different countries. A country with sophisticated technology can definitely produce at a lower cost as compared to a country with a low standard of technology.

Fifthly, the factors of inputs are highly mobile within a nation but they are immobile between the nations.

It has been a matter of controversy whether there is any difference between internal trade and international trade. The classical economists definitely held the view that there are certain fundamental differences. On this account they propounded a separate theory of international trade. According to them, basis of international trade was the comparative cost differences. On the other hand, modern economists like Bertil Ohlin, Haberler, etc., have regarded these two as similar. In the words of Ohlin, "International trade is but a special case of inter-local or inter-regional trade." Stating the difference between domestic trade and international trade as a difference of degree rather than a kind.

Nevertheless, there are several reasons to believe the classical view that international trade is basically different from internal trade. This led to a separate theory of international trade. According to Kindleberger, "International trade is treated as a distinct, subject because of tradition, because of urgent and important problems presented by international economic questions in the real world, because it follows different laws from domestic trade and because it studies, illuminates and enriches our understanding of economics as a whole." *The following are the reasons for a separate theory of international trade:*

1. Perfect mobility of the factors of production within the country but immobile between nations.
2. Different currencies.
3. Differences in natural resources.
4. Different national policies.
5. Exchange and trade control.
6. Separate markets.
7. Problem of balance of payments.
8. Different political groups.

Theory of Comparative Advantage in Nutshell

The theory of comparative advantage is used by economists to explain why international trade occurs and how the gains from trade are distributed.[1] The net gain from international trade results from specialisation that capitalizes on differences in the relative abundance of productive resources in the various locales. Differences in climate, natural resources, technology, capital, etc., provide regions with a comparative advantage over other areas in the production and sale of some goods. At the same time, other regions may have a comparative advantage in other goods. Although it is possible that a nation could produce every kind of good and service it requires, it cannot produce each with equal facility. Therefore, it is advantageous for a country to produce and sell those goods in which it is most productive (*i.e.*, has a comparative advantage) and purchase those goods in which it has a comparative disadvantage.

India furnishes some examples of this concept. A growing level of technology, a skilled labour force, and access to capital helps explain why India exports such products as tea, handicraft and handlooms. At the same time, India imports airplanes, fertilizers, sophisticated machinery which require more capital, more research and employ high manufacturing skills.

The theory of comparative advantage shows that though trade countries can obtain both more and different goods than might be available through home production, thus providing an improved standard of living to the consumers. This is the major argument favouring free trade among nations. A maximum social product would be available for the whole world if countries produced and traded those goods in which they had a comparative advantage when demand conditions warranted such trade.

The simple theory of international trade based on differences in natural factor endowments has come under increasing criticism. Economists have noted that trade in industrial goods can occur even in the absence of differences in factor endowments. Nations such as Japan, for example, have become important world traders without a rich base of natural resources. In fact, many of the important comparative advantages of industrial nations arise from economies of scale, product differentiation, technology gaps, and educational levels of the work force.

Furthermore, the theory does not adequately explain why firms choose to make investments to producer abroad rather than trade. This is a significant deficiency since international business has been characterized

1. The theory of comparative costs is developed more fully in all international trade textbooks. For a lucid explanation see Franklin R. Root, International Trade and Investment (4th ed., Cincinnati: South-Western Publishing Co., 1978), Chapters 2-4.

by substantial growth in direct investments in recent years. In a very real sense, decisions to invest or to export are strategic alternatives for servicing overseas markets. These decisions are influenced strongly by demand conditions as well as by cost.

There is, no doubt, that the modern theory suffers from a variety of drawbacks and shortcomings as detailed above. Yet it offers the best available explanation of the phenomenon of international trade. As such, it occupies quite a respectable place in the literature on international trade.

International Product Life Cycle Theory[2]

Figure 3.1 presents a simplified version of the international product life cycle concept. This concept builds on the research of both business and economics scholars and postulates a cycle in which products are first introduced in high income, advanced nations for use in the local market. Later the products are exported to other advanced countries. Later still, the initiating country loses some of its export market as other advanced nations initiate their own local production. (Some of this production is the result of direct investment by companies of the originating country). Finally, the initiating country loses additional export markets when less developed nations begin producing and exporting the product. Some of these last products become imports in the initiating country.

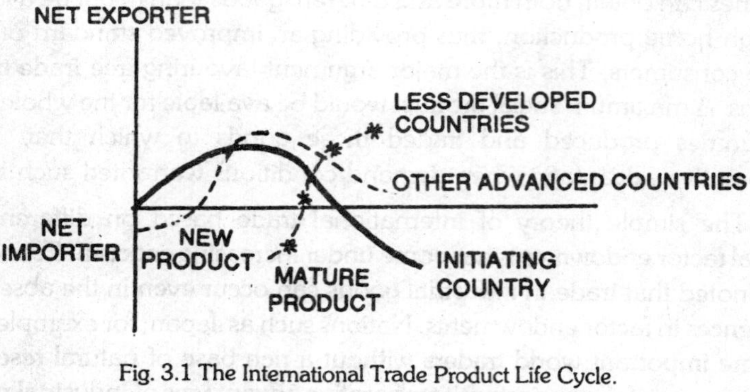

Fig. 3.1 The International Trade Product Life Cycle.

The International Trade Product Life Cycle

In the initial phase of the cycle, manufacturing occurs in a developed country (such as the United States) where the innovator is familiar with the

2. A more extensive coverage of the product life-cycle trade model may be found in Raymond Vernon, Manager in the International Economy (Englewood Cliffs, N.J.: Prentice-Hall, Inc., 1968), pp. 77-83; and in Louis T. Wells, Jr., (ed). The Product Life Cycle and International Trade (Boston: Graduate School of Business Administration, Harvard University, 1972). The Wells text contains a review of the theoretical contributions to the concept. Several examples in this section are drawn from this text.

needs of the market and senses that a potentially profitable market exists. Research and development (R & D) programme promote product development in the advanced country, and the risks of innovation are perceived as being lower. Also, it is advantageous to maintain close contact with the market during the initial stages when it is often necessary to adjust product and marketing programmes. This is accomplished by means of manufacturing and selling, primarily to the domestic market.

Other advanced countries may have needs similar to those of the initiating country. These countries form a potential export market. Later growth of demand in these importing nations may provide sufficient volume to justify local manufacture. Local production is specially likely to occur when the income level and the size of the local market are large and when tariffs and transportation costs are high. As production begins abroad, the exports of the initiating nation grow less rapidly, especially as other producing countries begin to export.

The product life cycle theorists hypothesize a third development as the product matures. The mature product uses an already established technology and a lower skilled labour content. Consumers are more apt to be price conscious because the product is no longer a novelty, and price competition will likely be prevalent. In this situation, the less developed nations may be able to undersell competitors by applying their less skilled labour to the sophisticated machinery already designed to the product. Lower production costs will be achieved if the machinery costs do not offset the labour cost advantage.[3] Thus, the less developed nations may become attractive production points and begin exporting the product to more advanced countries. Products such as textiles and electronic components are examples of products reaching this latter phase. In cases where marketing techniques are important to achieving adequate export volume, the exporter is often aligned with a foreign firm having expertise in the developed markets.

The product life-cycle concept has been found useful in explaining trade among nations.[4] In a study of the petrochemical industry, Stobaugh found that the theory explained international production and trade patterns. Looking to the future, Stobaugh saw evidence that nations having low cost raw materials based on oil and gas would become major exporters of the mature intermediate chemical products. The development plans of the Middle East countries currently reflect this potential.

The product life cycle theory, however, appears to be an incomplete explanation for the transfer of technology and the migration of industry.

---

3. R. Vernon, *op. cit.*
4. The following examples are drawn from Wells, *op. cit.*

There are historical exceptions to the sequence of the product life cycle. One recent exception is the calculator industry in which successive innovations have led to shifting dominance between the United States and Japan. As input requirements changed, the country favoured by the change became the dominant producer.[5] Because of this and other factors, researchers have sought a more general explanation of direct investment in the theory of oligopoly.[6]

Theory of Oligopoly Applied to Direct Investment

One explanation of direct investment relies on the theory of oligopoly. After considering the risks and costs of operating in a different political and legal environment in a foreign country, a firm may choose to invest overseas when it can earn a higher rate of return there than it earns at home. To be successful, the firm must have some advantage over its competitors in the foreign country that it can transfer from one country to another. Furthermore, this advantage must be such that it cannot be readily acquired by local firms. Direct investment requires some imperfection in markets for goods or factors. Kindleberger has itemized four types of monopolistic advantages that produce direct investment:

(*i*) Departures from perfect competition in goods markets, including product differentiation, special marketing skills, retail price maintenance, administered pricing, and so forth.

(*ii*) Departures from perfect competition in factor markets, including the existence of patented or unavailable technology, of discrimination in access to capital, of differences in skills of managers organised into firms rather than hired in competitive markets.

(*iii*) Internal and external economies of scale, the latter being taken advantage of by vertical integration.

(*iv*) Government limitations on output or entry.

Giddy likewise contends that international direct investment is a response to market imperfections. In the international market, cultural, informational, economic, and geographical distances, along with political and regulatory barriers, represent market imperfections and create uncertainties.[7] These imperfections motivate the firm to control and co-ordinate

5. Badiul A. Majumdar, "Technology Transfers and International Competitiveness: The Case of Electronic Calculators," Journal of International Business Studies (Fall, 1980), pp. 103-111.
6. Direct investments occurs when an investment in a firm is large enough to exercise control over company policy.
7. Ian H. Giddy, "The Demise of the Product Cycle Model in International Business Theory." Columbia Journal of World Business (Spring, 1978), p. 94.

international production and marketing. When external markets have severe enough imperfections, resources are allocated more efficiently by creating internal markets (within the firm) rather than relying on foreign firms to undertake production and/or marketing abroad. Thus, the firm begins overseas production and marketing. The firm's ability to compete internationally is dependent on having and maintaining a differential advantage over local firms.

This general approach recognises that the response of a firm to competitive threats is dependent on the nature of the barriers to entry upon which the firm's oligopoly position rests. The pattern of exports skills and technology; a lack of competition; government barriers; and the firm's managerial and marketing resources. The international product life cycle represents a special case of the more general oligopoly theory.

The Role of Multinational Enterprises

Much of the trade literature is concerned with the movement of goods on the assumption that factors of production such as labour, management, technology, natural resources, and capital are relatively immobile among nations due either to natural or political restrictions. However, data also show much growth of international production under the control of multinational firms implying at least some mobility of capital and management.

Some of the shift from international trade to foreign production reflects the rapid growth of markets abroad, such as that of the European Economic Community and Japan. In order to develop a market position or to retain an existing market share in these countries, Indian companies should acquire or establish production facilities abroad. The growth of these markets has been a major inducement for expansion by foreign companies not only because it provides enlarged scales, but also because the potential warrants economically efficient scales of operation. As markets grow the large-scale efforts of the firms permit use of the management and marketing techniques that have been tested and found successful at home.

Restrictions placed on the importation of goods and national economic development planning have given additional impetus to the rise of multinational firms. The existence of tariff and non-tariff barriers means that a firm must often establish production units within a country or region in order to compete effectively with local firms. Regional trading blocs, such as the European Economic Community (EEC), the Central American Common Market, ASEAN (Association of South-East Asian Nations), etc., have widened the market for local firms by removing many of the restrictions among the nations within the bloc, thereby making possible efficient scales of operation for local producers. Since no tariff is applied to trade within the bloc, but is applied to outsiders, trade may actually be diverted from the more efficient producer outside the bloc. For example, an Indian firm might have been the low-cost producer of certain machinery sold in West Germany prior to the formation of the EEC. Following formation of the Common Market, German industry might be served by French firms that face no tariff barriers. The Indian firm, though may be efficient, would have to overcome price resistance from the higher cost resulting from the tariff. In this instance, a possible response of the outsider is to establish production and marketing capabilities inside the Common Market. This strategy will preserve the firm's position by avoiding the tariff applied to producers outside the bloc.

Adverse reaction on a major scale to the growth of multinational companies is of relatively recent origin. However, multinational firms are currently under attack in many parts of the world, especially among the lesser developed nations including India. The Indian government has controlled foreign investments by foreign firms in order to improve the balance of payments, and Indian labour has become concerned about the effect that overseas production will have on employment. More recently, foreign investments in India have been under attack as protectionists have sought to retain foreign control over their industries.

The power of multinational firms relative to host country governments, the influence of the firms on employment and development policies, their ability to circumvent governmental policy through access to foreign capital, and their attempts to influence foreign politics are among the frequently mentioned concerns of host nations.[8]

The recency of multinational growth and the lack of data, together with differences among countries in the desire for economic development versus control of resources, makes it difficult to evaluate the merit of the arguments regarding the exact influence of the multinational firms. Various national governments and international groups continue to investigate the status and influence of multinational firms. The outcome of these investigations is resulting in policy measures aimed at strengthening national control over the activities of the firms within a country's boundaries.

International marketers need to be flexible in their use of various strategies for market entry to meet specific situations. The multinational firm employs several strategies in its approach. Emphasis shifts regarding the desirability of exporting, licensing, joint ventures, or the establishment of

8. The term host nation refers to the foreign country where production or marketing facilities are located or operative in contrast to the home country where company headquarters are located.

subsidiaries. For example, in 1973, the Arab countries established plans to reduce foreign ownership control over the production and marketing of crude oil, even though foreign investment had been encouraged earlier and had played a significant role in the development of some of these countries.

National Gains from International Trade

1. Nations gain from international trade and investment in many ways. The most obvious gain is that the variety of goods available in a country is increased. Often it is either impossible or not economically feasible to produce certain goods within a country, even though the demand for them may be great. Tropical fruits are an example. Although India might produce groundnuts, it is more economical to import them. Importation results in availability at a lower cost which, in turn, presents the possibility of more widespread consumption.

2. The increased variety of goods available through trade enhances the standard of living within a country. It provides new consumption experiences plus the possibility of buying products that more closely meet the requirements of varying life-styles. International trade opens the world market to producers of these goods, thereby allowing more efficient and profitable production than would be possible with only local sales.

3. Sometimes natural resources, or derived products, cannot be developed within the nation. Scarce resources such as tin, copper, and other basic commodities must be extracted where they are found. These commodities are essential for industial production and the only source of supply may be through trade. If the commodities are not imported, production of goods using these materials must obviously cease. Japan and the United Kingdom are good examples of countries that depend on such trade to keep their industrial plants in operation. The significance of imports is obvious where the country lacks a strong resource base, but similar conditions exist even in a more endowed nations. The production of many items in India, for example, depends on the importation of critical raw materials and energy supplies.

4. The quantity of goods available for consumption also can increase through trade. A nation, by concentrating production on the items having the greatest comparative advantage, can trade a portion of this output for goods that have a comparative disadvantage at home. The importation of goods that are produced more efficiently abroad results in a greater variety and quantity of goods on the local market than if resources were applied to the production of goods where the country does not have a comparative advantage.

5. Wider markets available through international trade lead to possible expansion of plant size. If such expansion in trade leads to scale economies, there is a good possibility that the benefits of lower cost will be available to either, or both, the domestic and foreign consumers. The presence and the degree of domestic competition will determine whether and how much of the savings will be passed on to consumers. This lower cost may further broaden the domestic market and make luxury products available to lower income segments.

6. Even when the foreign market is serviced by producing abroad, there are advantages for domestic consumers and producers since both gain from the transfer of products and technology among countries. Many companies think basically of selling technology abroad, but India also imports technology. Think of such technological imports as colour TV parts, chips, chemicals, fertilizers, etc.

7. While imports sometimes are viewed as competing with domestic products, it must be recognized that imports of goods, services, and capital are necessary to provide foreigners with the means of payment for domestically produced exports. Without imports a country merely sends away its resources and products without receiving usable products in return.

Gains for the Individual Firm through International Trade

1. The value of international marketing to individual producers, financial institutions, merchants, carriers, and other businesses is not difficult to understand. They are interested in foreign trade or investment because of the direct and indirect profits derived from it. Producers not only expect a profit on the commodities sold abroad, but they also see foreign markets as a basis for expanding production beyond the limits set by the domestic market. Export enable many industries to keep their labour and capital employed more fully and continuously, to expand their plants more rapidly than domestic commerce would warrant, to realize the lower costs of operating at a more efficient size, or to distribute sales more widely so the adverse effects of local or national business recessions are minimised.

2. Production and marketing abroad basically are geared toward expanding markets for the firm's products, but as we have seen, they may be only attempts to maintain existing markets by producing behind trade barriers. Early penetration of the foreign market may have as its goal the pre-empting of the market before local competition becomes established or rivals from another country secure a foothold.

3. Some international marketing activity takes place because a firm's customers have moved abroad. It may be necessary to establish branches or subsidiaries in the foreign nation to continue to serve these customers.

Advertising agencies, banks and marketing research agencies are examples of such expansion.

4. While many manufacturing industries in India historically have not been highly dependent on foreign markets, the significance of these foreign markets is growing. Despite this growth, it is possible to underestimate the effect of the foreign market on a firm's profits. A company may have only ten per cent of its output in foreign trade, yet the loss of that ten per cent may cause a much greater percentage loss in profits because of its effect on efficiency and overhead allocation. Some foreign sales may be made at higher profit margins than the sale of identical products in a highly competitive home market. Also, the establishment of foreign subsidiaries can expand exports to the domestic plant through the sale of both components and finished goods needed to offer a complete line of goods.

5. The worldwide location of production and marketing capacity provides opportunity for increased profits. An integrated logistic system can capitalize on the advantages of production and marketing in specific localities. Reduced transportation costs may result from overseas production. Advantages of scale may be achieved by concentrating production in one location and exporting to other countries.

6. There are other indirect methods by which profits are increased. The profits of the total company may be increased by the method of transfer pricing used when products or services are sold by one company unit to another. The subsidiary may pay royalties levied for management services from headquarters for needed services to improve the subsidiary's operation.

Conclusion

It is apparent that there are multiple avenues for gain through international operations. Many of these would remain inert if it were not for marketing. It is too frequently assumed that the products of an industry having a comparative cost advantage will flow automatically to foreign markets. Actually the size of the flow depends both upon the ability of the industry to produce and on marketing. Unless foreign markets can be developed, neither exports nor foreign investment will occur. Many exportable products will be legally excluded by potential importing countries in order to satisfy domestic employment and development policies. The foreign demand, even for necessities, may be at a minimum because of low purchasing power. However, the foreign demand for many products is subject to stimulation by effective marketing and trade promotion.

4

IMPORT AND EXPORT OF INDIA

For India rapid and sustained export growth remains the key to long term viability of the balance of payments and the reduction of foreign debt. It is possible to join the ranks of major exporters if the quality and cost structure of the whole economy is transformed. The remaining bias against exports provided by import licensing and high tariffs has to be eliminated over time. The handicap caused by fiscal distortions must be removed. A world class infrastructure and financial sector has to be built, and technical marketing and management skills upgraded. Labour laws must be changed to give greater flexibility to exporters to adjust their work force in line with export orders and to hire the thousands of workers needed for volume production, without fear of becoming sick with excess labour.

The long term sustainability of the balance of payments also depends on the stability of capital flows. Our strategy should be to shift the weight of financing, from borrowing to direct equity investment and to change the composition of commercial borrowing from short term and government guaranteed debt to long term debt with minimum reliance on government guarantees. During the current year steps have been taken to reduce short term exchange risk guaranteed FCNR debt and foreign investment (direct and portfolio) has increased rapidly. If this process continues in the next few years, as ongoing economic reforms, improve future economic prospects, the debt-GDP and debt service ratios could decline substantially. Within the overall emphasis on equity flows, a greater thrust to direct investment would be desirable, as such capital tends to be more stable and brings a number of other benefits such as marketing and technology.

With the Indian economy increasingly integrated with the world economy, the management of the balance of payments will pose major challenges. Careful attention will need to be given to exchange rate policy, external debt strategy and foreign exchange reserve management. For example, policy must ensure that exchange rate developments do not weaken the competitiveness of our exports. The large stock of external debt has to be carefully managed to minimize the potential for sudden pressures on liquidity of the kind that disrupted the economy in 1990-91. Foreign exchange reserves must be held at levels commensurate with growing trade and capital flows and the increasing diversity and flexibility of such flows. Anticipatory action will have to be taken to guard against shocks such as a sudden rise in petroleum prices or an agricultural drought. All this will call for a judicious mixture of boldness and vigilance.

VOLUME OF TRADE UNDER VARIOUS FIVE YEAR PLANS

VOLUME OF EXPORTS

1. In the First and Second Five Year Plans

Exports during first two plans remained stagnant largely due to country's narrow production base and lack of clear policy for exports. Annual average exports amounted to Rs. 609 crores during the first plan and Rs. 624 crores in the second plan period and the growth rate was 1% and 2.2% for its respective plans.

2. Third Five Year Plan

Average exports during the third plan amounted to Rs. 751 crores with a growth rate of 4%. The Indian government during this period took fiscal and financial and institutional measures to make exports an attractive proposition. Exports reached take-off stage during the third plan and got a big boost.

3. Three Annual Plans (1966-67 to 1968-69)

In June 1966 Government of India devalued Indian rupee as a measure to make exports cheaper and more competitive in global market. However, good results could not be achieved through devaluation because of cancelling out effect due to withdrawal of incentive schemes coupled with drought conditions and poor harvests during 1967-68.

The exports during the three years average amounted to Rs. 744 crores only. During this period trade deficit widened.

4. Fourth Plan

India's average exports amounted to Rs. 1,807 crores with the annual average growth rate of 14%. During fourth plan export sector was given a status of priority sector. Export policy resolution was approved in 1970.

Imports were liberalised to facilitate greater export production. Early 1970s witnessed a commodity boom in global markets due to emergence of oil rich gulf market and birth of Bangladesh coupled with the introduction of Generalised System of Preferences. India achieved for the first time a surplus trade balance of Rs. 104 crores in 1972-73.

5. Fifth Plan to Seventh Plan

Annual average exports during fifth plan from India amounted to Rs. 4,441 crores, during Sixth Plan Rs. 8,904 croresand during first year of 7th plan at Rs. 10,420 crores. During this period trade deficit tended to move upward. During 1988-89 exports were valued at Rs. 20,287 crores.

Table 4.1

India's Foreign Trade

Imports, Exports, Balance of Trade and Growth Rate (Plan Average) During Various Five Year Plans

(Value: Rs. crores)

Five Year Plan	*Exports*	*Imports*	*Balance of Trade*	*Exports as Percentage of Imports*	*Growth Rate (%age)*
First Plan (1951-52 to 1955-56)	609	723	–114	85	1.0
Second Plan 1956-57 to 1960-61	624	985	–361	63	2.2
Third Plan (1961-62 to 1965-66)	752	1,241	– 489	61	4.0
Three Annual Plans (1966-67 to 1968-69)	1,247	1,991	–744	63	—
Fourth Plan (1969-70 to 1973-74)	1,807	1,972	–165	91	14.0
Fifth Plan (1974-75 to 1977-78)	4,441	5,147	–706	—	86
Sixth Plan (1980-81 to 1984-85)	8,904	14,547	–5,643	—	60
Seventh Plan (1985-86 to 1989-90)					
1985-86	10,420	19,622	–9,202	—	53
1986-87	12,550	20,062	–7,512	—	62
1987-88	15,741	22,399	–6,658	—	70
1988-89	20,287	27,693	–7,406	—	73
1989-90	27,681.47	35,411.88	-7730.41	—	36.7
1990-91	32,553	43,193	–10,640	—	17.7
1991-92	44,292	47,301	–3,009	—	35.3
1992-93	53,688	63,375	–9687	—	21.9
1992-93 (April-Dec.)	42,182	51,477	–29.5	—	31.8

The depressed international economic and trading environment, a difficult balance of payments position and the dwindling foreign exchange reserves of the country continued to pose a serious challenge to the export promotion effort of India. To meet these challenges effectively, a multi-pronged and multi-faceted approach has been adopted in recent years in the form of innovative measures encompassing policy framework, institutional service support, export incentives and new tools of export promotion.

Volume of Imports

Average annual imports during first and second plan were to the tune of Rs. 723 and Rs. 985 crores. On account of limited available resources, efforts were made to strike a balance between imports and exports at a very low level, thus undermining the importance of higher inflow of key inputs as well as capital goods for generating export production.

During the Third Plan average imports amounted to Rs. 1,241 crores and trade deficit rose to Rs. 489 crores. Export earnings were able to meet 61% of expenditure on imports. Import policy was liberalised during the Third Plan and schemes of cash compensatory support, import replenishment and duty drawback schemes were introduced.

During Fourth Plan average annual imports amounted to Rs. 1,972 crores. It was realised for the first time that there was a close nexus between imports and exports. India's import policy was liberalised for generating export production. The adverse trade deficit was substantially narrowed to Rs. 165 crores compared to Rs. 489 crores in the Third Plan and Rs. 361 crores during the Second Plan.

During Fifth Plan annual average imports amounted to Rs. 5,147 crores leaving a trade gap of Rs. 706 crores. This deficit further widened to Rs. 5,643 crores in the Sixth Plan when average imports amounted to Rs. 14,547 crores. The trade gap an all time high of Rs. 9,202 crores during 1985-86 when imports were Rs. 19,622 crores. Trade deficit has witnessed an uptrend during 1988-89 when imports at Rs. 27,693 crores were recorded.

During early 1980s about 50% of total imports represented a single item — petroleum and petroleum products. The position was further accentuated on account of Iraq-Kuwaiti war due to hike in oil prices and global inflation which has been tolling on highly depleted position of India's balance of payment as it stands today when we go with begging bowl to International Monetary Fund.

Composition of Imports

Imports of Rs. 35,416 crores in 1989-90 showed an increase of 25.4 per cent in rupee terms and 9.1 per cent in US dollar terms. During 1990-

91 imports at Rs. 43,171 crores were higher by 21.9 per cent in rupee terms and 13.1 per cent in US dollar terms over the previous year. Analysis of import growth during 1989-90 and 1990-91 has been made after a discussion of trends in overall imports and structural changes in the composition of imports during the Sixth and Seventh Five Year Plans.

Table 4.2
Trends in Foreign Trade
Imports and Exports in Rupee and US Dollars

Year	*Imports*	*Exports*	*Trade Balance*	*Changes in Imports*	*Changes in Exports*	*Trade Balance as % of Exports*
1	2	3	4	5	6	7
	Rupees hundred crore			*Per cent*		
1986-87	201.0	124.5	– 76.4	2.2	14.3	61.4
1987-88	222.4	156.7	– 65.7	10.7	25.9	41.9
1988-89	282.4	202.3	– 80.0	26.9	29.1	39.6
1989-90	354.2	276.8	– 77.3	25.4	36.8	27.9
1990-91	431.9	325.5	–106.4	22.0	17.6	32.7
1991-92*	210.7	187.1	– 23.6	9.0	23.9	12.6
1992-93	218.82	185.37	–33.45	12.7	3.8	
1993-94	233.06	222.38	–10.68	6.5	20.0	
1994-95	286.54	263.31	–23.24	22.9	18.4	
1995-96	363.70	318.31	–45.39	26.9	20.9	
		Billion US Dollars		*Per cent*		
1986-87	15.7	9.7	–6.0	–2.1	9.4	
1987-88	17.2	12.1	–5.1	9.1	24.0	
1988-89	19.5	14.0	–5.5	13.6	15.6	
1989-90	21.3	16.6	–4.6	9.1	19.0	
1990-91	24.1	18.1	–5.9	13.2	9.1	–3.2
1991-92*	21.01	18.2	–1.0	–17.5	–6.2	–1.1
1992-93	23.21	18.83	–1.1	9.4	7.3	–2.0
1993-94	23.92	21.07	–2.2	8.3	7.8	–0.9
1994-95	31.84	26.85	–1.6	10.5	8.8	
1995-96	41.41	32.46	–2.7	12.6	9.9	

Source: (1) DGCI&S for trade data and RBI for exchange rate.
(2) RBI Currency and Finance Report 1995-96.
(3) Economic Survey: 1996-97, Government of India, New Delhi, 1997.

Table 4.3
India's Exports, Imports and Trade Balance

(in Rs. Crore)

Year	Exports (incl. re-exports)	Imports	Trade Balance	Rate of Change Export (per cent)	Rate of Change Import (per cent)
1	2	3	4	5	6
1949-50	485	617	–132		
1950-51	606	608	–2	24.9	–1.5
1951-52	716	890	–174	18.2	46.4
1952-53	578	702	–124	–19.3	– 21.1
1953-54	531	610	–79	– 8.1	–13.1
1954-55	593	700	–107	11.7	14.8
1955-56	609	774	–165	2.7	10.6
1956-57	605	841	–236	– 0.7	8.7
1957-58	561	1035	– 474	– 7.3	23.1
1958-59	581	906	– 325	3.6	–12.5
1959-60	640	961	– 321	10.2	6.1
1960-61	642	1122	– 480	0.3	16.8
1961-62	660	1090	– 430	2.8	– 2.9
1962-63	685	1131	– 446	3.8	3.8
1963-64	793	1223	– 430	15.8	8.1
1964-65	816	1349	– 533	2.9	10.3
1965-66	810	1409	– 599	–0.7	4.4
1966-67	1157	2078	– 921	42.9	47.5
1967-68	1199	2008	– 809	3.6	– 3.4
1968-69	1358	1909	– 551	13.3	– 4.9
1969-70	1413	1582	– 169	4.1	–17.1
1970-71	1535	1634	– 99	8.6	3.3
1971-72	1608	1825	– 217	4.8	11.7
1972-73	1971	1867	104	22.6	2.3
1973-74	2523	2955	– 432	28.0	58.3
1974-75	3329	4519	– 1190	31.9	52.9
1975-76	4036	5265	– 1229	21.2	16.5
1976-77	5142	5074	68	27.4	– 3.6
1977-78	5408	6020	– 612	5.2	18.6
1978-79	5726	6811	– 1085	5.9	13.1
1979-80	6418	9143	– 2725	12.1	34.2
1980-81	6711	12549	– 5838	4.6	37.3
1981-82	7806	13608	– 5802	16.3	8.4
1982-83	8803	14293	– 5490	12.8	5.0

1983-84	9771	15831	– 6060	11.0	10.8
1984-85	11744	17134	– 5390	20.2	8.2
1985-86	10895	19658	– 8763	–7.2	14.7
1986-87	12452	20096	– 7644	14.3	2.2
1987-88	15674	22244	– 6570	25.9	10.7
1988-89	20232	28235	– 8003	29.1	26.9
1989-90	27658	35328	–7670	36.7	25.1
1990-91	32553	43198	– 10645	17.7	22.3
1991-92	44041	47851	– 3810	35.3	10.8
1992-93	53688	63375	– 9687	21.9	32.4
1993-94	69751	73101	– 3350	29.9	15.3
1994-95	82674	89971	-7297	18.5	23.1
1995-96	106353	122678	-16325	28.6	36.4
1996-97	118817	138920	-20103	11.7	13.2
1997-98	130101	154176	-24075	9.5	11.0
1998-99(p)	141604	176099	-34495	8.8	14.2
1999-2000(p) (April-December)	118638	149087	-30449	16.5	12.6

P: Provisional.

Note: For the years 1956-57, 1957-58, 1958-59 and 1959-60 the data is as per the Fourteenth Report of the Estimates Committee (1971-72) on the Ministry of Foreign Trade.

Source: DGCI & S.

Table 4.4

India's Exports, Imports and Trade Balance

(in US $ Million)

Year	*Exports (incl. re-exports)*	*Imports*	*Trade Balance*	*Rate of Change (per cent) Export*	*Import*
1	2	3	4	5	6
1949-50	1016	1296	– 276		
1950-51	1269	1273	– 4	24.9	– 1.5
1951-52	1490	1852	– 362	17.4	45.5
1952-53	1212	1472	260	– 18.6	– 20.5
1953-54	1114	1279	– 166	– 8.1	– 13.1
1954-55	1233	1456	– 223	10.7	13.8
1955-56	1275	1620	– 345	3.3	11.3
1956-57	1259	1750	– 491	– 1.2	8.0
1957-58	1171	2160	– 989	– 7.0	23.4
1958-59	1219	1901	682	4.2	– 12.0
1959-60	1343	2016	– 674	10.1	6.0

1960-61	1346	2353	-1007	0.3	16.7
1961-62	1381	2281	-900	2.6	-3.1
1962-63	1437	2372	-935	4.0	4.0
1963-64	1659	2558	-899	15.5	7.8
1964-65	1701	2813	-1111	2.6	10.0
1965-66	1693	2944	-1251	-0.5	4.7
1966-67	1628	2923	-1295	-3.9	-0.7
1967-68	1586	2656	-1071	-2.6	-9.1
1968-69	1788	2513	-726	12.7	-5.4
1969-70	1866	2089	-223	4.4	-16.9
1970-71	2031	2162	-131	8.8	3.5
1971-72	2153	2443	-290	6.0	13.0
1972-73	2550	2415	134	18.4	-1.1
1973-74	3209	3759	-549	25.9	55.6
1974-75	4174	5666	-1492	30.1	50.8
1975-76	4665	6084	-1420	11.7	7.4
1976-77	5753	5677	77	23.3	-6.7
1977-78	6316	7031	-715	9.8	23.9
1978-79	6978	8300	-1322	10.5	18.0
1979-80	7947	11321	-3374	13.9	36.4
1980-81	8486	15869	-7383	6.8	40.2
1981-82	8704	15174	-6470	2.6	4.4
1982-83	9107	14787	-5679	4.6	-2.6
1983-84	9449	15311	-5861	3.8	3.5
1984-85	9878	14412	-4534	4.5	-5.9
1985-86	8904	16067	-7162	-9.9	11.5
1986-87	9745	15727	-5982	9.4	-2.1
1987-88	12089	17156	-5067	24.1	9.1
1988-89	13970	19497	-5526	15.6	13.6
1989-90	16612	21219	-4607	18.9	8.8
1990-91	18143	24075	-5932	9.2	13.5
1991-92	17865	19411	-1546	-1.5	-19.4
1992-93	18537	21882	-3345	3.8	12.7
1993-94	22700	23985	-1068	200	-6.5
1994-95	267.63	286.5	-2324	18.4	22.9
1995-96	323.11	436.7	-11359	20.9	12.5
1996-97	341.33	489.48	-14815	19.5	13.1
1997-98	356.80	511.87	-15507	4.3	6.1
1998-99	342.98	475.44	-13246	(-)1.2	(-)1.8

Source: DGCI&S and Economic Survey: 1999-2000 Government of India New Delhi.

India's Exports

The slow growth in total exports during 1992-93 was due to various economic and other factors combined to keep export growth down to 3.8 per cent. This was achieved despite a 62 per cent decline in exports to the Rupee Payment Area (mainly markets of erstwhile Soviet Union) which followed upon a decline of 42 percent in 1991-92. The collapse of India's exports to Russia and East European countries is best revealed by noting that monthly exports to these markets were on an average about $ 56 million (Rs. 162 crore) during 1992-93 as compared to $ 255 million (Rs. 458 crore) per month during the current and succeeding years.

Exports to the General Currency Area (GCA) increased by 10.8 per cent in dollar terms during 1992-93 which was a distinct improvement over a 6.3 per cent growth in 1991-92. Excluding the two months of December 1992, and January 1993, during which exports were adversely affected by post-Ayodhya developments, exports to GCA recorded an average growth of 13.1 per cent during 1992-93. This provided a sound basis to build up export performance during 1993-94.

The trade clearly indicates that export-import growth rates have fluctuated in post-liberalisation years largely due to South-East Asian crisis, devaluation of rupee against US $, U.S. Sanctions, W.T.O. code of conduct for global trade affected Indian exports and imports. However, the year 1998-99 showed negative growth rates of both exports and imports.

The current year started with export growth of 27.8 per cent, in dollar terms, during the first quarter. To some extent this was due to spill-over from the previous quarter when disturbances in Bombay had disrupted supplies and shipments. But it also represented the positive effects of policy changes of the previous two years. The export growth was adversely affected in August and September 1993 by the transporters' strike reinforcing the seasonal downturn. The exports growth of 19.9 per cent in dollar terms in the first nine months of 1993-94 is markedly higher than that of 3.4 per cent during the same period in 1992-93 and 9.2 per cent in 1990-91. Exports appear on track for a 20 per cent growth in 1993-94.

Manufactures accounted for 74.6 per cent of total exports in 1991-92. Their share increased to 76.3 per cent in 1992-93. Share of agricultural and agro-processed products declined from 17.9 per cent in 1991-92 to 16.4 per cent in 1992-93 (Table 4.7, Figure 4.1). These trends are apparently being reversed in 1993-94. Agricultural exports increased by 38 per cent while manufactured exports grew by 19 per cent during first half of 1993-94 (Table 4.8). Within manufactures, the highest growth was recorded by plastic and linoleum products (119 per cent), followed by gems and jewellery (37 per cent) and metal manufactures (30 per cent). A uniform incentive structure, comprising a favourable exchange rate and income tax exemption for all export earnings, provides greater incentives for promoting exports which have a high proportion of domestic value addition. This is a positive trend which needs to be strengthened. It generates backward linkages within the domestic economy and stimulates growth. This incentive structure may be expected to boost exports of agro-processed and labour-intensive and light engineering products, sectors in which the country has a distinct natural comparative and competitive advantage.

Trade in Nominal and Real Effective Exchange

Rate of Rupee *(Base 1995 = 100)*

Year	*NEER*		*REER*	
	5 Country Index	*10 Country Index*	*5 Country Index*	*10 Country Index*
1991-92	143.92	142.40	105.88	105.57
1992-93	118.75	117.37	96.06	95.52
1993-94	110.21	111.36	95.51	96.80
1994-95	106.31	106.80	101.17	101.72
1995-96	97.51	97.35	97.99	97.75
1996-97	95.68	96.52	101.12	100.78
1997-98	95.05	85.33	105.19	106.40
1998-99 (March)	83.14	84.93	101.17	102.53

Source: Economic Survey 1991-2000 Government of India, New Delhi.

Trends in Nominal Effective Exchange Rate (NEER) and Real Effective Exchange Rate (REER) notably affects balance of trade and balance of payment of India. The movement of Rupee against the currencies of major trading partners in 1998-99 have corrected for the appreciation of rupee. The table indicates that exchange rate has remained stable during post-liberalisation period in India. Downward movement of rupee against East-Asiam countries has been modest. Considering 1995=100 as base year, NEER and REER declined notably. Import growth as a result declined from 6% in 1997-98 to 0.9% in 1998-99. This has happened due to softening international oil prices and decline in import of capital goods, intermediate goods and slow down in local industrial activities.

Stability of exchange rates provide sound background to accelerate trade and new avenues for marketing by our corporates. The RBI tried its level best to maintain exchange rates without any controls and regulations. Free exchange rate and full convertibility of rupee on capital account will surely open new avenues in our trade.

Favourable change has been found in composition of India's exports after economic liberalisation policy in India's code of conduct of W.T.O. provided substantial change in export commodities also which enable Indian economy to be globalised through marketing of exports. This process encouraged exporters of medium and small scale industry to be quality conscious to participate in export marketing.

The ninth five-year plan envisages 22% growth in exports of aggregate level as per draft document of the plan. However, expenses of consumer goods and capital goods will have to be quality conscious.

Volume of Trade

India's exports aggregated at $ 18,420 million in 1992-93 registering an increase of 3.1% over 1991-92. This compared extremely well to a 1.5% decline in the previous year. In 1992-93, India's import bill grew by 11.9% to $ 21,725.54 million against a declining growth of 19.4% in 1991-92.

In dollar terms, exports grew by 6.14% compound per annum for the 13 year period from 1980-81 to 1992-93 while imports grew at only 2.45% during the same period.

India's share in world exports continues to be negligible despite the substantial growth in exports. The export growth however, as compared to the world exports growth, rate in India has lagged far behind. This resulted in India's share in world exports to come down from 0.65% in 1970 to 0.52 in 1990. While world exports grew at an annual rate of 4.97%, India's own exports grew at a much higher rate 7.09% between 1980 and 1990. Consequently India's share in 1980s improved from 0.42% in 1980 to 0.52 % in 1990.

The share of exports in India's Gross National Product (GNP) continued to be low with only 8.75% while imports accounted for 10.31% in 1992-93. However, when compared with previous years' figures, it was noted that while exports have constantly an increasing trend, by increasing from 5.47% of the GNP in 1980-81 to 8.75% during 1992-93, imports have actually declined from 10.22% in 1980-81 to 7.61% in 1987-88 but increased again to 10.31% in 1992-93, marginally higher than 1980-81.

This has happened largely due to liberalised efforts by the Government of India by reducing customs and excise duties and to prepare quality of manufactural good, it may necessary to import quality of raw materials.

Again GNP contribution of exports increased from 11% in 1994-95 to 12.9% in 1996-97. Moreover, rising level of exports helped to settle external debt payments and their servicing too. Post-liberalisation period in India provided a vital boost for export growth in general and emerging markets of Asia, Africa and Latin America in particular. This phenomenon allowed export houses and export consultants to develop their business. Exports as per cent of imports increased from 86.7% in 1991-92 to 88.5% in 1996-97. As a result current Account deficit of GDP in India declined from 1.5% to 1.1% in 1996-97.

To know exports by commodity group, Table 4.6 provides details of change in export-composition relative figures of tea and coffee have shown declines. Aggregate share of agriculture and allied activities declined, whereas, the share of manufacturer, items increased. These include gems and jewelleries, drugs and pharmaceuticals, machineries, transport equipments, electronic goods, handicraft and ready-made garments.

Looking to composition of India's exports in percentages, diagram provides percentage share in terms of dollars in principle group of exports, change is visualised than pre-liberalisation period.

Composition of India's Trade

In India's export basket oil meal topped the export ladder recording a growth of 41.9% followed by gems and jewellery at 11.5%, tobacco and ice at 9.1% and readymade garments at 8.5% in 1992-93 over the previous year. However, gems and jewellery accounted for the largest share of the total exports of 16.6% followed by readymade garments (12.9%), chemicals and allied products (7.6%) cotton made-ups (7.4%) and leather and leather manufactures (6.9%).

Table 4.5

Composition of India's Imports

(Percentage Shares)

Commodity	*1994-95*	*1995-96*	*April-Sept. 1995-96*	*April-Sept. 1996-97*
1	2	3	4	5
1. Food and allied products, of which	5.8	3.6	3.8	3.6
1. Cereals	0.1	0.1	0.1	0.1
2. Pulses	0.7	0.6	0.6	0.5
3. Casheunuts	0.8	0.6	0.5	0.4
4. Edible oils	0.7	1.8	2.1	2.5
II. Fuel, of which	23.2	23.0	21.5	28.0
5. Coal	2.5	2.5	2.3	2.5
6. POL	20.7	20.5	19.2	25.5
III. Fertilisers	3.7	4.6	5.0	2.1
IV. Paper board, manufactures and newsprint	0.9	1.3	1.4	1.5
V. Capital goods, of which	26.5	27.8	27.7	25.0
7. Machinery except electrical and machine tools	9.5	10.7	10.3	10.6
8. Electrical machinery and electronic goods	5.2	5.8	5.5	4.6
9. Transport equipment	3.9	3.0	3.0	2.7
10. Project goods	6.5	6.5	7.2	5.1
VI. Others, of which	24.0	23.5	24.1	24.8
11. Chemicals	10.3	9.9	10.4	9.7
12. Pearls, precious and semi-precious stones	5.7	5.7	5.7	6.9
13. Iron and Steel	3.8	3.7	3.5	3.8
14. Non-ferrous metals	2.5	2.5	2.5	2.9
15. Professional instruments optical goods, etc.	1.7	1.8	1.9	1.5
VII. Unclassified items	16.1	161	16.6	15.1
Grand Total	100.00	100.00	100.00	100.00

Source: DGCI & S. Calcutta.

The import data reveals that the maximum growth was in cereal and cereal and cereal preparation (35.7%), electrical machinery (30.4%), transport equipment (24.3%) pearls and precious stones (23.7%), non-electrical machinery (15.7%), manufacture of metals (14.6%), non-ferrous metals (13.5%) and crude oil and products (11.2%).

Table 4.6
Growth of India's Imports by Commodity Groups

(US$ Million)

Commodity	*1991-92*	*1992-93*	*Apr.-Sept. 1992*	*Apr.-Sept. 1993*	*Apr.-Sept. 1992 (per cent change)*	*Apr.-Sept. 1993 (per cent change)*
1	2	3	4	5	6	7
I. Food and allied products, of which	430.7	702.9	274.9	211.9	63.2	–22.9
1. Cereals	70.3	320.1	83.0	64.1	355.1	–22.8
2. Pulses	103.6	109.1	59.2	62.5	5.3	5.6
3. Edible oils	100.5	59.5	35.6	14.3	–40.8	–60.0
II. Fuel, of which	5784.4	6576.2	3415.0	3259.4	13.7	–4.6
4. Coal	420.4	476.2	282.0	214.4	13.3	–24.0
5. POL	5364.0	6100.0	3133.0	3045.0	13.7	–2.8
III. Fertilisers	954.2	976.1	612.9	386.8	2.3	--36.9
IV. Paper board, manufactures & newsprint	197.9	166.6	58.4	85.3	–15.8	46.1
V. Capital goods, of which	4231.8	4463.1	2191.2	2496.1	5.5	13.9
6. Transport equipment	371.1	461.2	172.1	302.6	24.3	192.0
7. Project goods	1470.5	1194.7	633.9	579.8	–18.8	–8.5
VI. Others, of which	4585.6	5274.9	2724.6	2601.1	15.0	–4.5
8. Chemicals	15151.1	1619.8	924.1	628.0	6.9	–32.0
9. Pearls, precious and semi-precious stones	1957.1	2120.6	1164.3	1428.3	23.7	22.7
10. Iron & Steel	706.4	722.3	391.0	314.7	2.3	–19.5
11. Professional instruments, optical goods etc.	407.1	512.3	245.2	230.1	25.8	–6.1
VII. Unclassified items	3225.9	3722.2	1872.0	1751.0	15.4	–6.5
Grand Total	19410.5	21882.0	11149.1	10791.6	12.7	–3.2

Source: DGCI&S, Calcutta.

COMPOSITION OF INDIA'S EXPORTS

(PER CENT)

A - AGRICULTURE AND ALLIED PRODUCTS

B - ORES AND MINERALS

C - MANUFACTURED GOODS

D - CRUDE AND PETROLEUM PRODUCTS

E - OTHERS

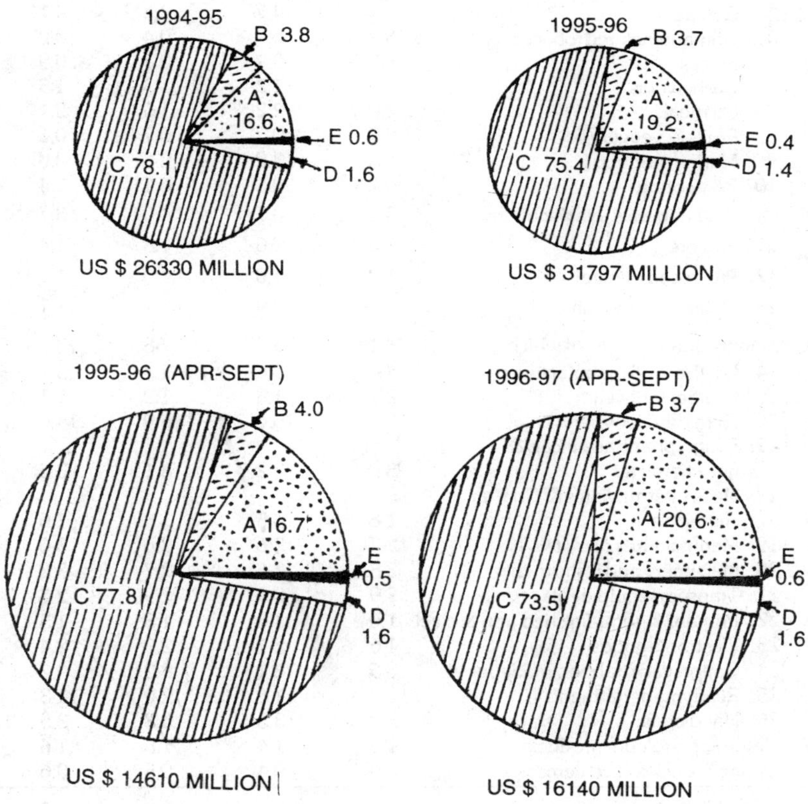

Fig. 4.1 Composition of India's Exports.

Table 4.7
Composition of Exports

(Percentage Shares)

Commodity Group	*1994-95*	*1995-96*	*Apr. - Sep. 1995-96*	*Apr. - Sep. 1996-97*
1	2	3	4	5
I. Agriculture & allied, of which	16.0	19.2	16.1	20.6
1. Tea	1.2	1.1	1.1	1.0
2. Coffee	1.3	1.4	1.6	1.6
3. Cereals	1.5	4.7	3.5	4.1
4. Unmanufactured tobacco	0.2	0.4	0.4	0.2
5. Spices	0.7	0.7	0.7	0.9
6. Cashewnuts	1.5	1.2	1.3	1.3
7. Oil meals	2.2	2.2	1.5	2.1
8. Fruits & vegetables	0.7	0.7	0.7	0.6
9. Marine products	4.3	3.2	2.8	3.0
10. Raw cotton	0.2	0.2	0.1	1.4
II. Ores and minerals, of which	3.8	3.7	4.0	3.7
11. Iron ore	1.6	1.6	1.8	1.4
12. Processed minerals	1.0	1.0	1.0	1.1
13. Other ores and minerals	1.0	0.9	1.1	1.1
III. Manufactured goods, of which	78.1	75.4	77.8	73.5
14. Leather and manufactures	4.0	3.6	3.8	3.1
15. Leather footwear	2.1	1.8	1.2	1.1
16. Gems and jewellery	17.1	16.6	16.9	14.0
17. Drugs, pharmaceuticals & fine chemicals	3.0	3.2	3.1	3.3
18. Dyes/intermediates & Coal tar chemicals	1.8	1.5	1.6	1.6
19. Manufactures of metals	2.7	2.6	2.6	3.0
20. Machinery and instruments	2.8	2.6	2.7	3.2
21. Transport equipments	2.9	2.9	2.9	2.7
22. Primary & semi-finished iron & steel	1.6	1.6	1.8	1.3
23. Electronic goods	1.6	2.1	2.0	2.4
24. Cotton yarn, fabrics, madeups etc.	8.5	8.1	8.2	9.2
25. Readymade garments	12.5	11.6	12.0	11.3
26. Handicrafts	3.9	3.5	3.8	3.5
IV. Crude & petroleum products	1.6	1.4	1.6	1.5
V. Others & unclassified items	0.6	0.4	0.5	0.6
Grand Total	100.0	100.0	100.0	100.0

Source: DGCI&S, Calcutta.

India's Imports

Imports reached a level of $ 21.9 billion during 1992-93 showing a growth of 12.7 per cent during that year. The current year is expected to end up with an import growth of less than four per cent. Imports during April-December 1993 were $ 16.4 billion as compared to $ 16.6 billion in the corresponding period of 1992. This represents a decline of 1.3 per cent. The overall trade deficit which stood at $ 3,556 million in April-December 1992 has dropped to $ 732 million during April-December 1993, showing an improvement of $ 2.8 billion.

POL imports reached a level of $6100 million during 1992-93 showing a growth of 20.9 per cent. During the first nine months of 1993-94, POL imports were $ 4,291 million representing a decline of 10.1 per cent over the corresponding period of previous year. Imports of POL have constituted an increasing share in total imports in the past few years. In 1989-90 they accounted for 17.8 per cent of total imports and this increased to 27.9 per cent in 1992-93 (Table 4.7 and Figure 4.2). During the first half of 1993-94, POL imports at $ 3,045 million accounted for 28.2 per cent of total imports. The increase in import share of POL has coincided with the decline in domestic production specially from offshore fields. It is important for balance of payment reasons to reverse the decline in domestic production. Other steps like rationalising the pricing structure of petroleum products, reducing subsidies and encouraging conservation through system of fiscal penalties and incentives will be required to bring down energy intensity in industry and agriculture.

Non-POL (DGCI&S) imports peaked in 1990-91 at a level of US$ 18.04 billion. These imports suffered a sharp decline of 22 per cent during 1991-92 as a consequence of import compression measures instituted in that year. They recovered in 1992-93 and grew by 8.7 per cent. During the first half of 1993-94, non-POL imports have declined by 3.6 per cent over the same period last year despite liberalisation of import policy and lowering of import duties. During the first nine months of the current year, non-POL imports have shown a growth of 2.2 per cent over the corresponding period of last year.

The composition of non-POL imports has remained virtually unchanged over the years. Capital goods, pearls, precious and semi-precious stones, chemicals, fertilisers and iron and steel together account for more than two-thirds of non-POL imports (Table 4.6). Imports of fertilisers, iron and steel and chemicals have declined during the first half of 1993-94. Consequently, the share of fertilisers has come down from 4.9 per cent in 1991-92 to 3.6 per cent during April-September 1993, of chemicals from 7.8 per cent to 5.8 per cent; and of iron and steel from 3.6 per cent to 2.9 per cent.

All such decline in imports cannot be explained away by pointing towards the slow recovery in industrial output. Fertiliser imports have declined as a result of decontrol of prices of phosphatic and potassic fertilisers, the resultant rise in prices and the subsidy in favour of domestic units. These imports will pick up again as the farmers revert to their use to

Table 4.8
Growth of India's Exports by Commodity Groups

(US $ million)

Commodity Group	1991-92	1992-93	Apr.-Sep. 1992-93	Apr.-Sep. 1993-94	Apr.-Sep. 1992-93 (per cent change)	Apr.-Sep. 1993-94 (per cent change)
1	2	3	4	5	6	7
1. Agriculture and allied of which	3193.5	3035.3	1338.3	1846.1	-5.0	37.9
1. Tea	491.5	335.8	158.1	164.5	-31.7	4.0
2. Tobacco manufactured	25.5	40.6	14.3	16.3	58.9	13.8
3. Oil meals	373.8	531.2	190.1	301.9	42.1	58.8
4. Sugar and molasses	63.8	37.1	21.5	46.5	41.8	116.3
5. Processed fruits and juices	33.8	42.9	21.7	23.7	26.9	9.1
6. Cotton raw incld. waste	124.1	67.5	8.1	164.7	-45.6	1920.9
II. Ores and minerals, of which	929.7	740.9	309.2	408.4	-20.3	32.1
7. Coal	6.1	17.6	2.8	3.9	188.6	40.4
III. Manufactured goods, of which	13325.5	14151.1	6567.8	7812.6	6.2	19.0
8. Leather and manufactures	804.9	867.2	427.3	410.4	7.7	-4.0
9. Footwear of leather	463.8	390.5	191.3	212.4	15.8	11.0
10. Gems and jewellery	2738.2	3051.9	1371.2	1875.0	11.5	36.7
11. Plastic and linoleum products	112.1	148.1	61.3	134.1	32.1	118.9
12. Manufactures of metals	484.2	585.5	251.3	325.7	20.9	29.6
13. Transport equipment	496.4	524.3	255.8	256.3	5.6	0.2
14. Iron and steel bar/ rod etc.	62.0	140.2	39.4	39.1	126.3	-0.7
15. Primary and semi-finished iron and steel	1299.3	1356.4	640.2	718.6	4.4	12.2
16. Readymade garments	2199.2	2388.7	1137.5	1215.7	8.6	6.9
17. Handicrafts	835.9	848.9	413.2	437.1	1.6	5.8
IV. Crude and petroleum products	414.7	476.2	237.2	236.7	14.8	-0.2
V. Others and unclassified items	2.0	17.1	82.0	47.3	743.8	-42.3
Grand Total	17865.4	18537.1	8534.6	10351.1	3.8	21.3

Source: DGCI&S, Calcutta.

correct the imbalance in use of nutrients. Imports of other commodities, which are largely in the nature of intermediate inputs, may have declined on account of weak industrial recovery but perhaps more so because of exchange rate changes. At the new exchange rates, domestic substitutes, whose quality is improving, have become more economical. Therefore, it appears that the decline in imports is attributable more to the exchange rate changes and lowering of import intensity of output rather than being primarily a result of industrial slowdown.

Direction of India's Trade

Direction of India's foreign trade has undergone a significant change with the collapse of Russian and some of the East European trading arrangements. This directional change both in exports and imports is reported in (Table 4.9 and Figures 4.3 and 4.4). Exports to Russia (former Soviet Union) accounted for as much as 16.1 per cent of India's total exports in 1990-91. This came down to 9.2 per cent in 1991-92 and further to 3.2 per cent in 1992-93. This decline continued during the first half of 1996-97 with exports to Russia now constituting only 2.4 per cent of total exports. The collapse of the Russian market has been a major shock to our export effort. However, exporters have demonstrated creditable flexibility and competitiveness in successfully switching exports to the General Currency Area and preventing the decline in exports to Russia from affecting the overall export performance. It is expected that as the Russian economy recovers and the working of the Indo-Russian Agreement is streamlined, exports to Russia will pick up in the second half of this year.

The data for the first half of 1996-97 indicate an increase in the share of developing countries, including OPEC, in India's exports. Their share increased to 27.7 per cent from 26.5 per cent in the first half of 1996-97 (Table 4.9 and Figure 4.3). The table reveals a substantial growth in dollar terms in India's exports to OPEC (24.8 per cent) and non-OPEC developing countries (54 per cent) during the first half of 1996-97. It may also be noted that exports to selected East Asian countries (Indonesia, Malaysia, Hongkong South Korea, Singapore, Thailand, and Chinese Tapei) have boomed, increasing on the average by 61 per cent in dollar terms during the first six months of 1993-94. The percentage export growth to these countries is about three times the overall export growth.

The share of foreign trade in the country's GNP has been rising over the years. It was 11.7 per cent in 1985-86, 14.5 per cent in 1990-91 and 16.9 per cent in 1992-93. In 1993-94 with plausible growth scenarios its share would be close to 19 per cent. It still remains one of the lowest in comparison with other developing countries (Table 4.11). With an increasing share in the country's GNP, foreign trade will have a more pervasive and significant effect on the country's economic performance in coming years than in the past. It is, therefore, important that trade performance and policies are now monitored closely and accorded high priority in policy making.

COMPOSITION OF INDIA'S IMPORTS

(PER CENT)

A - FOOD AND ALLIED PRODUCTS

B - FUEL

C - FERTILIZERS

D - PAPER BOARD, MANUF. AND NEWS PRINT

E - CAPITAL GOODS

F - OTHER BULK ITEMS

G - OTHERS

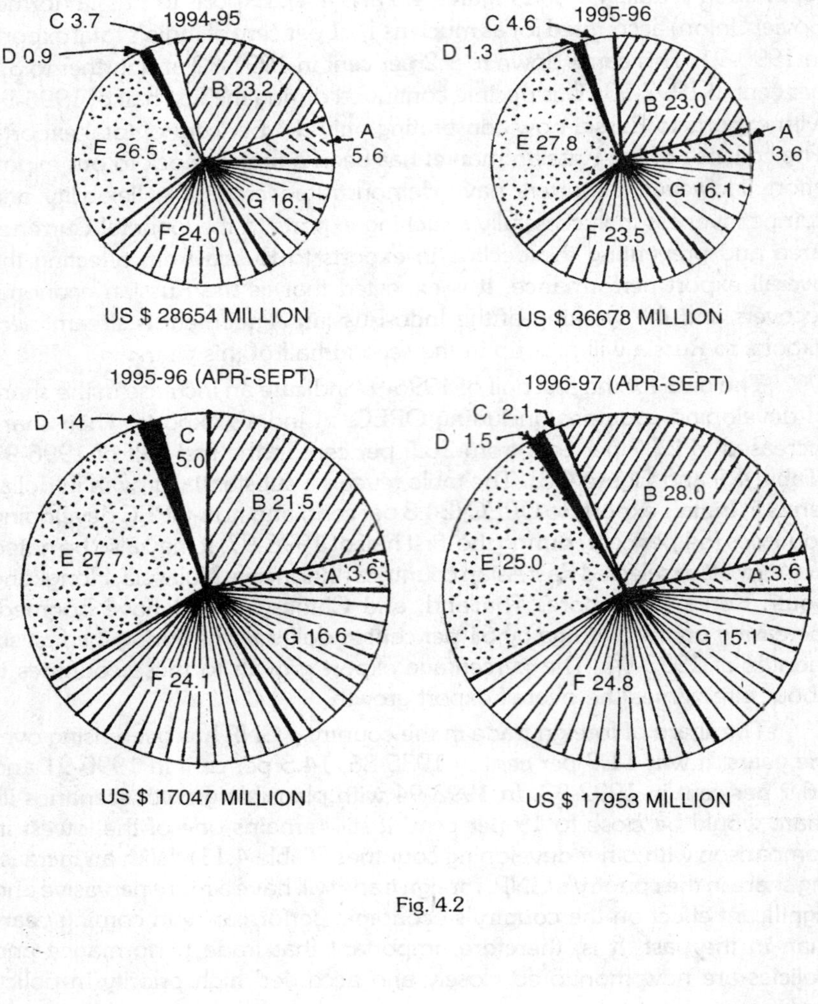

Fig. 4.2

DESTINATION OF INDIA'S EXPORTS
(PER CENT)

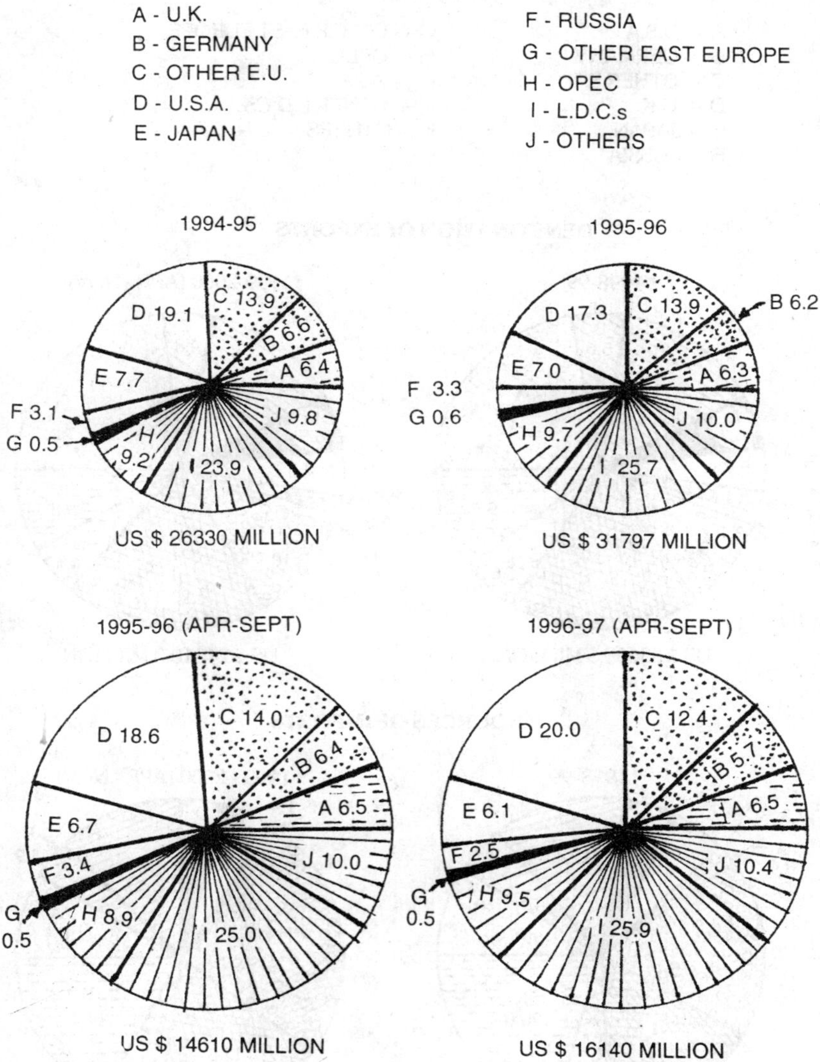

Fig. 4.3 Destination of India's Exports.

DIRECTION OF INDIA'S TRADE

(PER CENT)

A — U.S.A.
B — GERMANY
C — OTHER E.U.
D — U.K.
E — JAPAN
F — RUSSIA
G — OTHER EAST EUROPE
H — OPEC
I — ASIA
J — OTHER L.D.CS.
K — OTHERS

DENSTINATION OF EXPORTS

* 1998-99

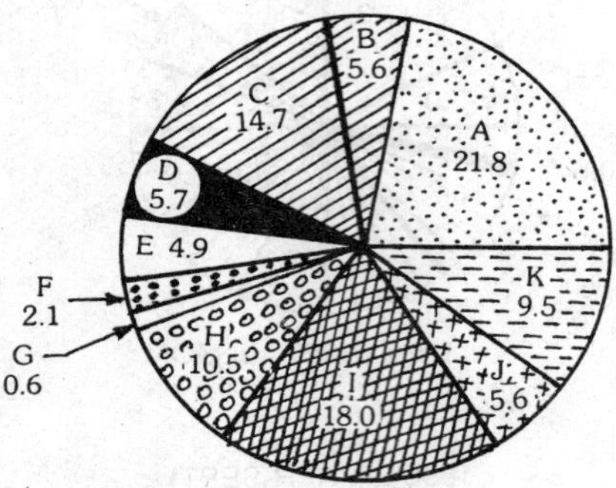

US $ 33658.5 MILLION

*1999-2000 (APR - NOV)

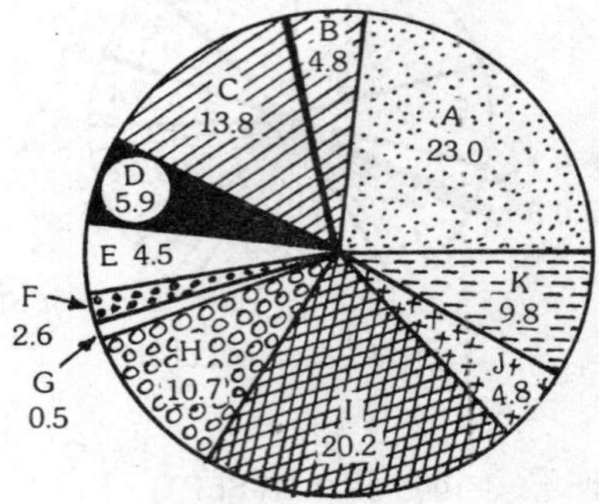

US $ 24210.3 MILLION

SOURCES OF IMPORTS

* 1998-99

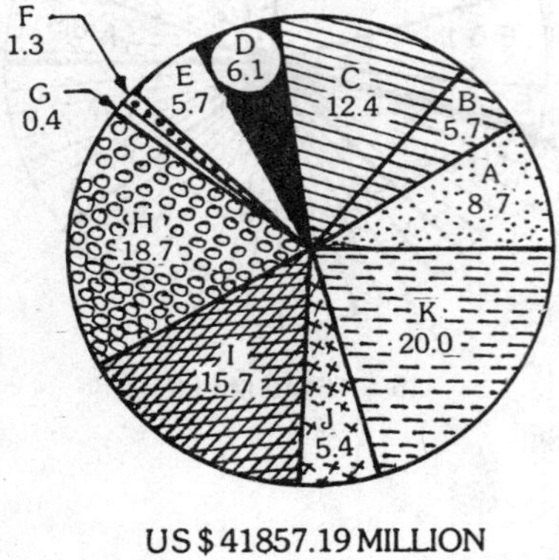

US $ 41857.19 MILLION

* 1999 - 2000 (APR - NOV)

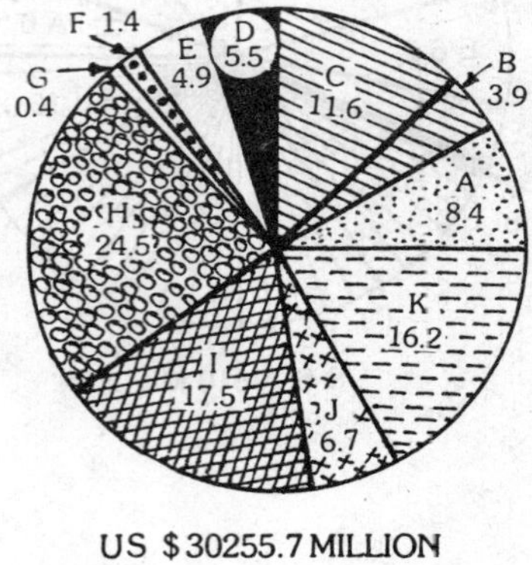

US $ 30255.7 MILLION

* PROVISIONAL

Fig. 4.4 Direction of India's Trade

SOURCES OF INDIA'S IMPORTS

(PER CENT)

A - U.K
B - GERMANY
C - OTHER E.U.
D - U.S.A.
E - JAPAN
F - RUSSIA
G - OTHER EAST EUROPE
H - OPEC
I = L.D.C.s
J = OTHERS

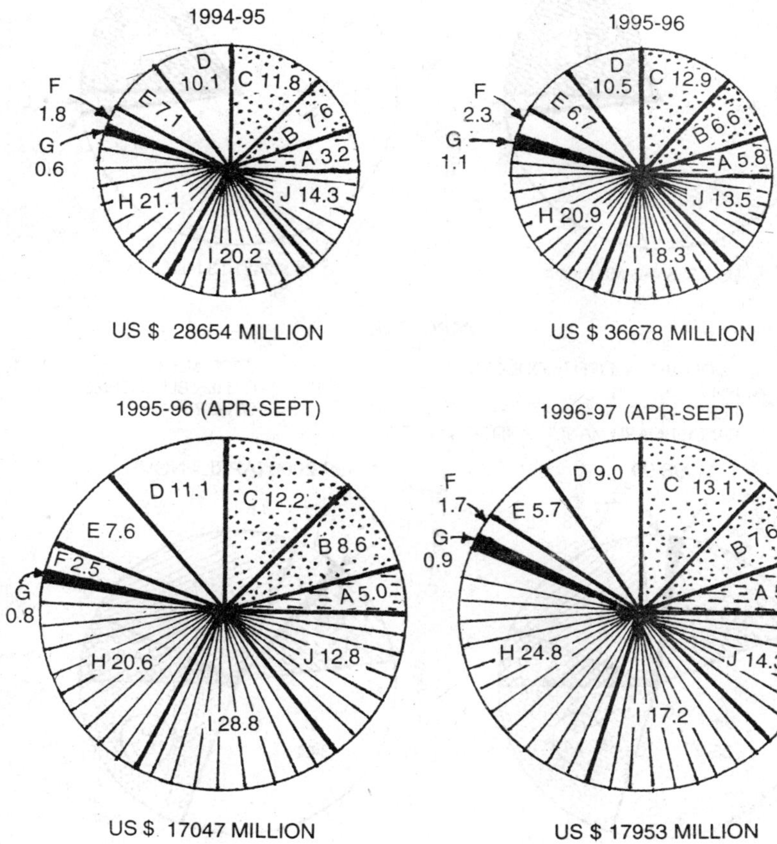

Fig. 4.4 Sources of India's Imports.

COMPOSITION OF EXPORTS & IMPORTS
(PER CENT)

EXPORTS

A — AGRICULTURAL AND ALLIED PRODUCTS
B — ORES AND MINERALS
C — MANUFACTURED GOODS
D — CRUDE AND PETROLEUM PRODUCTS
E — OTHERS

*1998-99

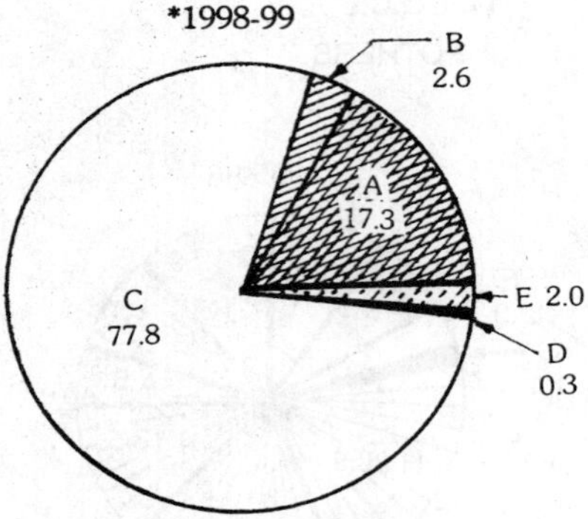

US $ 33658.5 MILLION

*1999-2000 (APR - NOV)

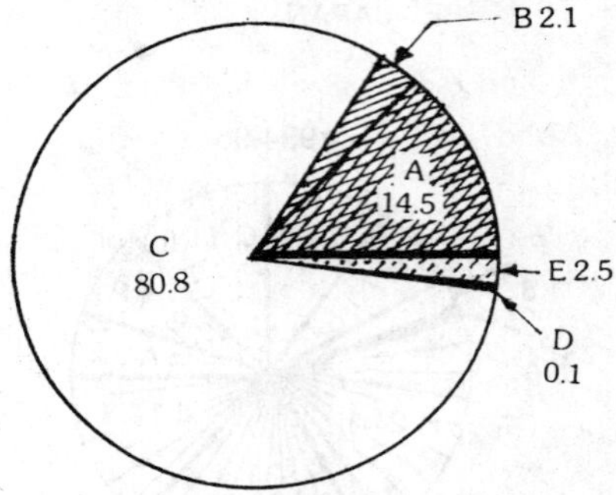

US $ 24210.3 MILLION

IMPORTS

A — FOOD AND ALLIED PRODUCTS
B — FUEL
C — FERTILISERS
D — PAPER BOARD MANUF. AND NEWSPRINT
E — CAPITAL GOODS
F — OTHER BULK ITEMS
G — OTHER

*1998-99

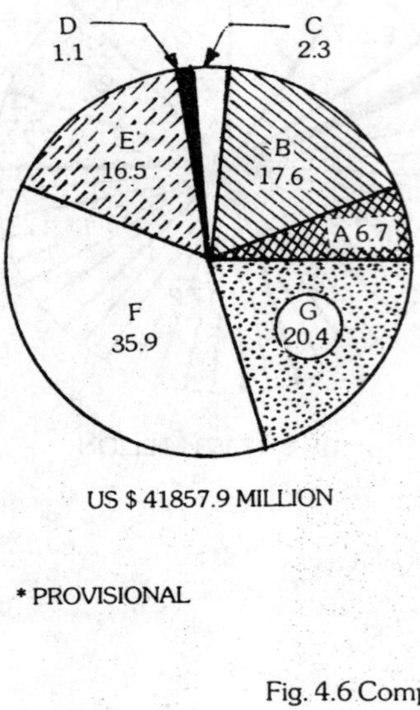

US $ 41857.9 MILLION

*1999-2000 (APRL - NOV)

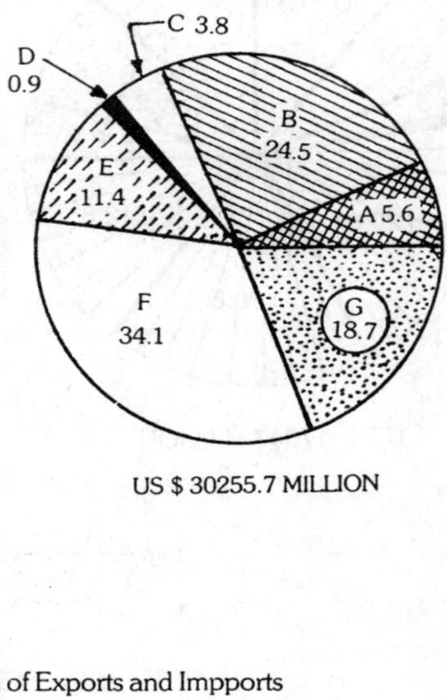

US $ 30255.7 MILLION

* PROVISIONAL

Fig. 4.6 Composition of Exports and Impports

36.6% of India's exports were directed to the countries of Asia and Oceania, 35.9% to Europe and 20.9% to America. Within Asia, and Oceanic region, the ESCAP countries shared the highest level of trade from India.

A major chunk of India's exports 49.63% was directed to six countries — USA (18.94%), Japan (7.79%), Germany (7.77%), U.K. (6.59%), UAE (4.41%), and Hongkong (4.13%). Most of the imports for India originated from the USA (9.77%) followed by Belgium (8.4%), Germany (7.59%), Saudi Arabia (6.87%), Japan (6.49%), UK (6.38%) and UAE (5.1%). India's consultancy exports have shot-up significantly from $36.6 million in 1980-81 to $ 286.92 million in 1992-93 clocking a growth of 18.49% during the period.

The import data reveals that the maximum growth was in cereal and cereal and cereal preparation (35.7%), electrical machinery (30.4%), transport equipment (24.3%), pearls and precious stones (23.7%), non-electrical machinery (15.7%), manufacture of metals (14.6%), non-ferrous metals (13.5%), and crude oil and products (11.3%).

Table 4.9
Direction of India's Trade

(Percentage Share)

	Exports				*Imports*			
Country	*1991-92*	*92-93 (Apr-Mar)*	*92-93*	*93-94 (Apr-Sep)*	*1991-92*	*92-93 (Apr-Mar)*	*92-93*	*93-94 (Apr-Sep)*
1	2	3	4	5	6	7	8	9
U.K.	6.4	6.5	7.4	6.3	6.2	6.3	6.6	6.9
Germany	7.1	7.7	7.5	6.9	8.0	7.5	8.3	7.3
Other EC countries	13.5	14.0	13.4	12.1	15.0	16.1	15.9	17.7
U.S.A.	16.4	18.8	19.5	18.6	10.3	9.7	10.1	10.4
Japan	9.2	7.7	7.7	7.7	7.1	6.4	4.3	5.8
Russia @	9.2	3.2	3.6	2.4	3.8	1.2	0.9	1.0
Other East Europe	1.8	1.1	1.3	0.9	1.4	1.4	1.4	0.6
OPEC	8.7	9.6	9.4	10.4	19.9	21.7	21.7	24.9
Other LDCs	17.5	20.3	19.4	24.3	17.1	15.1	15.5	13.7
Others	10.2	11.0	10.9	10.4	11.4	14.5	15.3	11.7
Total	100.00	100.00	100.00	100.00	100.00	100.00	100.00	100.00

@: Former Soviet Union for 1991-92.
Source: DGCI&S, Calcutta.

Table 4.10
Direction Of India's Trade With Selected East Asian Countries

(Percentage shares)

Country	Exports							Imports						
	1991-92	1992-93	1993-94	1994-95	1995-96	1995-96	1996-97	1991-92	1991-93	1993-94	1994-95	1995-96	1995-96	1996-97
	(April-March)					*(April-Sept.)*		*(April-March)*					*(April-Sept.)*	
A. Indonesia	0.8	0.7	1.1	1.1	2.1	1.6	1.5	0.3	0.3	0.5	1.1	1.3	1.1	1.5
B. Malaysia	1.1	1.0	1.1	1.1	1.2	1.2	1.5	2.0	1.9	1.1	1.7	2.5	2.6	3.0
C. Hong Kong	3.4	4.1	5.6	5.8	5.7	6.0	5.4	0.6	0.8	0.9	1.0	1.1	1.0	1.0
D. South Korea	1.4	0.9	0.9	1.3	1.4	1.3	1.5	1.7	1.6	2.4	2.2	2.2	2.3	1.9
E. Singapore	2.2	3.2	3.4	2.9	2.8	2.6	2.5	3.6	2.9	2.7	3.1	3.0	3.2	3.0
F. Thailand	1.1	1.4	1.6	1.5	1.5	1.5	1.3	0.3	0.3	0.2	0.9	0.5	0.5	0.5
G. Chinese Taipei	1.0	1.0	1.2	1.0	0.8	1.0	1.2	1.5	1.0	0.8	1.0	1.0	1.0	1.0
Total	11.1	12.3	14.9	14.6	15.6	15.1	14.9	9.9	8.8	8.6	11.1	11.5	11.7	11.9

Source: DGCI & S, Calcutta.

Direction of Trade with Selected Asian Countries

Post-liberalisation period opened new avenues for development of trade with emerging Asian markets. Table 4.10 provides a profile of direction of selected East Asian countries with their rising share year to year. Exports in aggregate increased from 11.1% in 1991-92 to 15.6% in 1995-96 and likely to be around 20% at the end of this century. Similarly, aggregate imports increased from 9.9% in 1991-92 to 11.5% in 1995-96, in South-East Asian countries in the table. Exports viewed that our imports may be around 22% in initial year of 21st Century with these countries. Hongkong, Singapore, Malaysia and China appear to be important countries as trade partners. Rising trade with South Asian block will provide to organise common forum and code of conduct within Asian countries by India. India's trade with SAARC countries increased notably during the last decade. Looking at the table, Hongkong, South Korea, Singapore and Malaysia appear to be strong trading partners. They are mutually useful and beneficial to India to expand business with such emerging markets. Diversified direction of trade has encouraged capital inflows from these countries. Foreign Direct Investment increased from US $ 0.05 billion to 2.16 billion in 1995-96. Similarly, Foreign Institutional investors have emerged as main source of such inflows a little over US $ 2 billion in 1995-96 from 1.5 in each of the preceding two years.

Table 4.11

Share of Merchandise Trade in GNP in Selected Countries, 1985-92

Country	*1985*	*1986*	*1987*	*1988*	*1989*	*1990*	*1991*	*1992*
1	2	3	4	5	6	7	8	9
India*	11.7	11.2	11.5	12.4	14.1	14.5	15.2	16.9
China	24.2	26.7	27.3	27.3	26.1	30.8	35.8	36.1
Malaysia	95.0	94.7	103.3	114.9	133.2	143.7	155.6	n.a
Mexico	20.6	23.2	25.4	24.4	23.9	24.7	23.4	23.1
Thailand	44.6	44.2	51.6	61.8	67.3	70.6	n.a	n.a
Indonesia	31.0	27.2	25.3	24.2	24.3	26.8	27.0	n.a
South Korea	68.4	64.5	68.4	65.2	58.6	55.7	54.6	53.8

* Data for India relates to financial years, April-March.

Source: IMF International Financial Statistics Year Book and Government of India.

India's Balance of Payments

The year saw a remarkable recovery in the balance of payments position. Exports have increased by 19.9 per cent in US dollar terms during April-December 1993. Imports have shown a decline of 1.3 per cent despite liberalisation of import policy and lowering of imports duties. The trade deficit at $ 732 million during April-December is less than a fifth of the level in 1992. By the end of the year, the trade deficit is expected to be about one billion dollars and a small surplus is expected on the invisible account. Based on this, the current account deficit in 1993-94 is likely to be less than 0.5 per cent of the GDP, the lowest since 1977-78.

Foreign currency reserves with the RBI stood at $ 10.9 billion on February 4, 1994. The year could end with reserves close to $ 12 billion. This represents nearly 6 months of import cover — as compared to 2 weeks of cover in May, 1991. The quality of these reserves has also significantly improved as outstanding swaps have been eliminated and short-term liabilities have been reduced.

A noteworthy feature of balance of payments situation is the response of foreign investors and portfolio managers to the policy reforms. Inflow of foreign investment at $390 million had almost doubled in 1992-93 over 1991-92. In the present year actual inflows were more than $ 1.7 billion by the end of December and are expected to exceed $ 2.5 billion by the end of the year. This comprises direct investment. Portfolio investment by foreign institutional investors and Euro-equity mobilised by Indian firms. If policy reforms are sustained and fiscal discipline maintained these private non-debt creating capital inflows can remain high.

The RBI has provided a revised format for data after 1990-91. However, the deficits in trade and current accounts of the balance of payments widened significantly after 1993-94. The current account of deficit, as a proportion of GDP rose from 0.5% in 1993-94 to 1.7% in 1995-96. Currency account deficit since 1993-94 reflects availability of foreign savings or external resources in order to bridge such higher savings-investment gap in our economy. Capital flows during 1993-94 and 1994-95 have not only financed the current account deficits but also led to a foreign currency assets build-up of US $ 14.4 billion. In actual practice, such assets increased from US $ 6.4 billion in 1992-93 to US $ 20.8 billion at the end of 1994-95. It is fact that foreign investment flows continued to dominate the capital account flows which helped to bring down pressure on current account and overall balance of payments in 1995-96. Foreign exchange management during the year played a vital role to reduce speculative pressures on exchange rate of rupee for tolerable situation in foreign exchange market. However, the Government of India made external payment worth of Rs. 10,761 for debt servicing, whereas, it picked to the level of Rs. 11,000 crores in 1996-97. Despite this, the net outflow was Rs. 2,772 crore in 1995-96 and gone down to Rs. 1,550 crore in 1996-97. Gross receipts of external aid increased from Rs. 7,989 crore which increased to Rs. 9,450 crore during the period. Thus, foreign exchange reserves and overall situation remained favourable during 1995-96 and 1996-97. However, the World Bank estimated that India will be required

Table 4.12
Direction of Trade: (A) Exports

(Rs. crore)
(percentage share)

		1960-61	1970-71	1980-81	1985-86	1989-90	1990-91	1991-92	1992-93	1960-61	1970-71	1980-81	1985-86	1989-90	1990-91	1991-92	1992-93
1	2	3	4	5	6	7	8	9	10	11	12	13	14	15	16	17	18
1	OECD	425	769	3126	5532	14743	17428	25481	32351	66.1	50.1	46.6	50.8	53.3	53.5	57.5	60.3
	of which:																
1.1	(*a*) EC																
	of which	232	282	1447	1929	6906	8951	11897	15166	36.2	18.4	21.6	17.7	25.0	27.5	27.0	28.2
1.1.1	(*i*) Belgium	5	20	145	255	1209	1259	1643	1962	0.8	1.3	2.2	2.1	4.4	3.9	3.7	3.7
1.1.2	(*ii*) France	9	18	147	203	638	766	1049	1351	1.4	1.2	2.2	1.9	2.3	2.4	2.4	2 5
1.1.3	(*iii*) Germany	20	32	385	513	1778	2549@	3131@	4149@	3.1	2.1	5.7	4.7	6.4	7.8	7.1@	7.7@
1.1.4	(*iv*) Netherlands	9	14	152	158	530	644	919	1202	1.3	0.9	2.3	1.5	1.9	2.0	2.1	2.2
1.1.5	(*v*) U.K.	173	170	395	524	1602	2128	2806	3513	26.9	11.1	5.9	4.8	.8	6.5	6.4	6.5
1.2	(*b*) North America	120	235	806	2106	4739	5077	7666	10659	18.7	15.3	12.0	19.3	17.1	15.6	17.4	19.9
1.2.1	(*i*) Canada	18	28	62	132	264	281	465	553	2.7	1.8	0.9	1.2	1.0	0.9	1.1	1.0
1.2.2	(*ii*) U.S.A	103	207	743	1974	4474	4797	7202	10106	16.0	13.5	11.1	18.1	16.2	14.7	16.4	18.8
1.3	(*c*) Other OECD	65	234	708	1304	3099	3401	4630	4916	10.1	15.2	10.6	12.0	11.2	10.4	10.5	9.2
	of which:																

Table 4.12 (Contd.)

1	2	3	4	5	6	7	8	9	10	11	12	13	14	15	16	17	18
1.3.1	(*i*) Australia	22	25	92	123	335	321	499	674	3.5	1.6	1.4	1.1	1.2	1.0	1.1	1.3
1.3.2	(*ii*) Japan	35	204	598	1164	2727	3039	4071	4153	5.5	13.3	8.9	10.7	9.9	9.3	9.2	7.7
II.	OPEC	26	99	745	835	1841	1831	3852	5156	4.1	6.4	11.1	7.7	6.7	5.6	8.7	9.6
	of which																
II.1	(*i*) Iran	5	27	123	95	132	141	302	329	0.8	1.7	1.8	0.9	0.5	0.4	0.7	0.6
II.2	(*ii*) Iraq	3	10	52	34	126	44	0	2	0.5	0.6	0.8	0.3	0.5	0.1	0.0	0.0
II.3	(*iii*) Kuwait	3	16	97	121	198	74	29	314	0.5	1.0	1.4	1.1	0.7	0.2	0.3	0.6
II.4	(*iv*) Saudi Arabia	3	15	165	221	429	419	866	1180	0.5	0.9	2.5	2.0	1.5	1.3	2.0	2.2
III.	Eastern Europe																
	of which:	45	323	1486	2294	5336	5819	4814	2276	7.0	21.0	22.1	21.1	19.3	17.9	10.9	4.2
III.1	(*i*) G.D.R.**	3	25	49	95	216	**	**	**	0.5	1.6	0.7	0.9	0.8	**	**	**
III.2	(*ii*) Romania	1	14	58	98	123	96	31	13	0.2	0.9	0.9	0.9	0.4	0.3	0.1	0.0
III.3	(*iii*) Russia@@	29	210	1226	2006	4463	5255	4043	1693	4.5	13.7	18.3	18.4	16.1	16.1	9.2	3.2
IV.	Others LDCs*																
	of which:	95	305	1286	1463	4246	5465	7712	10906	14.8	19.8	19.2	13.4	15.4	16.8	17.5	20.3
IV.1	(*i*) Africa	40	129	350	289	521	668	958	1411	6.3	8.4	5.2	2.7	1.9	2.1	2.2	2.6
IV.2	(*ii*) Asia	45	166	900	1156	3634	4665	6503	9091	6.9	10.8	13.4	10.6	13.1	14.3	14.8	16.9
IV.3	(*iii*) Latin America and Caribbean	10	10	36	18	93	132	251	403	1.6	0.7	0.5	0.2	0.3	0.4	0.6	0.8
V.	Others	51	40	68	771	1492	2010	2182	2663	8.0	2.6	1.0	7.1	5.4	6.2	5.0	5.0
VI.	Total	642	1535	6711	10895	27658	32563	44041	53688	100.0	100.0	100.0	100.0	100.0	100.0	100.0	100.0

Table 4.13

Direction of Trade (Contd.): (B) Imports

(Rs. crore)

(Percentage share)

		1960-61	1970-71	1980-81	1985-86	1989-90	1990-91	1991-92	1992-93	1960-61	1970-71	1980-81	1985-86	1989-90	1990-91	1991-92	1992-93
1	2	3	4	5	6	7	8	9	10	11	12	13	14	15	16	17	18
	OECD	875	1042	5740	10527	20224	23310	25943	35147	78.0	63.8	45.7	53.6	57.2	54.0	54.2	55.5
	of which																
1.1	(*a*) EC	417	320	2639	5234	11736	12680	13968	18976	37.1	19.6	21.0	26.6	33.2	29.4	29.2	39.7
	of which																
1.1.1	(*i*) Belgium	15	12	296	951	2696	2718	3422	5284	1.4	0.7	2.4	4.8	7.6	6.3	7.2	11.0
1.1.2	(*ii*) France	21	21	280	583	1612	1304	1516	1703	1.9	1.3	2.2	3.0	4.6	3.0	3.2	3.6
1.1.3	(*iii*) Germany	123	108	694	1544	2750	3473@	3846@	4776@	10.9	6.6	5.5	7.9	7.8	8.0@	8.0@	10.0@
1.1.4	(*iv*) Netherlands	11	19	215	296	549	793	689	1097	0.9	1.2	1.7	1.5	1.6	1.8	1.4	2.3
1.1.5	(*v*) U.K.	217	127	731	1251	2974	2894	2963	4016	19.4	7.8	5.8	6.4	8.4	6.7	6.2	8.4
1.2	(*b*) North America	347	570	1851	2515	4713	5804	5610	7285	31.0	34.9	14.7	12.8	13.3	13.4	11.7	15.2
1.2.1	(*i*) Canada	20	117	332	451	454	559	690	1138	1.8	7.2	2.6	2.3	1.3	1.3	1.4	2.4
1.2.2	(*ii*) U.S.A.	328	453	1619	2064	4260	5245	4919	6147	29.2	27.7	12.9	10.5	12.1	12.1	10.3	12.8
1.3	(*c*) Other OECD	80	122	932	2257	3775	4826	4988	6664	7.1	7.4	7.4	11.5	10.7	11.2	10.4	13.9
	of which																
1.3.1	(*i*) Australia	18	37	170	442	887	1464	1445	2411	1.6	2.2	1.4	2.2	2.5	3.4	3.0	5.0
1.3.2.	(*ii*) Japan	61	83	749	1774	2820	3245	3375	4081	5.4	5.1	6.0	9.0	8.0	7.5	7.1	8.5

Table 4.13 (cont.)

1	2	3	4	5	6	7	8	9	10	11	12	13	14	15	16	17	18
II.	OPEC	52	126	3488	3420	5074	7041	9499	13779	4.6	7.7	27.8	17.4	14.4	19.9	19.9	21.7
	of which:																
II. 1	(*i*) Iran	30	92	1339	885	390	1018	1435	1149	2.6	5.6	10.7	4.5	1.1	2.4	3.0	2.4
II. 2	(*ii*) Iraq	2	3	753	547	461	496	6	0	0.2	0.2	6.0	2.8	1.3	1.1	0.0	0.0
II. 3	(*iii*) Kuwait	0	6	338	340	1160	363	822	2765	0.0	0.3	2.7	1.7	3.3	0.8	1.7	5.8
II. 4	(*iv*) Saudi Arabia	14	24	540	794	1448	2899	3552	4330	1.3	1.5	4.3	4.0	4.1	6.7	7.4	9.0
III.	Eastern Europe	38	220	1296	2169	2990	3377	2444	1610	3.4	13.5	10.3	11.0	8.5	7.8	5.1	2.5
	of which:																
III. 1	(*i*) G.D.R.*	3	19	44	85	197	*	*	*	0.3	1.1	0.4	0.4	0.6	*	*	*
III. 2	(*ii*) Romania	5	17	97	144	106	50	62	159	0.4	1.0	0.8	0.7	0.3	0.1	0.1	0.3
III. 3	(*iii*) Russia@@	16	106	1014	1678	2038	2548	1796	745	1.4	6.5	8.1	8.5	5.8	5.9	3.8	1.6
IV.	Others LDCs**	132	239	1966	3466	6031	7965	8199	9592	11.8	14.0	15.7	17.6	17.1	18.4	17.1	15.1
	of which:																
IV. 1	(*i*) Africa	63	169	205	593	857	950	1961	2143	5.6	10.4	1.6	3.0	2.4	2.7	4.1	4.5
IV. 2	(*ii*) Asia	64	54	1431	2344	4452	6033	5365	6637	5.7	3.3	11.4	11.9	12.6	17.1	11.2	13.9
IV. 3	(*iii*) Latin America and Caribbean	5	16	313	529	723	974	873	813	0.4	1.0	2.5	2.7	2.0	2.8	1.8	1.7
V.	Others	25	8	60	75	1009	1505	1765	2795	2.2	0.5	0.5	0.4	2.9	3.5	3.7	4.4
VI.	Total	1122	1634	12549	19658	35328	43198	47851	63375	100.0	100.0	100.0	100.0	100.0	100.0	100.0	100.0

@ Figures for unified Germany.

* Included under F.R.G. (Item 1.1.3 above) with the reunification of Germany.

@@ Refers to former USSR before 1992-93.

** Excluding members of OPEC.

Source: DGCI & S, Calcutta.

total growth financing worth of 14 billion in 1997-98 and above $17 billion in subsequent years to building of reserves and modest current account deficit around 2% of the GDP.

The government has taken a conscious decision to reduce the quantum of short-term debt, especially components on which the exchange risk is to be borne by the RBI or government. The schemes under FCNR with less than one year maturity were withdrawn in May this year and those with maturity of one year and above but less than two years were withdrawn in October 1993. This measure, combined with others, including the elimination of the Foreign Currency (Banks and Others) Deposits Scheme in July last year, has resulted in a reduction of the share of short term debt in the total debt stock from 10.2 per cent in end March 1991 to 7.0 per cent by the end of March 1993. The increase in external debt in 1991-92 and 1992-93 has averaged about $3 billion per year, as compared to about $6 billion per year in the latter half of the eighties and over $8 billion in 1990-91. In the first half of 1993-94 the increase in external debt has been limited to less than $300 million. Major steps were taken during the year to promote exports. The Export-Import Policy announced on April 1, 1993, amended the existing policy to provide a greater thrust to exports from agriculture and labour intensive sectors in which the country has a strong comparative advantage. The negative list for exports was significantly pruned. A new Export Promotion Capital Goods Scheme permitting import of capital goods at a concessional 15 per cent duty rate was introduced for the services sector. EOU/EPZ units in agriculture and allied sectors were allowed to sell up to 50 per cent of their total output in the domestic market. During the year, the minimum export price for basmati rice was eliminated and export restrictions on superior quality of wheat were relaxed. Fiscal and financial policy was also deployed to support the export effort. The budget reduced import duties on capital goods used in textiles, readymade garments, leather, marine products, gems and jewellery, food processing and horticulture. The pre-shipment credit facility in foreign currency was greatly liberalised, thus, providing Indian exporters credit at internationally competitive rates of interest. A number of steps were taken to strengthen facilities and incentives available for export through Export Processing Zones, 100 per cent Export Oriented Units and Electronic Hardware Technology Parks.

The recently concluded Uruguay Round should enable India to expand its exports to developed country markets where tariffs will be further reduced. The phase out of the Multi-Fibre Arrangement over 10 years will enable our garment and textile exporters to increase their market shares in product categories where they have a competitive advantage. Similarly, the reduction of subsidies to agriculture in developed countries will benefit our emerging exports of agricultural and allied products. India will also benefit from a stronger multilateral discipline on unilateral measures which restrict trade. The successful conclusion of the Uruguay Round should strengthen the multi-lateral trading order which is in the overall interests of India and other developing economies.

Table 4.14

Balance of Payments

	1960-61		*1970-71*		*1980-81*		*1985-86*	
	Rs. Crore	*U.S. $ Million*	*Rs. Crore*	*U.S. $ Million*	*Rs. Crore*	*U.S. $ Million*	*Rs. Crore*	*U.S. $ Million*
1	2	3	4	5	6	7	8	9
1. Imports (c.i.f.)	1106	2323	1826	2435	12544	15862	21164	17298
(*a*) PL 480 Title I	185	389	50	67	—	—	—	—
(*b*) Others	921	1934	1776	2368	12544	15862	21164	17298
2. Exports (f.o.b.)	631	1325	1405	1873	6576	8316	11578	9463
3. Trade balance (2-1)	–475	–998	–422	–562	–5967	–7546	-9586	-7835
4. Non-monetary gold movement (net)		—	13	18	—	—	29	23
5. Invisibles								
(*a*) Receipts	260	546	496	662	5890	7449	7875	6437
(*b*) Payments	177	372	533	711	1580	1998	4245	3470
(Of which: Interest & service payments on loans and credits)	(34)	(71)	(204)	(272)	(282)	(357)	(1372)	(1121)
(*c*) Net	83	174	–37	–49	4311	5451	3630	2967
6. Current account (net)	–392	–824	–445	–594	–1657	–2095	–5927	-4845
7. Capital transactions								
(*a*) Private								
(*i*) Receipts	52	108	80	107	163	206	2567	2098
(*ii*) Payments	35	74	60	80	66	83	213	174
(*iii*) Net	17	35	20	27	97	123	2354	1924
(*b*) Government miscellaneous								
(*i*) Receipts	147	309	324	432	1011	1278	2233	1825
(*ii*) Payments	42	88	353	471	1247	1577	896	732
(*iii*) Net	105	221	–30	–39	–236	–298	1337	1093
(*c*) Amortisation payments (Gross)	–38	–79	–232	–309	–691	–874	–1465	–1198
(*d*) Rupee Debt Service*	—	—	—	—	—	—	—	—
(*e*) Repurchases from IMF	–11	–23	–154	–205	–8	–10	–253	–207
(*f*) Banking capital (net)	10	20	0	0	13	16	186	152
8. Errors & omissions	–6	–13	–67	–89	–158	–200	580	474
9. Total Surplus (+) or Deficit (-) (6 to 8)	–316	–663	–907	–1210	–2640	–3338	–3188	–2605
Financed By:								
10. External assistance loans	257@	539	743 @	991	1729**	2186	2481	3028
11. Drawings from IMF (gross)	—	—	—	—	274	347	—	—
12. Allocation of SDRs	—	—	75	101	121	152	—	—
13. Decline (+) or increase (–) in reserves	59	124	89	118	516	653	707	577
Total (10 to 13)	316	663	907	1210	2640	3338	3188	2605

Table 4.14 (Contd.)

	1987-88		1988-89		1989-90		1990-91	
	Rs. crore	*U.S.$ million*	*Rs. crore*	*U.S.$ million*	*Rs. crore*	*U.S.$ million*	*Rs. crore*	*U.S.$ million*
1	10	11	12	13	14	15	16	17
1. Imports (c.i.f.)	25693	19816	34202	23618	40642	24411	50086	27915
(*a*) PL 480 Title I	—	—	—	—	—	—	—	—
(*b*) Others	25693	19816	34202	23613	40642	24411	50086	27915
2. Exports (f.o.b.)	16396	12646	20647	14257	28229	16955	33153	18477
3. Trade balance (2-1)	–9296	–7170	–13556	–9361	–12413	–7456	–16934	–9438
4. Non-monetary gold movement (net)	—	—	—	—	6	4	—	—
5. Invisibles								
(*a*) Receipts	9279	7156	10926	7545	12484	7498	13394	7465
(*b*) Payments	6275	4840	8951	6181	11459	6883	13829	7707
(Of which: Interest & service payments on loans and credits)	(1949)	(1503)	(3731)	(2576)	(5095)	(3060)	(4958)	(2763)
(*c*) Net	3004	2317	1976	1364	1025	616	–435	–242
6. Current account (net)	–6293	–4853	–11580	–7996	–11382	–6837	–17369	–9680
7. Capital transactions								
(*a*) Private								
Receipts	3881	2993	7432	5132	11375	6832	10564	8395
Payments	966	745	2521	1741	6191	3719	10710	5969
Net	2914	2248	4911	3391	5183	3113	4354	2426
(b) Government miscellaneous								
Receipts	8499	6555	9466	6536	12015	7117	18594	10363
Payments	4838	3731	3572	2466	6153	3696	7383	4115
Net	3661	2824	5894	4070	5862	3521	11211	6248
(*c*) Amortisation payments (Gross)	–3611	–2785	–3924	–2710	–3773	–2266	–5725	–3190
(*d*) Rupee Debt Service*	—	—	—	—	—	—	–2140	–1193
(*e*) Repurchases from IMF	–1209	–933	–1547	–1068	–1460	–877	–1156	–644
(*f*) Banking capital (net)	75	58	–265	–183	59	36	–1134	–632
8. Errors & omissions	–948	–731	203	141	–720	–433	237	132
9. Total Surplus (+) or Deficit (–) (6 to 8)	–5410	–4173	–6309	–4357	–6231	–3742	–11721	–6533
Financed by:								
10. External assistance loans	4454	3435	4860	3356	4998	3002	6095	3397
11. Drawings from IMF (gross)	—	—	—	—	—	—	3334	1858
12. Allocation of SDRs	—	—	—	—	—	—	—	—
13. Decline (+) or increase (–) in reserves	956	738	1449	1001	1232	740	2293	1270
Total (10 to 13)	5410	4173	6309	4357	6231	3742	11721	6533

* As per the new balance of payments format starting from 1990-91

** Includes loan of Rs. 544.5 crore from the IMF Trust Fund.

@ Includes rupee loans under PL-480 Title-I. Figures from 1980-81 onwards are preliminary.

Notes.

1 Figures given in this table for some items of capital account do not correspond to similar statistics published by Reserve Bank of India. The difference is due to adjustments made in respect of loan drawings under external assistance and repayment thereof. The presentation of balance of payments statistic in the above table differs from the adjusted balance of payments statistics published in the previous issues of the Economic Survey.

2. The Rupee equivalent of all foreign currency transactions has been arrived at by applying the par/central rates up to June 1972 and thereafter on the basis of the average of RBI's spot buying and selling rate for sterling and the monthly averages of cross-rates based on London market for non-sterling currencies.

3. Grants received are covered under item 5 (a).

4. U.S. Embassy expenditures out of PL-480 counterpart funds are included under item 5 (a).

5. Receipts by way of loans by the private sector including loans out of Cooley Fund and amortization payments thereof are excluded from items 7 (a) (i) and 7 (a) (ii) and included under item 10 and 7 (c) respectively.

6. Receipts by way of loans received by the official sector under the External Assistance Programmes including Rupee loans out of PL-480 Title-I and corresponding amortization payments are excluded from item 7(b) (i) and 7 (b) (ii) and are shown under items 10 and 7 (c) respectively.

7. The movements in PL-480 Rupee balances are included under item 7 (b).

8. Since October-December 1986, data on credits under private long term capital and official loans include borrowings made to prepay earlier loans; debits against private long-term capital and official amortization cover such prepayments.

9. The balance of payments data in 1990-91 is based on new format as explained in Chapter 5.

Source: Reserve Bank of India.

Recent Trends in India's Foreign Trade

Encouraged by a growth of over 21% in the first 11 months of 1993-94, the commerce ministry of the Government of India plans to step-up exports by 25% in dollar terms during 1994-95, Exports in the first 11 moths (April 1993 to Feb 1994) have exceeded the $ 20 billion mark, with exports in February increasing by over $ 2 billion.

The target of $ 22.14 billion fixed for 1993-94 hopefully have already exceeded as exports in March invariably show a considerable rise over the previous months because exporters try to maximise shipments in the month of March generally. As already indicated exports in 1992-93 had amounted to $ 18.53 billion. Therefore, if a 25% growth in exports is planned for 1994-95 their target may have to be fixed around $ 27 billion.

Areas like textiles, agriculture and allied products, leather and leather goods, germs and jewellery as well as processed foods, are expected to improve further their export performance during 1994-95. Textiles exports in the first 10 months of the year 1993-1994, for instance, have gone up by 21.6% over the same period of 1992-93.

The Government of India is giving priority to exports to increase foreign exchange earnings. Apart from ensuring availability of inputs going into export production at competitive prices, steps have already been initiated to simplify procedures.

The amendments to the Exim Policy (1992-97) announced by the commerce ministry, are basically designed to provide a more conducive climate for enhanced exports. In order to simplify procedures and decentralise powers for giving licences within a time frame, the four regional offices of the Director General of Foreign Trade at Bombay, Calcutta, Delhi and Madras, will be authorised to issue licences under the EPCG Scheme.

Foreign Trade Ministry has recently announced the Exim Policy (1997-2002) for the years of the ninth five-year plan which is very progressive making tuning with diversification of Indian export marketing. Special efforts are made to develop trade with Asian countries and with emerging market countries.

Export Growth

The composition of exports has shown increase in the case of manufactured item which have consolidated from 75.4% in 1995-96 to 77.8% in 1998-99 and it is estimated about 80% in 1999-2000. The share of agriculture and allied producers was 20.4% in 1996-97 declined to 17.3% in 1998-99. In dollar terms, it fell from 16% to 11.7% during the period. This has happened largely due to declines in dollar value of 1.8% in the corresponding period of last year. Fastest growing commodities are cashew nuts, transport equipment, iron and sted, gems and jewellery, handicraft and electronics goods.

Direction of Exports

USA, EU and Japan are main areas of Indian exports. Africa and Latin American regions increased by 9.5 and 9.2% respectively. OECD countries increased their share from 55.7% in 1997-98 to 58% in 1998-99. Exports to the many developed countries declined include UK (-10.9%) Australia (-11.1%), Germany (-2.1%), Netherlands (-2.8%). Sizeable exports growth visualised in the case of USA (7.8%), Canada (10.1%), France (10.9%), Belgium (6.7%) during 1998-99. Exports to East Europe declined by 18.6% due to reduction in exports to Russia. A decline in exports to east Asia due to the Asian crisis.

Imports Growth

Imports in US value shows a downtrend, it has declined from 6% in 1997-98 to 0.9% in 1998-1999. This has happened largely due to decline in oil import bill and softening of oil prices at international levels. Growth in non-oil imports thus decelerated from 14.5% in 1997-98 to 6.3% in 1998-

TABLE 4.15

Balance of Payments: Summary

(in US $ million)

	1990-91 (P)	1993-94 (P)	1994-95 (P)	1995-96 (P)	1996-97 (P)	1997-98 (P)	1998-99 (P)	(Apr-September) 98-99 (P)	99-00 (P)
1. Exports	18477	22683	26855	32311	34133	35680	34298	16515	17808
2. Imports	27915	26739	35904	43670	48948	51187	47544	24663	25339
Of which : POL	6028	5754	5928	7526	10036	8164	6433	2910	4460
3. Trade Balance	**-9438**	**-4056**	**-9049**	**-11359**	**-14815**	**-15507**	**-13246**	**-8148**	**-7531**
4. Invisibles (net)	-242	2898	5680	5449	10196	10007	9208	5009	4073
Non-factor services	980	535	602	-197	726	1319	2165	1073	36
Investment income	-3752	-3270	-3431	-3205	-3307	-3521	-3544	-1412	-1848
Pvt. transfers	2069	5265	8093	8506	12367	11830	10280	5234	5762
Official Grants	461	368	416	345	410	379	307	114	123
5. Current Account Balance	**-9680**	**-1158**	**-3369**	**-5910**	**-4619**	**-5500**	**-4038**	**-3139**	**-3458**
6. External assistance (net)	2210	1901	1526	883	1109	907	820	-46	113
7. Commercial borrowing (net)@	2248	607	1030	1275	2848	3999	4362	4328	62
8. IMF (net)	1214	187	-1143	-1715	-975	-618	-393	-199	-156
9. Non-resident deposits (net)	1536	1205	172	1103	3350	1125	1742	46	932
10. Rupee debt service	-1193	-1053	-983	-952	-727	-767	-802	-588	-521
11. Foreign investment (net) of which:	103	4235	4807	4615	5963	5353	2312	868	2406
(i) FDI (net)	97	586	1228	1954	2651	3525	2380	1408	1057
(ii) FIIs	0	1665	1503	2009	1926	979	-338	-601	954
(iii) Euro equities & others	6	1984	2076	652	1386	849	270	61	395
12. Other flows (net) +	2284	2800	2604	-2235	-1131	-606	-174	-1352	1411
13. Capital account total (net)	8402	9882	8013	2974	10437	9393	7867	3057	4247
14. Reserve use (-increase)	1278	-8724	-4644	2936	-5818	-3893	-3829	82	-789

(P): Preliminary Actuals.

@ Figures include receipts on account of India Development Bonds in 1991-92 and Resurgent India Bonds in 1998-99 and related repayments, if any, in the subsequent years.

\+ Include, among others, delayed export receipts and errors and omissions.

Source: Economic Survey: 1999-2000, Government of India New Delhi p. 87.

Table 4.16

Selected Indicators of External Sector

Item/Years	1990-91	1993-94	1994-95	1995-96	1996-97	1997-98	1998-99	1999-00 (Apr-Sept)
1. Growth of Exports - BOP (%)	9.0	20.2	18.4	20.3	5.6	4.5	-3.9	7.8
2. Growth of Imports - BOP (%)	14.4	10.0	34.3	21.6	12.1	4.6	-7.1	2.7
(a) of which, POL (%)	60.0	-5.7	3.0	27.0	33.4	-18.7	-21.2	53.3
3. Exports/Imports - BOP (%)	66.2	84.8	74.8	74.0	69.7	69.7	72.1	70.3
4. Import cover of FER (No. of months)	2.5	8.6	8.4	6.0	6.5	6.9	8.2	7.9
5. External assistance (net) TC (%)	26.3	19.2	19.0	29.7	10.6	9.7	10.4	2.7
6. ECB (net)/TC (%)	26.8	6.1	12.9	42.9	27.3	42.6	55.4	1.5
7. Non-resident deposits/TC (%)	18.3	12.2	2.1	37.1	32.1	12.0	22.1	21.9
8. Short-term debt/FER (%)	146.5	18.8	16.9	23.2	25.5	17.2	13.5	13.9
9. Debt service payments as % of current receipts	35.3	25.6	26.2	24.3	21.2	19.1	18.0	18.7
				As per cent of GDP pmp				
10. Exports	6.2	8.3	8.4	9.2	8.9	8.8	8.2	
11. Imports	9.4	9.8	11.2	12.4	12.8	12.6	11.3	
12. Trade balance	-3.2	-1.5	-2.8	-3.2	-3.9	-3.8	-3.1	
13. Invisible balance	-0.1	1.1	1.8	1.6	2.7	2.4	2.2	
14. Current account balance	-3.2	-0.4	-1.0	-1.7	-1.2	-1.4	-1..0	-1.5*
15. External Debt	30.4	33.8	30.9	27.1	24.7	24.4	23.5	22.3@
16. Debt Service Payments	3.0	3.1	3.4	3.4	3.0	2.7	2.6	

* Annualised; @ Debt stock at end September, 1999 as a per cent of estimated GDP for 1999-2000.

Notes:

(i) TC: Total capital flows (net).

(ii) FCB: External Commercial borrowing.

(iii) FER: Foreign exchange rserves, Including gold and SDRs.

(iv) GDPmp: Gross domestic product at current market prices.

(v) As total capital flows are netted after taking into account some capital otuflows, the ratios against item no. 5,6 and 7 may, in some years, add up to more than 100 per cent.

(vi) Growth rate of exports and imports during April-Sept. 1999 are growth rates over April-Sept. 1998.

(vii) Rupee equivalents of BOP components are used to arrive at GDP ratios. All other percentages shown in the upper panel of the table are based on US dollar values.

Source: As per table No. 1

99. Industrial recovery in India had no impact on import rise. On the contrary in the case of capital goods imports declined due to restrictions on import of second hand capital goods. Due to liberalisation on gold and silver imports, they increase from $ 3.2 billion in 1997-98 to 4.9 billion in 1998-99. Decline in world prices of gold resulted many central banks to sell their gold reserves. Moreover, Union budget announced Gold Deposit Scheme 1999 to draw out privately held gold so as to reduce imports of gold.

Commodity-wise composition of imports reveals higher share of POL (54.3%), fertilizers (53.5%), wood and wood products and chemicals (4%) but in value chemical imports occupy larger share.

Balance of Payment

It can be observed from Table No. that trade balance has declined from US $ 15,507 in 1997-98 to US $ 13,246. Some trend is visualised sum April-Sept. 1999-2000. In 1998-99, current Account balance was US $ (-) 9,680 in 1990-91 which declined to (-) 4619 in 1996-97 as again US $ (-) 5,500 in 1997-98 and again it remained at US $ (-) 4,038 in 1998-99. Looking to capital account Indian balance of payment was $ 8,402 in 1990-91 to $ 10,437 1996-97 and $ 7,867 in 1998-99. As against this, reserve use indicate in 1990-91 $ 1,278 which declined to US $ (-) 3,829 in 1998-99. However, FDI net investment, but investments of FII declined US $ 1,665 in 1990-91 to US $ (-) 338 in 1998-99. Similarly, Euro equities and others decline from US $1,984 in 1990-91 to $ 270 in 1998-99. Thus, foreign investment in US $ declined in post-liberalisation period inspite of several steps taken by Government of India to boost foreign investment in India.

It is interesting to note that private transfer in India increased sizeably in $ terms from $ 2,069 in 1990-91 to $ 12,367 in 1996-97 and declined to $ 10,280 in 1998-99. However, due to financial crisis in Asia in July 1997 situation of balance of payment remained unfavourable all over the world. Indias balance of payment remained comfortable in both 1998-99 and 1999-2000.

It can be observed from Table No. 2 that the deficit in trade account of Balance of Payment declined 1% of GDP in 1998-99 as against 1.4% in 1997-98. Exports growth rate declined from 9% 1990-91 to - 3.9% in 1998-99, external assistance declined from 26.3% to 10.4% during the period. Short-term debt declined from 146.5 to 13.5 and debt services payment as percentage of current receipt declined from 35.3 to 18.0. External commercial borrowing increased from 26.8% to 55.4% during the period. Foreign currency reserves were $ 29.52 million in 1998-99 which climbed to about $ 36.00 billion in 1999-2000 as exchange rate remained stable. Exchange rate depreciation of Indonesian Rupiah since crisis to February 1999 was 17.6% to 65.8%, 32% in Thai baht, 35% in the Philippines peso, 33.8% of

Malaysian Ringgit, 21.8% of the Korean Won and 14.8% of Singapore dollar provided increased export markets and import competition in domestic markets of India. The slowdown and contraction of world trade positively affected Indian Balance of Payment during 1998-99 and 1999-2000.

BUDGETARY ACTIONS IN UNION BUDGET 1999-2000:

For managing global trade and conserving balance of payment situation following measures were taken by the Union Budget:

(1) Rationalisation of export-import duty structure and excise duty structure. Reduction in the 7 existing major ad valorem rates of customs to 5 basic rates.

(2) Special incentives provided to software sector known as information technology sector in terms of reduction in duty rates for critical inputs.

(3) Higher R & D incentives and establishment of a Technology Upgradation Fund Scheme.

(4) Entertainment industry permitted for tax benefits under Section 80 HHC to the exports of goods and services.

(5) New Gold Deposit Scheme under which selected banks permitted to accept gold deposits and issue intensive bearing bonds.

(6) Revamped export credit scheme in foreign currency to revitalise exports for preshipment and post-shipment credit needs with simplification of procedure.

(7) Setting up of high power committed to investigate high transaction for exporters to get suggestions to reduce such costs.

Measures Announced in Annual Exim Policy:

(i) Removal of quantitative restrictions, imports of 894 items made license free another 414 items against special import license.

(ii) A new chapter added on policy to boost export of services.

(iii) Free Trade Zones considered as outside the country's custom territory.

(iv) Duty Exemption Scheme made more flexible on the basis of self certificate.

(v) Zero duty export promotion capital goods with lower threshold limit of Rs. one crore extended to chemicals and textiles.

(vi) Entitlement of domestic tariff area sales for export oriented units.

(vii) Gem and jewellery sector permitted import and re-export through courier, personal carriage or diamond interest license for global business issue.

(viii) SAARC countries granted wide ranging concessions on preferential basis in custom duties on imports by ministry of Finance.

Emerging Export Markets

A sustainable higher rate of exports is a crucial element in Indian balance of payment situation and for stability also. Structural changes in global economy compel Indian economy to search for markets in emerging areas. Global competition for export drive led Indian economy to plan for hunting emerging markets of Asia and Latin America. However, events like disintegration of USSR, replacement of military alliances and blocks by economic and market alliances like EC and NAFTA opened new avenues and challenges to boost exports. Economic competition is replacing the cold war and new battle for export marketing place.

Emerging trade blocks like European Economic Community (EEC), European Economic Area (EEA), Asian Free Trade Association (AFTA) and North-American Free Trade Association (NAFTA) and many such other association formed in era of new World Trade Order (W.T.O.). In such a situation Indian Textile industry will have to face competition from Mexico. The same is the case with other export products also. A suitable export strategy is required for India so as to increase aggregate share of India in world trade which fell from 1.6% in 1960-61 to 0.6% in 1991-92. This has happened largely due to following factors which are overlooked:

1. Absence of historical common bonds, shared culture and colonial period not allowed to develop trade contracts or relationship between India and emerging markets.

2. Even language problem and legal system and commercial practices not allowed India to develop trade with Latin American and other countries. Indian exporters are without adequate market information and unable to undergo risk experimenting with unknown markets.

3. Political situation in the fifties, the sixties, and the seventies even in the eighties in the case of African countries was full of risk for Indian exporters.

4. Geographical distance in the case of Europe, Middle East and Far East with quick cargo facilities inhibited the growth of Indian exports.

5. Export competition adversely, affected underdeveloped countries like India largely due to agro-based export composition which consisted of primary agricultural, plantation, or mineral products in emerging markets and India.

6. Monetary factors like higher rate of inflation, large external borrowing, weaker currencies, devaluation of currencies, fluctuation in exchange rates could not encourage to boost exports from Indian exporters.

7. Due to tight fiscal policies for exporters, sometimes heavy tariff played vital role to block Indian exports. Post-liberalisation period after 1991 opened new avenues for export promotion and export market development.

8. Banking facility and convertibility of currencies was absence in initial decades of Indians independent which made restriction for trade between the south block and the north block of world trade.

Size of the market, size of the population, market segments like higher income and high purchasing power in the case of consumer goods marketing, rising volume of export trade with nations, inspite of United Front government consisted of different political parties welcomed peaceful co-existence and the best economic programme for political survival led liberalised export policy in the recent past. This phenomena compelled small, medium and large scale manufacturing units to go in for export business development in India.

Moreover, India attempted to develop cordial trade relation with SAARC countries so as to settle with crisis of external payment through export growth. Current Account convertibility of rupee from 1991 and still capital account convertibility from April 2000 provides vital boost to Indian export business development Indian increase 30% of total export business with countries of Association of South East Asian Nations (ASEAN). Collaboration efforts and absolutely necessary among ASEAN countries so as to cope with global competition.

The Strategy of the Ninth Five-Year Plan for External Sector

The Ninth Five-Year Plan (1997-2000) of the Government of India has emphasised viable external sector in the draft plan being an important component of a successful development strategy. The liberalisation of external sector following crisis in 1991-92 indicated substantial shift in the approach to India's external sector.

The eighth five-year plan achieved 6.8% of annual average growth rate with average annual 3.7% incremental capital output ratio, whereas, the ninth five-year plan has estimated 6.5 annual average rate of growth with 4.3% annual average rate of incremental capital output ratio service sector is about to contribute 42% of GDP at the end of 2001-02. Productivity of infrastructure sector and service sector is to be increased by privatisation and competition. Macroeconomic variables during the ninth-five year plan aim for reduction in trade deficit and budget deficit. In such a situation, export-import marketing will have to play a key role to achieve the targets of raising India's share in global trade. Deadline for complete removal of all quantitative restrictions will be effective from the tenth five-year plan. Successful management of open trade regime be created within ninth plan period. The Government of India will have to phase out quantitative restrictions on imports, replacing license protection by tariff protection, orderly adjustment of domestic producers with foreign investors. Capital goods industries will have to achieve efficiency and take full advantage of trading opportunities.

For improving balance of payment position during the plan, adequate rate of growth of exports need to be achieved. Thus, importance if sustained growth for maintaining overall growth rate of economy and 11.8% annual rate of growth in exports depend upon two factors: (a) the rate of growth of the tradable goods, and services sectors; and (b) the propensity to export of these sectors. The share of tradeables in GDP declined from 68.0% in the first plan to 49.9% in the eight plan. The marginal propensity to export necessary for achieving a growth rate of 11.8% with 2 a GDP growth of 6.5% at different terminal year shares of tradeable sector. The tradables is about to decline to 46% of GDP. 13.6% of the incremental value of production in the tradable sectors can achieve 11.8% growth rate of exports during the plan period.

Ninth Plan has estimated 10.8% annual rate of growth on an average as eighth plan achieved 11.7% rate of import growth. 10.4% rate of growth yielded an implicit elasticity of imports to GDP of 1.5% which is assumed to be rise 1.7% during the ninth plan period. At the end of terminal year of the plan import is expected in order of Rs. 220990 crore or US $ 60.7 billion at constant prices.

Exchange rate has emerged as an important instrument of policy. Steady sustainable growth of trade, investment and competition need to be achieved with full convertibility of rupee on current account and also partial convertibility on capital account. Sometimes exchange rates are uncertain instrument of export promotion but negative effects can be generated through cost-push inflation, retarding external capital flows. Stable exchange rate is conducive to attracting greater external flows by lowering the expected return dominated in foreign currency terms. During the ninth five-year plan, the exchange rate needs to be deliberately depreciated in terms of average level of prices in the country with about 5 to 7% per annum variation under normal circumstances. A depreciation of the real effective exchange rate in the region 2% to 3% per annum will not allow acceleration of inflation from 3 to 4% per annum to improve competitive price of Indian goods and services in the external market. It can be a part of development strategy during the plan. There is a need to have inflow of FDI to fund the plan.

It is expected to develop the trade under the plan as per provisions in WTO singed by India. Preferential tariff or customs unions are expected to have a common tariff at lowest rate to formation of trade block under free trade. The Ninth Plan will have to reduce balance of payment deficits. Balance of payment and its funding in the plan would be as under:

Funding of the Ninth Plan by External Sector

(Rs.'000 crore in 1996-97 prices)

Item	*1996-97*	*2001-2002*	*Ninth Plan*
Exports	117.3	205.1	800.9 (10.4)
Imports	132.2	221.0	936.1 (12.2)
Trade Balance	-14.9	-15.9	-135.2 (-1.8)
Net Invisibles	0.5	-2.0	-24.6 (-0.3)
Current Account Balance Financed by	-14.4	-17.7	-159.8 (-2.1)
Net external assistance	0.5	1.0	7.7 (0.1)
Net external debt	15.5	5.9	53.9 (0.7)
F.D.I.	8.7	10.7	92.3 (1.2)
Net F.P.I.	9.3	4.8	23.1 (0.3)
Total Capital Flow	34.0	22.4	177.0 (2.3)
Change in Reserves	20.8	4.5	17.2 (0.2)

Notes: (1) Repayment of IMF loan has been adjusted against external assistance in 1996-97.

(2) Net external debt includes NRI Deposits and short-term credit.

(3) Figures in brackets are percentages to GDP.

Source: Ninth Five-Year Plan: 1997-2000. Vol. I Planning Commission, Govt. of India, New Delhi, p. 140.

It is very clear from the table that balance of payment position in term of reserves will be 0.2% of GDP at the end of March 2002 which mean external sector will have to fund the plan at the cost of foreign exchange reserves. Absolute and relative figures show declining position during the plan as per table. RBI has outlined minimum conditions under which Capital Account convertibility can reasonably be considered. Inflation will be brought under control of 3 to 5%, external debt service raito is reduced to 20% of current account receipts, minimum foreign exchange resave during the plan period. For this, the committee on capital account suggested (a) availability and costs and prices of non-traded goods and services as against tradable goods sectors are not significantly as per prevailing international standard, (b) Indian exports are sufficiently robust so as to withstand periodic fluctuations in exchange rate and in international prices. Additional reserves of foreign exchange can be based on higher FDI flows to boost and maintain growth rate of the plan.

The Ninth Plan aims to achieve 4.1% gross fiscal deficit target for the entire plan period. Apart from earnings from visibles and non-visibles of trade disinvestment in public sector investment will help to develop infrastructure facilities, and process of fiscal consolidation in the plan.

Table 4.17
Import Projections for Ninth Plan

(Rs. Million)

Sector	1996-97		2001-02
	DGCI&S	RBI	
Wheat	3900	4279	4787
Other Cereals	5	5	8
Pulses	7069	7755	9384
Jute	780	856	960
Rubber	950	1042	1715
Other Crops	6937	7610	7125
Animal Husbandary	5649	6198	5440
Forestry & Logging	7119	7809	6009
Fishing	2	2	4
Coal and Lignite	30817	33808	45226
Crude Petroleum and N. Gas	158802	174214	333908
Other Metalic Minerals	57038	62573	72084
Non Metallic & Minor Minerals	110678	121419	12663
Sugar	31	34	38
Edible Oil	28268	31011	25874
Oth. Food & Beverage Ind.	858	941	1131
Wollen Textiles	2838	3114	3481
Silk Textiles	1313	1440	1613
Art. Silk and Synthetic Fibers	3818	4188	5629
Other Textiles	2267	2487	3344
Wood & Wood Products	9122	30711	50791
Paper and Paper Products	27994	30711	50791
Leather & Leather Prod.	4517	4955	5542
Rubber Products	5060	5551	6541
Plastic Products	3719	4080	3922
Petroleum Products	190284	208752	154400
Fertilizers	27977	30695	26854
Pesticides	1546	1696	1899
Synth. Fibre & Resin	27653	30337	31504
Paints, Drugs, Cosmetics	16038	17594	21644
Other Chemical	99223	108854	145617
Cement	20	22	0
Other Non-Mentallic Mineral Prod.	4201	4609	5155
Iron & Steel	50377	55266	35261
Non-Ferrous Metals	37900	41578	56349
Tractors & Oth. Agri. Machines	2517	2762	2509
Other Non-Electrical Machine	170271	2155125	306074
Electrical Machine	30483	47806	73644
Communications Equipment	51649	712026	64511
Rail Equipment	6613	7255	6589
Motor Vehicles	14089	44186	59886
Motorcycle, Scooter & Bicycles	701	769	861
Other Transport Equipment	24344	199081	302604
Other Manufacturing	83676	120523	179371
Total	1321940	1737530	2209860

Source: Ninth-five year plan, Vol. I, Planning Commission, Government of India New Delhi, p. 129.

This process will attend to achieve 11.8% rate of growth as projected by the Planning Commission. For this, the share of tradables in GDP was 54% with 8.2% marginal propensity to export in 1996-97 which is expected to change as 46% and 13.6% respectively during 2001-2002. Export incentive structure has to be re-oriented toward investment in tradable goods from non-tradables and relative profitability of exports via domestic sales need to be improved for sustainable growth of export rate. It is equally important that brought expenditure, flood expenditure, law and order expenditure for states by the Centre will remain in control in order to manage the plan financially viable. Such expenditure rises can nullify wastage of resources and now allowing expected rate of growth as per target of the Planning Commission.

Table No. 4.17 and Table No. 4.18 provides details of export and import projections for the Ninth Plan in Rs. million which has posed a challenge to professional international and national marketers and espouses to achieve the targets during the plan period. Both the tables reveal item-wise, sector-wise projections. As 64.5% of total investment is to be made by the private sector, privatisation process and the role of corporate sector will be vital to achieve the targets of exports and imports. Globalisation process will have to capture new markets by our industries and corporates for sustainable growth during the ninth plan and future plans of the Government of India. For this, export incentives and import concessions and facilities need to be gradually phase out as they have budgetary implications.

Table 4.18

Export Projections for Ninth Plan

(Rs. Million)

Sector	1996-97		2001-02
	DGCI&S	RBI	
Paddy	31458	32489	19670
Wheat	6790	7012	17503
Other Cereals	487	503	840
Pulses	1279	1321	0
Jute	158	165	275
Cotton	16042	16568	25495
Tea & Coffee	24059	24847	44104
Other Crops	17288	17855	23789
Animal Husbandary	8124	8390	14456
Forestry & Logging	649	670	1119
Fishing	40221	41539	75350
Coal and Lignite	766	791	1320
Crude Petroleum and N. Gas	1061	1096	1608
Iron Ore	17139	17700	29470
Other Metalic Minerals	3641	3760	4396

Non Metallic & Minor Minerals	7484	7729	11537
Sugar	6290	6496	8937
Edible Oil	9226	9528	10826
Oth. Food & Beverage Ind.	83552	86288	115869
Cotton Textiles	110365	113980	212194
Wollen Textiles	3553	3669	7254
Silk Textiles	4296	4436	4403
Art. Silk and Synthetic Fibers	25250	26076	59467
Jute, Hemp., Mesta Textiles	4582	4732	6364
Readymade Garments	132748	137095	249770
Other Textiles	40056	41367	78756
Wood & Wood Products	1333	1377	1549
Paper and Paper Products	5333	5508	9034
Leather & Leather Prod.	55089	56893	79512
Rubber Products	12086	12482	16708
Plastic Products	18833	19450	34825
Petroleum Products	17079	17638	22022
Fertilizers	0	0	5840
Pesticides	1198	1237	2064
Synth. Fibre & Resin	2946	3042	5076
Paints, Drugs, Cosmetics	53641	55398	99364
Other Chemical	48349	49933	88437
Cement	0	0	8000
Other Non-Mentallic Mineral Prod.	169360	174901	293782
Iron & Steel	27556	28459	42882
Non-Ferrous Metals	22613	23354	25051
Tractors & Oth. Agri. Machines	192	198	187
Other Non-Electrical Machine	39588	40885	71627
Electrical Machine	479	495	601
Communications Equipment	30403	31399	99024
Rail Equipment	328	339	405
Motor Vehicles	24504	25306	35952
Motorcycles, Scooter & Bicycles	7875	8133	8178
Oth. Transport Equipment	339	351	585
Oth. Manufacturing	37822	39061	75263
Total	1173510	1211940	2050740

Source: Ninth Five-Year Plan, Vol. I Planning Commission, Government of India, New Delhi, p. 137.

Action Plan for Global Marketing

It is necessary to glance through current situation of export-import trends during the post liberalisation period. India achieved 20% average annual rise during 1993-94 to 1995-96 which has declined in subsequent years. Same is the case with imports also as it has declined from 9.5% to 6% during the period. As a result trade deficit has increased (-) 3.3 to (-) 6.2% during the period. Similarly, foreign exchange reserves declined from US $ 1,278 million in 1990-91 to US $ -3,829 million in 1998-99. The deficit on trade account of balance of payment in 1998-99 had narrowed down to US $ 13.25 billion from US $ 15.51 billion in 1997-98 or from 3.8% of GDP to 3.1% of GDP in 1998-99. The world economy has slowed down from

3.2% in 1997 to 1.9% in 1998. Decline in export value is a matter of great concern to our marketers and traders. Imports from major trading partners have fallen and similarly, exports also fell to traditional countries and in traditional items. The movements of the Rupee against the currencies of India's major trading partners in 1998-99 is connected with depreciation of rupee is previous real effective exchange rate, whereas more stability is found during 1999-2000.

To reduce import of gold in the long-run, Union Budget 1999-2000 announced launching of the *Gold Deposite Scheme* 1999 to draw out privately owned gold stock for reduction in import of gold by India. Trade deficit during April-December 1999 was at $ 7039 million which was 40% lower than the deficit of $ 7328 million during April-December 1998. Exports in terms of unit value growth index considering 1978-79 as base years escalated from 292.5 in 1990-91 to 552.4 1998-99, whereas volume growth index of imports rose from 194.1 to 395.4 during the period which mean. This has happened largely due to low unit value realisation as decline in exports. It is a fact that despite significant policy and procedural simplifications, transaction cost in India is rising due to unspecified and unforeseen barriers from time to time.

In such a situation one can safely suggest following strategic action plan to boost our global marketing practices from managerial and economic point of view:

(1) It is most necessary to increase the efficiency of EPCG, export-oriented units, and export processing zones to boost exports and global marketing.

(2) Gradually phasing out of duty drawbacks.

(3) Stimulating exports and industrial growth. India has achieved 20% rate of growth of exports as against 8 to 10% industrial growth 1994-95 to 1995-96. Experience shows that 5% reduction in exports reflected 3.6% in slowing down of industrial growth.

(4) There is a need to correct the exchange rate mechanism leading to arrest in deceleration of rupee vis-a-vis doller rating in order to protect interest of exporters.

(5) A special drive to boost consume goods and capital goods item in the global markets.

(6) Compared with other countries, Indian industry is also handicapped owing to anamolies in that import duty structure. Raw material and components are facing higher rate of duty than finished products. Such anomolies need to be removed as Indian

industry is exposed to an uneven competition and is getting hurt in the process. A variety of sectors like steel, cement, engineering goods, textiles have been hit hard. Thus, tariff restructuring and phasing it appear to be most necessary.

(7) The Government of India need to follow export-oriented foreign investment policy. An appropriate policy package to attract FDI in export-oriented sector can boost production and exports too.

(8) Inter-country and inter-corproate collaborations are necessary white entering into joint venture for production. In this regard. India should follow experiments and experiences of the developed countries.

(9) India should forge new trading arrangements such as payment arrangement. Within South-East Asian countries, SAARC trade bloc along with new marketing and new production arrangement.

(10) Merchandise and services in which India has competitive advantages should be paid due attention with promotion packages to use indigenous materials and high value added exports.

(11) It is most necessary to have macroeconomic reforms in terms of cost disabilities arising out of infrastructure constraints, unbearable commodity taxes, redesigning duty drawback mechanism, advance licenses should be made transparent and export obligations under various schemes fixed and assessed time to time. Thus, policy should be a process to a built-in flexibility to cope with the changing marketing situation.

(12) WTO arrangement asked to phase out quantitative restrictions for agricultural products, consumers goods and other items. Indian enterprises should be prepared for necessary adjustment and tariff mechanism need to be effectively used to safeguard India's interest.

(13) It is most necessary to strengthen EPCG scheme. For this Assocham, FICCI and state level trade organisations represent for reduction n threshold limit in several industries cases. Lowering of duty rate should encourage zero window duty. There should not be harassment by the custom while evaluating the export under this scheme.

(14) For forex saving, it appears that a list should be prepared of items having potentiality of exports or deemed exports.

(15) Export processing zones and export oriented schemes found rewarding for export earning rise. Such zones should be allowed for the sale in Domestic Trade Area of specified portion. Flexibility

in export market conditions is necessary to maintain production growth rate of such units.

(16) Deregulation of interest rate is necessary for pre-shipment and post-shipment facilities required by the exporters. 100% Modvat credit facility should be available to them.

(17) Exporters should produce exportable surplus as part of global standards for achieving sustainable marketing of exports. Other norms like environment audit, cost audit, I.S.O. need to be maintained by them.

5

POST-LIBERALISATION EXPORT-IMPORT POLICIES

(A) Exim Policy: 1992-1997

In March 1992, Government of India decided to make the earlier policy of five years and extend the period to 1992-1997. So the earlier policy's period turned out to be of one year that is 1990-91 to 1991-92. However, it is an extension of earlier policy. The policy has the following objectives:

(*i*) To establish the framework for globalisation.

(*ii*) To augment exports by facilitating access to raw materials and other inputs including capital goods.

(*iii*) To promote modernisation and competitiveness by recognising the growing interdependence among technology, investment and production to further the prospects of trade.

The policy aims at:

(*a*) Stability by providing a validity period of five years *i.e.,* co-terminus with 8th Plan.

(*b*) Greater consistency by endeavouring to undertake changes only once in every quarter.

(*c*) Simplification by condensing the policy package to just one book of 85 pages and delineating the specifications in simple language which makes it easy to understand.

The new 5-year Exim Policy gives a further push to liberalisation by freely allowing imports of all items except a negative list, decanalising a large number of raw materials including non-ferrous metals and further liberalising import of capital goods against export obligation.

Continuing the liberalised trade regime, new Exim Policy substantially eliminates licensing and discretionary controls by introducing negative lists of import of capital goods including second-hand items and offers a great deal for the 100% export oriented units and export processing zones. The new policy is co-terminus with the 8th Five Year Plan and attempts to make imports-exports account for as much as 20% of the gross domestic product in the coming years. Thus, new policy stipulates fewer restrictions, gives greater freedom to trade and reduces administrative controls.

The new policy is intended to give a significant boost to India's exports. It contains a number of new incentives for generation of exports. Duty-free imports, related to export production have been liberalised. The import duty on capital goods has been reduced with increased export obligation.

Thus, new policy enlarges the scope of duty-free imports under advance licences, special benefits for deemed exports and more incentives for 100% export-oriented units and those located in free trade as well as export processing zones. The policy has introduced a Foreign Trade (Development and Regulation) Bill which would replace the Import and Export (Control) Act 1947. It incorporates the new policy and imposes monetary penalties, confistication of goods and suspensions or cancellation of licence for violators of the law.

Exporters have been given special incentives to maximise foreign exchange earnings in the coming years. Thus, import-export controls have been substantially reduced. Only two types of import licences (advance licences and special import licences) now remain against several licences including the Open General Licence in the earlier timings. As per the new policy, the negative list would be administered as far as possible not through case-by-case licensing but by general schemes. The negative list of imports is smallest ever and consumer goods continue to be under restraint. Import of only three items were banned, 68 items restricted and eight items canalised. The pruned negative list of exports banned seven items, restricted 62 items and canalised ten items. The policy allows special import facilities for the hotels and tourism industry and for sports bodies and permitted export of 46 items with minimum regulations. The new procedure of exports-imports has come into operation with effect from May 1, 1992. In future, it would be the policy of the government to prune the list from time to time as exports gather momentum. As indicated earlier new Exim Policy has given greater autonomy and flexibility for export-oriented units (EOUs) and Units located in the country's export processing zones (EPZs). These units are now allowed to install not only own machinery but also machinery taken on lease. They are also permitted to export their productions through export houses, trading houses or star trading houses. The novelty of the scheme in relation to an EOU/EPZ Units is that it may on the basis of a firm contract between the parties acquiring the capital goods from a domestic leasing company and will be eligible to import the capital goods free of duty and supply it to the EOU/EPZ Units on such terms and conditions as might be mutually agreed upon between the two parties. The capital goods should, however, remain as a part of the capital assets of the EOU/EPZ Units till the export obligation is discharged by the Units and they should not be diverted for any other purpose. The deemed exports have been accorded favourable treatment, except for some petroleum products, edible oils, fertilizers and cereals, all other items have now been decanalised. Newsprint has not only been decanalised, but the procedure for its import has been considerably simplified. Import of all items including capital goods are freely allowed. The negative list contains consumer goods, barring 28 specific items and 70 other items whose imports have been restricted. In addition imports of three items namely, tallow, animal rennet and unmanufactured ivory have been prohibited. Import of a number of items including newsprint, non-ferrous metals, natural rubber, intermediates and raw materials for fertilizer have been decanalised. Petroleum products, edible oils, fertilizers and cereals, however, continue to be on the canalised list under the new policy. Similarly, exports of all items are free except a negative list. Export of items like beaf and tallow is in the negative list which contains items like raw silk, certain minerals, pulses, military stores, milk, coconut and copra is allowed subject to licensing.

Salient Features of New Exim Policy 1992-97

1. Under the new policy the scope of duty exemption scheme has been enlarged by introducing value-based advance licensing besides the quantity-based advance licence. This will give greater flexibility to the exporter to import and export goods within the overall value limits and without any quantity restrictions except in the case of sensitive goods.

2. New policy sheds the mood of export pessimism. The policy has a pronounced bias towards exports and strengthens special schemes directed towards exports.

3. The scope of duty exemption has been enlarged by introducing value-based licences besides the quality-based ones. This gives greater flexibility to the exporters to import and export goods within the overall value limits and without any quantitative restrictions except in the case of sensitive goods.

4. The export houses, trading houses and star trading houses will be eligible for the facility of self-certification under the advance licence scheme. Exports of specified products will be brought under the self-certificate scheme later.

5. The export promotion of capital goods (EPCG) Scheme has been liberalised and two windows are now available for import of capital goods at concessional rates of customs duty of 25% or 15% with corresponding export obligations. Both new and second-hand capital goods may be imported under the scheme. Domestic manufacturers of capital goods, who may require to import components may also avail themselves EPCG Scheme at the concessional rate of customs duty at 15% of CIF value. The export obligation for import at 25% duty will be four times of CIF value of capital goods over a five year period.

6. The Gem and Jewellery Scheme is continued with little modifications.

7. Under the new policy, the 100% EOUs and EPZs will be allowed to install not only own machinery but also machinery taken on lease. They may also export their productions through export houses, trading houses or star trading houses. The EOU/EPZ Schemes have been extended to agriculture, horticulture, acquaculture, poultry and animal husbandry. The new policy also allows inter-unit transfers. These units could also be considered for taking up services as an area of activity on merits.

8. Deemed exports have been defined and benefits such as duty exemption schemes, duty drawback schemes and exemption from terminal excise duty have been extended to deemed exports. Certain categories of exports and exporters will be eligible to receive special import licences. These include deemed exports, export houses, trading houses and star trading houses and manufacturers who acquire ISO 9000 (gems) or BIS 14000 (gems) certification of quality.

9. The important role of export promotion councils, export houses, trading houses and star trading houses has been reiterated. The registration-cum-membership certificate (RCMC) issued by EPCS will continue to be the essential requirement for any importer to avail of the benefits or concessions or to apply for any licence under the new policy.

10. The handbook of procedures has been published on May 1, 1992. The procedures are simple, transparent, and easy to administer. The simplified procedure relates for both imports and exports of a number of items including cameras, motor vehicles, air craft and helicopters and delegated considerable powers to the regional licensing authorities. Only one application form each has been prescribed for exports and imports, as

also for legal undertakings and bank guarantees as against several set of application forms earlier. The procedure for project exports has been clearly defined and the terms and conditions in respect of 46 items in the negative list, which might be exported without a licence have been simplified. The multiplicity of controlling agencies have been considerably reduced.

11. The licence for import of cameras with accessories upto Rs. 60,000 by accredited correspondents and camera and other equipment by accredited foreign correspondents of foreign TVs and new agencies has been done away with. These could be imported on the recommendation of the Press Information Bureau now.

12. The Foreign Trade (Development and Regulation) Bill 1992 would replace the Import and Export Control Act, 1947. The new Bill relating to foreign trade comprise the new Act, the rules and orders made thereunder and the new export and import policy. Violation of the law would attract monetary penalties, confiscation of goods and/or suspension or cancellation of licence.

13. The list of canalised items has been drastically reduced in the new Exim Policy for 1992-1997, with only 8 items on import side and 10 items on the export side, throwing certain canalising agency partially and others fully out of job on this count. In the import category, the major items which have been decanalised include newsprint, natural rubber, cinematographic films and all kinds of steel and pig iron. On the import side, there would only be four canalising agencies which include Indian Oil Corporation (IOC), Minerals and Metal Trading Corporation (MMTC), State Trading Corporation (STC), and Food Corporation of India (FCI). Earlier there used to be about a dozen agencies for importing canalised items. The canalised items on the import side include petroleum products, all types of nitrogenous, phosphatic, potassium and complex fertilizers, drugs, edible oils, seeds and oil seeds, fatty acid oils and cereals. On the export side sugar, iron and steel, railway wagons, passenger coaches and locomotives, exposed cinematographic films and raw jute are few of the major items which have been taken out of the canalised list. The reduced canalised list for exports include petroleum products, butter, gum karaya, gum resin, mica waste and scrap, rare earth minerals, iron ore, chrome ore, all grades of bauxite, manganese ores, iron ore concentrate and pallets, major seeds, onions, powdered milk and pure milk ghee. Subsequently, a lesser number of agencies will be engaged in handling canalised items.The agencies which shall lose all strength on account of canalisation include Project and Equipment Corporation (PEC), Steel Authority of India Ltd. (SAIL), National Film Development Corporation (NFDC), Jute Corporation of India, Indian Petrochemicals Corporation Limited (IPCL) and Metal Scrap Trading Corporation (MSTC).

14. The import of newsprint has been decanalised. Certain conditions have been set out for the newsprint import to which the user will have to hold a "Certificate for Entitlement to Import of Newsprint" issued by the Registrar of Newspapers for India (RNI). The imported newsprint will be subject to actual user condition and will have to be used only for the publication for which the entitlement has been issued. The quota for entitlement will be determined by RNI. The new Policy while decanalising import of newsprint removes it from the Open General Licencing (OGL) list and places it under the restricted items. It restricts the import of glazed newsprint to only those periodicals which are regularly published and which have multicolour printing requirements. Under the new rule no sale, loan, transfer or disposal of newsprint in any other manner will be permissible without prior written consent of the RNI. Any violation of the prescribed norms and conditions will disqualify the newspaper concerned for future import entitlement certificate.

Highlights of New Exim Policy 1992-97

I. General

(i) Stable Exim Policy for 5 years from 1992-97 subject to policy changes only once in a quarter.

(ii) Trade to be free, subject only to a negative list of imports and exports.

(iii) National campaign for quality awareness to be launched.

II. Exports

(i) Negative list of exports curtailed. 7 items banned, 62 items subject to restrictions, 10 items canalised.

(ii) Export of 46 items permitted with minimum regulation.

(iii) EOU and EPZ schemes liberalised.

(iv) Crucial role of EPCs, export houses and star trading houses recognised.

III. Imports

(i) Smallest-ever negative list of imports.

(ii) Consumer goods to continue under restraint.

(iii) Import of 3 items banned, 70 items restricted, 8 items canalised.

(iv) Special import facilities for hotels, tourism industry and sports bodies.

(v) EPCs Scheme liberalised; two windows opened for concessional duty imports.

IV. Licensing

(*i*) Negative list to be administered by general scheme.

(*ii*) Actual user condition eliminated, except in special cases.

V. Capital Goods

(*i*) Capital goods no longer in negative list.

(*ii*) Import of capital goods liberalised.

(*iii*) Second-hand capital goods allowed.

The new policy is noteworthy but its efficacy will largely depend on actual implementation and generation of additional exports in a substantive way.

The negative list continues to be large. Even decanalised items like fertilizers and newsprint have been brought in its fold. Restrictive regime continues despite open and free policy frame.

Export of many items like rice and cotton yarn are being subjected to certain terms and conditions.

Trading with RPA and ACU countries has not been given the attention it deserves. The exports to Asian Clearing Union countries will generate exchange at official rate only.

There are several other areas which need urgent attention. These include re-structuring of customs duty especially with regard to capital goods, removal of export duties, allowing all export linked imports at official exchange rate. In addition, there needs to be liberal facility for trading and re-export. In regard to shipping freight, there are obvious exchange anomalies — while freight is determined at market rates, the shipper is allowed at 60:40 ratio and this tends to make the exports non-competitive. The new policy is likely to boost exports of agro-products rather than value added goods.

The success of the new reform measures largely hinges on the acceleration in exports to the tune of 16 per cent postulated in the IMF/World Bank perspectives and a reigning in of inflation to single digit in 1992-93.

Greater transparency since case by case licensing will be replaced by a general scheme of guidelines and flexibility as the actual user condition is being withdrawn except in a few cases. The realisation of ambitious export growth rate in a recessionary climate prevailing in OECD countries is daunting.

A facility of self-certification and self-declaration under advance licence scheme is being made available to export houses, trading houses and star trading houses. Export of specified production will be brought under the scheme later.

The advance licensing scheme announces the concept of broad-banding of exports and imports by providing licence for a class of products instead of individual items.

All licences under duty exemption schemes are to be made transferable.

Special Import Licence

Three categories namely deemed exports: export houses, trading and star trading houses; manufacturers with ISO 9000 and BIS 14000 certification to be made eligible for special import licence.

Special incentives will be made available to exporters for achieving internationally acceptable quality standards. The incentives include recognition/reward to manufacturers who have acquired internationally recognised certification of quality *e.g.,* ISO 9000 (Series), BIS 14000 (Series) etc. Upgradation of laboratories/trading houses, role of export houses/trading houses/star trading houses.

The catalytical role of Export Promotion Councils, Export Houses, Trading Houses and Star Trading Houses has been recognised.

Exim Policy 1992-97: Some Limitations Remain

While the new Exim Policy has several bold initiatives, it is not sufficient to ensure export dynamism. There is room for both exports and imports to grow in a developing country like India.

The first stage of latest Exim Policy related to abolition of controls and licensing and simplification of procedures. The second stage involved making the rupee partially convertible. The third stage related to the simplification of the Exim Policy and the fourth stage pertains to tariff reforms. The trade policy is not complete without tariff reforms.

Evaluation of the New Export and Import (EXIM) Policy: (1992-1997)

1. Significantly this policy has the longest ever validity period of five years which is co-terminus with the Eighth Five Year Plan (1992-97).

2. The Exim Policy builds on the major directional shifts in the trade policy regime. Mr. Chidambaram, the then commerce minister deserves to be complimented for taking several bold and imaginative initiatives in the new Exim Policy.

3. These initiatives go a long way in further freeing India's foreign trade from many discretionary bureaucratic controls.

4. The new policy attempts to establish a future framework for more effective globalisation of India's foreign trade by increasingly subjecting it to the rigours of the market forces in a phased manner.

5. The underlying vision of globalisation includes raising the combined contribution of exports and imports to Gross Domestic Product (GDP) from its present level of about 15 per cent to 20 per cent in the next five years. The policy claims to have a "pronounced bias towards exports and strengthens special schemes directed towards exports." Despite several initiatives contained in the policy for promoting exports mainly via easier and more profitable access to imports and dismantling of controls, they are by themselves insufficient for achieving a self-sustaining growth of exports required by the nation. What are the strengths and the weaknesses of the new Exim policy. Also, what complementary measures are required which will help to achieve the "overall objective of promoting foreign trade to the advantage of the country."

It is necessary to point out that the new Exim Policy should be evaluated in conjunction with the overall economic policy reforms in the fiscal, industrial, exchange rate and other related areas being put in place since June 1991 and further evolved in the Union Budget for 1992-93. The Exim Policy is to be seen in tandem with other policies aimed at short-term fiscal correction and the medium term restructuring of the economy.

6. These economic reforms have been necessitated by the most binding balance of payments constraints, to save the country from the brink of defaulting on its external debt servicing obligations in June 1991. The rupee devaluation helped the government in eliminating the cash compensatory support (CCS) to exports thereby reducing the budget deficit.

7. The new Exim Policy also ensures that budgetary subsidies are not used as a means for financing export promotion measures at the micro level. The policy has scrapped the instrument of exim scrip introduced in August 1991 in favour of the 'partial convertibility of the rupee' (PCR) scheme introduced in the Union Budget for 1992-93 as a means for increasing export earnings.

8. The new Exim Policy has been formulated as a corrective measure to the relatively unsatisfactory growth of exports especially during 1991-92 in view of the several adverse developments in the external environment.

The most important adverse external development relates to the breakup of the former Soviet Union and continuing global recession. Savage import cuts and high interest rates have also adversely affected India's exports. Thus, it was necessary to provide stimulus to the growth of exports and relax import controls in the new Exim Policy.

While formulating the new five year Exim Policy, the ministry of commerce accepted the widely acknowledged view that "trade can flourish only in a regime of substantial freedom." There is room for both exports and imports to grow in a developing country like India.

9. The policy makers recognised the vital role of imports in promoting existing import-linked exports on a competitive basis as well as in generating higher value added exports especially in the richer and growing markets of the world. Imports of technology were also required to modernise Indian industry and make it cost-competitive in the context of efficient import substitution. *The new policy had to redeem the pledges made in the trade policy announcements made on July 4, 1991 and August, 13, 1991 to further liberalise the trade policy regime and to take steps to move to a fully convertible rupee on trade account in the next three to five years.* The new policy has shown boldness in taking major initiatives towards those ends. It rightly claims that the "fundamental feature of the new policy is freedom." It drastically reduces the existing areas of licensing, quantitative restrictions, other regulatory and discretionary controls including canalisation of imports and exports. Most goods can now be imported and exported freely subject to two small negative lists, one for imports and the other for exports. These negative lists are the smallest ever. Thus, this policy shows genuine efforts to unshackle Indian trade and industry from trade controls. These changes together with the promised drastic simplification of the procedures from May 1, 1992 will help to reduce the prevalent areas of "export prevention".

10. What is more heartening is the promise contained in the policy for the further gradual pruning of the negative lists by permitting the import of consumer goods as the balance of payments position improves. Hopefully, this will be effected in a selective manner after reconciling it with the national interest (and not just the interests of foreign suppliers). Again, even though the policy has not explicitly stated so, an additional justification for selective import liberalisation is to use import competition as a credible tool to compel the overprotected Indian industry to improve its international competitiveness both in the national and international markets.

11. A suitable downward revision of tariffs will have to be relied upon as a major instrument for doing so. This is particularly appropriate and feasible as the rupee depreciates further towards its longer term sustainable level in the freer foreign exchange market. Similarly, tariffs will have to be selectively revised in cases where foreign suppliers may misuse the provisions of a fairly liberal import policy by dumping their products in India. An independent Tariff Commission must be set up by the government with inter-ministerial powers for tailoring future import policy in national interest.

12. The new policy has taken several initiatives to provide a boost to exports. The partial rupee convertibility of rupee over time will favour exporters. The direct measures adopted by the new policy to give a positive push to exports rely heavily on providing preferential and more lucrative access to imports mainly to several categories of committed exporters who

are in the business of exporting as their major activity. The MOC has also entrusted them with self-certification in utilising special import facilities under duty exemption schemes subject to audit later. A promise has been made to keep the new policy stable with as fewer changes as possible. This should facilitate export planning by the units (including investment planning) on longer basis.

13. Some of the initiatives taken by the new Exim Policy directly related to export promotion are listed below: The import of second hand machinery has generally been permitted for export oriented industries. The duty exemption (DE) scheme has been strengthened under which imports are allowed at two concessional rates of 15 per cent and 25 per cent subject to appropriate export obligations. The exporters have been given a choice to opt for advance import licences under the DE scheme either under quantity based or (for the first time introduced) value-based norms. The norms have already been set out for over 1500 items and separately published. For these items, advance import licence has been promised in a maximum of 15 days.

14. The policy appropriately recognises the importance of deemed exports and restores benefits for such exports. It rightly confers higher benefits to 100 per cent export-oriented units (EOUs) and units in the export processing zones (EPZs) over those exporting from the domestic tariff area (DTA). The EOU and EPZ schemes have now been extended to newer activities including software, horticulture, agriculture, aquaculture, animal husbandry and related activities and services. By a separate notification, such units dealing with broad agro-based products can sell 50 per cent (twice the normal) output in the DTA. This can prove to be a powerful initiative for boosting exports. The policy document has for the first time devoted an exclusive chapter to quality and provided for special benefits to the Indian manufacturer-exporters who adopt ISO 9000 and/or BIS 14000 standards mandatorily required for exports to the European Community after 1992.

15. Despite the above listed measures towards export promotion, the new Exim policy does not measure up to the tasks of ensuring a quantum jump in India's exports on a self-sustaining basis. This would be critical for meeting the challenge of balance of payments during the Eighth Five Year Plan. The policy document does not clearly specify any such objective. Nor does it incorporate any targets towards increasing the market share of India's exports in the world markets in its vision of globalisation of our foreign trade. The concepts of thrust products (and within those, products with 'extreme focus') and thrust markets being reviewed by the Board of Trade are not made an integral part of the policy document.

16. The contribution of exports in generating employment do not even find a mention in the new policy. A balanced policy towards RPA is called for. There is inadequate stress on maximising net foreign exchange earnings from exports in general. No monitoring system or trade information system has been planned to review relative profitability of exports and develop the foreign trade for achieving the "national objectives". Additional reward should be provided for exports of new products and services to new markets. Too much faith has been put in the capacity of the existing export promotion councils to provide professional services to their members.

17. The biggest weakenesses of the new policy lie in the near total neglect of developing infrastructural supporting activities related to exports including modernisation of ports, airports, warehousing, airconditioned road transport, telecom and development of management capabilities for an export revolution. The development of an indicative microlevel plan with commmitment for targeted exports by products, services and destinations consistent with the macro-economic requirements of the external sector during the Eighth Five Year plan should be taken up soon. The MOC should more actively lobby for support to strengthen export production base of the country on the basis of competitive advantage.

Modifications in Exim Policy announced on July, 1992 widens the definition of manufactured and capital goods for achieving further value addition to earn more foreign exchange through exports.

The modifications removed certain anomalies in the international price reimbursement and duty drawback schemes gave triple weightage to net foreign exchange earned on exports and allowed import of computer software under advanced licensing scheme.

This is not an export-import policy. It is rather an import policy. It is not true that we cannot export unless we import. Why should import of capital goods be allowed? Why can't we import technology instead?

The small exporters has not been benefited from the new policy. They got some subsidies from the government but how are they to increase exports when the GCA importers are facing recession? They will have to make extra efforts to sell more, and that can be possible only if they get some incentives.

Indian exporters are mostly in the manufacturing sector and compete with the world's best. This requires import of capital goods.

Now we can import freely, but the tariffs are still quite high unless the importer is prepared to export a bulk of his products. As it is, we need double digit growth in exports to keep up with what we have achieved for the last few years. That seems an unlikely proposition because in 1986-87, we had achieved over 17 per cent rise in exports over the previous year.

When the recently abolished pre-shipment inspection was in force, inspection of goods was restricted to consignments the small exporter wanted to send. Export houses were exempted. This was a clear case of discrimination against the small exporter.

How will import for re-export benefit the small exporter? He has to have a bank guarantee of 250 per cent if he imports, even if it is for re-export purposes? Even after the export order is fulfilled, the guarantee is not released by the bank. How are the really small exporters to survive and let alone thrive in such conditions?

Many manufacturing units are not direct exporters. They export through merchant exporters, get orders in dollar value, but is paid in rupee at the market rate.

Capital goods exports have been permitted against export obligations. But importing capital goods is not all that simple. The policy allows export houses to import capital goods at concessional rates, but that is only a one time duty. When it comes to spares, however, only a small amount is allowed the concession. A similar concessional duty could be applied to spares and that the government could demand an export obligation on exports of spares. That way, exports will rise.

There is a clause in the policy which says that if the value of the duty drawback is less than two per cent of the FOB value, one would not receive any drawback. That means that if one decides to export at a higher price and earn more foreign exchange for the country, he looses out. This should be corrected.

Conclusions

(*a*) On the whole it seems as if for the first time, industry and government are working together on the same side.

There were still some pinpricks, being attended by the government after presentations made by the association or individual exporters.

(*b*) The duty reduction on customs will have much impact on exports. For this imports will have to be financed by dollars bought at the market rate, which is nearly 15 to 20 per cent higher than the official dollar rate. Further there has been devaluation of nearly 18 per cent. The net gain may be zero if not negative on this count. For import intensive exports to be made easy, bureaucratic norms have to be relaxed. Duty drawback must be simplified, customs clearance should be made easy, and interest rates must be brought down. These are the greatest irritants to an exporter.

(*c*) Seventy five per cent of India's garment exports are in the quota countries, and the country has been using up its entire quota. Why does the country export very little of non-quota items or to non-quota countries?

(*d*) After so many years we are still commodity exporters. What we need to do is gather these millions of small exporters under one umbrella like Japan and Korea have done, establish brand names and concentrate on marketing. Only a large exporter will have the marketing skills or the money to advertise. Take Van Heusen, for instance, it is the name that fetches the mark-up that consumers pay. The Indian supplier or the Chinese supplier is like a dispensable commodity who is willing to supply goods for only slight mark-up.

The small scale sector counts for over 45 per cent of the country's exports, but this can go up if they get together. We must give special incentives to really large export houses, say those which export goods worth Rs. 10,000 crore a year.

Till then, what are the problems the small scale sector is bound to encouter?

(*e*) If the export credit interest rates have gone up, so have the options.

Now an exporter can borrow in FOREX designated export at 6.5 per cent and medium term deferred credit at 7.8 per cent. Export credit in Indian rupees carries interest as high as 15 per cent. Exporters have not been taking advantage of this.

(*f*) A currency is convertible when it can be exchanged against any other currency. In the case of the rupee, it can be exchanged only against the dollar, and that too through the banks.

This partial convertibility has led to discrimination. Earlier at least all exporters got the same amount for the dollar. Now on some days the dollar rules higher than on other days.

It is expected that exports will sustain a 10 per cent growth during 1992-93. More important is to sustain a high level of capacity utilisation. Only a healthy domestic economy will give India the export push it needs.

The Exim Policy (1992-97) was modified in March 1993, giving a new thrust to exports for agricultural and allied sectors, and services in which the country has comparative advantage. The Budget for 1993-94 made substantial reduction in customs duties on capital goods, ferrous and non-ferrous metals and chemicals. Import duties on specified capital goods for export thrust areas such as textiles, leather, marine products, gems and jewellery, food processing, horticulture and floriculture industries were reduced. The Budget also announced a reduction in maximum import duties to 85 per cent and a cut in the duties on personal baggage to 150 per cent from 255 per cent. Tariffs applicable to personal baggage were lowered again in June 1933 to 100 per cent. Commercial policy measures announced during 1993-94 included the following:

(i) Decanalisation of imports of kerosene oil, liquefied petroleum gas, low sulphur heavy stock/low sulphur waxy residue amongst petroleum products and of phosphatic and potassic fertilizers;

(ii) Abolition of minimum export price for basmati and reduction in minimum export price of non-basmati rice from $275 to $200 per tonne;

(iii) Permitting the export of 50000 tonnes of sunflower seeds and superior (Durum) quality of wheat;

(iv) Permitting export-oriented units engaged in agriculture and allied activities to avail of duty-free capital goods imports under the EOU/EPZ scheme even if they export only 50 per cent of their output;

(v) Pruning of negative list of exports by removing 146 entries;

(vi) Introduction of a new scheme called the Export Promotion Capital Goods Scheme for the Services Sector which permits import of capital goods at 15 per cent import duty by professionals on an undertaking to meet a stipulated export obligation;

(vii) Enlarging the definition of capital goods so as to include sectors like agriculture, mining and services;

(viii) Removing the value of domestic inputs from the calculation of value-added criterion for EOU/EPZ units;

(ix) Change in the criterion for recognition as an export or trading or star trading house from net foreign exchange earned to the gross F.O.B. value of physical exports. The award of Special Import Licences for these houses as well as for the electronic sector will also be caused on this criterion;

(x) Permitting large units in ready-made garrnents — an item so far reserved exclusively for small/ancillary units — subject to 50 per cent export obligation, and overall investment limit of Rs. 3 crore in plant and machinery and 5 per cent of the export obligation to be achieved in nonquota markets;

(xi) Announcement of duty drawback rates for 333 new items and improvement in rates for 84 products. Drawback on packing materials used in the export of all commodities has been made payable by making a special provision to that effect and individual rates for different packing materials have been announced;

(xii) Introducti n of electronic hardware technology park (EHTP) scheme which permits 100 per cent foreign investment in electronic sector and provides benefits on par with EOU/EPZ units;

(xii) Setting up of an exporters' grievance cell in the Ministry of Commerce to facilitate action on problems being faced by exporters; and

(xiv) Lifting of ban on trading with South Africa.

The above policy changes, admittedly incremental in nature have helped to maintain the momentum of trade policy reforms. Our trade reforms received across the board recognition from GATT contracting parties at the first trade policy review for India which was completed by GATT in September 1993. Yet, there is substantial ground still to be covered. Our agricultural and allied exports continue to be severely constrained by policy-imposed restrictions. These exports pose no danger to the objective of food security and will in fact help the processes of capital formation and productivity enhancement in agriculture. Removal of these restrictions will provide our farmers with fresh incentives to increase output and put agriculture at par with the industry. On the other hand, a major share of bulk imports continues to be canalised and more than a third of our tariff lines are still covered by some from of licensing. Quantitative restrictions on import of consumer goods provide very high levels of effective protection to these sectors. This results in mis-allocation of investible resources away from sectors where the country may possess a competitive advantage. Overall, it can be concluded that while significant progress has been made in trade policy reforms since July 1991, large areas still remain to be covered. Given that achievement of export competitiveness and export expansion is perhaps the most important policy objective, policy reforms in the above-mentioned and related areas merit urgent and coordinated Government action.

It is important to focus attention on the infrastructual requirements for export expansion. Exports will rise above $22 billion (Rs.69,000 crore) for the first time in 1993-94. Facilitating a further expansion by 15-20 per cent in dollar terms in 1994-95 will expectedly put a severe strain on country's infrastructural facilities. It will also require that internationally competitive infrastructual services, in terms of both prices and quality, are available for exporters. Therefore, to prevent physical infrastructural facilities and their quality from emerging as binding constraints on the country's export effort, policy action has to be urgently initiated in these sectors. An increasing share of foreign trade in national output calls for a corresponding reorientation and development of the economy's non-tradable sector.

New Exim Policy Liberalised 1992-97 Further Liberalised to Boost Exports on 30-3-1994

Government of India further liberalise of the Export-Import Policy (1992-97) to give boost to exports. The major amendments to the policy include expansions of the list of items to be imported against special licences, creation of a new super star trading house category with higher import entitlement, removal of maximum age limit for import of second-hand machinery by actual user, continuation of the value-based advance licensing scheme (VABAL) and broadening of operational areas in export processing zones (EPZs) to include trading as well.

Moreover, the Export Promotion Capital Goods (EPCG) scheme has been simplified and third party exports have been permitted for purposes of fulfillment of export obligation. Also handicapped persons have been allowed to import freely certain specified items. Besides procedures have been simplified to facilitate exports including those from EPZs and Export Oriented Units (EOUs). More benefits have also been given for deemed exporters.

It is hoped that the tempo of export growth achieved in 1993-94 of about 21% will not only be sustained but accelerated in the coming years.

The negative list of imports has been pruned by taking out some components required for the manufacture of finished products in the electronic industry. Also, fisherman can now import outboard motors freely.

Apart from broadening the list of items under special import licences, gold and silver can now be imported against them on payment of concessional rate of customs, duty in foreign exchange, as applicable to incoming passangers, by the holders of EEFC (Exchange Earners Foreign Currency) account. To make these licences "financially more attractive", a number of items relating to health care, sports, communication and office equipment, some consumer goods/consumer durables not reserved for small-scale units, and spares and components have been added to the shopping list.

A new category of super star trading houses has been created and all those exporters with average free on board (FOB) trade turnover of Rs 750 crore in the preceding three years or Rs 1000 crore during the preceding year are eligible for such a status. These houses will be entitled to membership of apex consultative bodies concerned with trades policy and promotion, representation in important business delegations, special permission for overseas trading and special import licences at enhanced rate.

The provided further incentive to export houses, trading as well as star trading and super start trading houses certain types of service exports like software, profes- onal services rendered abroad including overseas consultancy services contracts, will now be counted for purpose of eligibility for the grant of such status to exporters.

The areas of activity in Export Processing Zones (EPZs) have been broadened by providing for trading, re-export after repacking and labelling and also repairs, reconditioning and reengineering.

The requirement of prior approval of Development Commissioner of EPZs for inter-unit transfer has been dispensed with. Debonding modalities have been liberalised and procedures for third party exports by EOU/EPZ units have been further simplified.

The requirement of supporting manufacturer to be indicated in the DEEC (duty exemption entitlement certificates) book has been dispensed with. The Duty Exemption scheme has been further simplified and input-output norms have now been finalised for 3,383 export items as against 2,200 on March 31, 1993. These should help in rendering efficient service to the exporting community.

As regards deemed exports some more facilities are being given to indigenous manufacturers in order to strengthen the industrial base. Here after, the duty -free licence holders will be able to source their goods from local manufacturers instead of importing the same with an added advantage of deemed export benefits. The facility of advance release order has also been extended to special imprest liences, advanced intermediate licences, transferred advance licences and sensitive list items in terms of value. The additional 20% flexibility permissible on such items on value-based licensing will now be permitted to advance release order also.

In order to provide quick and efficient service to the exporters, the powers to grant Export Promotion Capital Goods (EPCG) licences, which were centralised in the office of the Director General of Foreign Trade, have been decentralised. Regional offices can henceforth permit imports upto Rs. 25 lakh. For fulfillment of the obligation under this scheme third party exports have been permitted and the obligation will be based on the exports of same product having nexus with the imported capital goods.

The Government of India has also decided to simplify procedures under the duty exemption seheme. Minimum value addition under the advance customs clearance permit has been reduced from 15% to 10%. Third party exports will now be permitted. Zonal licensing committee have been set up at Bombay, Calcutta, Delhi and Madras, which will permit licence up to Rs 1 crore in respect of cases where norms have not yet been fixed. These committees can also permit licence up to Rs. 10 crore where norms have already been fixed.

Under the simplified policy, second-hand capital goods can now be imported by actual users at normal duty without obtaining a licence, provided they have a minimum residual life of 5 years. The condition of maximum 7 years age as well as submission of chartered engineer certificate has been dispensed with. However, in case of machinery of value exceeding Rs. 1 crore, certificates of reputed international agency has been prescribed.

It may be pointed out that it would not affect the indigenous machinery manufacturers as the import continues to be restricted to actual user only but at the same time it would provide freedom of commercial judgement to the industry about the choice.

Some components required for the manufacture of finished products in the electronic industry have been taken out of the negative list of imports. Moreover relaxation has been provided for the import of prototypes/sample for product development. For the import and export of items which are not covered by the negative lists of exports and imports, the restriction of value additions etc, which was acting as an irritant has been removed. To provide matching facilities to the foreign exhibitors participating in international fairs being held in India, facility to sell items of restricted list up to CIF (Cost, Insurance and Freight) value of Rs 5 lakhs. On payment of normal customs duty has been provided.

In Nutshell Changes in Exim Policy (1992-97) are as follows:

(i) A new category of Super-Star Trading Houses have been introduced.

(ii) Gold, Silver and some consumer goods may be imported under special import licences: items reserved for small scale industries sector not included.

(iii) Deemed exporter status to local manufacturers supplying to duty-free licence holders.

(iv) Duty Exemption Scheme further simplified and import-export norms for 3383 items finalised.

(v) Third party exports permitted under Export Promotion Capital Goods (EPCG) scheme.Negative list further proved.

(vi) Advance release order facility extended to special import licences, advance intermediate licences and transferred advance licences.

(vii) LUT limit further rationalised

(viii) Value-based advance licence scheme to continue with safeguards.

Evaluation of New Exim Policy

The new Exim Policy could be expected to be called as "Export-industrial growth oriented" which is expected to accelerate globalisation of the Indian economy.

Measures such as expansion of shopping list under special import licence creating new category of super star trading houses, decentralisation of EPCG licensers, simplification of duty exemption scheme, pruning of negative list and deemed exporter status to local manufacturers supplying to duty free licence holders, better facilities to the EOUs and EPZs will take care some of the pressing problems of the exporters and will give push to India's exports.

However, the new Exim Policy could have given more export incentive in sectors such as agriculture and food processing gems and jewellery, garments and leather manufactures. The Exim Policy continues a steady progress of economic reforms and trade liberalisation which has been the hallmark of the Government policies since June, 1991. The new policy is supposed to strengthen the hands of exporters to meet the challenge not only to maintain tempo of export but also to accelerate growth in achieving higher export targets. The changes effected in the export Import Policy (1992-97) should help to accelerate the pace of exports and will give impetus to the industrial and trading activities in the country.

Setting-up of super star trading houses has been a welcome feature, but the threshold limit should have been brought down to Rs. 500-700 to crore to enable big exporters to excel their performance. Regarding import of second-hand machinery, interest of the indigenous machinery manufacturers should be safeguarded. Now the steps should be taken to see that import of certain consumer goods and relaxation in import of second-hand machinery do not affect the domestic industry.

APPENDIX A

Definitions of Important Words in Exim Policy: (1992-97)

For the purpose of this Policy, unless the context otherwise requires, the following words and expressions shall have the meanings attached tc them:

(1) "Accessory" or "Attachment" means a part, sub-assembly or assembly that contributes to the efficiency of effectiveness of a piece of equipment without changing its basic functions.

(2) "Act" means the Imports and Exports (Control) Act 1947.

(3) "Actual User" means an actual user who may be either industrial or non-industrial.

(4) "Actual User (Industrial)" means a person who utilises the imported goods for manufacturing in his own industrial unit or manufacturing for his own use in another unit including a jobbing unit.

(5) "Actual User (Non-Industrial)" means a person who utilises the imported goods for his own use in

(*i*) any commercial establishment carrying on any business, trade or profession; or

(*ii*) any laboratory, scientific or Research and Development (R &D) institution, university or other educational institution or hospital; or

(*iii*) any service industry.

(6) "Capital Goods" means any plant, machinery, equipment or accessories required for production, directly or indirectly, of goods or for rendering services, including those required for replacement, modernisation or expansion.

(7) "Canalisation" of exports and imports means exports and imports only through the agencies designated by the Central Government.

(8) "Competent Authority" means an authority competent to exercise any power or discharge any duty or function under the Act or the Rules and Orders made thereunder or under this Policy.

(9) "Component" means one of the parts of a sub-assembly or assembly of which a manufactured product is made up and into which it may be resolved. A component includes an accessory or attachment.

(10) "Consumables" means any item which participates in or is required for a manufacturing process, but does not form a part of the end-product. Items which are subsantially or totally consumed during a manufacturing process will be deemed to be consumables.

(11) "Consumer Goods" means any consumption goods which can directly satisfy human needs without further processing and include consumer durables.

(12) "*Counter Trade*" means any arrangement under which exports/imports from India are balanced either by direct imports/exports from the importing/exporting country or through a third country under a Trade Agreement or otherwise. Exports/Imports under Counter Trade may be

carried out through Escrow Account, Buy Back arrangements, barter trade or any similar arrangement. The balancing of exports and imports could wholly or partly be in cash, goods and/or services.

(13) "Drawback" in relation to any goods manufactured in India and exported means the rebate of duty chargeable on any imported materials or excisable materials used in the manufacture of such goods in India.

(14) "Excisable goods" means any goods produced or manufactured in India and subject to a duty of excise under the Central Excise and Salt Act 1944 (1 of 1944).

(15) "Exporter" means a person who exports or intends to export and holds an Importer-Exporter code number.

(16) "Export House/Trading House/Star Trading House" means an exporter holding an Export House/Trading House/Star Trading House certificate issued by the Chief Controller of Imports and Exports.

(17) "Export Obligation" means the obligation to export the product or product covered by the licence or permission in terms of quantity, value or both, as may be prescribed or specified by the licensing or competent authority.

(18) "Importer" means a person who imports or intends to import and holds an Importer-Exporter code number.

(19) "International Price Reimbursment Scheme" means any scheme providing for reimbursment of an amount equivalent to the difference between domestic and international prices, as determined by the Central Government from time to time, in respect of specific input used in the export product.

(20) "Licensing Authority" means the authority competent to grant a licence under any law for the time being in force.

(21) "Licence" means a licence granted and includes a Customs Clearance Permit or any other permission granted by the licensing authority.

(22) "Licensing year" means the period beginning on the 1st April of a year and ending on the 31st March of the following year.

(23) "Life Saving Drug" means a drug necessary for saving life and includes a sight-saving drug and notified as such by the Chief Controller of Imports and Exports.

(24) "Life Saving Equipment" means an equipment (including spares) necessary for saving life and notified as such by the Chief Controller of Imports and Exports.

(25) "Manufacture" means to make, produce, fabricate, assemble, process or bring into existence, by hand or by machine, a new product having a distinctive name, character or use.

(26) "Manufacturer-Exporter" means a person who manufactures goods and exports or intends to export such goods.

(27) "Merchant Exporter" means a person engaged in trading activity and exporting or intending to export goods.

(28) "Notification" means a notification published in the Official Gazette.

(29) "Part" means an element of a sub-assembly or assembly not normally useful by itself and not amenable to further disassembly for maintenance purposes. A part may be a component or an accessory.

(30) "Person" includes an individual, firm, society, company, corporation or any other legal person.

(31) "Policy" means the Export and Import Policy 1992-97 as amended from time to time.

(32) "Prescribed" means prescribed under the Imports and Exports (Control) Act 1947 or the Rules or Orders made thereunder or under this Policy.

(33) "Public Notice" means a notice published under the Policy for the information of the public.

(34) "Raw material" means

(*i*) basic materials which are needed for the manufacture of goods, but which are still in a raw, natural, unrefined or unmanufactured state; and

(*ii*) for a manufacturer, any materials or goods which are required for his manufacturing process, whether they have actually been previously manufactured or are processed or are still in raw or natural state.

(35) "Registration-cum-Membership Certificate" means the certificate of registration and membership granted by any Export Promotion Council listed in Chapter XIII.

(36) "Spares" means a part or a sub-assembly or assembly for substitution, that is, ready to replace an identical or similar part or sub-assembly or assembly. Spares includes a component or an accessory.

(37) "Specified" means specified by or under the provisions of this Policy.

APPENDIX 1B

Export-Import Policy (1997-98 to 2002-3)

The Government of India declared new export-import policy for 1997-2002 in order to raise India's share in global trade. The export-import policy of 1992-97 resulted in rise of Indias share in global trade from 7.3% in 1991-92 to 9.9% in 1995-96. Moreover, the ministry of commerce has set an ambitious target of attaining an export level of US $ 90 - 100 billion by 2002 so as to achieve 1% share in world Trade. Keeping in mind the fact, an effort is made in the new policy to deregulate and simplify the procedures after organising a number of seminars/workshops at different places in India to know expectations and aspirations of traders.

The policy has following objectives:

(1) To accelerate the country's transition to a globally-oriented vibrant economy with a view to derive maximum benefits form expanding market opportunities.

(2) To stimulate sustained economic growth by providing access to essential raw materials. Intermediaries, components, consumables and capital-goods required for augmenting production.

(3) To encourage the technological strength and efficacy of Indian Agriculture, industry and services, thereby improving their competitive strength while generating new employment opportunities and encourage the attainment of internationally accepted standard of quality.

(4) To provide consumers with good quality products or reasonable prices.

Thus, the policy aims at:

(a) Growth with stability in global trade of India during the period of the ninth five-year plan.

(b) Simplification of the policy package only in a 77 pages book by easy language.

(c) Explanation of the value addition technique in over export earning.

(d) Showing ways and means to boost export against advance license.

The present New Exim Policy 1997-2002 has bridged the gap of missing links in policy measures in earlier policy of liberalisation period. It also indicates future happening of evenses by full-convertibility of Rupee. This is so, capital account convertibility of Rupee will substantially affect foreign exchange reserves as well as foreign exchange earnings also.

The exporters and export houses will be benefitted a lot as the present policy gave a significant boost to Indian export business duty free imports related to export production have been liberalised and provision for duty free license so as to raise 22% of gross domestic products in the coming years of India.

Negative list of imports contains 3 prohibitive items in the case of consumers goods Tallow, fat, oils of any animal, animal rennet, wild animals whereas, restricted items number electronic goods, consumes tele communications equipments, telephone instruments watches in SKD/CKD or in assembled condition, manmade and blended fabrics, concentrated alcoholic beverages, wines and saffron. For precious, semi-precious and other stones import permitted for export against a license or in accordance with a public notice issues in this behalf safety, security and related items, the same position remained in the case of paper for security printing, stamp paper, fire arms, Ammunation, explosives and acetic anhydrides, same position remained in the case of other imported item except raw material for production.

Salient Features of 1997-2002 Exim Policy

One can safely draw following features of the policy:

(1) under the policy, conscious effort is made to dismantle various protectionist and regulatory policies and accelerate the country's transition towards a globally-oriented economy. Introduction of value-based advance licencing over and above quantity-based advance licence will give greater flexibility in the trade in the case of sensitive goods.

(2) New policy tunes with export target of the ninth five-year plan which is about 22% in order to strengthen special schemes directed towards diversification of export business from India.

(3) The earlier policy 1992-97 enlarged export business without any quantitive restrictions except in the case sensitive goods, whereas, the present policy of 1997-2002 seeks to consolidate the gains of the previous policy and to further to carry forward the process of liberalisation.

(4) The new policy tries to create congenial environment for export community by simplifying procedure.

(5) Import of computer systems may be imported under the Export Promotion of Capital Goods (EPCG) scheme. Import on concessional duty is applicable to capital goods including spares upto 20% of cif value of the capital goods.

(6) More clarity is given on 'Duty' exemption scheme to permit duty free licence for MODVAT, Special imprest licence, Advance licence, export obligation and transferability with clear formula of value additional purpose as well as net foreign exchange earnings as a percentage of export calculation method is given in the policy.

(7) Quality conscious in the new policy highlighted to acquire ISO-9000 or BIS 14000 certificate of quality for export houses, trading houses, for professional dynamic institution.

(8) Diamond, gems and jewellery export promotion schemes for importing their inputs by obtaining Replenishment licence. Items not sold abroad shall be reimported within 45 days of the close of the exhibition. Similarly, the gold/silver/platinum content items may be reimported as replenishment not later than 60 days.

(9) Export-oriented units and Export processing Zone are encouraged for more amount of exports for Gems and Jewellery and software technology part units. Only 5% of rejected value of the production may be sold in Domestic Tariff Area, 25% of the production in value terms may be sold in the area subject to payment of applicable duties.

(10) The policy has highlighted important role of Export promotion councils. Export Houses, Trading Houses and star trading houses is kept continued. They can also avail benefits of concession under the new policy.

(11) The list of canalised items indicate marginal change as 8 items on important side and 6 items on export side, whereas, in the case of earlier Exim policy, there were 8 items on import side 10 items on export side. Limited number of Indian corporation are permitted for the business.

Highlights of New Exim Policy 1997-2002

I. General:

(i) Stable and diversified policy for five years from 1997 April to 2002 March, subject to marginal change once in a quarter.

(ii) Basic philosophy of free trade tuning with New World Trade Order (W.T.O.) so as to raise Indian percentage share in global trade.

(iii) Competition, cost consciousness with level of quality to develop business.

(iv) Trade to be free subject to negative list of both export and imports considering capital convertibility of rupee from April 2000.

II. Exports:

(i) Negative list of exports contain 10 prohibitive items, 32 restricted items and 6 canalised items.

(ii) Now Export business promoted with minimum regulation.

(iii) All export contracts and invoices shall be denominated in freely convertible currency and export proceeds shall be realised in freely convertible currency. The central government may relax for contracts through Asian clearing union in Acu dollar.

(iv) Export of Gift including edible items of value shall not be exceeding Rs. 15,000/- in a licensing year.

(v) For raising export performance level FOB criterian and NFE criterion for export houses, trading houses, star trading houses and super star trading houses.

(vi) Role of Export-oriented units, Export processing Zones and export promotion councils liberalised and made effective.

III. Imports:

(i) 542 items of import exempted from special import licence, 150 items permitted import under special licence scheme, 60 items totally exempted form licence and 75% of total are free from controlled licence. Only five items bear import restriction due to environment control, safety, strategic and also in the interest of public health.

(ii) Import or export basis are permitted along with import of gift in Baggage Rules.

(iii) Negative List of imports include 3 prohibitive items five Restricted items in consumers list insecticide and chemical items.

(iv) Concessional duty imports will continue under EPCS schemes.

Evaluation of the Policy: (1997-2002)

(1) The provision of the new exim policy is valid for five years of the ninth five-year plan period.

(2) An effort is made in the policy by commerce Ministry for bold and imaginative initiatives in the policy as India is marching towards 21st century.

(3) The new exim policy has provided firm steps in rising Indias exports to boost its share.

(4) The partial convertibility of the rupee scheme was introduced in the union budget 1992-93 so as to increase export earnings in revenue account, whereas, capital account convertibility as contained in Tarapore Committee Report of RBI (July 1997) will surely open new avenues of trade.

(5) The policy has emphasised quality consciousness for sustainable growth of Indias trade considering external environment in initial years of 21st century. It will surely contribute to balance of payment situation, particularly for external payment of debt and its servicing.

(6) Sufficient trade reforms are offered since 1992-97 policy to meet with global challenges. Indian trade community will have to take advantage of the new policy so as to make India on global map as an authority.

(7) The new exim policy need to raise gross domestic product from present 18% to 23% in the next five years and must help to bridge gap of budget deficit for at sustainable level.

(8) The success of the new exim policy lies with efficient operation of monetary policy, fiscal policy, foreign exchange Management Policy by the Government of India during the years of the ninth five-year plan. Moreover, trade organisations and Associations expect quick and efficiency services to the exporters.

(9) For export processing Zones, areas of activities are broaden by providing for trading, re-export after repackaging and labelling. Moreover, repairing, reconditioning, and re-engineering are also included to broaden their functioning.

Thus, policy makes of India offered on excellent new exim policy and it depends upon exports and super-exporters to exercise the policy in order to correct Macroeconomic imbalances by diversifying the trade and substantial contribution to make India as a leading nation in global trade.

Role of Capital Account Convertibility in Globalising Trade

Dr. Manmohan Singh Ex. Finance Minister declared current account convertibility as a measure of liberalisation. Still, it was expected capital account convertibility of Indian rupee so as to make it fully convertible in any currency of the world. However, convertibility helped Indian Traders to boost overseas markets.

Reserve Bank of India appointed a committee on Capital Account Convertibility (CAC) of the Rupee under the chairmanship of Mr. S.S.Tarapore. The committee submitted report June in 1997 and pleaded full convertibility of rupee on capital account from April 2000 A.D. From marketing and payment point of view, CAC has two important implications.

(1) Macroeconomic equilibrium in India will be characterised by net inflow of capital.

(2) Any effective constraint on outflows result in a corresponding reduction in gross inflows and higher domestic interest rates.

(3) Fear about volatility of exchange rate may affect cross-country payment mechanism.

(4) Convertibility on capital account means that households and firms of India are not forced to meet each other through Indian financial system. It will be direct route for global payment mechanism in such cases and private sector payments.

CAC means rupee can be converted to dollars for acquisition of capital Assets abroad which include both financial and real assets. It is an exercise to make free Indian banks and corporates from various FERA Regulations. Convertibility means that households and firms of India are not relied to meet each other through India's Financial system. The GDR Market is one of the alternatives to meet with foreign investors through markets outside India. Convertibility to meet with foreign investors through markets outside India. Convertibility will make Indian firms to interact with Indian households in markets of singapore. This would provide alternatives to India's households and firms, generate competition for India's financial industry. For example, if derivatives on the dollar rupee start trading in Singapore or Chicago. Thus, convertibility means we in India would be able to use them.

Convertibility would generate mossive flows of funds to and out India as Indians and foreigners modify their portfolio to reflect new investment possibilities. It will allow Indian nationals to hold internationally diversified portfolios thereby decreasing their vulnerability to domestic shock. This may encourage Indian entrepreneurs to seek a global presence without interference from government or regulatory authority/agencies. Convertibility open up new avenues for a narrowing of the tax base and hence upgrades the priority of harmonisation of taxation in India with international standards.

The foreign market will be specially in the spotlight since increased flows of funds will have to go to through the dollar-rupee market. An illiquid dollar-rupee market will display spurious volatility under pressure. For this, it appears that two alternative approach to be followed:

(1) Transition of the spot market away from the interbank market to modern screen based trading that is country-wide accessible, and,

(2) Transition away from the inter-bank dollar — rupee forward market to a modern dollar rupee future market without entry barrier.

However, experts of the foreign market viewed that capital account convertibility increase the volatility of the rupee exchange rate and second there is a fear that capital flight can take place. Enormous amount of Indian capital has gone out during the previous restrictive regimes. Our foreign exchange reserves are not high to cope with requirements of servicing existing debt and current Account Deficits. Approximates per annum at $ 45 billion for 1998-99 and 1999-2000. Tarapore committee reviewed and reacted that restriction on current account and then liberalise policy for investment abroad by sound export growth and transparent financial system. Operational controls on banks need to removed with sound capital base of banks by lower level of non-performing assets of banks from 13.5% in 1996-97 to 5% in 1999-2000.

Capital account convertibility will require new exchange rate policy as a part of convertibility plan. For this, Tarapore Committee Report (1997) suggested a Real

Effective exchange Rate as a primary indicator of the market and the exchange rate, to be aligned to it. Movement of exchange rate and its monitoring require 5% variations on each side of neutral Real Effective Exchange rate with minimal inntervention from the RBI. The Real Effective Exchange rate as if stands now: Rs. 37 to Rs. 37.25 to a dollar and if we compare net effective exchange rate stands at Rs. 35.85 to a dollar. For exporters, it will be quite depreciated rate. Tarapore committee recommended that as a part of exchange rate management greater attention should be focussed on ensuring the forward exchange markets reflect interest rate differentials. Thus, credibility of exchange rate policy would be vital in the context of Capital Account Convertibility. This is so as developments in the forex market will move the money market as well. It appears that capital account convertibility would be a right step by the government of India to tune with new World Trade Organisation to develop trade of developing countries in 21st century. Therefore, if may dismantle binding outflow restriction before allowing inflows, instead of simultaneously removing both curbs as planned. It can be argued that Capital Account Convertibility will lower total savings. Artificially boosting GDP growth by curbing resident out flows is neither desirable nor likely to be sustainable in the long run. Thus, capital account convertibility posed challenges to Indian economy for serious financial and export business preparation to match with the prevailing situation of 21st century.

APPENDIX - II

Definitions

3.1 For the purpose of this Policy, unless the context otherwise requires, the following words and expressions shall have the meaning attached to them.

3.2 "Accessory" or "Attachment" means a part, sub-assembly or assembly that contributes to the efficiency or effectiveness of a piece of equipment without changing its basic functions.

3.3 "Act" means the Foreign Trade (Development and Regulation) Act, 1992 (No.22 of 1992).

3.4 "Actual User" means an actual user who may be either industrial or non-industrial.

3.5 "Actual User (Industrial)" means a person who utilises the imported goods for manufacturing in his own industrial unit or manufacturing for his own use in another unit including a jobbing unit.

3.6 "Actual User (Non-Industrial)" means a person who utilises the imported goods for his own use in:

(*i*) any commercial establishment carrying on any business, trade or profession; or

(*ii*) any laboratory, Scientific or Research and Development (R & D) institution, university or other educational institution or hospital; or

(*iii*) any service industry.

3.7 "ALC" means the Advance Licensing Committee in the Directorate General of Foreign Trade for recommending grant of licences under Duty Exemption Scheme.

3.8 "Applicant" means the person on whose behalf the application is made and shall, wherever the context so requires, include the person signing the application.

3.9 "Canalisation" of exports and imports means exports and imports only through the agencies designated by the Central Government.

3.10 "Capital Goods" means any plant, machinery, equipment or accessories required for manufacture or production, either directly or indirectly, of goods or for rendering services, including those required for replacement, modernisation, technological upgradation or expansion. Capital goods also include packaging machinery and equipment, refractories, refrigeration equipment, power generating sets, machine tools, catalysts for initial charge, equipment and instruments for testing, research and development, quality and pollution control. Capital goods may be for use in manufacturing, mining, agriculture, aquaculture, animal husbandry, floriculture, horticulture, pisciculture, poultry, sericulture and viticulture as well as for use in the services sector.

3.11 "Competent Authority" means an authority competent to exercise any power or discharge any duty or function under the Act or the Rules and Orders made thereunder or under this Policy.

3.12 "Component" means one of the parts of a sub-assembly or assembly of which a manufactured product is made up and into which it may be resolved. A component includes an accessory or attachment to the component.

3.13 "Consumables" means any item which participates in or is required for a manufacturing process, but does not form a part of the end-product. Items which are substantially or totally consumed during a manufacturing process will be deemed to be consumables.

3.14 "Consumer Goods" means any consumption goods which can directly satisfy human needs without further processing and include consumer durables and accessories thereof.

3.15 "Counter Trade" means any arrangement under which exports/imports from/to India are balanced either by direct imports/exports from the importing/exporting country or through a third country under a Trade Agreement or otherwise. Exports/Imports under Counter Trade may be carried out through Escrow Account, Buy Back arrangements, Barter trade or any similar arrangement. The balancing of exports and imports could wholly or partly be in cash, goods and/or services.

3.16 "DEEC" means Duty Exemption Entitlement Certificate issued under Duty Exemption Scheme.

3.17 "Designated Authority" means an officer of the Directorate General of Foreign Trade not below the rank of Deputy Director General of Foreign Trade, for operating the Pass Book Scheme.

3.18 "Drawback" in relation to any goods manufactured in India and exported means the rebate of duty chargeable on any imported material or excisable material used in the manufacture of such goods in India. The goods include imported spares, if supplied, with capital goods manufactured in India.

3.19 "EOU" means Export Oriented Unit.

3.20 "EPZ" means Export Processing Zone.

3.21 "Excisable goods" means any goods produced or manufactured in India and subject to a duty of excise under the Central Excises and Salt Act,1944 (1 of 1944).

3.22 "Exporter" means a person who exports or intends to export and holds an Importer-Exporter Code number.

3.23 "Export House/Trading House/Star Trading House/Super Star Trading House" means an exporter holding an Export House/Trading House/Star Trading House/Super Star Trading House certificate issued by the Directorate General of Foreign Trade.

3.24 "Export Obligation" means the obligation to export the product or products covered by the licence or permission in terms of quantity, value or both, as may be prescribed or specified by the licensing or competent authority.

3.25 "Form" means a form prescribed under the Foreign Trade (Development and Regulation) Act, 1992, or the Rules and Orders made thereunder or a form provided in the Handbook (Vol.1).

3.26 "Handbook (Vol.1)" means the Handbook of Procedures (Vol.1) and "Handbook (Vol.2)" means Handbook of Procedures (Vol.2) published under the provisions of the paragraph 4.11 of the Policy.

3.27 "Importer" means a person who imports or intends to import and holds an Importer-Exporter Code number.

3.28 "Jobbing" means processing or working upon of raw materials or semi-finished goods supplied to the job worker so as to complete a part or whole of the process resulting in the manufacture or finishing of an article or any operation which is essential for the aforesaid process.

3.29 "Licensing Authority" means the authority competent to grant a licence under the Act/Order.

3.30 "Licensing Year" means the period beginning on the 1st April of a year and ending on the 31st March of the following year.

3.31 "Manufacture" means to make, produce, fabricate, assemble, process or bring into existence, by hand or by machine, a new product having a distinctive name, character or use and shall include processes, such as refrigeration, repacking, polishing, labelling and segregation. Manufacture, for the purpose of this Policy, shall also include agriculture, aquaculture, animal husbandry, floriculture, horticulture, pisciculture, poultry, sericulture, viticulture and mining.

3.32 "Manufacturer Exporter" means a person who exports goods manufactured by him or intends to export such goods.

3.33 "Merchant Exporter" means a person engaged in trading activity and exporting or intending to export goods.

3.34 "Notification" means a notification published in the Official Gazette.

3.35 "Order" means Order made by the Central Government under the Act.

3.36 "Part" means an element of a sub-assembly or assembly not normally useful by itself and not amendable to further disassembly for maintenance purposes. A part may be a component or an accessory.

3.37 "Person" includes an individual, firm, society, company, corporation or any other legal person.

3.38 "Policy" means the Export and Import Policy, 1997-2002 as amended from time to time.

3.39 "Prescribed" means prescribed under the Foreign Trade (Development and Regulation) Act, 1992 (No. 22 of 1992) or the Rules or Orders made thereunder or under this Policy.

3.40 "Public Notice" means a notice published under the provisions of paragraph 4.11 of the Policy.

3.41 "Raw material" means:

(*i*) basic materials which are needed for the manufacture of goods, but which are still in a raw, natural, unrefined or unmanufactured state; and

(*ii*) for a manufacturer, any materials or goods which are required for his manufacturing process, whether they have actually been previously manufactured or are processed or are still in a raw or natural state.

3.42 "RALC" means the Regional Advance Licensing Committee in the office of the Regional Licensing Authority.

3.43 "Regional Licensing Authority" means a licensing authority exercising powers in respect of any area of region specified in this behalf by the Director General of Foreign Trade.

3.44 "Registration-cum-Membership Certificate" (RCMC) means the certificate of registration and membership granted by an Export Promotion Council or other competent authority as prescribed in the Policy or Handbook (Vol. 1).

3.45 "Rules" means Rules made by the Central Government under section 19 of the Act.

3.46 "SALC" means the Special Advance Licensing Committee in the Directorate General of Foreign Trade for recommending Input-Output Norms to be notified by Director General of Foreign Trade.

3.47 "Service Provider" means a person providing —

(*i*) supply of a service from India to any other country;

(*ii*) supply of a service from India to the service consumer of any other country in India; and

(*iii*) supply of a service from India through commercial presence in the territory of any other country.

3.48 "Services" include computer software.

3.49 "SIL" means freely transferable Special Import Licences issued under the Policy.

3.50 "Spares" means a part or a sub-assembly or assembly for substitution, that is ready to replace an identical or similar part or sub-assembly or assembly. Spares include a component or an accessory.

3.51 "Specified" means specified by or under the provisions of this Policy.

3.52 "Wild Animal" means any wild animal as defined in section 2(36) of the Wildlife (Protection) Act, 1972.

3.53 "ZALC" means the Zonal Advance Licensing Committee in the office of Jt. Director General of Foreign Trade at Mumbai, Calcutta, Delhi and Chennai for recommending grant of licences under Duty Exemption Scheme.

6

GOVERNMENT REGULATIONS — EXCHANGE CONTROL, FERA 1973, CUSTOMS LAW

Statutory Basis for Exchange Control on Exports

Section 18(1) of FERA 1973 empowers Government of India to prescribe a condition precedent to any export of goods from India that a declaration should be furnished by the exporter that *(i)* the full export value of the goods, or *(ii)* if the full export value of the goods is not ascertainable at the time of export, the value which the exporter, having regard to the prevailing market conditions, expects to receive on the sale of the goods in the overseas market, has been or will be paid, within the prescribed period and in the prescribed manner. In exercise of powers conferred by this sub-section, Government of India have issued Notifications No. F1/67/EC/73-1 and No. F1/67/EC/73-2 both dated 1st January 1974 prohibiting the export of any goods directly or indirectly or indirectly to any place outside India, other than Nepal and Bhutan, unless a declaration in the prescribed form is furnished to the prescribed authority.

Exemptions for Goods sent Otherwise than by Post

In terms of Government of India Notification No. F1/67/EC/73-1 dated 1st January 1974 (as amended) the requirement of declaration on one of the prescribed forms does not apply to the following:

(a) Trade samples supplied free of payment.

(b) Personal effects of travellers, whether accompanied or unaccompanied (Articles covered by this exemption are strictly limited to *bona fide* personal effects and will not normally include

unused carpets, silverware and other such articles of high value. Shipment of such articles will not be permitted by Customs Authorities except when they are within the permissible limits, if any, laid down under Export Baggage Rules unless they are accompanied by specific waiver issued by Reserve Bank.)

(c) Ships' stores carried on board vessels for their own use during voyages.

(d) Transhipment cargo *i.e.,* goods shipped from countries outside India and transhipped at Indian ports for destinations outside India.

(e) Goods shipped under orders of Central Government or of such officers as may be appointed by Central Government in this behalf or of Military, Naval or Air Force authorities in India for Military, Naval or Air Force requirements.

(f) Goods, other than sample of journals and periodicals, despatched by air freight and accompanied by declaration by sender that they are less than Rs. 200/- in value and that their despatch does not involve any transaction in foreign exchange.

(g) Samples of journals and periodicals despatched by air freight and accompanied by a declaration by the sender that they are less than Rs. 250/- in value and that their despatch does not involve any transaction in foreign exchange.

(h) Goods despatched by air freight and covered by certificate issued by an authorised dealer that their despatch does not involve any transaction in foreign exchange.

(i) Goods in respect of which Reserve Bank has waived requirement of declaration.

Exemptions for Parcels sent by Post

In terms of Government of India Notification No.F1/67/EC/73-2 dated 1st January 1974 (as amended) the requirement of declaration on the prescribed form does not apply to the following:

(a) Postal packet accompanied by declaration by sender that the contents are less than Rs. 200/- in value and that its despatch does not involve any transaction in foreign exchange.

(b) Postal packet covered by certificate issued by an authorised dealer that the despatch of the parcel does not involve any transaction in foreign exchange.

(c) Goods in respect of which Reserve Bank has waived requirement of declaration.

Exports by U.N.O. and its Affiliates

Exports of goods by United Nations Organisation (U.N.O.) and its affiliate bodies in India for their official use abroad are exempt from the requirement of declaration on prescribed from if the body concerned certifies that the export is for official use and exemption is claimed in terms of paragraph 7(b) of Article II of United Nations (Privileges and Immunities) Act, 1947. Customs will permit such exports on production of the certificate without insisting on declaration on prescribed from or production of a waiver from Reserve Bank. This exemption does not apply to exports of goods by exporters on account of U.N. Agencies where payment will be realised by the exporters in rupees from funds held by these U.N. Agencies in India or in free foreign exchange by means of cheques drawn by UNICEF on their overseas bank account/s in respect of goods exported to UNICEF assisted projects/ programmes in third countries. In such cases, the exporters should declare the exports on prescribed declaration form and also obtain prior permission of Reserve Bank for the method of payment.

Foreign Exchange Regulation Rules

In exercise of powers conferred by Section 79 of FERA 1973 Government of India have framed the Foreign Exchange Regulation Rules. 1974 vide Notification No.F1/67/EC/73-3 dated 1st January 1974 (as amended). The various forms in which the declaration referred to in paragraph 11A.1 should be furnished have been prescribed in the Second Schedule appended to the Rules. These Rules also lay down regulations applicable to various matters such as allotment of code numbers too exporters, prescribed period for realisation of export proceeds, manner of payment of export value of goods, etc. These subjects are dealt with at appropriate places in this Part.

Export Declaration Forms

The Foreign Exchange Regulation Rules, 1974 (as amended) prescribe export declaration forms called GR, PP and VP/COD forms. All exports to which the requirement of declaration applies must be declared on appropriate forms as indicated below:

(a) *GR Form:* Exports to all countries made otherwise than by post.

(b) *PP Form:* Exports to all countries by parcel post, except when made on 'value payable' or 'cash on delivery' basis.

(c) *VP/COD Form*: Exports to all countries by parcel post, under arrangements to realise proceeds through postal channels on 'value payable' or 'cash on delivery' basis.

Note: Export declarations are to be made in a set of two copies (original and duplicate) of GR or PP form. VP/COD forms are to be submitted in a single copy.

Numbering of Forms

GR and PP forms are printed by Reserve Bank for sale to authorised dealers for supply to their customers. VP/COD forms are sold directly to exporters by the offices of Exchange Control Department of Reserve Bank. GR/PP forms are printed in distinctive colours and each set bears a printed number which appears on both copies in it. Each GR form also bears a superscription indicating the date before which it should be used. In all remittance applications and correspondence with Reserve Bank relating to any export transaction, the printed number of GR/PP form on which relative export was declared should invariably be cited. In case of export declared on GR form, the number allotted to the GR form by Customs at the time of shipment should also be cited in full.

Exporter's Code Number

(i) Every person/firm/company engaged in export business in India should obtain a code number from Reserve Bank. Application for this purpose should be made by the Head/Registered Office of the exporter in form CNX in duplicate to the office of Reserve Bank within whose jurisdiction the Head/Registered Office of the applicant is situate. Such applications may preferably be routed through the bankers of the applicant in the interest of speedy disposal. Reserve Bank will return to the exporter the duplicate of the form with the code number indicated thereon. The Head/Registered Office as well as its branches in India should invariably cite the code number so allotted by Reserve Bank on GR, PP or VP/COD forms used for declaration of exports. Customs will not entertain any export form which does not bear the exporter's code number allotted by Reserve Bank.

(ii) In order to avoid delay in obtaining code numbers, exporters should be advised to ensure that form CNX is properly completed and the information is complete and precise. Particular attention should be paid to the following requirements:

(a) Exporters should furnish the full Income-Tax Permanent Account Number on the form. In case Permanent Account Number has not been allotted by Income Tax authorities, the application may be supported by an undertaking to the effect that the Permanent Account Number will be intimated to Reserve Bank as soon as it is allotted.

(b) Exporters should indicate full postal addresses of their bankers against the respective column.

(c) The application firm/company should submit a separate declaration to the effect that its proprietor, partners or directors, as the case may be, is/are not associated as proprietor/partners directors in a firm/company which has been caution-listed by Reserve Bank.

(*d*) If the applicant is a firm or company the signatory should indicate his designation and affix the stamp of the firm/company at the place provided therefore.

Authorised dealers should forward the application without any delay together with their confidential reports on means and standing of the applicants indicating, *inter alia* date of establishment of the firm/company, names/addresses of the proprietors/partners/directors, nature of business and period for which they have been bankers to the applicants. Exporters should be advised that the code number allotted by Reserve Bank is for the common use of all their offices/branches in India and in no circumstance should the same exporter apply for more than one code number at the same office or any other office of Reserve Bank.

Time Limit for Realisation of Export Proceeds

The amount representing full export value of the goods exported must be realised by exporters within six months from the date of export in respect of all shipment to all countries. However, in respect of exports to Indian-owned warehouses abroad, a maximum period of 15 months is allowed for realisation of export proceeds.

Methods of Payment

(*i*) The basic rule governing payment for exports is that it must be received through the medium of an authorised dealer in foreign exchange in a currency or through an account appropriate to the country of **final destination** of the goods as declared on GR etc. forms, irrespective of the country of residence of the buyer. For example, if goods are shipped to West Germany on the order of a buyer in East Germany, payment must be received only in permitted currency or in rupees from a bank situated in a country in the External Group.

(*ii*) Financing of exports in a manner other than a permitted method will require prior permission of Reserve Bank. Reserve Bank will normally permit methods of payment which are beneficial from the angle of Exchange Control, such as where a convertible currency is offered against export to a country in the Bilateral Group, provided the payment is voluntarily offered by overseas importers. While referring applications to Reserve Bank, reasons why financing is not being done in one of the approved methods should be explained. Suitable documentary evidence in original should, as far as possible, be forwarded along with the application.

(*iii*) Exporters are not generally permitted to receive payments for exports **directly** from the buyers in the form of cheques, bank drafts, pay orders, foreign currency notes or foreign currency travellers cheques. As an exception to this rule, Reserve Bank will be prepared to consider applications from exporters to receive directly from their overseas buyers drafts and bankers; cheques/pay orders, for a sum not exceeding U.S. $ 15000 or its equivalent (per export shipment) (Amended vide ADMA 17 of 1994)in payment for exports made to them, provided such payment is received in a currency or though an account appropriate to the country of final destination of the goods as stated in sub-paragraph (*i*) above. Payments in the form of foreign currency notes or foreign currency travellers cheques tendered by buyers while on visit to India would also be permitted up to a limited extent. For this purpose, the concerned exporter should designate a branch of an authorised dealer to whom documents in respect of all shipments effected by him will be delivered and instruments such as bank drafts and bankers' cheques/pay orders received towards payment for exports will be tendered within one week of receipt thereof. The application to Reserve Bank should be submitted through the designated branch of authorised dealer.

Participation in Trade Fairs Abroad

(*i*) Firm and companies wishing to participate in fairs and exhibitions (other than book fairs and exhibitions) to be held abroad should apply for their foreign exchange requirements direct to *Trade Fair Authority of India (TFAI),* New Delhi who will make suitable recommendations to Reserve Bank. Such applications should, *inter, alia,* give the following particulars:

(*a*) Extent of space that the firm/company is booking at exhibition and rent payable for it.

(*b*) Quantity and value of goods that the firm/company proposes to send for purpose of display.

(*c*) Incidental expenses for decoration, display of exhibits and labour charges.

(*d*) Number of representatives intending to visit the foreign country for work connected with the exhibition and negotiation of trade and their period of stay there and daily expenses of each.

(*e*) Cost of advertisement if the firm/company intends to have special advertisements other than what will normally be available through the exhibition.

(*ii*) Private publishers, printers, etc. wishing to participate in book fairs/ exhibitions to be held abroad should apply for their exchange requirements to Ministry of Human Resources Development (Department of Education), Government of India, New Delhi who will make suitable recommendations to Reserve Bank.

(*iii*) Trade Fair Authority of India/Ministry of Human Resources Development will endorse copies of their sanction to respective offices of Reserve Bank under whose jurisdiction participating firms/companies are situated.

Reserve Bank will release exchange up to the amount recommended and subject to conditions imposed by the above Authority/Ministry.

Exports under Trade Agreements/Rupee Credits

(*i*) Exports of goods under special arrangements or rupee credits extended by Government of India to foreign governments will be governed by terms and conditions set out by Export Trade Control authorities in the relative Public Notices. These notices will cover various aspects such as type of goods eligible for export, procedure for obtaining approval for individual export contracts, manner of receiving payment and other matters. Important instructions relating to such exports will also be communicated by Reserve Bank to authorised dealers in the form of A.D. (G.P. Series) Circulars. Authorised dealers should refer to these Public Notices and A.D. (G.P. Series) Circulars while handling documents covering exports under these arrangements and ensure that prescribed procedure is meticulously followed.

(*ii*) The Export-Import Bank of India (Exim Bank) also extends, from time to time, lies of credit to commercial banks/financial institutions in foreign countries for financing exports from India to those countries. Terms and conditions governing such credits are communicated by Reserve Bank to authorised dealers by means of A.D. (G.P. Series) Circulars. Authorised dealers should be guided by the instructions contained in such circulars while handling documents covering exports under these arrangements and should meticulously follow the procedure prescribed therein.

Insurance on Exports

Insurance premium on export cargo should be paid by exporters in rupees in India. Wherever such charges are not be borne by the exporter in terms of sale contract between him and the overseas buyer and the exporter is defraying the insurance charges on account of overseas buyer, he should add the amount on the invoice and recover the payment so made from the buyer in an approved manner.

Protection Against Risks Under F.O.B., C.and F. Contracts

In case of exports contracted in F.O.B., C. & F., etc. terms and not covered by irrevocable letter of credit opened by buyers, exporters will be well advised to ensure even before cargoes are shipped that the shipment has been adequately insured against all risks of loss or damage during the entire course of transit and that such insurance cover incorporates seller's interest clause in the relative policy, permitting claims being paid to exporter in India in the event of loss/damage to the shipment before ownership in the good passes to buyer.

Export Trade Control

(*i*) Export Trade Control authorities issue, from time to time, Export Trade Notices containing instructions regulating export of commodities.

These instructions may prohibit export of certain commodities, make export of any commodity subject to licence from Export Trade Control, prescribe minimum export prices or methods by which payments for exports of some commodities will have to be received or lay down special procedures for settlement of claims on export of certain commodities or otherwise regulate exports. Nothing in the Exchange Control regulations or procedures outlined in this Manual shall relieve the exporter from fulfilling the conditions laid down by Export Trade Control authorities in regard to export of goods.

(*ii*) Authorised dealers should also keep themselves informed of the provisions of the notices etc., issued by Export Trade Control authorities from time to time so that procedures, conditions, etc., if any, laid down in such notices insofar as they relate to authorised dealers' business may be complied with.

Certification of Exports for Incentive Purposes

Under the policy formulated by Government for grant of export incentives, Registered Exporters are entitled to obtain import replenishment licences and cash assistance from Government against exports of certain specified commodities. Applications for grant of replenishment licences and cash assistance are required to be made to the licensing authorities, supported by, among other documents, bank certificates issued by authorised dealers. Authorised dealers may issue bank certificates on appropriate forms prescribed by the licensing authorities and also attest invoices wherever required. Details (*i.e.,* number and date of the certificate and the name and address of the licensing authority to whom the duplicate certificate has been sent) should be recorded by the authorised dealers in the export bills register against the relevant entries. Authorised dealers may also register export contracts under the scheme introduced by Government in order that exporters may obtain import replenishment and other benefits as were permissible on the date of such contract with overseas buyers. If any clarification is required in regard to issue of bank certificates or registration of export contracts, authorised dealers may approach Export Trade Control authorities directly.

Bid Bonds and Other Guarantees against Commodity Export

(*i*) Authorised dealers may furnish bid bonds, performance bonds and guarantees (including those in lieu of earnest money) in favour of overseas buyers on account of Indian exporters without prior reference to Reserve Bank in all cases of commodity exports, provided they are satisfied about the bona fides of the applicant and his ability to perform the export contract, and the terms agreed to between the exporter and foreign buyer are in accordance with Exchange Control regulations. In those case where exporters find it necessary to furnish bank guarantees for an amount slightly in excess of what is asked for in tender invitation.

Note: Authorised dealers must ensure, while issuing bid bonds and other guarantees that the value for which they are issued as a percentage of the value of the tender or contract is reasonable and according to normal practice in the trade. Any request containing unusual features should be referred to Reserve Bank. Requests for executing performance guarantees on behalf of exporters placed in the Exporters Caution List should also be referred to Reserve Bank for prior approval.

(ii) Authorised dealers should forward to Reserve Bank monthly statement in form GTE 1 in duplicate giving details of bid bonds/tender guarantees.**

(iii) Authorised dealers may also issue, subject to compliance with conditions laid down in sub-paragraph *(i)* counter-guarantees in favour of their branches/ correspondents abroad in cover of guarantees required to be issued by the latter on behalf of Indian exporters, in cases where guarantees of only resident banks are acceptable to overseas buyers in accordance with local laws as giving full regulations. Details of such counter-guarantees should also be reported to the Reserve Bank in the monthly statement in form GTE-1. Remittances arising on account of invocation of such counter-guarantees may also be made to the non-resident beneficiaries and reported to Reserve Bank as indicated in the sub-paragraph *(iii)* above. All other counter-guarantees to be issued by the authorised dealers will require prior approval of Reserve Bank.

Minor Guarantees

Authorised dealers may freely give on behalf of their customers and overseas branches and correspondents, guarantees in the ordinary course of business in respect of missing or defective documents, authenticity of signatures and for other similar purposes.

PROCEDURE FOR DECLARATION OF EXPORTS

GR/PP Form Procedure for Export of Goods

Customs will not permit a shipment to be made if it is not covered by any of the exemptions listed and unless appropriate declaration form duly signed by the exporter is lodged with them. Since declarations made on GR etc. forms are binding on the exporter, every care should be taken to complete

---

Note: **A.D. if asked for can issue counter guarantee in favour of their branch correspondents abroad to enable them to furnish bank guarante in favour of overseas beneficiaries as per local Law.

all the columns in the form correctly. In particular, the following requirements should be carefully observed by exporters while competing the forms:

(*a*) Name and address of authorised dealer through whom the proceeds of the export have been or will be realised should be specified in the space provided in the form.

(*b*) Details of commission and discount due to foreign agent or buyer should be correctly declared on the form. Exporters have been cautioned that if declaration is not correctly made, inconvenience is likely to be caused as applications for remittance of commission are liable to be rejected and documents allowing discounts to buyers are liable to be refused to be handled by authorised dealers.

(*c*) Where goods are being exported against a firm order or sale contract, the word 'CONSIGNOR' appearing in the declaration part of the form and the entire (*b*) thereof should be struck out. If on the other hand, goods are exported on consignment basis at the risk of exporter for eventual sale and remittance of proceeds by consignee to exporter, the word 'SELLER' appearing in the declaration and the entire clause (*a*) thereof should be struck out.

(*d*) Under the item 'Analysis of full export value', a break-up of the full export value of goods under F.O.B value, freight and insurance should be furnished in all cases, irrespective of the terms of contract.

Disposal of Copies of Export Declaration Forms — GR Form

Copies of export declaration forms should be disposed of as under:

(*i*) (*a*) GR forms should be completed by the exporter in duplicate and both the copies submitted to Customs at the port of shipment. In certain cases (*e.g.*, export of jewellery by air), GR forms are required to be countersigned by an authorised dealer before being presented to Customs. Customs will give their running serial number on both the copies of the GR forms in the space provided for the purpose after verifying the particulars in both the copies and admitting the corresponding shipping bill. The Customs serial number will have ten numerals denoting the code number of the port of shipment, the calendar year and a **six digit** running serial number. Customs will certify the value declared by the exporter on both the copies of the GR form at the space earmarked and will also record the assessed value. They will then return the duplicate copy of the form to the exporter and retain the original for transmission to Reserve Bank. Exporters should submit the duplicate copy of the GR form again to Customs along with the cargo to be shipped. After examination of the goods and certifying the quantity passed for shipment on the duplicate copy, Customs will return it to the exporter for submission to the authorised dealer for negotiation or collection of export bills. Where the forms are countersigned by an authorised dealer prior to submission to Customs, the duplicate copies of the forms must be submitted to the same authorised dealer who countersigned the forms.

(*b*) Within **twenty one** days from shipment of goods, exporter should lodge the duplicate copy together with relative shipping documents and an extra copy of the invoice with the authorised dealer named in the GR form. As soon as documents have been negotiated/sent for collection, the authorised dealer should report the transaction to Reserve Bank in statement ENC under cover of appropriate R-Supplementary Return, The duplicate copy of the form together with a copy of invoice will be retained by the authorised dealer till full export proceeds have been realised and thereafter submitted to Reserve Bank duly certified under cover of appropriate R-Supplementary Return.

Note: In the case of exports made under deferred credit arrangement or to joint ventures abroad against equity participation or under rupee credit agreement, the number and date of Reserve Bank approval and/or number and date of the relative A.D. circular should be recorded against item 16 of GR form.

PP Form

(*ii*) The manner of disposal of PP forms is the same as that for GR forms save that postal authorities will allow export of goods by post only if the original copy of the form has been countersigned by an authorised dealer or Reserve Bank except where Reserve Bank has specifically waived the requirement of countersignature in the case of the concerned exporter. PP form should, therefore, be first presented by exporter to an authorised dealer for countersignature. Authorised dealers will countersign the forms in accordance with regulations explained in paragraph 11C.1 and return the original copy to exporter, who should submit the form to the post office with the parcel. The duplicate copy of PP form will be retained by the authorised dealer to whom the exporter should submit relevant documents together with an extra copy of invoice for negotiation/collection, within the prescribed period of **twenty one** days.

Note : Where PP forms cover export of jewellery or precious stones, the parcel will have to be first produced for valuation to Customs who will seal the parcel and stamp the invoice. The extra copy of invoice submitted to the authorised dealer should have also been duly stamped by Customs.

VP/COD Form

(*iii*) In the case of VP/COD form, only one copy is required to be completed and submitted to post office along with the relative parcel at the time of despatch.

Date of Export

The method of arriving at the date of export in respect of shipments effected by various modes of transport is explained in the Hand Book of Import-Export Procedures issued by Trade Control authorities from time to time. In respect of shipments effected by sea, the date of bill of landing/mate's receipt will be taken as the date of export while in case of export by air, the date of airway bill or the date of loading of the goods as certified by Customs, whichever is later, will be taken as the date of export. In cases, where the goods are despatched from an Inland Container Depot (ICD) and the shipment is not covered by a letter of credit which calls for a Combined Transport Document (CTD), drawn subject to FEDAI Rules for CTD in force from time to time, and bears the Combined Transport Operator's undertaking to get it replaced by an Ocean Bill of Lading soon after the goods are loaded on board an ocean going vessel, the date of the Ocean Bill of Lading will be taken as the date of export. In cases where the export from ICD is covered by a letter of credit which calls for a CTD drawn subject to FEDAI Rules without such an undertaking, the date of CTD will be taken as the date of export.

Submission of Shipping Documents

Under Rule 6(3) of Foreign Exchange Regulation Rules, 1974 it is obligatory for exporters to submit all shipping documents pertaining to every export passed by Customs or postal authorities to the authorised dealer mentioned on relevant declaration form, within **twenty one** days from date of export of goods.

Shut out Shipments and Short Shipments

(i) When part of a shipment covered by a GR form already filed with Customs is short-shipped, exporter must give notice of short shipment to customs on prescribed form in the manner prescribed. Customs will then verify that the goods were actually short-shipped and forward a certified copy of short shipment notice to Reserve Bank. Exporter should record the analysis of export value of the goods **actually shipped** on the duplicate of G R form. A copy of the Customs-certified short shipment notice should be attached to the duplicate GR form while submitting it to authorised dealer. In case of delay in obtaining short shipment notice from customs, exporter should give an undertaking to authorised dealer to the effect that he filed the short shipment notice with Customs and that he will furnish it to the authorised dealer as soon as it is obtained. Authorised dealer should send the shipment notice along with the relative GR duplicate to Reserve Bank. When the short-shipped portion is subsequently shipped by another vessel, a fresh set of GR forms to be used for declaring the residual shipment.

(ii) Where a shipment cannot be sent by the vessel named in GR form but is being shipped by another vessel, exporter will make an application in

duplicate in the manner and form prescribed for the purpose to Customs for permission to amend the name of the vessel on GR form and shipping bill. Customs will verify the particulars and will certify the copy of the application as correct and forward it to Reserve Bank for necessary action.

(iii) Where a shipment has been entirely shut out and there is delay in making arrangements to re-ship, exporter will give notice in duplicate to Customs in the manner and in form prescribed for the purpose attaching thereto the unused duplicate copy of GR form and the shipping bill. Customs will verify that the goods were actually shut out, certify copy of the notice as correct and forward it to Reserve Bank together with unused duplicate copy of the GR form. In this case, the original GR form received earlier from Customs will be cancelled and if shipment is made subsequently, a fresh set of GR form must be completed.

(iv) The procedure set out in sub-paragraph *(iii)* will also be followed where a consignment is entirely shut out and will not be re-shipped.

Exports by Air

In the absence of negotiable shipping documents in case of air consignments, exporters sending goods by air run the risk of losing value of goods, if they are consigned directly to overseas buyer/consignee and not to the overseas branches/correspondents of an authorised dealer, except where they are covered by irrevocable letter of credit opened by buyer for the full value of the goods or payment towards the full value of the goods has been received in advance. Exporters will, therefore, be well advised to consign the goods in such cases to the concerned overseas branch/correspondent of the authorised dealer through whom shipping documents will be forwarded for collection, to enable the latter to instruct the overseas branch/correspondent to arrange for issue of delivery order in favour of buyer on payment or acceptance of bill drawn by the shipper.

Consolidation of Air Cargo

(i) Where air cargo is shipped under consolidation, the Airline Company's Master Airway Bill will be issued to the Consolidating Cargo Agent who will in turn issue his own House Airway Bills (HAWBs) to individual shippers.

Authorised dealers will negotiate HAWBs only if relative letter of credit specifically provides for negotiation of these documents in lieu of Airway Bills issued by airline company. Authorised dealers will, however, accept freely HAWBs where documents are to be sent on collection basis. Exporters wishing to ship air cargoes through consolidators will be well advised to provide in the relative sale contracts with their overseas buyers for payment being made against either HAWBs or the customary airline company's

Airway Bills. When, however, a letter of credit has been opened it is the duty of the exporter to ensure that it provides for negotiation of HAWB before forwarding the consignment.

(ii) While handling export document, authorised dealers should verify that consignee shown on HAWB is the overseas correspondent of the authorised dealer through whom payment will be realised, except in following cases where authorised dealer may handle HAWBs showing the overseas buyer or his agent as consignee, as desired by exporter:

(a) an irrevocable letter of credit for the full value of the shipment has been opened in favour of the exporter and has been advised through the authorised dealer concerned;

or

(b) the full value of the shipment has been received in advance by exporter through an authorised dealer;

or

(c) special permission of Reserve Bank has been obtained by exporter for consigning the cargo direct to overseas buyer. Additionally, HAWBs should bear number and date of approval granted by Reserve Bank to the air cargo agent in regard to consolidation of air cargo.

Exports by Barges/Country Craft/Road Transport

Following procedure should be adopted by exporters for filing original copies of GR forms where exports are made to neighbouring countries by road, rail or river transport:

(a) In case of exports by barges/country craft/road transport, the form should be presented by exporter or his agent at the Customs station at the border through which the vessel or vehicle has to pass before crossing over to the foreign territory. For this purpose, exporter may arrange either to give the form to the person in charge of the vessel or vehicle or forward it to his agent at the border for submission to Customs.

(b) As regards exports by rail, Customs staff have been posted at certain designated railway stations for attending to Customs formalities in respect of goods consigned to Pakistan, Afghanistan or Bangladesh. They will collect the GR form in respect of goods loaded at these stations so that the goods may move straight on to the foreign country without further formalities at the border. The list of designated Railway Stations is obtainable from Railways. In respect of goods loaded at stations other than the designated stations, exporters must arrange to present GR forms to the Customs Officer at the Border Land Customs Station where Customs formalities are completed.

Sending Jewellery Etc. Out of India

Reserve Bank has granted general permission vide its Notification No. FERA 60/81-RB dated 23rd February 1981 (as amended) to any person to despatch by post out of India, precious stones or jewellery without any gold content or jewellery of which the value of gold content does not exceed ten per cent of the value of such jewellery, to countries and to the extent as specified below:

Country	Value
Nepal	Up to Rs. 2,000/- in value on any one day
Any country in the External Group	Without limit provided the exports are declared on PP forms or are accompanied by either a certificate issued by an authorised dealer or a PP waiver issued by Reserve Bank.

For export of precious stones and jewellery not covered by the above general permission, of Reserve Bank is required to be obtained. Applications for this purpose should be made on form J 1.

Export of Jewellery Etc. by Air

The general permission covers export of jewellery and precious stones by post only. Export of jewellery and precious stone **by modes other than post** *e.g.,* by air freight, requires a specific licence from Reserve Bank. With a view to facilitating export by air freight of precious stones and jewellery without gold content or jewellery in which the value of gold content does not exceed ten per cent of the value of such jewellery, Reserve Bank grants to established exporters whose past record in regard to realisation of export proceeds is good, exemption from the licensing requirement in the case of such exports by air freight, subject to the condition that GR forms on which such exports are declared will require countersignature of an authorised dealer prior to export. Exporters have to apply for such exemption by letter to Reserve Bank through their bankers furnishing details of their past record of exports. Export of jewellery or articles in which the value of gold content exceeds ten per cent of its value is not permitted under this scheme.

Export of Jewellery under Special Schemes

(i) The Handicrafts and Handlooms Export Corporation of India Ltd. (HHEC) operates a scheme under which export of gold jewellery is permitted by air freight without any restriction as to the value of its gold content against gold supplied by the foreign buyers through HHEC. Reserve Bank has granted general permission in favour of HHEC to import gold and to export

gold jewellery with or without precious stones studded in it, against gold supplied by the foreign buyers in respect of orders received through HHEC or its associates. Similarly, export of gold jewellery irrespective of the value of its gold content and with or without precious stones studded in it is allowed under the scheme known as 'Gold Jewellery Export Promotion and Replenishment Scheme' formulated by Ministry of Commerce. *Slip No.3 AD/M.A 14/1988.*

(ii) Government of India have introduced scheme for export of gold and silver articles from Export Processing Zones and 100 per cent Export Oriented Complexes. Under the Scheme, the jewellery manufacturing units set up in the Zones/Complexes have been permitted to import into India raw materials, intermediates and components made out of gold or silver including gold alloys, carat gold, coloured gold, silver as well as sockets, frames, mountings and findings made of gold and silver for manufacturing and exporting jewellery. Government have also permitted State Bank of India to make available gold imported by it under the Gold and Silver Jewellery and Articles Export Promotion And Replenishment Scheme to the eligible units in Free Trade Zones/100 per cent Export Oriented Complexes. The Minerals and Metals Trading Corporation of India Ltd. (MMTC) has also been permitted to import gold into India for supply to such units. In order to obviate the needs for securing specific export licences from the Reserve Bank under Section 13(2) of FERA 1973 the Reserve Bank has granted special permission to the eligible units to export plain and studded jewellery made out of gold/silver/raw materials imported by them or gold procured from State Bank of India and MMTC authorities, Reserve bank has authorised certain Export Trade Control officials to allow export of precious stones studded in silver jewellery/articles exported under the scheme.

Valuation of Jewellery/Precious Stones by Customs

All parcels containing articles of jewellery or precious stones of over Rs. 200/- in value, by whatever mode exported, must first be produced for valuation to Customs who will seal the parcel and stamp the invoice. This implies that in case of exports of jewellery or precious stones by air where GR forms require countersignature of authorised dealers in terms of exemption granted by Reserve Bank vide paragraph IIB.10 as well as exports of such articles by post, exporters should first have the parcels valued and sealed by Customs and the invoice stamped by them and then approach an authorised dealer for countersignature of GR/PP forms.

Note: Prior approval of Reserve Bank must be obtained for allowing any reduction in the declared value as assessed by Customs even in cases where exports have been made on consignment basis.

Re-export of Synthetic Stones Etc. after Processing

Sometimes, synthetic stones, pearls, diamonds and other precious stones are imported into India on free-of-payment basis for cutting, polishing, etc. and subsequent re-export. In such cases, the only foreign exchange to be recovered would be the processing charges. Applications from exporters concerned for countersignature of PP forms in such cases should be referred to Reserve Bank with full particulars including names of consignor and consignee, number of import licence and amount due towards processing charges. Authorised dealers will thereafter be given permission to countersign the forms against their undertaking to ensure realisation of the processing.

Export to Indian-owned Warehouses Abroad

(i) In order to enable Indian exporters to arrange off-the-shelf sales for achieving greater penetration of overseas export markets, some Indian organisations have been permitted by Reserve Bank to establish warehouses for stocking the goods. Considering various stages in the cycle of despatch of merchandise to an overseas warehouse for eventual sale to buyers from different parts, the prescribed period for realisation of proceeds of export consignments to any Indian-owned warehouse established abroad with the permission of Reserve Bank has been fixed at fifteen months from the date of shipment.

(ii) Shipments to an Indian-owned warehouse will be declared on GR/PP forms in the usual manner but the exporters will furnish an undertaking therein to realise the export proceeds within fifteen months from the date of shipment. GR/PP forms covering such shipments will be superscribed at the top with a notation 'Export to .at. . . . . .'. Exports
(Name of Indian-owned warehouse)
will be on C.I.F. basis as in case of consignment exports. Exporters will have to designate a branch of an authorised dealer for the purpose of submission of shipping documents and GR/PP forms relating to all exports to Indian-owned warehouses abroad. While the designated branch of the authorised dealer will report particulars of shipments made under this scheme in the relative fortnightly ENC statements in the usual manner, they will continue to hold the relative duplicate GR/PP forms till full export proceeds are realised through normal banking channels and thereafter submit them to Reserve Bank, duly certified.

ADMA seeks, 1 of 1988, The Electronic Trade and Technology Development Corporation Ltd, a Government of India undertaking has since been permitted to establish a warehouse at USA for promoting export of Indian electronic goods, to that country. Instructions contained in paragraph above would apply mutatis mutands to export.

Bill Purchases Subsequently Treated as on Collection Basis

(*i*) Where shipping documents drawn against letters of credit and negotiated 'under reserve' are not accepted by overseas buyers, authorised dealers may reverse the relative entry or recredit the amount to the account of the foreign branch or respondent concerned, as the case may be. They should also immediately send an invoice to concerned overseas branch / correspondent to treat the bills as on collection basis. The duplicates of relative GR/PP forms should be held until full realisation of export proceeds. Authorised dealers should furnish on form A2 to be completed at the of reversal of entry, details of GR/PP form numbers, amount of bill purchased, supplier and particulars of R Return in which earlier purchase was reported to Reserve Bank. A similar procedure may be followed in case of export bills purchased and dishonoured by drawees.

(*ii*) All other cases involving refund of export proceeds to foreign buyers or their bankers should be referred to Reserve Bank with full particulars for prior proval.

Change of Tenor of Bill

Authorised dealers may accept substitution of D.P. bills by D.A. bills provided the date of maturity of the D.A. bill falls within the period prescribed for realisation of proceeds of export. In case of commodities subject to floor price restrictions, authorised dealers should permit such substitution only if a 'no objection certificate' has been produced from appropriate authority enforcing the floor price unless overseas buyer has agreed to pay interest for usance period.

Change of Buyer/Consignee

Prior approval of Reserve Bank is not necessary if, after goods have been shipped, they are to be transferred to a party other than the original buyer in the event of default by the latter, provided the goods are sold to the other party on the same terms and conditions on which they were initially sold, no reduction in value is involved and prescribed period for realisation of export proceeds is not extended in anyway.

Extension of Time Limit

In cases where exporter has not been able to realise proceeds of a shipment made by him within the period prescribed, for reason beyond his control, but expects to be to realise proceeds if extension of the period is allowed to him, necessary application (in duplicate) for the **purpose should be made to Reserve Bank in form ETX together with appropriate documentary** evidence. Extension will not ordinary be granted unless Reserve Bank is satisfied that the exporter is in no way directly or indirectly responsible for the delay in realisation of proceeds and that by grant of a short extension the exporter will be able to realise proceeds.

Re-import of Unsold Goods and Surrender of Cash Incentives

(i) Prior approval of Reserve Bank is not necessary when exporter desires to reimport the goods exported by him for any reason such as refusal of buyer to take delivery of the goods. Sometimes Reserve Bank may also direct an exporter to reimport the goods if he has, in its opinion, failed to take necessary steps to ensure their prompt delivery to the buyer and/or timely sale of the goods and realisation of export proceeds. Whenever exported goods are reimported, authorised dealer should satisfy himself by verification of Customs Bill of Entry/postal wrapper that goods to the extent claimed to have been reimported have actually been reimported. In all such cases, a report giving reasons for reimport should be submitted to Reserve Bank, along with the relative duplicate copy of GR/PP forms suitably certified; where the value of the shipment is in excess of Rs. 5,000/-, Customs Bill of Entry or postal wrapper, as the case may be should also be forwarded as evidence of re-import.

(ii) Whenever goods exported are re-imported, authorised dealers should advise the exporters to surrender cash incentives/other benefits, if any, availed of by them in respect of the re-imported goods. Authorised dealers should also send a special report in the matter to the office of Joint Chief Controller of Imports and Exports of that area in cases where the invoice value of goods re-imported is rupees one lakh and above.

(iii) Airline/shipping companies have been authorised to accept payment of freight in rupees in respect of goods re-imported, provided the prescribed certificate is completed by the exporter concerned. If freight on re-import is required to be paid abroad by remittance from India, the application for remittance should be forwarded to Reserve Bank for prior approval, together with exporter's explanation for not arranging freight payment in India.

Shipments Lost in Transit

When shipments from India for which payment has not already been received either by negotiation of bills under letters of credit or otherwise are lost in transit, authorised dealer must see that insurance claim is made as soon as loss is known. The duplicate copy of GR/PP forms should be forwarded to Reserve Bank with following particulars regarding insurance:

(a) Amount for which shipment was insured.

(b) Name and address of insurance company.

(c) Place where claim is payable.

In cases where claim is payable abroad, authorised dealer must arrange to collect the full amount of claim due on the lost shipment, through the medium of his overseas branch/correspondent and forward the duplicate copy of GR/PP forms to Reserve Bank only after the amount has been collected. A certificate for the amount of claim received should be furnished on the reverse of the duplicate copy.

Note: Sometimes claims on shipments lost in transit are also partially settled directly by shipping companies/airlines under carriers' liability. Authorised dealers should ensure that amounts of such claims if settled abroad are also repatriated to India by exporters.

Payment of Claims by ECGC

Where export has been covered by a policy issued by ECGC, settlement of a claim by the Corporation does not absolve the exporter of the obligation to Exchange Control undertaken on the GR/PP form to realise proceeds of the export within prescribed period. In such cases exporter should, in consultation with ECGC take all necessary steps for realising the proceeds. Authorised dealers should also continue to hold the duplicate copies of GR/PP forms in their custody and initiate follow-up measures in the normal manner.

Return of Documents to Exporters

The duplicate of GR/PP forms and shipping documents on submitted to authorised dealers for negotiation, collection, etc. should not ordinarily be returned to exporters for rectification of error and resubmission.

Exporters Caution List

(i) In terms of Section 18(9) of FERA 1973, Reserve Bank may subject exports of certain exporters who have come to its adverse notice in regard to realisation of export value, to the conditions stipulated in clauses (*b*) and (*d*) thereof, in order to ensure that the full export value of further exports to be made by them will be realised in proper time or without delay as required under the law. In such cases Reserve Bank will issue caution listing order directing that the exporter should submit GR/PP forms through an authorised dealer to Reserve Bank for its prior approval, supported by documentary evidence to show that the exporter has received advance payment or an irrevocable letter of credit in his favour covering the **full** value of goods to be exported. Copies of caution-listing orders will be furnished, among others, to all Customs authorities in India, for the purpose of ensuring that the conditions of the orders are fulfilled. Authorised dealers will also be advised whenever exporters are caution-listed. Authorised dealers should not accept for negotiation/collection, shipping documents covering exports declared on GR forms completed by such exporters nor countersign PP forms completed

by them unless the GR/PP forms bear approval of Reserve Bank. If a caution listed exporter presents documents to authorised dealer together with the GR form which does not bear the approval of Reserve Bank, authorised dealer should withhold the documents and not handle them in any manner without prior approval of Reserve Bank.

(ii) Ordinarily, Reserve Bank will include in the caution listing order, not only the names of the exporters (including proprietor/partners in case of firms) but also their associate concerns. If authorised dealers come to know of other associate firms who are in the export field, they should bring the matter to the notice of Reserve Bank promptly.

(iii) When firms and companies included in the caution list are removed from the list by Reserve Bank, the relative de-listing orders will also be forwarded to Customs authorities and authorised dealers will also be advised. Shipping documents etc. submitted by de-listed exporters may be dealt with by authorised dealers according to normal regulations.

EXPORT OF COMPUTER SOFTWARE

Export of computer software is undertaken in **physical form** *i.e.,* software prepared on magnetic tapes and paper media as well as in **non-physical form** *i.e.,* direct data transmission abroad through dedicated earth station/satellite links. As far as export of computer software in physical form is concerned, the procedure relating to declaration of shipments on GR/PP forms, handling export documents by authorised dealers and other allied matters is the same as applicable to export of other goods as set out in Parts A, B and C of this Chapter. The procedure to be followed in respect of export of computer software in non-physical form is set out in this part.

Declaration of Software Exports

(i) Exports of computer software in **non-physical form** should be declared on SOFTEX Form. Each set of SOFTEX forms comprises **three copies marked** Original, Duplicate and Triplicate which carry an identical pre-printed number. All three forms in each set should be completed and the entire set submitted for the purpose of valuation together with relevant documents.

(ii) Each exporter will have to designate a single branch of an authorised dealer to whom export documents in respect of all software exports made *via* dedicated earth stations/satellite links will be submitted by him together with the relative SOFTEX forms for negotiation/collection. The work of handling of the shipping documents and realisation of export proceeds will have to be entrusted only to the designated bank branch.

Valuation of Software Exports and Certification of SOFTEX Forms

Valuation of exports of software through satellite links **will be done by officials of the Department of Electronics,** Government of India, designated for the purpose. Exporters should submit completed sets of SOFTEX forms to the designated officials together with other export documents like invoices, copy of letter of credit, etc., and such other documentary evidence as may be specified by the designated officials in order to be able to value the exports and certify the relative SOFTEX forms. After certifying all the three copies in sets of SOFTEX forms, **the designated officials will directly forward all the originals to the office of Reserve Bank** under whose jurisdiction the exporters are situated, on the dates of their certification. The certified duplicate SOFTEX forms will be returned to the exporters together with all supporting documents for being submitted to the designated branches of authorised dealers and the triplicates will be retained by the designated officials for record of Department of Electronics.

Terms of Payment

(*i*) Exports of computer software through dedicated earth stations/ satellite links have to **be made against full advance payment or irrevocable letters of credit covering the full export value.** Exporters should enter into proper agreements/ contract with their overseas buyers providing, *inter alia*, for payment of the export value by one or the other of the above two methods. **A copy each of the agreement/contract should be submitted by the exporter to the designated official of the Department of Electronics** and to the office of Reserve Bank under whose jurisdiction he functions.

(*ii*) If any overseas buyer is not in a position to accept either of the above two modes of payments for any reason, Reserve Bank will be prepared to consider the exporter's application for permission to send the export documents on collection basis, provided an irrevocable bank guarantee for a suitable amount is arranged in favour of the exporter from an acceptable bank to guarantee payment of the export value within the prescribed period in case of each export declared on SOFTEX forms. The application should be submitted in duplicate to the concerned office of Reserve Bank along with a copy each of the export contract and draft of the guarantee document.

Time Limit for Realisation of Proceeds of Software Exports

The amount representing the full value of each export of software, whether made in physical form or in non-physical form, must be realised within six months from the date of export.

Duplicate SOFTEX Forms and SNC Statement

(i) Exporters should submit duplicate copies of SOFTEX forms to the designated branches of authorised dealers soon after their certification by the designated officials of Department of Electronics together with copies of invoices and bill/s of exchange drawn on the overseas buyer.

(ii) Authorised dealers will submit to the concerned office of Reserve Bank at fortnightly intervals, a statement **in form SNC** (in duplicate) containing details of all SOFTEX forms handled by them during the course of the preceding fortnight. Entries in the SNC statement should be made in strict chronological order of the transactions as recorded in the Bills Registers of authorised dealers. **As in the case fortnightly statement in form ENC relating to export of goods declared on GR/PP forms, statements in form SNC should be forwarded to Reserve Bank along with the R Supplementary Returns for the relevant fortnight.**

(iii) The duplicate copies of SOFTEX form should be retained by authorised dealers till full export proceeds have been realised and thereafter sent to Reserve Bank, duly certified, under cover of appropriate R Returns along with copies of the respective invoices attested by the Department of Electronics.

REMITTANCES CONNECTED WITH EXPORTS

This part deals with regulations to be followed by exporters and authorised dealers while applying for and effecting remittances abroad for various purposes connected with exports. Exporters holding blanket exchange permits are not eligible to obtain separately release of foreign exchange either from Reserve Bank or from an authorised dealer for effecting remittances on account of export claims, charges for testing of samples abroad, legal expenses, export of trade samples, advertisements abroad, participation in trade fairs abroad or similar approved purposes. Holders of blanket permits should utilise these permits for effecting remittances to meet the foreign exchange expenditure towards all approved purposes covered by the Blanket Permit Scheme.

Agency Commission on Exports

(i) Remittances by exporters to their selling agents abroad towards commission payable for business booked through them normally require prior approval of Reserve Bank. Authorised dealers have, however, been permitted to remit commission dues against irrevocable letters of credit opened in favour of exporters and providing for payment of agency commission to overseas agents, subject to fulfillment of conditions laid down. Similarly, authorised dealers handling export documents can allow remittance of commission up to rupees one lakh in respect of shipments of goods

falling under the 'select list' of export products and upto Rs. 50,000 in respect of shipments of other ('non-select') export products.

(ii) To facilitate prompt payment of commission, Reserve Bank also operates a scheme for registering selling agency agreements and issuing Agency Agreement Registration Certificates against which remittances can be made by authorised dealers without reference to Reserve Bank. It would, therefore, be in the interest of exporters to conclude agreements with their selling agents abroad to the extent possible and to have them registered with Reserve Bank. Sometimes exporters may agree to pay commission to overseas agents on export orders secured through them on a case-to-case basis. In the absence of agency agreements, remittances of commission in such cases will require prior approval of Reserve Bank unless authorised dealers are able to effect remittances under powers delegated to them. At times, an export order involves several shipments and commission is required to be settled every time a shipment is made. If amount of commission in respect of various shipments is expected to exceed the ceiling prescribed for authorised dealers for allowing remittances on this account, exporters may approach Reserve Bank in advance, through the authorised dealer who will be handling the export documents, for permission to remit commission as and when due without further reference to Reserve Bank. Approval granted in such case will be restricted to the particular export order for which application is made. Such approval will not be necessary where the exporter is in possession of a valid Agency Agreement Registration Certificate.

Note: Remittance of commission in advance (*i.e.,* before shipment is made) is not permitted.

(iii) Application for remittance towards agency commission on exports financed under rupee lines of credit extended by Government of India to foreign government as well as lines of credit extended by Exim Bank to financial institutions/ banks abroad upto a maximum of 5 per cent of the F.O.B. value of exports, will be considered by Reserve Bank on merits of individual cases, subject to the conditions, *inter alia,* that the export contracts provide for appointment of agents abroad for rendering after-sales service in respect of goods exported and the credit agreement provides for an advance/ down payment of not less than 10 per cent of f.o.b. value of the goods by the overseas buyers.

Declaration of Commission to Customs

Remittance of commission is permissible only if it was declared on the relative GR/PP forms. It is for this reason that authorised dealers have been required to record in Export Bills Register at the time of handling GR/PP forms and documents, amount of commission declared by exporters on the export declaration form. If therefore, the export involves payment of commission to an overseas agent, the exporter must declare it on the GR/PP forms.

Procedure for Registration of Agency Agreements

Application for registration of agency agreement should be submitted to Reserve Bank through an **authorised dealer in form RCX accompanied by the agency agreement** (correspondence exchanged where formal agreement does not exist), in original, together with a certified copy. On approval of the application, Reserve Bank will issue a Registration Certificate authorising concerned exporter to make remittances (through an authorised dealer) towards commission due to the selling agent on business booked by him, provided the terms and conditions of the Registration Certificate are complied with.

Procedure for Remittance of Commission

(i) Application for remittance of commission should be made by exporters to authorised dealers on form **A2 together with the commission statement in form CDX, duly completed in duplicate and accompanied by documents indicated therein and also documentary evidence to show the rate of commission agreed upon.** In cases where relative agency agreement has been registered with Reserve Bank, the Registration Certificate should be submitted in support of the application together with proof to show that the order on which commission is required was booked through the agent. Applications for remittance of commission must clearly indicate whether the commission is payable on F.O.B., C.I.F. or C.& F. value of the export.

(ii) Ordinarily, commission will be remitted through the authorised dealer through whom relative bills were negotiated/sent for collection. In such cases, the certificates in Parts A and B of the commission statement should be furnished by the authorised dealer. In cases where remittance is made through an authorised dealer other than the one who handled the bills, the certificate in Part A should be completed by the authorised dealer through whom the relative bills were negotiated/sent for collection and that in Part B by the remitting the authorised dealer. Before furnishing the certificate in Part A, the authorised dealer should verify the particulars shown in the statement with relative entry in Export Bills Register and ensure that they agree. The fact of remittance of commission should also be noted in Export Bills Register to preclude possibility of commission being remitted again on the same shipment. One copy of the commission statement duly certified as indicated above should be attached in all cases to the form A2 on which the remittance is reported to Reserve Bank. Remittances made on the strength of Agency Agreement Registration Certificates should be endorsed on the certificates.

Currency of Settlement of Commission

Remittances towards commission to selling agents abroad should be made in a manner conforming to country of residence of the agent irrespective of the currency in which payment for the export is realised. However, remittance of commission in free foreign exchange for exports to countries in the Bilateral Group or to countries with which Government of India have entered into trade agreements containing special provisions for settling trade payments is not permissible unless specifically approved by Reserve Bank.

Payment of Commission from Bill Proceeds or by Deduction from Invoice Value

(i) In cases where exporters desire that agency commission should be deducted from the bill proceeds and paid to the agent direct by overseas branch or correspondent of the authorised dealer, authorised dealer may convey instructions to this effect while forwarding documents, provided the agency agreement has been registered with Reserve Bank or the payment of commission has been specifically approved by Reserve Bank or where authorised dealer can remit agency commission in terms of above paragraph. **Full value of the bill should be reported as purchase in the relative R Return and commission as sale on form A2 under the same Return. Exporters should also complete the prescribed commission statement in form CDX which should be forwarded to Reserve Bank along with the relative from A2, after due certification by authorised dealer.** Authorised dealer should certify this suitably on the duplicate copy of the relative GR/PP forms before forwarding it to Reserve Bank.

(ii) Authorised dealers may likewise accept invoices showing deductions on account of commission in cases where the relative agency agreement has been registered with Reserve Bank or the payment of commission has been specifically approved by Reserve Bank. The authorised dealer should authenticate the deduction by affixing his stamp and signature on the copy of the invoice and also furnish suitable remarks on the duplicate copy of GR/PP forms citing reference to the Agency Agreement Registration Certificate or the approval of Reserve Bank, as the case may be, before forwarding the duplicate to Reserve Bank, as the case may be, before forwarding the duplicate to Reserve Bank. Completion of the commission statement form is not necessary in such cases.

(iii) Commission paid/adjusted in either of the above ways should be recorded in Export Bills Register. Where such payment/adjustment has been made on the authority of Registration Certificate, it should also be endorsed on the certificate.

Note: Payment of commission out of export proceeds or by deduction from invoice value is permissible only if it has been declared on the relative GR/PP forms and accepted by customs.

Letter of Credit Providing for Payment of Commission

Where an **irrevocable letter of credit** covering exports to be made from India provides specifically for payment of commission to an overseas agent, the authorised dealer through whom the bills are negotiated under letter of credit may either remit the commission abroad or accept deduction from proceeds of the bill without reference to Reserve Bank, provided the following conditions are fulfilled:

(a) The rate of agency commission indicated in the letter of credit is the normal rate of commission for the commodity in question according to prevalent practice in the **trade and does not in any case exceed 7.5%** (of commission enhanced 5% to 7.5% vide MA 4 of 1989).

(b) The commodity exported under letter of credit is not one in respect of which **payment of agency commission is not permissible (e.g. gold and silver jewellery).** If the commodity to be exported is one which qualifies for a rate of agency commission which is lower than 7.5 per cent of invoice value in terms of special guidelines issues by Reserve Bank to authorised dealers from time to time, remittance or deduction of commission does not exceed the sub-ceiling applicable to the commodity.

(c) The commission amount pertains to the actual value of export documents negotiated under the credit and the amount is correctly arrived at in conformity with the provisions of the credit.

(d) The commission has been declared on the relative GR/PP forms and has been accepted by Customs.

(e) There are no grounds to believe that the beneficiary is not entitled to receive the commission abroad.

(f) Prescribed commission statement in form CDX has been completed by the exporter.

Note: Remittance of commission should not be allowed if documents are negotiated under 'reserve' or sent on 'collection basis' due to discrepancies or non-compliance with letter of credit terms.

Authorised Dealers' Powers to Allow Remittances Towards Agency Commission

Authorised dealers negotiate/send for collection documents pertaining to export shipments may allow remittance of agency commission or convey instructions to their overseas branches or correspondents to deduct the amount of agency commission from the bill proceeds and pay it to the agents direct, without reference to Reserve Bank, in cases where relative agency agreements are not registered with Reserve Bank or in respect of shipments which are not covered by irrevocable letters of credit providing for payment of agency commission, subject to the conditions that *(i)* the amount of agency commission remitted/deducted from the bill proceeds of the relative shipment does not exceed rupees one lakh in respect of goods included in the 'select list' of export products and Rs. 50,000/- in respect of other goods falling under the 'non-select list' of export products and *(ii)* the rates of commission are within the prescribed ceilings, except in the following cases:

(a) Payment of commission in free foreign exchange in respect of exports to the Bilateral Group countries.

(b) Exports made by Indian partners towards equity participation in an overseas joint venture.

(c) Export financed under Rupee Line of Credit extended by Government of India to any foreign government.

(d) Payment of commission in a manner other than deduction from invoice value of individual shipment in cases where exports are financed under Rupee Line of Credit extended by financial institutions like Exim Bank to foreign governments/financial institutions.

(e) Remittance of commission before relative shipments are made and/or where commission is payable to more than one overseas agent in respect of same shipment.

(f) Method of payment of commission is not in conformity with the country of residence of the overseas agent.

The rates at which agency of commission could be allowed by authorised dealers in respect of different export products will be advised to them by Reserve Bank from time to time. Applications for remittance of agency commission under this arrangement have to be made by exporters to authorised dealers **on form A2 (in duplicate) along with statement of agency agreement/correspondence, cables, etc.** evidencing the fact that the export order in question was booked through the concerned agent. Before allowing remittance of commission, the authorised dealers **should ensure** that the particulars mentioned in form CDX, form A2 and relative invoice agree with those recorded in **Export Bills Register,** the amount of commission has been declared on GR/PP forms and has been accepted by Customs, appropriate rate of commission is applied and the amount of commission has been correctly calculated. Authorised dealers should refer to the current. **Import-Export Policy Book issued by Trade Control**

authorities for classification of export commodities into 'select list' export products and other ('non-select') export products. The amount of commission allowed to be remitted/deducted from invoice value should be noted against relative entry in Export Bills Register. **Authorised dealers should forward duplicate copy of form A2 together with copies of supporting documents including statement of commission in form CDX to Reserve Bank along with R Return in which relative sale transaction is reported.** A statement should also be submitted to Reserve Bank in form CRX on monthly basis giving details in respect of commission allowed in terms of this paragraph so as to reach Reserve Bank by 15th of the month following the one to which it relates. Cases not covered by above provisions may be referred to Reserve Bank for prior approval.

Overprice

Overprice arrangements by exporters are prohibited and no remittance towards overprice on exports will be permitted by Reserve Bank. Cases having exceptional features may be referred by Reserve Bank. Cases having exceptional features may be referred to Reserve Bank explaining why the exporter is unable to remunerate overseas intermediary by payment of agency commission instead of overprice.

Export Claims

(i) Applications of exporters for remittances in settlement of claims made by overseas buyers **on account of compensation for non-fulfillment of contracts, shortage in weight/length, inferior quality of goods supplied, penalty for late shipment, etc. should normally be referred to Reserve Bank in form REX together with the documents specified therein.** Authorised dealers who have handled the relative export documents may, however, allow remittances in settlement of small value claims on behalf of their exporter clients upto 15% per cent of the invoice value of the relative shipment or Rs 1,00,000/-, whichever is less. Applications for this purpose have to be made by the exporters **in form REX along with from A2 duly completed (both in duplicate) together with a certified copy of original sale contract, survey/inspection/analysis/weighment report, as appropriate to the commodity exported, debit note or documentary evidence received from the overseas importer in lieu thereof and bill of lading** (where claim is on account of penalty for late shipment). Before allowing any remittance towards export claim, authorised dealers should ensure that full export proceeds of the relative shipment have been repatriated to India in an approved manner, amount of claim agrees with the amount of debit note/amount arrived at on the basis of survey/inspection/weighment report

submitted by the exporter and does not exceed Rs 100,000/-. Authorised dealers should also satisfy themselves in respect of claims arising on account of non-fulfilment of contracts, penalty for late shipment, etc., that failure/ delay in honouring the commitment was on account of circumstances beyond the control of the exporter.

(ii) Details of remittances in settlement of export claims should be noted against the relative items in the Export Bills Register. The concerned exporters should be advised in writing to surrender to the local Trade Control authorities proportionate **export incentive,** if already received, and a copy of the advice should be endorsed to the concerned Trade Control authorities. Authorised dealers should also forward to Reserve Bank, at the time of reporting the transaction through **appropriate 'R' Return, a copy of form REX and a copy of the advice to the exporter regarding surrender of proportionate export incentives, together with the documents on the basis of which the remittance has been allowed. A statement in form XCL should also be submitted to Reserve Bank on a quarterly basis so as to reach it by the 15th day of the month following the calendar quarter to which the statement relates.** Authorised dealers should refer to Reserve Bank, with full details and their comments, case of doubtful nature or those which do not satisfy fully the above requirements.

Charges

There are various charges from exporters for remittances or controlling charges like fees for general superintendence, submission of weight certificates, quality reports, etc., may be approved by authorised dealers provided they are supported by debit notes and other supporting documents. The relative form A2 should bear a certificate to the effect that —

(*a*) the bills covering the shipments declared on GR form No. . . . . . . in respect of which charges are being remitted were negotiated/ accepted for collection on . . . . . . (date);

(*b*) the proceeds of the shipments have been/will be receive in an approved manner; and

(*c*) satisfactory documentary evidence has been seen in support of the remittance. (Documents examined to be specified).

Reimbursement of Expenses Incurred on Dishonoured Export Bills

Authorised dealers may reimburse to their branches/correspondents abroad, expenses in insurance, storage, demurrage and other incidental expenses incurred by them on goods covered by dishonoured/unaccepted export bills. However, if the total amount reimbursed exceeds 10 per cent of the C.I.F. value of the consignment, a report should be furnished to Reserve Bank by letter giving full particulars of the relative GR/PP forms, the reason for dishonour of the bill and steps already taken and/or proposed to be taken by exporter to protect his interests. In order to avoid unnecessary expenditure of foreign exchange and to ensure that corrective steps are taken in time by the exporter, such cases should be taken up by authorised dealers promptly with exporters and followed up systematically. If exporters do not take necessary steps, the matter should be reported to Reserve Bank. **Exporters holding valid Blanket Exchange Permits issued by Reserve Bank should be asked to utilise blanket allocations of exchange for marking the remittances.**

Legal Expenses Against Dishonoured Export Bills

In the case of dishonoured export bills, authorised dealers may permit their overseas branches/correspondents to incur expenses not exceeding U.S. $1,000 or its equivalent per export bill for instituting legal proceedings against the drawee. Exporters holding valid Blanket Exchange Permits issued by Reserve Bank should be asked to utilise their blanket allocations of exchange for making the remittances. A special report should, however, be furnished to Reserve Bank giving full details of the case. Developments in the case should be regularly reported to Reserve Bank. Where the cost of legal proceedings is likely to exceed U.S . $1,000 or its equivalent per bill, prior approval of Reserve Bank should be taken.

Testing Charges

(i) Occasionally, export-oriented firms and companies may require to have samples of raw materials, semi-finished and fininshed products used/ manufactured by them, tested in overseas laboratories/manufacturing units to establish that the products to be exported will meet quality etc. standards set by overseas buyers. Remittance of charges, if any, payable for such testing requires prior approval of Reserve Bank. Applications should be made by exporters through an authorised dealer supported by original correspondence with the overseas laboratory/manufacturing unit/buyer together with information on the export performance/potential of the product. If similar testing facilities are available in India, reasons for not availing of them should be explained.

(ii) Holders of valid Blanket Exchange Permits are permitted to make remittances towards testing charges against such permits.

Remittances towards Advertisement Abroad, Cost of Export Information, Tender Documents, Etc.

Power have been delegated to authorised dealers to effect sundry remittances on behalf of their exporter-clients towards cost of various ancillary services obtained by them from abroad in connection with their export promotion efforts.

Note: The monetary ceilings specified in various items of the above-referred Table do not apply to holders of blanket permits.

Earnest Money

Remittance of earnest money by exporters to overseas tender-inviting bodies requires prior approval of Reserve Bank. Applications should be made on form A2 together with supporting documents and an explanation why bank guarantee in lieu of earnest money cannot be issued.

DESPATCH OF GOODS NOT INVOLVING FOREIGN EXCHANGE (WAIVER OF GR/PP FORM PROCEDURE)

Personal Effects of Travellers

Travellers proceeding out of India are allowed by Customs to take out their *bona fide* personal baggage within limits, if any, prescribed by Export Trade Control authorities in the Export Baggage Rules. Articles such as unused carpets which are easily saleable abroad as well as silverware and similar other articles of high value carried by travellers in excess of the limits are not considered by Customs as personal effects. Any person wishing to take such articles out of India should apply to Reserve Bank by letter in duplicate for grant of GR waiver giving full particulars of articles to be taken out and value of each article at the time of purchase. This application should be made simultaneously with application, if any, for taking out jewellery in excess of prescribed limits.

Gift Parcels

(*i*) In terms of Government of India Notifications No.F 1/67/EC/73-1 No. F1/67/EC/73-2 both dated 1st January 1974 (as amended) the requirement of declaration on GR/PP form is not applicable to exports by **air freight** and **post parcel** which are covered by certificates issued by authorised dealers confirming that the exports do not involve any transaction in foreign exchange. Authorised dealers may issue to their **regular constituents,** on application, certificates stating that the export does not involve any transaction in foreign exchange, to enable them to send out gift etc., parcels abroad, provided, *inter alia,* the following conditions are fulfilled:

(a) Export is made only by post parcel or air freight.

(b) Authorised dealer is satisfied that the export does not involve any transaction in foreign exchange

and

(c) A declaration is furnished by the sender of the gift stating that the aggregate value of gifts despatched by him during the calendar year does not exceed the limit of Rs. 4000/-.

The certificates issued by the authorised dealers should also carry a notation to the effect that the value of gift shall be subject to acceptance by Customs. A quarterly statement in form XGS covering certificates issued during each calendar quarter should be sent to Reserve Bank before 15th of the month following the quarter.

Note: Authorised dealers should not issue certificates if gifts are intended for official use of Indian Missions abroad.

(*ii*) All other cases where waiver of GR/PP from formalities is required should be referred to Reserve Bank. Applications for sending gift parcels should be made in form WXG in duplicate.

Tourist Purchases

Bona fide foreign tourists are permitted by Customs to take out of India good, other than those specified in Part 'A' of Schedule I to the Exports (Control) Order, 1977, to their countries of residence up to the limits, if any, and the procedure laid down in the Export Baggage Rules, on production of documentary evidence to show that the goods have been purchased against payment in foreign exchange. Bona fide foreign tourists are not required to apply to Reserve Bank for permission to take out articles purchased by them, irrespective of the value of the articles.

Note: As far as commercial purchases of Indian goods by foreign buyers' representatives on short visits to India are concerned, the normal procedure of declaring them on GR/PP form would apply for their export.

Replacement Part Articles

(*i*) Exporters of engineering goods may sometimes have to provide in respect of their exports, free supplies of spareparts or free replacement of articles damaged in transit or during warranty period. Exporters should apply in such cases to Reserve Bank on a set of shipping bills (or by letter) for waiver of GR/PP form formalities, furnishing full particulars of the export in respect of which free supply/replacement has arisen.

(*ii*) Sometimes the overseas buyers may find it convenient to replace the defective parts of small value by purchasing them from local market where standby spares are available instead of obtaining them from the Indian exporter under warranty clause. Reserve Bank would be prepared to consider, on merits, applications from Indian exporters of engineering goods for effecting remittances towards reimbursement of actual cost of spares purchased by the foreign buyers locally (and not from third country sources) to a reasonable extent in relation to the value of the relative shipment. Exporters holding valid Blanket Exchange Permits issued by Reserve Bank should utilise their blanket allocation of exchange for making such remittances.

Export of Defective Goods for Replacement or Replacement or Repairs and Return

(i) Firms/companies wishing to re-export defective goods for replacement/repairs and subsequent return should apply to Reserve Bank for waiver of GR/PP form formalities furnishing an undertaking to produce in due course evidence of reimport. **Export will be permitted, provided an import licence has been obtained from the Import Trade Control authorities for reimport of the goods unless such goods are covered by Open General Licence.** Where reimport involves payment to the overseas firm/company towards repair, freight, etc., charges, it will have to be covered by an import licence issued with Exchange Control copy permitting remittance of the charges. **Where value of the defective goods to be shipped exceeds Rs. 5,000/- applicants should complete a set of GR/PP forms.** Shipment of the defective goods may be made after Reserve Bank's approval has been secured on the form. The duplicate copy of the form should be resubmitted directly to Reserve Bank within the stipulated time limit together with Customs Bill of Entry/post parcel wrapper evidencing reimport of the goods after repairs/replacement.

(ii) In case of articles such as cameras etc., which are to be sent to original manufacturers by **post parcel** for repairs and return by individuals, Reserve Bank will grant permission on being satisfied that reimport will be allowed by the Postal Customs without an import licence. While applying for such permission, applicants should state whether the repairs will be undertaken by the manufacturer free of charge or any repair charges will be payable and in the latter case, whether the repairs cannot be made in India. Supporting correspondence should be produced.

Newspapers, Magazines and Periodicals

Publishers of newspapers/magazines/periodicals will be granted, on application, general permission to export their publications to subscribers residing abroad either by air freight or post parcel **without completion of GR/PP form formalities, subject to compliance with prescribed conditions.** This facility is also available to agency firms of standing who wish to export publications of their principals too subscribers abroad.

(iii) Exporters making exports under the Scheme will submit to Reserve Bank through the designated branches of authorised dealers a half-yearly statement in form ECW in duplicate giving details of all shipments made to any Indian-owned warehouse abroad. The designated branches will forward the statements to the concerned offices of Reserve Bank after carefully checking the particulars furnished and completing the certificate incorporated therein.

AUTHORISED DEALERS' OBLIGATIONS REGARDING EXPORTS

Countersignature on PP Forms

(i) PP form will be presented by the exporter to an authorised dealer for countersignature. Authorised dealers should countersign PP forms after ensuring that the parcel is being addressed to their branch or correspondent bank in the country of import. The concerned overseas branch or correspondent should be instructed to deliver the parcel to consignee against payment or acceptance of relative bill. Authorised dealers may, however, countersign PP forms covering parcels addressed direct to the consignees, provided —

(a) an irrevocable letter of credit for the full value of the export has been opened in favour of exporter and has been advised through authorised dealer concerned;

or

(b) the full value of shipment has been received in advance by the exporter through an authorised dealer;

or

(c) exporter has obtained prior approval of Reserve Bank for addressing parcel direct to consignee.

In such cases, particulars of advance payment/letter of credit/Reserve Bank's approval should be furnished on the form, duly authenticated by the authorised dealer. Any alteration in name and address of consignee on the PP form should be authenticated by the authorised dealer under his stamp and signature.

(ii) Where authorised dealers are not in a position to countersign PP forms for reasons such as *(a)* they cannot undertaken to collect the export proceeds in the absence of banking facilities in the country of destination or *(b)* payment has been received otherwise than through an authorised dealer (*e.g.,* by foreign postal orders, money orders). Reserve Bank will, on application by the exporters and subject to being satisfied about realisation of value of the goods in an approved manner, countersign PP forms.

Note: Where an exporter has obtained general permission from Reserve Bank to receive payment direct from overseas buyers in terms of provisions of paragraph 11A.10 (iii), the designated branch of an authorised dealer may countersign the relative PP form, provided the exporter has already delivered the instruments such as bank drafts or pay orders to the authorised dealer.

Counter Signature GR Forms Pertaining to Export of Precious Stones; Jewellery by Air

(i) Approved exporters will be permitted by Reserve Bank to export by air precious stones and jewellery without any gold content or the value of gold

content of which does not exceed ten per cent of its value without having to obtain specific export licence for each export in terms of Section 13(2) of FERA 1973, provided the GR forms are countersigned by an authorised dealer prior to export. Authorised dealers should countersign GR forms submitted by exporters who have obtained the special permission from Reserve Bank only after the parcels containing jewellery, precious stone, etc. have been valued and sealed by Customs and Customs-stamped copies of invoices have been produced as required. Authorised dealers should also ensure that the parcel has been addressed to their branch or corespondent in the country of import. The concerned overseas branch or correspondent should be instructed to deliver the parcel to consignee against payment or acceptance or relative bill. Authorised dealers may, however, countersign GR forms covering parcels addressed direct to the consignees provided —

(a) an irrevocable letter of credit covering the export has been opened in favour of exporter for the full value of the shipment and has been advised through authorised dealer concerned;

or

(b) the full value of the shipment has been realised in advance by the exporter through an authorised dealer;

or

(c) exporter has obtained prior approval of Reserve Bank for addressing the parcel direct to consignee.

In these cases, particulars of advance payment/letter of credit/ Reserve Bank's approval should be furnished on the GR forms, duly authenticated by the authorised dealer.

(ii) Authorised dealers should ensure that the exporters submit to them the duplicate copies of GR forms and the relevant shipping documents for negotiation or collection within five working days from the date of countersignature. Cases of default should be promptly reported to Reserve Bank.

Exports by Air

(i) Since airway bills issued by airline companies are not negotiable documents, authorised dealers should advise exporters that they should, in their own interest, consign air cargo to overseas branches/correspondents of authorised dealers in order to obviate possibility of loss arising from non-payment by buyers, except where irrevocable letter of credit has been opened by buyer or advance remittance has been received.

(ii) In case of air cargo moving under consolidation, authorised dealers should abide by procedure laid down while handling HAWBs.

Delay in Submission of Shipping Documents By Exporters

In case where exporters present documents pertaining to exports after the prescribed period of twenty one days from date of export authorised dealers may handle them without prior approval of Reserve Bank, provided delay is only of a few days and they are satisfied that it was due to reasons beyond the control of the exporters. If, however, the delay exceeds seven days, while documents may be handled by authorised dealers, circumstances of the delay should be ascertained and a report furnished to Reserve Bank giving full details and enclosing the exporters' explanation for the delay.

Check-list for Scrutiny of Forms

(*i*) When duplicate copies of GR and PP forms are handed over by exporter with relative bills for negotiation or collection, authorised dealers must check the bill and other documents with particulars stated on the form to see the *prima facie* they are in order. Additionally, authorised dealers should call for original sale contract entered into between exporter and overseas buyer and verify essential particulars like description, quantity, value (including unit price, wherever applicable), etc. with the declaration on GR/PP forms and export documents. In the absence of sale contract, authorised dealers may accept any of the undernoted documents:

(a) Order of overseas buyer together with order confirmation of exporter.

(b) Proforma invoice of exporter duly countersigned by overseas buyer.

(c) Indent/order from overseas buyer or his authorised agent.

(ii) A list (which is illustrative and not exhaustive) of checks to be applied is given below for general guidance of authorised dealers:

(*a*) All columns of the duplicates should have been completed fully and properly by exporters. The number of the duplicate copy of a GR forms presented to them is the same as that of the original which is usually recorded on the Bill of Lading and the duplicates have been duly verified and authenticated by appropriate Customs authorities. (Where any form has not been properly filled on or where the duplicates do not appear to have been verified and authenticated by Customs or where any material particulars on the forms have been altered but the alterations have not been authenticated by Customs, the forms should be returned to exporter for resubmission after due rectification).

Note: The export realisable value may be more than what was originally declared to/ accepted by Customs on the GR form in certain circumstances such as where in C.I.F. or C.& F. contracts, part or whole or any freight increase taking place after contract was concluded is agreed to be borne by buyers or where as a result of subsequent devaluation of the currency of the contract, buyers have agreed to an increase in price. In such cases, the total realisable value will be amended by exporters on the duplicate copy. Authorised dealers may handle documents in such cases without insisting on authentication of increased value by Customs after verification by reference to original correspondence between exporters and overseas buyers that the latter have agreed to the increase and invoices/bills have been prepared for the full increased value. A suitable certificate to this effect should be provided in the duplicate copy of the GR form as well as on the extra copy of invoice submitted to Reserve Bank.

(b) Exporters have correctly completed the declaration on the GR etc., form as required.

(c) Declaration made on GR etc., form is correct and the value declared on the form is the same as that contracted for.

(d) Amount for which the bill is drawn and the invoice is made out is the same as the value declared on the form.

(e) Documents do not reveal any material *interse* description of goods exported, export value or country of destination.

(f) Method of payment proposed is a permitted one.

(g) In case of usance bills date of maturity is such as would enable proceeds being realised within prescribed period.

Scrutiny of Documents

(i) Freight on exports is permitted to be paid in rupees in India by exporters only if liability on account of freight on the shipments is to be borne by exporters in terms of the sale contract with overseas buyers or the export has been made on consignment basis. If the Bill of Lading, Airway Bill, etc., has been issued on 'freight prepaid' basis authorised dealer should verify that freight is for account of exporter in terms of the sale contract unless the export has been made on consignment basis.

(ii) As an exception to the above general rule, authorised dealers may accept Bills of Lading/Airway Bills issued on 'freight prepaid' basis even if the sale contract between exporter and overseas buyer is on F.O.B. or F.A.S. or such other terms under which freight would be to the account of overseas buyer, provided the actual amount of freight has also been included in the invoice and the bill and will be recovered from overseas buyer in an approved manner.

Note: Where the export is made to a country in the Bilateral Group, authorised dealers should not accept Bills of Lading/Airway Bills in terms of this paragraph if the carrying vessel or airline belongs to a country other than India and the country of import, unless such freight will be recovered from buyers separately in a permitted currency.

(*iii*) In case of shipments under contracts on C.I.F., C. & F., etc., terms freight may occasionally be arranged to be paid at destination, the equivalent amount being deducted on the invoice. Authorised dealers may accept Bills of Lading/Airway Bills issued on 'freight payable at destination' basis is such cases, provided the deduction from invoice value is only to the extent of freight element declared by exporter relative GR form or actual amount of freight indicated on Bill of Lading/Airway Bill whichever is less. However, in order to avoid delay in handling documents, authorised dealers may also accept, at their discretion, deductions on account of actual freight if it exceeds the freight element declared on the GR form marginally, *i.e.*, by not more than 5 per cent of the freight element: declared on the GR form marginally, i.e., by not more than 5 per cent of the freight element. All other cases will require prior approval of Reserve Bank.

(*iv*) If liability on account of marine insurance on the shipments is to be borne by overseas buyers in terms of the sale contract with the latter and insurance is taken by exporter on buyer's account, authorised dealers should verify that the actual amount of insurance premium paid to the General Insurance Corporation of India or its subsidiaries by exporter has been included in the invoice and the bill and will be recovered from buyer in an approved manner. In case of goods exported on consignment basis marine insurance must be arranged in India.

Transfer of Documents

(*i*) Authorised dealers may accept from their constituents, for negotiation or collection, shipping documents covering exports even where the original declaration or GR forms had been signed by some other party, provided —

(*a*) the constituent has been allotted an exporter's code number by Reserve Bank;

(*b*) the constituent drawing the bill countersigns (citing his exporter's code number) on the duplicate copy of GR form, the undertaking to deliver to authorised dealer the foreign exchange proceeds of the shipment within prescribed period;

and

(*c*) the constituent furnishes the following declaration on the duplicate copy of the GR form:

'I/We am /are resident in India or I/we have a place of business in India and I/we have become entitled to sell the goods exported or to procure their sale; and

I/We am/are not on the Exporters Caution List of the Reserve Bank'.

(ii) Where the constituent is on Exporters Caution List, he will be unable to furnish the latter part of the above declaration. Authorised dealers may, however, negotiate documents in respect of GR forms countersigned by an exporter who is on Exporters Caution List where the full export value is covered by advance remittance or by irrevocable letter of credit, provided in the latter case the documents conform strictly to the terms of the letter of credit.

(iii) In all cases where authorised dealers are unable to handle the documents submitted by a countersigning exporter in this manner, the constituent should be advised to retransfer documents back to the original exporter. Simultaneously authorised dealer should issue a suitable advice to the original exporter. Simultaneously, authorised dealer should issue a suitable advice to the original exporter advising him it is his responsibility to account to Exchange Control for the export proceeds.

Trade Discount

(i) Bills in respect of exports by sea or air which fall short of the value declared on GR forms on account of trade discount may be accepted for negotiation or collection by authorised dealers only if the discount has been declared by exporter on relative GR form at the time of shipment and accepted by Customs.

(ii) In case of exports by parcel against declaration on PP forms, post offices will not undertake scrutiny of trade discount deductions, if any, declared on the forms. Authorised dealers may accept deduction towards trade discount in such cases, provided the discount declared is in conformity with the normal level of discount usually offered in the particular line of export trade, subject to maximum of 40 per cent in the case of books and periodicals, 25 per cent in case of drugs and medicines and 5 per cent in all other cases. All cases where discount offered by exporter does not conform to the above stipulations should be referred to Reserve Bank.

Deductions Arising out of Quality Analysis and Late Shipment Penalty

In certain lines of export trade, final settlement of price may be dependent on the results of quality analysis of samples drawn at the time of shipment; but the result of such analysis will become available only after the shipment has been made. Sometimes, contracts may provide for payment of penalty for late shipment of goods in conformity with trade practice concerning the commodity. In these cases, while exporters declare to Customs the full export value based on the contract price, invoices submitted along with shipping documents for negotiation/collection may reflect a different value arrived at after taking into account the results of analysis of samples or late shipment penalty, as the case may be. As such variations stem from the terms of contract, authorised dealers may accept them on production of documentary evidence after verifying that the arithmetical calculations showing the variations are correct and are based on the terms of underlying contracts. Authorised dealers should record a certificate in such cases on the extra copy of invoice submitted to Reserve Bank to the effect that (*a*) deductions shown therein are based on pre-shipment analysis/late shipment penalty, (*b*) necessary documentary evidence has been verified, and (*c*) the deductions are in accordance with the terms of relative contract. Where such deduction exceed 5 per cent of invoice value, a special report should be sent to the office of Reserve Bank under whose jurisdiction the Head/Registered Office of the exporter is situated, giving full details along with copies of relative contract, analysis report, etc., immediately after negotiating documents.

Advance Remittances

(*i*) Where part of the invoice value of goods exported has been received in advance by exporter, authorised dealer who negotiates for the balance should certify on the duplicate copy of the GR/PP form amount so received and method by which it was received, provided (*a*) the advance remittance had been received through his medium for payment to exporter and not to some other party, (*b*) he has no grounds to suspect that the remittance was intended for some other purpose, and (*c*) the advance remittance does not involve payment of interest to overseas remitter. In cases where advance remittance covers the full invoice value of the export, the duplicate copy of the form should be certified and sent to Reserve Bank. Such certificates on forms should not be furnished on the strength of certificates issued by other authorised dealers except as indicated in sub-paragraph (*iii*).

(*ii*) In cases where invoices indicate that the advance remittance received by exporter involves payment of interest to overseas remitter, authorised dealers should obtain prior approval of Reserve Bank before undertaking negotiation/collection of documents. Where, however, exporters have obtained Reserve Bank's permission for receiving interest-bearing advances and shown such interest as deduction in the invoice, authorised dealers may certify the deduction on the reverse of the relative duplicate copy of the GR etc., form citing the number and date of Reserve Bank's approval.

(*iii*) When remittances are received from abroad with specific indication that the amount represents advance payment for exports to be made by the beneficiary to the remitter, authorised dealers may issue certificates on security paper stating purpose and other relevant particulars. Exporter's bankers may certify GR etc., forms on the strength of the original of such certificates, provided conditions (*b*) and (*c*) of sub-paragraph (*i*) are complied with. The appropriations made against every shipment must be endorsed on the original certificate under stamp and signature of handling authorised dealer.

Advances against 'Red Clause' Letters of Credit

Authorised dealers may freely grant pre-shipment advances against 'Red Clause' letters of credit opened by overseas buyers in favour of their exporter-constituents. Advances made by the letter of credit opening bank will, however, be treated as advance remittances against exports. If the advances are interest-bearing, they will require prior approval of Reserve Bank in terms of paragraph 11 C.10(ii).

Note: Advances made by auathorised dealers to FERA Companies in terms of this paragraph will also be subject to regulations laid down.

Part Drawings

(*i*) In certain lines of export trade, it is the practice of exporters not to draw bills for full invoice value of the goods but to leave a small part undrawn for payment after adjustment due to differences in weight, quality, etc., ascertained after arrival and inspection, weighment of analysis of the goods. In such cases, authorised dealers may negotiate bills, provided —

(*a*) undrawn balance is in conformity with the normal level of balance left undrawn in the particular line of export trade, subject to a maximum of 5 per cent of the full export value;

and

(*b*) an undertaking is obtained from exporter that he will surrender/ account for the balance proceeds of the shipment within the period prescribed for realisation.

Authorised dealers should obtain the above undertaking from exporter on the duplicate copy GR/PP form.

(*ii*) All cases where the balances required to be left undrawn by the exporters do not conform to the above stipulations *e.g.,* tenders for supply of goods to overseas projects financed by international financing agencies like World Bank, Asian Development Bank, African Development Bank, etc., should be referred to Reserve Bank. Where, however, it is not the practice in the particular line of export trade to leave a part of the export value undrawn, authorised dealers should advise exporters to draw the bills for the full export value.

Follow-up of Undrawn Balances

(*i*) Authorised dealers should enter all undertakings relating to undrawn balances against exports in a special register and maintain a watch through the register on the realisation of the balances before expiry of the prescribed period. On receipt of the amount in settlement of undrawn balance, the duplicate copy of the relative GR/PP forms should be forwarded to Reserve Bank duly certified for the total amount received against the shipment together with original documents in support of adjustments, if any, made on account of differences in weight, quality, etc. Before certifying the forms in the above manner, authorised dealers should verify the terms of relative sale contract and ensure, by reference to the weight certificate, analysis report, etc., that the full amount payable by the buyer has been realised according to those terms.

(ii) In cases where exporter has failed to fulfil his undertaking within the prescribed period, authorised dealer should take up the matter suitably with him and if he fails to comply with the requirements within twenty one days, authorised dealer should report the case to Reserve Bank with full details. The duplicate copies of GR/PP forms should continue to be retained by authorised dealers.

Note: As an exception to the above rule, in cases where exporter has not been able to arrange for repatriation of the undrawn balance in spite of his best efforts, authorised dealer on being satisfied about the bona fides of the case, may submit duplicate copies of GR/PP forms to Reserve Bank duly certified for the amount actually realised, provided the amount outstanding does not exceed 2.5 per cent of export value declared on the form or the equivalent of Rs. 5,000/-, whichever is less, and a period of one year has expired from shipment. The items should, however, continue to be reported in the quarterly statement of outstanding export bills.

Export of Films

(i) Films can be exported from India against declaration on GR/PP forms in the usual manner only if exports are to be made on **outright sale** basis. In these cases, exporters are required to give the name of the film to be exported on both copies of GR/PP forms and indicate thereon clearly the number of quota prints and/or extra prints/trailers with the value thereof separately. Authorised dealers should ensure that the name of the film and the number of prints are invariably indicated on both copies of GR/PP forms before accepting shipping documents for negotiation/collection. Where exports are to be made on fixed or variable rental/distribution basis, exporters are required to apply to Reserve Bank and obtain waiver of the GR/PP form formalities.

(ii) At the time of submitting bills for collection/negotiation to authorised dealer in case of export of films on outright sale basis, exporters should also submit the original sale contract or agreement with overseas buyer relating to sale of the prints and/or rights of exhibition and distribution, duly approved by the National Film Development Corporation Ltd. (NFDC) along with annexures issued by it authorising export of prints. These documents

(together with an extra copy of each) should be forwarded to Reserve Bank along with the duplicate copy of GR/PP form duly certified and accompanied by a copy of the relative invoice as usual. The original sale contract/ agreement will be returned undue course to authorised dealer by Reserve Bank for return to exporter.

(iii) Prior approval of Reserve Bank must be obtained in case rights of exploitation of a film already exported on outright sale basis are desired to be transferred to another party on rental/distribution basis.

Consignment Exports

(i) When goods have been exported on consignment basis at the risk of exporter for sale and eventual remittance of sale proceeds to him by the agent/consignee abroad, authorised dealer, while forwarding shipping documents to his overseas branch/correspondent, should instruct the latter to deliver them only against trust receipt/undertaking to deliver sale proceeds by a specified date which should be within the period prescribed for realisation of proceeds of the export. This procedure should be followed even if according to the practice in certain trades, a bill for part of the estimated value is drawn in advance against the exports.

Notes: *(A)* Exports of engineering goods on consignment basis are permitted to be made to a warehouse maintained at Rotterdam by the Engineering Export Promotion Council and the time limit for realisation of proceeds of such exports is fifteen months.

(B) Exports of jewellery, precious stones, etc. made on consignment basis are also subject to the directions. 11B.12.

(ii) The agents/consignees may deduct from sale proceeds of the goods expenses normally incurred towards receipt, storage and sale of the goods, such as landing charges, warehouse rent, handling charges, etc., and remit the net proceeds to the exporter. Any commission due to overseas agents/ consignees may be deducted in Accounts Sales only if relative agency arrangement has been registered with Reserve Bank.

Note: In case of goods exported on consignment basis, freight and marine insurance must be arranged in India.

(iii) Duplicate copies of the GR/PP forms covering consignment exports must be retained by authorised dealers until all the goods declared on the form have been sold and sale proceeds have been repatriated to India. When this is completed, the form should be forwarded to Reserve Bank duly certified for the total amount realised, together with original Accounts Sales received from agent/consignee. Deductions in Accounts Sales should be supported by bills/receipts in original except in case of petty items like postage/cable charges, stamp duty, etc.

(*iv*) Authorised dealers should maintain a special register in which they should enter full details of all exports on consignment basis whether or not bill of exchange has been drawn. The register should contain a column showing date on which the period prescribed for realisation of proceeds of the export will expire. They should watch realisation of proceeds through this register and follow the procedure laid down, as if a bill had been drawn covering the export. Quarterly statement as prescribed therein in respect of overdue bills should also be forwarded to Reserve Bank.

Despatch of Shipping Documents

(*i*) If after scrutiny, GR/PP forms and shipping documents submitted by exporters are found to be in order, authorised dealers should despatch shipping documents to their overseas branches/correspondents as expeditiously as possible. As delay in transmission of shipping documents may result in avoidable demurrage payments at destination and also quite often in refusal of the consignments.

(*ii*) Authorised dealers may despatch shipping documents direct to the consignees in cases where advance payment or an irrevocable letter of credit has been received for the full value of the export shipment and the underlying sale contract letter of credit provides for despatch of shipping documents direct to the consignee or claims for reduction from overseas buyers on grounds of delayed delivery, authorised dealers should streamline their internal procedure for handling documents at the offices in order that despatch of documents is not delayed. Authorised dealers should ensure, particularly in case of exports to neighbouring countries, that shipping documents are despatched to their overseas branches/correspondents expeditiously so that documents reach the buyer before the carrying steamer discharges the cargo at port of destination.

Geographic Delivery Orders

Consignors of cargo to nearby countries such as Sri Lanka, Malaysia, Indonesia, Gulf countries, Kenya, Tanzania, etc. may at times find it necessary to have Telegraphic Delivery Orders (TDOs) issued to shipping agents at port of delivery to enable overseas consignees to obtain delivery of the goods in the absence of shipping documents. Issue of TDOs by shipping companies or their agents directly in favour of consignees is prohibited. TDOs should be issued only through the medium of the authorised dealer through whom proceeds of the export have been or will be realised. In cases where issue of TDOs is necessary, exporter should obtain the signed telecommunication (TDO) from the shipping company/agent addressed to their agent at port of delivery. The TDO should direct the agent to deliver the goods to the order of a bank in the country concerned, who should be the correspondent bank of the authorised dealer through whom exporter intends to forward remaining documents (*i.e.*, bill, invoice, etc.,) relating to the shipment for collection. Exporter should, thereafter, hand over the TDO to the authorised dealer along with his invoice, etc. Authorised dealer should prepare his own telecommunication to his overseas correspondent and despatch his telecommunication and the TDO prepared by the shipping company/ agent simultaneously. In his telecommunication to the correspondent bank, authorised dealer should issue suitable directions regarding handing over of the delivery order to consignee and payment to be obtained against the shipment.

Handing over Negotiable Copy of Bill of Lading to Master of Vessel/ Trade Representative

At times, letters of credit opened in respect of exports to certain land-locked countries, particularly in Europe, may stipulate that one negotiable copy of Bill of Lading should be delivered to the Master of the carrying vessel or Trade Representative of the country concerned. Authorised dealers may deliver one negotiable copy of Bill of Lading to the Master of the carrying vessel or Trade Representative, provided the letter of credit is irrevocable and the documents conform strictly to the terms of the letter of credit.

Export of Perishables to Bangladesh

Special facilities are allowed to exporters of perishable commodities to Bangladesh for sending direct to importer, railway receipt/steamer receipt/ bill of lading/airway bill or any other document conveying title to the goods, so as to enable the latter to take delivery of the goods immediately on arrival at destination. Exporters desiring to avail themselves of these facilities should be asked to apply to Reserve Bank stating name and address of authorised dealer through whom they propose to negotiate bills covering such shipments and nature of goods to be exported. They should also furnish an undertaking that the covering bill and invoice for the value of goods exported will be sent by them through an authorised dealer for realisation of proceeds in prescribed manner. If the application is approved, authorised dealer concerned will be advised by Reserve Bank and it will then be in order for him to accept for negotiation/collection from exporter, clean bills drawn on importer in Pakistan or Bangladesh for the value of goods, provided they are accompanied by invoices and the duplicate copies of the relative GR form. In case letter of credit has been opened in favour of exporter, it should permit documents of title to the goods being sent by exporter direct to consignee.

Submission of ENC Statements and Certification of Duplicate Copies of Export Forms

(i) Simultaneously with the despatch of shipping documents abroad, authorised dealers should submit to Reserve Bank a statement **in form ENC**

(in duplicate) in respect of export transactions handled by them. Such statements are required to be submitted on a fortnightly basis **along with R-Supplementary Returns,** and the serial number of relative GR/PP forms should be listed therein in the serial order of the bill numbers as appearing in the Export Bills Register. In case of exports on consignment basis as also cases where bills are not drawn for full invoice value but a small part is left undrawn, authorised dealers should record full invoice value while reporting transactions in ENC statements. Similarly, where part or full invoice value of goods has been received in advance by the exporter, authorised dealers should report the full invoice value of the goods in ENC statement although shipping documents may have been negotiated for the balance amount only or no amount is to be realised thereagainst.

(ii) The duplicate copy of GR/PP forms should be retained by authorised dealer until actual realisation of full proceeds of the export. When full payment is received, appropriate certificate on the duplicate copy should be completed and the form forwarded to Reserve Bank. Ordinarily, proceeds of exports will be realised by the authorised dealer who handled shipping documents, either by credit to a foreign currency account maintained by him overseas or by debit to a rupee account maintained by an overseas correspondent bank with him. In some cases, proceeds may be realised through another authorised dealer *i.e.,* by credit to a foreign currency account maintained by the other authorised dealer or by debit to a rupee account maintained by the overseas bank with the latter. Certification of the duplicate GR/PP forms should be made even in such cases by the authorised dealer who forwarded documents abroad after ensuring that payment has emanated in an approved manner. Where, however, one authorised dealer forwards documents to another authorised dealer for negotiation under a letter of credit restricted to the latter, certification will be made by the authorised dealer to whom negotiation under the credit is restricted except where payment is made by the latter in foreign currency to enable the exporter to deliver foreign currency to his banker under a forward contract fixed with him.

Export Bills Register

(i) Authorised dealers should provide columns in their Export Bills Register for recording GR/PP form number, date on which period prescribed for realisation of export proceeds will expire, the fortnightly period of R Supplementary Return with which ENC statement covering the transaction was sent to Reserve Bank and the period of R Supplementary Return with which the duplicate copy of GR/PP form is submitted to Reserve Bank. These entries will enable authorised dealers to watch closely realisation of bills and also to ensure that they have reported all transactions to Reserve Bank.

(ii) Authorised dealers should ensure that all types of export transactions are entered in the Bills Register and are given bill numbers. The bill numbers should be recorded in ENC statement and other relevant returns submitted to Reserve Bank.

(iii) While handling documents against exports, authorised dealers should record against relative entry in Bills Register, the amount of commission and/or discount declared by exporters on GR/PP forms to facilitate reference while dealing with applications for remittance/deduction from the invoice on account of commission/discount.

Follow-up of Overdue Bills

(i) Authorised dealers should closely watch realisation of bills through Bills Register and, in cases where 'bills remain outstanding beyond the period prescribed for realisation of export value, they should take up the matter promptly with exporter concerned. If exporter fails to arrange for delivery of the proceeds within twenty one days, the matter should be reported to Reserve Bank by letter stating, where possible, the reason for the delay in realisation of proceeds of the exports unless exporter has sought permission for extension of time. The duplicate copies of GR/PP forms should, however, continue to be held by authorised dealer until full proceeds are realised except in case of undrawn balances covered by Note under paragraph 11 C. 13 *(ii)*. Authorised dealers should follow up export outstanding with exporters systematically and vigorously so that action against defaulting exporters does not get delayed.

(ii) **Authorised dealers should furnish annually to Reserve Bank a consolidated statement in form XOS giving details of all export bills outstanding beyond the prescribed period of realisation as at the end of March every year.** They should also submit quarterly statements in form XOS for the subsequent three quarters ending 30th June, 30th September and 31st December giving separately only details of the additions and deletions of outstanding export bills during the relative quarter and the net position of such bills. Details of certificates, if any, issued to exporters for claiming export incentives should invariably be indicated in the respective column in XOS statement. The statement should be submitted by 15th day of the month following the close of the quarter to which it relates.

Notes: (A) Separate statements on the lines indicated above should also be furnished in respect of exports on consignment basis (including exports to Indian-owned warehouses abroad) for which payment is outstanding beyond the prescribed period, although no bills were drawn.

(B) Authorised dealers should indicate prominently with an asterisk, items in the quarterly statements against which they have issued to exporters certificates in accordance with the procedure laid down by the Import

Licensing Authorities to enable exporters to secure export incentive benefits from Government. Serial number of such items should also be underlined in the XOS statements. Since such items are required to be extracted from the statements and advised to Import Trade Control Authorities for purpose of adjusting incentive benefits available to concerned exporters, authorised dealers should exercise good care while preparing the quarterly statements.

Reduction in Value

When Bills of Lading have been negotiated or sent for collection, the amount thereof is desired to reduced for any reason except in cases covered by sub-paragraph *(ii)* and *(iii)*. All applications for reduction in invoice value must be made in form X, in duplicate, explaining fully the circumstances necessitating the application supported by appropriate documentary evidence, and submitted to authorised dealer who had handled the relative shipping documents. Whenever an application has to be forwarded to Reserve Bank because it is not referred by provisions of sub-paragraph *(ii)* below, the authorised dealer should — on its merits furnishing information on export realisation of the applicant during the previous two years and export outstandings, if any, particularly whether the exporter has been frequently seeking approval for reduction in invoice value. Where the commodity in question was subject to floor price restrictions at the time of shipment, the authorised dealer should also indicate whether the net realisation after the reduction asked for should conform to the floor price requirement. In cases where the reduction has permitted, the exporter will have to surrender to the Trade Control priorities export incentives proportionate to the percentage of reduction in invoice value allowed.

(ii) Authorised dealers handling shipping documents may accept requests of their exporter constituents for allowing reduction in invoice value up to 10 per cent of the value of shipment or Rs. 20,000/-, whichever is less, and issue necessary instructions to their overseas correspondents to accept short payment, subject, among others, to the following conditions:

(a) Reduction in invoice value is insisted upon by the overseas buyer as a precondition for accepting the shipping documents and/or clearance of goods for reasons such as delay in shipment of goods, apparent damage to the consignment in transit, fall in demand for goods in the local market, etc. and documentary evidence in support thereof is produced.

(b) The commodity in respect of which reduction is sought to be allowed is not one the export of which is regulated by the system of allocation of export quotas by Government of India. The request for reduction should not also involve gold or silver jewellery and articles made out of cut and polished diamonds, which calls for

special examination by Reserve Bank in consultation with Customs.

(c) In respect of those commodities the export of which is subject to floor price stipulations, the export value to be realised after reduction should continue to satisfy such floor price requirements. Similarly, exports from Free Trade Zones and 100% Export Oriented Units which are subject to stipulation of minimum value addition to the export items made out of imported materials, the export value to be realised after the proposed reduction should continue to satisfy the requirement of minimum value addition laid down by the concerned authorities.

Authorised dealer should record against the relative entry in the Export Bills Register the amount of reduction agreed to. Authorised dealer should forward to Reserve Bank relative case papers including copies of correspondence between the exporter and the overseas buyer for *post facto* scrutiny. In cases where certificate of export has been issued by the authorised dealer to enable exporter to claim export incentives from Trade Control authorities, he should advise the exporter to surrender export incentives proportionate to the reduction in invoice value agreed to by him and forward a copy of such advice directly to the Trade Control authorities for necessary action.

(iii) Exporters availing themselves of tariff concessions under the Generalised Scheme of Preferences (GSP) established by certain countries like Japan, E.E.C. countries, etc., may at times be exposed to uncertainties about availability of tariff concessions as exports to these countries are eligible for the concession depending upon whether the ceiling applicable in the importing countries have been reached or not at the time consignments land there. If sale contracts were entered into and invoices drawn by Indian exporters on the assumption of availability of tariff concessions but on account of the ceilings having been already reached by the time goods reach destination, importers abroad will be required to pay the duty and claim it from Indian exporters either by reduction in invoice value or remittance from India for the equivalent amount, depending upon whether payment against the export has been made or not. Authorised dealers may allow reduction in invoice value to the extent of duty paid abroad without reference to Reserve Bank, provided exporter produces the following documents:

(a) Certificate from certifying agency in India that the product in question is covered by GSP Scheme of the importing country,

(b) Certificate from the Indian Mission in the importing country indicating date on which the quota level for the commodity in question under GSP was reached,

and

(c) Suitable documentary evidence regarding the duty paid/payable by importers abroad.

Authorised dealer should also certify on relative GR form amount of short-fall accepted by him and confirm that necessary supporting evidence in terms of this paragraph has been seen. Where export proceeds have already been realised by exporter, the amount of duty paid by importer may have to be refunded by remittance from India. Applications for such refunds should be referred to Reserve Bank together with documents specified above and authorised dealer's certificate for realisation of export proceeds.

Rebate on Pre-payment of Usance Export Bills

Occasionally, drawees of usance export bills negotiated by authorised dealers may offer to pay the bills before maturity on a rebate being allowed on the value of the bills. Authorised dealers may accept pre-payment of usance bills in such cases and allow rebate for the actual unexpired usance of the bills at the discount/rebating rate prevailing in the country of payment, provided the rate does not exceed the concessionary ceiling rate of interest stipulated for post-shipment credit in India or any lower rate actually charged by the bank in India on such post-shipment credit, and no interest subsidy is claimed for the unexpired period. The rebated bills will not be eligible for refinance from Reserve Bank. While certifying realisation of proceeds in such cases on the reverse of the duplicate copies of GR/PP forms, authorised dealers should indicate amount of rebate allowed and also and a confirmation that the conditions in this paragraph have been fulfilled. Authorised dealers may also permit pre-payment of usance bills sent on collection basis if conditions laid down in this paragraph are fulfilled.

Customs Rules Simplified

Controversies over valuation, classification, and other customs matters are common; therefore, a procedure for resolution has been established. An importer may protest a decision and get an administrative review by the customs authorities.

In a significant extension of liberalisation schemes, which the government has been following over the past one year, Government of India have simplified and rationalised customs laws and procedures as part of the liberalised economic, industrial and trade policies of the government in June 1992.

The following is the gist of official announcement on simplification of customs rules and procedures, both for goods and passengers.

— Self-assessment of import documents by which importer of proven identity with unblemished record of past conduct to self-assess the goods, determine duty liability and disburse the duty.

— This is applicable to government departments and undertakings.

— Any breach of trust to attract penalty.

— Green channel for clearance of cargo under which cargo imported by persons of proven identity with unblemished record as well as private sector units to be cleared without scrutiny.

— Only 10 per cent consignments to be selected at random for physical verification.

— Chemical test of samples to be extended to other institutes and laboratories in view of the congestion in the central revenues control laboratory.

— The powers of assistant collectors and deputy collectors enhanced. Export documents in certain prescribed categories not required to be put up to assistant collector.

— Import documents up to a value of rupees one lakh to be assessed by the appraisers.

— Greater facility to imports through international courier service to be provided. The level of duty cut and value up to which the articles to be imported through courier raised.

— Bonafide commercial samples restricted to Rs. 200 for duty free imports allowed up to Rs 1300.

— Passenger clearance rules simplified and inconvenience and irritants eliminated.

— Duty-free allowance to passengers enhanced from Rs 2000 to Rs. 3000. This includes those arriving from Sri Lanka and Maldives provided their stay abroad is more than three days.

MAJOR CONCESSIONS IN CUSTOMS DUTY

In a further bid to boost exports and bring tariffs down to international levels, the government of India have announced major concessions in customs duty for capital goods and their components.

The first notification prescribes a concessional rate of customs duty of 25 per cent ad valorem or 15 per cent ad valorem on capital goods imported under the Export Promotion Capital Goods (EPCG) scheme, subject to specified conditions.

The second notification prescribes customs duty at a concessional rate of 15 per cent ad valorem on components imported for the manufacture of capital goods to be supplied to the manufacturers-exporters under the EPCG scheme, subject to specified conditions.

The third notification fully exempts capital goods and components imported under the scheme from auxiliary duty to customs.

According to the first notification, an importer undertaking an export obligation equivalent to three times the CIF value of the capital goods over a period of four years would attract customs duty at the rate of 25 per cent ad valorem.

Imports undertaking an export obligation equivalent to four times the CIF value of the capital goods over a period of five years would have to pay customs duty at the rate of 15 per cent ad valorem.

Capital goods include plant, machinery, equipment or accessories required by an importer for manufacture of goods and also machinery for packing goods, testing equipment and equipment required for research and development activity.

The second notification prescribes a concessional rate of customs duty of 15 per cent ad valorem on components imported for the manufacture of capital goods.

All such imports of capital goods and components have also been fully exempted from the additional customs duties.

WHAT FACTORS INFLUENCE EXCHANGE RATES?

To cover all the factors influencing exchange rates in detail would require a separate workbook on economics. Instead, we will look at the main influences to give you a broad overview.

Fundamental Issues

1. Balance of payments — generally a surplus leads to a stronger currency, while a deficit weakens a currency.
2. Economic growth rate — high growth leads to rise in imports, and a fall in the currency.
3. Fiscal policy — an expansionary policy, *e.g.*, lower taxes, can lead to a higher economic growth rate.
4. Monetary policy — the way a central bank attempts to influence and control interest rates and money supply.
5. Interest rates — high domestic interest rates tend to attract overseas capitals thus the currency appreciates in the short term. In the longer term, however, high interest rates slow the economy down, thus weakening the currency.
6. Political issues — political stability is likely to lead to economic stability, and hence a steady currency, while political instability would have the opposite effect.

Technical Issues

1. Government controls — can lead to an unrealistic value of a currency, resulting in violent exchange rate movements.
2. Charts — are used to predict future short-term rates, based on the premise that history tends to repeat itself. By looking at past upper and lower limits the "support" (lower) and "resistance" (upper) limits of interest rate movements can often be predicted.

Speculation

Speculative forces can have a major effect on exchange rates. Say, for example, there are expectations that a currency will be devalued, the speculator will then start selling the currency in-preparation for buying it back later at a cheaper rate. This very act can be self-fulfilling, however, if the selling pressure from speculators extends to other market participants. It should be noted that forex traders create position through the process of speculation. This activity creates liquidity in the foreign exchange market.

Spot Dealing

In this section, we will look at spot dealing. The foreign exchange market, like so many other markets and industries, is full of jargon. So, before we start, let us define what we mean by a spot deal.

A spot deal is one executed today to buy one currency for another currency with settlement in two business days.

The rate used in a spot deal is the sport rate. This is the rate you see quoted on bank dealing screens and in newspapers.

At this point, you may find it helpful to refer to the Glossary at the need of this workbook which defines several other terms used in the foreign exchange market. The most commonly used terms include "short", "long", "square" and "value date". Understanding what these mean will help you proceed through this workbook.

Methods of Quoting Rates

Many people find foreign exchange confusing, particularly the difference between direct and indirect rates, and the method used to quote rates in the foreign exchange market. Below we clear up this confusion.

A direct is a fixed amount of a foreign currency quoted against your home currency.

For example, if you live in West Germany:

FFr 100 = DM 29.32

An indirect rate is the mirror image of a direct rate, i.e. it quotes a fixed amount of your home currency compared to a variable amount of foreign currency.

An example of an indirect rate, again in West Germany, would be:

DM 100 = FFr 341.02

As you can imagine, if a dealer in Frankfurt called a dealer in Brussels for a quotation on a rate, it could be confusing if the Brussels dealer quoted his direct rate, which would be the indirect rate for the Frankfurt dealer. To eliminate any confusion, a common standard was adopted and is known as the "dollar rate".

The dollar rate is when a variable amount of foreign currency is quoted against one unit of the US dollar, regardless of where the dealer is located or in what currency he is requesting a quote. The exception is the sterling/US dollar rate (commonly called "cable") which is quoted as units of the US dollar to sterling and is a result of the method of trading before decimalisation.

Since banks deal in the foreign exchange market to make a profit, there is a difference between the rate at which they will buy a currency and the rate at which they will sell it. This difference is referred to as the bank's "spread", or profit. How does a bank decide which rate to use?

A bank will buy US dollars for another currency at a low rate (its "bid rate") and sell US dollars for another currency at a high rate (its "offered rate"). The exception is sterling where the bank will buy sterling for US dollars at the bid rate and sell sterling for US dollars at the offered rate. To put it simply, a bank will always deal at the most advantageous rate to itself so that it can make its spread.

Below we give an example of how spot rates are quoted in the foreign exchange market against the US dollar.

Currency	*Bid*	*Offer*
US dollar/Deutschmark	1.8225	1.8235
US dollar/yen	126.20	126.30
US dollar/Swiss franc	1.5560	1.5570
US dollar/guilder	2.0570	2.0580
US dollar/French franc	6.2100	6.2150
US dollar/Belgian franc	38.25	38.35
US dollar/Lire	1345.75	1346.25
Sterling/US dollar	1.7525	1.7535

Source: Financial Times, closing rates on February 24, 1989.

To help you understand how rates are quoted, you should now study the following examples, which are based on the rates quoted in the table above. Remember, the rates are those at which the bank will buy or sell US dollars for another currency, except for sterling in which case the bank will buy and sell sterling for US dollars.

A German shoe maker sells shoes to a US importer and invoices in US dollars. What rate does bank quote the shoe maker to convert the US dollars into Deutschmarks?

The bank is buying US dollars, therefore it will quote 1.8225.

A Belgian supplier of dental equipment wishes to import a new range of chairs from the US. What rate does the bank quote the Belgian supplier to convert his Belgian francs into US dollars to for the equipment?

The bank is selling US dollars (buying Belgian francs), therefore it will quote 38.35.

A bank sells pound 5m for US dollars. How many US dollars does the bank receive?

The bank is buying US dollars (selling sterling) with the rate being 1.7535; therefore it will receive 8,767,500.

Cross Rates

Cross rates are another area of foreign exchange that can confuse the amateur. Again, once you understand the meaning of the term, you will have no problem working with cross rates. A cross rate is the exchange between the currencies of two centres from the point of view of a third centre; for example rate of exchange between French Francs and Canadian dollars quoted in London.

In the international market, however, cross rates have come to mean any rates do not involve dollar, thus the above rate, even when quoted in Paris or Toronto, would be a cross rate.

Cross rates are obtained by dividing the rate for one currency by the rate for the other, with the exception of sterling, where the rates are multiplied.

Before going on, the following example will help you understand cross rates. The rates for sterling French francs and Canadian dollars are available in London. To find out the rate for selling French or Canadian dollars you would first have to sell French Francs and buy sterling and then use that sterling to buy Canadian dollars.

One complication with cross rates is the rate between two currencies will be quoted differently, depending on who is quoting it. For example, the French franc/Deutschmark cross rate will be different, depending on whether it is being quoted in France or West Germany. In Paris, the quote will be in numbers (French francs per 100 Deuschmarks, say, FFr 300 whereas in Frankfurt it is the number of Deutschmarks per 100 French francs, or DM 33.3. In other words, the rates are quoted in direct terms. The numerator (upper part of the fraction) determines from whose perspective the quote is made. Rates involving sterling are always quoted in terms of units of foreign currency to one unit of sterling.

For cross rates not involving sterling, to convert the foreign currency into the home currency, divide the foreign currency by 100 and multiply by the rate. To convert the home currency into a foreign currency, divide by the rate and multiply by 100.

Think about this formula for a moment, and then study the examples below, using the rates quoted in the table which you used for Exercise 1.

A Japanese radio maker sells radios to a French retailer and is paid in French francs. What rate will a Japanese bank quote the radio maker to convert the French francs into yen?

The bank is buying French francs, *i.e.*, selling dollars, and selling yen, *i.e.*, buying dollars. Therefore the customer has to pay the most French francs (6.2150) to receive his dollars. He gets the smallest number of yen (126.20) for his dollars.

$$\frac{126.20}{6.2150} \times 100 = ¥\,2{,}030.57 \text{ per FFr } 100$$

A German tyre maker sells tyres to a Japanese car maker and agrees to accept payment in yen. The Japanese car maker pays him ¥ 150m. What rate *(i)* does the bank quote the tyre maker and *(ii)* what does the tyre maker receive from his bank when he converts the yen into Deutschmarks?

The bank is buying yen, *i.e.*, selling dollars, and selling Deutschmarks, *i.e.*, buying, dollars. Therefore:

(i) $$\frac{1.8225}{126.30} \times 100 = \text{DM } 1.4430 \text{ per } ¥\,100$$

(ii) $$\frac{150{,}000{,}000}{100} \times 1.4430 = \text{DM } 2,\,164{,}500.00$$

A Dutch bank tells a customer that the rate at which it will buy guilders against Belgian francs is 5.3804 guilders per 100 Belgian francs. The customer wants to exchange 300,000 guilders. How many Belgian francs does he get?

$$\frac{300{,}000}{5.3804} \times 100 = \text{BFr } 5{,}575{,}793.62$$

Risks in Spot Transactions

The risks inherent in spot transactions are related to the payments made to settle the transaction. These risks are described briefly below.

Settlement Two Days After the Deal is Struck

The potential risk here is that one of the counterparts to the transaction could become bankrupt between the time the deal is struck and settlement. This would leave the remaining counterparty with an obligation in theory to deliver one currency, but with no certainty that the counterparty would deliver another currency.

Global Time Differences

In certain situations, such as selling US dollars and buying Deutschmarks, one currency is delivered several hours before the other.

Payment Confirmation Not Received Until the Following Day

This occurs because the correspondent bank cannot tell an account holder that funds have not been received until the end of the bank's business day.

FORWARD DEALING

Let's now move on to forward foreign exchange and forward dealing. First of all, what is forward foreign exchange transaction? It is a transaction executed today to buy, one currency for another currency at a rate agreed today, with settlement at an agreed future time, for example in six months.

What Determines Forward Rates?

In theory, there is no reason why the spot and the forward rate are not the same. However, remember that in the Introduction we looked at the factors influencing exchange rates and indicated that high interest rates lead to a weaker currency. But do we know by how much the currency will weaken? Is it just a guess? Those of you who have studied economic theory will know there is a great debate about precisely how the forward rate is created. In practical terms, banks, wishing to manage their risk, calculate the forward rate by taking the spot rate today and adjusting it by the differential of the interest rate on the two currencies.

Take the following example. Say the spot and forward rates between US dollars and yen were the same at 125, but US dollar interest rates were at 10% while yen interest rates were only at 4%. Japanese investors would than buy US dollars for the higher yield. When the funds were required again, the investors would be able to convert the US dollars into yen and end up with more yen than if they had invested directly in Japan. In this case, an investor with ¥ 125,000 could convert this to US $ 1,000, invest it for one month at

10% per annum, giving him US $ 1008.33 at the end of the month. This would then be converted back to yen to give him ¥ 126,041. In contrast, if he had invested directly in yen at 4%, the amount would only have been Y 125,417.

In a free market, the advantage of the higher US dollar interest rate will be neutralised by a lower value of the US dollar in the forward foreign exchange market should the investor wish to agree at a rate today for converting US dollars into yen at the end of the investment period. As we mentioned above, this future value will be calculated by taking the current spot rate, and adjusting it by adding or subtracting an amount to allow for the interest rate differentials. These adjustments are called forward points.

It is important to grasp one basic principle here. The forward points are only a reflection of the relative interest rates of the currencies. They are not an indication of what the future spot rates of the currencies will be. For instance, during 1983 and 1984 the US dollar continually strengthened against most other hard currencies, despite the fact that it was quoted at a discount in the forward market. A more recent example is that between July 1987 and December, 1987 sterling was quoted at a discount to the US dollar in the forward market, but in early July 1988 the exchange rate was around 1.61, whereas in early December 1988 it was around 1.80.

Why Use Forward Foreign Exchange?

Why would an institution agree to exchange a currency in future at a rate agreed today? For two major reasons : first, to hedge an exposure and, second, to take advantage of forward exchange rates not truly reflecting interest rate differentials between currencies.

To Hedge an Exposure

Consider an American importer of German cars. The importer will be paying for the cars in Deutschmarks but selling them in US dollars. The importer will have to agree a price with the manufacturer when the order is placed, and will have to decide his US dollar selling price so that he can arrange his sales campaign. As you can see, the importer runs the risk that in the time between agreeing the Deutschmark price and selling the cars in US dollars, the US dollar could decline. As a result the importer might not earn enough US dollars to cover the cost of the Deutschmarks. However, by entering into a forward foreign exchange contract, the importer will know exactly how many US dollars he will need to buy the Deutschmarks, and at what price he needs to sell the cars to make a profit. These transactions, where there is only a single forward transaction, are often referred to as "outrights."

To Take Advantage of Interest Rates and Currency Differentials

In practice, the interest and exchange rate differentials rarely cancel each other out. Dealers can take advantage of these imperfections through a money market operation and a simultaneous spot and forward transaction. These transactions are referred to as "*swap transactions*" and are discussed later in this workbook.

Premiums and Discounts

Forward exchange rates are not quoted in the same way as spot rates. Instead, forward rates are quoted in terms of "forward points". There are 10,000 points to each whole unit of a currency. The forward points are the difference between the spot rate and the forward rate. These differences are called "premiums" or "discounts". Some dealers refer to the difference as "the swap rate", but this can be confusing since all forward transactions are not the swap transactions mentioned above.

How do we decide if the currency is at a premium or a discount? (Just remember that the high interest rate currency is expected to depreciate, therefore more of it will be required to buy the same amount of the low interest rate currency. So, the high interest rate currency is at a discount to the low interest currency in the forward market. The opposite will be the case for a currency at a premium.)

In the next section we will explain how to calculate forward points and how to work out the forward exchange rate to be used in a transaction.

Calculating Forward Points and Rates

In order to know what the rate in a forward transaction will be, we first have to calculate the forward points using a simple arithmetic formula. All the formula does is to take the interest rate differential per year, convert it into a differential for the period of the forward contract, and then express the spot rate, the forward contract, and then express the spot rate of the currency as a percentage of the differential the period.

The formula for a US dollar versus other currency forward is:

$$\text{Spot Rate} \times \frac{\text{No. of Days}}{360} \times \frac{\text{US\$ Int. Rate} - \text{Other Currency Int. Rate.}}{100}$$

$$1 + \frac{(\text{US\$ Interest Rate}}{(100} \times \frac{\text{Number of Days})}{360)}$$

=Number of Forward Points of Spot Currency

* make value positive

The same formula can be used for any currency against another by substituting the appropriate spot interest rates.

At this point, you should be aware of the conventions used in the foreign exchange and money matter for the number of days. All calculations are based on the actual number of days elapsed, divided or multiplied by 360, except for sterling and some other currencies which use 365 days. Furthermore, the value date is the last business day of a month, the corresponding day in any future month is also last business day. For example, if the spot value date is 28th February, the value date in a one-n forward transaction would be 31st March, and, if the spot value date was 31st May , the forward date in a six-month transaction would be 30th November. If the last day of the month is not a business day, then the value date is the next preceding business day. For simplicity, we will show 360 days formulae given in this workbook. It may look complicated, but using the interest rate provided let us work through an example and see how easy it is.

Currency	*One-month Interest Rate*		*Three-month Interest Rate*	
	Offer	*Bid*	*Offer*	*Bid*
Deutschmark	6.6875	6.5625	7.00	6.875
Yen	4.5	4.375	4.875	4.75
Swiss Franc	5.9375	5.8125	6.125	6.00
Guilder	6.875	6.75	7.125	7.00
French franc	9.5	9.375	975	9.825
Belgian franc	8.25	7.875	8.5	8.125
Lire	12.00	11.50	12.50	12.00
Sterling	12.875	12.75	13.1875	13.0625
US dollar	9.8125	9.6875	10.125	10.00

Source: Financial Times, closing rates on February 24, 1989.

First we calculate the forward points applicable to the one-month forward Deutschmark against the US dollar.

$$\frac{1.8225 \times \frac{31}{360} \times 0.031250}{1 + 0.096875 \times \frac{31}{360}} = \frac{1.8225 \times 0.08611 \times 0.03125}{1 + (0.096875 \times 0.08611)}$$

$$= \frac{0.004904}{1.008342} = \text{DM } 0.0049$$

or, as a dealer would say, 49 points.

Just as there is a bid and offered rate in the spot market, there is a bid and offered rate in the forward market. This means that the forward points for both sides of the exchange rate must be quoted. In practice, banks only quote forward points for even period of time *i.e.,* one month, two months, three months.

A typical example of how forward points are quoted is given below:

Currency	*One-month Forward*			*Three-month Forward*		
	Bid		*Offer*	*Bid*		*Offer*
US dollar / Deutschmark	0.50	—	0.49 pfpm	1.43	—	1.39 pfpm
US dollar / Yen	0.58	—	0.56 ypm	1.69	—	1.66 ypm
US dollar / Swiss franc	0.53	—	0.50 cpm	1.53	—	1.49 cpm
US dollar / Guilder	0.50	—	0.47 cpm	1.49	—	1.44 cpm
US dollar / French franc	0.22	—	0.12 cpm	0.65	—	0.50 cpm
US dollar / Belgin franc	7.00	—	4.00 cpm	20.00	—	12.00 cpm
US dollar / Lire	2.00	—	3.50 ldis	7.00	—	9.00 ldis
Sterling / US dollar	0.44	—	0.41 cpm	1.22	—	1.17 cpm

Source: Financial Times, closing rates on February 24, 1989.

Note that the quotes in the above example are not in points, but in pfennings or centimes or lire. Usual market practice is to refer to 1/100th of a lire, or 1/100th of a yen as points, whereas for most other currencies 1/10,000th is a point. This will cause you no problem, provided you remember to convert the centimes into points when undertaking calculations.

How do we apply the forward points to the spot rate to arrive at the forward rate? We either have to add them to, or subtract them from, the spot rate depending on whether the currency is at a premium or discount in the forward market. There are two simple rules of thumb to decide if a currency is at a premium or discount, and what to do with the forward points. Remember, exchange rates are quoted as units of that currency which equal one US dollar (except for sterling).

If the forward points decline from left to right, the US dollar is at a discount to the currency (except sterling where it is at a discount to the US dollar) and the forward points are deducted from the spot rate.

If the forward points rise from left to right, the US dollar is at a premium to the currency (except for sterling where it is at a premium to the US dollar) and the forward points are added to the spot rate.

The following examples, using the spot rates in the section on Spot Dealing and the forward points will make this clear.

What rates would a bank quote for a three-month forward US dollar/lire transaction?

The forward points rise from left to right, therefore, the US dollar is at a premium to the lire, so the points are added to the spot rate. Therefore:

1352.75 – 1355.25

A bank customer wants to sell 2m guilders one-month forward for US dollars. How many US does he receive from the bank?

The forward points decline left to right, therefore, the US dollar is at a discount to the guilder, so the forward points on the offer side are deducted from the offer spot rate. Therefore:

$$\frac{2,000,000}{2.0533} = \text{US\$}974,041.79$$

Forward Cross Rate

Forward cross rates are worked out in the same way as spot rates. First, we work out the forward rate from the spot rate and the forward points. Then we decide what currency is being bought, and what is being sold. Finally we divide or multiply the one rate by the others as appropriate.

To reinforce your understanding of the concepts just presented, work through the following which are based on the preceding tables.

What would be the three-month forward Deutschmark/yen rate from the point of view of a corporate company looking to sell Deutschmarks?

The corporate is looking to sell Deutschmarks (for US dollars) and buy yen (with US dollars).

$$\frac{126.20 - 1.69}{1.8235\text{-}0.0139} \times 100 = ¥\,6,880.5 \text{ per DM } 100$$

What would be the one-month forward Swiss franc/Belgian franc rate from the point of Belgian investor looking to sell Swiss francs?

The investor is looking to sell Swiss francs (buy US dollars) and buy Belgian francs (for US dollar. Therefore:

$$\frac{38.25 - 0.07}{1.5570 - 0.0050} \times 100 = \text{BFr } 2460.05 \text{ per SFr } 100$$

Note: In many local markets the participants do not have to physically calculate the cross rates because agencies such as Reuters provide computer-driven information for treasurers and bankers.)

Changes in Exchange Rate and Other Government Policies

The year 1993-94 started on a high note with the announcement of the unification of the exchange rate and the floating of the Rupee. The exchange rate was henceforth to be determined by demand for and supply of foreign exchange in the market. This marked the culmination of a policy sequence which had started with the two-step downward adjustment of the exchange rate and the introduction of 'exim scrips' in July 1991. It included a year-long experience with the dual exchange rate regime under the Liberalised Exchange Rate Management System (LERMS). The exchange rate unification and floating of the Rupee provide the basis for a phased shift to full convertibility of the Rupee. This can be achieved once the remaining controls and restrictions on the current transactions have been eliminated and the crucial macro-economic parameters like the fiscal deficit, the growth of money supply and inflation rate are firmly under control.

After an initial depreciation during February-April, 1993 the nominal effective exchange rate for the Rupee (NEER) held steady. As a result of this stability in the nominal exchange rate, the real effective exchange rate (REER), has tended to appreciate since May 1993. The index for 10-country REER for 1993-94 has recorded an appreciation of 9.6 per cent from May till December 1993 and crossed the 1992-93 level in July this year. It will be important to maintain a stable REER so as to prevent an erosion in incentives available to our exporters.

The premium in the 'hawala' market for the US dollar had come down sharply by the end of 1992-93 to about ten percent. It reached its historically lowest level of 6 per cent in mid-June 1993. This was a result of exchange rate policy and the liberalisation of bullion imports. The premium temporarily went up during August to October 1993 when it reached 13 per cent. It has declined during the subsequent months. The six-month forward rate quoted by authorised dealers for the US dollar has come down to below on per cent recently which is significantly lower than the interest rate differentials between global and Indian markets. This represents a market confidence that the Rupee will retain its position vis-a-vis the major currencies.

The unification of the exchange rate and floating of the Rupee, have provided new opportunities for the foreign exchange market to develop and mature. Recently, banks were permitted by the RBI to deploy funds held in foreign currency accounts of their customers in certain kinds of overseas investments. Banks have also been allowed to rediscount export bills abroad without the prior approval of the RBI with certain interest rate ceilings.

Another important development in the area is the permission given to banks to write cross-currency options for their customers by resorting to arrangements with their overseas branches or other banks abroad.

Another major policy initiative with regard to the external sector includes the extension of dollar-denominated credit facilities for pre-shipment finance. Under this scheme of pre-shipment credit in foreign currency (PCFC) announced by the RBI in October 1993, exporters with confirmed/firm orders and/or letters of credit can avail of credit in major currencies at LIBOR-related interest rates. In conjunction with the facility for post-shipment credit in foreign currencies at a fixed rate of 6.5 per cent. PCFC will now provide Indian exporters access to credit at globally competitive rates. The RBI has also, since November 1992, taken steps to ensure that credit availability for exports is in line with expanding requirements and that commercial banks have sufficient incentives to increase the share of export credit in total advances. As a result, export credit as a percentage of total net bank credit increased from 8.8 per cent on March 20, 1992 to 10.8 per cent on March 19, 1993. The share of export credit in total net bank credit was 10.5 per cent on November 12, 1993. The Government, along with the RBI, has been closely monitoring the export credit and other aspects of banking operations to ensure that the country's export effort is not constrained by inadequate credit availability or the inferior quality of banking services.

Foreign Exchange Management Act: (FEMA)

Foreign Exchange Regulation Act (FERA) 1973 was designed to have a code of conduct for receipt and utilization of foreign exchange for individuals, corporates, traders, bankers. It was pertaining to practices of foreign exchange in day-to-day life contain circulars issued by the RBI. These provisions cannot be changed unless guidlines and circulars are changed. However, there are several changes of procedure to hold foreign exchange and intersaction within immediate effect and relevance particularly relating to certain subjective matters and contraventions and punishment.

At present all transactions in foreign exchange and all transactions with non-resident (whether in rupee or in foreign exchange) are absolutely prohibited except where specific relaxations are made. It is equally necessary to consider by Act regarding transaction involving foreign exchange and foreign securities for non-residents and non-resident Indians. This is so as post-liberalisation period in India highlighted security scam, Hawala scam and intermediaries engaged in bigger transactions involving utilisation of foreign exchange. Financial sector reform in India required legal changes in the statutory provisions of the old FERA Act 1973 in changing circumstances. As a result after 25 years Foreign Exchange Management Act (FEMA) 1998 came into existence as a part and parcel of external sector reform to boost higher rate of growth with stability in exchange reserves and exchange rate management.

The main objective of FERA was to conserve foreign exchange. The provision of the act considered foreign exchange crime is civil than that of criminal. The money laundering bill takes away more rights than even FERA. More powers are given under FEMA (Foreign Exchange Management Act). Any person can be arrested and kept for any period as requirement under the Act is to produce arrested person before the Magistrate without any delay. Crimes may be drugs or kerosene related or even minor offences are enough for government to put innocent citizen in jail so that true culprits can rest easily as money laundering bill made the street safe for true culprits.

FERA contains elaborate and overlapping provisions to cover every conceivable transaction in foreign exchange, transaction with and by non-residents making the law fairly lengthy and complex. The FEMA contains to cover most of such transactions as regulations notified by the RBI. The category of authorised dealers and money changers have been merged under a common category of "authorised persons." Off-shore banking units and authorised persons are permitted to deal in foreign exchange/foreign securities. FEMA has made no provision for imprisonment for contravention of any of the provisions. Only punishment is made of penalty and non-payment of penalty can lead to provision of imprisonment as contained in the new law.

Section 5 of FEMA to make free current account transaction as drawer may be authorised person. This section seems to be the primary motivation behind FEMA to free current account transfer. Under section 41 the central government may give directions to the RBI as it thinks fit. The objective of FEMA is to simplify FERA (1973) with removal of special restrictions, regulation on foreign exchange investment, removal of restriction on companies.

FEMA states FERA had outright utility on account of significant development since 1993 which led to increase in Forex resources, trade negotiation of tariffs, current account convertibility, liberalisation abroad, increased access to external commercial borrowing of Indian companies and participation of Foreign Institutional Investors (FII). FEMA aims at simplification, consolidating, amending laws related with forex business, facilitating external trade and payment mechanism for promotion of orderly forex markets in India.

FEMA simplified definition of person residence in India but also delink from the citizenship aspect to denote a person residing in India more than 182 days. Sub section 6(4) and (5) provides the necessary permission for person resident in India to hold, own, and transfer or invest their foreign property acquired when they were resident outside India or inherited it respectively.

Section 8 to 31 of FEMA deals with excessive regulation and controls, restrictions on use of foreign exchange FEMA provide more liberal and orderly regulatory framework conducive to economic growth by limiting its ambit to current account transaction or payment due to concentration with foreign trade. Other current business, service, short-term bank credit facilities.

FEMA has given code of conduct for fair transaction as payment due on interest on loan as net income from investment, remittances for living expenses of parents, spouses, children residing broad and expenses in connection with foreign travel.

Regarding capital account transfer FEMA provided meaning of assets, liabilities in India or outside India of person resident of India. Borrowing/ Lending, foreign security holding, transfer, deposit in India and outside India are clearly defined and explanation is given pertaining to giving surety of debt obligation or of other liabilities in India and outside India by FEMA.

The Act provided provisions for foreign exchange transactions for export of goods and services, realisation and repatriation of foreign exchange, excuse of realisation and repatriation where foreign currency is involved in transaction. FEMA has provided rules, regulations, level of penalty for contravention of any provisions of FEMA. It is Rs. 5,000 per day of contravention. Clause 13 of FEMA provides provisions of penalty related with contravention not quantifiable and containing contravention.

Critical Aspect of FEMA

Activists laywers and legal experts viewed that foreign exchange market development is missing in the Act as it is superior to FERA. Perhaps FEMA treated the RBI as a sole authority for it.

Section 35 of the Act empowers directorate of enforcement to control and regulate all Individuals and corporates dealing with forex.

An absurd dimension is that all branches outside India owned or controlled by a person of resident in India. Section 2(i) of Act and (iv) mean existing on proposed wholly owned subsidies (W.O.S.) abroad of India will henceforth as treated as 'Persons Resident in India.' This means India's foreign trade will fall as W.O.S. operating will be no longer permitted in law to hold, own, transfer, process, acquire any foreign exchange.

This section reveals that no person shall acquire and foreign exchange holding security, transfer of foreign securities or immovable property situated outside India. This means inevitably it implies that W.O.S. outside India will have to wind up their obligations. Approval of the RBI/central government appears necessary before such transactions.

Corporate experts viewed that FEMA violation will affect Indian companies/branches abroad. Directorate of Enforcement is entitled for taking up investigation about forex dealings for Indian companies/branches abroad also.

It appears that entire FEMA is based on investigation, regulation, control, empowers officials to investigate international trade authority. FEMA needs to be broaden in terms of customs, excise and other laws in connection with development of Indian foreign exchange market perspectives. However, India's share in global trade and global forex market is steadily declining with the controls and license raj. FEMA has completed ignored macro perspective while ushering in a new forex era. Members of Parliament who passed the bill could not differentiate FEMA provisions and money laundering bill. Capital account convertibility report was not published by the RBI at the time of FEMA bill. Thus, vision for 21st century in forex dealing growth, corporate autonomy, globalisation of Indian market and actual foreign exchange management and development aspects are not given due wieghtage. For period revision in such Acts, it is most necessary to mobilise public opinion, corporate opinion and practitioners in forex markets.

However, revision of FERA into FEMA is a part of legal reform ancillary to financial sector reforms in India. In this fashion, it is most necessary to revise Income Tax Act 1961, Corporate Act 1957 and the RBI Act with respect to foreign exchange transactions for sustainable growth of Indian forex markets.

APPENDIX 6.1
FORM ETX
Application for permission to extend the period for Realisation of export proceeds

---

1. Particulars of exporter:
   - (i) Name of the exporting firm/company (i)
   - (ii) Address in full (ii)
   - (iii) Exporter's Code Number allotted by Reserve Bank (iii)

---

2. Full particulars of shipment:
   - (a) Name and address of the overseas buyer/consignee (a)
   - (b) Commodity (b)
   - (c) Quantity (c)
   - (d) Distinctive Number/s of GR/PP form(s) (d)
   - (e) Date of shipment (e)
   - (f) Invoice value (f)
   - (g) Country of destination (g)
   - (h) Terms of payment (specify whether D/P, D/A or L/C etc.) (h)

---

3. Whether goods were shipped on outright sale or consignment basis.

---

4. (a) Reasons for non-payment of bill/s (a)
   - (b) If the goods, have remained unsold, present condition/position thereof. (b)
   - (c) Steps taken or proposed to be taken by the exporters to realise the export proceeds. (c)
   - (d) If the buyer has deposited the sale proceeds with a local bank in the currency of the country to which export has been made, the possibility of externalisation *i.e.,* the time likely to be taken for conversion of the proceeds into foreign exchange. (d)

---

5. Particulars of previous approval/s, if any, for extension obtained from the Reserve Bank.

---

6. Further period for which extension is sought.

---

7. In case part payment has been received against the bill in question —
   - (a) When and how much proceeds realised so far (a)
   - (b) Amount yet to be realised (b)

---

8. Export performance during last 3 years

Year	Amount (Rs.)
Exports made	(1)
	(2)
Export outstanding, if any:	(1)
	(2)
	(3)

---

9. Any other information which exporter deems necessary to furnish in support of the request.

We declare that the particulars given above are true and correct to the best of our knowledge and belief.

Place: . . . .

Date: . . . .

Stamp

. . . .

Signature of Authorised Official

Name: . . . .

Designation: . . . .

(The signature on behalf of the firm/company should be that of the senior partner/proprietor or authorised signatory of the exporting firm or company, as the case may be)

(Space for use of Authorised Dealer)

We hereby certify that the bills pertaining to shipments declared on the above GR/PP form/s was/were included in ENC statement for the fortnight ending . . . .

Any other comments (Please mention here special features like delays on account of externalisation, payments in local currency, settlement of claims by ECGC, etc.

Place:. . . . .

Date: . . . .

Stamp

. . . .

(Signature of Authorised Official)

Name: . . . .

Designation . . . .

Name and Address of Authorised Dealer. . . . . . .

. . . .

(Space for use of Reserve Bank of India)

APPENDIX 6.2

FORM EFC

Application by Exporter for Opening of Foreign Currency Account with a Bank in India or Abroad

(i)	Name and Address of the exporter			
(ii)	Exporter's code number			
(iii)	Name and address of the bank/branch with which foreign currency account is proposed to be maintained.			
(iv)	In case the account is to be maintained with a bank outside India, name and address of the branch of a bank in India which will monitor the transactions put through the foreign currency accounts.			
(v)	Details of export proceeds realised during each of the preceding 3 years and outstanding export bills.	Year	Amount Rs.	Outstanding Rs.
(vi)	Details of imports made during the preceding 3 years (yearwise) in respect of imports from countries in External Group.	Year	Country	Amount Rs.
(vii)	In case the account is proposed to be opened with a bank abroad, indicate the details of arrangements made for availing of loans/overdrafts/lines of credit from the bank with which the account will be maintained.			
(viii)	Quaterwise projections of export receipts to be credited to the account and payments in foreign exchange (item wise) to be made from the account under various heads, during the next year.			
(ix)	Whether the applicant's name has been/was placed on exporter's caution list at any time.			

(x) Details of foreign currency loan raised by the exporter and their maturity patterns.

(xi) Any other information that the applicant may like to provide in support of this application.

Place: . . . .

Date: . . . .

. . . .

(Signature of the authorised official)

Name: . . . .

Designation: . . . .

(Space for Authorised Dealer's comments)

Comments for the branch of the bank in India with which the account is proposed to be maintained or which will monitor the operations on account maintained with a bank abroad, as the case may be.

Place: . . . .

Date: . . . .

Stamp

(Signature of the authorised official)

Name: . . . .

Designation: . . . .

APPENDIX 6.3

FORM REX

Application For Remittances on Account of Claims Against Exports For Nonfulfillment of Contract, Shortage in Weight/Quantity, Inferior Quality of Goods Supplied, Penalty for Late Shipment, Demurrages, etc.

A. General Hints to Applicants

1. The application should be completed in duplicate and submitted to an authorised dealer in foreign exchange.
2. Please give clear and complete particulars against each item. If any particular item is not applicable, please write 'N.A'. against it.
3. If space is not sufficient for giving full information particulars against any particular item, a separate sheet may be attached to the application and serially numbered as an annexure.
4. The application should be submitted well in time to avoid delay in granting approval.
5. Where specially mentioned, originals of documents may be submitted together with photo-copies thereof. Original documents would be returned to the applicants unless it is absolutely essential to retain any of them with Reserve Bank.
6. The exporter should give a brief history of the case stating the circumstances in which the claim has arisen and enclose the original correspondence exchanged by him with the parties concerned regarding the claim. In cases where arbitration had been resorted to the original award of the arbitrator, with a certified copy thereof, must be attached.
7. Holders of Blanket Exchange a permits are required to use their permits for making remittances for this purpose. They should not, therefore, apply to Reserve Bank in this form.

B. General Instructions to Authorised Dealers

1. The authorised dealers should refer to Reserve Bank for prior approval only cases not covered by the powers delegated to them.
2. Before forwarding the application to Reserve Bank, authorised dealer must properly scrutinise it to ensure that it is complete in all respects.
3. Where comments certificates from authorised dealers are necessary, the same should be precise and clear.
4. Wherever applicable, reference numbers and dates of RBI's letters of permission be quoted in full. References to the Exchange Control Manual should also be quoted in full.

C. Documentation

(i) Form A2 duly filled up and signed by the applicant and countersigned by the authorised dealer.
(ii) Certified copy of the Invoice.
(iii) Certificate in original from the authorised dealer in support of realisation of full export value of the shipment in question.

(iv) Original Debit Note, If any, (together with a copy) received from the claimant.
(v) Original sale contract with a certified copy of the same.
(vi) Survey/Inspection/Analysis/Weight report as may be relevant to the type of claim. (In case no Survey Report is available, state the reasons for dispensing with the Survey).
(vii) Copy of relative Bill of Lading in case the claim is on account of late shipment penalty.
(viii) In case of claim on account of nonfulfillment of the contract, a copy of contract, correspondence exchanged with the overseas party and Arbitration award (in original).
(ix) Details of remittances, if any, allowed on account of quality claims during last 2 years.

The above documents may please be submitted neatly placed in a file.

---

1. Full name and address of the claimant.

---

2. (a) Number of the GR/PP forms on which the export was declared
   (b) Date of shipment
   (c) Nature of goods exported

---

3. Invoice value of the goods exported

---

4. Grounds on which claim has been made

---

5. Amount for which claim is being settled

---

6. Basis on which the amount of claim has been settled

---

7. Exporter's comments regarding the claim: [If the claim is pertaining to quality, state whether the goods exported are covered under scheme of pre-shipment inspection under the Export (Quality Control and Inspection) Act, 1963]
   (a) Name of the exporting firm/company
   (b) Address in full
   (c) Exporter's Code Number (allotted by the Reserve Bank)

---

8. Export performance for the last three years. @ (Enclose bank certificates from all your banks)

Year	Total Export	Amount Outstanding

9. Whether you hold any blanket permit issued by Reserve Bank; if so, number and date of permit

---

10. Whether the buyer has been allowed any reduction for the shipments effected under captioned GR/PP forms.

@ This information is required in case where survey report/inspection report is not available.

We declare that the particulars given above are true and correct to the best of our knowledge and belief and we confirm that the present claim has neither been settled nor adjusted in any other manner.

Place: .... **Stamp** ....

(Signature of Exporter)

Date .... Designation ....

The signature on behalf of the firm/company should be that of the Proprietor/ Partner or authorised signatory of exporting firm or company as the case may be.

(To be completed by Authorised Dealer)

Certified that the aforesaid information/documents submitted are in order and to reduction or remittance has been allowed on this shipment by us under any of the powers delegated to us or under the blanket permit held by the exporter.

Our further comments on this application are as under:

Date ....

(Signature of Authorised Official)

Stamp

Name ....

Designation ....

Name and Address of

Authorised Dealer ....

APPENDIX 6.4
FRC (X) 1

Certificate to be Given by Exporters in Support of Payment of Freight in Rupees on Exports or Reimport of Goods Previously exported

To

(The Airline/Shipping Company or its agent)

Dear Sirs,

(A)* We hereby certify that the shipment, in respect of which a sum of Rs. . . . .) (Rupee is the freight, has been passed by the Customs authorities for shipment without declaration on a GR form.

and

(B)* We hereby certify that the shipment in respect of which a sum of Rs. . . . .) Rupees is the freight, has been passed by the Customs authorities for shipment without declaration on a GR form.

and

(C)** We further certify that the shipment referred to above has not been sold to any party, resident outside India on F.O.B., F.A.S. or any other terms under which freight on the shipment has to be borne by the non-resident party and that the payment is not being made by us on behalf of any non-resident.

or

(D)** We further certify that payment of freight is being made by us on behalf of the non resident buyer against contract with the buyer on f.o.b. f.a.s. or similar terms, under which freight on the shipment has to be borne by the non-resident party and we undertake to add the amount on the invoice and recover the payment so made from the buyer in an approved manner.

or

(E)** We attach hereto the Reserve Bank's approval obtained for payment of the above freight in rupees by us.

(F)*** We hereby certify that the sum of Rs.. . . . . (Rupees . . . .) represents freight on . . . . imported per
(particulars of cargo)
. . . . The goods were previously exported against a declaration
(name of vessel/airline)
of form GR No. . . . .

Yours faithfully

Date:. . . . .

(Signature of Exporter/Authorised Official)
Name: . . . .
Designation: . . . .
Name and Address . . . .
of Exporter . . . .
Exporter Code No. . . . .

---

* Cancel (A) or (B) whichever is not applicable.
** Cancel (C) or (D) or (E) whichever is not applicable.
*** (F) to be completed only in case of reimport of goods previously exported.

APPENDIX 6.5

FRC (X) 2

Certificate to be Given By Exporters in Support Of Payment of Freight to Consolidator of Air Cargo in Rupees

(The Consolidating Air Cargo Agent in India)

Dear Sirs,

(A)* We hereby certify that the shipment, in respect of which a sum of Rs. . . . .(Rupees . . . .) is the freight, has been declared on Form GR No. . . . .

or

(B)** We hereby certify that the shipment in respect of which a sum of Rs. . . . .(Rupees . . . .). is the freight, has been passed by the Customs authorities for shipment without declaration on a GR form.

and

(C)** We further certify that the shipment referred to above has not been sold to our overseas buyers on C.I.F/C & F terms and not on F.O.B. etc. terms under which liability for payment of freight has to be borne by the non-resident party.

or

(D)*** We further certify that payment of freight is being made by us on behalf of the non-resident buyer against contract with the buyer on F.O.B., F.A.S.or similar terms, under which freight on the shipment has to be borne by the non-resident party and we undertake to add the amount on the invoice and recover the payment so made from the buyer in an approved manner.

or

(E)** We attach hereto the Reserve Bank's approval obtained for payment of the above freight in rupees by us.

Yours faithfully,

Date: . . . .

. . . .

(Signature of Exporter/Authorised Official)

Name:. . . . .

Designation: . . . .

Name and Address . . . .

of Exporter . . . .

Exporter Code No. . . . .

---

* Cancel (A) or (B) whichever is not applicable.

** Cancel (C) or (D) or (E) whichever is not applicable.

7

AGENCIES HELPING INTERNATIONAL MARKETING AND MEASURES TAKEN FOR EXPORT PROMOTION

To stimulate and support the international marketing efforts of the country, various organisations and institutions have been established. These organisations and institutions aim at the development of specialisation in specific spheres of commodities and products and the provision of various services. The activities of important organisations and institutions which have been involved in the export effort have been briefly described and evaluated in this chapter.

Department of Commerce (Ministry of Commerce) Government of India

The Department of Commerce in the Ministry of Commerce is headed by a Secretary. The Department is responsible for the country's external trade and all matters connected with it such as commercial relations with other countries, state trading export promotional measures, and the promotion, development or regulation of certain export oriented industries and commodities. The Department of Commerce formulates policies in the sphere of foreign trade particularly the import and export policy of the country. The Secretary is assisted in the discharge of duties by Additional Secretaries and a number of other senior officers functioning as Division Heads.

Chart 7.1

A STRUCTURE AT THE GOVERNMENT OF INDIA

MINISTRY OF COMMERCE
DEPARTMENT OF COMMERCE

I. *Trade Policy Division Tasks include:*	II. *Exports Products Division pays attention:*	III. *Export Services Division* deals with the problems of export assistance including —	IV. *Economic Division:* It is headed by the Economic Adviser. He is responsible for:	V. *Administrative and General Division:*	VI. *Foreign Trade (Territorial Division)* is entrusted with:	VII. *Export Industries Division is responsible* —	VIII. *Finance Division:*
1. To keep abreast of the developments in the International Organisations, like: (*a*) UNCTAD (*b*) GATT (*c*) Economic Commission for Europe, Africa, Latin America, Asia and Far East (ESCAP). 2. Division is also responsible for India's relations with the (*a*) European Economic Community (EEC) (*b*) European Free Trade Association (EFTA) (*c*) Latin American Free Trade Area (LAFTA)	1. To the problems connected with: (*a*) Production (*b*) Generation of surplus (*c*) Development of markets for the various products under its jurisdiction. These products are: All agricultural commodities, marine products, chemicals, plastics, leather and leather goods, sports goods, films, steel, metals, engg. products, minerals and ores, coal, petroleum products, mica, salt, etc. 2. Although in administrative terms the responsibility for these products remains with the Ministries concerned.	Import replenishment, licensing, export credit, export houses, marketing development assistance (any grants etc.), transport bottlenecks, free trade zones, dry ports, quality control and preshipment inspection, guidance to Indian entrepreneurs to set up joint ventures abroad, capacity creation in export oriented industries, assistance to Import capital goods and essential raw materials.	Formulation of export strategies, export planning, periodic appraisal and review of policies, maintaining coordination and constant contacts with the other divisions which have been set-up under the Commerce Department to assist the export drive. The division also monitors work relating to: (*i*) Technical assistance, (*ii*) Management Services for export and overseas investment by Indian entrepreneurs.	General administration and co-ordination with other divisions.	1. The work relating to the development of trade with different countries and regions of the world. 2. The division also handles matters pertaining to — (*i*) State trading (*ii*) Barter deals, (*iii*) Organisation of trade fairs and exhibitions, and	1. For development and regulation of — (*i*) Rubber, (*ii*) Tobacco, and (*iii*) Cardamom. 2. The division is also responsible for handling export promotion activities relating to — (*i*) Textiles (*ii*) Woolens (*iii*) Handlooms (*iv*) Ready-made garments (*v*) Silk and cellulosie fibres (*vi*) Jute and jute products	Financial co-ordination and policy formulation for ECGC etc.

Chart 7.1 (Contd.)

(*d*) Other regional Groupings and Commonwealth. 3. It also looks after the generalised system of preferences and non-tariff and tariff barriers. 4. International trade and commercial policy. 5. International commodity agreements.	The Export Product Division keeps itself in close touch with them to ensure that production is sufficient to realise the full export potential. 3. The division is also responsible for the working of export organisations and corporations dealing with these products.			(*iv*) Commercial publicity abroad. 3. It also maintains contracts with Indian trade missions abroad. 4. Attend to the connected administrative work as also the protocol functions.	(*vii*) Handicrafts (*viii*) coir and coir products.

(This is the main organisations to formulate and guide India's Trade Policy and Programmes, Commercial Relations with other countries, State Trading, Trade Promotional Measures, Development and Regulation of certain Export Oriented Industries).

1. Director General of Foreign Trade (DGFT)

DGFT is responsible for the execution of the export and import policies of the government. Now the role of DGFT would be to promote exports and to remove controls. India now needs promoter of exports and not the controller of exports.

DGFT's supporting offices are located at important port towns and commercial centres of the country. They include:

Agartala, Ahmedabad, Amritsar, Bangalore, Bombay, Calcutta, Cuttack, Chandigarh, Ernakulam, Guwahati, Hyderabad, Jaipur, Kandla, Kanour, Madras, New Delhi, Panjim, Patna, Pondicherry, Rajkot, Shillong, Srinagar, and Visakhapatnam.

Advisory and Policy-Making Organizations

These have been set up to ensure that the collective advice of the commercial interests is available to the Government of India:

(*a*) for framing and formulating export promotion and import policies; and

(*b*) for successful implementation of these policies.

2. Cabinet Committee on Exports

The cabinet committee under the chairmanship of the Prime Minister expedites decisions on important policy matters relating to exports.

3. Board of Trade

It has been reconstituted on 13 August 1991 by the Union Commerce Ministry with the Minister for Commerce as its Chairman. The Deputy Minister of Commerce is the Board's Vice-Chairman.

(*i*) The Board consists of 28 members including representatives from different organisations and individuals with business standing and expertise in the field of commerce;

(*ii*) The Board has powers to co-opt additional members;

(*iii*) The members of the Board hold office for two years; and

(*iv*) The Board ordinarily meets twice a year and advises the government on matters relating to:

- (*a*) export and import policy and programmes;
- (*b*) the operation of export and import controls;
- (*c*) organisation and development of commercial services;
- (*d*) organisation and expansion of export production;
- (*e*) the Board of trade ensures continual dialogue between industry and trade on the one hand, and the government on the other;

(*f*) the Board advises the government on policy measures for preparation and implementation of both short and long term plans for increasing exports in the light of national and international economic scenario;

(*g*) the Board also reviews export performance of various sectors, identifies constraints and suggest measures to be taken by the government and industry and trade consistent with the need to maximise export earnings and restrict imports;

(*h*) in addition Board also examines existing institutional framework for exports and suggest practical measures for reorganisation or streamlining it with a view to ensure co-ordinated and timely decision-making;

(*i*) the Board will review policy instruments, package of incentives and procedures for exports and suggest steps to rationalise and channelise incentives to areas where these are most needed.

The Board reviews half yearly the performance of the country's economy in its commercial aspects and considers policies relating to the expansion of exports, regulation of imports and the operation of import and export controls.

It provides a form for discussion of the export policy and the export promotion measures taken by the government.

4. Zonal Export and Import Advisory Committees

In order to make a detailed study of the export possibilities of the commodities exported from different regions and to advise the government on specific problems of exports from these regions, Regional Export Promotion Advisory Committees have been set up:

Western Zone (Bombay)	Southern Zone (Madras)	Eastern Zone (Calcutta)	Northern Zone (Kanpur)

These committees were set-up in July 1968 to consider:

1. Difficulties faced in the operation of prevailing import and export policies and procedures and to suggest measures for improvement in disbursement of various assistance;
2. Difficulties in the matter of:

   (*i*) Customs clearance;

   (*ii*) Shipping;

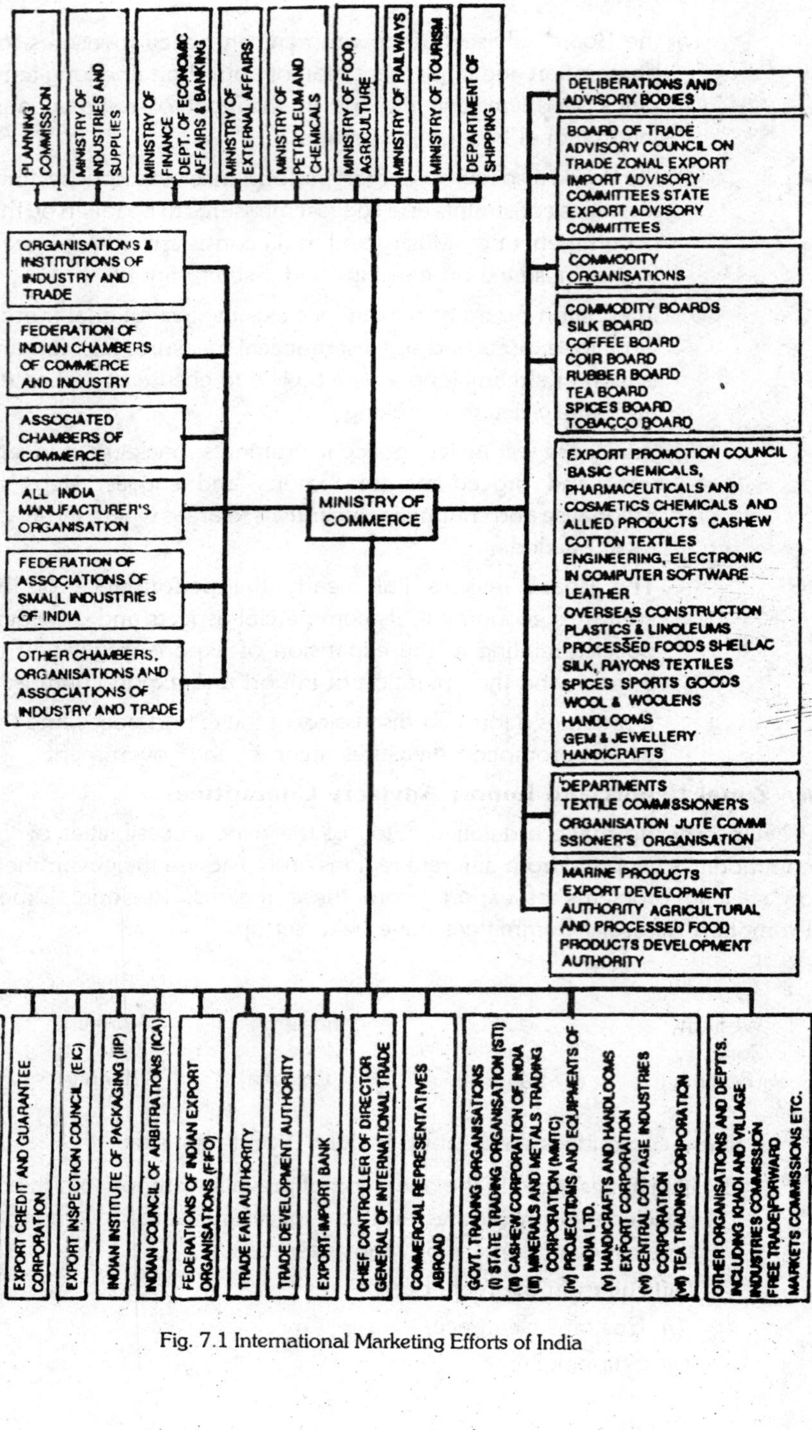

Fig. 7.1 International Marketing Efforts of India

(*iii*) Credit;

(*iv*) Insurance; and

(*v*) Export inspection and to suggest measures for improvement therein.

3. Suggest improvements in the methods of working and public relations of the DGFT organisation and other government departments, concerned with trade and industry; and
4. Representatives of State Governments and the Customs and Central Excise Department are included in these committees.

A. State Government

State Government Liaison Officers

State Governments have appointed liaison officers in charge of export promotion, whose main function is to develop the exports trade in the goods produced in their states, in consonance with the policies of the Central Government. The machinery provided by the State Liaison Officers, on the one hand, and on the other, the Honorary Export Promotion Advisors and the Regional Export Promotion Officers are particularly useful in the solution of the problems affecting the exports from these states.

B. Commodity Organisations

(*i*) Export Promotion Councils

EPCs are supported by financial assistance from the Central Government.

Under the administrative control of Ministry of Commerce, EPCs are registered as nonprofit organisations under the Companies Act or Societies Registration Act, as the case may be. The EPCS perform both advisory and executive functions. The councils are also the registering authorities under the import policy for registered exporters. On being admitted to membership the applicant is granted a Registration-cum-Membership Certificate.

With a view to secure the active association of growers, producers and exporters in the drive for export promotion, a number of export promotion councils have been set up, which look after the export problems of specific commodities. The functions of these councils are broadly to advise the government, the local authorities and public bodies on the policies to be pursued and the steps to be taken to expand the exports of the commodities grown and/or manufactured in their states. The councils also performs some other promotional functions, such as a study of foreign markets through periodical market surveys and market research, sending of trade delegations abroad, participation in exhibitions, conducting publicity, disseminating information, administering export promotion schemes, taking measures to ensure quality control, etc. There are 19 export promotion councils covering such items as engineering, leather exports, shellac, sports goods, basic chemicals, pharmaceuticals and cosmetics, cashews, chemicals and allied products, plastics and linoleums, overseas construction, electronics and computer software, apparel handicrafts, handlooms, silk, rayon textiles, wool and woollens etc.

Some of these councils have opened branches or regional offices in places other than their headquarters, and overseas offices in selected foreign countries.

Functions of Export Promotion Councils (EPC)

EPC's main function is to project India's image abroad as a reliable suppliers of high quality goods and services.

1. Advise the government of current export problems and measures necessary for the growth of exports. Promote interaction between the exporting community and the government both at the central and state levels.
2. Assist individual exporters on specific problems confronting them and help them to overcome these problems. Provide commercially useful information and assistance to their members in developing and increasing their exports.
3. Offer services for the development of overseas markets.
4. The council deregisters any defaulting exporter.
5. Disseminate amongst registered exporters the trade enquiries received from abroad, giving information on overseas markets, market leads, export-import procedures, customs tariff, GSP facilities. To build statistical base and provide data on the exports and imports of the country, exports and imports of their members as well as other relevant international trade data.
6. To offer professional advice to their members in areas such as technology upgradation, quality and design improvement, standards and specifications, product development, innovation etc.
7. To organise visits of delegations of its members abroad to explore overseas market opportunities.
8. Resolving trade disputes between exporters and importers.
9. Help exporters in shipping and transport problems.
10. Help exporters in obtaining licenses, duty-drawback etc.
11. To organise participation in trade fairs, exhibitions and buyers and sellers meet in India and abroad.

Advantages for Units Registered with Export Promotion Councils

There are many advantages that accrue to an exporter when he is a member of export promotion councils. Some of these are:

(*a*) Trade enquiries received by the councils from commercial representatives abroad are circulated among members, much in advance of their publication in the usual course;

(*b*) The bulletins and publications issued by the councils contain useful information on trade conditions in different markets;

(*c*) Exporters may ask for inclusion in trade delegations and study teams sponsored by the councils. They organise commercial publicity abroad;

(*d*) Exporters may have their products displayed or advertised in any particular country under the council's plans for publicity abroad, including participation in exhibitions, hold exhibitions within India for the benefit of foreign visitors;

(*e*) In case of a survey in a foreign country arising from a dispute, the exporter may ask for the overseas officer or correspondent of the council to witness the survey in order that his interests may be safeguarded;

(*f*) The exporter may take any difficulty of a general nature to the council which, in appropriate cases, will make recommendations to the government suggesting measures to remove such difficulties; and

(*g*) Encourage individual exporters to develop new products for export.

(*ii*) Commodity Boards

Commodity Boards have been set up to help in the development of certain commodities. The Commodity Boards deal with the entire range of problems of production, development and marketing etc. Tea Board has opened an office in London to promote consumption of tea. They, too, have taken measures to promote the export of commodities with which they are concerned. They advise the government on policy matters, such as fixing the quotas for exports, the signing of trade agreements with foreign countries, etc. They also undertake promotional activities, such as participation in exhibitions and trade fairs, sponsoring delegations, quality inspection etc. Commodity Boards, which deal with the commodities that are important from the point of view of exports, are:

(*i*) Tea Board;
(*ii*) Coffee Board;

(*iii*) Coir Board;
(*iv*) Central Silk Board;
(*v*) All India Handicrafts and Handloom Board;
(*vi*) Tobacco Board;
(*vii*) Rubber Board; and
(*viii*) Spices Board.

The Textile Commissioner and the Jute Commissioner are respectively concerned with the development (including exports of textiles machinery and jute and jute machinery). The Indian Jute Mills Association looks after the exports of jute and jute products. Similarly, the Indian Sugar Mills Association is associated with the development of exports of sugar.

(*iii*) Marine Products Exports Development Authority (MPEDA)

This authority came into being in September 1972. It is concerned with the organisation, co-ordination, regulation and growth of the export of marine products with special reference to the quality of the material, processing, packaging, storage, transport shipment, marketing and attendant investigation.

The authority serves the sea food industry from fishing to processing down to marketing all over the world. Importers and exporters both could obtain information relating to the markets and marine products from MPEDA. It has regional offices at major sea food processing and export centres and a foreign office at Tokyo. The authority is entrusted with the task of ensuring a healthy growth of the industry through judicious regulations, conservation and control.

(*iv*) Agricultural and Processed Food Products Export Development Authority (APEDA)

APEDA came into being on 12th August, 1986. It serves as the focal point for agricultural exports, particularly the marketing of processed foods in value added forms with a view to increase the exports of agricultural and processed food products. Government of India has established this authority.

C. Service Institutions

(*i*) Indian Institute of Foreign Trade (IIFT), New Delhi

The Indian Institute of Foreign Trade, set up by the Government of India in 1964, is acting as a nucleus for human resource development in the fields of foreign trade, international business and marketing through specialised training programmes.

The main activities of the IIFT include training *i.e.*, training of personnel in modern techniques of the international trade and research into problems of foreign trade, commodity studies, overseas market surveys in India. It provides consultancy to export enterprises. It distributes market information through "Foreign Trade Review" and "Foreign Trade Bulletin."

Over the past twenty-six years of its existence, the Institute has organised nearly 640 programmes with the participation of about 22,300 personnel including 780 foreign nationals, and completed over 500 research studies.

(*ii*) Trade Development Authority, New Delhi

The TDA, set up as a Registered Society, induces and organises entrepreneurs, largely in the medium and small scale sectors to develop their individual export capabilities. It provides assistance in a personalised form to individual exporters from the stage of intention to export through collection of information, product development, market research and analysis. It also advises them on export finance and asssits them in securing and implementing export orders.

It was set up in 1970, it undertakes export development of industrial products. It deals with the package assistance to enterprises at micro level after identifying the potential of their products and their requirements for assistance. It arranges commercial contacts between Indian units and foreign buyers and helps in conclusion of contracts. Its offices are located at Frankfurt, New York, Tokyo and Stockholm.

TDA strives to concentrate on specific products, specific exporters, specific markets and specific buyers.

Being a non-trading institution, TDA does not enter into direct commercial transactions but confines itself to a catalyst's role. As such, TDA does not charge any commission from its members for specific business secured by them for its help.

(*iii*) Export Inspection Council of India, Calcutta

The EIC, a statutory body, is responsible for the enforcement of quality control and compulsory preshipment inspection of various exportable commodities.

This Council organises thorough inspection all over the country, preshipment inspection of the products and commodities notified for compulsory inspection. 850 items are subjected to compulsory inspection. It establishes labs and test-houses throughout the country.

(*iv*) Export Credit of Guarantee Corporation of India Ltd., Bombay (ECGC)

The ECGC was incorporated in 1957. It is a company wholly owned by the Government of India, functioning under the administrative control of the Ministry of Commerce and managed by a Board of Directors representing the Government, Banking, Insurance, Trade and Industrial Sectors.

The primary goals of ECGC is to support and strengthen the export promotion drive in India, by providing a range of credit risk insurance covers against loss in export of goods and services and also by offering guarantees to banks and financial institutions to enable exporters obtain better facilities from them.

ECGC helps exporters to cover both the commercial and political risks involved in the export trade and also possible losses in the development of new export markets. Facilities for export credit though such schemes as packing credit guarantee, post-shipment export credit guarantee, export finance guarantee, export production finance guarantee, export performance guarantee and export finance guarantee (overseas lending) are also provided.

The guarantees are provided by ECGC with a view to assist exporters to maximise their turnover through its guarantees which it issues to the commercial banks in India. The guarantees reduce the lending risk of the banks, create an environment in which exporters get easier access to export finance which is a critical factor for the rapid expansion of business.

Over the years ECGC has evolved a number of special schemes to suit the particular needs of the exporting community. Many of these schemes have no parallel elsewhere in the world. These special schemes include insurance cover for buyer's credit and lines of credit, transfer guarantee, overseas investment insurance, guarantees short terms exports, guarantees project and term exports and exchange fluctuation risk cover.

(*v*) Indian Institute of Packaging, Bombay

The IIP is registered under the Societies Registration Act. It undertakes research on raw materials for the packaging industry. This organisation effects improvements in packaging standards, providing consultancy services, organising training activities and rendering testing facilities in respect of packages. The main objective of IIP is to stimulate consciousness of the need for good packaging amongst Indian exporters.

(*vi*) Indian Council of Arbitration, New Delhi

The Indian Council of Arbitration, set-up under the Societies Registration Act, promotes arbitration as a means of settling commercial disputes and popularises arbitration among the trades particularly those engaged in international trade.

This Council provides facilities of effecting arbitration in cases of commercial disputes in relation to foreign trade.

(*vii*) Directorate-General of Commercial Intelligence and Statistics, Calcutta

DGCI&S is the primary government agency for the collection, compilation and publication of the foreign, inland and ancillary trade statistics and dissemination of various types of commercial information. The Directorate brings out a number of publications, particularly on trade statistics, which are utilised in framing economic policies, formulating trade agreement in foreign countries and monitoring these agreements. The Directorate conducts studies on various topics relating to promotion of trade. It helps in the settlement of commercial disputes and provides Indian businessmen going abroad with letters of introduction to Indian commercial representatives concerned. It also maintain a commercial library which is widely used by the exporters, importers, research scholars and others.

This organisation collects and disseminates statistics relating to imports and exports.

(*viii*) Trade Fair Authority of India (TFAI)

It was set up in 1977. Its main functions include organising, promoting and participating in industrial trade fairs and other exhibitions, setting up showrooms in India and abroad, to undertake trading activities in items related with such fairs, to promote exports of new items and diversify India's exports. The journals it brings out include (*a*) Journal of Industry and Trade, (*b*) Udyog Vyapar Patrika, (*c*) Indian Export Service Bulletin, and (*d*) Economic and Commercial News. These periodicals brought out by TFAI provide information on the country's economy, business possibilities offered by foreign markets, government's trade policies, facilities available for exports and important tenders floated by other countries. They also provide material to Indian mission for their publicity effort.

(*ix*) Federation of Indian Export Organisation (FIEO)

It is an apex body of various export promotion organisations. It was set up in 1965. This Federation is a common co-ordinating platform for the various export organisations, including the commodity councils and boards, and service institutions and organisations. It is the primary servicing agency to provide integrated assistance to government and organised export houses. FIEO is the central co-ordinating agency in respect of export promotional efforts in the field of consultancy services. It serves generally as a common forum for the national export promotion effort.

(*x*) Export-Import Bank (EXIM Bank)

The Export-Import Bank of India is a public sector financial institution, established on January 1, 1982. It was established by an Act of Parliament, for the purpose of financing, facilitating and promoting foreign trade of India. It is the principal financial institution for co-ordinating the working of institutions engaged in financing exports and imports. The EXIM Bank Act also empowers the bank to finance export of consultancy and related services, assist Indian joint ventures in third world countries, conduct export market studies, finance export oriented industries and provide international merchant banking services.

The EXIM Bank grants in and outside India, loans and advances by itself or in participation with any bank or financial institution for the purpose of export or import.

The present focus of EXIM Bank is on export finance. The Bank finances export of Indian machinery, manufactured goods, consultancy and technology services, on deferred payment terms. EXIM Bank's finance is also available at export production stages. EXIM Bank undertakes co-financing with global and regional development agencies, and assists Indian exporters in their efforts to participate in such overseas projects.

EXIM Bank's advisory services provide access to Euro financing and global credit sources for Indian companies engaged in exports. The Bank works closely with Indian companies in designing financing packages for export oriented industries in India, overseas joint ventures and projects.

As on March 31, 1990 the Bank had a paid-up capital of Rs. 233.80 crores. The Bank raises loan resources from domestic and international markets.

D. Export Corporations

I. The State Trading Corporation of India Ltd. (STC)

The Corporation was set up as a Private Limited Company in 1956 and later converted into a Public Ltd. Company in 1959. The Corporation helps the development and promotion of exports of commodities on a long term basis, exploring new markets, canalising import of bulk commodities to bridge temporary gaps between supply and demand in commodities essential for the economic and industrial development of the country, internal distribution of any commodity in short supply with a view to stabilise prices and rationalise distribution. The Corporation has five subsidiaries:

(*i*) The Handicrafts and Handlooms Export Corporation of India Ltd.

(*ii*) Projects and Equipment Corporation of India Ltd.

(*iii*) Cashew Corporation of India Ltd.

(*iv*) Central Cottage Industries Corporation of India Ltd., a subsidiary of HHEC.

(*v*) Tea Trading Corporation of India Ltd.

(*i*) *The Handicrafts and Handlooms Export Corporation of India Limited (HHEC)*

HHEC undertakes exports of handicrafts and handloom products including hand knitted woolen carpets and readymade garments, gold jewellery and woollen knitwear.

(*ii*) *Projects and Equipment Corporation of India Limited (PEC)*

The main objective of PEC is to give a fillip to export of engineering equipment and project. It identified the technological competence of manufacturers of goods and of other agencies for services and ensures through organised monitoring, planning and control, fulfilment of contractual obligations in respect of quality and delivery schedules.

(*iii*) *Cashew Corporation of India Ltd.*

The Cashew Corporation of India is the canalising agency for import of raw cashewnuts to the export oriented sector of the cashew industry.

(*iv*) *Central Cottage Industries Corporation of India Ltd.*

Central Cottage Industries Corporation of India Ltd. provides marketing support for products from cottage and small scale sector.

(*v*) *Tea Trading Corporation of India Ltd.*

The Tea Trading Corporation of India was established in 1971 to create a stable export market for Indian tea, particularly in their value added forms, namely, packed tea, tea bags, instant tea. Other activities of this Corporation include marketing of tea for domestic consumption, management of tea gardens, warehousing of tea and establishment of other facilities beneficial to the tea industry.

II. Minerals and Metals Trading Corporation (MMTC)

The Minerals and Metals Trading Corporation deals with export and import of canalised items like iron ore, manganese ore, coal, chrome ore, bauxite and non-canalised items like barytes, diamonds and import of non-ferrous metals, industrial raw materials, steel, raw materials for fertilizer and finished fertilizers, sulphur and rock phosphate. In addition, the MMTC is providing valuable market support to the manufacturers and exporters of various products from the country.

E. Indian Government Trade Representatives Abroad

The Government of India's Trade Representatives (Trade Commissioners, Commercial Counsellors and Commercial Secretaries) function in almost all the important trading centres of the world as the government's "eyes and ears" and help in furthering trading relations between India and the countries falling within their jurisdiction. They report periodically on the economic, financial and commercial conditions of the country in which they are stationed; attend to trade enquiries from this country; acquaint importers in those countries with the kinds of goods available for export from India, and assist visiting Indian businessmen with suitable introductions. They also help in the settlement of trade disputes.

F. Other Committees and Agencies

(*i*) *Drawback Committee*

Problems relating to rebate of excise duty on export or drawback of customs and excise duty on the export of manufactured products, and procedural difficulties in exports, are looked after by a Drawback Committee in the Ministry of Finance (Department of Revenue), with a Deputy Secretary of that Ministry as Chairman and with representatives of the Department of Commerce, the Directorate-General of Technical Development and others as members.

(*ii*) *Freight Investigation Bureau*

A Freight Investigation Bureau has been set up in the office of the Director-General of Shipping, Bombay, to look into the problems of high or discriminatory ocean freight rates, the non-availability of shipping space or shipping services and other allied problems. The Freight Investigation Bureau has a branch in Calcutta. The Director (Transport) in the Department of Commerce under the Ministry of Commerce may also be approached in regard to shipping problems.

(*iii*) *Railway Freight Committee*

A Committee in the Ministry of Railways, with representatives of other Ministries, considers requests from exporters for reduction in railway freight for the export of goods. Requests for railway freight concessions as well as for priority in the movement of export cargo may be made to the Director (Transport) in the Department of Commerce.

(*iv*) *Customs and Central Excise Department*

All the exports from the country have to pass through the Customs. There are Customs Houses at Bombay, Madras, Calcutta and Cochin and at a number of smaller centres, land customs offices at border stations and foreign post offices at Bombay, Madras, Calcutta and New Delhi. The procedures for the examination of export cargo are constantly reviewed and simplified. Rebates on exports, like drawback, are paid by the Customs Houses. Rebate of Central Excise duty on the exported products subject to Central Excise duty is allowed by the Central Excise Department.

(*v*) *Reserve Bank of India (RBI)*

The Reserve Bank of India is concerned with the administration of the Foreign Exchange Regulation Act. Exporters have to satisfy it (under the

G.R., etc., form procedure) about the receipt of foreign exchange on exports, such payment being collected through banks authorised to deal in foreign exchange. Applications for the sanction of foreign exchange for business visits and for opening foreign offices have to be made to the Reserve Bank, which has its major offices at Bombay, Calcutta, Madras and New Delhi.

(vi) Central Warehousing Corporation

This government corporation maintains a chain of warehouses run along scientific lines at important centres, including port towns. Warehousing is particularly important for exports in cases where the availability of shipping and rail transport to a port cannot be exactly co-ordinated. The Corporation considers requests from the trade for putting up or increasing warehousing facilities at any centre.

World Trade Organisation for Global Marketing

Since 1995, all the countries of the world transformed the General Agreement on Trade and Tariff. (GATT) into World Trade Organisation. The main objective of (W.T.O.) are same as in the case of GATT: raising standard of living and income of people, ensuring full employment, expanding production and trade, optimal use of world's resources. It aims to services for sustainable development by recognising the need for positive efforts for developing countries. Rapid growth in economic belts countries can reap better benefits by trading with the neighbouring countries. The Indian ocean rim countries like India and South Africa can develop their trade very profitably.

General Council of W.T.O. decided that in the interim period the provision of multinational agreements lapsed on 1st Jan. 2000. W.T.O. being rules-based organisation the voice of the developing countries' call for observation of the rules is being heard. The decisions like the fate of moratorium on tariffs, e-commerce, the Singapore working parties on four issues and work programme was discussed in the council. Due to "subsidy war" between United States and the European Community and "trade war" between United States and Japan delayed operation of W.T.O.

World agriculture has remained weak, inelastic and more than stagnant in terms of comparative advantage or fulfilment of basic needs. There is a limit to food as a basic need but not in the sphere of industrial consumers goods. This factor has compelled the developed countries to oversubsidise and control the surplus production in the farm sector. Reduction of tarif on one hand and disciplining of controls in many sectors like agriculture on the other became imperative in arriving at a concensus trade agreement.

The export share of India in world export trade has been slowly declining and this has to be arrested by a combination of new trade and liberalisation strategies. India had signed Dunkel proposals to be the member of WTO. It is an institution for arbitrating between the countries where there is a problem in their trading transactions. Almost all countries, rich and poor, have become members of WTO.

Looking to globalisation of trade of the developing countries and W.T.O., it is necessary to glance through social "backwash effect" on the economies of the third world. There has been in the strong "other" point of view about WTO that in the bargain between the rich and the poor countries in any bilateral trade agreement, the rich and powerful in the class structure always benefit more. There are genuine reasons for these apprehensions. In the past, it is observed that GATT became a club for rich countries. Trade between unequals, ultimately lead to unequal exchange between the nations, and the resultant exploitation of the poor by the rich. Consequently, economic strife, rich-poor gap, social tensions increased in the society. Multinational companies (MNCs) essentially come for trade purpose not for welfare of the people obviously their objective is maximisation of profits. Such MNCs are likely to bring more pressure on developing countries like India through WTO to liberalise completely to ensure free market. It is presumed that as a result industry will suffer, labour will be exploited, whereas, power and wealth will be concentrated in the hands of fewer. Champions of free market forget that unless the power is decentralited towards a larger section of society, the equi-distribution of the benefits of development is nearly impossible. Free market unleashes the aggressive competition among unequals leading to a jungle law. It is necessary that WTO should allow foreign investors in our country for basic industries and great caution is required before allowing foreign goods in our markets as it may hamper the growth of indigenous industries. It appears that the market expansion activities under the umbrella of WTO is good and useful instrument in the process of growth but its strengths and weaknesses in ensuring just and equal society should be understood.

However, sudden building of common concern over the WTO appears that it is World Trade Organisation or International Trade Organisation as proposed in Havana Charter. It has a vital role to implement its work programme since inception of WTO created an impression being a global government regulating the world trade by impunging on the national sovereignty. The "time out" period should be utilised in strengthening developing countries' unity and bargaining position and carrying out trade reforms that would bring visible gains from trade expansion. NGOs of the developing countries posed challenges to WTO that the developing countries will need to strengthen their own civil society institution. It is expected that Director General of WTO will have to revive a deliberate process which is open, accountable, development focused and responsive to the needs and aspirations of four-fifth of mankind.

Geneva based WTO proposed agreement on Trade Related Intellectual Property Rights (TRIPs) which are world class legislation in copyrights. India has also had a patent regime through standard in this area. TRIPs agreement allows the patenting of only processes (and not production) in pharmaceuticals, chemicals and food. As a result, Indian industries diversified and newly discovered medicines rapidly accessible to the poor which is sizeable low-cost. Under intellectual property rights "technology," "brain," "material" have become important service for global marketing. Economists like Michael Finger and Philip Schuler estimate that the cost of legislation required to implement the TRIPs Agreement alone would cost about $150 million per country. This is unbearable for African countries having no potentitality for benefits.

The principal objective of WTO is to remove trade barriers. But Intellectual property rights can hardly be construed as trade barriers and as such constitute what many of us call "non-trade agenda." Balance the rights of innovators against benefits from innovators in the light of the prevailing social and ethical norms rather than to acquire any 'unfair' advantage in international trade. Economists viewed that TRIPs Agreement has become an effective instrument for labour and environment groups for promoting more non-trade agenda. They maintained that WTO must now do for workers and nature, whereas, ti has protected interest of corporate culture.

The General Agreement on Trade in Services (GATS) provides flexibility in timing and choice of service to be opened up. GATS can help better access for information technology network, distribution channels, and new technology. In actual practice GATS appears to be titling more in favour of developed than developing countries. Indian companies will have to face global competition in marketing of products. They will have to achieve size or critical mass in the shortest possible time to face global competition. Acquisitions, mergers, strategic alliances, joint ventures, co-operatives all these avenue need to be explored.

WTO has completed five years of its existence. Uruguay Round Agreements Act (URAA) is administered by the WTO so as to have an assessment of the domestic legislation of the US in a regime and use of Section 301 for identifying countries that were seen as violating US trading interests. WTO must supervise and responsible for ensuring fair trade.

WTO is one kind of an NGO engaged in world trade order. Greater involvement of civil society would help make India's negotiating position more comprehensively viable. India has an option of working towards making this involvement democratic or strengthening the impression that its government has reason to fear civil society. Thus, participation in the world economy through WTO will protect the interest of 135 countries. ILO should be allowed and empowered to do as much as it possibly can. WTO working group needs to discuss issues like development related aspects of trade, social related aspects of trade and work towards multilateral consensus.

Progress in fulfilment of India's commitments to W.T.O.*

(1) Quantitative Restrictions: (QRs)

Quantitative Restrictions on imports maintained on Balance of Payments grounds were notified in WTO in 1997 for 2714 tariff lines at the eight digit level. The committee on BOP Restriction had asked India for a phase out plan for quantitative restrictions. An agreement was reached with those countries except USA to phase out restrictions over a period of six years beginning 1997. India and USA have agreed to a bilateral settlement for determination of a reasonable period of time up to 1-4-2001 within which India has to implement the rules and recommendations to the Dispute Settlement body to remove existing quantitative restrictions in a phased manner. As on date, number of tariff lines on which QRs exist have come down to 1429 at eight digit level.

(2) Trade Related Intellectual Property Rights (TRIPs):

The agreement sets out the minimum standards of protection to be adopted by the parties, in respect of (a) copy right (b) trade marks (c) geographical indications (D) industrial designs (e) patents (f) lay out designs of related circuits and (g) protection of undisclosed information (trade secrets) and the enforcement of these. A transition period of five years. However, they have to provide exclusive marketing right for products which obtain patents after 1-1-1995. As per our obligations under the WTO agreement, the Patents (Amendment) Act 1999 was passed in March 1999 to provide for exclusive marketing rights.

(3) Patents

The basic obligation in the area of patent is that invention in all fields of technology, whether products or processes, shall be patentable if they meet the three tests of being novel, involving an invention step and being capable of industrial application. In addition to general security exemption which applies to the entire TRIPs Agreement, exclusion from patentability are permissible for inventions whose commercial exploitation is necessary to protect public order or morality, human, animal, plant life or health or to

* Taken from Economic Survey, 1999-2000: Government of India, New Delhi, 2000.

avoid serious prejudice to the environment. Diagnostic, therapeutic and surgical methods for the treatment of human or animals and plants and animals other than micro organism may also be excluded from patentability.

The patent term provided for in the TRIPS agreement is 20 years. A Bill to make these and other changes was introduced in Parliament and has been referred to a joint select committee of the House.

In respect of plant varieties, then is an obligation to provide for protection by patents or by an effective sui generis or by any combination there of. The agreement does not spell out the elements of a sui generis system as it is left to the government to decide the elements which could be deemed to be providing effective protection. A decision has been taken to put in place a sui generis system as it is perceived to be in our national interest. A legislation to this effect tabled in the parliament by the Ministry of Agriculture has been referred to a joint parliamentary committee of the houses.

In respect of plant varieties, there is an obligation for protection or by an effective sui generis or by any combination thereof. The agreement does not spell out elements of a sui generis system and it is left to each government to decide the elements which could not be deemed to be in our national interest. A legislation to this effect tabled in the Parliament by the ministry of agriculture has been referred to a joint parliamentary committee.

Layout Designs of Integrated Circuits

India is a signatory to the international agreement (the Washington Tready) administered by the WIPO. The main obligations of the Washington Treaty are also incorporated in the TRIPs Agreement with some enhancement and cover the protection of the intellectual property in the respect of lay-out design that are original in the sense of being the result of their creator's own intellectual efforts. The obligations include national treatment to foreign right holders and a term of protection of 10 years. A legislation giving protection to lay-out designs, was introduced in the Rajya Sabha on 20 December 1999 by the Department of Electronics.

Copyright and Related Rights

In the area of copyright and related rights, i.e. right of performers, producers of phonograms and broadcasting organisations, the Agreement require compliance with the provisions of the Berne Convention. Computer programmes are to be protected as literary works. The term of protection for copy rights and the right of performer and producers of phonograms is to be no less than 50 years. In the case of terms of protection of performer's rights. In case of broadcasting organisations, however, the term of protection is to be at least 20 years.

India is a signatory to the Berne Convention. The Copyright Act, 1957 as amended in 1994 talks of our own concerns and meets with the requirements of TRIPs Agreement except in the case of terms of protection of performer's rights. A bill to increase this term to 50 years was passed by Parliament in December, 1999.

Trade Marks

Our trade Marks law, the Trade and Merchandise Marks Act (TMMMA), 1958 is in its essential features, in accordance with International Law. A bill to amend the TMMA was introduced in Parliament in 1993 so as to provide for protection to service mark also. The bill could not be passed and subsequently lapsed. A bill in their regard, however, was passed by Parliament in December, 1999 which, inter alia, provides for protection to service marks.

Geographic Indication

The agreement contains a general obligation that parties shall provide the legal means to interested parties to prevent the use of any means in the designation or presentation of a good that indicates or suggests that the good in question originates in geographical area other than the true place of origin of the good. In India, we don't so far have any specific law on geographical indications. Case Law, however, enables legal action for protection of geographical indications. It was decided to enact a new law not the subject to take advantage of the provisions of the TRIPs Agreement. A Bill in this regard was passed by the Parliament in December 1999.

Industrial Designs

Obligations envisaged in respect of industrial designs are that independently created designs that are new or original shall be protected. There is an option to exclude from protection, designs dictated by technical considerations, as against aesthetic considerable which constitutes the coverage of industrial designs. Our law, the Design Act, 1911 is a very old enactment and needs updating. The department of industrial development prepared a bill in this regard, which was passed by the Rajya Sabha in December, 1999 and will now have to passed by the Lok Sabha.

Trade Related Investment Measures (TRIM)

Under the TRIM Agreement, developing countries have a transition period of 5 years up to 31, December 1998, during which they can continue to maintain measures inconsistant. With the agreement provided there are duly notified. We notify two TRIMs, viz., the relating to local inconsistent requirements in the production of certain pharmaceutical products and divided balancing requirement in the case of investment in 22 categories of consumer items. In view of the inconclusiveness of the Seattle ministerial conference, where no final decision on request of developing countries for extension of transition period for elimination of the notified TRIMs was taken, it needs to be seen what final decision is taken by General Council on this issue.

Tariffs

Our commitment to reduce tariffs to the bound levels by 1-3-2000, exists in respect of non-agricultural and non-textile items and necessary action will be taken to fulfil these obligations.

8

MARINE INSURANCE

What is Marine Insurance?

Marine insurance is a contract of indemnity whereby the assurer or underwriter agrees, for a stated consideration, known as the premium, to protect and indemnify the shipper and/or owner of the goods against loss, damage, or expense in connection with the goods at risk, if the damage is caused by perils specified in the contract known as the policy of insurance.

When the goods have left the shipper's plant or warehouse and are in the course of transportation, shipper has no physical means for the protection of these goods and must rely upon the ability of the transportation company to which he entrusts them for safe delivery at their intended destination. In addition, there are perils and hazards which the goods may encounter and which are beyond control of the carrier. Hence the importance of marine insurance can well be appreciated.

The carrier in export trade is not an insurer of merchandise. He is exempted by law from certain causes of loss as well as from the conditions and stipulations which may be entered in the contract of carriage between the shipper and the carrier. For these reasons, the merchant must have some means of protecting himself against losses which he may not be able to recover from the carrier under his bill of lading. He, therefore, insures himself against loss or damage.

Despite the fact that they are covered by clean bills of lading indicating that they were apparently in good order and condition when received on board, the damage to the goods might occur in transit, especially if it encounters hazardous conditions during the journey. The buyer may have to pay for the goods before he sees them; or even after he sees them in the customs shed at his end, the goods may be damaged or pilfered before reaching his warehouse. Another point to be considered is the fact that where no letter of credit has been established, the goods most probably remain the property of the exporter until the buyer takes up the documents; and if that buyer gets to know that the goods have been damaged in transit, he may refuse to retire the draft.

Although a bill of lading are the title to the goods, that title is only worth as much as the goods themselves; and if the goods are worthless because of the damage caused to them, the title to them, too, is worthless. But if the goods are properly insured, then, irrespecuve of whether they suffer damage or not, the worth of the title remains; and, for this reason, goods cannot be shipped abroad unless they have full insurance cover. In most cases, the insurance is the responsibility of the exporter; and he must arrange to insure the goods on C.I.F. transactions.

Insurance is a system of financial protection against the happenings of accidental or fortuitous events.

(*a*) During sea transportation, the *goods may be lost due* to sinking of the vessel.

(*b*) *Goods may be damaged* due to incursion of sea-water into the holds of the ship during heavy weather.

(*c*) During land transit the goods may be lost or *damaged by derailment of railway* wagons or collision of motor goods vehicle.

(*d*) During transit and whilst in storage incidental to transit, the *goods may catch fire or may be stolen*. These hazards or causes of loss referred to as perils or risks in insurance terminology, may result in the following type of losses.

(*i*) *Total loss* — *e.g.*, an entire shipment is lost due to the sinking of the vessel or due to out-break of fire.

(*ii*) *Partial loss* — cargo is damaged by sea-water. During heavy weather cargo is jettisoned to save the marine voyage threatened by heavy weather.

(*iii*) *Expenses* — The insured may incur certain expenses to prevent aggravation of loss or damage *e.g.,* hides slightly damaged by sea water may be re-conditioned at an intermediate port to reduce the loss or even prevent total loss.

Upon total loss of the entire cargo by an insured peril the sum insured is paid in full. If part of the cargo is a total loss, the appropriate proportion of the insured value is paid.

Claims for damage are settled by ascertaining the percentage of depreciation and applying this percentage to this insured value. The percentage of depreciation is calculated by comparing the value the goods would realise in their damaged state with their gross sound value on the date of the sale. The same date is used for both values in order to avoid distortion of the result arising from fluctuations in the market.

In marine insurance it is customary to issue agreed value policies. The agreed value is conclusive between the insurer and the assured except in the event of the unintentional error or where fraud is alleged.

"Duty" and "Increased Value" policies are not agreed value policies. They provide pure indemnity only.

(2) Insurable Interest

The Marine Insurance Act contains a very clear definition of insurable interest. It states that there must be a physical object exposed to marine perils and that the insured must have some legal relationship to the object, in consequence of which he benefits by its preservation and is prejudiced by loss or damage happening to it or where he may incur liability in respect thereof.

Whereas in fire and accident insurance an insurable interest must exist both at inception of the contract and at the time of loss, the interest in respect of a marine contract need only exist at the time of loss. This is necessary when one considers maritime commerce where goods are bought and sold whilst in the course of transit.

"Lost or not lost": The former "lost or not lost" provisions of the Policy are given effect to by clause No. 11.2 of the Institute Cargo Clauses. They render the protection of the contract where the voyage has commenced retrospective to the commencement of the risk. Thus where property suffers loss before the assured acquires his interest, he is protected by the policy, provided the risk in the goods has passed to him. Arising from this, both a contingent and a defeasible interest are insurable. A partial interest is also insurable.

A Marine Cargo Policy is freely assignable either before or after loss provided of course the assignee has acquired insurable interest.

When the assured has no interest at the time of the loss, he cannot acquire interest by any act or election after he is aware of the loss.

(3) Good Faith

Every contract of insurance is a contract "uberrimae fidei" *i.e.,* one which requires utmost good faith on the part of both the insurer and of the assured. In marine insurance it is the duty of the proposer to disclose clearly and accurately all material facts related to the risk. A material fact is a fact which would affect the judgement of a prudent underwriter in considering whether he would enter into a contract at all, or enter into it at one rate of premium or another and subject to what terms. Apart from the duty of disclosure the insured must act towards the insurer in good faith throughout the duration of the contract.

It is customary to classify breaches of the duty of utmost good faith under four headings — non-disclosure, concealment, innocent misrepresentation and fraudulent misrepresentation. The first two are termed passive breaches and the other two are termed active breaches. The Marine Insurance Act places a statutory duty on the assured to disclose to the insurer all material circumstances known to the assured or which should be known by him in the ordinary course of his business.

Whether non-disclosure is intentional or inadvertent, the effect is the same and the policy may be avoided, although deliberate and material non-disclosure would usually amount to fraud and render the policy void.

Over-valuation, for example, must be communicated to the insurers; if it is not so communicated, it is a concealment of a material fact and voids the insurance.

(4) Proximate Cause

"Proximate cause means the active, efficient cause that sets in motion a train of events which brings about a result, without the intervention of any force started and working actively from a new and independent source."

Insurers are liable if an insured peril is the proximate cause of the loss. If an insured peril is only the remote cause of the loss, the proximate cause being an uninsured or excepted peril, the insurers are not liable.

The proximate cause is not necessarily that which is proximate in time, but that which is proximate in efficiency. It is the dominant, effective and operative cause of the loss.

In the case of concurrent causes, following rules apply:

(*a*) If one of the causes contributing to the loss is an insured peril, and no excepted peril is involved the loss is covered.

(*b*) If one of the causes is an expected peril, the loss is not covered at all, unless the consequence of the insured peril can be separated from those of the uninsured peril, in which event the former, but not the latter, is covered.

(5) Subrogation

"Subrogation is the right which one person has of standing in place of another and availing himself of all the rights and remedies of that other, whether already enforced or not."

Subrogation is a corollary of the principle of indemnity and the right of subrogation therefore applies only to policies which are contracts of indemnity. Subrogation is a matter of equity, the purpose of which is to ensure that the insured is not over-indemnified for the same loss.

(*i*) In marine insurance, where an insurer pays for a total loss:

(*a*) he is entitled to take over the interest of the assured in whatever may remain of the subject-matter so paid for (abandonment);

(*b*) and he is subrogated to all the rights and remedies of the assured as from the time of the loss (subrogation).

(*ii*) Where an insurer pays for a partial loss, he acquires no title to the subject-matter insured or to such part of it as may remain, but he is subrogated to all the rights and remedies of the assured as from the time of the loss, and in so far as the assured has been indemnified.

In marine insurance subrogation applies only after payment of a loss. The insurer is entitled to recover only upto the amount which he has paid, in respect of rights and remedies.

On payment of a total loss, the insurer is entitled to assume rights of ownership of the subject-matter insured. The right is conferred upon him by virtue of abandonment (not by rights of subrogation) and the effect is that if the property is subsequently salvaged or recovered the insurer is entitled to retain the whole of the proceeds of sale even though they may exceed the sum paid out under the policy, always assuming the property is fully insured and that the assured was not bearing part of the risk himself.

In addition to this right of exercising ownership of the property, the insurer is subrogated to "all rights and remedies of the assured as from the time of casualty causing the loss." This simply means that if the loss has been caused by the negligence of a third party, against whom the assured has the right action in tort — say, against a carrier or bailee — then the insured is entitled to succeed to any recovery (whereby the loss is reduced) the assured may effect from such third party. This principle applies equally to total and partial losses and has nothing whatever to do with the doctrine of abandonment.

(6) Contribution

Sometimes one risk may be covered by more than one insurer. In that case it is desirable not only to ensure that the insured does not receive more than indemnity but that any loss is fairly spread between all the insurers involved. The principle of contribution is a method of distributing fairly among insurers the burden of claims for which each shares some responsibility.

Following factors are required to exist before a loss is shared among the insurers.

(1) There must be at least two policies of insurance.

(2) All insurance must be policies of indemnity.

(3) The policies must cover:

(*i*) The same interest.

(*ii*) The same subject matter.

(*iii*) The same peril.

(4) A loss must occur.

(5) The policies must be in force at the time of loss.

(6) All policies must cover the loss.

(7) The policies must be legally enforceable.

Marine Insurance Act provides that —

(*a*) Where the assured is over-insured by double insurance, each insurer is bound, as between himself and the other insurers, to contribute rateably to the loss in proportion to the amount for which he is liable under his contract.

(*b*) If any insurer pays more than this proportion of the loss, he is entitled to maintain an action for contribution against the other insurers, and is entitled to recovery from them of their share of the loss.

(*c*) Where the assured receives any sum in excess of the indemnity allowed, he is deemed to hold such sum in trust for the insurers, according to their right of contribution among themselves.

The Subject Matter of Insurance

The subject matter of insurance may be any property of intrinsic value, or any event the happening of which will cause the loss of a legal right or the creation of a legal liability. The subject matter is described in the policy but it should be remembered that insurance is operative in respect of the interest of the assured in the property concerned and it is this interest which is the subject matter of the insurance contract. It is the pecuniary interest of the insured in the property exposed to peril that is insured. Therefore, while the subject matter of the insurance may be property or liability, the subject matter of the contract is the insurable interest therein.

Subject Matter of Marine Insurance

There are three classes of properties which are the subject matter of marine insurance:

(*i*) Cargo insurance;
(*ii*) Freight insurance; and
(*iii*) Hull insurance (insurance of the ship).

In the C.I.F. price quotation, it is only the cargo which is insured because the freight has already been paid. However, freight insurance may be taken out either by the cargo-owner or by the shipping company if freight has not been paid.

The exporter, who only makes occasional shipments, advises the insurance broker or company of the full details of the goods to be shipped, giving the number of cases, a brief description of the goods themselves, the markings on the cases, the name of the ship, the port of shipment and the place of destination to which he is sending the goods, and the value for which he wants the goods covered. At the same time, he has to state the risks which are to be covered. The insurance broker, or company, then issues the appropriate policy of insurance to cover the shipment; and this policy is required in duplicate. As this policy is issued in the name of the shipper, it must be endorsed by the shipper before it is handed over to the bank so that, whoever has the benefit of the bills of lading, may also have the benefit of the insurance cover and can claim reimbursement for any damage or shortage.

It may occasionally happen that a letter of credit asks for insurance policies in favour of the bank which originally opened the credit; and this can be arranged either by asking the insurance company to make out the policy in favour of the required party or by the exporter endorsing the policy as follows: "Pay any claims arising under this policy of insurance to the order of. . ." and then signing the endorsement.

When the exporter has done a fair amount of export trade with several shipments per month, arrangements for an insurance cover can be speeded up and simplified by the exporter having an "open cover" with the insurance broker or insurance company. The exporter tells the insurance broker what his estimate of the total value of his export shipments for the next twelve months and also what he anticipates will be the value of the largest single consignment which he is likely to ship.

The insurance brokers for insurance company then agree to give the exporter an insurance cover for any shipments made within the limits estimated without the necessity of the exporter having to advise them in advance. The exporter is issued a pad of certificates and he himself fills in the details of each shipment, which is to be covered for insurance — the details being the same as those of which he would advise the insurance brokers if he wanted a policy as described earlier. These certificates are in sets of four — the first two are the originals and the other two are non-negotiable copies. The originals valid as part of the shipping documents, whilst one of the copies is sent to the brokers or insurance companies that they are advised of the risk that has been covered and can make the appropriate charge for premium. The other copy is retained in the exporter's file for reference and for checking the insurance broker's bill for premiums. These certificates of insurance have to be endorsed in the same way as insurance policies are endorsed.

Care to be Exercised

Care must, however, be taken to see to it that insurance policies or certificates are properly initiated because they are legal documents. If, with an open cover, the exporter has an order which is larger than the one he originally estimated, care must be taken to see to it that the limit amount for any one shipment, which is shown on the certificates, is altered and it is necessary to send all the four copies of the certificates to the insurance company or brokers for an official approval of the alteration.

If the exporter has underestimated the total yearly value of his shipments, he would ask, before the total value has been reached, for the total cover to be extended, and the insurance company or brokers will be glad to agree, provided that there has not been any excessive number of claims against the earlier shipments.

10 PER CENT EXTRA OF THE ACTUAL C.I.F. PRICES

It is usual to cover 110 per cent of the actual C.I.F. prices of the goods. The reason for this is that, in addition to having paid for the C.I.F. cost of the actual goods when he retires the drafts (or makes payment, or has accepted to make payment in any other way), the buyer has probably also paid for the customs clearance and for the unloading and transit of the goods to his warehouse. There are a few instances when these charges have been exceptionally heavy or when the customs duty cannot be reclaimed even though paid on worthless goods, in consequence, the shipper will be asked to cover the goods for up to 150 per cent of their C.I.F. value. The exporter must bear in mind that, where such heavier than normal cover is requested, the premium for insurance is considerably higher, and the buyer should be asked to confirm that he will pay the cost of the excess premium.

The exporter should also remember that it is as well to cover for 110 per cent for his own sake, especially when the shipment is not covered by a letter of credit because it may so happen that the buyer, instead of himself collecting the insurance payment for damaged or missing goods, may send the certificate or the policy back to the exporter, asking the latter to replace the damaged or missing goods and reimburse himself by collecting the insurance money. Such a procedure will mean a higher transit cost to the exporter; and this is covered by the extra 10 per cent cover.

Types of Risks Insured

There are many possible risks for goods that are shipped abroad, apart from the possibility of the sinking of the ship itself. She may run into a heavy storm, and the cargo may be damaged by rain or sea-water. There is always the risk of fire or of some of the goods being stolen. Some letters of credit specify the risks which must be insured against. The usual procedure, therefore, is to have an "all risks policy". It is not worthwhile for an exporter to try to save on premium payments and hence a less comprehensive policy because a few banks, negotiating letters of credit, accept such a policy. A reputable insurance company or a reputable firm of insurance brokers will give the "standard all risks cover" and issue polices and certificates to that effect which will be acceptable by any bank.

The standard "all risks" cover, however, is not quite sufficient for this policy which covers only normal civil happenings. Cover will also be invariably required against "war risk" even in peace time. The exporter should, therefore, instruct the insurance brokers or the insurance company to include a war risk cover, which they will do by endorsing the policy and/or certificates.

As already indicated, damage or pilferage may occur while the goods are on board. In fact, much of the damage and pilferage occurs during loading or unloading or in transit to the docks in the country of shipment or in transit from the docks at the destination. The exporting manufacturers see to it that the goods are packed safely and in good order at his warehouse; and in normal circumstances, the goods are not seen again until the cases are unpacked in the buyer's warehouses. The exporter cannot reasonably have all the cases examined immediately before the goods are loaded on board; and the buyer cannot open all the cases for a thorough examination at the docks at his end. Yet goods are damaged by being left out in the rain on the dock, or by being loaded with hooks when they should not be so loaded, or by pilferage by dock workers and dock-side thieves. To cover these risks, it is advisable to have a "warehouse-to-warehouse" cover, which is quite normal and which covers all the risks from the time the goods leave the exporter's warehouse up to the time they arrive at the buyer's warehouse. This is usually modified slightly by limiting the period of cover after the arrival of the ship at destination to 30 days irrespective of whether the goods have reached the buyer's warehouse or not.

Marine Insurance Claim

Under an ordinary marine insurance cover, if the goods have been damaged or pilfered or lost, the buyer reports the fact immediately to his local agents or the local branch of the insurance company or to the firm of insurance assessors. They examine the goods and certify the extent of the loss. The buyer then works out his claim on the basis of the proportion which the damaged goods bear to the whole consignment. For instance, if the exporter's invoice value for the goods which are damaged is Rs. 400 and the total of the exporter's invoice is Rs. 40,000 (*i.e.*, 110 per cent of invoice value), the amount to be claimed will be:

$$\frac{\text{Rs. } 400 \times \text{Rs. } 44{,}000}{\text{Rs. } 40{,}000} = \text{Rs. } 440$$

If the goods have been invoiced on F.O.B. value plus the cost of marine freight, insurance and shipping charges, the buyer is entitled to claim a proportion of such charges. For instance, the total F.O.B. value of goods shipped is Rs. 2,000; Rs. 400 has been added for the charges mentioned, making the invoice total Rs. 2,400. The insurance cover would normally be for Rs. 1,640. If Rs. 200 worth of goods are damaged or lost, the claim will be for Rs. 264, which is represented by:

$$\frac{\text{Rs. } 200 \times \text{Rs. } 1{,}640}{\text{Rs. } 2{,}000} = \text{Rs. } 264$$

The buyer would send the original insurance certificate or policy to the broker or company which issued it, with a statement of the claim and the latter would send him the money. Alternatively, the buyer may send these papers to the exporter and ask him to make the claim on his behalf, and either credit the amount to the buyer's account or remit the money to him.

This claim procedure may be quite a nuisance; and a certain proportion of the claim is lost in the costs of transmission and exchange into the buyer's currency. To avoid this nuisance and expense, therefore, it is usual to have a C.P.A. policy for marine insurance. The letter of C.P.A. is referred to *claims payable abroad.* This facility costs a little extra but it is well worth paying for it. On a certificate or a policy of insurance, when the C.P.A. arrangements have been made, there will be words to the effect that insurance agent — is authorised to settle any claims arising under this certificate or policy of insurance; and, in the empty space, will be filled in the name of the town or city at which the insurance agent nearest to the buyer is located (usually the port to which the goods are consigned). Under these arrangements, the buyer can get his claim paid in his own currency on the spot.

It might be advisable even in some cases of cost and freight (C & F) shipments that the exporter should also get an insurance cover. This should be done when the exporter ships goods without being covered by a letter of credit. The goods are still the exporter's liability until buyer has taken up the documents; and if he (the exporter) fails to do so and damage or loss occurs, the exporter will suffer, for he will find it difficult to make a claim under the buyer's insurance agreements.

The cost of marine insurance premium is quite low, and reliable exporters, doing a fair amount of business, can probably get all the risks covered by paying 1/2 per cent and 1 per cent of the value insured, depending on the type of goods that are insured and the type of containers in which they are shipped. For instance, the insurance premium on goods packed in glass bottles is considerably higher than on the same goods packed in tin cans. It is quite possible to get a standard rate, irrespective of the destination of the goods. In addition, there may be an extra premium on war risks cover, which varies considerably according to the country of destination and in the light of the political conditions prevailing in the country of destination or in countries en route at the time of shipment. A small extra fee is payable for C.P.A. facilities. On normal goods to normal destinations, it should be possible to secure an insurance cover for all the risks including war risks under C.P.A. at an average cost of about one per cent to 1¼ per cent.

Some Practical Suggestions

The following suggestions are likely to be helpful to the exporter who wants to protect himself against marine and related risks:

(*i*) Employ the most experienced and most reputable marine insurance broker who can be found.

(*ii*) Take out an open or floating marine insurance policy.

(*iii*) Insist that the terms of the policy be made as broad as possible, not only from the point of view of the types of merchandise to be shipped but also in respect of the areas covered, the elapsed time and other provisions.

(*iv*) In the case of loss:

- (*a*) Notify your broker;
- (*b*) Do it immediately; and

(c) Move without delay. The collection of an insurance loss may be vitiated by postponement.

(v) Marine insurance never covers what is known as "inherent vice", which means deterioration such as spoilage due to the character of the merchandise.

(vi) See to it that all the insured goods are moved promptly. They must not be allowed to remain on docks, in trucks, or in unprotected places.

(vii) Invariably add at least 10 per to the invoice price of the merchandise — sometimes more.

(viii) If the total risk exceeds the amount of insurance named in the policy, the limit should be immediately increased.

Marine insurance companies and underwriting organisations are keenly interested in export packing methods and make recommendations based on their experience. One of the basic factors considered by an underwriter in quoting a marine insurance premium is the loss experience of the shipper. This is a tangible measure of the packing problems of every shipper and offers a reward to effect improvements in the loss and damage record.

Marine insurance to cover cargo risks is commonly place on all shipments moving in international seaborne trade. The insurance may be placed for the exporter's account or for the account of the buyer, or it may be placed by the importer who has selected a particular underwriter. This is not as simple as it may sound. For example, the importer may agree to take care of the insurance. In this case, let us say that the purchase is made under a letter of credit. The letter calls for furnishing an on-board bill of lading in order to collect under the credit. If a loss should occur between the time the goods leave the exporter's warehouse and before the on-board bill of lading is issued, the credit could not be used and the insurance taken out by the importer probably would not cover the loss.

There are certain advantages to the exporter who takes marine insurance. For example, when the sale is F.O.B.vessel Bombay, the importer's insurance may become effective only when the goods are loaded aboard ship; hence, any loss to the shipment between the exporter's warehouse and the vessel may not be covered. To protect against such a risk, the exporter would need to purchase an inland marine policy or a special endorsement for an open cargo policy.

What Policy Must Specify?

In terms of Section 25 of the Marine Insurance Act, 1963 a marine policy must specify:

(i) the *name of assured*, or of some person who effects the insurance on his behalf;

(ii) the *subject-matter* insured and the risk insured against;

(iii) the *voyage or period* of time or both, as the case may be, covered by the insurance;

(iv) the sum or *sums* insured;

(v) the name and *signature of* the insurer;

(vi) the place where claims are payable together with details of the agent to whom claims may be directed;

(vii) the *declaration of the assured*, where applicable. His endorsement on the reverse of the document is also required so that the rights to claim may be transferred to another party (usually the importer);

(viii) the *date of issue.* This must be the same as or earlier than the date of the document evidencing despatch except where warehouse to warehouse cover is indicated.

Assignment of Marine Cargo Policies

In terms of Sections 52 and 53 of the Marine Insurance Act, 1963 a marine cargo policy *is freely assignable to any one, who may acquire insurable interest as there are no terms in the marine cargo policy expressly prohibiting assignment. A marine cargo policy can be assigned either before or after a loss.*

Who can Issue?

Contracts for sale and purchase of goods in international trade may take various forms because the sellers and buyers may like to incorporate terms and conditions in the contract to suit their requirements. *The type of sale contract will determine as to when the risk of loss or damage falls on the seller or on the buyer and who should therefore arrange insurance protection.*

C.I.F. (Cost Insurance and Freight): In the absence of any specific advice from the *buyer the seller is required to arrange insurance of the C.I.F. value of the goods plus 5% to 10% towards incidental charges.* It is a prevalent practice that insurers are generally agreeable to grant insurance cover upto 10% extra over and above the C.I.F. value of the goods.

C & F (Cost and Freight): The responsibility of arranging insurance is on the *buyer.*

C & I — (Cost and Insurance): The responsibility of arranging insurance is on the seller.

F.O.B. -- (Free On Board): *The buyer is obliged to arrange insurance.* As soon as the seller has fixed up the ship, he will advise the buyer immediately so that he could arrange for insurance before commencement of risk (before the vessel sails).

F.A.S. (Free Along Shore): The seller's obligation is to bring the goods at the shore by the side of the ship. It is the responsibility of the *buyer to* arrange for shipment and insurance.

What are the Special Features of Marine Insurance?

(a) *Marine cargo policies are freely assignable* because the interest in the goods pass through various hands till final delivery is taken by the ultimate consignee. A cargo policy may be assigned either before or after a loss. Since the *policies are freely assignable the existence of the insurance interest of the claimant should exist at the time of loss.* There is no need of insurable interest to exist at the time of taking up the policy. However, the insured should have reasonable expectation of acquiring such interest at a later date.

(b) *The sum insured indicated in the policy is the value agreed between the insured and the insurer.* Hence the policies are on Agreed Value basis. The value so agreed upon cannot be reopened unless fraud is suspected. In addition to cost, insurance and freight a percentage loading is effected to arrive at the agreed value. An element of anticipated profit can also be added to arrive at such an agreed value. The indemnity provided by the policy is of course subject to the actual amount of the loss or damage and is also subject to the overall limit. *i.e.,* the sum insured. *The marine insurance contract is a contract of commercial indemnity and not of pure indemnity as in other classes of business.*

(c) *The duration of cover in a marine policy is subject to the transit clause of the respective cargo clauses.* This differs from one mode of transit to another (sea, rail, road and air). While the duration of cover in other clauses is fixed at the time of the issue of the policy itself, in marine insurance it is governed by the nature of transit , *the time of discharge and the time of arrival at the destination.*

With Whom to Insure?

Exporters/firms in *India are expected to take general insurance business only with GIC or its four subsidiaries in India.* They are not permitted to take marine insurance cover with insurance companies in foreign countries without prior permission of RBI and Government of India.

How to Pay Premium?

Payment of premium on marine insurance policies *can be made in rupees,* on exporter furnishing to insurer a certificate to the effect either *(a)* that insurance charges on the shipment in question have to be borne by him in terms of contract with overseas buyer and that he is not making the payment on behalf of any non-resident; and *(b)* that he is defraying insurance charges on the shipment in question on account of overseas buyer of the goods and he undertakes to add the amount on the invoice and recover the payment so made from they buyer in an approved manner.

Disclosure of Material Facts

An insurance is a contract of *"Uberrima Fides" — a contract of utmost good faith.* Hence the exporter has to declare all the material facts about the shipment at the time of getting the insurance cover. If any material information is concealed/withheld or an incorrect statement is made by him, the insurer may repudiate the claim.

Types of Policies

The different types of marine insurance policies can be divided into three broad groups — (1) Individual shipment policy, (2) Open policy, and (3) Floating policy.

Individual Shipment Policy: Taken for *every individual shipment* can be categorised into (*a*) *Restricted policy,* (*b*) *All risk policy,* and (*c*) *All risk comprehensive policy* depending upon the nature of risk covered.

(a) Restricted Policy may be of 4 types:

(i) *Total Loss of Vessel Only (TLVO)* — provides cover only if the *total vessel is lost.*

(ii) *Total Loss Only (TLO)* — Loss is indemnified only if goods insured against *maritime perils are totally lost* irrespective of the fact whether the vessel is lost or not.

(iii) *Free from Particular Average (FPA)* — Coverage is provided against (*a*) *total* loss, (*b*) *general* average loss; (*c*) partial particular loss caused by marine perils in case the ship is stranded, sunk or burnt, and (*d*) *loss due to fire, explosion, contact* of vessel with outside substance, etc.

(iv) *With Particular Average (WPA)* — Besides the losses *covered under FPA,* coverage is provided against the loss/damage caused *by heavy weather or sea water* provided it reaches to a specified percentage.

'Average' is a common word used in marine insurance, denoting loss.

(*b*) *All risk policy against all risks of loss or damage to the subject matter — not covers loss,* damage or expense proximately *caused by inherent vice or the nature of the subject-matter insured — also excludes war risks and risks/damage by Strikes, Riots and Civil Commotion* (SRCC).

(c) *All risks comprehensive policy coverage the widest— includes all risks of loss or damage to the insured* subject matter caused by marine perils, war risks, SRCC, extraneous losses like theft, pilferage and non-delivery, fresh water/rain water, hook holes, oil damage etc.

Open Policy: Individual policies are issued for single shipments. Regular exporters with sizable volume of operations usually insure under long-term policies. *Open cover insurance contracts may run for a fixed period, such as 12 months.* Under an open cover, the assured has *automatic protection for all his shipments.* Generally a *maximum limit of cover is set for a shipment on any one vessel.* It is important to note that *under an open cover contract the assured is obliged to declare to the insurers all shipments.* Big exporters prefer this method as it *saves them* the trouble of having to arrange for protection before a shipment is made and more importantly *it enhances their competitiveness by obtaining special premium rates* (where these are not predetermined by statutory authorities) and being *able to quote an accurate sales price inclusive of known insurance costs.*

Floating Policy: It describes the insurance in general terms and leaves the name or names of the ship or ships and other particulars to be defined by subsequent declaration.

What Risks Can be Covered?

Institute Cargo Clauses (C): This cover is *granted by attaching Cargo Clauses* (C) *to the policy of insurance.* The policy covers loss of or damage to the goods *insured caused by*:

(a) fire or explosion,

(b) *stranding,* grounding, sinking or capsizing of the vessel,

(c) *overturning* or derailment of land conveyance,

(d) *collision* or contact of vessel, craft or conveyance with any external object other than water,

(e) *discharge of cargo* at a port of distress,

(f) *general average* sacrifice,

(g) *jettison.*

The *cover extends over the entire period of transit* from the time the goods leave the warehouse at the place of commencement of transit and continues during such transits including transshipment, deviation (not within the control of insured) and terminates on delivery of the goods at the warehouse at destination named in the policy or on expiry of 60 days after the completion of discharge from the vessel at the final port, which shall first occur. The policy will not cover the following risks:

(a) Loss, damage or expense *caused by delay and inherent vice or* nature of the subject-matter,

(b) Loss, damage or expense attributable to *willful misconduct of the insured,*

(c) *Ordinary leakage, ordinary loss in weight or volume or ordinary wear and tear* of the subject-matter insured,

(d) Insufficient or *unsuitability of packing,*

(e) Deliberate damage to or *deliberate destruction of the* goods,

(f) Loss, damage or expense arising *from insolvency or financial default of the owners,* managers, characterers or operators of the vessel, and

(g) Loss, damage or expense arising *from the use of atomic weapons or nuclear fusion* and/or other like reaction or radioactive force.

Institute Cargo Clauses (B)

This cover is granted by attaching Institute Cargo Clauses (B) *to the policy of insurance. In addition* to the risks covered under Institute Cargo Clauses (C), *the following risks are covered:*

(a) Loss of or damage to the goods *attributable to earthquake, volcanic eruption or lightning,*

(b) *Washing overboard,*

(c) Loss of or damage to the goods *caused by entry of sea, lake or river water into vessel, craft,* hold conveyance, container lift - van or place of storage, and

(d) Total loss of any package lost *overboard or dropped whilst loading on to, or unloading from, vessel or craft.*

This policy also will not cover the excluded risks mentioned under Institute Cargo Clause (C).

Extraneous Perils: As the goods in transit are subject to a large number of non-maritime extraneous perils, it is possible to extend the policy issued on Institute Cargo Clause (B) to *cover any or all the following extraneous perils by payment of suitable extra premium:*

(a) Theft, pilferage and non-delivery,

(b) Fresh and/or rain and/or river water damage,

(c) Hook, oil, mud, acid and damage by other cargo,

(d) Heating and sweating,

(*e*) Breakage, denting, chipping, scratching and blending,
(*f*) Breakage,
(*g*) Bursting and tearing.

Institute Cargo Clause (A): This insurance covers all risks of loss or damage to the subject matter except those specifically excluded under the Exclusion Clause.

The risks excluded are same as for ICC (C) and ICC (B) except that the exclusion No. 8 on "*malicious damage*" does not apply to this cover.

In other words *ICC (A) includes malicious damage also.*

Malicious damage cover can be taken under ICC (B) or (C) on payment of appropriate additional premium. Similarly the extraneous perils-theft, pilferage and non-delivery, can also be included in these restricted types of covers where the insured does not require the widest cover as per Institute Cargo Clauses (A).

Trade Clauses: There are also specially designed clauses to meet requirements of certain trades. They are based on provisions of *'Trade Clauses'* drafted by the Institute of London Underwriters in consultation with the relevant trade associations. *Though they are not commonly used in India*, if an export contract requires insurance on these lines it can be obtained in Indian insurance market on payment of suitable premium.

War and SRCC Cover: The shipper/exporter can obtain war, riots, strike and civil commotion cover *along with all the three types of policies* by payment of an individual premium. The above cover is granted by attaching Institute War Clauses (Cargo) to the policy of insurance.

Insurance of Air Freight: Air freight consignments are *covered under three sets of clauses*:

(i) Institute Cargo Clauses (Air) *excluding sending by post*;

(ii) Institute War Clauses (Air Cargo) excluding sending by post; and

(iii) Institute Strike Clauses (Air Cargo).

For Registered Postal Sendings: The cover is provided to *cater to special needs of import/export in diamonds and precious stones by air freight* parcels or registered post parcels by air under a special insurance scheme designed by the General Insurance Companies in India.

The insurance is against all risks of physical loss or damage as per Institute Cargo Clauses (A) for registered insured post parcels, and as per Institute Cargo Clauses (Air) for sending by air-freight.

This cover generally incorporates the door to door clause similar to transit clause in ocean cargo.

Exclusions listed under Institute Cargo Clauses (A), (B) and (C) also apply with certain changes due to special mode of transport.

Inland Transit Policies (rail/road): There are two types of covers available to *insure goods transported by the railways or motor vehicles.* The Inland Transit Clauses (*A*) cover all risks of loss or damage to the *insured goods whereas Inland Transit Clauses* (*B*) provide cover for fire, lightning, breakage of bridges, collision, overturning of the vehicles, *derailment or accidents of like nature.*

Duty and Increased Value Insurances

Any cargo landed at the port of destination is subject to the *payment of duty and this goes to increase the value of* the imported item. *Such duty can also be insured separately.* Similarly in some cases the market value of the goods at destination on the date of *landing is higher than the CIF* and duty value of the cargo. *Then a separate insurance on the increased value can be effected.* These two specialised insurances *are governed by specific provisions of the All India Marine Cargo Tariff. The important features of these insurances are summarised below.*

1. *This can be given only when a policy for the CIF value of the cargo has been taken.* The perils covered under the cargo policy and the increased value policy *should be identical.* Where, however, there is *an unavoidable contractual obligation* to insure abroad, this restriction does not apply.
2. The insurance can be granted *only to the holder or assignee of the import licence or the actual user who has* purchased the goods from a recognised export house/channelising agency.
3. *The policy is not assignable.*
4. The policy is *not a valued policy* and hence claims are payable on the basis of the *actual duty paid,* or on the basis of the *sum insured whichever is less.*
5. No claim shall be paid for duty until the claim under the *C.I.F. value insurance is payable and proof of liability for loss under that policy shall be furnished to the company.*
6. *No cover can be granted after arrival of the ship at the port of destination.*
7. *The indemnity provided shall be 75% of the liability,* the balance 25% must be borne by the insured himself, in the case of increased value policy.
8. For the issue of duty and increased value insurances, a proposal form has to be filled in by the insured in *which he must declare all other insurance in respect of consignment.*

9. Insurance on cargo in inland transit in excess of established market value, cannot be granted under any circumstances.
10. The rate of premium for insurance of duty shall be 75% of the rate charged for covering the C.I.F. value of cargo itself.

Marine Cum Erection Insurance

When a project is under execution, a number of items are imported and numerous items are purchased locally. A few of these items undergo some fabrication/modification before being sent to the project site. At the project site the material is kept in storage pending erection. This storage may be extended to as long as a year or even two years depending on the size of the project, the arrival of erection personnel, arrival of the other connected materials/machinery/equipments etc. After completion of erection the plant is handed over after a test run.

During this entire period starting from the time of procuring the materials from the manufacturer's warehouse, during the transit, during the storage, while undergoing erection and till handing over after successful completion of the test run, the entire value is at risk. To ensure that there is a continuous insurance cover for the project materials in transit, in storage and while undergoing erection and test run, *two types of policies are issued.*

A combined *marine-cum-erection policy* can be taken incorporating the ocean transit and inland transit risks to the storage and erection portion. *As an alternative, separate policies can be taken for the transit portion and the storage cum erection portion of the risk.* It is usual to incorporate an excess on loss during erection and testing to avoid small claims. The premium rates for marine-cum-erection and marine-cum-storage-cum-erection are tariffed. Projects costing over Rs. 25 crores are specially rated.

Insurance Documents

(1) Letter of Insurance: This is analogous to cover note issued by the broker. It states that particular subjects are placed under insurance and *certificate/policy of insurance will be issued latter on.* It does *not contain full details of the* insurance and *is not acceptable* because the broker acts for the insured and not for the insurer.

(2) Broker's Certificate: This is *also not acceptable as the same is issued by broker, as broker acts for the insured and cannot compel insurer to accept the proposal of insurance; any action for claim in the event of damage to the subjects of insurance would be against broker and not insurer.*

(3) Insurance Certificate: *The insurer issues an open cover or 'floating' policy covering all shipments on certain terms and subject to* *conditions laid down. The insurer furnishes pre-signed blank declaration forms to the insured and insured in turn declares value of each shipment and signs such declaration.* The declarations are now issued in aligned document format with effect from 1.10.1991. *Unless the insurance certificate* gives details of the conditions of cover it is not of too much value to third party who negotiates the shipping documents. *Besides the insurance policy is necessary for filing a claim for indemnity, and the holder* of the certificate may have to secure the assistance of the shipper who retains the custody of the policy to file claim with the insurer. *The document is not generally accepted under letter of credit unless expressly permitted.* The insurance certificate is issued in Aligned Document form as per form given in Appendix 25. II.

Insurance Policy: This is a *basic legal document evidencing contract of insurance between the insurer and insured. It gives full details* of all the risks covered. Marine or transit insurance policies can be assigned by the insured merely by endorsement and delivery.

Insurance policies are issued in different forms like floating policy, open policy or *cover specific policy* etc. *A floating policy* is a contract of insurance for covering number of shipments, the details of which are not finalised when the contract of insurance is concluded. The relevant details like name of the vessel, destination, description of the cargo etc. are therefore required to be declared subsequently and endorsed in the policy. An open cover or policy is valid for a given period of time or is permanently open. As per this policy the insurer undertakes to insure all the shipments for which the details are already intimated to the insurer. *A specific policy covers* specific shipment and such policy is readily available for submitting with the export documents.

Insurance policies can also be classified as per the risks they cover. Accordingly, policies are available in the form of FPA (Free of Particular Average), *WA* (With Average), *All Risks* etc. The *coverage of risks is classified into categories,* A, B, C etc. and the insurance policies are issued accordingly.

When the export is covered under L/C the *insurance document must be as stipulated in the L/C and must be issued and or signed by insurance company of under-writer of their agent.* Cover note issued by the broker is not accepted unless specifically authorised by L/C. Similarly, unless otherwise stipulated in the L/C, the insurance document must be expressed in the same currency as the L/C and shall be effective latest from the date of shipment/taking in charge of the goods.

Seller's Contingency Insurance

Because of statutory regulations prevailing in certain *countries such a Nigeria* where all exports to such countries have necessarily to be on *FOB or C & F basis insurance is to be effected on goods shipped from India* by the overseas buyers with insurers registered in that country. *Under the foreign exchange regulations* prevailing in some countries the sale proceeds on good exported can be remitted only when goods reach the buyers at the destination in sound condition. It is possible that goods may be lost or damaged due to marine peril before arrival of the vessel or before discharge of goods overside the vessel of final destination. *The overseas buyer in that case may not honour the contract and may not negotiate the documents and hence the exporters in India would not be able to obtain the sale proceeds from the overseas buyers.* In that event the insurable interest in the goods will revert back to the exporters in India. Loss or damage to the cargo would remain uninsured since the Indian exporter would not have obtained the insurance as he was not obliged to, under the contract of sale of goods (*i.e.*, F.O.B. or C & F basis). The Exchange Control Manual prescribes that in such cases the exporters in India should obtain *Seller's Contingency Policy in order to protect his interest from any loss of or damage to the goods taking place before the insurable interest passes on to the buyers.* Accordingly, the exporter or shipper in India can avail of a Seller's Contingency Policy covering his interest subject to either Institute Cargo Clauses (A), (B) or (C).

This policy, however, is not negotiable to the overseas buyers and claims under this policy can be paid in India in Indian rupees only.

Types of Risks

Marine insurance differs from many other forms of insurance in that the insured has a choice of a vast variety of risks against which insurance can be effected. In broad categories, the risks that are commonly insured against are:

(1) *Free of damage insurance.* This is a very limited form of insurance and covers only *total* loss of the goods; partial losses are not covered.

(2) *Fire and sea perils.* Under this coverage, FPA (Free of Particular Average) insurance, claims are paid only in case the vessel is standard, sunk, burned, on fire, or in collision.

(3) *Named perils.* This includes the fire and sea perils as explained directly above, and a number of additional perils may be added, such as fresh water damage, hook damage, fuel oil damage, theft, pilferage, nondelivery, or breakage.

(4) *All risk insurance.* This is the most complete coverage commonly written, but it is confined to losses from physical loss or damage from any *external* cause, exclusive of war, strikes, and riots. This coverage does not include loss due to the inherent nature of the goods, nor does it cover market losses due to delays in shipment,

for example, missing the Diwali sales season. If insurance is desired to cover excluded perils, under certain very limited circumstances they can be included in the insurance policy by endorsement, except for war risk insurance, which requires a separate policy.

All of these coverages include general average and salvage charges. Marine insurance is one of the few kinds of insurance where it is permissible, in addition to insuring the value of the goods themselves, to insure profit. While the sales price of goods usually includes the exporter's profit, it does not include import duties or the importer's anticipated profit. In practice a common rule is to insure for an amount equal to all known costs plus 10 percent.

Loss Covered Under Marine Policies

Basically, there are two types of losses under marine insurance policies: (1) particular average, and (2) general average.

Particular Average. Damage to the goods themselves is known as *particular average* and may be classified as follows:

(1) *Total loss.* The amount stated in the insurance policy is paid.

(2) *Total loss of part of a shipment, for example, by theft or pilferage.* The policy pays the insured value of the past lost.

(3) *Repairable loss.* The fender of an automobile is crumpled; it is repaired in the country of importation. Loss paid is the amount of the repair bill.

(4) *Replaceable loss.* The fender must be replaced by a new one which must be shipped by the exporter. Loss paid is the total cost of a new fender, packing, freight, etc.

In all of these situations, the limit of liability, of course, is the face amount of the insurance policy.

General Average. Loss or damage common to the entire venture is known as *general average.* If a voluntary sacrifice is made in face of impending disaster, and that sacrifice is successful in preserving at least a part of the common venture, then all who survive (ship and cargo) contribute pro rata in accordance with the value saved in order to make up the value of whatever was sacrificed.

A classic example of general average loss is by jettison, or throwing overboard certain cargo to save the ship. If 10 percent of the combined value of ship and cargo is thus sacrificed, all owners, including the owner of the jettisoned cargo, contribute 10 percent of their respective values to reimburse for the loss of the cargo that was jettisoned.

More common today is the case of water being used to extinguish a fire. The common sacrifice here is damage to cargo by water; cargo damaged by fire or smoke is not damaged as a result of a voluntary sacrifice and therefore is not subject to general average adjustment.

Classificatiion of Losses

·The various types of losses in marine expert can be classified as below:

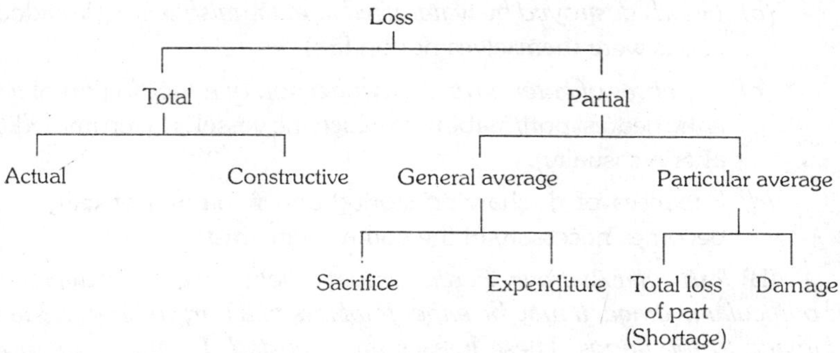

These can be briefly explained as below:

Total Loss: As indicated above this could be either actual or constructive total loss.

Actual Total Loss: This occurs when the *cargo suffers irreparable pysical destruction* and becomes no longer the cargo which was initially insured or where once and for all, the *insured has lost use of the commodity.*

Examples: A ship carrying salt or sugar sinks resulting in the soluble cargo being lost permanently. When a vessel sinks in mid-ocean the shipment cannot be salvaged. So it is permanently lost to the insured.

Constructive total loss: This is also known as *Commercial Total Loss.* In this the *insured loses possession of the goods* and is not likely to recover the same. Even if it can be recovered, the *cost of such recovery will be far higher* compared to the value of the goods after recovery, *e.g.,* if Rs. 1,000/- has to be spent to save the cargo worth Rs. 900/-, definitely it is uneconomical and would be treated as a Constructive Total Loss.

Partial Loss: This is *referred to as 'Average'* in marine terminology. It *could be either a General or Particular Average* depending on the manner in which it happens.

(A) *General Average*: The *principle* of General Average is *very old and dates back to 9th century B.C. This affords idemnity only when losses are incurred voluntarily* — for example, deliberately throwing cargo overboard in an attempt to save the ship from sinking. This loss is brought about to save the ship, freight and other cargo in it. Naturally these saved interests have to share the loss due to which, their safety has been ensured. *This is called General Average Sacrifice.* Insurers are liable for such General Average contributions or General Average loss even under policies issued under I.C.C. (C).

A few examples are:

(a) Cargo jettisoned in an attempt to refloat the vessel.

(b) *Goods destroyed by water used to extinguish a fire* (Provided the goods were themselves not on fire).

(c) *Expenses of entering and leaving a port of refuge* (a port of refuge is the nearest port/harbour to which the vessel is taken immediately after a casualty).

(d) Expenses of discharging storing and reloading of cargo which becomes necessary in the common interest.

(B) *Particular Average: Particular loss other than general average loss is particular average. It may be either total loss of a part such as shortage or damage to the goods.* These lossses are *adjusted* for the proportionate insured value. In the case of damage, a *degree of depreciation is applied* to the insured value to ascertain the loss. If repairs are effected to set right a damage, the actual repair charges are paid. Any frachise or excess stipulated in the policy, is taken into account before the claim is arrived at.

Sue and Labour Charges: These are expenses incurred by the insured or his agent *for the purpose of minimising the loss or damage caused by the insured peril.* They are *payable in full.* These are *paid in addition* to the loss or damage payable under the main policy including a total loss.

Extra Charges: Survey fees, settling agent's fees etc., which are *incurred by the insured to prove the loss,* are paid if the claim itself is admitted.

Procedure and Documentation When a Loss Arises

(a) *Give immediate notice of loss to the insurance company* and/or their agents mentioned in the policy giving the details of loss.

(b) *Ensure that all rights against carriers,* bailees or other third parties are properly preserved and exercised.

(c) If the packages show any outward sign of loss or damage, *insured and/or their agents must call for a detailed survey by ship surveyors on such packages and also lodge a proper monetary* claim on the shipping company for loss or damage found in the packages.

(d) *If the ship survey is time barred then insured and/or their agents must call for an insurance survey on such packages before effecting delivery.* If the packages are found in apparently sound *condition*

but on unpacking any loss or damage is found, insured and/or their agents must *inform* immediately the insurance company and obtain an insurance survey. *Insured should keep the goods as well as the contents with its packing materials intact for inspection by the surveyors for proper assessment of loss or damage.*

(e) In case of *packages which are found to be missing,* insured must *lodge a proper monetary claim* for full value of the missing packages with the shipping company and also with the bailees, and obtain a proper acknowledgement from them.

(f) In terms of Carriage of Goods by Sea Act, 1925, *the time limit for filing suits against shipping companies is one year from the date of discharge.*

The following *documents* have to be submitted in support of the claim:

(a) *Original Policy:* Duly endorsed. This is the document of title establishing the *right to claim*. If the original is not available, *duplicate may be accepted* on the insured/claimant *furnishing a Letter of Indemnity.*

(b) *Copy of Invoice:* This serves the purpose of providing the *basis of valuation* as well as *details of goods despatched.*

(c) *Copy of Bill of Lading:* This would show *in what condition the goods were despatched.* It also contains the *conditions of carriage,* which enable the insurer to decide whether, after paying the claim, he can hope to recover the loss from the carrier.

(d) *Survey Report:* As stated above, this shows the cause of loss, which enables the insurer to decide *whether a loss is payable,* as well as the *extent which determines the amount payable.*

(e) *Letter of Subrogation:* This is a document *supplied by insurers* which transfers the right of insured against the carrier to the insurer, so that he can make a claim on the carrier to recover the loss.

(f) *Copies of Notice to or Correspondence with the Carrier:* As referred to in the Duty of Assured Clause and under the law, the *insured is required to serve notice of damage* on the carrier within certain time limits. *Copies of these are required by the insurers to follow up recovery.*

(g) *Claim Bill:* This sets out the *actual claim:* Survey fees have to be shown as an additional item. The practice is that, if the claim is paid, *these fees are also reimbursed.*

(h) *Other Documents:* Depending upon the nature of claim, the insurers may require certain other documents such as *Bill of Entry* (for imports), *Special Power of Attorney* (for railway claims), various types of *certificates issued by port authorities,* etc.

The following documents, as applicable, are required to be submitted to insurers in support of claims under rail/road policies:

1. *Original Policy* or Certificate of Insurance duly endorsed.
2. *Original Railway Receipt* (non-delivery cases).
3. *A Copy of the Railway Receipt* (damage claim).
4. *Original Consignment Note* (non-delivery cases — Road Transit Claim).
5. A Copy of the *Consignment Note* (damage claim — Road Transit).
6. *Invoice* (original or copy)/packing list/ weight specification.
7. *'Non delivery'* or *'Partial Delivery'* Certificate from the railways/ road transport operators.
8. Open Delivery/*Assessment Delivery Certificates* (rail/road).
9. *Certified* Copy of the Remarks in the Railway Delivery Book (Damage Claims).
10. Certified Copy of the *Remarks in the Delivery Challan* (Road Transit Claims).
11. *Independent Surveyor's Report, if any.*
12. *Copy of:* (*a*) Notice of claim lodged on the carriers (Rail/Road).
    (*b*) Relative Postal Registration Receipts and A.D. Cards.
    (*c*) *Subsequent correspondence* with the carriers.
13. *Letter of Subrogation.*
14. *Special Power of Attorney* (Rail Transit Claims).
15. *Letter of Authority* (Rail Transit Claims).

Duties of the Insured (Preservation of Recovery Rights)

In the case of a claim it has to be ensured by the *claimants that the right of recovery against the carrier is properly preserved.* In the absence of the same, recovery action against the carrier becomes prejudiced. This will adversely affect the right of the insured to claim under the policy. This has been incorporated as a specific provision in the Institute Cargo Clauses (A), (B) and (C) under the heading 'Duty of Assured.'

Insured should insist on a carrier's survey, if they observe any damage to the goods while taking delivery. They should *demand an open delivery certificate* indicating the condition of the goods before delivery is taken. *No clean receipt should be issued to the carrier, when the goods are in an apparently damaged condition.* The *carrier may refuse* to give a Damage Certificate/Open Delivery Certificate. Then the insured or his representatives, should send a letter stating that he is arranging for a survey to be conducted. If the *carrier does not join* with the surveyor insured/claimant should serve a notice on him that the findings of such a survey will be binding on him (carrier). When damage is noticed in the case of an inland transit, the insured must give only a qualified receipt or he can write about the damage upon the delivery challan. Underwriters must also inform the insured of the period within which they have to issue notice of claim against the carrier.

Claims Against Marine Policies

Claims against marine insurance policy when *payable to exporters in India will be paid only in rupees by GIC and its subsidiaries irrespective of the currency of the relative policy.* When claimant is not a resident of India, *claims may be settled in foreign currency provided* GIC and its subsidiaries are satisfied that ownership of the goods lost, damaged, etc., vests in such claimant.

GIC will settle claims in rupees in favour of Indian exporters even in cases where the title of goods has passed on to foreign buyer, if a request to the effect has been made by the non-resident claimant. *In such cases a certificate indicating full particulars of the transaction including number of relative GR/PP form and amount paid in settlement of claim will be issued to the exporter to enable him to obtain necessary approval of RBI for making replacement shipments.*

Insurance Agents and Brokers

Marine insurance may be obtained from an insurance agent or insurance broker. The agent or broker will help to select reliable marine underwriters and arrange the amount and kind of protection that is required. Brokers and agents represent the policy holder and help in the presentation of losses. They often use their experience to make suggestions that lower a firm's losses. Since marine insurance rates are not standardized, but are determined by the risk experience and judgement of the underwriter, the reduction in losses could help justify reduced rates.

There is no proposal form for marine insurance. But for the insurance underwriter to assess the risk, a form known as "Declaration Form" is generally used. Full particulars should be given in the standard form supplied by the company. It is designed to include the following essential details, and be signed by the proponent.

1. The name of the party who effects insurance or on whose behalf insurance is effected.

2. If the payment on account of claims is desired in any foreign currency, it should be stated accordingly.
3. Name of the steamer and voyage. For cargo normally shipped via Suez Canal but not via Cape of Good Hope, a surcharge of premium is added by the insurance company. Rates are applied for the vessels of less than 2000 G.R.T. vessels under "Flags of Convenience" like Librarian, Panamanian, Greek, etc., yield high loss ratio, hence recovery of claim is difficult. Therefore, the insurance underwriter charges extra premium for shipments to Greece, Panama, China, Poland, Bulgaria and East European countries.
4. Strike, riots and civil commotion risks should be included wherever necessary. War/SRCC rates are charged extra in accordance with the rules framed by the Institute of London Underwriters.
5. Description of goods and their packing details should be furnished. Sound packing attracts lower rates.
6. Details of risks to be covered should be given — F.P.A., W.A., W.A. Comprehensive. All Risks, and Inland Transit.

All the above types of insurance cover loss or damage, to the cargo caused by marine perils, *i.e.*, perils of seas, fire acts of thieves and pirates, jettison barratry, etc. Inland transit risks are not covered, unless specifically provided for.

F.P.A. Covers

(Free of Particular Average)

The following losses are covered:

1. If the ship is stranded, sunk or burnt.
2. If packages are totally lost during loading, unloading or transhipment.
3. If the goods are damaged due to fire, collision, explosion or due to ship's contact with any fixed object and/or if the ship is damaged at the port of refuge.

W.A. Policy Covers

(With Particular Average)

In addition to the losses under F.P.A. policies, loss or damage to the cargo caused by heavy weather or sea water, is also covered provided the damage reaches the percentage of franchise specified in the policy. Percentage clause could be deleted at the request of the insured on payment of extra charges. There are numerous non-marine perils also which could be covered under W.A. Comprehensive or All Risks policies.

Extraneous Risks

Due to rapid growth of the international trade and as a result of progressive curtailment of their liability by shipping companies under the terms and conditions of bill of lading, a demand has gradually arisen for cover against many extraneous risks like:

1. T.P.N.D. (Theft, Pilferage and Non-Delivery).
2. Fresh Water or Rain Water Damage.
3. Hook Damage.
4. Oil Damage.
5. Damage by Mud or Acid.
6. Heating.
7. Sweating.
8. Damage by other Cargo.
9. Leakage.
10. Breakage.

All Risks Cover

This is an all embracing cover and includes all the extraneous risks as mentioned above, but does not include War or SRCC Risks. Loss or damage due to inherent vice, or losses proximately caused by delay are not covered.

War and SRCC Risks

Cover is given for capture, seizure, arrest, restraint, detainment, hostilities, civil war, revolution, civil strike or war like operations.

War risks are covered only when the cargo is water borne and for fifteen days on land at a port of transhipment from the date of arrival of the steamer.

Inland Transit Cover

Cover is granted for rail as well as road risks against fire, collision, breakages of bridges, derailment or accident of like nature. According to the rail tariff clause, insurance commences with the loading of each package into the railway wagon and terminates three days after arrival of the train at the destination or on delivery of the goods by railways, whichever is earlier.

Warehouse to Warehouse Cover

This cover is granted on payment of extra premium. No liability is attached to the company in respect of goods damaged or lost while in custody of the transport carrier unless a provisional claim is lodged with the carriers.

Tariff Rates

Some of the voyages are governed by the Tariff, *i.e.*, (1) India to Japan (Cotton); (2) India to Burma; (3) Coastal Ports of India, Ceylon and Pakistan; (4) India to Persian Gulf, Red Sea Ports, Egypt, East and West Africa, Ports like Alexandria, Colombo, Free Town, Indonesia, Pakistan, Red China, or Israel will attract more rate of premium because of the difficult and insecure port conditions. Similarly, commodities like cement, sugar, household goods, second hand machinery, vegetables, bricks, tiles, crockery and bullion or jewellery attract a higher rate of premium.

Types of Policies/Covers

There are three types of policies/covers. These are discussed below:

Specific Policy

Marine insurance policy in respect of individual shipments is issued by the insurance underwriter on application from the exporter giving details of the consignment to be insured, risks to be covered, value for which the cover is required and the name of the country and the currency in which claims are payable. On receipt of these details the insurance company issues a stamped insurance policy in duplicate.

Open Cover

At the outset it should be emphasised that open cover is not a policy. It is a contract for a period of time (usually twelve months) whereby the insurance underwriter agrees to grant insurance during that period not exceeding the agreed limit per vessel with a view to avoiding accumulation of liability in any one vessel or location.

Open Policy

It is cargo policy expressed in general term and effected for an amount sufficient to cover the number of shipments. It covers all shipments of the insured until the sum insured is exhausted. The names of the steamers may not be available when the open policy is effected. Therefore, the company stipulates that the shipment should be made by first class steamer (not over 20 years old) carrying highest class in any one of the classification societies mentioned in clause. Further the vessel should not be more than 15 years old.

CLAIMS

In case of railway claims the consignees should be advised to lodge claim on railways within six months of the issue of railway receipt.

The following documents are necessary in case of marine claim.

1. Policy.
2. Bill of Lading.
3. Invoices.

4. Letter of Subrogation.
5. Survey Reports.

Survey Reports

The following details are necessary in the survey report:

1. Whether packing was sufficient?
2. If not, what improvements are recommended?
3. How claim could have been minimised?
4. Was there failure of insured to protect interest by not taking measures to avoid or minimise loss or not protecting the rights of recovery from carriers/port, etc.?

The Statutory Time Limits for Lodging Notice of Claim and Filing Suits

	Time Limit for Lodging Claim	*Time Limit for Filing Suit*
Steamer	Within the period of *3 days* from date of discharge of cargo from overseas vessel.	*Within one year* from the date of discharge from overseas vessel.
Port Trust Authorities	For "short landing" and "Landed but missing." Within *7/5 days* from the General Landing date (Bombay Port within 7 days of landing). (Calcutta and Madras Ports within *5* days of landing.)	*Within 6 months* from the date of discharge, 6 months from the date of accrual of the cause (Bombay and Madras Ports). *3 months* from the date of accrual of the cause (Calcutta port).

In all cases, one month's notice of intention to file suit must be given.

Notices against the Port Authorities Customs/Carriers must be by Registered Post (A.D.) copies sent to the insurers, to enable them to decide on questions of eventual recovery.

The above are as per provisions of the Indian Carriage of Goods by Sea Act 1925 and provisions of the Major Port Trust Act.

Rail Carriers	*6 months* from date of booking. (As per Sec. 78 B of the Indian Railway Act)	*3 years* from date of delivery or date when consignment ought to have been delivered.
Motor Lorry Carriers	*6 months* from the time loss or damage came to knowledge. (Sec. 10 of the Carriers Act).	-do-
Air International	*14 days* from the date of delivery of cargo.	*2 years* from the date of arrival at destination or the date on which aircraft ought to have arrived (as per Indian Carriage by Air Act).
Domestic	*7 days* from the date of delivery of cargo.	- do-
Non-Delivery International	*21 days* from the date of booking of cargo.	- do -
Domestic	*14 days* from the date of booking of cargo.	- do -
Postal Authorities	*Immediately.*	*3 years* from the date of postal receipts.

9

CLEARING AND FORWARDING OF CARGO

A. CLEARING OF GOODS

The first step toward the import of goods from abroad into India will be to set-up an establishment for importing things and secure recognition from the government as an importer. A person or a firm can import goods only on the strength of an import licence issued by the Controller of Exports and Imports. If the firm imported goods of the class in which it is interested during the basic period prescribed for such class, it will be treated as an established importer. In such cases, application can be made to secure a quota certificate. For this the intending importer furnishes details of the goods imported in any one year in the basic period prescribed for the goods together with documentary evidence including the Bill to Entry/Postal Declaration forms and Customs Duty receipts with relevant invoices and Bank Drafts/Chartered Accountant's Certificates in the prescribed form certifying the C.I.F. value of the goods imported in the selected year. The quota certificate entitles the established importer to import up to the value indicated therein which is calculated on the basis of past imports. In case the importer is an actual user, that is, one who requires raw materials, accessories, machinery, and spare parts for his own use in an industrial manufacturing process, he has to secure licence through the prescribed sponsoring authority which certifies his requirements and recommends the grant of licence. The sponsoring authority for Scheduled Industries borne on the Register of the Director-General of Technical Development have to move through the Director-General of

Technical Development (Technical Cell), New Delhi, and others have to move through the authority prescribed for them. Small industries (with a capital of less than Rs. 5 lakhs) have to apply for licence through the sponsorship of the Director of Industries of the State where the factory is located unless some other authority is expressly prescribed by the Government. For other categories of importers — (*a*) those importing against exports made under a scheme of export promotion, and (*b*) others — licences have to be secured from the Office of the Chief Controller of Exports and Imports. The import licences are usually issued for a period of one year at a time.

Stages in an Import Transaction

The following stages mark the various steps involved in importing goods into India under an import licence and quota:

1. Placing the Indent

The importer places order for the goods he requires, and for which he holds an import licence. The order is called 'indent' and may be placed either directly or through specialised intermediaries called "indent houses". The word "indent" is used for import of goods, according to which two or three copies of the order are prepared and indented. An indent may be 'open' or 'closed'. An open indent is one which does not specify the price and other details of the goods ordered but leaves them to the discretion of the buyer in the exporting country. A closed indent, on the order hand, specifies the brand of the goods ordered, the price at which they are to be purchased, and the details of packing, shipping and insurance, etc. If an indent specifies the price at which goods are sought to be imported, it may give rise to negotiations between the parties. In such a case, the indent incorporating the price finally settled is called a 'confirmatory indent'.

Though one can order goods directly, generally importers prefer to make use of the services of indent houses or Clearing Agents for this purpose. The indent firms or clearing agents serve as middlemen between the exporters and importers and charge a certain percentage of commission from the importer. In India, many of the big indent houses (clearing agents) have their offices in port towns like Bombay, Calcutta, Madras, etc.

The indent houses (Clearing houses) maintain close touch with the well-known foreign firms who send the samples of their products to them. Their salesmen take these samples to the intending importers and book orders from them. The details of the order taken down by the salesmen in their note-books are entered in the indent form. Two copies of the indent form are sent to the importer for his acceptance. The importer returns one of the copies duly accepted and signed to the indent house which then sends a copy of the indent to its agent in the foreign country concerned.

If an importer does not act through an indent house, he may place an order directly with the exporter.

2. Obtaining Foreign Exchange

The foreign exchange reserves of any country are controlled by the Government and are released through the central bank. In India, the Exchange Control Department of the Reserve Bank of India deals with applications for the release of foreign currency. However, an importer is able to get the foreign exchange only from an exchange bank approved and recognised by the Reserve Bank of India for dealings in foreign exchange. The importer has to produce the import licence along with the prescribed form for securing foreign exchange required to pay for the goods ordered from another country. The exchange bank through which the payment is proposed to be routed puts its endorsement on the application form. On the strength of the application and the licence and the exchange policy of the Government of India in force at the time of application, the Reserve Bank of India sanctions the release of a certain amount of the desired foreign currency. This paves the way for the importer to go ahead with the other formalities in connection with an import transaction. It must be noted that while licence is issued by the Government for all imports during the period of its validity, exchange is released and made available only for a specific transaction for which an order has been placed.

3. Arrangement for Payment

After the importer has succeeded in securing the requisite amount of foreign exchange from the Reserve Bank of India, he has to make arrangements for paying for the goods ordered. This may be done through an L/C where it is intended to enable the shipper to obtain payment for the goods immediately on surrendering a documentary bill to a bank in his own country.

Another method will be to request the exporter to forward the documentary bill through his banker to the importer for being delivered to him either against acceptance of the bill of exchange or against its payment. In such cases, when the shipper (exporter) has shipped the goods, he sends an advice note to the importer stating the date of shipment of goods and the probable date when the ship is expected to reach its destination. At the same time he draws a bill of exchange on the importer (also called indentor) for the full invoice value of the goods. Various documents like master document, insurance policy, bill of lading and certificate of origin are attached to this bill. That is why it is called the "Documentary Bill". A Documentary Bill may either be D/A or D/P, *i.e.*, the banker through which it is sent may be instructed to deliver the documents against the acceptance of the bill by the importer or against the payment by him. (D/A= Documents against Acceptance: D/P = Documents against Payment).

The bank's branch in the importing country, or its agent there, arranges for the bill to be presented to the drawee (importer). The attached documents are handed over to him immediately thereafter if it is a D/A bill; in case of a D/P bill, the bank delivers the documents only after the importer pays the amount of the bill on maturity. Generally, indent house is mentioned as the 'Referee in case of need' on the bill. In case, the importer cannot comply with the requirements regarding acceptance or payment, the indent house does so on his behalf.

4. Clearing the Goods

Assuming that the importer has taken possession of the various documents relating to the goods shipped, he will have to comply with the formalities prescribed for clearing the goods. When the ship carrying the goods touches at a port, it is notified in the newspapers and the importer has to secure the release of cargo from the custody of the customs authorities. The first thing for him to do is to obtain the '*Endorsement for Delivery' Delivery or Order* on the back of the Bill of Lading which is the document of title to the goods. The shipping company will make such endorsement only if it is satisfied that the freight has been paid. If freight has not already been paid by the shipper or exporter, the importer will have to make the payment on this score before he can be given a green signal by the shipping company. The importer then presents two copies of the Port Trust Dues Receipt and three copies of the Bill of Entry to the Port Trust Office to obtain clearance regarding dock dues, etc. Thereafter, one copy of the first form and two copies of the second are presented to the Customs Office.

Bill of Entry. The Bill of Entry, drawn in triplicate, attests the fact that goods of specified quantity, value and description are entering the bounds of the country. Separate forms of the Bill of Entry are used for each one of the three classes of good: (*i*) free goods which are exempted from customs duty, (*ii*) goods for home consumption, and (*iii*) bonded goods.

5. Payments of Customs Duties

If the goods are free, no import duty is to be paid at the Customs Office. On dutiable goods, the importer or his agent will pay the import duty which may be specified, *i.e.,* based on weight, measurements, etc. It may be *ad valorem, i.e.,* according to the tariff value or the market value of the commodity or its invoice value.

Payment of customs duty can also be made under the system called the "*Permanent Deposit System*". Under this system, an importer may maintain a running account with the Customs Office and make deposits from time to time. The duty payable on a particular consignment of goods received at the customs is charged to the account and the importer is informed of this.

In case the importer is not in a position to pay the customs duty on the whole of imported goods, he may apply to the customs authorities to get them placed in the 'Bonded Warehouse'. He can then pay the duty on each instalment of goods that he withdraws from time to time.

To save themselves from the botheration of going through all the above-mentioned formalities, the importers may entrust the job to clearing and forwarding agents. In such a case, these agents will take it upon themselves to deliver the goods at the exporter's warehouse. Clearing agents charge commission for their services.

IMPORT PROCEDURE SIMPLIFIED

As per the new Import Policy 1992-1997 Import procedure has been simplified:

(1) Against seven application forms required for import of various items in the negative list only one form will now be required.

(2) Most of the imports are now free from licensing. However, where licensing is required — cases like duty-free imports for export production— considerable delegation of powers has been made to the regional licensing authorities.

(3) Under the new procedure, import licences/customs clearance permits will have validity of 12 months. However, capital goods licences and customs clearance permits will be valid for 24 months. Revalidation may be granted on merits.

(4) Other highlights of import procedures are: grant of licences for certain items of raw materials, components and consumables in the negative list of imports, decentralised application for second hand capital goods up to a CIF value of Rs. 50 lakh to be considered by the regional licensing authorities;

(5) Imports through courier service up to a value of Rs. 5,000 at a time can be made in accordance with the policy.

(6) Licences for import of cloves, cinnamon and cassia to be granted to the extent of 10 per cent of best year's imports in value in any of the preceding 5 licensing years, subject to fulfillment of export obligations. Items qualifying for exports include tea, coffee, tobacco and certain spices.

(7) Dealers of books may be granted licences on the basis of 20 per cent of the purchase turnover for import of fiction and other books.

(8) Import of motor vehicles including tourist coaches and air-conditioning units will be permitted within the entitlement of the licences given to hotels, travel agents and tour operators.

(9) The import entitlement of any one licensing year can be carried forward, either in full or in part and added to the entitlement of the two succeeding licensing years.

(10) A special licensing committee headed by the Director General of Foreign Trade may consider applications for advice on the grant of licence for import of restricted items.

(11) Import of spares for imported motor vehicles and tractors up to a maximum value per year of Rs. 20,000 (for motor vehicles) and Rs. 10,000 for tractors for each imported vehicle can be made without a licence.

(12) Similarly, aircraft spares can also be imported without a licence on the basis of the manual of the aircraft or on the recommendations of the Department of Civil Aviation.

(13) Goods imported without restrictions may be transferred to others. However, in the case of goods imported with actual user condition can be transferred only with the prior permission of the licensing authority.

(14) Import licences issued under various provisions of the policy will indicate the value both in rupees and in foreign currency at the exchange rate prevailing on the date of the issue of licence. No enhancement of rupee value will be necessary if the imports are covered by the amount of foreign currency indicated in the licence.

(15) Authorised dealers of foreign exchange will indicate the value in foreign currency as well as in rupees determined on the basis of the market and official exchange rate in the letters of credit opened for import of freely importable items or the items proposed to be imported against a licence.

B. FORWARDING OF CARGO

Having sent out letters and leaflets, it is necessary to be prepared to answer in a proper manner the enquiries which will be received as a result of these first efforts. No price lists would have been sent in the first instance, and interested parties abroad will ask for these and also for payment terms, and possibly for agency conditions. There will also be requests for samples. The forwarding or export procedure starts right from the time of the registration of the exporter with different organisations. The registration makes it possible for exporter to enter into export business and obtain export orders. In this direction the exporter must obtain a code number from the Reserve Bank of India.

SEVENTEEN STEPS OF EXPORT PROCEDURE

Step I: Receipt of an Enquiry

It is impossible to attend personally to all of these enquiries, as it would not be economical to do so; but there may be several enquiries from one country and all of them asking for sole agency rights. It is of no use in wasting time and money if the enquirer is not in a position to give proper representation or does not have adequate finance to conduct the business or pay for the goods he orders. There will always be a certain number of enquiries from firms which import the same product or products from competitors and merely want to have information to serve their own ends. It is, therefore, important to find out who these enquirers are and what their status is. The best way to do this is to ask the enquirers themselves to supply information about their business, stating

(*i*) Whether or not they already handle any competing products;

(*ii*) How long they have been in that business;

(*iii*) What area of their country they cover for sales purpose;

(*iv*) Whether they intend to purchase goods on their own account or whether they intend to act only as commission agents;

(*v*) What other products they already sell; and

(*vi*) The names and addresses of at least two firms which they already represent or have represented in the past.

If the enquirer is well established, he will be glad to give the information asked for, but if he refuses to do so, than that in itself is fairly good evidence that his intentions are not good.

When the aforesaid information has been supplied, it is advisable to write to the firms whose names are given as references and ask for the following information, giving the full name and address of the party about whom the enquiry is made:

(*i*) How long they have dealt with the party about whom the enquiry is made?

(*ii*) Has the party been their sole agent for the concerned territory?

(*iii*) Does he order goods for himself or does he merely act as a commission agent?

(*iv*) If he orders for himself, does he pay through a letter of credit, through a sight draft or by 30 days or 60 days term draft, or in any other way?

(*v*) If he is allowed to pay through a sight or term draft, it has to be seen whether the party honours draft drawn on him according to the conditions specified therein?

(*vi*) Has the party in the past done good work in promoting sales?

The answers received will show whether the enquirer is responsible and whether he will do business only against a letter of credit. If, however, no information on the score is received, the aforesaid information to some extent may be had from the Indian Embassy or Consulate or from an export promotion council. A banker's reference can also be obtained through the exporter's own bank. However, the references given by banks and governmental bodies are necessarily guarded and somewhat brief and should only be taken into account as an adjunct to commercial references.

The provision of a first class leaflet can often induce a foreign buyer to place at least a trial order without his having first seen the samples. Most buyers and agents will nevertheless still want samples to ensure that the goods match up to their description and illustrations. To send samples to every enquirer is a costly business, especially as samples should always be sent by air, if possible, so that the interest of the prospective buyer or agent is maintained; but to refuse samples to everyone results in lost opportunities. Therefore, the enquirer should be asked to pay for the samples plus the cost of despatch (or at least be asked to pay half of the costs); and if he is really seriously interested, he will do so. The normal procedure is to ask for payment and at the same time promise to refund such payment by credit against the first reasonably sized order. In most cases, where such an order is refused, it may be taken as an indication that business relationships with the party abroad are not likely to be satisfactory.

It must be remembered that during this initial process of investigation, the worth of the enquirer abroad should not be prejudged and that any letter from the enquirer should be promptly dealt with.

The exporter, after having satisfied himself that the enquirer abroad is a fit person to represent him and is capable of meeting his obligations, should provide him with a price list, giving details of the terms of business and payment which he is expected to adhere to.

Step II: Check on Restrictions on Foreign Exchange and Import in Importer's Country

When an order is received, the first decision as to whether it will be filled is based upon the approval of credit. The approval of the order for shipment should also be contingent upon the ability of the customer to secure foreign exchange in those countries where there are exchange restrictions. A list of such countries should be kept, and whenever an order comes in from one of these countries, a special approval on the exchange should be required. This is a matter which naturally does not concern the credit standing of the individual customer but does bear specifically upon the customer's ability to secure the necessary foreign exchange with which to pay for the order when the merchandise is received by him.

The same reasoning applies to merchandise destined for those countries where there are import quotas and import licences. It is necessary, however, to have the information in hand before the order is acknowledged or put into production.

If the exporter is dealing with an experienced importer in a foreign country, the latter will undoubtedly furnish full information with reference to both foreign exchange restrictions and import licences while placing the initial order.

Step - III: Scrutinise the Order

The exporter should carefully scrutinise and check the contents of an export order before its confirmation. It should broadly be in accordance with the 'elements of contract' which might have been conveyed to the overseas buyer, and received along with the duplicate copy duly signed, of the export contract, in case such contract was sent by the exporter. In particular, the export order should be scrutinised on the following aspects.

(A) Terms of Payment: The buyer should have agreed to the terms of payment conveyed to him. Where a letter of credit (LC) has been received, it should provide that:

(*a*) Payment will be available in India. It implies that L/C issued by a foreign bank must be confirmed by Indian bank;

(*b*) Documents stipulated in L/C will be submitted to an Indian Bank in India.

(*c*) Drafts to be drawn under L/C are to be Usance or Sight drafts, and to be drawn on the bank or the buyer.

(*d*) Credit validity period is sufficient for the collection of relevant documents.

(*e*) Payment is permissible according to exchange control regulations.

(B) Documents: What are the documents required by the buyer along with the bill of exchange (draft) to be drawn on him? These documents could be either Master document or

(*a*) Commercial and/or consular invoice and customs invoice.

(*b*) Clean on board bill of lading.

(*c*) Certificate of origin in general, or for availing GSP concessions.

(*d*) Packing list.

(*e*) Marine insurance policy.

(C) Delivery Schedule: It should be in conformity with the exporter's manufacturing/procurement programme.

Inspection Of Goods. The preshipment inspection stipulated by the buyer is to be effected by the Export Inspection Agency (EIA) and/or any other agency.

(D) Packaging: It has to be seen whether labelling/packing requirements are usual or some special type of packing is to be effected.

An exporter has to strictly follow the regulations of both the exporting country and the importing country. The export procedure starts right from the time of the registration of the exporter with different organisations. *e.g.*, EPC or CCI&E makes it possible for him to enter into export business and obtain export orders.

Step IV: Acknowledgement of the Order

Another step in filling the order is to acknowledge it. It may seem pointless to acknowledge an order before the manufacturer or exporter is able to state definitely when or, in fact, whether he will be able to fill it. This situation is one which is likely to arise and to occupy more time in the case of the initial order received from a new customer, because if the customer is an established one, a credit limit would already have been established for him, and because of his previous experience he will understand that he must submit with his order information on exchange restrictions and import licences. Therefore, in the case of old established relationships, the acknowledgement of the order is almost coincidental with the decision to fill it.

The acknowledgement of the order should contain the following specific facts:

(*i*) A courteous acknowledgement of the receipt of the order and "thank you letter".

(*ii*) The expected date of shipment from the factory and from the seaboard.

(*iii*) The price which should, of course, correspond to the original quotation or established price list, and if there is any variation, a sound explanation for the same.

(*iv*) Credit terms under which the merchandise will be shipped. This, too, should correspond with the original quotation.

(*v*) The method of shipment, that is, whether it is by ship, railway, air, parcel-post or any other mode.

(*vi*) Method of packing.

(*vii*) Marks, which will be placed on the package, should be shown in the acknowledgement.

(*viii*) If the shipper must apply for an export licence, a statement to that effect should be made and shipment should be contingent upon the shipper's ability to secure the export licence.

(*ix*) The name of the bank, which will be used for the purpose of collecting the drafts; or if some special bank is preferred for a letter of credit, this fact should be mentioned.

In short, the acknowledgement should contain the essential facts concerning the shipment which the importer should know. It should reassure him that any special instructions, which he may have given, have been properly complied with. It should indicate to him approximately when his shipment may be expected to arrive and through which bank he is likely to receive his documents.

If all of the above-stated information is not available within a time which will enable the exporter to make a reasonably prompt acknowledgement of the order, an interim acknowledgement should be sent simply stating that the order has been received and prompt attention will be given to it, but not committing the exporter to fulfil the order by particular time.

On receipt of an export order from a new customer abroad the exporter should examine the terms and conditions to determine as to what the requirements are in regard to documentation.

The exporter sends a quotation generally C.I.F. The quotation is given in the currency acceptable in the importer's country. A standard contract form may be sent to the importer to give him an idea of the terms relating to payment, packing, settlement of disputes, etc.

Sometimes a *proforma invoice* giving exact specifications of goods and its price and other costs is also sent to give the importer an exact idea of the terms on which the exporter can supply his requirements. Proforma invoice is a preliminary, provisional, temporary invoice covering a contemplated shipment which may or may not be made in future. Such proforma invoices are always made out on the exporter's own commercial invoice forms and contain estimate only and are not intended to have the status of the bill of payment. Proforma invoice serves many useful functions.

Proforma invoice enables the importer to take care of certain requirements before his order can be placed. For instance, importer may first have to obtain an import licence and not being fully familiar with the packing details — some of which may have to be shown on the import licence application — the importer might ask the Indian exporter to let him have a proforma invoice for the merchandise he intends to order. Sometimes the authorities in the importing country insist on the licence application being accompanied by a proforma invoice by the exporter. Another advantage of proforma invoice can be found when a letter of credit is to be established by the overseas buyer. If a proforma invoice is issued by the exporter, it can be supplied to the bank with instruction that the letter of credit be opened in accordance with it. This procedure will help to eliminate some of the common mistakes, *e.g.,* incorrect spelling or description of merchandise, etc.

The proforma invoice takes the form of an offer from the exporter to the importer containing the name and address of the buyer, description of the goods, the price and other conditions of sales, delivery schedule, payment terms, etc. When the proforma invoice is accepted by the importer, it becomes a confirmed order. Customarily, the duplicate copy of the proforma invoice is duly signed by the importer, accepting the conditions therein and the indent or order of the foreign buyer must be received in detail by the exporter, who must specify the particulars of the goods he is willing to buy and he must specify the particulars of the goods he is willing to buy and the price range, etc. An *indent* is an order for the supply of certain goods placed by an importer with an exporter. An export transaction starts with the receipt of such an order by the exporter. The indent contains all the details in respect of the goods required as well as the various instructions regarding packing, shipping, insurance, etc. Indents are of two types, *i.e.,* closed and open. A closed indent contains specific details of everything. In an open indent, some details are found lacking, and further negotiations take place till there is an acceptance of the offer. The proforma invoice could also serve as an indent if the conditions on which exporter has made an offer have been accepted by the importer and it has been sent back to the exporter for compliance. The exporter should strictly comply with the requirements laid out in the indent.

Step V: Arranging the Goods — Export Production/Procurement

As soon as the export order has been confirmed or finalised, preparations are made for the production or procurement of the goods to be exported. The manufacturer-exporter has to raise an internal indent on the production department/division, which may also be sent either to the Works Manager or the Factory Manager. The indent should contain the description of the goods given in the export order, together with a copy of the instructions given by the importer. The other details, such as the date by which the goods must be manufactured, the date by which the necessary formalities must be completed, the date of shipment, etc., are also mentioned. A merchant-exporter has either to obtain the required goods from the market or to get them manufactured from other domestic manufacturers.

Step VI: Export Licence

If the item being exported requires an export licence, the same should be procured by the exporter from the licensing authority, *i.e.,* Chief Controller of Imports and Exports.

Step VII: Central Excise Clearance

The excisable goods can be exported outside India either under claim for rebate of excise duty or under bond. The difference between these two procedures is that in the case of former the duty is first paid and its refund claimed after exportation, and in the latter case the goods are allowed to be exported without payment of duty provided a bond is executed in form B-I (General Security) or form B-I (General Surety).

Before excisable goods are removed from the factory for export, each consignment is required to be presented to the Central Excise Officer having jurisdiction over the factory together with an application in form *AR-4* for claiming rebate of excise duty. When the goods have been removed from the factory, a copy of this application together with the goods is then presented by the exporter to the customs collector at the port who will certify that the goods have been actually exported. On the basis of this endorsement the exporter will claim the rebate of excise duty if he has already paid, or discharge his obligation to that extent in case he has executed the bond.

Step VIII: Apply to Export Inspection Council for Inspection

Exporter should apply to EIC for preshipment inspection. Under the Export (Quality Control and Inspection) Act, 1963, the EIC will depute an inspector for carrying out quality control and inspection of exportable products. After carrying out the inspection, if the consignment is found to conform to the prescribed specification, each package in the consignment is sealed by the inspecting officers. For each consignment declared export worthy, a certificate of inspection is issued by the inspection agency, in which the details of each consignment are incorporated. The original copy of the certificate is valid for the customs authorities, who ensure that only the consignment whose details are given on the certificate is permitted for shipment. The goods are then despatched to the port of shipment and railway receipt is obtained by the exporter. Pre-shipment inspection for export houses and large houses stands withdrawn under the New Exim Policy. However, small units are still subjected to it. Government of India has introduced a scheme to recognise and suitably reward manufacturers who have acquired the ISO 9000 (Series) the BIS 14000 (Series) or any other internationally recognised equivalent certification of quality. Such manufacturers will be eligible for grant of special import licences.

Step IX: Apply for Marine Insurance Policy, if it is a C.I.F. Quotation

As soon as the goods are ready for export, the exporter has to apply to insurance company for an insurance cover/policy as the case may be. Where an insurance policy is insisted upon by the importer, an insurance cover will not do. The policy would be for C.I.F. value plus 10 per cent to cover expenses. The insurance policy should be obtained in duplicate by the exporter.

At this stage all formalities in relation to floor price regulations, Certificate of Origin, Export Credit and Guarantee Cover etc., should be completed.

Step X: Issue Instructions to the Clearing and Forwarding Agent

A detailed note is prepared for the clearing and forwarding agent, giving instructions regarding the shipment of the consignment (*e.g.,* the shipment may be made under claim for drawback). Along with this note, a master document and form of bank guarantee should be forwarded to the forwarding agent.

Step XI: Clearing and Forwarding Agent's Role for Shipping and Customs at the Port

On receipt of the above documents, the clearing and forwarding agent takes delivery of the consignment from the railway road authorities and arranges for its storage in a warehouse.

The clearing and forwarding agent then prepares the shipping bill and presents them along with the above documents to the export department of the customs house. The customs appraiser examines these documents and appraises the value of the goods. If everything is in order, he endorses the duplicate copy of the shipping bill and indicates the extent of physical examination to be carried out at the docks. All the documents, except the GR-I form, the original shipping bill and a copy of the master document are returned to the clearing and forwarding agent for presentation to the dock appraiser.

The clearing and forwarding agent presents the port trust copy of the shipping bill to the shed superintendent of the port trust and obtains a carting order. This enables him to cart the cargo to the transit shed for physical examination. If satisfied, the dock appraiser makes an "out of charge" endorsement on the duplicate copy of the shipping bill and returns it with the other documents.

The duplicate copy of the shipping bill is now presented to the preventive officer of the custom department, who endorses it with "Let Ship" order.

It is then handed over to the agent of the shipping company in token of authorisation by the customs to accept the cargo on board the vessel. As soon as the goods are loaded on board the ship, the captain issues a receipt, known as the "mate receipt", to the shed superintendent.

The clearing and forwarding agent then pays the port charges and takes delivery of the mate receipt, which is presented to the preventive officer, who records the certificate of shipment. This certificate is recorded on all the copies of the shipping bill, AR-4/AR-4A form (original and duplicate copies) and railway freight rebate application (triplicate copy) and returned to the clearing and forwarding agent. The mate receipt is presented by him to the shipping company for the issue of a bill of lading.

Step XII: Documents Returned by the Forwarding Agent

The master document is returned by the clearing and forwarding agent to the exporter at this stage along with:

(*a*) Shipping bill;

(*b*) Original L/C (Contract) Order;

(*c*) AR-4/AR-4A form in duplicate;

(*d*) Full set of clean-on-board bill of lading together with the required number of non-negotiable copies.

Step XIII: Shipment Advice to Importer

An intimation is sent to the importers, indicating the date of despatch of goods and the name of the ship by which they have been sent. The following documents are also enclosed:

(*i*) A non-negotiable copy of the B/L;

(*ii*) Master Document copy.

Step XIV: Presentation of Documents by the Exporter to Bank

The following documents are now presented by the exporter for negotiation/collection:

(*a*) Master Document;

(*b*) GR-I form (duplicate and triplicate);

(*c*) Full set of clean-on-board bill of lading (all negotiable copies plus one non-negotiable copy):

(*d*) Original L/C;

(*e*) Bank certificate in prescribed form (in duplicate);

(*f*) Marine Insurance policy (in duplicate);

(*g*) Export contract/order; and

(*h*) Bill of exchange.

Step XV: Processing of Documents by the Bank

Bank examines the documents with reference to the terms and conditions of the original order and also of the letter of credit. The exporter's bank screens the above documents and sends a set of the following documents to the importer's bank:

(*a*) Master Document (Original copy);

(*b*) Marine Insurance Policy;

(*c*) Negotiable Bill of Lading (original copy);

(*d*) Bill of Exchange (original copy).

The banker sends GR-I form (duplicate copy) to the exchange control department of the Reserve Bank of India. The triplicate copy of the form is sent to the Reserve Bank of India on receipt of payment from abroad.

The banker returns the following documents to the exporter:

(*i*) Original copy of the bank certificate; and

(*ii*) Attested copies of the Master Document

The exporter receives payment against the above documents.

The banker also sends to the concerned Joint Chief Controller of Imports and Exports a duplicate copy of the bank certificate.

Step XVI: Central Excise Rebate

A claim is filed by the exporter with the concerned Maritime Collector of Central Excise for rebate on the central excise duty or for getting credit in his bond account, as the case may be.

Step XVII: Advance Licence/Special Licence

The exporter should file an application to the licensing authority for an advance licence/special licence in accordance with the export-import policy of the country at that point of time.

New Exim Policy — (1992-97) Simplifies Export Procedure

The Government of India on March 31, 1992 notified in the new Hand Book of Export-Imports procedures (May 1, 1992 to March 31, 1997) which has reduced the number of forms and delegated more powers to regional authorities to help exporters and importers by quick clearance.

The 256-page new Hand Book of Export-Import procedure contains simple and transparent procedures which are easy for compliance and administration.

1. Against seven application forms required for import of various items in the negative list only one form will now be required. Similarly, for exports only one application form has been prescribed. Besides, legal undertaking and bank guarantee forms have been reduced to one.
2. Most of the exports and imports are now free from licensing. However, where licensing is required — in cases like duty-free imports for export production — considerable delegation of powers has been made to the regional licensing authorities, according to a press release issued by the Chief Controller of Imports and Exports.

3. For exports — duty exemption scheme (advance licence, intermediate and special imprest licence) — application format has been simplified and the number of enclosures has been reduced to two only.
4. There is now no need to submit copies of applications to various authorities. The regional authorities have been given powers to grant extension in export obligation period.
5. For project exports, the procedure has been clearly defined. These proposals will be considered by the projects committee in the commerce ministry, on production of a copy of the turnkey project approved by Exim Bank, contract documents and an essentiality certificate from a chartered engineer.
6. Export procedures for trade samples have been further liberalised and the value increased to Rs. 25,000 from Rs. 10,000.
7. Moreover, terms and conditions in respect of 46 export items/categories mentioned in Part 5 of the negative list has been simplified considerably.
8. The export obligation in respect of import of second-hand capital goods under the export promotion capital goods scheme as a multiple of the value of the capital goods as given in Para 38 of the policy will be reckoned with reference to the CIF value of the corresponding new capital goods.
9. Applications for grant of special licences by the exporters of TV sets, TV picture tubes and two-in-ones will be made to the regional licensing authorities or to the development commissioners of export processing zones.

Exporting is not always feasible or desirable, even when a firm has a product suited to the needs of consumers in other countries. A company may not be able to export because of the relatively high costs of domestic production and marketing abroad, or because of trade barriers in the foreign market. The cost structure of a firm may be so high that it cannot effectively compete in foreign markets. This high cost may be due to many factors. Competing producers located abroad may have access to lower cost raw materials, components, and labour. Foreign producers may also have higher levels of productivity, lower transportation costs, or a well-established market position. In instances such as these, the off-shore producer may be effectively excluded from the market so long as exporting is relied upon as the primary strategy. The off-shore producer may, however, be able to compete by moving at least part of an operation abroad to a location with lower costs. The long transportation routes and attendant inventory problems also may be reduced by this approach.

Tariffs

Even very efficient producers marketing products in high demand may be excluded from markets by artificial barriers designed to protect local producers or to furnish the government with revenue. The most obvious of such barriers are the *tariffs* established by individual countries or by common markets. A *tariff* is a tax levied on goods entering the market. It may be a *specific tariff assessed per unit of the import, or an ad valorem tariff* based on the value of the imports. It might even be a combination of the two. Regardless of the type, the effect of the tariff is to make imported items more expensive and to reduce their ability to compete with local products. Substantial progress has been made recently in reducing tariffs. The General Agreement on Tariffs and Trade (GATT) has provided a forum for negotiating multilateral tariff reductions among the member nations. Despite these negotiating efforts, however, many tariffs still exist and much effort is still required to lower these barriers.

What is Tariff?

Tariffs or duties are taxes levied on imports. In other words, a tariff is a tax on the goods which one nation imports from another. Many nations use tariffs to protect their own industries from foreign competition. Tariffs provide such protection in by raising the price of imported goods, and encourage people to buy the goods produced in their own country. Governments rarely place tariffs on exports because nations want to sell as much as possible in other countries.

A nation may use tariffs to influence political and economic policies of other countries. For example, a nation may raise its tariffs to protest against tariff increases by others.

Nations fix their tariff rates in various ways. Two or more nations may sign a reciprocal trade agreement to fix tariff rates for one another. Such an agreement may include a most favoured nation clause. This clause requires the countries involved to use their lowest tariff rates on all products when dealing with one another. Nations may also set tariffs by forming a free trade area, a customs union, or a common market. The members of a free trade area have no tariffs among themselves; but they establish a common set of tariffs for non-members. A common market has the same tariff policies as a customs union, but it provides for greater economic co-operation among its members.

Kinds of Tariffs

Tariffs may be classified according to:

(i) The purpose of the taxes;

(ii) How they are levied.

A tariff levied to restrict imports is called a *protective tariff*. A tariff levied simply to raise a government's income without protecting any industry is called a *revenue tariff*.

In some cases, a *revenue tariff* may serve as a *protective tariff*. For example, if domestic and foreign companies both produce woollen sweaters, a revenue tariff might give the domestic firms an advantage. Such a tariff would raise the price of imported sweaters and reduce their sale and thus protect domestic firms.

Through the years, many governments have used revenue tariffs to increase their income. But protective tariffs usually play a more important role in a nation's economy than revenue tariffs.

How Tariff Systems Operate?

A tariff or customs duty is imposed by a government on physical goods as they move into or out of a country. Tariffs have been used extensively as a protective measure against foreign competition.

(i) Specific duties;

(ii) Ad valorem;

(iii) Compound duties.

A specific duty is expressed in terms of amount of money per quantity of goods. If they are imposed on the basis of the physical quantity of an import (so much per ton, per metre, per item, etc.), they are called *specific duties.*

If they are levied on the basis of a percentage of the value of the imported article they are known as *ad valorem tariffs.* Ad valoram duties on manufactured goods are obviously more than specific duties as the cost of import increase.

When a combination of specific and ad valorem duties is used, we call them *compound duties.* These are levied on certain manufactured products on the basis of the weight of the raw material used in them and the value of the finished article.

Tariffs may differentiate among the countries from which imports are obtained. They may, for instance, be lower between countries that have previously entered into special arrangements, such as the trade preferences accorded by members of the British Commonwealth.

Tariffs may affect the economy of the country imposing them in a number of ways. By raising the prices of imported goods, tariffs may encourage domestic producers to increase production. As the expenditure on domestic products rises, domestic employment tends to go up. This is why tariffs are favoured by industries that find themselves hard pressed by foreign competitors. Tariffs may also encourage tendencies towards a monopolistic market structure to the extent to which they lessen foreign competition, with the resulting decrease in the incentive to modernize or innovate. But a tariff by increasing the price of a commodity may also reduce its consumption, depending on how consumers react to the higher price. If enough of them curtail their purchases, the decrease in demand may be large enough in relation to the world market to force down the price of the imported product. This would register as an improvement in the tariff imposing country's terms of trade. In other words, if export prices remained stable, the country would be paid the same amount for its exports, but would pay less for its imports.

In order to facilitate the administration and negotiation of tariff agreements and give international marketers the assurance of uniform classification of their goods, a common worldwide customs nomenclature is necessary. Today, the Brussel's tariff nomenclature, which classifies the thousands of products that move in world trade, has been adopted by more than 100 countries.

Disagreements about Tariffs

Many people believe that tariffs enable a nation to improve its economy. On the other hand, most economists argue that tariffs lower the standard of living in a country by forcing its citizens to pay higher prices for goods. Most economists also believe that tariffs lower the standard of living throughout the world by reducing trade.

Arguments for Tariffs

The supporters of tariffs claim these taxes help provide:

(i) Domestic job protection;

(ii) Aid to industrial development; and

(iii) A strong national defence.

Tariff policies reflect the economic and political conditions in various countries. Throughout history, nations have changed their tariff policies to keep in step with their economic and political goals.

Arguments against Tariffs

There is a belief that tariffs result in:

(i) Higher prices;

(ii) Industrial inefficiency;

(iii) Reduction in trade.

Many economists, therefore, believe that they lower the standard of living of the trading nations.

The advocates of protection often argue that new and growing industries, particularly in less developed countries, should be shielded from foreign competition. They contend that costs decline with growth and that some industries must reach a minimum size before they are able to compete with well-established industries abroad. Tariffs can protect the domestic market until the industry becomes internationally competitive. It has often been argued that the costs of protection can be recouped after the industry has reached maturity. This justification of tariffs is often abused. In many developing countries, industries have failed to attain international competitiveness even after 15 to 20 years of operation; they would not survive if protective tariffs were removed. The infant industry is probably better aided by production subsidies than by tariffs. Production subsidies do not raise prices and, therefore, do not curtail domestic demand, and the cost of protection is not concealed in higher prices to consumers. Production subsidies have the disadvantage of drawing upon government revenue rather than adding to it, which may be a serious consideration in countries at lower levels of development.

Tariffs raise import prices and tend to shift demand from imported to domestic products. They may, therefore, stimulate domestic employment. In developing countries, protection for the purpose of increasing employment may involve a misuse of scarce resources, such as capital and entrepreneurship; but it is defensible if the employment objective is of paramount importance. In trade among developed countries, however, the imposition of tariffs for employment reasons means exporting unemployment to other countries. It, therefore, invites retaliation.

One hypothesis in the theory of trade is that countries tend to specialise in producing those commodities that use relatively more factors of production than they have in an abundant supply. For instance, a country with relatively more capital than labour tends to specialise in goods that require more capital per visit of labour than other goods and to import labour-intensive goods. If, however, imports are restricted by tariffs, production will shift towards labour-intensive industries, increasing the demand for labour, and hence the wage rate.

Economists in developing countries have argued that, in order to attract labour, industry has to pay higher wages than agriculture and that tariffs are necessary to compensate the manufacturing sector for the higher cost of labour. Empirical evidence for such differential wages rates, however, is not definitive, and therefore, the worth of this argument must be evaluated case by case. Another frequently used argument for protection is based on the need for maintaining the so-called key industries that are vital for national defence. Domestic industries can be protected equally well, however, by subsidies. If the objective is to reduce dependence on foreign products tariffs may be appropriate, for they reduce both imports and the total consumption of the commodity in question. But the argument has lost much of its force in a world threatened by nuclear warfare.

A country may be able to use tariffs to improve its terms of trade. But other countries may retaliate; and, moreover, such power is not usually available to many countries over a long period. To the extent they restrict imports, tariffs reduce the outflow of funds, and may help remedy balance of payments deficits. This objective has been important in less developed economies. A serious deficit in the balance of payments, however, calls for a more fundamental treatment, such as the devaluation of the currency.

In advanced industrial nations, tariffs result mainly from the political pressures of producers in particular industries. The costs of such protection are borne by consumers in general. The pressures of special interests on parliaments and legislatures of industrialised countries are far more intense and sustained than the counter pressures from consumers, both in establishing tariffs and maintaining them once they exist.

Measuring the Effect of Tariffs

It is difficult to gauge the effect of tariff barriers among countries. First of all, how import demand responds to change in tariffs depends on a variety of factors. Some of these are:

(i) The reaction of producers and consumers to price changes;

(ii) The share of imports in domestic production and consumption; and

(iii) The substitutability of imports for domestic products.

The responsiveness to tariff levels differs from country to country as well as from commodity to commodity. For one thing, the amount of tariff does not necessarily determine its restrictive effect. For another thing, such comparisons must be restricted to commodities for which tariffs are a major protective device. This is generally true for non-agricultural commodities in developed countries; but other devices are often employed to protect agricultural production. A tariff levied upon imports of raw materials will protect domestic raw material producers but will increase the costs of the manufacturers who use those raw materials. It is necessary, therefore, to distinguish between nominal and effective rates of protection.

One way of measuring effective protection is to take the value added in domestic production, *i.e.*, the value of output minus the costs of materials after the imposition of tariffs and other protective measures to compare it with the value added before protection. The effective rate of protection depends on the share of value added in the product price. Effective rates can be very high if the value added to the imported commodity is a small proportion, or they can be very low if the value added is a large proportion of the total price. Effective protection in one country may be much higher than that in another, even though its nominal tariffs are lower, if it tends to import commodities of a high level of fabrication with correspondingly low ratios of value added to product price.

How to measure the Trade and Protection Effect of National Tariff Systems?

This is very difficult. The most naive approach is to divide a country's custom revenue by the total value of all dutiable imports. This is an aggregative method and seldom gives a correct picture, especially as production costs often differ between countries.

Another approach is to add up all the duties in a tariff system and then calculate the unweighted average. A superior version of this is to calculate an average of all duties weighted by the country's imports of each dutiable product. Thus, if product A had imports of Rs. 4 lakhs it would be given twice the weight of B with imports of Rs. 2 lakhs. This measure retains a downward bias. A high tariff that kept out a lot of imports would have a low weight.

Nominal vs. Effective Tariff Rates

An import tariff duty raises the domestic price of the imported product, thereby encouraging domestic consumers to shift from the foreign good to a domestic substitute. Therefore, the import duty rate, together with demand and supply, determines the consumption effect. A decrease in consumption results from the tariff. Thus, for domestic consumption, effective and nominal tariff rates have the same impact. For domestic producers, however, an effective tariff is the level of protection on the value added component, and it can be markedly different from the nominal tariff rate. A nominal tariff rate is the named duty, that is, the import duty rate. Assume that a country places a 10 per cent tariff duty on certain imports, which are also made within the country. The raw material/intermediate goods required to make the product are imported duty free and cost 60 per cent of the final product value. Then the value added component of the final product value is 40 per cent (100 minus 60). Therefore, the effective rate of protection is 10 on 40, or 25 per cent, which is higher than the nominal rate of 10 percent. The rich industrialized countries, in general, admit raw materials and other intermediate goods either duty free or at a lower rate than finished goods in order to encourage local manufacturers. Therefore, effective tariff rates in these countries are usually higher than nominal rates.

It can be seen from the example that weighted averages are not the best measure of the protection level but there is no suitable alternative measure. The correct measure would be the duty on each category weighted by the goods that have been kept out by the height of the tariff. The previous weighted-average method could be improved if one, instead of using as weights the value of national imports, used the value of world trade in these products. But one cannot use as weights the value of world trade in each product since lack of trade data and lack of comparability due to different custom nomenclature make it impractical to use such statistics.

To determine the actual level of effectiveness, one would be forced to do a product/industry study by sector. This, though, is impractical for all products and industries in so many countries.

Non-Tariff Barriers

Other government regulations and practices may also act as barriers to trade. In some countries, *sales and turnover taxes* are imposed on imports but are rebated on goods destined for export; if such taxes apply at identical rates to domestically produced commodities, foreign goods receive equal treatment. By contrast, *excise taxes* discriminate against foreign goods if they are levied on commodities that cannot be produced domestically.

Quotas or quantitative restrictions may prohibit the import of certain commodities or limit the quantities of imports. Such quotas are usually administered by requiring importers to have licences to bring in particular commodities. Quotas raise prices just as tariffs do; but, being set in physical terms, their impact on imports is direct, with an absolute ceiling on supply.

Increased prices will not bring in more goods. There is also a difference between tariffs and quotas in their effect on revenues. With tariffs, the government receives the revenue; under quotas, the import licenceholders obtain the revenue in the form of the difference between the high domestic price and the low international price of the import. Quotas may be used to protect agriculture, and in a number of developing countries they are used in place, or in conjunction with, tariffs to prevent the outflow of money. Still other barriers include State trading organisations and government procurement practices that may be used preferentially. Finally, customs classification and valuation procedures, health regulations and marking requirements may have restrictive effect on trade.

Nations and companies have begun to seek reductions in other barriers that may be even more significant in their effect on world trade. These so-called non-tariff barriers are common. Their effects are extremely difficult to evaluate and, as might be expected, their diversity makes it difficult to negotiate reductions, though strong efforts are now being made to incorporate these matters into GATT trade negotiations among nations.

The *import quota* is a prevalent non-tariff barrier encountered by exporters. It places a limit on the amount of a commodity that is permitted to enter the country. The quota may be an absolute limit placed on imports so that all imports stop when the quota is filled, or it may be combined with tariffs so that a limited amount enters the country duty free with a higher rate on further imports. *Boycotts* have been employed by governments to exclude goods of companies or countries with whom they have political differences. For example, Coca-Cola and Ford Motor Company were boycotted by Arabs because of their operations in Israel. *Exchange barriers* exist in numerous forms. Importers may not be able to get exchange to pay for their purchase, they may have to pay a premium for foreign exchange used to import luxury items, or they may have to make deposits of local currency long before the goods arrive and the foreign exchange is required. Even more insidious are the myriad of *administrative and legal barriers* involving customs procedures and delays, health and safety regulations, antidumping regulations, subsidies paid to local producers, governmental procurement regulations, and an array of taxes.

Most of the major trading nations, including India, employ a variety of measures similar to those described. Exporters who hope to penetrate these markets must cope with these barriers. Even though effort is made to reduce their significance, there is no hope that they will disappear. It is small wonder, then, that firms also seek strategies other than exporting as a means for carrying on international business.

Codes on Non-Tariff Barriers

A central feature of the Tokyo Round has been the negotiation of multilateral codes of conduct governing various non-tariff barriers. The areas concerned were subsidies and countervailing duties, standards, customs valuation, government procurements, and import licensing.

Countries adhering to the new code will now be prohibited from using export subsidies for industrial products and primary mineral products. Further, the GATT discipline over export subsidies on primary, generally agricultural products will also be greatly improved through a prohibition on the use of export subsidies for products destined for a particular market in a way which will result in prices materially below those of other suppliers to the same market. The code also requires signatory countries to structure their internal subsidy program to avoid having import substitution effects, causing injury to domestic industries of other countries, and to avoid prejudicing the interests of other suppliers to a third-country market.

The code provides for two routes of redress. The first route is domestic action intended to prevent injury to their industry through the traditional means of countervailing duties. The second route provides a multilateral mechanism through which signatory countries can enforce their rights under the codes. The second route would be used, for instance, when a country is losing a share of a third-country market to subsidized exports from another country. In the second route the code provides for mandatory consultation between interested parties. If these parties cannot reach an accommodation through consultation, multilateral procedures to settle disputes would be invoked.

Standards

Several devices have been used in the recent past to exclude exports from foreign markets. Product standards, ranging from permissible auto exhaust emission levels to wine labeling requirements, have been manipulated to discriminate against foreign goods. The purpose of the agreement on technical barriers to trade, known as the standards code, is to discourage discriminatory manipulation of product standards, product testing, and product certification systems. The code would prevent countries adopting new standards without consultation and without considering their import blocking effects. It would require that imports be no more harshly treated in testing procedures than domestic goods and that an importing country accept the exporting one's certification that the goods met the importer's standards.

The code also establishes international procedures by which countries may complain of code violation by other countries, may secure reviews of their complaints, and may ultimately take some type of retaliatory action.

Customs Valuation

The countries of the EEC and many other countries base customs valuation on the relatively simple Brussels Convention of 1950. The US has a different, highly complex system that includes the notorious American Selling Price (ASP) device, which values certain imports, notably benzenoid chemicals, canned clams, tennis shoes, and woollen gloves at the highest wholesale price of the competitive US product.

The customs valuation code lays down new international rules which should result in uniform and equitable evaluation for duty purposes of all classes of trades. This agreement will provide major benefits to exporters by bringing an end to the common practice of customs authorities arbitrarily lifting the dutiable value of goods. The code also requires that the US eliminate the controversial ASP method of valuation.

The primary method of valuation under the new code is *transaction value* which is based on the price actually paid or payable for the imported goods, with additions for those costs, charges, and expenses incurred that are not reflected in the price. A hierarchy of fallback methods is provided for instances in which transaction value cannot be used. Under this hierarchy, valuation is based on the first of the following, whichever can be determined:

1. price of identical goods,
2. price of similar goods,
3. resale price of the goods, with allowances for factors such as profits and costs associated with resale of the goods,
4. cost of producing the goods.

When value cannot be determined by using these fallbacks, customs officials must use other means with the proviso that no method can be used if its results are unreasonable. There are also provisions guaranteeing the right of importers to an impartial appeals procedure; and establishing a dispute settlement mechanism to guard against breaches of the agreement procedures.

Government Procurement

The government procurement issue has been a thorny one. All governments and their satellites discriminate in favour of national suppliers. The Europeans do it through administrative decisions. The EEC has only recently decided that the public sector market should be open even to intra-EEC competition; and even that excludes public works, transport, telecommunications, power equipment and, for the moment, computers. The Americans do it administratively and through buy American legislation that gives local suppliers a preference of 6 percent, 12 percent, or even 50 percent in some instances.

The agreement on government procurement provides for non-discrimination on government purchases covered by the code. This will open a $ 20 billion market which has hitherto been closed to international competition. The coverage extends to contracts valued at $ 190,000 or more. It does not apply to service contracts, except those incidental to the purchase of goods, construction contracts, national security items, or purchases by state and local governments or by entities which have not been specified.

Other Codes

An agreement on import licensing procedures has been made for automatic licensing so as to have no restrictive effects on imports. On certain types of goods where there was non-automatic licensing, government agreed that this would not have any indirect discriminatory effects in addition to the direct effects of the restrictions themselves.

Foreign Exchange Control

Foreign exchange deals with the means and methods by which rights to wealth in one country's currency are converted into right to wealth in terms of the currency of another country. According to Indian exchange control regulations, "foreign exchange" means foreign currency and includes all deposits, credits and balances payable in any foreign currency, and any drafts, travellers cheques, letters of credit and bills of exchange and promissory notes.

Every deal in export trade is a two-way transactions, *i.e.,* the buyer pays the consideration money and the seller receives the value of merchandise sold. Thus, the importer has to arrange for foreign currency (by converting his home currency) through his bank, which asks its foreign branch or correspondent at the exporter's place of domicile for ultimate payment to the exporter. The purchase and sale of foreign currencies take place in two different countries. Therefore, to bridge the gap, there is the need for a foreign exchange market, which plays the part of a clearing house, through which the twin purposes of purchases and sales of foreign exchanges are offset against each other.

Transactions in foreign exchange are effected broadly at four different levels:

(i) Between the banks (which are authorised to deal in foreign exchange, *i.e.*, authorised dealers) and their customers;

(ii) Between the banks themselves in the same market (*i.e.*, inter-bank) at times supplemented by the central banks;

(iii) Between the banks and their branches in different foreign centres; and

(iv) Between the central banks.

The activities in first two levels are, in fact, confined to the local or domestic markets while the dealings at the other two levels are an international plane.

Under the Foreign Exchange Regulation Act (FERA) all receipts from exports and other sources have to be surrendered to the Reserve Bank of India.

Aims of Foreign Exchange Control

The objectives of foreign exchange control are:

(i) To restrict demand for foreign exchange;

(ii) To give protection to industries;

(iii) To maintain over-valued exchange rates;

(iv) To have independent monetary and fiscal policies;

(v) To check the flight of capital; and

(vi) To earn revenue.

If foreign exchange control is effective and if strict measures are taken to implement it, a lot of evasion could be avoided which takes place in our country by way of overvaluation of imports, undervaluation of exports, taking domestic currency while going abroad and retaining foreign exchange receipts in foreign countries over a longer period of time than is ordinarily allowed by the Reserve Bank of India.

Exchange Control Rules Liberalised

(1) Chief executives of export houses, trading houses and star trading houses would now be allowed entertainment expenses up to US $ 5,000 per trip, while the amount for other businessmen would continue at the existing limit of $ 2,000 per trip.

Foreign exchange would now be allowed at a rate not exceeding US $ 300 per day for business visits of up to 45 days abroad, as against the earlier limit of 20 days.

The limits of allowable exchange were enhanced in a few cases further to the RBI's attempt to liberalise exchange control regulations.

(2) The RBI allowed authorised dealers in foreign exchange to release foreign exchange without the RBI's approval for certain purposes.

Foreign exchange for medical treatment abroad would now be released by authorised dealers against medical certificates in prescribed forms from the physician or surgeon. The earlier requirement, of counter-signing the form by a competent authority, has been done away with.

(3) There would be no ceiling on remitting exchange abroad by Indian parties towards legal proceedings in respect of all trade proceedings in respect of all trade disputes.

(4) There would be no limits on remittances for various other purposes, such as admission fees for overseas universities, advertisements, membership fees of scientific and technical institutions abroad, purchase of copyright material and registration fees for conferences.

This would, however, be subject to fulfilment of satisfactory documentary evidence.

Dealers may also allow remittances up to $ 100 per calendar year for gifts from parents to sons and daughters. Other bonafide sundry personal and commercial remittances (except gifts) would be allowed up to $ 300 or its equivalent.

(5) There would be no limit on remitting exchange for meeting the cost of repairs to imported machinery or capital equipment abroad. For repairs to personal articles like cameras, binoculars and watches, remittances up to $ 300 or its equivalent would be allowed.

(6) Foreign nationals employed in India can now be permitted by authorised dealers to remit up to 75 per cent of their monthly net income on a recurring basis, against the earlier limit of 50 per cent on such remittances.

Per diem rate for foreign technicians engaged by the Indian companies has been enhanced to $ 1,000, against the earlier limit of $ 500. This, however, is subject to the condition that the total duration of the technicians engaged by the Indian company does not exceed 12 man-months in a calendar year.

In case the period of engagement of individual technicians exceeds three months, period clearance of the Ministry of Home Affairs is to be obtained.

In the case of engagement of foreign technicians from a firm outside India, the total remuneration should not exceed \$ 20,000 or its equivalent in a calendar year. The earlier limit for this purpose was \$ 50,000.

In case tariffs, quotas and exchange controls fail to achieve equilibrium in balance of payments, a country might be compelled to adjust its exchange rate. An upward adjustment is called revaluation and may be resorted to by a country having a persistent balance of payments surplus. A downward adjustment is called devaluation and is often resorted to by countries suffering from deficit in their balance of payments. As a deficit in balance of payments creates more serious problems, devaluation is more frequently resorted by a country like India having a consistent adverse balance of payments position.

SECTION - II

10

TRADE POLICIES: A BASE FOR INTERNATIONAL MARKETING

International marketing of commodities and goods solely depend upon trade policies or strategies to boost trade by a particular nation or a group of nations, United Nations conference on Trade and Development (UNCTAD), Uruguay Round, World Trade Order (WTO) provided vital boost for trade growth. Very recently, trade liberalisation policies adopted by developing countries, positive trade policies by the developed countries towards the developing countries gave a needful new shape to global trade development. Liberal and outward-looking trade policies can lead to higher economic growth through efficient industrialisation of developing countries. Keeping this view in mind inflow of investment in emerging market economies of Asia, Africa, Latin America and Caribbean nations, succeeded in opening new avenues for market of manufactured goods and services.

Most of the trade policies aim to earn maximum gains of trade by the speed of reforms and their sequencing. Liberal trade policies replaced with equivalent tariffs, reasonable rate of tariffs to encourage entrepreneurs and traders. The liberalisation of capital flow, provided development of manufacturing activities. Such policy has succeeded for improved allocation efficiency of credit and better utilisation of financial resources. Such liberalisation process for trade development is linked with (a) An appropriate exchange rate regime (b) maintenance of fiscal stability (c) floating exchange rate policy used to manage exchange rate regime.

Economists have maintained that complete liberalisation of all markets appear to be vulnerable strategy to boost trade. This has led international marketing process from unilateralism to multi-lateralism. However, it is maintained that the superiority of multilateral trade liberalisation can lead world markets towards trade liberalisation with expanded trade and marketing.

Globalisation process include, trade flows and capital flows, technology flows for expansion of markets. World exports increased from $61 billion in 1950 to $ 315 billion in 1970 and again climbed to $ 3447 billion in 1990. It is estimated that world exports in 1997 were around $5200 billion. The share of world exports in world GDP rose from about 6% in 1950 to 12% in 1973 to 16% in 1992, whereas, this proportion increased for industrial countries from 12% in 1973 to 17% in 1992. Integration of world eocnomy through international trade and rising awareness in international marketing remained the same as it was in the beginning of this century. Therefore, trade policies were framed and reframed in changing circumstances. The past two decades have witnessed an explosive growth in international finance, transaction of tarde in foreign exchange market, rose from $ 15 billion per day in 1973 which increased to $ 800 billion per day in 1998. Investment flows changed the direction from the developed countries to emerging market economies. The principal recipients are China, India, Argentina, Brazil, Mexico and other Asian and Latin American countries. The Uraguay Round of multilateral trade to reshape international trading system. The multilateral regimes for trade related investment measures, trade related intellectual property rights, trade in service are under W.T.O. International trading and marketing process is managed by transnational corporations which are transnational in operation also. A level playing field for direct investment world wide seeking to create multilateral regimes in W.T.O. However, researchers, observed that globalisation process resulted in uneven growth and it can widen the gap between the rich and the poor nations. The benefits of integration within world economy, through globalisation would be in favour of those nations having sound base of industrialisation policies of state would be vital and economies are moving from plan to market.

Exported Growth and Growth-led Exports

International marketing of exports involve export pessimism and export optimism. Economists and marketing consultants viewed that higher the level of export growth is necessarily linked with higher growth of GNP.

Normally, in consumption-oriented growth of a nation, government finds itself in problems such as shift/change of resources from consumption to investment as this act will reduce inducement to investment, whereas export-led growth is free from such problems as investment is export-oriented. Therefore, the rate of growth of a nation is higher with export led growth largely due to higher capital formation and rising share of manufacturing in the growth of output. Agriculture-demand-led industrialisation as an alternative to export-led growth and industrialisation to boost structural changes.

Marketing managers will have to seek new potential market in these countries, so as to earn benefits of economies of scale in international marketing which is suited to marketing managers of the developing countries.

Similarly, strategy of growth-led expenses reveals technological advancement under which manufacturing sector will go under thorough changes. Efficient corporates can face global competition to earn advantage of international export marketing. This means, countries having higher ratio of growth can successfully hunt international markets largely due to technological growth which may lead to cost reduction in manufacturing with quality of services. Moreover, higher rate of growth to the developing countries allow them to invest in technological upgradation in manufacturing through rising capability for investment in technology.

Import-led Growth:

There are countries having philosophy to build infrastructure and to achieve growth by imports. Developing countries need to build up infrastructure like, roads, railways, power, water, drainage and sanitation facilities. International marketing practices can be enlarged in these countries largely due to rising opportunities of investment in such critical projects.

Theory of Strategic-Trade Policy:

The theory holds the view that significant imperfection in the product markets and factor markets create monopolistic and oligopolistic market structure in product markets to generate profit above normal profits then, trading country will have to suitably design appropriate policy interventions to use longer share of profits to improve national welfare.

The Theory of Strategic trade policy is some sort of reincarnation of earlier theories to protect trade of home industries. Thus, the theory involve proper sectoral targetting, proper timing, sequencing and proper choice of subsidies, Taxes and protectionist policies. The common denominator of this policy is interventionism that the industries are induced to be engaged in an investment race aided by the government policy. Industrial risk is minimised by the governance support. It is visualised that the nature of policy intervention was "market-conforming" and not "market-regressive." Experience shows that state intervention being highly market regressive has miserably failed and it was targetted to specific sectors. The protection of domestic market and tax enforcement of the anti-trust statutes are supposed to significantly boost industrial and market structure.

World Development Report (1996) viewed that trade policy reform and performance of trade are highly associated. Rapid liberalisation in trade pays off in the case of newly independent states which removed restrictions on exports and quantitative restrictions on import. It helped to reorient trade, quality standards and boosted hand currency revenues. Export growth was necessarily linked with higher GDP growth rate. Thus, export performance has been phenomenal.

Similarly, slow trade liberalisation imposes high costs, administrative controls kept domestic prices below world prices. Tight-export control sought to prevent producers from selling subsidised goods abroad. Exporters had to surrender foreign exchange earnings at below market exchange rates. Non-transparent reference price system continued to restrain exports below a minimum price, encouraging rent seeking corruption and decline in exports.

11

INTERNATIONAL TRADE AGREEMENTS AND AGENCIES FOR PROMOTING INTERNATIONAL CO-OPERATION

(A) GATT (GENERAL AGREEMENT ON TARIFFS AND TRADE)

GATT is a multilateral treaty between governments that lays down rules for international trade. Its basic objective is to liberalise world trade. The most fundamental principles of GATT is non-discrimination between the contracting parties. GATT contains rules relating to tariffs, quantitative restrictions, trade measures for balance of payment purposes, export subsidies, anti-dumping and counter-vailing duties, customs valuations, state trading etc. Special provisions have been made for few developing countries. GATT also provides a forum for dispute settlement among member countries.

When GATT was concluded by 23 countries at Geneva in 1947 (to take effect from January 1, 1948), it was considered an interim arrangement pending the formation of a UN agency to supersede it. When such an agency failed to emerge, GATT was amplified and further enlarged at several succeeding negotiations. It has since proved to be the most effective instrument of world trade liberalisation.

In short, GATT is an international agreement to reduce trade barriers among member countries. The GATT is really a code of conduct to which members, called the contracting parties, subscribe. Since it was signed in 1947, it has become the chief international agreement on world trade.

The GATT deals with a wide range of commercial policies. The contracting parties meet from time to time to negotiate the removal of barriers to international trade. They also review complaints against violations of GATT rules. These meetings have reduced tariffs and other trade obstacles on thousands of products. GATT rules specify that a party granting a trade advantage to one country must grant the same advantage to all the contracting parties. The rules limit the use of import quotas and other restrictions on the flow of goods among GATT nations. The GATT grants special privileges to developing nations without requiring these nations to observe all the GATT rules.

GATT includes a long schedule of specific tariff concession^ for each contracting nation, representing tariff rates that each country has agreed to extend to others. It sets forth the general rules that are, in effect, a code of commercial policy. They provide for unconditional most favoured nation clauses (which guarantee to other GATT countries the extension of any tariff concessions granted to non-GATT countries), elimination of quantitative trade restrictions, uniform customs regulations, and the obligation of each contracting nation to negotiate for tariff cuts upon the request of another. An escape clause allows the contracting countries to alter agreements if their domestic producers suffer excessive losses as a result of trade concessions. The countries which are members of a customs union or free trade area are permitted to grant preferential tariff rates to each other; the resulting external tariffs of such unions, however, cannot be greater than the average of all the tariffs of those countries prior to the formation of the unions.

Trade Ministers of 124 governments, on April, 15, 1994, signed a historic pact, which embodies the results of Uruguay Round of multilateral trade negotiations and paves the way for setting up of the World Trade Organisation (WTO) with effect from January 1, 1995. The Ministers also adopted, what is being describe, the Marrakesh Declaration, which veriterates their commitment to the new multilateral trade framework envisaged under the Uruguay Round Final Act.

The signatories which included Government of India gave their approval to about 20 decisions accompanying the Uruguay Round Final Act. These relate to various issues that will be taken up for discussion and debate at various forums in the coming matters.

The 20 decisions adopted by ministers include one on defining the relationship between the IMF and the WTO, one of outlining steps to neutralise the possible negative effects of the reforms programme on least developed and net food-importing developing countries, one on notifying the action to be taken by developed countries on integrating textiles into the multilateral framework, one on the proposed understanding on WTO-ISO standards information system and one on discussing the problem of circumventing anti-dumping measures.

Several other decisions were taken by the trade ministers. These included:

* Decision regarding cases where customs administration have reasons to doubt the truth or accuracy of the declared value;
* Decision on texts relating to minimum values and imports by sole agents, sole distributors and sole concessionaires;
* Decision on institutional arrangements for the general agreement on trade in services;
* Decision on certain dispute settlement procedures for the general agreement on trade in services;
* Decision on trade in services and the environment;
* Decision to hold negotiations on movement of natural persons;
* Decision on monitoring progress of talks on trade in financial services; and,
* Decision on starting talks on maritime transport services basic telecommunications and professional services.

The Declaration welcomed the stronger and clearer legal framework of the Uruguay Round, global reduction by 40 per cent of tariffs, wider market-opening agreements on goods and the establishment of multilateral framework of disciplines for trade in services and for protection of trade-related intellectual property rights in agriculture, textiles and clothing.

The ministers expressed their determination to resist protectionist measures and agreed to undertake, with immediate effect and until the entry into force of WTO, not to take any trade measures that would undermine or adversely affect the Uruguay Round results. They also resolved to enhance cooperation between WTO, the IMF and the World Bank.

The Declaration dwelt on the role of developing countries in making the Uruguay Round a success and agreed to review regularly the impact of the Uruguay Round results on the least developed countries and the net-food importing developing countries. The need for WTO to provide such countries with technical assistance was also recognised.

The ministers bound themselves to ratify the WTO agreement in such a manner that it could enter into force by January 1, 1995 or as early as possible thereafter.

The following are the main elements of the Final Act:

Market Access: This is the backbone of the act.

Countries have pledged to cut tariffs on industrial and farm goods by an average of about 37 per cent.

The US and the European Community have agreed to trim tariffs between them by one half.

Services: For the first time, rules will govern an estimated $4 billion in annual trade in services like banking, insurance and travel, as well as the movement of labour.

However, only minimal market liberalisation commitments were made.

This was largely because Washington and Brussels could not iron out disagreements over audio-visual products like television programmes and films, financial services and shipping.

The US reserves the right to deny other countries favourable access to the lucrative US financial services market, but will hold off for at least 18 months.

Washington has threatened to challenge EC curbs on audio-visual goods.

Countries could demand an exemption from the obligation to offer Most Favoured Nation (MFN) treatment to service trade partners.

Agriculture: Also, for the first time, agriculture has been folded into the GATT.

The blueprint is the 1992 Blair House accord reached between the US and the EC, as amended in talks last December. The accord:

(*a*) Converts all non-tariff barriers, like quotas, into tariffs, which are reduced by 36 per cent for industrialised countries and 24 per cent for poor nations.

The cuts will be implemented over six years for rich countries and 10 years for others.

(*b*) Forces countries with closed farm markets to import at least 3 per cent of domestic consumption of the product, rising to 5 per cent over six years.

Japan will import 4 per cent of its rice, rising to 8 per cent.

South Korea will import 1 per cent of its rice, rising to 2 per cent in 1999.

Cuts trade distorting support for farmers by 20 per cent over six years in rich countries and 13.3 per cent for the developing world.

Cuts the value of direct export subsidies by 36 per cent over six years and volume by 21 per cent.

The base period is 1989-90, or 1991-92, if exports were higher in that period.

Exempts the poorest nations from farm reforms.

Textiles: Import quotas on textiles and clothing, in place under the Multi-Fibre Arrangement (MFA) since 1974, will be phased out over 10 years.

Anti-Dumping: Rules on anti-dumping — imports priced below their value in the domestic market — have been clarified.

Intellectual Property: The treaty toughens up protection for patents, copyrights, rights of performers and producers to sound recordings, trade-marks, and labels of origin.

Expanding GATT: Set up as a temporary body in 1947, the GATT will be transformed into a permanent watchdog, called the World Trade Organisation (WTO), with status equal to the International Monetary Fund and the World Bank.

The WTO will start operations between January and July next year. GATT has created a new multilateral trading system slashing tariffs by up to 40% in the biggest package of market access concessions ever negotiated. The Marrakesh Declaration include agreements on the establishment of the preparatory committee for the World Trade Organisation (WTO), acceptance of the agreement establishing the WTO as well as pacts on trade and environment, and organisational and financial consequences following from the setting up of the WTO. The Marrakesh Declaration calls for common action on the trade front with no retaliatory measures till the establishment of the WTO in January 1995.

The deal will lead to the replacement of GATT by the WTO in 1995. The WTO will oversee a comprehensive set of rules and disciplines covering every aspect of world commercial, including trade in services and intellectual property protection. In addition it will have a dispute settlement system to ensure adequate redress for bilateral trade problems. The most important decisions will be the one concerning the establishment of the preparatory committee (PREPCOM) for the WTO. All the existing members of GATT would be members in this body that would draw the outline for the WTO. The Prepcom, which will arrive at decisions by consensus, will deal with the social clause issue for the first time in multilateral trading system; there will be general agreement on trade in services which will open up commercial activity worth up to $ 3,000 billion a year.

GATT also establishes new rules for the protection of intellectual property besides bringing textiles and clothing within the framework of multilateral trading system. Apart from ratification of final act of Uruguay Round, five plurilateral agreements, which constituted part of GATT, were also signed. India is, however, not a signatory to plurilateral agreements as it has not taken any decision to join it so far.

The Prepcom will deliberate at Geneva in the coming months on together social policy issues like labour standards and immigration policies, be linked to trade policy or not.

Whatever may be the intensity of the forthcoming battle, there is now no uncertainty about WTO becoming the apex institution for world trade, almost on par with the Bretton Woods institutions such as the World Bank and the IMF. The challenges before WTO are indeed daunting. It has its task cut out: making sure that GATT members fulfil their promise of reducing subsidies on agriculture; ensuring that the new treaty on patents and copyrights is honoured; enforcing the opening up of textile markets over the next 10 years as per the accord, and clamping down on abuse of anti-dumping laws in member nations.

Quite apart from this, the WTO will have to start negotiations on financial services where member countries are yet to arrive at an agreed framework; basic telecommunication services, where many countries are reluctant to end public sector monopoly; and shipping services. All these will be a difficult job for the WTO.

The lifting of all restrictions on Indian handloom exports to the USA removes the major stumbling block to the resumption of negotiations on textiles between the two countries.

However, the signing of the historic Uruguay Round trade agreement in Marrakesh marks the beginning, not the end of bitter trade disputes in the world. There would be disputes between the US and other countries like Japan, China and Europe, and between developed and developing countries. Now there would be move than five billion people competing for their share in the international trade, and that makes conflict all the more inevitable. It may again be pointed out that thing would have been still worse but for the Uruguay Round. The world would have been carved into spheres of influence, or regional trade blocks, which ultimately would have proved self destructive. It may be concluded by saying that for India after signing Uruguay Round trade agreement that there is now a sense of shared dissatisfaction.

(B) UNCTAD (UNITED NATIONS CONFERENCE ON TRADE AND DEVELOPMENT)

The United Nations Conference on Trade and Development (UNCTAD) was established by the U.N. General Assembly in 1964. The ma function of the UNCTAD is to promote international trade with a view to accelerating economic development and to formulate principles and policies on international trade and related problems of economic development. UNCTAD is the principal instrument of the General Assembly for deliberations and negotiations in the field of international trade and development and related issues of international economic cooperation. The activities of UNCTAD cover a wide area which include trade in commodities, trade in manufactures, invisibles and financing related to trade, transfer of technology, shipping and economic cooperation among developing countries.

The less developed countries contended that the terms of international trade were against them. They complained that the prices of the manufactured goods they had to import from industrialised countries were high, whereas the prices of the primary commodities that they produced for export were low, thus frustrating their efforts to achieve a rapid growth. Although they became parties to the General Agreement on Tariffs and Trade (GATT), they were critical of it, insisting that more was required than the application of the Most Favoured Nation principle and the mere reduction in tariff. They demanded a conference to consider means for the removal of obstacles to the trade of developing countries. A United Nations Conference on Trade and Development (UNCTAD) met in Geneva in the early months of 1964, chiefly to consider the trade needs of the developing countries, and came to the following decisions:

(*i*) A continual United Nations Conference on Trade and Development to promote international trade, especially with a view to accelerate economic development;

(*ii*) A Trade and Development Board, composed of 55 members, to be elected by the Conference;

(*iii*) A permanent and full-time secretariat, and a secretary-general to be appointed by the UN Secretary-General with the confirmation of the General Assembly.

The UNCTAD has proposed a variety of means, such as agreements on commodity trade and tariff rates favouring the exports of developing countries.

We may, therefore, say that main purposes of UNCTAD are:

(*a*) To promote economic development through international trade;

(*b*) To formulate new principles and policies in international trade and related economic fields; and

(*c*) To negotiate multilateral trade agreements.

The *major activities* of UNCTAD include:

(*i*) Research and support in connection with the negotiation of commodity agreements;

(*ii*) Technical elaboration of new trade schemes, such as a new import preference system; and

(*iii*) Various promotional activities designed to assist developing countries in the area of trade capital flows.

UNCTAD has no direct official relationship with individual business firms.

The UNCTAD comprises all members of the United Nations as well as states which do not belong to the United Nations but are members of one or more specialised agencies. UNCTAD considers a wide range of problems relating to trade, aid and related areas.

In the trade field, one of the UNCTAD's principal tasks has been to secure remunerative, equitable and stable prices for primary products of export interest to developing countries. Securing improved access by the elimination of tariff and non-tariff barriers to trade is another important objective.

On the positive side, it should be recognised that UNCTAD succeeded in launching the Generalised System of Preferences (GSP) in 1970 by most of the developed countries — designed to give developing countries wider export opportunities for their manufactured products. This represented, perhaps, the only important advance in that the UNCTAD had been able to secure implementation of an important principle, deviating from the GATT's original principles relating to strict reciprocity and the Most Favoured Nation treatment in international trade matters.

Another important matter which has received UNCTAD's attention, is the promotion of trade among countries having different economic and social system such as the East-West trade, as well as the expansion of trade between developing countries and socialist countries of Eastern Europe and Asia.

In the past UNCTAD had a number of achievements to its credit. For example, the Generalised System of Preferences under which tariff perferences are being granted by the developed to the developing countries is the result of a decision taken in UNCTAD in 1968. In 1974, the convention on a Code of Conduct for Linear Conferences was adopted which seeks to promote an equitable balance of interests between shippers and shipowners and between traditional shipowners in developed market economy countries and new shipowners in developing countries. In 1976, the Integrated Programme for

Commodities was launched in UNCTAD with the objective of dealing with price instability and other problems faced by primary commodities exported by developing countries. The Common Fund is the key element of the Integrated Programme and is intended to assist in the financing of buffer stocking as well as financing of other measures such as research and development, market promotion, etc., under international commodity arrangements. The agreement on Common Fund was reached in June 1980. The other achievements of UNCTAD include the agreement on the set of Multilaterally Agreed Equitable Principles and Rules relating to Restrictive Business Practices in 1980 and the Convention of Conditions for Registration of Ships in 1986.

The policy guidelines for UNCTAD are laid down at the Session of the Conference which generally takes place every four years. So far eight conferences have been held.

As in the recent years, various negotiations in UNCTAD have made little progress and the stalemate continued. In the area of commodities, since the launching of the Integrated Programme only three new international commodity arrangements, *viz.*, rubber, jute and tropical timber have been concluded. Efforts to conclude international commodity arrangements for tea, iron ore, cotton, hard fibre, vegetable oils, etc., have not succeeded so far. It has also not been possible to evolve measures to secure for developing countries a greater share in the processing, marketing and distribution of primary commodities. In the meanwhile prices of primary commodities continued to be depressed having serious implications for developing countries significantly dependent on commodity exports. Negotiations for the establishment of an International Code of Conduct for Transfer of Technology and further improvement of the set of Agreed Principles and Rules relating to Restrictive Business Practices have not yielded any result.

UNCTAD VII provided an opportunity to discuss the problems confronting developing countries in the area of trade and development and to arrive at international policy measures to seek solutions to the problems. The subjects discussed were financial resources for development, commodities, international trade and the problems of the least developed countries.

Economic Co-operation among Developing Countries (ECDC)

The developing countries are becoming increasingly aware that trade and economic co-operation among themselves could be a powerful mechanism to promote their economic development and collective self-reliance. The importance of such co-operation is enhanced on account of the current environment of protectionism which has been seriously impeding their export efforts. Trade preference agreements have been one of the major instruments for expanding trade and economic links among developing countries. There are already a number of such trade preference agreements. The agreements of which India is a member are: (*i*) The Trade Expansion and Economic Co-operation Agreement between India, Egypt and Yugoslavia (popularly known as the Tripartite Agreement), (*ii*) the Bangkok Agreement; and (*iii*) GATT protocol relating to preferential Arrangement among developing countries.

The most significant step taken by developing countries for expanding mutual trade and economic co-operation was the launching of the first round of negotiations under the Global System of Trade Preferences (GSTP) at the ministerial level meeting held in Brasilia in May 1986. It may be recalled in this connection that a ministerial level meeting of developing countries was convened in New Delhi in July, 1985 with a view to providing political thrust to GSTP which enabled the completion of the preparatory process and paved the way of commencing the negotiations. The ministerial meeting held in Brasilia adopted the Agreement on GSTP which provided the legal framework for the conduct of the negotiations. According to the time frame agreed upon the negotiations in principle were to be concluded by September 1987. About 60 developing countries, including India had notified their intentions to participate in the negotiations. India has also submitted its request lists for trade concessions on other participating developing countries.

Recent years have witnessed yet another important development in the area of trade expansion among the developing countries themselves. The special treatment to be extended to the least developed countries is entirely due to the efforts made by UNCTAD.

Several initiatives have been taken in the field of development such as aid, debt explosion, shipping and technology, but it cannot be said that much success has been recorded as a result of these initiatives.

The regional groups, which make up UNCTAD, utilise a consensus-formation process of negotiations to alleviate adverse economic conditions in major areas of concern to the LDCs. UNCTAD's agenda has, therefore, included, over the years, a plan for a "New International Economic Order" (NIEO), liberalised trade policies towards the LDCs, attempts to stabilise commodity prices, a means to finance the external debt of Third World Countries, and proposals to improve the terms of trade of LDCs, in general.

According to the Brandt Commission, UNCTAD has become a principal forum for important international debates and negotiations for change in world economic system. Unlike GATT, it has universal membership. The developing countries raised their major proposals for restructuring and reforming of UNCTAD.

Whatever is debated and negotiated in UNCTAD may have to be implemented by other international agencies like IBRD, IMF and UNIDO.

However, one cannot but feel that the results achieved are not commensurate with the efforts put in. The theme of UNCTAD all along has been commodities, trade, money and finance. This has to be made meaningful in reality.

Problems and Failures of UNCTAD

(1) UNCTAD has had problems from its inception, which have kept the organisation from being fully effective in achieving its objectives. It has been dominated by two organisational problems: the UN-type grouping which permeates most UN agencies and the overbearing role of the Group of 77. UNCTAD's membership is broken down into four diverse groups, only two of which have much in common. Thus, vested interests of each of the major political-economic classifications create so much friction that the rule-by-consensus method of negotiating issue results in few concrete accomplishments.

(2) Very often, the socialist governments support Group of 77 resolutions. The resolutions may be passed by votes, for example, of 120 or so in favour to one dissenting vote (usually the United States) but the financial support for most of the major issues debated in UNCTAD conferences must come from the developed nations. Thus, a stalemate occurs.

(3) In addition, UNCTAD, as stated in the introduction, lumps all poor nations in the same boat. This may result in viewpoints, which become splintered or confused because of wide diversity within groups.

UNCTAD's record has had mixed results. Some successes can be identified. Some limited success in the commodities area has come from UNCTAD debates. At least two agreements to stabilise prices, those for sugar and cocoa, have come from UNCTAD. The organisation has gained acceptance from ICs for the Generalised System of Preferences whereby developed nations give a preferential rate of duty for their exports. UNCTAD also negotiated a Code of Conduct for Linear Conferences and had had some limited success in the monetary reform and trade negotiations areas.[1]

(4) UNCTAD has, on the other hand, failed to adopt or implement a trade policy for development—in short, the New International Economic Order in which the worldwide economic system will be restructured on a grand scale. This proposal appears to have gone too far for both the industralised and socialist nations.

(5) UNCTAD seems to be an international organisation which, rather than do a proper job with short meetings and a clear focus of its objectives

1. Gamani Corea, "Commodities — A Key Issue at Nairobi Conference: Long Neglected Area Needs to be Rectified", *United Nations Monthly Chronicle,* Vol. 13 (April. 1976). p.47.

and international realities, appears to be among those institutions which "huff and puff for weeks while revealing their own importance."[2] It would seem that UNCTAD ranks high among the huffers and puffers.

These problems could be alleviated. UNCTAD was given no executive powers in 1964 when it began operations. It undertakes no projects or advisory work, as does the UN Development Programme. GATT and the IMF are already performing some of the same functions which UNCTAD has been doing. Finally, UNCTAD seems to take a Don Quixote attitude to world economic problems, *i.e.*, it looks at global issues when many if not most of the LDC's economic problems stem from domestic policies. In the 1983 report by UNCTAD to the delegates, only four of 123 paragraphs were devoted to domestic policies. UNCTAD tends to ignore these problems.

It has been recommended that UNCTAD should narrow its agenda to one narrow goal, *e.g.*, commodities, and/or spend more time on domestic economic policy issues. Or if it desires to retain its focus on a full range of issues, it should abandon its executive ambitions. In other words, it should be a catalyst to cajole countries and international agencies into adopting development objectives. At the present time UNCTAD, regardless of its few successes during the first two decades, meets neither recommendation.

UNCTAD which is now composed of over 120 member states assumes importance since it affords an opportunity to the majority of developing countries to firm up their stand on vital issues before the Uruguay Round.

The dual challenge of the process is to attract the full adherence of stronger trading partners, whose autonomous actions can undermine the system and to make the system more responsive to the needs of the weaker partners. A positive outcome, which meets this challenge will be a decisive blow against protectionism and possible fragmentation of the trading system and will counter recessionary tendencies in the world economy.

The implementation of the commitments contained in the final act of UNCTAD VII to advance structural adjustment as well as halt and reverse protectionism will have to be intensified. UNCTAD VIII was held in Columbia in February, 1992. The broad scope of the Uruguay Round called for a coherent and integrative approach, supportive of national development efforts.

(C) INTERNATIONAL TRADE CENTRE (ITC)

The ITC is of particular interest to developing countries, for it has been set up to help these countries to promote their exports. To achieve this objective, the ITC engages in two major activities:

2. "Uncreative UNCTAD", *The Economist*, Vol. 287 (11 June 1983), p.14.

(*a*) It collects and disseminates information on potential markets and on marketing techniques that will be successful in these markets; and

(*b*) It trains export promotion personnel, and assists governments in developing adequate export promotion services. To carry out this activity, the ITC created a special section in mid-1966, known as TPAS (Trade Promotion Advisory Services).

TPAS suggests to the developing countries how to use successfully such promotion methods as export credit and insurance, trade fairs and exhibitions abroad.

(D) WORLD BANK

International Bank for Reconstruction and Development (IBRD)

This is popularly known as the World Bank. It has its origin in wartime preparations for post-war international financial and economic cooperation that culminated in the United Nations Monetary and Financial Conference which was held in July, 1944, at Bretton Woods, New Hampshire, and attended by 44 nations. The principal purposes of the World Bank, set forth in its articles of agreement (charter), are:

(*i*) To assist in the reconstruction and development of its member countries by facilitating the investment of capital for productive purposes, thereby promoting the long-range growth of international trade and improvements in standards of living;

(*ii*) To promote private foreign investment by guarantees of, and participations in, loans and other investments made by private investors; and

(*iii*) When private capital is not available on reasonable terms, to make loans for productive purposes out of its own resources or the funds borrowed by it.

The World Bank came into existence on December 27, 1945, when its articles of agreement were signed by 29 governments in Washington, D.C. By 1972, the Bank had 119 members. The largest of these, in terms of capital subscribed, were the USA, the UK, West Germany, France, India, Canada and Japan. Among the bank members are many other countries, such as Iceland, Israel, Lebanon, Sri Lanka, Indonesia, Afghanistan, Libya, Lesotho, Somalia, Ghana, Yugoslavia, and all the Latin-American republics, except Cuba.

The World Bank's charter authorises it to engage in the following types of financing:

(*a*) It may lend funds directly, either from its capital funds or from the funds that it borrows from private investment markets;

(*b*) It may guarantee loans made by others; or it may participate in such loans; and

(*c*) Loans may be made to member countries directly or to any of their political subdivisions or to private business or agricultural enterprises in the territories of members.

When a member government, in whose territory the project is located, is not itself the borrower, its government must guarantee the loan.

The World Bank obtains its funds for loans from paid-in capital subscriptions, from borrowings in the capital markets of the world, and from net earnings. Sales to investors of portions of the Bank's loans portfolio and repayments of loans to the bank, while representing only a recovery of funds originally derived from one of the above sources, have the same effect as new capital in that they reduce the amount the bank would otherwise have to obtain from other sources. The capital markets of the world provide the largest amount of funds for loans.

Because the World Bank is primarily a source of long-term loan capital, its resources have been used largely to assist in the financing of investments for which large amounts of long-term loan capital are required and for which this method of financing is appropriate. For this reason, a large part of the bank's portfolio consists of loans to publicly and privately owned utilities, such as undertakings for the generation and distribution of electric power, rail road, ports and inland waterways, airlines and airports, telecommunications and pipelines.

The World Bank and its subsidiaries, the International Development Association (IDA) and the International Finance Corporation (IFC), are a group of supernational financial institutions which offers aid to governments, governmental agencies and private business firms. The World Bank and its subsidiaries are specialised agencies of the United Nations. In contrast to certain other organisations of the United Nations, *e.g.,* UNCTAD and UNIDO, the World Bank group generally does not impose political sanctions or other requirements on aid recipients. The group is generally oriented toward development lending, with the great bulk of funds directed to the less developed countries of the world.

The World Bank makes loans to governments, governmental agencies and private business firms of member countries for productive development projects. Loans are also made to the IFC. The primary emphasis by the IBRD is placed on the development of a country's infrastructure. In general, the IBRD makes loans only when private funds are not available on reasonable terms. If a private company requests funds, it must obtain a guarantee from the member government involved. The total cost of a project is never financed by the IBRD. Generally speaking, only the foreign exchange costs of imported products or services are covered.

Payments are made only as required by the receiver of a loan; thus the loan is disbursed over a period of time, and only in accordance with a previously agreed upon "list of goods". Membership of the World Bank is limited to countries which are members of the IMF.

There is a distinct shift from agriculture to industry in the World Bank's lending to India, its largest single recipient. The emphasis on lending for infrastructure development was also expected to continue, particularly in the power sector.

In line with India's policies, the Bank's objectives in lending to these sectors would not only be the expansion of capacity but also the attainment of a more efficient utilisation of the existing assets.

So far agriculture has had a larger share in India's borrowings from the World Bank and its soft lending affiliate, the International Development Assistance (IDA). Over the years, lending by the IDA, which was on soft terms, had decreased and by the IBRD, which was on harder terms, increased.

The World Bank is now expanding its lending to the industrial sector in India through support for programmes that stressed export development and the development of an efficient "industrial base".

The Bank had been concerned that the rate of return on investment in India had been less than what the government had projected. There has been a systematic tendency of projects taking longer than what was planned. The high rate of investment of 24 to 25 per cent has not been producing the desired results. The relationship between India and the World Bank is a mature one and the Bank's objectives in its lending programme was being met to the extent of 70 to 80 per cent.

India's repayments had been regular. The ability to service debts depended on export performance and the World Bank is quite confident that India could reverse the declining trend in exports in five to seven years and sustain a higher debt burden.

There was a loss of non-project lending by the World Bank where the body did not take a direct participation, like its loan to the NABARD (National Bank for Agriculture and Rural Developments).

Lending to the social services sector, which includes population control, water supply and sewerage, was also likely to increase from 6 per cent at present at 10 per cent.

Aid India Consortium at its Paris meet in September 1991 pledged $ 6.7 billion for India for fiscal year 1991-92 which is 0.4 billion more than what was pledged last year.

Steps taken for structural reforms, financial package, investment in different sectors and project issues were discussed by the Indian Finance Minister with World Bank officials in October 1991 at Bangkok. India has expressed concern over the negative outflow of the World Bank and has urged World Bank to make a study of the causes of negative flow of $ 1 billion in 1991-92. The World Bank's outflow by way of credit is less by $ 1 billion as compared to the inflow by way of repayment of loans and interest.

Government of India has got an assurance for about $ 6 billion assistance annually in the coming years from the IMF to carry out the government's massive structural reforms and tide over the balance of payment crisis. Although World Bank is insisting on monetary reforms to improve the working of the banking sector by the next budget, however, it is left to the Indian government to take steps in this regard.

The Asian Development Bank has stepped up substantially to $ 1 billion for 1991-92, including a $ 150 million fast disbursed aid to tide over balance of payment crisis.

As a result of the Indian government's decision to close down 50 sick public sector undertakings the World Bank agreed to give second structural adjustment loan of about $ 600 million in early 1992. The money to be utilised for the creation of a social security net to the employees of the closed sick public sector units. The loan to be utilised to finance the national renewal fund announced in this year's budget for tackling the problem of sickness in public sector units.

The World Bank would periodically assess the degree to which country's development strategy, expenditure policies, programmes and institutions were consistent with poverty reduction and help through its assistance programme to support and complement India's efforts to reduce poverty.

World Bank of late is keen in helping India in its efforts to create a social safety net that was essential to implement its structural reforms. World Bank sources indicate that second structural adjustment assistance of about Rs. 200 crore to India would provide money for the national renewal fund to help the modernisation efforts of the sick public sector units. India's quota is likely to go up about 2.200 million special drawing rights to 3.055 SDRs.

The World Bank has announced an increase in the capital of International Finance Corporation, the lending arm of the private sector.

This would greatly benefit India as it has taken a policy decision to encourage the private sector.

World Bank's prescription for India is that our country should dismantle all laws and rules governing industry and trade except for a gentle regulating and legal framework and confine all government work to social infrastructure like education, health, nutrition, family planning and poverty alleviation. It is predicted that the wide gap in foreign trade and the acute shortage of hard currency will continue for atleast three years. So will the need to make repeated pilgrimage to the World Bank and IMF, seeking more loans and bail outs. Two devaluations which have taken place in our country in 1991 have pushed up the cost of imported items. Coupled with the second source of trouble — inflation. Reduction in various subsidies has also magnified the ill effects of price rise. The rich countries should keep trade fully free so that export earnings of poorer and developing countries may go up by $ 55 billion, almost the same amount that they receive as loan. The rich nations like USA should also keep interest rates low, otherwise the real burden of the poor countries will go up. Therefore, rich countries should narrow down their fiscal deficit. India should push up farm output. Agriculture is one area where our country is uniquely placed to record dramatic improvements. Liberal reforms adopted by the Government of India have of late facilitated the country's development. However, the question is of pace and depth of the reform. It is one thing to pass laws, another to change thinking.

(E) THE INTERNATIONAL MONETARY FUND (IMF)

The IMF was designed to stabilise international monetary rates. It came into existence in March, 1946, after the ratification and appropriation of funds by national governments had been completed; but the Fund was not actually opened until March 1947, and the first transactions were made in May of that year. The funds of the IMF are subscribed to by member governments. Each member has a quota, of which an amount equal either to 25 per cent of the quota or 10 per cent of the member's holdings of gold and US dollars, whichever is smaller, is subscribed in gold and the remainder in national currency.

The IMF was designed to stabilise exchange rates by assisting members to tide over temporary difficulties in their international balance of payments. It does so partly by consultation and technical advice, but also by allowing members to purchase from it with their own national currencies the gold or foreign exchange they require. In principle, not more than 25 per cent of the member's quota may be purchased in any one year; but in an emergency, this limit may be, and often is, waived. Not more than 125 per cent of the quota may be purchased in all. Charges begin at ½ per cent for the first year, rising by ½ per cent for each additional year, with a limit of 5 per cent. Members may arrange standby credits to use as and when necessary. If demands for any currency outrun the IMF's resources, it may be deleted, scarce and rationed. Members may then impose discriminatory exchange controls against it. Members are required to repurchase the excess of their own currencies over their quotas within an agreed period (three to five years) as their balances improve. They agree not to alter the exchange value of their currencies (except once by not more than 10 per cent) without prior IMF agreement.

The expansion of world trade, however, coupled with a succession of international financial crisis, has created a demand for additional reserves that can be used in settlement of international balances. In October, 1969, the IMF voted to distribute a total of $ 9,500,000,000 in Special Drawing Rights. These served, in effect, to enlarge the members' quotas without any additional subscription either in gold or in national currencies and thus created a base for new credit expansion. But demands upon international liquidity continued to increase. A realignment of currencies, which was agreed upon in December, 1971, included an effective 11 per cent devaluation of the US dollar and the upvaluation of other major currencies. Another realignment came after the USA announced a new devaluation of 10 per cent in February 1973. A number of countries allowed their currencies to "float", *i.e.*, to change in value according to market conditions and without a formal announcement. In 1991, Indian government devalued Indian rupee against the major currencies of the world by approximately 23 per cent to cope up with balance of payment crisis.

As already indicated, the IMF was formed for the purpose of promoting international monetary co-operation and a balanced growth of world trade. Its articles of agreement came into force in December, 1945.

According to Article 1 of the IMF, the main purposes of the IMF are:

(*i*) To promote international co-operation;

(*ii*) To facilitate the expansion and balanced growth of international trade and to contribute thereby to the promotion of organisations, and maintenance of high levels of employment and real incomes;

(*iii*) To promote exchange stability, to maintain orderly exchange arrangements among members;

(*iv*) To give confidence to members by making funds available to them; and

(*v*) To shorten the duration and lessen the degree of disequilibrium in the balance of payments position of members.

Among supernational the IMF is unique in that it combines three major functions:

(*a*) Regulatory;
(*b*) Financial; and
(*c*) Consultative.

(*a*) *Regulatory.* In its regulatory aspect, the IMF administers a code of good behaviour in international payments. Of primary interest are the exchange rate practices and restrictions on international payments.

(*b*) *Financial.* As a financial institution, the IMF has resources to make short to medium term loans to national monetary authorities to enable them to meet their balance of payment deficits. The IMF's resources come from the subscriptions of member countries based on an established quota; and these subscriptions are paid in the form of gold and each member's own currency. The IMF may borrow from its industrial member countries under certain conditions set forth in the "General Arrangements to Borrow".

(*c*) *Consultative.* As a consultant the IMF provides a forum for international cooperation and is a source of counsel and technical assistance to its members.

The financial operations of the IMF are in the form of drawings and standby credits to member nations. A member country makes a drawing when it purchases the currency of other members (*i.e.*, foreign exchange), paying to the fund an equivalent amount of its own currency. The maximum amounts of various currencies that a member may draw are linked to the size of its quota and to the amount of the IMF's holdings of its currency. A drawing must be reversed when the problem for which the member drew has been solved; and within a period of three to five years at the latest, the repurchase of its own currency must be with gold or convertible currency.

Under the standby credit arrangement, a member country gets an assurance that, during a fixed period of time, generally a maximum of one year, which is renewable, requests for drawing up to a specific amount will be honoured when need is shown. This arrangement, in essence, establishes a line of credit. Such financial operations by the Fund are carried on only with national governments. They are designed primarily to correct or prevent short-term balance of payment problems, *i.e.*, only short-term financial aid is provided by the IMF. Although the Fund does not lend for specific projects, it promotes international economic and exchange stability in its member countries. In other words, it contributes invaluably to the quality of international investments.

India has received the first instalments of a standby loan from the IMF $ 2.2 billion in November 1991. It is one-third of this amount and around

$ 800 million. IMF is appreciative of various steps taken by India to deal with the balance of payment position and certain medium-term problems.

India as a member of IMF is fully entitled to seek conversion of the 20-month upper tranche standby loan into an EEF assistance (Extended Fund Facility) under which it can draw $ 2.2 billion annually for three years in soft terms.

IMF's, Managing Director has made a plea to the donor countries to pledge additional $ 700 million to tide over the balance of payment crisis of India. Usually Aid India Consortium pledges loans for specific projects and this year's $ 6.7 billion aid pledged included $ 700 million. India is staking its claim for the concessional Extended Structural Facility loan (ESAF) which it had not utilised. So far India being a low income country, is entitled to avail of ESAF to tide over the balance of payment crisis.

IMF's strong support for the far reaching measures initiated by India are there for helping India to achieve macro-economic stabilisation.

The IMF had during September 1991 sanctioned India a loan of $ 635 million under the Compensatory and Contingency Financial Facility (CCFF) to help it tide over the balance of payments crisis. This was India's third credit since January 1991 when India got the first credit of $ 1.09 billion. The second loan of $ 220 million came in July, 1991. In addition, the IMF had made available to India $ 777 million in January 1991. Under the first credit tranche standby arrangement for three months.

Meanwhile, India's quota in the IMF is expected to go up from the present 2.2 billion Special Drawing Rights (SDRs) to SDR 3.05 billion, an increase of nearly 40% by January 1992. This will mean a corresponding increase in India's voting power in the IMF. its access to the Fund's resources and its share of allocations of SDRs by the IMF.

IMF would extend assistance to create more effective social safety nets and maintain education and health care at acceptable levels.

The IMF of late wants India to have a contraction of money in circulation to reduce demand, to keep prices under check and to make surplus available for export and then to hit the road to a high growth rate.

12

TRADE BLOCKS

What is Economic Integration?

The economic integration of several countries or states may take a variety of forms. The term covers preferential tariffs, free trade zones, customs unions, common markets, economic unions, and full economic integration. The parties to a system of preferential tariffs levy lower rates of duty on imports from one another than they do on imports from third countries. For example, Great Britain and its commonwealth countries operated a system of reciprocal tariff preferences after 1919. In a free trade zone, duty is levied on imports from members, but different rates of duty may be charged freely by each member on its imports from the rest of the world. The European Free Trade Association is an example. A further stage is the customs union, in which free trade among the members is sheltered behind a unified schedule of customs duties charged on imports from the rest of the world. The 19th century German Zollverein was a customs union. A common market is an extension of the customs union concept, its additional feature being that it provides for the free movement of labour and capital among the members; an example was the Benelux common market until it was converted into an economic union in 1959. The term economic union denotes a common market in which the members agree to harmonise their economic policies generally, as is the case with the European Economic Community. Finally, total economic integration implies the pursuit of a common economic policy by the political units involved. Examples of this integration are the USA and the countries of the Swiss Confederation.

The Regional Approach

Regional integration has been increasing, both in incidence and significance, throughout the world. In its broadest sense, economic integration of groups refers to the unification in some way of separate individual economies into a large single economy. Consequently, regional economic integration schemes are arrangements designed to promote close economic ties with an area which is composed of several politically independent countries, and which serve to minimise the economic consequences of political boundaries. From the point of view of export trade, the extreme case of integration is one in which the entire world is one big trading block, *i.e.*, free trade exists among all the nations of the world.

The basic assumption underlying the regional approach is that higher levels of output can be obtained by national states if the size of the market in which their products are freely exchanged is extended beyond national boundaries to include major trading partners. It is the contention of the proponents of the regional approach that, as the market is enlarged, two positive effects are likely to occur. First, there will be an increase in efficiency because the pool of existing resources is re-allocated. It involves increases in output stemming from an enlarged scale of production, specification of labour and capital and standardised parts and products. It has been contended that economies of size and specialisation cannot be achieved by small nations with limited markets; but a combination of markets would make these possible.

Second, there will be more rapid technological progress and a higher level of investment. It may be argued that regional integration, like free trade, may result in a greater volume of trade, better allocation of resources and a higher standard of living. Considering international trade alone, these benefits will accrue as a direct result of the removal of trade barriers within a region. Of course, whether such effect of regional integration will, in fact, be favourable depends upon a number of factors, including, for instance, the extent to which the products produced in the various countries involved overlap. The greater the overlap, the more likely it is that a meaningful internal re-allocation of consumption and production pattern will occur.

Types of Regional Arrangements

Various schemes for achieving regional economic integration have been tried, or are operational or have been suggested. These range from rather loose bilateral arrangements to elimination of trade barriers, to complete economic integration with supernational institutions. In general, regional arrangements may be categorised into:

(*i*) Free trade areas;
(*ii*) Customs unions;

(*iii*) Common markets; and
(*iv*) Economic unions.

(*i*) *Free Trade Area:* This is the least complex and exacting of the regional integration schemes. Is provides for internal free trade by the abolition of trade restrictions among the member countries. However, each member is allowed to determine its own commercial policies with respect to non-members. The best known examples of free trade areas are: EFTA (European Free Trade Association) and LAFTA (Latin American Free Trade Association); there are no restrictions on the flow of trade between the member countries, but they are free to maintain their own tariffs and to follow their own commercial policies vis-a-vis third countries.

The *European Free Trade Association* (EFTA) is an organisation of seven West European nations. The association regulates and promotes trade among its members. Austria, Norway, Portugal, Sweden and Switzerland are associated with the EFTA since it was established in 1959. Finland became an associate member in 1961. Iceland joined the association in 1970.

The members of the EFTA have eliminated almost all tariffs and other restrictions on imports of manufactured goods from one another. During the organisation's first 33 years of existence, the members' standard of living increased greatly and their exports increased substantially. The EFTA works to increase free trade in Western Europe.

The EFTA ranks as the second largest trade association in Western Europe. The largest is the European Economic Community, a group of eleven nations which have united their economic resources into a single economy. Unlike the European Economic Community, the EFTA does not regulate its member's agriculture, economy, or trade outside the group. Two original EFTA members, Great Britain and Denmark, resigned in 1972 and joined the European Economic Community in 1973.

The EFTA began operating in 1960. Its constitution, called the Stockholm Convention, provides that each member should send a representative to the EFTA Council which makes policy decisions for the organisation. Policies are carried out by a Secretary-General and the Secretariat is at EFTA headquarters in Geneva, Switzerland.

The EFTA has encouraged trade between its members who exchange such complementary, rather than similar, products as Swedish and Finnish timber; Portuguese tungsten, wine, cork, canned fish; and Swiss watches and food products. The accession of Norway, Ireland and the UK to the Common Market in January 1973 was expected to alter substantially the volume and direction of some trade patterns both within and between the EFTA and Common Market blocs. This was expected to be especially true for agricultural commodities and for Commonwealth trade with Britain.

ASEAN (The Association of South-East Asian Nations)

This group comprises six countries. They are Indonesia, the Philippines, Brunei, Thailand, Malaysia, and Singapore. The economies of the ASEAN group of countries have grown as rapidly as any region's in the world. They have skilled and well-educated population and have made major strides in industrialisation. The per capita GNP ranges from $ 520 in Indonesia to $ 5,100 in Singapore. The ASEAN group members are oil surplus, rich in many minerals and agricultural commodities and diversifying into manufacturing at a rapid pace. These countries are openly encouraging foreign investors. Regional cohesiveness and joint industrial planning are providing further incentive to growth. Thus, the ASEAN group provides an expanding market for international marketers across a very broad product range.

Asean group of nations established the trade block for their identity as a group of nations in their geographical contiguity. The countries of this region have a common Historical background of recent vintage in terms of a colonial past. For cultural and philosophical encouragement. Asear Trade block established for Asian "unity and solidarity." Asian Economic Area is a notion. But acceptance of its existence by the economic agents in the region, governments and intellectuals would bring a paradigm of development.

The ASEAN has adopted India as its sectoral partner recently, as far as its relations to trade, investment, science and technology and training are concerned. ASEAN has reached an accord in January 1992 for the establishment of the common effective preferential tariffs (CEPT) plan designed to create an ASEAN free trade area in 15 years starting from January, 1993. The CEPT will cut existing tariffs up to 20% to a 0.5% beginning with 15 products.

ASEAN of late is concerned with the growing wave of protectionism in the USA and the European Community's pre-occupation with the emerging economies of eastern Europe and for that matter emergence of economic blocks throughout the world. It may undermine and erode the fledgling economies of Asia. ASEAN is opposed to the establishment of a naval base by Americans in Singapore. ASEAN desires south-east Asia a nuclear weapons free area and a zone of peace, freedom and neutrality.

Asean Free Trade Area (AFTA)

In the beginning of the 1990s, the ASEAN countries have armed themseives against a number of changes in the international environment. They had to establish AFTA in Sept. 1994 for 10 years to develop inter-ASEAN Trade. Liberalisation of intra-ASEAN Trade stimulate foreign investment in the region, the Asean group of countries established free Trade Area in Asia. The AFTA agreement allows member countries to exclude sensitive, products from tariff under the 'normal track' or 'fast track'. Tariff reduction will apply to the products of ASEAN countries origin. ASEAN origin is obtained 40% of value of a product originated in ASEAN countries.

Latin American Integration Association (LAIA)

The growth of manufacturing in Latin America resulted in many conferences during the 1950s which aimed at increasing trade among the Latin American countries. Finally, in February 1960, at a meeting in Montevideo, Uruguay, the LAFTA was formed. Seven countries signed the LAFTA agreement — Argentina, Brazil, Chile, Mexico, Paraguay, Peru, and Uruguay. In 1961, Colombia and Ecuador joined the LAFTA. Venezuela jointed it in 1966 and Bolivia in 1967. Later Colombia and Ecuador also joined. These countries agreed to end by 1980 most of the restrictions on trade among them, such as customs and tariffs. The tariffs are being lowered gradually. The LAFTA was modelled on the European Free Trade Association. Later LAIA replaced LAFTA.

In December 1960, four Central American countries formed an organisation similar to that of the LAFTA. El Salvador, Guatemala, the Honduras and Nicaragua signed a treaty of Central American Economic Integration. In 1963, Costa Rica joined the organisation, usually referred to as the *Central American Common Market* (*CACM*).

In spite of many problems, trade among the Latin American nations has increased under the two free trade agreements. For example, Chile imports cotton from Mexico and Brazil. In the past, Chile bought cotton from the United States. Mexico sells steel to several South American countries, and Brazilian manufactured products, such as typewriters, are sold in Chile.

The structural organisation of LAIA includes a Council of Ministers, composed of Foreign Ministers of member countries; a conference of contracting parties, which makes decisions on questions requiring a joint resolution of the members; a permanent Executive Committee, which supervises the treaty's implementation; and a secretariat, which performs technical and administrative functions.

Tariffs and other restrictions on trade were to be reduced over a period of 12 years; each country was to present annually a list (national list) of commodities on which it would concede duty reductions. A common list of products to be completely exempt from tariffs (in trade within the area) was to be negotiated every three years; almost all of the intra-area trade was to be on this list. Provision was also made for special lists granting more favourable terms to the relatively less developed countries.

Tariff reduction within the group have not moved along as per schedule. Some observers have attributed the lack of progress to the high transportation costs within the area, contentment with sheltered markets, and the forces of nationalism.

In realising the problems of implementing the original treaty, the members of the LAIA adopted the Protocol of Caracas during the ninth session in 1969; the protocol moved the date of achievement of a free trade area forward to 1980, suspended the requirements for a common list, and reduced the required tariff reductions on the national lists.

In May 1969, Chile, Colombia, Ecuador, Peru and Bolivia (the Andean group) signed the Cartagena Agreement calling for the elimination of all barriers to trade within the area by December 31, 1980, and for the establishment of a common external tariff. These five Andean pact signatories hoped that their organisation in a common market might enable them to compete with the larger economies in Latin America (Mexico, Argentina, and Brazil) and that the expansion of the market might draw new industry into the area. The sub-regional pact has raised a number of questions that remain to be answered regarding the relationship of these countries to the LAIA as a whole.

The achievements of the LAIA, compared to those of the EFTA, have been modest. Other free trade areas include New Zealand/Australia Free Trade Agreement, the Caribbean Free Trade Area (composed of Antigua, Barbados, Guyana, Trinidad and Tobago), the Arab Free Trade Agreement (composed of all the Arab countries except Egypt). Each of these groups has different objectives and characteristics, but all are part of the general movement to break down the world into small national markets so that business can serve a large area and achieve the maximum economies of production.

(*ii*) *Customs Union*. It is an association of two or more countries to encourage trade. The countries making such an arrangement agree to eliminate duties and other restrictive regulations on trade among them. The members of the union apply a single set of tariffs to all the countries outside the union. A free trade area is like a customs union, except that the members of a free trade area may apply separate tariffs against non-members.

A customs union does away with restrictions on trade among participating nations; but, unlike a free trade area agreement, they are no longer free to determine their own tariffs and quotas with nonparticipating nations. A customs union aims at establishing common tariffs and quotas with the rest of the world on behalf of all its members, though there may be concessions and considerations in respect of some members for a limited period, till they are fully integrated. Thus, a customs union is a closer form of integration than the free trade area.

The best known customs unions include the Zollverein, the Benelux, and the European Economic Community (EEC). The Zollverein was formed by the German States in the 1830s. These States became the German nation in 1871. Belgium, the Netherlands, and Luxembourg established the Benelux in the 1940s, Belgium, France, Italy, Luxembourg, the Netherlands and West Germany set up the European Economic Community in 1957. Britain, Denmark and Ireland joined the Community in 1973. Greece and Turkey are the associated members.

(*iii*) *The Common Market.* The European coal and steel community was only the initial step in the movement for European integration. On March 25, 1957, its six member governments signed the Treaty of Rome, under which they agreed to establish the European Economic Community, or "common market", which came into being on January 18, 1958. In 1973, it was enlarged with the entry of Great Britain, Ireland and Denmark. The EEC is the most far-reaching attempt at economic integration among sovereign countries. Its founding treaty has been the model, in whole or part, for all subsequent attempts at economic integration. The Treaty of Rome aimed to "establish a common market" and "progressively bring the economic policies of members into alignment so as to promote the harmonious growth of economic activity in the Community as a whole, regular and balanced expansion, augmented stability, a more rapidly rising standard of living, and closer relations between the participating States." The treaty pledged the signatories to abolish customs duties and quantitative restrictions on the entry and outflow of merchandise, to abrogate all other measures having an equivalent effect, and to fix a common customs tariff for imports from non member States. They also agreed to abolish, as between members, all barriers to the free movement of persons, services and capital. This was to be accomplished during a transition period of 12 years. The transition period ended on January 1, 1970. The Community then entered into its definitive phase.

In short, we may say that a common market or economic community goes a step further than the customs union. It provides a free market for the goods of all the member countries and facilitates the free mobility of all the factors of production within the economic community. Labour, capital and enterprise have unrestricted freedom to go where they can be most productive and most profitable. Thus, the productive efficiency of all the member countries, and the allocation of resources among them, are both sought to be optimised. The outstanding examples of the common market are the ECM (European Common Market), the EEC (European Economic Community) and the CACM (Central American Common Market).

The *European Community* is a group of West European nations working to unite their economic resources into a single economy. The original members of the Community are Belgium, France, Italy, Luxembourg, the

Netherlands and West Germany. Denmark, Ireland and Great Britain became members on January 1, 1973.

The European Community is based on the treaties of three organisations:

(*i*) The European Atomic Energy Community (Euratom)

(*ii*) The European Coal and Steel Community (ECSC)

(*iii*) The European Economic Community (EEC).

Both the *European Community* and *the European Economic Community* are sometimes known as the *European Common Market.*

In 1968, the six original members of the European Community abolished all the tariffs affecting trade among themselves. They have set up a common tariff on goods imported from other countries by any member of the community. The group hopes to eventually remove all the barriers to the free movement of capital, goods, services and workers among its members. These economic resources will move freely among the members of the community.

The Community co-ordinates the member nations' legislation on health, food, industrial standards, taxes and other issues. It protects the social security rights of workers of member countries who take jobs in other member countries. The group hopes that it will eventually have a monetary union and a common currency for all its members. The European Community gives financial aid to developing countries.

There is active trading within groups of countries that have associated primarily for this purpose to rationalise and to increase profitability. The *European Economic Community (EEC) has directed its efforts toward economic specialization* in increasingly interdependent member countries. Germany supplies coking coal and chemicals to France, which provides Belgium with iron/ore from the Lorraine region; steel is moved to extranational markets; Dutch natural gas is piped to France, Belgium and Germany. Speciality foodstuffs, wines, cheeses, spring vegetables and fruits find an enlarged market far beyond their production centres, as do such manufactured items as fashion goods, automobiles and washing machines etc.

European Economic Integration (European Common Market)

A significant development during 1989 was European Economic Integration. The European Community (EC) has decided to move towards a single market by the end of 1992. Significant progress was made in 1989 towards establishing this goal of a common market in which goods, labour and capital would move freely. In fact the first step had already been taken by removing obstacles to financial integration and including all EC currencies in the exchange rate mechanism of the European Monetary System (EMS). In May 1992 Denmark had objected to have one single currency. To decide on an issue is one thing and to implement and to accept it is another. Time will tell whether European Economic Integration turns out to be a reality. If it does, it would pose a challenge and opportunity for the rest of the nations in terms of international trade.

(*iv*) *Economic Unions.* An economic union may be described as the fourth form of international arrangement between nations. Once an economic union becomes a fact, the participating nations may move to have a common currency for the entire union. In this way, an economic union may lead to a monetary union. Economic unions require among the signatory nations a general harmonisation of national economic policies. They work out common rules covering such matters as competition, taxation, and economic legislation. They also call for the development of common policies in such areas as foreign trade, agriculture and transportation. Members may be asked to concert their economic policies in fiscal and monetary fields, balance of payments and social welfare.

There is no major economic union in existence. However, it is said that EEC is moving in this direction.

There is another type of regional economic integration scheme which is a hybrid and which involves the political union of economic affairs, either voluntary or forced. An example of a voluntary political union is the British Commonwealth of Nations. Another example of forced political union is the COMECON (Council for Mutual Economic Assistance, which is composed of the Soviet Union and the countries of Eastern Europe). These examples in a way are not regional integration schemes; but they ultimately do depend on certain economic issues for their success.

Some diversified companies will be affected by the preference and the growth effect of regional economic integration. To companies located outside any particular region, the existence of a preference effect means that there will be a decrease in their exports to that region because of the preferential treatment given to competing producers located within the region. Therefore, an outside company interested in maintaining its markets within the region might seek ways to be more competitive. To an extent, the preferential effect on an outside company may be offset by the growth effect. The joining together of several countries tends to create a larger market. This fact, coupled with the increased rate of economic growth, means that people within the region will have more money to spend on products from abroad.

Now the question arises as to how are export marketers affected by the changing facets of trade protectionism both at the regional integration level and directly? And how should export marketers respond?

The export marketer must study economic and political trends in relevant countries and industries. Being aware of these trends will help to forewarn of the possibility of governments resorting to protectionism. This should provide the export marketer the time needed to study strategy alternatives and to implement contingency plans. With the establishment of World Trade Organisation on 1-1-95 replacing GATT, many of these trade blocks effectively would get reduced or they may disappear as the world moves towards globalization.

The global trading system post-1990 was founded as the principles of liberal internationalism — Multilateralism, non-discrimination and based purely on the economic theory of compositive advantage. Trade agreements in the 1990s are conceived on very different grounds. What NAFTA and the EU share in common is that both an incredibly bold attempts to enlist external markets to obtain political ends. Conceptually, they owe much to the Regan-Thatcher-Mulroncy monetary experience but they go beyond the previous model of political co-operation in dramatically new ways. The fundamental change (i) that-they are investment-driven initiatives to accelerate regional economic integration around a Triad member and require a high level of Itali and market co-ordination to bring new market relationship. Trade blocks are constructed on given principles:

(1) They are designated to be intrusive legally. They are comprehensive agreements that cover almost all areas of public decision-making as well as private sector activities. Public wealth creation is to be subordinate to the private work of investment and commerce.

(2) The trade block having highly sensitive in public policy like environment, culture work, employment, social policy etc. It is possible that the government of the country cannot join in area of environment and social policy innovation and labour market of another country.

(3) Each signatory has prescribed rights and responsibilities and there is a mechanism of enforcement to settle trade dispute, between members with a range of sanction available for non-compliance.

(4) Power asymmetry is legitimized because the dominant members of the block, be it Germany of the U.S., controls the key level of fiscal and monetary policies of other members.

(5) Public accountability through an elected legislature is minimal while most crucial decisions are not subject to public reviews.

(6) Only minimal provision is provided for redistribution of trade-generated benefits or the sharing of costs of adjustment through the EU has made some progress in this area.

(7) Finally, the entire agreement is subject to legal review and arbitration by non-elected judges and tribunals. Increasingly, democratic institutions are marginalised by the transfer of public policy making to an elite-based judiciary.

NAFTA and European Union (EU) are prototype economic projects questionable for economic integration process. Fifteen European Nations building a common future with a super national authority having a full range of administration, legal, and fiscal instruments. Each block wants to use trade to restructure market-state relations to promote trade-led development. Such blocks are designed to promote capital movements and foreign investment, transfer of technology and location of future production activities.

Table 12.1
Major Regional Market Groups

Organization	*Members*	*Population (millions)*	*GDP ($ billions)*	*GDP per Capita*
EEC (European Economic Community)	Belgium	9.8	110.9	11260
	Luxembourg	0.4	3.5	9723
	Denmark	5.1	66.2	12925
	France	47.6	573.3	10720
	Germany	61.3	761.8	12419
	Ireland	3.4	14.8	4412
	Italy	56.9	323.6	5686
	United Kingdom	55.9	401.9	7192
	Netherlands	14.0	149.1	10624
	Greece (Assoc)	9.4	38.6	4093
	Turkey (Assoc)	44.2	50.1	1161
EFTA (European Free Trade Association)	Austria	7.5	68.4	9107
	Iceland	0.2	2.5	10739
	Norway	4.1	46.7	11486
	Portugal	9.9	17.8	1816
	Sweden	8.3	106.4	12831
	Switzerland	6.3	95.0	15006
	Finland	4.8	41.4	8701
COMECON (Council form Mutual Economic Assistance)	Cuba	9.8	102.3	1041
	Czechoslovakia	15.2	87.4	5770
	German Dem. Repub.	16.7	91.4	5489
	Hungary	10.7	17.7	1673
	Poland	35.2	62.2	1780
	Romania	22.1	30.3	1314
	U.S.S.R	264.1	693.3	2419
	Bulgaria (Assoc)	9.0	23.6	2611
Arab Common Market	Iraq	12.8	19.3	1604
	Kuwait	1.3	23.3	18370
	Jordan	3.1	2.1	931

Table 12.1 (Cont.)

Organization	*Members*	*Population (millions)*	*GDP ($ billions)*	*GDP per Capita*
	Syria	8.3	10.0	1199
	Egypt	41.0	25.0	628
ASEAN (Association of South East Asian Nations)	Indonesia	148.5	49.1	331
	Malaysia	13.3	13.1	1045
	Singapore	2.4	9.0	3829
	Philippines	47.7	30.1	640
	Thailand	46.1	27.2	590
NAFTA (New Zealand-Australia Free Trade Agreement)	Australia	14.4	127.4	8836
	New Zealand	3.1	21.4	6896
ECOWAS (The Economic Community of West African States)	Benin	3.5	0.7	221
	Guinea	4.9	0.6	130
	Ivory Coast	4.9	7.7	1014
	Mali Republic	6.5	0.5	87
	Mauritania	1.6	0:8	500
	Niger	5.2	0.7	160
	Senegal	5.5	2.4	436
	Togo	2.5	1.0	406
	Upper Volta	6.7	0.8	126
	Gambia	0.6	0.2	256
	Ghana	11.3	9.7	913
	Nigeria	74.6	50.2	717
	Sierra Leone	3.4	0.9	283
	Liberia	1.6	0.8	480
	Guinea-Bissau	0.6	0.1	208
CACM (Central American Common Market)	Guatemala	7.1	6.9	977
	El Salvador	4.7	3.5	755
	Costa Rica	2.2	4.0	1843
	Nicaragua	2.6	2.1	889
	Honduras	3.6	2.2	608
LAIA (Latin American Integration Association) replaced LAFTA (Latin American Free Trade Association)	Argentina	26.7	36.8	1448
	Brazil	118.6	214.6	1809
	Colombia	26.4	28.1	1064
	Paraguay	3.0	3.4	1150
	Uruguay	2.9	7.6	2397
	Chile	10.9	11.5	1078
	Ecuador	8.1	9.3	1137
	Mexico	69.4	121.3	1749
	Peru	17.3	12.4	716
	Venezuela	13.5	49.0	3622
	Bolivia	5.4	5.0	924
ANDEAN Common Market	Bolivia	5.4	5.0	924
	Chile (has withdrawn)	10.9	11.5	1078
	Colombia	26.4	28.1	1064
	Ecuador	8.1	9.3	1137

Table 12.1 (Cont.)

Organization	*Members*	*Population (millions)*	*GDP ($ billions)*	*GDP per Capita*
	Peru	17.3	12.4	716
	Venezuela	13.5	49.0	3622
CARICOM (Caribbean Common Market)	Barbados	0.3	0.7	2659
	Guyana	0.9	0.4	540
	Jamaica	2.2	3.3	1554
	Trinidad Tobago	1.1	4.9	4355

* The COMECON GDP figures are actually Net Material Product. This is GDP minus (value of government services expenditures on social and community services, financial services and real estate transactions).

Sources: UN, *Statistical Yearbook 1980/81, Yearbook of National Statistics 1980,* Vol. II (New York: United Nations: 1981 and 1982, respectively); and International Monetary Fund. *International Financial Statistics,* November 1982.

13

OVERSEAS MARKETING COMMUNICATION

(A) WHAT IS OVERSEAS MARKETING COMMUNICATION

Overseas marketing communication includes the same activities of the home trade. These activities are the marketing and merchandising functions which are completely controlled by the manufacturer and exporter and which assist in the development of sales. Such activities differ from advertising in that the advertising is generally placed in media which are not controlled by the advertiser, the manufacturer, or the exporter. Sales promotion activities differ from selling in that they aid and assist selling rather then participate in selling.

International promotion extends beyond advertising to many other promotional tools. The trade fair has assumed increasing importance as a specialized international market which facilitates the meeting between informed buyers and sellers. Another interesting vehicle is international direct mail for certain specialised products offerings and for specialised international market segments, such as the East European governments, buyers of Western goods. Other promotional tools are more for use in localised foreign market situations. These relate to POP, especially when used in-store.

Characteristics of Foreign Buyers

In the area of promotion, the effects of family, education, religious and social systems are strongly felt. In creating promotion for export markets, the following *characteristics of foreign buyers must be carefully considered:*

I. Capacity to Purchase

— Size of income
— Consumption pattern
— Distribution of income
— Rate of change
— Extent of consumer financing

II. Motivations of Purchasers

— Religious system
— Family system
— Educational system
— Social system
— Economic system
— Geographic characteristics
— Economics and daily living

III. Purchasing Practices

— How the decision is made
— Sophistication of product qualities.

The difference between sales promotion activities in export and in home trade is based on the differences in business methods encountered in overseas markets. Usually it requires only a little ingenuity to adopt domestic materials to use even in the farthest and strongest markets with the greatest varieties of language. Language is always the first stumbling block. Hence the greater the emphasis on pictures or visual demonstration, the better it would be from every point of view.

FORMS OF OVERSEAS MARKETING COMMUNICATION

Export Catalogues

Like every catalogue for home trade, the export catalogue is the ever present silent, accurate salesman. It is erroneous to think of an export catalogue merely as a condensed card index of products and prices. It must be considered as an active, vital, sales-making force in the export business.

The objectives of export catalogue are listed below:

(i) It should invite perusal.

(ii) It should express and impress the personality of the Indian exporter.

(iii) It should carry domestic goodwill into the world markets.

(*iv*) It should simplify purchase procedures.

(*v*) It must create the desire to purchase.

(*vi*) It should speak louder than the salesman.

The export catalogue should be a separate, different and distinct catalogue from the domestic catalogue and should not be merely a domestic catalogue printed in a foreign language.

Domestic trade terms and references to methods and practices peculiar to India should be carefully and rigidly avoided, and words and phrases with doubtful or double meanings should be eliminated. The writer of an export catalogue must know the product fully and visualize its use in foreign markets, and the arrangements used in its sales abroad. If any new words or phrases are used, their meaning must be made clear.

Accuracy in an export catalogue is much appreciated and is very important. The following points must be borne in mind while preparing an export catalogue:

(*i*) The export catalogue should be so constructed that through its use alone the buyer in a foreign market may adjust his buying to his capacity to sell or his capacity to pay.

(*ii*) Every point of importance should be emphasized, *e.g.,* a product saves time, temper and money, and will sell on sight for these reasons.

(*iii*) Each item should be analysed to determine its best export selling points.

(*iv*) It should state facts — neither exaggerate nor understate them.

(*v*) It should make it easy for the foreign dealer to place an order.

A loose-leaf type of export catalogue is recommended. It should not be too large or bulky. An attractive set-up of the catalogue should be an important consideration.

House Magazine

While a few manufacturers publish highly creditable house magazines for the special use of the export trade, there is, in general, no more commonly neglected sales aid in the entire field of export marketing.

The following suggestions, if kept in mind while publishing a house magazine, would really help as an effective export sales aid:

(*i*) Incorporate illustrations in the house magazine; they are interesting and need not be translated;

(*ii*) The typography should be excellent and easily readable;

(*iii*) Do not criticise one area or distributor in a direct way;

(*iv*) Tie in new products at every reasonable point but not in a strictly selling style;

(*v*) Write about those things which normally a salesman cannot say; and

(*vi*) Last, but not the least, always keep in mind that customer house organ should be edited for the reader. Whether the customer be actual or prospective, he is the person at whom all export salesmanship is directed.

(B) ADVERTISING IN WORLD MARKETS

The function of advertising in trade is precisely the same as its function in domestic trade. Advertising may be used as a means of creating dealer demand, dealer preferences, or consumer demand or acceptance. It may be used to prepare the way for the salesman to enable him to make a greater volume of sales than would otherwise be possible. Advertising may be used likewise to help move the products from the dealers' shelves. Naturally many problems confront the manufacturer and exporter who undertakes to advertise his products in foreign markets — the formulation of an advertising policy, the estimates of appropriations, the selection of media and the preparation of advertisements.

The formulation of policy depends largely upon the opinion of the export manager as to the efficacy of advertising a particular product in a given market. The appropriations to be made for foreign advertising depend, of course, upon the general financial budget and the amount which can be allocated to the development of foreign sales. Foreign advertising campaigns may be planned for as wide a range of objectives as in domestic selling. The variation from modest initial advertisements to world-wide campaigns offers the possibility of meeting any set of conditions imposed by the character of the products, the size of concern, or other factors. Keeping in mind the differences in purchasing power, purchasing habits, and methods of thought, the same principles apply to the preparation of foreign advertising as to those of domestic advertising. However, that does not mean that an advertisement which ranked high in selling power in India would so rank in the USA. In illustration and wording, the appeal must be consistent with the customs and habits of the country in which the advertising is used.

The manufacturer is separated from the foreign consumer by a long chain of middlemen. The exporter, instead of relying only on personal selling, resorts to advertising to stimulate demand. Advertising methods help the exporter to present facts to the foreign buyer. Advertising in foreign countries fails because, at times, it does not recognize merchandising and marketing functions in a foreign country; it fails to maintain more than a tenuous relationship with the economics of the product and it falls short of perfection in its technique. The problem of advertising in foreign markets is the problem of adapting Indian advertising to conditions that are different. Conditions are highly variable in different markets, and each market must be considered, to a large degree, as a separate and a distinct unit. Indian advertising practices may be 25 years behind American standards.

The use of available media, the size of the column, and the use of colour are the technical details of foreign advertising. In every essential respect — method, appeal, continuity, coverage, relation to merchandising and marketing, employment of research, principles of getting attention, use of a sound layout and good art — advertising is the same the world over because people in every land respond to the same general kind of stimuli and react to the same visual appeals and to the same economic motives.

The problem of advertising in foreign markets, therefore, is not the problem of the creation of new and different advertising but the problem of adaptation of domestic advertising to conditions found in overseas markets. Export advertising expenditures are growing rapidly as products compete for world market share. A large number of international marketing segments cross many national boundaries. The growth in expenditures is also occurring due to the availability, increasing capacity, and diversity of media vehicles.

The problem to be solved by export marketers is whether to follow an international advertising strategy of standardization or to adapt advertising to satisfy the needs of local foreign markets. The principal reasons for employing standardized advertising are cost savings and a reduction of message confusion in areas where their is media overlap or country-to-country consumer mobility. According to an estimate, German TV broadcasts are received by forty percent of Dutch homes with TV sets. Also, *Paris Match* has a circulation of 85,000 in Belgium, 26,000 in Switzerland, and substantial readership in Luxembourg and other countries of West Europe. The risk of confusion that may result from reaching such audiences with different brand names and advertising appeals has led to the standardization approach which does not sacrifice local adaptability. Examples are the Esso "Tiger in Your Tank" campaign and the Playtex brassiere ads which feature the same stop-action photographic demonstrations of the product strength. Exporters will plan more and more global brands, TV and communications generally will reach further across the world, and standardization is bound to grow.

The choice being exercised today by many exporters is between prototype versus pattern advertising. To a major extent, the choice is product dependent. This involves consideration of the needs satisfied by the product.

In deciding on export advertising strategy, two further main factors have to be thought through. These factors are interactive. One is the position of the product in its life cycle in different foreign markets. The second is the role and responsibility of export advertising in the marketing mix abroad. Some large exporters have developed a benchmark strategy which involves similar advertising themes and basic copy across multiple markets. In most cases, these multiple markets span the advanced industrialized countries, including Japan.

Exporters can either adopt the same promotion strategy they used in the home market or change it for each local market.

Consider the message. The exporters can change the message at three different levels.

(*a*) The exporters can use one message around the world by varying only the language, name, and colours.

(*b*) The next possibility is to use the same theme globally.

(*c*) Finally, some exporters encourage their advertising agencies to make a full adaptation of theme and execution to local market.

The use of media also requires international adaptation because media availability varies from country to country. Commercial radio or TV is not even available in some Scandinavian countries and Middle Eastern countries. In Germany, advertisers have access to commercial TV only during a few preannounced short time blocks, none of which interrupt the program. As a result, viewership of these commercial time blocks is low. Yet companies complain that they must buy time months in advance and have little control over when their ads will be broadcast. Certain countries add restrictions as to what can be advertised, often not allowing cigarette or alcoholic beverage advertising on TV. The rapid growth of VCR usage in Europe has cut further into the size of TV audiences. Another medium, magazines, varies in its effectiveness; magazines play a major role in Italy and a minor one in Austria. Newspapers have a national reach in the United Kingdom, but the advertiser can buy only local newspaper coverage in Spain.

Management of the export advertising function encompasses the setting of objectives; the process for the formulation of strategy; implementation of the strategy; choice of advertising agency; decisions on whether and to what extent to conduct export advertising research; the setting of budgets; and establishing control.

Communication Strategy

Positioning the advertising theme for a product may vary from one nation to another. Other phases of advertising also may have to be modified as a result of culture. For example, words and symbols may connote different things in different cultures. In a new car promotion, Chrysler-France translated the phrase "the original" that had been used in England to "the example" for its advertising campaign in Germany. The problem was that "die original" in German has a connotation of strange or odd, which was not what the firm was trying to communicate to the German public.

The choice of advertising media is also subject to culture. The British airline, BEA, found that its promotional theme emphasizing the reliability of British pilots was very successful when displayed in print media in all Western European countries with the exception of Italy. Research showed that it was less successful in Italy because of the importance of oral communication to Italians.

The first day of the new moon in India is considered a very bad day for conducting business. Many otherwise Westernized well-educated Indians simply will not become involved in nor associated with business affairs at this time, as they feel it is bad luck.

It would be considered very poor planning to advertise a product in a birthday or wedding setting with the models wearing black dresses or suits. It is simply not considered auspicious to display black at such pleasant occasions.

According to Hindu mythology, Diwali, is considered an excellent time to do business and the Hindus makes it a specific point to transact a piece of business on that particular day for good luck, to open the way for good tie-in promotions and a receptiveness to forceful promotions at that time.

While English is widely used throughout India, for vernacular authenticity it is best to tailor the approach. For example, an advertiser could generally use Tamil dialect in South India, Hindi in North India, and Gujarati around Bombay.

The cow is a sacred animal to the Hindus in India. It would be extremely unwise for a food product manufacturer to extol the joys of a beef sandwich. Similarly, Muslim beliefs preclude promotion in settings where ham or bacon is shown.

It would be a mistake to show a Hindu god in any kind of deodorant promotion. This would be the equivalent of running an ad in Western media for boot polish with the trade name of Jesus.

In many cases, it is possible to standardize the buying proposal. Appeals such as the cosmetic benefits of toothpaste, the conservative management of bank departments, and the heavy-duty cleaning power of detergents are practically universal. However, the actual creative presentation used to present the buying proposal may have to be modified to fit local conditions.

The status of advertising in a society sets broad limits for promotion programmes. The economists with socialistic views have deterred the development of advertising in their countries because advertising expense is looked upon as a waste.

Indian advertising agencies are in their infancy. Advertising agencies in overseas markets perform the function of the placing of an advertisement, *i.e.*, the agency takes the advertisement already fully developed, and buys the space in which it is to be inserted. Sometimes the agency offers a translation service; this is usually the maximum service that may be expected from a foreign advertising agency.

In the development of an advertising campaign in foreign markets, the choice, therefore, of the right agency is more than important; it may mean the difference between success and failure. The following should be considered in selecting an advertising agency:

(*a*) Choose an agency to which export advertising is the main business and not a side business;

(*b*) Its method of operation must fit in with your conditions;

(*c*) If local knowledge and contacts are of importance in selling your product, ensure that the agency chosen has these contacts;

(*d*) Make sure that information about media, markets, etc., is concentrated where it is quickly available;

(*e*) Confirm whether the agency has sufficient executives to pay attention to your account;

(*f*) Audit the agency's financial standing; and

(*g*) Look into the experience the agency has had in your product line.

Export Advertising Media

One should ask which is the most effective medium in reaching to the customer abroad with a specific message. All media in all the countries are not available because of governmental restrictions and the general low opinion about advertising. The aspects of coverage, economics and effectiveness have got to be carefully considered while selecting a medium.

The following questions must be asked by the exporter while selecting a medium:

(*a*) Whom does it reach?

(*b*) How much does it cost to reach the customer?

But these are difficult things to ascertain in many foreign markets. Therefore, in foreign advertising, the following problems arise:

(*i*) How to secure national coverage;

(*ii*) How to get the facts about the amount and quality of circulation; and

(*iii*) How to get the facts on rates.

In general, the same types of media are available to Indian advertisers in foreign markets that are available to them in the home market. The conditions that strike the Indian advertiser as different are the variations of development, the quantity and character of application, and frequently the difficulty of reaching and using them.

Practically all the various media, which are available in India, are also available in foreign markets. The important ones are:

(*i*) Newspapers

These play a far more important role in advertising in some foreign markets and a far less important part in some others. In the markets which are fairly literate, newspapers play a relatively more important part in advertising. This is true because of the absence of, or the comparatively limited influence of magazines and periodicals, because of the highly specialised character of outdoor advertising and because of the lack of, or the comparatively restricted application of, radio advertising. In markets which are composed largely of illiterate persons, newspapers play a relatively less important role for the simple reason that the people cannot read them and their circulation is greatly restricted.

(*ii*) Magazines

Foreign magazines may be divided into two classes:

(*a*) Legitimate; and

(*b*) Illegitimate.

(*a*) A legitimate group of publishers are in a position to flinch payment from Indian advertisers for worthless advertising. These magazines do not last long but they make boundless promises which are never fulfilled. They fold up and are never heard of again, at least not under the same garb or under the same name. Some survive by a process of never ending effrontery. Some have been known to print only a sufficient number of copies to provide tear sheets for the advertisers. There is only one defence against shysters and that is the employment of someone who knows the foreign media.

(*b*) The illegitimate magazines in general have a limited circulation and they reach a highly selected upper class people or some selected circles devoted to a cause, a party, a religion, sports, or some other objectives. They vary greatly in size and hence the plates suitable for one are seldom suitable for another. Trade papers are useful, and advertisers sometimes believe that they are an indispensable advertising medium.

(*iii*) Posters

Printing or lithographed posters monopolise foreign outdoor advertising. Foreign advertisers use posters of every size and shape. The design of the poster largely decides its size and shape. Given a total lack of uniformity of boards or hoardings, there is no particular reason for any definite size or shape of poster. The only limitation is that posters should be of a size that can be conveniently affixed to any upright structure. The great majority of posters ultimately find their way onto walls, sides of new unused buildings, temporary structures, and the like. If the space for the poster is too large, a simple device is used — the same poster is repeated twice, thrice or a dozen times until the available space is completely occupied. The effect, far from being ludicrous, is distinctly arresting and effective.

(*iv*) Wall Writings

A type of outdoor advertising, which has been very generally used both in India and abroad, is that used on what are called "painted walls or wall writings." In practically every country, blank walls of one kind or another are available for painted signs. These walls are frequently larger and are, therefore, suitable for bigger designs and layouts. It should be recognised, however, that in many countries, skilled sign painters are not available, and that, therefore, the posters or layouts, the human body, and particularly the human face, cannot be used. Colours can be reproduced, however, and lettering can be well done in almost any country. Painted walls should be renewed at least once every six months, and more often in some climates, where paint quickly loses its luster, brightness and effectiveness. It should be remembered that after the public has seen a given arrangement or a given combination of colours on wall too often, they are likely to go past it without seeing it at all. Therefore, the longer the same illustration remains on a wall, less its effectiveness.

(*v*) Electric Signs

These are used practically in every country. They are mainly of three types:

(*a*) *Illuminated painted signs:* Painted or paper signs are illuminated by the electric lights thrown upon them.

(*b*) *Electric signs in which the important features are outlined in electric light bulbs:* The electric lights are so arranged that their flashing gives the impression of movement.

(*c*) *Neon signs* are considered to be an effective method of advertising at night in foreign markets.

(*vi*) Handbills

A minor form of advertising, which is employed to a considerable extent in most foreign countries, is the distribution of handbills.

(*vii*) Public Conveyance Advertising

These advertisements, known as car cards, are used on buses, trains, etc. The size of the cards may vary. It is in many respects, the best form of outdoor advertising that is available in overseas markets.

(*viii*) Direct Mail

With the increasingly perfected technique of direct mail, it is used widely and more intensively in connection with the development of sales. The difficulty or handicap is that some of the effect upon the prospect is dulled because he receives too much direct mail material. In many foreign countries, it is both difficult and costly to send direct-mail material. However, practically any person abroad is flattered by the receipt of a letter from another country. Smart, colourful material with beautiful printing can make a tremendous hit in most overseas markets. Such advertising is successful not only in calling attention to Indian products but also in actually making sales because it is so far in advance of anything that ordinarily appears in the form of advertising material in overseas markets.

(*ix*) Radio and TV Advertising

Radio and TV advertising in markets abroad seems to run to two extremes. Either the programme is all advertising, or there is no advertising. Both of these extremes have considerably reduced the effectiveness of radio and TV advertising abroad. Another contributory cause is the fact that there are fewer receiving radio or TV sets in many countries and that government restrictions and regulations have further reduced their distribution. It should be noted that because of the number of language groups to which radio and TV advertising must appeal, this type of advertising is not very successful in many markets even as newspaper advertising is not. In radio or TV programmes, some of the following difficulties may be encountered.

(*a*) The broadcast or telecast of the kind of programme which will appeal to a foreign audience;

(*b*) The large number of different programmes which must be developed because of differences in language and local tastes; and

(*c*) The disorganised condition of radio and TV advertising in many foreign countries.

(*x*) The Cinemas

Cinema advertisings, by which it is meant the use of motion pictures for the advertisement of products, is at best a limited and usually an expensive form of advertising. A short length movie, even a silent one, must be titled in the languages of the countries in which it is to be shown. This invariably adds substantially to the expense. In general, the motion picture as an advertising medium should be used only after a complete and thorough campaign has been launched in other media.

(*xi*) Shows and Expositions

In overseas markets, expositions and shows of all kinds appear to be growing in favour as advertising media. Actually, a show or exposition and the method of participation becomes a test of the manufacturer's export organisation and what he can do with it.

PRODUCTION OF INTERNATIONAL ADVERTISING

There are certain conditions in overseas markets that limit the freedom of the advertiser, the artist, the copywriter, and the production man. Some of these are:

(*i*) Inadequate mechanical equipment;

(*ii*) Lack of unusual and important type faces as well as lack of variety of type faces;

(*iii*) Poor quality of paper;

(*iv*) Great variety of periodical and newspaper page size as well as column widths;

(*v*) Small circulation of many newspapers and practically all magazines;

(*vi*) Lack of trained commercial artists;

(*vii*) Shortage of trained copywriters;

(*viii*) Shortage of creative advertising agencies;

(*ix*) Variety of languages which not only pose copy problems but involve constant variations in the length of headlines and copy;

(*x*) Widespread illiteracy in many countries; and

(*xi*) Lack of uniform poster sizes in outdoor advertising.

Whenever possible, the Indian campaign should be adapted, re-worked, and re-thought out for use abroad. In this way, the best of the Indian campaign can be utilised and much of the illustrative material and copy can be salvaged and put to good use, thus reducing the production costs of overseas advertising which, under any circumstances, will be large as compared with the space costs. The subject of Indian advertising in export markets may be divided into three main categories:

(*a*) Copy;

(*b*) Art, including layout; and

(*c*) Mechanics of reproduction.

(*a*) *Copy.* The adaptation of copy to conditions in foreign markets means rewriting as well as translating both for English and non-English speaking countries. The translation of any piece of writing from one language to another is difficult and requires complete familiarity with both languages. The copy should not merely be "translated." The ideal method is to have the copywriter who knows the language in which it is intended to advertise. When any copy is translated, it almost inevitably has the flavour of the language from which it has been translated. To those familiar with a foreign language, a piece of English copy translated into almost any language can be spotted without failure. If, however, the copywriter has simply used the Hindi or English text to get the idea and then writes the copy in the foreign language, the "smell" of Hindi or English will almost entirely disappear. If this method of writing copy in foreign languages is followed, all the other problems involved in translations, such as "localism," the use of direct command, technical terms, and the like will be resolved. If the copy is actually written in a foreign language, the copy writer follows the usual and customary practices of the country in whose language the copy is written.

One economical way of preparing foreign language editions of catalogues, announcements, illustrative price lists, and the like is to devote the principal position of the booklet to material that can be picturised or tabulated.

Advertising must adapt itself to the marketing machinery which it finds in foreign markets. Copywriters should be particularly careful and guard against the use of "localism" in their copy. All types of "localism" should be scrupulously removed from foreign advertising copy. The characteristics of the people themselves must be taken into account in the writing of advertising copy.

Avoid direct commands and overemphasis. Phrases such as "Buy now", "Only 10 days left", should be rigorously excluded. People abroad are naturally suspicious, their money is hard-earned and they spend it carefully. It is dangerous in most overseas markets to mention fixed prices in advertising.

Testimonial advertising should be used with caution in the export market. It is useless to use Indian personalities in Germany. In other words, if a testimonial campaign is to be carried out, it must be carried out with the personalities of the country in which the advertisement appears. Testimonials must be tailor-made. If testimonials are to be used at all in overseas markets, they must be the testimonials of highly placed persons. If not, the testimonials will have little or no value. Testimonials are always suspect because they are known to have been bought and paid for. This is particularly true of overseas markets. People generally believe that such testimonials are not an expression of the truth. A copy written for the Indian audience should never be used in the markets abroad. "To sell them you must know them" should be the main consideration in writing the copy.

(*b*) *Art and Layout.* It is equally if not more important that art and layout should be adapted to the peculiarities of the market in which the advertisement is to be used. But the emphasis here should be on the adaptation and not upon the ideas put across or the fundamental conceptions. All markets will not require the same degree of either change or adaptation.

The following considerations may be kept in view for export newspaper and magazine advertising as it relates to art and layout:

(*i*) Art work should be foolproof from the reproductive standpoint.

(*ii*) All figures and background should be non-committal. They should be suggested rather than drawn out in detail. It is dangerous to go into background detail to any extent whatsoever. The product should be given prominence with as little background as possible.

(*iii*) The layout of the advertisement must necessarily be kept simple and dignified to allow for the insertion of translated headlines in the copy. There must not be too much variety or too much individuality from the standpoint of types, for there are definite limits in securing certain varieties of type faces in most localities. There should be enough white space so that they can be increased or reduced in size without affecting the essential integrity of the advertisement.

(*iv*) Get commercial work done in India, reproduced and sent abroad.

(*v*) It is advisable to explain in the actual illustration, or in an accompanying instruction sheet, the various possibilities in case changes are required.

(*vi*) In no case should the headline be made part of the illustration.

(*vii*) Local colour or local atmosphere in advertising intended for overseas markets should be completely avoided. It is undoubtedly more generally acceptable to get something neutral or something symbolic into the background illustrating pleasure, enjoyment, strength, action and the like.

(*viii*) The story should be told in pictures. The illustration tells the story in every language. The idea behind the advertisement should be expressed in the technique of advertising. For example, a strong, rugged technique should be used in truck advertising, whereas a lighter or more delicate technique should be used in cosmetic advertisement. The message can be changed in each market but the illustration and the technique cannot be changed.

(*ix*) In poster advertising, no attempt should be made to tell the whole story in a single poster. Each poster should express one idea. Posters are attention-getting; they feature a single colourful motif or figure or idea with the name of the product, or they feature an illustration with keen humorous interest, with two or three words of copy and the name of the product. You get the idea in a flash and it remains with you.

Frequently, the observer finds it difficult to read all the material on the poster even if he has to stand there for five minutes. Posters should be build on the principle: Read as you run.

Window displays are a special problem because the picture actually has to tell the story. Window displays for use in overseas markets can and should be so arranged that the dealer can write his own message, naturally, in his own language. In many cases, this can be done with a window-writing pencil.

The use of other types of sales promotional material — such as window stickers, banners, car cards, street banners and all kinds of decorative material — has proved to be very popular. Advertisers find that the demand for these types of displays and promotional material is increasing rapidly. It takes ingenuity, however, to design attention-getting window displays without the use of a single word of copy. It must be remembered that such material, when produced in small lots in different languages, is costly. In addition, the advertiser takes the chance of having his material seriously mixed up when despatched to a large number of overseas countries.

(*c*) *Mechanics of Reproduction:* Great care should be used in the selection of material furnished to distributors and dealers for reproduction because not in every country are all the facilities for reproduction available. The use of colour demands special attention to advertising in export markets. The more lavish the use of colour, the greater the advertiser's chances of attracting attention. The advertiser should use all the colour which his advertising budget will permit. Naturally, this colour should not be splashed indiscriminately over a page simply to enhance the conspicuousness to the advertisement; instead the layout man should be instructed to make his colour a definite part of the layout scheme.

Exporters should consider the possibilities of cooperative campaigns where they have two or more distributors in one country or in one language section.

In foreign markets, there appears to be a far more general use of advertising stunts. The exporter must create repeated effects in order to accomplish the desired result. Some of the representatives of foreign media can be exceedingly useful to Indian exporters in guiding them not only in the use of media but also in the character and nature of the advertising which should be used.

There are almost as many methods of control in handling and placing advertising in overseas as there are advertisers. The following methods are generally used by Indian advertisers:

(*i*) The advertiser places his advertisement in foreign media either directly or through his advertising agency;

(*ii*) The advertiser allots his representative, agent, distributor or dealer a lumpsum to be spent on advertising; and

(*iii*) The advertiser allows a special advertising discount on sales of merchandise to a distributor, agent or dealer in a particular market.

Indian exporters should deviate as little as possible not only from the practices and methods which they use in domestic advertising but as little as possible from the form of presentation of the actual advertisements. The differences which exist between Indian and foreign advertising are mostly on the surface and arise out of the variations in the conditions of production rather than in matters of fundamental advertising principles.

(C) SALES MANAGEMENT FOR PERSONAL TRADE VISITS AND INTERNATIONAL MARKETS

Beyond management of the advertising function lies management of other forms of promotion. Then there is management of the vital area of export sales forces, which operate from corporate headquarters. The export sales people visit foreign markets, distributors, and large end-user customers. They are usually employed by two types of firms: those which market big ticket items, or by exporters who have yet to set up subsidiaries or affiliates abroad. Other sales forces in whose management exporters may directly involve belong to the subsidiaries and affiliates and operate in local foreign markets. The problems of export management of them arise since the personnel often come from and operate in culturally and economically different environments. Therefore, the questions of recruitment, compensation, training, measurement of comparative performance, and control are complicated.

Due to cultural differences in dealing with buyers suggests that the tactics of a sales persons will differ from country to country. A big problem that an Indian salesman will face is impatience; negotiations with buyers from many foreign countries will seem quite slow or too fast. And it may even take some time to get down to taking business. The sales force is truly an area where adaptation is wiser than standardization.

International Sales Organisation's Objectives

(*i*) To find the prospective buyer;

(*ii*) To sell him the product(s); and

(*iii*) To create goodwill.

A company's export sales organisation has at its disposal more or less the same techniques as its home trade organisation has. But an export sales organisation has certain unique problems which come in the way of export business.

Difficulties in International Sales Organisation

These are:

(*a*) Large distances;

(*b*) International boundaries;

(*c*) Customs formalities;

(*d*) Differences in language; and

(*e*) Differences in business psychology.

Important Rules for International Sales Management

These are:

(*i*) Do not call yourself an Indian where the buyer prefers to call you an Asian (Bangladeshi or Pakistani). The Middle East countries are an example. The advice is: "When in Rome, do as the Romans do".

(*ii*) Try to know something of the history and background of each of the countries and cities you propose to visit for business purposes. In your business talks show that you know quite a bit about their country.

(*iii*) Learn something about the popular pastimes of each country you visit.

(*iv*) Respect the religious customs of the peoples in the countries you propose to visit — whether they are Islamic or Christian. If you cannot say something polite, keep quiet.

(*v*) Do not boast about your country.

(*vi*) Be sure to respect the language of the people of the country you visit. The Kurd would much rather have you make a feeble attempt in Kurdish, or strain his ears in trying to understand your English, than to have you talk Arabic to him.

(*vii*) Respect local customs and dresses.

(*viii*) Do not comment upon the slowness of the pace of industrial development in the country you visit for business. For example, do not tell an Iraqi businessman that they do not have any industry except petrol refineries and dates.

(*ix*) No matter how tough a break you may think you have received, do not make a scene. May be you very wrong. If you were not, put your trip on the expense account, and profit by the experience.

(*x*) Be always courteous. If you want to win business and influence people in Latin America, be constantly courteous, kind and considerate. Don't be ashamed of putting your arms around their shoulders, of giving them a hug, and of asking about their wives and families and friends.

Fundamentally, selling is much the same everywhere. The difference between the Indian market and other markets is largely a question of degree. Experience shows that the best methods of selling in foreign markets are not unlike the methods used in the domestic market for the simple reason that all business is conducted along certain basic lines, which are fundamentally similar. The mainsprings of business are the mainsprings of economic life in general; the same fundamental appeals and the same fundamental methods of selling are likely to be successful everywhere. Economic life, whether in its simplest or more complex form, is merely the gaining of the wherewithal to purchase the necessities and luxuries of life. Therefore, if the digging goes deep enough, the same motives are likely to be uncovered.

Sales Methods

In the development of a foreign market — let us say Iraq — instead of sending a representative to survey the prospective market, the exporter would perhaps content himself with reading surveys by IIFT or Export Promotion Councils. He would then write to the Commercial Secretary in the Indian Embassy in Iraq and request that a list of persons in Iraq be sent to him, who, in the opinion of the Commercial Secretary, would be likely to buy his products or he would consult Trade Directions of Iraq available in the Embassy of Iraq in New Delhi.

Most exporters would probably then write or circulate their export materials to the addresses of the business houses thus obtained — almost inevitably in Arabic (get it translated from English to Arabic in the Embassy of Iraq) and send the catalogues and price lists.

International Sales Fundamentals

These fundamentals are:

(*i*) The international marketers should follow, as closely as possible, the methods which he has used in the home market. He should modify them or adapt them to the conditions in the foreign market only in so far as it is absolutely necessary to do so.

(*ii*) The international marketer should never switch over to making inferior products simply because a certain foreign market seems to be willing to take that kind of product. This does not mean, however, that if a market requires a less expensive product because of the low purchasing power of the people or because of the special conditions which exist in that market, such a less expensive product should not be developed by the manufacturer.

(*iii*) Capitalise on mass production. It is far better for the manufacturer to sell the products which he produces in large quantities and therefore at relatively lower prices than to manufacture a small quantity of some other product which almost invariably raises the price of the other products or may raise the prices of all his products.

Available Sales Methods

The normal sales methods available to the exporter are:

(*i*) Mail campaign — sending circulars, engaging in correspondence, sending samples;

(*ii*) Advertising — using various media, periodicals, posters, sending gifts;

(*iii*) Salesmanship — solicitation by a salesman;

(*iv*) Resident representatives — who utilise salesmanship, advertising and other promotional activities;

(*v*) Branch selling offices;

(*vi*) Investments in distributing and related organisations in foreign countries.

Samples

The use of samples in export trade is quite frequent. Sampling is the universal means of conveying information about products to a foreign buyer. The samples used in the export trade are classified as *analysis* samples, *standard* samples, *shipping* samples and *selling* samples.

The exporter must decide upon his sample policy. If the product is new, if its use is not well known, samples must be placed in the hands of prospective buyers. In placing these samples, however, it is possible to incur great waste. All over the world, there are persons who are known as sample collectors, whose interest in the product persists only until free samples are secured. They can do little or nothing for the sale of the product; and samples sent to such persons are a total loss. Where the product is one of value, it is best to charge for the sample.

A liberal discount may be given on such samples. Under such conditions, a request for samples indicates some real interest of the overseas buyer in the product.

Linking Sales and Advertising

The success of an international marketer in developing his export business depends on the care with which he handles both the salesman and the advertising and how he correlates their efforts.

The international marketer must first decide what types of salesmen he wants to employ. The usual type of export salesman is one who operates as a sales representative of only one house; but there are a number of so-called "combination salesmen" who represent more than one concern.

Having taken a decision upon the type of export salesman he wants to employ, the exporter must attempt to form some definite basis for his selection. Most export salesmen have been selected by a process of "trial and error."

Classes of International Marketer

Exporters may be divided into two distinct classes:

(*i*) Accidental International Marketers

In this case, foreign sales come largely from unsolicited orders. This class includes those manufacturers who have no export departments; or if they have someone to take charge of exports, they have no definite or concrete export policy and certainly no plan for export sales.

(*ii*) International Market Hunters

Such persons are definitely seeking to develop their export business. In this class are to be found those exporters who are doing not only a substantial and profitable export business but their export organisation is well and carefully planned and integrated into their total business, both domestic and foreign.

Successful exporting demands the correct use of every form of the sales attack, separately and in combination, which should be properly timed and intelligently directed, including the development and concentration of a selling force to meet any unusual situations that may arise. A sound export practice multiplies the effectiveness of the techniques of modern scientific selling by surprise measures, by unusual attacks, by adroit manoeuvring and by taking advantage of the competitors' mistakes or wrong tactics.

An intensive sales campaign is an exhaustive sales campaign, and it should be based on an exhaustive study of the chosen market. No intensive campaign is without its value elsewhere. A good export man studies his market not only before, but also during and after, each and every campaign. He is not content with a statement of results from his fieldmen — he asks for detailed reports. He does not entrust the analysis of these exports to clerks, but considers them himself because they guide him in estimating the expense incurred by him, enabling him to compare the expense with the results achieved and realising for him his real goal — that of making profits. To clerks may be left the task of recording the essential facts of the campaign. But only an executive can be entrusted with an evaluation of the facts presented to him.

One of the hardest tasks for man is to complete what he has begun well. When the success of an export sales campaign has been demonstrated by pleasing profits, the temptation is always to relax. But investment in a sales endeavour should follow commonsense planning. The gleaners must follow the reapers if full profit is to be realised. It is a growing and wise custom to have the missionary salesman remain in the territory for several weeks after the active campaign. This method ensures the completion of half-made sales, the gleaning of orders from merchants who are overflow buyers and the re-enthusing of salesmen who have lost their interest when the spectacular task changes to a routine one. A second and a vital reason for planning for the continued presence of the salesman is to correct any mistakes and rectify any failure, to live up to promises fully, and to handle any criticism which is the inevitable aftermath of any selling effort involving many human beings, in many walks of life. The salesman's presence definitely links the past with the future. It is natural that the transition from the introductory period to the era of regular and increasing sales at normal expense should invariably bring with it problems, which must be tackled; and remedies must be applied before the scratch becomes an infected wound.

The selling services performed by export organisations in foreign markets may be absorbed by:

(*a*) The manufacturer's export organisation;

(*b*) The combination export manager or manufacturer's export agent;

(*c*) The export commission house; and

(*d*) The export merchant.

Sales Records for International Markets

From the exporter's point of view, a satisfactory system of control is one which not only permits detailed direction of all operations but also fixes accountability for the results that have been obtained. Hence the gathering and recording of all available data concerning the success of sales policies and sales programmes are of basic importance.

If the overseas market is to be aggressively and thoroughly developed, export sales records must include considerably more than a simple tabulation of orders and sales.

The sources of records include:

(I) Internal Records

(*a*) Research department;

(*b*) Reports of salesmen, agents and representatives, and branch offices located in foreign markets; and

(*c*) Accounting records.

(II) External Records

These cover the facts supplied by outside agencies. Usually information can be most efficiently filled in a series of card catalogues listed below:

(*i*) Country guide cards;

(*ii*) City guide cards;

(*iii*) Customer cards;

(*iv*) Prospective customer cards; and

(*v*) Cards on indirect sales.

(*i*) Country Guide Cards

One card should be used for each country. Information on the following points must be entered:

(*a*) Agency relations,

(*b*) Customs duties,

(*c*) Classification for invoicing,

(*d*) Salesmen's visits,

(*e*) Mail campaigns,

(*f*) Competition,

(*g*) Government requirements.

The general rule covering entries here should be — record everything (except items of regularly published information) which applies to the whole country.

(*ii*) City Guide Cards

Whether there should be city cards or not would depend largely on the form of sales organisation in foreign areas. City cards should include information on the following points:

(*a*) Competition,

(*b*) Salesmen's visits,

(*c*) Agency relations,

(*d*) Other local campaigns.

(*iii*) Customer Cards

These should be entered and should cover all the information the exporter has gathered about customer's character and business practices. The following information may be included in these cards:

(*a*) Data on the relative importance of the firm;

(*b*) Its line of business;

(*c*) The terms of sales;

(*d*) Discounts and special prices;

(*e*) The leading competitive brands; and

(*f*) Any special requirements in packing, invoicing or handling of deliveries.

(*iv*) Prospective Customer's Card

On this card, the following information should be recorded:

(*a*) His line of business;

(*b*) The occasion for the entry;

(c) Efforts already made to sell a product to him, with dates; and

(*d*) All general data which should be recorded for any actual customer.

Record only the names of firms, with their addresses which have shown interest in the exporter's items.

(*v*) Cards on Indirect Sales

On these cards, the following information may be included:

(*a*) Sales through domestic wholesaler;

(*b*) Sales through export commission houses; and

(*c*) Sales to non-competing manufacturers, to be passed on to their customers.

International Salesmen

In international marketing, a salesman is the man who has the ability to make the opportunity to present his full argument in favour of a product under favourable circumstances. This quality differentiates him from the salesman in domestic trade. In export trade, distances are far greater than in domestic trade. The time which elapses between the sales effort and sales consumption cuts into profits. It requires only a few questions to delay the opening of business relations for a full year. The point is particularly worth earnest thought when there is doubt as to the extra worth of the export

Table 13.1
Comparative Attitudes Towards Business

USA (American)	*Europe (European)*	*Spain (Spaniard)*
1. Not interested in property for property's sake — Desirability of greater rewards — Increase his income from property.	1. Interested in the property for property's sake — Emphasise safety — preserves the property.	1. Pleasure before business.
2. Family basis in business is not important.	2. More of the European business is on family basis.	2. Customer-is-never-right approach.
3. Selling is the mainspring of all business — High pressure selling is resorted.	3. Buying is the more important business activity.	3. Businessman will not sacrifice pride, dignity, opinion, or comfort to make a sale. In other words, he places principle above business.
4. Eager for innovations.	4. Relatively conservative in so far as innovations are concerned.	4. The Spaniard is by habit courteous, sometimes too extreme, and at times becomes hostile in business.
5. Far too business-like — placing business above everything else.	5. Service is not relatively important. Take-it-or-leave-it approach.	
6. The idea of service in business is fundamental — the legal doctrine of caveat emptor is not that important.	6. Competition is largely based on price cutting. However, it may be emphasised that the U.K. enjoys a reputation for reliability, quality and trustworthiness in the business world.	

salesman in preference to the most skilful use of export sales correspondence. The international salesman thrives on cooperation and suffers from neglect. He is at his best when he forms the keystone of the arch of a well-balanced sales campaign. He should be supported by the best of export correspondence, the best of export advertising, and the best of export samples or testimonials.

TYPES OF SELLING IN INTERNATIONAL MARKETS

There are three broad types of selling in export markets:

(*i*) Personal selling — through a representative sent out from the home office;

(*ii*) Selling through representatives — selling through agents, distributors and dealers; and

(*iii*) Selling by correspondence.

The following are some of the problems which arise in the development and management of an export sales force:

(*i*) Selection of export salesmen;

(*ii*) Training and preparation of export salesman;

(*iii*) Equipping the export representative;

(*iv*) Planning itineraries;

(*v*) Preparing the field for the salesman;

(*vi*) Travelling expenses, etc.;

(*vii*) Co-operating with the export sales force;

(*viii*) Export traveller's records;

(*ix*) Compensation of export salesmen;

(*x*) Combination export salesman; and

(*xi*) The salesman's first trip.

The international manager will find the selection of good export salesmen a challenging test of his judgement. Good export salesmen cannot be picked off the streets, nor is it possible to find them as easily and with as little outlay of energy and resourcefulness as in the case of salesmen for the domestic trade.

CHARACTERISTICS OF INTERNATIONAL SALESMAN

The desired characteristics of an export salesman may be divided into two broad categories:

(A) Basic Qualifications

(*a*) Sales ability;

(*b*) Honesty;

(*c*) Loyalty;

(*d*) Courage;

(*e*) Instincts of a gentleman; and

(*f*) Self-control.

(B) Education and Experience

(*a*) Formal education (preferably IIFT diploma or any certificate of export marketing from a university or institution of repute);

(*b*) Export practice;

(*c*) Clerical training;

(*d*) Knowledge of the product.

Recruitment and Training of International Salesman

All the desirable qualities may not be found in an export salesman. It is, therefore, desirable to train the salesman after hiring him.

The chief sources through which an export salesman can be found are:

(*i*) Commercial organisations, both national and international, marketing and local chambers of commerce;

(*ii*) Advertisements placed in national dailies, commercial journals or trade magazines devoted to international marketing; and

(*iii*) Export managers of other companies who have already travelled abroad.

It is often better to appoint the natives of the country in which you want your company to be represented for the simple reason that they know the language and trade customs of their country. In general, a knowledge of the business, the product, and the manufacturer's methods of doing business as well as knowledge of the territory to be covered must be acquired.

An export salesman should be trained under the supervision of the exporter. He should:

(*a*) make a thorough study of the product;

(*b*) be given a thorough training in the exporter's methods of doing business;

(*c*) receive language training; and

(*d*) acquire knowledge of export techniques.

Preparing the International Salesman for the Field

In preparing the salesman for the field, care should be taken:

(*a*) To plan the business equipment and personal effects which the salesman should carry with him;

(*b*) To prepare a workable and detailed itinerary; and

(*c*) To prepare the field for the salesman.

An international salesman should also receive a thorough physical examination.

EQUIPMENT OF INTERNATIONAL SALESMAN

(*a*) Equipment Relating to Business

(*i*) Samples of the products,
(*ii*) Advertising specimens,
(*iii*) Copies of invoice,
(*iv*) Book of instructions,
(*v*) Standard agency contract,
(*vi*) Stationery,
(*vii*) Catalogues,
(*viii*) Cable code,
(*ix*) Letters of introduction,
(*x*) Letter of authority,
(*xi*) Motion picture and slide film equipment,
(*xii*) Customers' records,
(*xiii*) Prospective customers' sheets.

(*b*) Other Equipment

Personal Effects

(*i*) Clothing,
(*ii*) Passport,
(*iii*) Medicines.

(*c*) Personal Addresses Notebook

(*d*) Bonding the International Salesmen

(*e*) Planning the Itinerary

Routing of International Salesman

For an efficient routing for an international salesman, the following should be considered:

(*i*) The time to be devoted to the entire trip;
(*ii*) The approximate period to be spent in important centres;
(*iii*) Specific matters requiring attention in the various territories;
(*iv*) Time elapsed since last visit;
(*v*) Seasons best suited for business travel.

IMPORTANT CONSIDERATIONS

(I) Preparing the Field for the Salesman

The best single way is by correspondence. Each prospective customer, long in advance of the salesman's arrival, should be sent the following information:

(i) The responsibility of the exporter;

(ii) His ability to export;

(iii) His desirability as a source of supply;

(iv) His policy of assisting dealers in making sales;

(v) The value of the visit of the salesman;

(vi) The quality of the products offered;

(vii) The profit to the buyer; and

(viii) The appeal of the products to the consumer.

A single letter covering the above information should precede the salesman's visit.

(II) Travelling Expenditure

(i) Define exactly what the salesman is permitted by way of expenses.

(ii) Money for travel should be carried either:

(a) in the form of travellers' letter of credit, or

(b) as travellers' cheques.

(III) Co-operate with the International Salesman

(i) The salesman should be provided full information.

(ii) After the salesman has left the territory, every customer should be followed up by mail.

(IV) Post-travel Discussions for International Salesman on the Following Points Should Take Place:

(i) Analysis by salesman of each city and country he has visited.

(ii) Analysis by customers, checking up records, including individuals within firms to whom correspondence should be addressed and diagnosis of buyer's preferences and dislikes.

(iii) Adjustment of any claims not already a matter of record.

(iv) Salesman's criticism on general export sales helps advertising plans, and past or proposed sales policies.

(v) Salesman's criticism of past or proposed promotion work in his territory.

(vi) Betterment of any practices or forms affecting territory as a whole.

(vii) Review of use of samples carried and decision on samples for succeeding trip.

(viii) Salesman's estimate of sales possibilities in his territory and his suggestions as to the methods to be employed in order to develop these possibilities both rapidly and economically.

(ix) Cities not visited within territory which should be visited on succeeding trips and method for preparation of these new fields.

(x) Necessities for salesman's territory as a whole to be sent before succeeding trip.

(V) The Salesman Should Submit a Separate Credit Report on Each Customer in his Territory.

(VI) Ask the Salesman to Submit a Report on Each Territory Visited.

(VII) The export salesman's compensation will largely depend on the character of business and the type of man required for its representation. The export salesman gives up, to a great extent, home ties, comforts and the joys of a fixed residence. For these sacrifices, he deserves adequate compensation.

(VIII) Decide on Vacations

At least one month after one year's work.

(IX) Decide on Bonus if to be paid

This can take the form of a percentage of the total volume of the business in his territory over a given period.

(X) Ask for Expense Accounts

There are two types of combination of export salesmen:

(*i*) Salesmen who return to the country of their employers at regular intervals; and

(*ii*) The combination salesmen who reside abroad.

A combination salesman has all the qualities of a good salesman. He is intimate with established trade outlets and is fully aware of export techniques.

14

INTERNATIONAL MARKETING IN SERVICE SECTOR INDUSTRY (E-MARKETING)

International marketing strategy emerging from the Uruguay Round centered around Patent regime, and constitution governing asymmetric negotiations. Considering international marketing in 21st century, industrialised countries determined that intellectual property rights is an increasingly important component of their national wealth and an article of international trade. There are really two forces operating for marketing: first science and technology have become major factor in international economic competitiveness and national wealth, second rnore efficient communication and transportation have stimulated global interaction of knowledge and technology. United States have lost their supremacy in many manufactured goods sectors and their economics have evolved towards more knowledge based and service-based or service-oriented activities. And hence they have intensified their efforts to expand trade in services and protect intellectual property around the world.

Dunkel Draft proposals having more than 400 pages and contains 25 sections which are organised under four Annex headings:

1. Trade in goods
2. Trade in services
3. Trade related intellectual property rights
4. Agreement establishing the multilateral trade organisation.

Dunkel proposal has prepared competition policy based on comparative trade advantage. In Indian context, service sector growth is commandable during the years of the nineties. This chapter deals with trade in services or global marketing for service sector, by using E-marketing practices.

What is E-Marketing

Electronic marketing is known as e-marketing where marketing/ business processes are made through electronic media, paperless business like scriptless transaction in capital market. E-marketing brings together real time interaction between producer and sellers and sellers and buyers and transactions are made on electronic marketing through Internet or web sites. E-marketing or e-commerce is the umbrella term for an entire group of activities such as EDI, electronic payment systems, inventory, order management, information delivery through Internet, bar coding, e-mail, smart cards, CD-ROMs etc. Market information will be complete through such media for marketing purpose. Emerging e-commerce or e-marketing technologies help ultimate buyers and sellers. It is a form of "cybermellas" and online services to radically change marketing or business direction. E-marketing is an instrument through which traders respond to their trading partners very fast as per their needs. Trading partners include not only customers and suppliers but also transport carriers, banks, insurance companies, health care providers, government organisations as well as any other organisation interested in exchanges of information about marketing or business. World Wide Web and Internet are important technologies providing essential services. Instead of personal contact for marketing these tools through computers can do better than intermediary people.

Looking to marketing practices e-marketing can affect producers or selling companies as well as society at large. E-marketing offers the possibility of changes that so radically alter consumer expectations that they redefine market or create entirely new markets. Companies those which are deprived of such latest information and ignore the new technologies will be adversely affected by changes in markets and customers expectations.

E-marketing improves data accuracy, increase productivity, promote loyalty of trading partners, customer orientation as well as in maximising profits of marketing individuals or organisation. It is estimated that business to business (B2B) transaction are worth about us $ 220 billion and business to customers (B2C) worth about US $ 30 billion in value. Under the leadership of the USA, Europe and Japan has followed such marketing practices.

Let us examine economics and management of e-marketing by Internet.

Entertainment through electronic media has gained acceptance following rapid urbanisation, rising income levels and alignment of Indian media with global trends. Service sector like media service providers have vast potentiality in new marketing area. Information technology has to play a definite and determination role to boost Indian service sector. The advertising expenditure is 0.40% of GDP in India which is very low compared with other countries. The covergence in India has arrived faster than expected. The covergence would help in web costing, video on demand, internet via cable. The much awaited delivery of internet through cable network has already started in Delhi and Mumbai. The technological advancement in terms of direct-to-operator and direct-to-home is taking off indicating rapid growth towards convergence. It can open subscription revenue stream for channels. With more than 40 channels telecast by the broadcasters in India, media sector has emerged as a profitable business.

Advertising Marketing and Internet

Advertising is a major source of revenue to media sector which has fetched about Rs. 94,171 million in 1999-2000 to reach about Rs. 1,43,223 million indicating 15% rate of annual growth. Indian advertising to GDP ratio is considerably low at 0.39% in India, 1.6% in Brazil, 0.88% in Germany and 1.34% in the USA. This represents a widespread potentiality in Indian case. The Government of India's commitment to WTO and agreement to GATT can open new avenues for multinationals in India. The pay subscription market offers huge opportunity for India in terms of additional and stable revenue streams. Cable operators have gained significant importance in an era of convergence.

Cost Economics of Internet Marketing

The internet market is easier for both buyers and sellers to compare prices. It reduces transaction cost and barriers to entry. It has also experienced in Japan and USA that reckon the huge marketing and

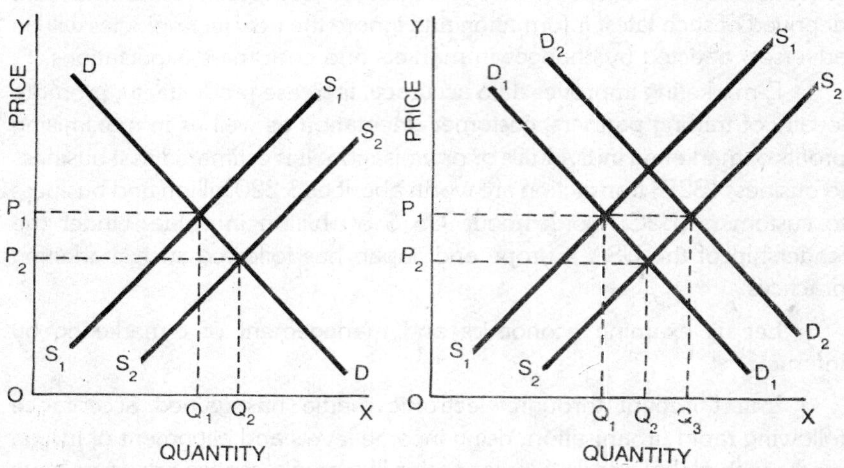

technical cost for setting business. The internet offers even clearer savings in services such as banking. B2B e-commerce cuts companies' cost in three ways:

(1) it reduces procurement costs, making easier to find supplier and cutting cost of processing transactions,

(2) encourages better chain for management

This means, the economy's supply curve will shift to the right. The following diagrams show the fact about internet business demand and supply curves.

The above charts clearly indicate a shift in supply curve at given price level from S_1 to S_2 as lower cost encourages firms to produce more and long-run equilibrium level of output will rise and price level will fall. Hence, it should be noted that price will not fall below the level of inflation. The second diagram indicates that on long-run, there will be change in supply and demand of internet services as new equilibrium indicate a fall in both price and inflation in an economy. It inflation drops below level target because the internet pushes prices down and the central bank will reduce interest-rates allowing faster growth of internet services leaving inflation unchanged. If equity investors expect faster rate of growth in output and profits, the prices of shares of internet services will go up and household sector will be encouraged to spend more. This means higher share prices, cheaper cost of capital and production too will boost investment in such service sector. Hence, the second chart shows a shift in demand curve from D_1 to D_2 in the chart. The internet may yield smaller benefits in more tightly regulated economies with rigid labour and capital markets and inefficient capital markets which normally prevent labour and capital shifting in response to new opportunities.

The longer run supply chain, the bigger potential gain from B2B e-commerce, since it allows internet service provider firms to eliminate the many layers and middlemen that hamper economic efficiency.

Thus, internet, services can boost growth in emerging economy like India which may accelerate the process of economic catch-up speeding up the diffusion of information through new technologies. It expresses that the internet is spreading very fast throughout Asia, Latin America and European countries. It will take time to make use of internet services in developing countries like India in infrastructure sectors like railways, electricity and telephone providing vital services. A developing country like America gained from Inforamtion Technology and internet services having comparative advantage in global marketing of such services.

Internet Training Market

Marketing of e-commerce training also draw attention of marketers. Example of Asset International, the corporate training arm of Aptech Ltd. launched the second wave in e-com training arena. It has started advance course in alliance with IBM. This has happened largely due to rising demand of properly trained e-com professionals. There is a vital company for a graduate, engineer, MBA or C.A. in branches of finance and accounts, sales and marketing, software or management e-com and internet can open new info jobs and career avenues for them we have blue chip companies like Indiainfo.com, bababazar.com, indiamart.com, healthcarehouse.com, Net solutions, PMG on the net, ESP Interactive, Ernst & Young, Standard and Chartered, Syntal, Deutsche Bank, Adit technologies, Zap Technologies, Microland, Aptech, Cybertech, Wintech with internet access and availability of advanced web development tools.

Internet Trading and Broking

It is a fact that no company can get more business except internet and web sites. Online trading has shown outstanding growth. In American economy 5 million online brokers are there. One in every six share traders now takes place over internet. The number has increased from 50,000 to 100,000 traders from 1997 to 2000. E-broking has had a huge impact on the cost of trading. The average commission for each online trade is around $ 15, compared with $ 100 to 300 at full service brokerage. E-broking is very competitive at global level capital and trading markets. E-broking minimises actual contact by doing all work on online.

Dot com means: An internet globalisation, as the net knows no geographical boundaries, an initiate ability to grow overnight thousands of customers. Technology translated to business with real benefits relatively easier. The internet allows small and medium sized business to make good use of Electronic Data Interchange which links all computers of all trading partners to transmit orders and invoices.

Internet can also help for component of supply chain management known as enterprise resources planning which provides companies with historical status of their business which allows them to capture and control the transactional data related with their operations. Most of the manufacturing business organisations are at some stage of a major supply chain optimisation project. Services on internet like business environment, customers, demand service, and cost-effectiveness will surely help the organisation. It appears that 21st century will shift from "hard" to "soft" even within IT industry and we will have to move from *Knowledge Age* to *Information Age*.

World Trade in Services Through Internet

Economists have viewed that our participation in the world trade in services would mainly depend upon Internet marketing information growth along with the efficient financial systems. Screen-based automated trading, transactions on internet, infortainment services, in-house R & D growth required such physical infrastructure to boost exports and overseas business. The transformation of PC, CDs, and internet have well began. States like Karnataka and Andhra Pradesh are leading in service providing. Now, it is most necessary for India to go in for efficient service trade as 40% of world trade composed of communication, construction, insurance, finance, computer and inforamtion, royalties and licenses. The internet has been hailed as a development of far greater significance, then either the automobiles or the PC. It has created an electronic economy that will fundamentally re-shape business relationship.

Distribution from Net

Advances in video technology have increased market demand for higher markets with high-speed, direct access, storage capabilities. Storage Area Network and Network attached storage can help companies feed the growing bandwidth needs applicable to video operation. By employing long wave fibre-optic cable between cascaded switches, servers storage array can access data up to 200 MB/s in a full duplex configuration. Availability and performance are two of the key factors Internet customers think of as we glance through important issues surrounding the Net and business needs. Network Attached storage is designed to provide easy, cost-effective, virtual snap-in, shared storage to both clients and servers in Windows NT, UNA, or mixed existing environments. Typical application include file server consolidation, Web server, simple data-base, software development, CAD/CAM/CAE, disaster recovery and even back-up. Network Attached Storage is a high-performance, platform independent data store technology that uses hardware and software can be optimised to perform specific task-file services. Their efficient, optimised architecture, allows them to offload many of the file management operation. Network Attеched storage architecture, is both competitive and complementary to Storage Area Network as prone to centralised data storage consolidation and efficient file access. Thus, e-transforming corporate Information Technology infrastructure is possible to Network. To gain the benefits of distribution on internet Gujarat Narmada Velley Fertilizer has gone for Infor-Towers for business development and sharing of global marketing information.

Inforamtion Technology Bill

E-commerce transactions could rise from the present Rs. 450 crore to Rs. 2500 crore in 2000-01 if the bill is passed and implemented in the next

1 or 2 months (end of December 2000). It contains a comprehensive piece of legislation with thirteen chapters dedicated to everything from electronic records to cyber crimes. The proposed bill has provisions regarding the attribution of an electronic record to a person as well as provisions regarding the time and place of dispatch, receipt of electronic records and electronic contracts. US, Malaysia, Singapore and India has chosen to base its electronic transaction law on public key infrastructure model.

Any person may apply for digital signature certificate from a certified authority along with necessary fees and a certification practice settlement. Our proposed bill must include these things and amendment is necessary before notification. For regulation of certification authority a licensing system is necessary for operation. At present the bill has not specified threshold standards for an applicant for net worth, track record or even practices.

The controller will also monitor and oversee activities of certification authorities. The bill has provision about this and necessary to make rules and regulations, for several aspects of certification authorities.

Looking to liability of network service providers, the bill has defined "network service providers" as intermediaries. Chapter XI of the proposed bill shows several offenses and prescribes imprisonment and penalties. These include unauthorised copying, destroying information or damage to it, unauthorised access to records, publication and transmission mechanism. For this, the controller is given wide powers to ensure compliance. Police officers of specified ranks are empowered to enter any public place to search and arrest. The bill has provided adjudicating officer and his order can be appealed at the level of Cyber Regulations Appellate Tribunal.

E-markets and Business Alliance

It appears that e-markets will hold the key to all future business alliances and beginnings have already been made in some industries. The global B2B (business to business), internet transactions that will happen by 2003. Fortune, Bank of America securities has forecasted B2B transaction to grow 650 fold to nudge the $ 13 trillion mark by 2004. Global companies of chemicals like Dupont of USA, BP Amoco of the U.K., Misui Chemicals and Mitsubishi Chemicals of Japan are going to trade on line marketplace. Similarly, automobile industry and airlines are to create an e-market place linking buyers and sellers as well as providers and receivers of related services. E-markets are acting as an excellent intermediaries which develop chain and squeeze out significant time and cost. Technology behind e-market is extremely sophisticated and above capability of individual company to create market. E-commerce transactions during 1998-99 were of Rs. 131 crore and in 1999-2000 are estimated to be Rs. 300 crore in India.

E-markets are B2B e-speak, e-markets known as hubs, vortals, exchanges, value-added communities electronic business hubs, "Net-markets," "vortexes," and "butterfly markets." Portals differ from e-markets/hubs as typically structured so as to serve one to many. Portals typically combines portfolio of basic content, communication, commerce and services. Direct portal is connected with a customer to support order management, whereas, an indirect procurement portal to aggregate and manage purchases across its employees. For this, companies have developed e-markets like vertical-Net Chemdex and General Motors' Trade X change which actively crossed $ 100 billion in market capitalisation. E-markets have winner-take all characteristics and advantages like market place liquidity, for land-grab, Meta-markets will emerge vertical e-markets will form a patchwork of alliance with horizontal e-markets. E-markets are offerings to provide value added fulfilment and productivity enhancing services. Such services include, Information Technology related services like system integration and hosting, financial services such as payment processings and receivables management, credit analysis, logistic services warehousing and inspection as well as risk mitigation services.

Functioning of e-markets in trade blocs in cyberspace, buyers can pool their collective strengths to create e-markets. Similarly, sellers can play the same game. Small and medium enterprises can team up to figure the collective might of e-markets. Once both buyers and sellers create their own markets as e-markets trading will take place between these blocs, competition in rival bloc can place of similar industry marketing.

Very recently, Deputy Prime Minister of Singapore declared ambitions plan at CommunicAsia and Broadcast Asia 2000 about inforcom technologies as under as an e-government experiment:

1. Punishing the envelop of electronic service delivery and marking electronic services integrated and customer-centric.

2. Building up new capability and new capacity to allow people to do the things they had not been able to do before and to create new value for customers.

3. Innovating with infocom technologies by adopting, a "creative destruction" approach is the government policies, regulations and work process to keep up with rapid development in global economy.

4. Being proactive and responsive with public servants being savvy-technology users, keeping in touch with national and international trends.

5. Developing tough leadership on e-government.

The internet is transforming the world's biggest market that is bond market. Larger transformation is to sweep over the bond market. Most of the institutional investors use Trade Web between 20% to 80% of their Treasury market trends as they find better prices. Competition across the Atlantic from the growing market for euro dominated debt, the e-bond revolution will help keep the US bond market No.1 place to raise money. Now highly frangmented bond market underwent a transformation. Electronics technology is charging balance of power. There is a shift from sellers' side to buyers' side with institutional investors gaining a lot. Issuers are also incorporating electronic road shows into their debt offerings. As it has been found cost-effective and efficient in services. Tradeweb has emerged as most powerful system in the secondary markets. There are winners and losers in e-bond revolution. Dealers understand that they must restructure their bond business, cut costs by embracing new technology.

For better operation of internet, companies using the services must keep in mind six "Cs" of e-business: computers, connectivity, content, cyber laws, costs and common sense. It is estimated that there will be 3 million users by the year 2002 as there is powerful thrust in e-commerce application in business practices by Indians. One can observe growth of capital market in India through online trading as a most dynamic innovation in the market. The US experience also shows higher growth in online trading as investors are doing more trade on internet rather than from e-broker. Most of online firms in the US are converting themselves into electronic financial services companies offering a range of detail products. Internet trading in capital market has lower transaction costs, office costs setup, wider client reach and ability to concentrate on core business with a variety of services.

Indian Companies with e-commerce

It is a fact in the case of Indian corporates that ignorance is bliss. The second global Information security survey (1999) was conducted by Ernest and Young's Information Systems Assurance and Advisory Group. It reveals that there are 4300 information technology professionals in 35 countries. It has been observed from the survey in India that 2% of total companies are conducting electronic commerce in some form or other within the country and 3% are conducting it in transactions originating outside our country. 9% of total respondents expressed that barriers in using electronic commerce in their organisation as they fear Internet transaction. 25% cost-benefit ratio which encourage them to move to e-commerce. Indian corporate regarding e-commerce also feel that they are unaware of the dangers that the Internet could pose to their companies about system, data base, etc. Most of Indian companies Internet is accessed through the local area network. The results of the survey indicate that through e-commerce is being pushed as a glamorous activity in the country and slower growth in India than in the developing countries. One can observe that the "initial thrust cost" to institutionalise an e-business, the long-run benefits which accrue to the business is recouped many times over. Manufacturing, sales, distribution, receivables, vendor management, purchase and every other aspect of the operating cycle can be taken care by electronic media. However, hacking of website is one of the biggest nightmare of any organisation in India hosting a web site for e-commerce. There is a need for Internet usage policy to govern it about who can do e-business and on what and which connection besides content monitoring, traffic analysis and conduct for the users.

Software exports

The Government of India has set up a new Ministry of Information Technology (IT) in November 1999 as the nodal agency for facilitating all initiatives in the Central Government, State Government, private sector and academia. In order to make India a super power in IT in 21st century, it has estimated exports of software target of US $ 50 billion, by 2008. It has emphasised Internet revolution, IT-enabled services, IT education, electronics and computer hardware manufacturing, silicon facility e-commerce and internet-based enterprises. IT ministry has initiated institutional mechanism towards greater utilisation of IT. Action plan is prepared to develop a road map for India in e-commerce. The government has approved setting up an IT venture capital fund of Rs. 100 crore for software companies. Software is fastest industry having 50% compound annual rate of growth in the last five years in India and exports worth of US $ 2.6 billion in 1998-99. The Indian electronic industry is estimated to have production worth of Rs. 4,140 crore in 1998-99, compared to Rs. 32070 crore in 1997-98, which indicates 28% rate of growth. GDP of India, likely to grow to Rs. 18000 crore by Infotech in 1999-2000. The following table shows top 20 exporters in software industry:

Top 20 Exporters of Software Industry

Name of Company	*Rank (1995-96)*	*Revenue (1995-96) (Rs. in crore)*	*Rank (1994-95)*	*Revenue (1994-95) (Rs. in crore)*
1. Tata Consultancy Services	1	420.52	1	286.00
2. Wipro	2	163.90	2	850.60
3. Pantafour software	3	102.03	4	55.26
4. Tata Unisys	4	94.00	3	83.50
5. Silverline Industries	5	81.49	5	51.40
6. Inforsys Technologies	6	80.65	6	50.90
7. Fajitsu-ICIM	7	66.46	8	42.00
8. Square-D software	8	62.10	9	38.10
9. Patni Computer System	9	56.00	10	35.20
10. Satyam Computer Services	10	50.47	15	25.40
11. Information Management Resources	11	43.94	12	28.82
12. Tata Inforamtion System	12	38.77	14	27.03
13. Mahindra BT	13	38.63	16	24.21
14. Siemens Information	14	36.75	17	21.81
15. Larsen & Toubro	15	36.59	20	19.98
16. Digital Equipment	16	35.70	7	44.54
17. Rolta India	17	32.95	-	-
18. IIS Infotech	18	32.90	18	20.80
19. Mastek	19	31.78	-	-
20. Citicorp Information	20	31.06	19	20.40

Source: The Economic Times (Ahmedabad) 8th July 1996 p.6.

The National Association of Software and Services companies hold the view that India exported software worth of Rs. 14.50 crore in 1995-96 which has increased $ 2.6 billion in 1998-99 having remarkable rate of grwoth as mentioned earlier. The off-shore services increased 120% of total exports, whereas on-site services contributed to 130% of export revenues. 132 companies already acquired ISO 9000 certificate for quality business in software. Software Technology Parks of India is an autonomous organisation established by the Government of India. It is a scheme to promote development and exports of computer software. Such organisation is helping software companies procure projects, approvals, import certificate, software valuation, export of software, technology assessments, Marketing and market analysis, supportive services. Software Technology Park, Pune completed 10 years of its establishment. The concept of an Incubation centre has been introduced for the very first time in Pune park. Such parks are encouraging *'single window'* system, promote concept activities, help participation in shows abroad. Now, the parks have decided to provide services in support areas like web-hosting, designing and e-commerce also.

Presently, 65 cities have Intelligent Network Services in India. Indigenous technology is developed by Indian prime research institute

Centre for Development of Telematics (C-DOT), which has 512 SBM exchange with the help of Mahanagar Telephone Nigam Ltd. The multinationals are now approaching C-DOT for IN-technology because of its quality and cost effectiveness. No doubt, 14 out of 26, state governments have already announced Inforamtion Technology Policy and formed task force for IT. It is estimated that infrastructure investment in IT industry required annual investment worth of Rs. 10,000 crore in India and Indian computer industry will face shortfall of 1.8 million professionals by 2008. Therefore, venture capital funding for local entrepreneurs is an urgent need which may be in different forms. Then India can achieve position of superpower in software industry so as to capture a sizeable segment of the emerging e-commerce and e-business segment by 2010.

Most of the corporate are approaching softare companies for training requirements and some of them have started their own institutes. Outside training services offers training in operating system, languages and four ends; database, quality and validation. This is so as project management linked with interpersonal skills and communication and performance management which can be met by software services. It appears that content is a king of the Internet as several web companies aspire to become media power. For this, they will have to evolve sustainable revenue models to capture e-commerce. Mere distribution devices cannot make web companies profitable but content segment is strategically important for profit generation and survival of web companies in Information Technology market. Information Technology and its transformation and innovation help obviously a positive development in general and software growth in particular. There will a shift of resources to this new sector. Economists viewed that there is a need for software-led growth than growth-led software in the case of emerging country like India. Growth-led software can be suited to the developed country like the USA.

Software-led economy expands software industry growth for output, employment and income generation. The government initiatives in education, workforce planning will be more compatible with a software-led economy. It has been observed by the Reserve Bank of India that 60% of total expenditure of Infosys in the quarter ending December 1999 was in foreign currency, up from around 45% in the same quarter of 1998. Software professional moving abroad cannot invest in long-term fixed assets in India, like houses etc. within country. It is most necessary to shift workforce from traditional industry to software industry so as to make use of local software professional in hi-tech inputs like software industry so as to stop their migration to USA, UK, Australia and Japan.

15

METHODS OF PAYMENT FOR SETTLEMENT

International Commercial Payments

International commercial payments may be broadly grouped into the following categories: (1) cash, (2) open accounts, (3) bills of exchange, and (4) letters of credit.

Cash

Cash is both a method of payment and a term of payment, but as a method of payment it is rarely used in international marketing. As a method of payment, the international marketing firm may use cheques like domestic trade. If accounts are maintained in banks in various countries, cheques may be drawn and paid in a variety of currencies. Or cash may be remitted by means of an international money order for small amounts.

Banks in India have deposit accounts abroad, and foreign banks have deposit accounts in Indian banks. Funds may be paid from any of these accounts for purposes of financing trade, yet an exporter in India receives rupees for the merchandise that is sold, regardless of whether the price was stated in Indian rupees or in some other currency. If, for example, the price was stated in Italian lira, then the Indian bank's lira account in Italy is increased and the Italian bank's rupee account in the Indian bank is reduced. The conversion of the lira into Indian rupees is a foreign exchange transaction taken care of by banks. Of course, exporters can accept foreign currencies in payment, but they usually do not care to do so.

Cash is also a term of payment. Cash may be called for with the order, or against certificates of manufacture as work on a complicated piece of equipment progresses. Today credit is increasingly demanded. Cash payment is not attractive to buyers since they bear the entire burden of financing the shipment. The buyer loses the use of funds for a considerable time before the goods are received, incurring a loss in the use of working capital as well as loss of interest. There may also be resentment of the view that the buyer is unworthy of credit. Furthermore, the buyer is dependent upon the honesty, solvency, and promptness of the exporter in the business deal. Today cash payment will probably be used when the importer is of doubtful credit standing, when the exporter is financially weak, on orders requiring special construction, or when the exporter is not cognizant of the competitive situation faced by manufacturers of other countries.

Open Account

The open account method of payment for export shipments is the opposite of the cash method. Under the open account, goods are shipped without documents calling for payment — the commercial invoice of the exporter indicating the liability. Since no documentary evidence of ownership or obligation exists, the open account presents difficulties because of differences in the laws and customs of countries which make it difficult to safeguard the interests of the exporter. In the open account method, the burden of financing rests upon the exporter. This requires a greater amount of working capital than other forms of payment and the exchange risks are assumed by the exporter. Despite the disadvantages of the open account, competitive pressures have forced many producers to use this method after years of selling on more secure terms. The Indian government has recognized the competitive advantage of this form of credit in the system of credit guarantees, it has established to aid Indian producers in competing with their European and American counterparts.

Channels for Financing

These channels are:

(*i*) *By the Exporter Himself.* This method is most unusual because comparatively few manufacturers and professional exporter either have sufficient capital or wish to employ their capital in this manner. Even if manufacturers and exporters have ample capital, it is to be doubted whether this is the wisest policy to employ it in this manner. Not only are the interest rates charged by banks comparatively low, not only are the fees for negotiating drafts usually quite small, but in refusing to use the facilities offered by banks, the manufacturer or exporter deprives himself of constant contact with a source of information covering a wide range of countries and subjects which may be of importance to him in deciding whether or not to extend credit in some particular instance.

(*ii*) *By the Export Middleman.* The export middleman, particularly the export merchant or export commission house, finances export shipments. The manufacturer may have his shipments to overseas markets financed by paying the export middlemen a fee. The fee usually charged by a middleman for services of this nature is comparatively high. Credit risks which are not ordinarily acceptable to banks naturally gravitate towards this type of financing. Usually, the middleman turns around and refinances his own drafts through a bank. The manufacturer, therefore, is paying the middleman a profit for the use of his credit. If the manufacturer is able to present a reasonably sound financial position to a bank, there seems to be every reason why he should finance his export business direct, provided that he is qualified by experience and training to judge the credit risks involved in the export trade.

(*iii*) *By Banks.* The financing of export shipments is usually done through the discount of documentary drafts by banks. In Indian case, Export-Import Bank of India (Exim Bank) provides refinance for export business development to nationalised banks having foreign currency chest.

(*iv*) *By Importers.* When the exporter insists upon letters of credit or cash in advance with the order, he is virtually asking the importer in the overseas market to finance the transaction. The importer does this either by placing the actual cash in the hands of the exporter or by establishing a letter of credit with some bank. In either case, the effect is the same — the importer has financed the transaction.

(*v*) *By Factors.* This method is useful to those exporters whose working capital is limited. The factor is a combination of mercantile and banking house which finances manufacturers, exporters, commission houses and selling agents through the purchase and discount of receivables created by sales of merchandise. They are documentary drafts and transactions related to Letters of Credit. Charges for factoring export transactions are generally assessed on a percentage basis. But because little or no cash is required, this type of financing is attractive to many manufacturers and exporters.

Terms of Credit

The terms of credit are contractual matters of prior arrangements between buyer and seller, and their determination depends upon a number of such factors as the type of merchandise to be shipped, the availability of the merchandise, the amount involved, the market customs, the credit standing of the buyer, the country in which the consignee is located, the exchange restrictions existing in that country, the amount due from the buyer at the time the shipment is, the availability of freight space to the country of destination, whether the account is a new one or an old one, and many other considerations.

The terms of sale should be carefully distinguished from the closely related "terms of credit". The terms of sale are the conditions of content, time, place and delivery of the merchandise, and only indirectly affect the extension of credit or the length of time for which credit is allowed. The terms of credit are the expression of the extent of trust, the seller (exporter) is willing to place in the buyer.

TERMS OF CREDIT IN EXPORT TRADE

(*i*) *Consignment.* This method is probably used in the export trade, possibly because export transactions are always wholesale transactions. In the end, payment is frequently made by means of a clean draft, that is, a draft without any documents attached, and, therefore, a draft which the buyer may honour or not as he sees fit.

(*ii*) *Open Account.* It may be liquidated by means of a clean draft.

(*iii*) *Sight Draft.* This refers to documents against acceptance (D/A). In this case, credit is extended on the basis of the buyer's "acceptance" of a draft calling for payment within a specified time.

(*a*) This specified time may be expressed as a certain number of days after sight, that is, after the draft is first presented to the consignee.

(*b*) This specified time may be expressed as so many days after the date on which the draft is drawn. Date drafts are preferable because they indicate a definite date for their maturity.

(*c*) Generally, the drawee is permitted to examine the merchandise before he accepts the draft; but in some cases this is not allowed.

(*iv*) *Letter of Credit.* Payment is made against the documents surrendered to the named bank. The buyer arranges for the establishment of a Letter of Credit through his local bank and specifies the conditions under which payment may be made to the seller. Upon the arrival of the credit, the Indian bank notifies the Indian exporter that the credit is at his disposal, and upon what terms. To secure payment, the exporter in India simply presents the necessary or specified documents covering the shipment to the notifying bank, either directly or through his own bank in India. If the documents are in order, they are accepted by the bank, and the exporter receives the payment in full. As far as the exporter is concerned, the transaction is closed. Great care, however, must be taken by the

Indian shipper to comply with all the conditions set forth in the original Letter of Credit. Even experienced exporters occasionally get into difficulties by overlooking some item.

(*v*) C.O.D. (Cash on Delivery). This may be worked out in one of the several ways:

(*a*) *Cash against documents at the point of shipment (usually at the port of shipment):* This involves advance payment. The goods are not released for shipment until the buyer pays for them. Part payment may be made in advance and part payment against documents.

(*b*) *Cash against documents at destination (sight draft):* The goods are shipped without repayment but the buyer must take up the draft and pay the face amount of it upon presentation.

(*c*) *Document against payment (time draft):* The goods are shipped without pre-payment, with a draft calling for payment within thirty, sixty, ninety or one hundred and twenty days from the date or sight. On arrival, the merchandise is placed in a warehouse. Payment may be made at any time within the period specified in the draft, at which time the buyer may take possession of his goods. Partial deliveries, against proportionate payments, can usually be arranged under this method.

(*vi*) *Cash with Order (C.W.O.).* Although once a practically unknown procedure, due to difficulties currently encountered by foreign importers in securing merchandise, this may now be a practice which is used at times. It may be accomplished either by actual remittance of cash by a bank draft, or by a cheque on an account in India, or by an available letter of credit.

It should be emphasised that the terms of sale virtually represent a contract between the buyer and the seller and include the "terms of credit". "Terms of sale", when once agreed upon between buyer and seller, should include every condition on which the sale has been made.

INSTRUMENTS USED IN FINANCING INTERNATIONAL TRADE

(*i*) Letters of Credit

Letters of credit are the most important single factor in the export trade. They form the basis of a very large portion of world trade, and give security to both buyer and seller. Letters of credit are much more than a means of arranging payment between the two parties to a transaction: they also set out the ways in which the contract between the two parties is to be performed.

A letter of credit has been defined as a written instrument issued by the buyer's bank, authorising the seller to draw in accordance with certain terms, and stipulating in a legal form that all such bills shall be honoured. Letters of credit are also known as commercial credits and banker's credits.

The terms of *letters of credit* vary greatly,because alterations are made to suit the requirements of each individual transaction. All such credits, however, have certain characteristics in common; all contain an authorisation for some seller of goods to draw on a bank which promises to honour the drafts, although in the case of revocable credits, this promise is contingent upon the cancellation of the letter of credit or its not having been received. The bank thus places the security of its name behind the buyer. In the case of irrevocable credits, this security cannot be taken away, except with the consent of the beneficiary. Herein lies the main point of attractiveness of letters of credit from the exporter's point of view — he is assured of obtaining payment for his goods, provided that he lives to the terms specified therein. On the other hand, the buyer, provided that he is able to satisfy his local bank as to his standing and the legitimacy of his requirements, can have his orders accepted by almost any firm in any country of the world.

It may be pointed out here that the bank issuing the letter of credit is the stake-holder in the transaction and is acting on behalf of the buyer who opens the credit. It is not a party to, and knows nothing about, the negotiations between the parties, and is not interested in the goods as such. In issuing a letter of credit, the bank is acting in accordance with the instructions which have been given to it by the buyer. The bank is not in a position to modify any of the details contained in the credit, whatever the reasons given by the exporter. This position must be clearly understood before describing the usual letter of credit requirements. Every little detail must be complied with by the exporter to enable him to obtain payment against the letter of credit and one small (and often apparently senseless) divergence will lead to considerable complications, entailing extra expense, delay in payment, or non-payment and, probably also, offence to the buyer who opened the credit. The letter of credit must be minutely studied by the exporter; and if there are any details, however small, which call for adjustment, the exporter must ask the buyer to amend his instructions to the bank and the exporter must wait until the bank, which issued the credit to him, notifies him that the letter of credit has been amended as required. The amendments must follow the same channel as the original credit; it is no use for the exporter to ask the bank at his end to make the amendments. The form and actual wording of a letter of credit vary from bank to bank; but the basic contents are the same.

It is a frequent practice among exporters to request their foreign buyers to arrange with their local banks for the establishment of credits through a designated preferred bank in India. Commercial letters of credit used in connection with exports fall into the following three principal categories.

(*i*) An irrevocable letter of credit (L/C) issued by a foreign bank and confirmed or guaranteed by an Indian bank. This type of letter of credit is referred to as a "confirmed irrevocable letter of credit", and becomes the irrevocable obligation of the confirming Indian bank.

(*ii*) An irrevocable letter of credit issued by a foreign bank but without the responsibility of an Indian bank. It simply transmits advice of the issuance of the letter of credit. This is called an "unconfirmed irrevocable letter of credit".

TYPES OF LETTERS OF CREDIT

In accordance with their terms, letters of credit may be classified as:

(*i*) *Clean and Documentary Letters of Credit*

Letters of credit may be either clean or documentary.

A clean letter of credit is one in which payment is made to the beneficiary against his receipt or against his clean draft. Most commercial letters of credit are documentary, the payment being made by the notifying bank against the beneficiary's draft accompanied by the delivery of the full set of documents called for by the terms of the letter of credit.

(*ii*) *Revocable and Irrevocable Letters of Credit*

It is obvious from the above classification of letters of credit that they may be either revocable or irrevocable.

Irrevocable letters of credit may be either confirmed or unconfirmed. A confirmed letter of credit is one which is the irrecovable engagement of the issuing bank and which has been guaranteed to the beneficiary by another bank. The Indian bank gives its undertaking that drafts drawn in accordance with the terms of the letter of credit will be duly honoured. For confirming a credit, the confirming bank charges a commission; for that reason, confirmation is usually avoided unless it is necessary or desirable. It would be necessary, for example, when the bank establishing the credit is practically unknown in the beneficiary's country'; in such a case, confirmation of the credit by a local bank would enable the beneficiary to negotiate drafts drawn under it much more readily.

Revocable letters of credit are obviously never confirmed, since confirmation would render them irrevocable so far as the confirming bank is concerned.

It should not be assumed that revocable credits carry no obligation on the part of the bank which establishes them. The bank cannot cancel transactions, under revocable letters of credit, after they take place — that is, after the drafts are negotiated.

Revocable credits are invariably addressed to a bank and not to the beneficiary. Under some circumstances, the exporter may be satisfied and accept the irrevocable letter of credit of a foreign bank without confirmation by an Indian bank.This form may provide for drafts drawn on the Indian bank; but in either case, the Indian bank has no obligation to honour the drafts. The revocable letter of credit is less frequently used than the irrevocable letter of credit. The revocable form serves only as a means of arranging payment, for it affords the exporter no protection prior to payment and may be amended or cancelled without the consent of the beneficiary and without placing him on notice of changes or cancellations. As a matter of courtesy, however, banks generally notify beneficiaries of changes or cancellations; but there is no obligation on their part to do so.

(*iii*) *Assignable and Non-Assignable Letters of Credit*

Letters of credit may also be divided into two groups, depending upon their assignability. An assignable letter of credit is one which may be assigned by the beneficiary to some other party. A non-assignable letter of credit is one which may not be transferred by the beneficiary named in the letter of credit. An assignable letter of credit is usually issued to a representative of the importer whom he does not know at the time he requests the letter of credit who will actually be the exporter of the merchandise. Once the representative of the importer has found a suitable person or firm which is able and willing to ship the goods on the terms specified by the importer, the letter of credit will be assigned to that party, who becomes the exporter, ships the merchandise, and collects under the terms of the letter of credit which has been assigned to him.

(*iv*) *Revolving Letters of Credit*

A revolving letter of credit was devised to meet the needs of firms in different countries whose business transactions with one another were more or less regular and continuous, at least over a certain period of time. A firm in Iraq, for example, which expects to buy a substantial quantity of fertilizers in India over a period of 4 or 5 months, may not find it convenient to establish a separate letter of credit covering each transaction. It can, however, arrange with a bank in Baghdad to establish a letter of credit with a bank in New Delhi to be availed of against sight documentary drafts, with the provision that not more than $ 100,000 is outstanding at one time. Two common types of revolving letters of credit are:

(a) *Revolving Cumulative Letters of Credit.* A letter of credit which indicates the maximum amount of drafts which may be outstanding at any time. When once this maximum is reached, the paying bank may negotiate fresh bills only to the extent that those previously negotiated have been paid, and advise to that effect received from the bank which established the credit.

(b) *Revolving Non-Cumulative Letters of Credit.* A credit which provides for a certain maximum payment in any one month (or some other period of time). It is a normal precaution in establishing such credits to indicate that if the credit is not drawn against during one month (or the period of time specified), the amount not availed of cannot be availed of subsequently.

(v) *Foreign Currency Letters of Credit*

Letters of credit may specify the currency in which drafts against them shall be drawn. The currency specified depends on the arrangements made between the seller and the buyer at the time the sale is effected, and these arrangements vary according to the countries in which the seller and the buyer are located.

(vi) *Cable Credits*

Under arrangement, these letters of credit are opened by cable.

(vii) *Ancillary Letters of Credit (Back to Back Letter of Credit)*

These assisting letters of credit are based on the original letters of credit.

Suppose our exporter in India has received a letter of credit for the shipment of sports goods. The exporter has no funds and no line of credit with a bank, and consequently is unable to buy the sports goods ordered by the importer. He, therefore, requests the bank, which has notified him, of the letter of credit to open its own letter of credit to a third party (the seller of sports goods) under the identical terms contained in the importer's letter of credit. If the importer's letter of credit is irrevocable, the bank may issue its own letter of credit (ancillary letter of credit), honour the drafts of the seller (the owner of the sports goods) on receipt of the shipping documents and cancel the ancillary letter of credit. The exporter presents his draft for the amount of the original letter of credit, but receives only the difference between the amount of the draft and the amount paid by the bank on the draft drawn under the ancillary letter of credit.

Discrepancies

The discrepancies most frequently found in documents scrutinised by the paying bank are:

(*i*) The letter of credit has expired, or the time of shipment specified in the letter of credit has expired.

(*ii*) The invoice of the draft exceeds the maximum amount specified in the letter of credit.

(*iii*) The charges included in the invoice are not authorised in the letter of credit.

(*iv*) The insurance coverage supplied by the consignor is not complete, either as to amount or as to the risks covered.

(*v*) The date of the insurance certificate is later than the date indicated on the bill of lading.

(*vi*) The bill of lading is not "clean".

(*vii*) The bill of lading does not include the "on board" endorsement, or changes on the bill of lading have not been signed by the shipping company or have not been initialled by the same party who signed the bill of lading.

(*viii*) The bill of lading is made out to "order" whereas the credit stipulates a "straight" bill of lading, or *vice versa.* Bills of lading to some countries are prohibited and heavy penalties or additional duties are imposed for failure to ship on a straight bill of lading.

(*ix*) Description marks and numbers of the packages are not exactly the same on all documents presented, or as called for in the letter of credit.

(*x*) All the documents required under the letter of credit have not been presented.

(*xi*) The invoice does not set forth the terms of shipment as stipulated in the letter of credit, such as C & F, CIF, FOB, FAS, etc.

(*xii*) Documents are "stale dated", *i.e.*, not presented to the opening bank promptly after date of their issuance.

(*xiii*) The bill of lading does not indicate "freight prepaid," when freight charges are included in the invoice.

It is difficult to exaggerate the importance of carrying out all these stipulations to the last detail. The bank must thoroughly satisfy itself as to the accuracy and completeness of the documents attached to the drafts presented for discounting. Once the drafts under a letter of credit have been accepted or paid, the bank is committed. If an error has been made, the party for whom the credit was originally established is not considered to be liable in any way and cannot be forced to take up the drafts so accepted or paid by the bank.

The bank negotiating, accepting and paying the drafts under a letter of credit covering shipments of merchandise is not responsible for the quantity or quality of the merchandise. The buyer must be satisfied as to the integrity of the exporter before he closes the transaction. But the bank is entirely responsible for the fulfillment of the conditions specified in the letter of credit itself.

Main Parties to a Letter of Credit

There are four main parties to a letter of credit. They are:

(*i*) The importer or buyer on whose account the letter of credit has been opened.

(*ii*) The seller or beneficiary who is authorised to draw against it.

(*iii*) The bank which opens or establishes the credit, called the "issuing bank".

(*iv*) The paying or accepting bank, frequently called the "advising" or "notifying" bank, on which the beneficiary is authorised to draw.

A third bank may become a party to this transaction when, under an irrevocable letter of credit, the beneficiary chooses to present his drafts, drawn against the letter of credit, for negotiation to a bank other than the notifying bank.

When opening a letter of credit, it is necessary to state:

(*i*) Whether the letter of credit is revocable or irrevocable, and whether confirmed or unconfirmed.

(*ii*) The name of the beneficiary.

(*iii*) The person on whose account the credit has been opened.

(*iv*) The tenor of the drafts to be drawn.

(*v*) Description of the goods.

(*vi*) How goods are to be consigned and bills of lading drawn.

(*vii*) Details of documents required and the disposition to be made of them.

(*viii*) Where and how insurance is to be placed and to whose order it is payable.

(*ix*) Expiry date.

(*x*) The number of the letter of credit and instructions that bills drawn under it shall bear the clause "Drawn under (the name of the issuing bank) Letter of Credit No.........."

Drafts or Bills of Exchange

A draft or a bill of exchange, as it is known throughout the world; is an unconditional order in writing, addressed by one person to another, signed by the person giving it, requiring the person to whom it is addressed to pay, on demand or at a fixed or determinable future time, a definite sum in money to, or to the order of, a specified person or the bearer.

An accepted draft or an accepted bill of exchange is called an acceptance. The person to whom it is addressed is called the drawee, and if he signifies his assent to the order in due form, he is called the acceptor. Such assent usually consists of the acceptor writing across the face of the bill, the date, "accepted payable at ...." and affixing his signature.

A draft is payable to the bearer when it is expressed to be so payable or when the only or last endorsement is an endorsement in blank. This endorsement in blank is one in which the name of the company only is shown, with the name of signatory and his title. For example:

Indian Export Company,
B.S. Rathor
Finance Officer.

The form of endorsement conveys title to the bearer.

A special or direct endorsement would read as follows:

Pay to the order of Joe Macanzie & Co.
Indian Export Co.
B.S. Rathor
Finance Office

The sum payable is a definite and specified sum, although it is required to be paid with interest or with collection charges, or according to an indicated ascertainable rate of exchange.

No special form of words is essential for the validity of a draft, provided that the sense is clear and the bill conforms to the provisions laid down in the definitions given above.

Drafts are usually drawn in pairs, one of which is the "first of exchange" and the other the "second of exchange". It is customary to send the first of exchange by the first mail and to send the second of exchange by a subsequent mail. If the first of exchange is lost, the second of exchange then becomes negotiable. However, if the first of exchange is negotiated, the second of exchange ceases to have any value.

It is drafts or bills of exchange, drawn by the shipper of goods or the provider of services in one country, on people in another country who are buying the goods or using the services, that constitute the chief supply of international currency.

A draft or a bill of exchange performs two or three functions. A draft payable at first sight is a demand for payment due and a receipt for payment made. A draft payable at some future period after sight becomes a demand for payment by the seller, a promise of payment by the buyer on the agreed date, and a receipt for payment after such payment has been made.

The person who makes out the draft (*i.e.*, the person who receives the money) is said to draw the draft and is called the drawer. The person to whom the draft is addressed and from whom payment is demanded is called the drawee. When the drawer expects the drawee to make payment immediately, the draft is presented to him and this draft is called a "sight draft" which is said to be "drawn at first sight" or "on demand" or on presentation." In its strict technical meaning, a sight draft should be retired or honoured (meaning thereby the payment demanded should be made) by the drawee immediately it is presented to him; but in export trade, most drawees wait until the vessel carrying the goods arrives at the port of destination before doing so.

The bank in the buyer's country normally receives a sight draft and the shipping documents which accompany it sometimes before the goods arrive, as these documents are sent by air mail; but whilst the bank will notify the buyer that the documents have been received and are due for payment, it will not take any further action to obtain payment until it knows that the vessel has arrived. This notification to the buyer that the draft is with the bank awaiting payment is called presentation; and when the buyer pays the draft, the bank will hand over the shipping documents (*i.e.*, the bill of lading, invoices, insurance certificates, etc.) to him. The buyer is then said to have taken up the documents.

Unless and until the sight draft has been returned, the bank will not hand over the shipping documents and the buyer cannot, therefore, obtain the goods which can only be released by the shipping company in exchange for one of the copies of the bill of lading. If the exporter has been paid through a letter of credit, the bank making the payment will own the goods if the drawee does not pay. If the exporter has agreed to send the goods abroad on D/P terms (documents against payment terms) without asking for credit to be opened, the goods will remain the exporter's property until the drawee has paid.

When the draft is drawn for payment at any date later than the presentation, it is called a *usance draft* or a *usance bill.* When the exporter has agreed to give credit to the foreign buyer for a certain number of days or weeks, the exporter will draw such a usance draft on the buyer. Similarly, the buyer may be able to arrange with his bank to advance the money for the goods and to pay the bank back, sometimes after he has received the goods.

In this case, the bank will open a letter of credit and arrange to pay the seller, but will require the seller to submit drafts at 30 days' sight or 60 days' sight or after the number of days they have arranged to allow credit to the buyer. The period which is allowed between presentation and payment is referred to as tenor of the draft. When a draft is drawn at 30 days' sight, it means that the drawee has to retire it thirty days after it has first been presented to him. What in fact happens is that, as soon as the draft is received by the bank abroad, it will be handed over to the drawee, who will then write upon the word draft accepted with the date and his signature. The actual wording will, in all likelihood, be: "Accepted payable at ....," and in the blank space will be inserted the name of the drawee's own bank, thereby converting the draft into a post-dated cheque.

As soon as the bank abroad receives the accepted draft from the drawee, it will hand over the shipping documents to him and this is the explanation of the term, "D/A or documents against acceptance." When the exporter has already been paid under letter of credit, the bank abroad will recover the payment after 30 days, or whether other tenor is allowed, have elapsed from the date on which the drawee signed this acceptance.

If there is no letter of credit, the bank aboard will notify the exporter that his draft has been accepted and give the date of acceptance, unless instructions have been given to the contrary that the bank should hold the accepted draft as agent for the exporter and recover payment from the drawee after the appropriate number of days has expired. The bank will then remit the money to the exporter after deducting its own charges.

While it is usual for usance drafts to be presented and accepted immediately they arrive abroad, there are some cases where buyers will not sign their acceptance until the vessel carrying the goods has arrived at their port. As the documents are sent by air mail and reach the foreign bank within three or four days, the goods many take four or five weeks to reach the foreign port. The acceptance of a draft only on the arrival of the vessel will, therefore, give the buyer credit for another four to five weeks.

Once the draft has been accepted, the exporter can, if he wants to get his money quickly, discount it. If he has sent the draft and documents direct to the foreign bank, he can instruct that bank to send the bill back after acceptance; and when he receives it back, he can hand it over to his own bank, or to a discounting firm, which will pay the amount of the draft, less a commission for discounting, which will vary according to the tenor of the draft and the amount of risk involved in obtaining payment from the drawees when it becomes due. In the alternative, the exporter, without asking for the draft to be sent back, may request the foreign bank to do the discounting and remit the proceeds to him. In actual fact, drafts are normally and preferably handed over by the exporter to his own bank, which sends them abroad to the bank with which they have dealings; and the bank abroad will notify the exporter's own bank of acceptance. In this instance, the exporter's bank will arrange for the discounting of the bill for him. Commercial practice, in fact, goes a stage further; the exporter's bank will normally discount the bill at the time it is handed over to it for transmission abroad and will not wait for a notification of acceptance. Whether the bank will do this depends largely upon how well the bank knows the exporter and how much it trusts his commercial acumen and morality.

Such discounting of bills costs the exporter money in bank charges, and these charges vary and depend upon whether the draft is discounted with recourse or without recourse. The term with recourse means that if the draft is not paid by the drawee, the bank or discounting house can claim back the money paid to the exporter when it discounted the draft. The term *without recourse* means that the bank or discounting house takes the full risk of not being able to get its money back from the drawee. Drafts presented against a letter of credit are almost always without recourse (even though the phrase is not mentioned on the actual draft). If with recourse drafts are asked for in a letter of credit, the exporter is advised to obtain an amendment before taking action to ship the goods.

In some countries, it is customary to allow the drawee three days in which to make payment after the due date of a usance draft. These days are called *grace days*, and a drawee, who has accepted a draft for payment in 60 days after sight, will in fact make payment on the sixty-third day after the date on which it was accepted. Such grace days are not allowable on at sight or on *presentation* drafts. In India, no stamp duty is required on but usance drafts must be stamped legally acceptable. The amount of tenor of the draft — whether it is 3 sight — but is calculated on the amount.

While it should not happen if proper care and attention is taken, there may be an instance when the drawee does not make payment against the draft even if it is a draft which he has signed as accepted. In such a case, the first procedure is to have the bill noted. This means that the unpaid draft is handed over to a Notary Public (who is a specially authorised lawyer) who again presents it to the drawee (or to the bank at which he accepted the draft as payable) for payment. If payment is not made, the Notary Public will note the fact on the draft, giving also the reasons why payment has not been made.

After the draft has been *noted*, the same Notary Public will draw up a formal document known as protest. The protest is legally necessary to enable the drawer to enforce payment from the drawee. The bank abroad will see to it that the unpaid draft is not noted and is unprotested if instructions to do so have been given by the exporter.

Noting and protesting can also be done if the drawee refuses to accept the bill. The consequences then will be the same for the buyer who refuses acceptance.

In most countries there is a time limit for noting and protesting. Care must, therefore, be taken to ensure that if such action is necessary, it is taken within the legal period, which may be within one week or within one month after the date on which payment should have been made.

While the main reason for noting and protesting an unpaid or unaccepted draft is to enable the drawer to sue the drawee or a proven debt, it often happens that the effect of noting and protesting is to frighten the buyer (or the drawee) into honouring his obligations because if he allows the noting and protesting to be carried out, his credit and reputation with other possible suppliers will be badly damaged.

It is not usual for drafts and documents to be sent direct to a collecting bank abroad. The exporter hands over the drafts and shipping documents to his own banker and usually fills in a special form, supplied by the bank, which provides space for the exporter's instructions to be filled in, including space headed "If paid" and "If unpaid" and it is in these spaces that the exporter will fill in the words protest or no protest he wants the bank abroad to note and protest in the case of non-acceptance or non-payment. If the word protest is filled in, the exporter will be responsible for the payment of the noting and protesting fees, which he may or may not be able to recover from the drawee. However, all this may not happen if drafts are drawn under a letter of credit.

One more fact should be borne in mind in connection with D/P and D/A terms of payments — and that is that both the exporter's bank to which the documents are handed and the foreign bank which collects from the drawee will make a charge for their own services. The charges are not excessive, but are certainly worth considering, especially when the exporter wishes to have the money remitted by cable as soon as it is collected from the drawee. The banks also charge extra for sending the documents by air mail. As the actual amount of these costs is not known to the exporter before the transaction is finalised, he may, instead of adding a calculated amount to the total of his invoice, as he would when drawing against a letter of credit, add the words *plus bankers'* collection, air mail and remittance charges immediately following the amount of draft.

Credit Extension

One of the ever-present problems in international marketing is the extension of credit. Whenever international marketing people assemble and the subject turns to marketing conditions in particular countries, the question inevitably raised is: "What terms do you grant?" The differences in the terms are often due to the products for which the terms are cited. There is also difference in the way marketers appraise a particular market. Therefore, it would appear that the appraisal of the credit situation of a buyer in a particular market is determined by a number of factors. Before looking at these factors, however, it would be well to examine closely the meaning of credit.

The Meaning of Credit

Credit usually refers to the procedure of surrendering title to merchandise without immediate payment. In other words, credit means trusting the buyer to pay for goods after title to them has been obtained by the buyer. Under the various credit and payment terms described earlier, a buyer would receive credit under open account and under all draft transactions. Under a letter of credit, the exporter (beneficiary) is assured of payment; therefore there is no credit risk.

There is another aspect of credit, however, that should also be considered. That is the credit needs of the firm which is engaged in exporting merchandise, because there is a period of time elapsing between the shipment of the order and the time that payment is received. A payee of a draft may discount or borrow against the draft before its maturity but in doing so, interest for the period of time for which the funds are advanced must be paid. Moreover, there is no assurance that the draft will eventually paid by the drawee.

The inference may easily be drawn that under all credit and payment terms except open account, a payee (exporter) can make use of valuable documents to obtain immediate finances, if such finances are required. However, banks will not discount or loan against accepted drafts beyond a certain limit set by the line of credit that the bank has set up for each individual customer. The line of credit establishes a maximum amount that will be loaned to a customer. A limit may be placed on the rupee value of discounting or borrowing that an exporter will be permitted to receive.

Conditions Influencing Foreign Credit Extension

There are several conditions peculiar to international marketing that require an exporting firm to view foreign credit differently from domestic credit. These conditions are:

(*i*) Supply of banking capital.

(*ii*) Interest rates.

(*iii*) Diversification of production.

(*iv*) Time in transit and business turnover.

(*v*) Exchange rate fluctuations.

(*vi*) Competition.

(*vii*) Customs.

At the outset, it is well to emphasize that the influence of these conditions varies from country to country. While in Canada credit conditions are practically identical with those in the United States, except for foreign exchange rates and tariffs, the conditions influencing credit extension are different in Mexico. The supply of capital varies greatly among countries and is highly dependent on the nation's natural resources and past production.

Importers located in underdeveloped areas have depended upon foreign sellers to finance their purchases of consumer goods, transportation, automobiles, or infrastructure improvements because local bankers were unable to provide the financing. The supply of capital is quite meagre in these countries.

Interest rates in non-industrial areas may be substantially higher than in industrial countries. In such circumstances, the wisdom of an importer borrowing abroad at relatively low interest rates and lending the funds at home becomes apparent.

The lack of developed business system is another factor entering into the foreign credit situation. In underdeveloped or developing areas of the world, intensive specialisation in commodity or functional lines may not be warranted, and the business person may frequently combine several types of business ventures in order to earn an adequate income. This imposes a heavy financial responsibility. Another factor accentuating this condition is the lack of diversified production. Many countries have only certain primary products for export such as sugar, rubber, coffee, etc. It is quite conceivable that a crop failure or a low price could cause an economic collapse. If this occurs, not only the growers, but also businesses, bankers, and others may be placed in precarious positions.

Because of the length of time elapsing between the date of shipment by the exporter and the time when goods are received by the importer, there may be a considerable period during which, in the case of cash payment, the importer is without both — funds and goods. If credit of sufficient duration is granted to enable the importer to obtain the goods before making payment, the exporter bears the financial burden of the import transaction, but the sluggishness of turnover may leave the goods in the hands of the buyer for a considerable additional period of time, during which the buyer's funds would also be tied up. This condition is of little significance in domestic trade where shipments may be made quickly, but in international marketing it presents an important problem. It may be weeks or months before the importer located at an inland destination receives the merchandise. Moreover, customs duties and transportation charges may be paid before delivery. In addition, distance and time compel importers to place orders for substantial quantities of goods long before the selling season opens.

Still another condition influencing credit extension in international marketing is the fluctuation in foreign exchange rates. Whenever a buyer receives quotations and accepts prices in a currency other than the native currency, the buyer assumes a speculative risk against which protection may or may not be obtained.

If the buyer has agreed to pay for the purchases by sight draft, utmost the that payment can be postponed and possession of the goods received is upon their arrival. An exchange loss sufficiently great to eliminate the anticipated trade profit may be incurred.

Finally, credit may also be extended for competitive reason. As a means of promoting sales, liberal credit terms may be offered. Moreover, it may be difficult for an exporter to refuse credit terms at least as liberal as those granted by rival suppliers.

Credit extension is influenced by the credit customs of the foreign market. Certain terms are often established in each market along commodity lines, and they are to be recognized by exporters selling in those markets.

Counter Trade (Barter)

Most international trade involves a cash transaction. The buyer agrees to pay the seller in cash within a certain stated time period. Yet many nations today lack sufficient hard currency to pay for their purchases from other nations. They want to offer other items in payment, and this has led to a growing practice called countertrade. Approximately 40 percent of trade with Communist-block nations in yester years was handled through countertrade. Less developed countries are also pressing for more countertrade agreements when they buy. Although most companies dislike countertrade deals, they may have no choice if they want the business.

Countertrade takes following forms:

(*i*) **Barter**. Barter involves the direct exchange of goods, with no money and no third party involved. For example, the Germany agreed to build a steel plant in Indonesia in exchange for Indonesian oil.

(ii) **Compensation deal**. Here the seller receives some percentage of the payment in cash and the rest in products. A British aircraft manufacturer sold planes to Brazil for 70 percent cash and the rest in coffee.

(iii) **Buyback arrangement**. The seller sells a plant, equipment or technology to another country and agrees to accept as partial payment products manufactured with the equipment supplied. For example, a U.S. chemical company built a plant for an Indian company and accepted partial payment in cash and the remainder in chemicals to be manufactured at the plant.

(iv) **Counterpurchase**. The seller receives full payment in cash but agrees to spend a substantial amount of money in that country within a stated time period. For example, Pepsi-Cola sold its cola syrup to the USSR for roubles and agreed to buy USSR vodka at a certain rate for sale in the United States.

More complex countertrade deals involve more than two parties. For example, Daimler-Benz agreed to sell thirty trucks to Romania and accept in exchange 150 Romanian made jeeps, which it sold in Ecuador for bananas, which in turn it sold to a German supermarket chain for Deutsch marks. Through this circuitous transaction, Daimler-Benz finally achieved payment in German currency. Various barter houses and countertrade specialists have emerged to assist the parties to these transactions. Everyone agrees that international trade would be more efficient if carried out in cash, but too many nations lack sufficient hard currency. Sellers have no choice but to learn the intricacies of counter trade, which is a growing phenomenon in world trade.

European "Euro" — New Currency for global payment

Since January 1, 1999, the "Euro" has became single common currency of 11 European countries those who are members of European Monetary Union (EMU) which include Austria, Belgium, France, the Netherlands, Germany, Italy, Luxumbourg, Portugal, Spain and Ireland. Britain has adopted a policy of wait and watch regarding operation of the new currency.

There is a talk of the Euro replacing world's most widely used currency — Dollar- (US $), as a transaction currency, as a reserve currency and as an investment currency. It appears that "Euro" can be alternative currency to US $ in global payment mechanism and its value fluctuation will affect transaction and willingness of trading partner for settlement in Euro. According to figures available with the RBI at the end of 1996 the US $ had a 47% share in trade invoicing among the major currencies, the

Deutsch mark 15.7% and French franc followed with 65% shares in global payment settlement. European Union countries united in single currency have combined strength as a strong currency. The distribution rate of each currency is governed by the economic strength of the country at global level.

An important consideration, of course, is the interest rate and exchange rate movements of the "Euro" after the monetary union. A debate pertaining to Euro reveals that whether a strong or weak Euro is appropriate against the US dollar. It Euro is meak, dollar holders will start buying Euro which means that debt in dollar terms would increase.

According to official release by the IMF and the World Bank settlement figures with the RBI in 1975, 79% of official reserves were held in dollars against 61.5% in 1995 the share of Japanese Yen escalated from 0.5% to 7.5% during the period. Trade development within Asian countries will not be affected by the Euro. Economists forecasted 30% decline in the demand for dollar reserves if the European Central Bank models itself along the lines of the Bundesbank. Most of the currency follow a policy of pegging their exchange rate against single currency or a basket of currencies. Thus, policy can be dictated by trade considerations and inflation control.

The process of "Euro" as a new currency having following background:

Countdown to Euro

May 1-3-1998	• Decision on final list of EMU participants. • Methodology for bilateral conversion rates between EMU currencies fixed
July 1998	• Formal Establishment of European Central Bank.
Jan. 1, 1999	• Fixing conversion rate of participating currencies versus Euro • European Central Bank assumes responsibility for the Euro and Germany assumes presidency of the EU.
Jan. 4, 1999	• Redenomination of government debts of EMU participants into Euro
Jan 2, 2002	• European Central Bank issues Euro Bank notes and coins and the physical exchange programme begins

Source: HSBC Markets

Looking to currency emergence and benchmark for bond dominated in Euro, the sovereign yield curves acts for bond in that currency. Possible benchmark under French sovereign yield curve, the Euro swaps curve (which uses the LISOR) or mixture of all sovereign bond yields of different government bonds for different maturies. But European Union has not settled the issue before actual operation of Euro.

Now European Central Bank will issue coins and notes of Euro into circulation by 2002 will bind together European block founded 50 years ago on the hope that economic co-operation could prevent any repetition of war. However, financial analysts have warned that the failure to agree on the European Central Bank job could dent the Euro's credibility before it starts by highlighting perceived fundamental differences in approach to economic policy among the countries of EMU. EMU has started mergers and corporate consolidation in sectors like airlines and there will be market integration for payment in single currency. Economists in Europe viewed that a single currency would also give industrial management a better insight into costs, margins, and price structure across the continent.

For better operation of EMU trade block and new currency euro, the following criteria are kept to be member of European Monetary Union:

1. Low inflation rate not more than 1.5% above the best performing countries.
2. Low interest rate not move than 2% above the best performing countries.
3. The Government debt should not exceed 60% of GDP.
4. The budget deficit should not exceed 3% of GDP.

There is three-year transition period (1999-2001) when both nationals and the euro currency will co-exist. Industry and trade will have to indicate prices both in Euro and national currencies. Hence, it should be noted that the European currency unit (ECU) is a basket of currencies, whereas, the Euro will be currency in its own rights managed by European Central Bank. The new currency will be traded between banks in electronic form only until Euro coins and notes will be introduced in Jan. 1, 2002.

Looking to behaviour of currencies like European Euro and Japanese Yen have some economic problems, still, however, both the currencies are behaving differently. Europe has a weak but improving economy, structural problems, financial assets are cheap, bond yield rose much more of late than America. Japan has also some characteristics but interest rate is for lower than those obtained in Europe. Japan has made external sector very strong.

Basic issues in Management of Euro as a currency:

(1) EMU and ECB will have to check variations in real value of Euro before its actual operation as it can affect real transactions in markets. Such as nominal exchange rate will be adversely affected.

(2) EMU will have to protect member countries as against competitive devaluation to manage external payment.

(3) Apart from trade transactions, global capital market and other payment will have to convert US $ into Euro ₵.

(4) Banks will have to update conversion and settlement of accounts as PC linked clients expects immediate conversion in order to know their balance.

(5) An entry of Euro will affect liquidity accounts in IMF, IBRD and other regional global, institutions.

(6) ECB will have to manage liquidity and efficient payment mechanism to cope with global situation.

(7) There is a need to develop hedging market against currency value changes in world currency markets. Money exchangers in foreign exchange markets can be protected if "spot" and "future" price of Euro is declared for transactions.

(8) Economists hold the view that Indian exporters and importers have 20% of total transactions in European currency, whereas, larger share about 70% in dollar area, still, however, the RBI will have to direct Euro price daily to the Indian banks.

Worries of Professional Bankers:

(1) Paying Bank will face difficulty at initial stage for fall in inter-bank dollers-per-Euro quote in customer driven market.

(2) Banks will have to re-programme computers to cope with conversion of prices of European shares and bonds into Euro.

(3) Management Information System of Indian banks abroad need thorough change for clients and PC-based banking system.

(4) Conversion process will keep financial staff very busy to maintain accounts in two currencies.

(5) Accounts in single currency in Euro can save to run 10-12 accounts in European currency after 2002, meanwhile, they will have to manage accounts in different currencies and Euro.

(6) Bankers will have to see from efficiency point of view accounts realisation process to manage Euro-cash efficiency and cost of operation of a branch of the bank.

(7) Indian banks and financial institutions need to prepare ready reckoners with Euro transaction value as it is emerging counter currency to dollar and trade invoice will shift from dollar to Euro.

(8) Foreign banks in Europe will have to open Rupee accounts against Euro. Prompt settlement with branches of Indian banks abroad.

(9) For the settlement of payment in capital market transactions, value of portfolio management for transactions in Euro need to be made in bank accounts.

European economists viewed that implications of Euro on business is reduction in transaction costs and elimination of exchange rate uncertainty in Euroland. Euro currency will be used in financial markets to manage monetary policy. Local currency will have to be withdrawn by EMU member countries by Jan 1, 2002 and replaced by notes and coins of new Euro-currency. Under Euro-currency system, however, Knediet-bank risk losing much of its clout. Giants like Deutsche Bank will be dominant in future Euro-currency system. Existing loan contracts will have to be reviewed with options for automated-teller machines to switch over to the single Euro-currency. Barriers to banking competition would be removed, making it easier for banks in one country to offer products and services in others. This can happen if the political and economic hurdles can be crossed.

It will be very interesting to know about the position of Euro in global currency with Indian Rupee and US Dollar:

Period	*Euro/Rupee*	*Euro/Dollar*
Jan. 4 1999	50.34	1.1842
March 31	45.41	1.0702
June 30	44.79	1.0327
Sept. 30	46.39	1.0641
December 31	43.89	1.0085
March 31, 2000	43.80	0.9584
May 12, 2000	39.50	0.9027

Source: The Economic Times 12 May 2000

It can be observed from the table that there is a watch of traders on the youngest currency Euro. Forex market reveals that there is unnoticed gain against Euro for Indian traders. The rupee which has slipped by a little below 4% against the greenback since January 2000 and has inched up 21% over the Euro during the past 14 months as mentioned in the table. European Central Bank has kept inflation low and not exactly defend the exchange rate. There is a feeling that the fall is over, and Euro might just being to gain as a result avenues for investment in the market is drying up. It appears that there will be a gradual fund reallocation in favour of European Markets. Euro has failed to live up to the expectations that was created during 1998-99. The pressure on Euro also emanates from the single interest rate and a bigger bond market.

Implications on Indian Economy

In India, the real effective exchange rate used by the central bank has 36 currencies in its basket, which is trade weighted. Emergence of Euro as a single currency peg is more effective than a basket peg. A basket peg has advantage of stability and helps the countries avoid country-specific factors. These include, political, institutional upheavals from influencing the exchange rate. There will be implications on exchange rate management with the single peg. The introduction of Euro will help countries enjoy the advantages of both single peg. as well as basket peg. There will be a definite role of the Euro during Capital Account convertibility period. Exporters and importers have concentrated on Dollar than Euro.

Bankers already expect the invoicing of trade in dollars to go up considerably. Companies are more comfortable tracking the dollar-rupee rates rather than dollar-rupee, dollar-euro and finally calculating Euro-DM rate. The small countries of Europe can prove to be a source of FCNR (B) deposit for India as their real investment will be in Euro. Bankers have viewed negative implication on banks as portfolio of the banks would end up concentrating on the risk rather than diversify it. Banks will have to carry risk just with single currency Euro in European Markets. Public sector banks in India will have to update their dealing room software to delete currencies from their trading system.

The EMU involves nostro accounts and correspondence banking in many countries of Europe, now with the advent of Euro just one Euro nostro account will be sufficient for banking needs all over Europe.

Euro investment in South-East Asia and SAARC countries will be development oriented for the nations an Asia-European Fund is likely to develop in Euro in emerging Asian markets.

The federation Chairman Alan Greenspan said EMU will come to the subject of US interest rates. He expressed that EMU can raise living standards in Europe if it succeeds in Europe. EMU and Euro can survive for first two or three years but beyond 2005 there are divergent views. For this, Greece has decided to join after 2001.

16

SOUTH-EAST ASIAN FINANCIAL CRISIS AND MARKETING

Much of the South-East Asian financial crisis is viewed by financial and marketing consultants as its analysis is based on weakness of financial sectors of the crisis-hit economies. These include Indonesia, Thailand, Korea, Malaysia and Taiwan. Economists viewed currency crisis for external payment emerged as financial crisis largely due to lending rates of banks exceeded the US rate through nineties which exceeded the changes in normal exchange rates. A country's risk was low because growth rate of such economy was higher. The governments of the crisis-hit currency committed to stipulate exports not allowed in appreciation of exchange rates and the large foreign inflow ruled out an immediate depreciation. This phenomenon provided incentives to the private corporates to borrow from aboard in the short-run without hedging. On account of market weakness in general and financial markets in particular, as there was rapid collapse after mild shocks. Normally, depreciation of exchange rate can occur under low monetary growth.

East-Asian crisis is a direct consequence of the fast success of the said economies based on outward-oriented thrust represented by aggressive export promotion. Such crisis adversely affected payment mechanism of money markets, capital markets and banks as monetary and exchange policies were not well co-ordinated. Exchange rate management becomes difficult in the presence of higher capital inflows to the worst hit countries during the crisis. Macroeconomic policy need to be in open nature keeping high mobility of capital, domestic interest rates must be linked to foreign interest rates. The crisis in stock and currency markets was accompanied by problems in banks and other financial institutions of these countries. In Thailand 58 out of 90 financial firms had to be suspended by July 1997, 16 large banks were closed in Sept. 1997 in Indonesia and corporate firms were seeking survival all among default to large payments after sudden depreciation of exchange rates. South-East Asian financial crisis aggravated as fall in securities prices with larger outflow of short-term portfolio investment. Investors from abroad gained a lot due to exchange rate variations in those countries which helped capital flight. Local and external environment in the countries created the crisis largely due to external shocks, financial structure and illiquidity resulted into insolvency, along with depreciated exchange rates of the currency of the concerned countries hit by the crisis.

Payment Settlement in Era of Currency Crisis in Asian Countries

Since 1995, Asian currencies like Thailand Baht, Korean Won, Indonesian Yen, Chinese Yuan, Mexican Peso, Indonesian Rupiah facing international financial crisis and now Indian rupee has experienced falling external value. Floating exchange rate system accepted by these countries under W.T.O. sizeably affected external value of these soft currencies and affected export earnings in terms of U.S. dollars. Economists have exam ined alternative models and policy options through in connection with structural reform and showing Capital Account convertibility.

Fall in value of rupee affects foreign exchange reserves and management of exchange rates for efficient payment mechanism in external currency. International marketing experts and financial consultants try to examine real rate of growth of exports in an era of persistently falling of a particular currency. Most of the studies reveal that nations which are facing currency crisis having weak fundamentals and excessive reliance on investment flows in emerging market countries of South-East Asia. They have not sufficiently increased their repaying capacity.

A depreciation of nominal exchange rate is expected to increase incentives for exports and reduces incentive for imports. Such nominal exchange rate can be adjusted for difference between inflation rate of foreign countries and provides real effective exchange rate. A depreciation of rupee actually helps only a few exporters and that too in traditional exports like gems and jewellery, leather garments and appanels. A competitior aggregate benefits arising from a depreciating rupee which to a foreign buyer means cheaper imports which is not sustainable. On long-run manufacturers of other countries will also follow in the same footsteps and they will outbid India in price and technological parity.

The exchange rates are one of the important predictors of a country's export performance. After currency crisis period, from Jan. 1996, export level has fallen. The Government of India targeted 20% rate of growth in exports during Ninth five-year plan period and estimated 12% rise during 1997-98 but in actual practice it has remained below 10% level. This means price elasticity pegging against wrong. Bhalla estimated 1.4% against each 1% increase in relative price is accompanied by a 1.4% decline in export volume. Similarly, 1% decline in exports of industrialised countries, import results in a 0.7% decline and export fundamentalists view that a strong rupee can hurt exports and hold the view that RBI funded depreciation will be beneficial to the exporters rather than export industries. Export transaction expenses of foreign exchange constitute very small portion in India's total transactions in foreign exchange. Due to currency turmoil, monthly variations in exports registered 2.6% than 10% during April 1997 and 1998 respectively. India's rate of growth of exports fell by 16.8 per cent point in the first nine months of 1996 and lower price realisation accounted for a fall of 7.4% points in export growth, while export volume declined 9.4% points. It is estimated that average decline in export growth rate was 12.6% point in 1997-98 as rupee fluctuated between Rs. 39.2 to Rs. 41.2 against the U.S. dollar. It is appears that most of the competitive gains of a weaker currency has eaten away by dearer import costs. Indian exports are not responsive to changes in real effective exchange rate but can build infrastructure through low cost of import which may lead to rise in real output and exportable surplus at competitive cost.

The table given after this page reveals comparison between domestic and USA interest rates with change in exchange rate for South-East Asian countries. There is much higher changes in exchange rates in Indonesia, Philippines, Thailand and India and Singapore, whereas, in the case of Malayaisa and Korea such difference remained higher for some periods only. Normally, fixed exchange rate gives assurance against immediate depreciation but positive interest differential led foreign investors, domestic corporation and banks to borrow short-term loans. This had led to the real sector depending upon borrowed short-term debt and imperfect financial structure among uncertainty.

One can safety draw the event as under:

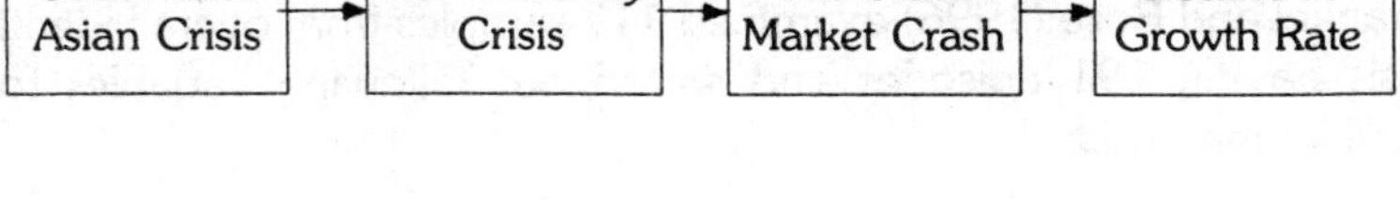

Indian could escape from the crisis largely due to tight money policy, high revenue deficits, which kept interest rate far above the prevailing rates in foreign markets.

Weaknesses of South-East Asian Financial Crisis:

1. Directed credit and administered interest rates in worst-hit countries.
2. Lack of international level standard in bank supervision by the central banks as large amount of non-performing assets created by banking sector in the countries.
3. Similarly, the central banks of worst-hit countries ignored supervision of financial market which was very poor and non-transparent.
4. There was a crisis of liquidity in both local currency as well as foreign currencies to manage payment mechanism and sustainable debt market.
5. Scarcity of adequate equity in both the financial and corporate sector.

However, the above reasons for the crisis are highly debated by the financial consultants that the crisis can be interpreted as a consequences of growth strategy race to achieve higher rate of growth by the countries caught by the crisis.

Moreover, World Bank economists hold the view that South-East Asian crisis emerged largely due to following *structural factors*:

(1) Move of the countries from labour-intensive technology to capital intensive technology. Such technology resulted into rapidly rising wage cost affected structure of production process.

(2) Japan is leading nation in Asia in the region. Japanese production and exports have dominant effect in neighbouring countries, the impact of Japanese economic slowdown adversely affected the worst-hit countries.

(3) According to Krugman's hypothesis in the absence of productivity growth, East Asian performance was not sustainable. As a result slow down in exports seriously affected financial sector and payment mechanism.

(4) Slowdown in exports markets adversely affected the equity and capital market growth in an era of capital flight by FII.

Frankel and Rose (1996) examined 117 samples from overall identified crisis having 191 episodes and sorted out following variables for behaviour of the crisis:

Comparison of Difference in Domestic and US Interest Rate with Change in Exchange Rate for South East Asian Countries

Year	Hong Kong		Indonesia		Korea		Malaysia	
	Interest Rate Differential	Change in Exchange Rate	Interest Rate Difference	Change in Exchange Rate	Interest Rate Difference	Change in Exchange Rate	Interest Rate Differential	Change in Exchange Rate
1990 Q1	-10.04	0.01	10.96	1.45	-0.04	3.24	-3.04	0.00
1991 Q1	0.81	-0.09	16.81	1.63	0.81	1.26	-1.19	0.00
1992 Q1	2.50	-0.54	18.50	1.26	3.50	1.84	2.50	0.00
1993 Q1	1.00	-0.14	16.00	0.44	3.00	0.76	4.00	0.00
1994 Q1	0.98	0.03	11.98	1.56	2.98	-0.12	2.98	0.00
1995 Q1	0.17	-0.06	9.17	0.86	0.17	-2.15	-1.83	0.00
1996 Q1	0.67	0.03	10.67	1.26	0.67	1.03	0.67	0.00
1997 Q1	0.73	0.18	10.73	1.51	0.73	6.28	-0.27	-33.33
1997 Q2	0.50	-0.04	10.50	1.28	-0.50	-1.00	-0.50	50.00
1997 Q3	0.50	-0.12	14.50	33.67	-0.50	3.04	-0.50	0.00
1997 Q4	1.50	0.10	-1.50	71.76	1.50	85.36	-1.50	33.33

Year	Phillippines		Singapore		Thailand		India	
	Interest Rate Differential	Change in Exchange Rate	Interest Rate Differential	Change in Exchange Rate	Interest Rate Differential	Change in Exchange Rate	Interest Rate Differential	Change in Exchange Rate
1990 Q1	11.96	4.55	-3.04	0.00	-2.04	0.00	6.96	0.00
1991 Q1	16.81	0.00	-2.19	0.00	2.81	4.00	6.81	11.11
1992 Q1	14.50	-7.41	-0.50	0.00	4.50	4.00	13.50	0.00
1993 Q1	11.00	4.00	-1.00	0.00	5.00	-3.85	12.00	19.23
1994 Q1	9.98	0.00	-0.02	0.00	2.98	-3.85	8.98	0.00
1995 Q1	5.17	8.33	-2.83	0.00	2.17	0.00	6.17	3.23
1996 Q1	6.67	0.00	-2.33	0.00	2.67	0.00	8.67	-2.86
1997 Q1	5.73	0.00	-2.27	0.00	2.73	0.00	6.73	0.00
1997 Q2	4.50	0.00	-2.50	0.00	2.50	0.00	5.50	0.00
1997 Q3	8.50	30.77	-2.50	100.00	4.50	42.31	5.50	0.00
1997 Q4	-1.50	17.65	-1.50	0.00	-1.50	27.03	-0.50	8.33

Source:IMF and World Bank Publications 1999.

(1) Foreign Direct Investment flow dry-up as foreign investors withdraw their investment and flight of capital is visusalised.

(2) There will be declining trend in foreign exchange reserves and liquidity crisis for external payment.

(3) Experience show that there will be higher domestic credit growth as against absorbing capacity of real sector.

(4) Fluctuations in exchange rate lead to overvaluation shown by real exchange rate.

(5) There will be a rise in "Northern Interest Rate" which may affect cost structure in the economy.

(6) Industrial recession is visualised but causality remain unclear.

(7) Financial crash is not a result of neither current account or budget deficit in the economy.

IMF and World Bank Economists sorted out

(A) Financial (Proximate) Factors

Such factors can make larger outflow of foreign exchange. Vulnerability to large outflows are due to (i) short-term debt, (ii) importance of portfolio investment, (iii) levels of forex resources, (iv) weakness of domestic portfolio can lead to a crisis.

It has been visualised in the case of Korea and Taiwan where net investors abroad and FDI issue is only relevant to Thailand and Indonesia in our case. East Asian picture is not matching with the fact stated by Frankel and Rose. Expansion in financial intermediation activities that is higher rate of growth of domestic credit, appear relevant reason for the crisis. It is also a fact that US interest rate of varying maturities bottomed in 1993 and steadily rose in subsequent years which has affected increased risk premiums demanded of the East Asian countries than movement in northern interest rates.

(B) Structural Factors

These factors can be represented by variables are:

(i) Nature of domestic financial system in crisis affected countries.

(ii) Institutional mechanism of supervision by the central bank.

(iii) Opportunities for diversification.

(iv) External factors include; the role of Japan and China as a major external factor in many of the commodities market where they dominated in the world market.

(v) Internal factors include cost competitiveness in global market with currency movements. These include banking system, stock market, portfolio investors's decision to exit crisis-hit countries.

These evidences provide a clue to believe that South-East Asian crisis is based on neglect of restriction on interest and exchange rates policies due to arbitrage in a global market by domestic and foreign investors which led to depreciation of exchange rates positively.

The East-Asian crisis took place largely due to:

(i) sudden and deep devaluation of national currencies
(ii) affected prices of stocks and nominal stock markets
(iii) steep climb in interest rate
(iv) decline in foreign exchange reserves in Indonesia followed by South Korea and Thailand.

The currency crisis spread due to:

(i) fall in value of Thai Baht by 18% in relation with US $.
(ii) speculative currency pressures in Brazil, South Africa, and Czech Republic as they concentrated in these emerging market economies.
(iii) stock markets of Tokyo, London, Frankfurt, Paris and New York were severely affected.

The stock market crisis or crash due to:

(i) Negative movement of exchange rates in the region
(ii) Swing in cross-border capital flows
(iii) Resulted in short-run return to short-term portfolio.
(iv) Domestic and financial markets/sectors showed signs of distress
(v) Rising non-performing assets of banks in crisis hit countries.
(vi) There was a decline in performance of real sector.
(vii) A fall in secondary and property markets.

Decline in GDP Growth Rate

GDP growth rates were 8.2%, 10.1% and 8.7% in the case of Indonesia, Malaysia and Thailand respectively during pre-crisis period which dropped to around 1%. Exports fell from 24% in 1996 to 0.9% in 1997, 3% to 9% for Thailand and Malaysia respectively. Similarly, trade deficits of these three countries increased by $ 17.8 bn, $ 16.6 bn and $ 8.0 bn respectively.

Implications for India

Due to massive depreciation of currencies of the neighbouring countries, India lost export markets, growing significantly our portfolio investment flows obviously increased our exposure.

Financial sector allocation of resources based on signals that did not have built-in incentives to efficiency in the East-Asian economies. As a result, quality of bank portfolio have a serious problem and inadequate opportunities that exist for hedging them. It appears that in interpreting this crisis from Indian perspective moved away from currency aspect to banking/credit aspect for different reasons.

It is viewed that the crisis as emerging from structural factors to export performance and proximate factor relating to moral hazard problem faced by domestic and international financial intermediaries. India escaped from the crisis because its financial markets were not fully integrated with each other and world market. India had enough volatile funds, at margin to allow arbitrage as full Capital Account convertibility was absent during the period of crisis. India's short-term debt was 5% of total debt hence depreciation in exchange rate could not be affected as RBI announced low interest rate during the period.

India has not a policy framework to improve its competitiveness to cope with future crisis. India needs national competition policy keeping is mind financial and real sectors, removing barriers to entry for domestic and foreign entrants in the markets, announcing a takeover code, evolving consensus on reducing government deficits, removal of administrative price mechanism and strong legal base for orderly output and income growth.

South-East Asian financial crisis created tension for worst-hit countries. It is a fact that currency value fell against US $. Economists viewed that USA's budget deficit was 20%, totally financed by external lenders from East-Asia and Japan. It is a capital flows into US in the form of deposits of reserves of various countries including Asia. If any of the Asian countries withdraws its reserves from the US and deposits them in securities of other Asian economies, the US will surely face a crisis.

It is viewed that risk management system and the rating agencies operating in South-East Asian countries could not warn the nations about the financial crisis. They have been blamed about this by commercial banks. The Bank for International Settlement viewed that undue reliance may have been placed by financiers on rating for the pricing of credit. It is also argued that negative rating would have triggered a crisis which otherwise could have been avoided.

It is necessary to maintain interest of foreign investors interested in India for foreign investment. Indian economy is trying to rebuild fundamentals for stability to pose confidence among the investors during post-crisis era. Economic fluctuation of stock markets in India never reflected the fundamentals of Indian economy. A fall in value of the rupee needs to be arrested by limited downward adjustment in its value. The role of FIIs in stock market appears to be artificial. To save India from future currency war, needs for realistic approach by the government for stability in output, exchange rates and level of inflation to cope with global competition.

Lessons of South-East Asian Crisis

(1) Compared to the turmoil in South-East Asia, India is in area of economic tranquility and foreign investors are looking at India with respect for preferred investment destination in Asia. India should target the growth rate within its reach in order to save the rupee and devaluation of exchange rates.

(2) An Indian growth rate of 5.5% plus looks pretty one. Higher growth rate expectation through FIIs and foreign investment can give a jump in growth rate but full caution is required to protect the currency of our nation and countries of Asia. China expected 6.5% rate of growth having higher foreign exchange reserves than India. Taiwan's foreign currency reserves were thrice in 1998 than that of India still expected 5% rate of growth. If India will expect to achieve 6% rate of growth can invite currency war. If all nations in Asia will be crazy for relatively higher impressive growth, they will have to pay the cost for it.

(3) Indonesian experience reveals that it expected to contract by 16.6% with population growth rate of 1.6% as a result there was a fall in per capita income by 18.1%. During the period of crisis Indonesia's per capita GNP fell from $ 981 to 803. It is very difficult to achieve above 7% annual rate of growth and 5% per capita that demolished Indonesia. Future growth need to be targetted with consideration of expected real growth rate. Economists observed that it will take more than 35 years to achieve 7% rate of growth of GDP per capita income level of a depressed Thailand and 46 years to reach Malaysias current level.

4. Experience reveals that East Asian collapse and capital flight had nothing to do with uncontrolled growth in government expenditure and scams by ministers and political leaders. Indonesia, Malaysia and Thailand had surplus budgets, whereas Korea's deficit was 0.2% of its GDP. IMF's formula could not deliver the expected result what it worked for Chille and Argentina in mid-1980s and 1994 respectively.

Now Asian countries should strongly check their banks and financial institutions with proper supervision for short-term dollar denominated commercial debt, non-performing assets of banks and financial institutions. India needs pump priming in central government fiscal overhang. A special drive is necessary to check fiscal deficit in federal budget of Government of India with reasonable check on unfavourable balance of payment situation so as to manage macroeconomic variables in proper direction.

(5) Leading countries of East Asia affected by greater global pressure to world trade than India, Malaysia, Thailand and Korea had recorded substantial growth rate of export. Now Korean won, Thailand baht and Malaysian ringgit have stabilized and attempted to diversify exports. Still, however, these currencies will go flat out to sell textiles, garments, steel, plastics, polymers, electronics and man-made fibres. They will have to establish their entity to give sufficient confidence to their trading partners to boost exports.

(6) Recovery in stock market of currency hit nations and capital appreciation via export growth can encourage foreign investors to re-establish their investment tempo for further recovery. India will have to keep continued reform process to maintain output and export growth. For this, industries associations, RBI should prepare transparent guidelines for foreign investment. There is no need for foreign investment promotion Board but legal and statutory provisions required

(7) The Government of India should sell shares of public enterprises worth of Rs. 10,000 crore with full of caution than fully go in privalisation process of central and state government enterprises. Some portion should be sold in India, whereas, some portion of the sale needs to be in GDR and strategic sales required by establishing a national Trust.

(8) Privatisation process need to go gradually, the government should provide a wide spectrum to the capital market by allowing buy back of shares which will not harm investors in the market. Corporate Act needs revision in changing circumstances by merging section 370 and 372 regarding corporate loans and investment. There is a need to raise ceiling according to company bill.

(9) The Government of India should execute insurance sector reforms by establishing Insurance Regulatory Authority, amendment in LIC and GIC Acts.

As such insurance sector reforms are ancillary to industrial sector, trade sector and financial sector reforms. Nationalised insurance companies should be phased out by reducing overstapping and face open competition of about 20-25 joint venture insurance companies to re-shape our economy. It is a fact that insurance companies in India only collected higher premium than globally operating companies and not found with innovative service to their customers. Banks and insurance companies should be allowed in hedging business, to manage all types of market efficiently and to boost output and exportable surplus in real sector of our economy.

(10) Thailand had maintained a quasi-fixed exchange rate system with the US $ as the main peg over the past decade when dollar had a secular down trend against other major currencies like the Japanese yen over the same period. The fixed relationship of Thai Baht with the dollar became main culprit in driving Thai exports growth down to a negative range. Number of investors and speculators betting that Thai authority need restore Thai export competition during the period of crisis. The central bank was forced to maintain higher than trend interest rate to check speculative transaction on the currency. Thai financial system could not rescue banking, finance, property and exchange vote. Thailand had huge foreign currency dominated commercial loan portfolio depending upon arbitrage between lower US interest rate vis-a-vis higher Thai interest rates which was adversely affected during the crisis period. India can learn a lot from Thai currency crisis in order to protect the rupee in future.

(11) To stop big currency crash in future, investment banks, credit rating agencies and academic economists need to formulate suitable models to predict currency crash. They must develop indicators to guide hedging decisions as developed by J.P. Morgan. Moody's and other companies for Asian countries in the first two decades of 21st century in order to gauge the risk of crisis, currency, exchange rate. IMF, World Bank and Asian Development Bank economists can concentrate in predicting timing of crashes and economic fluctuations. There is a need to establish Asian Monetary Union (AMU) like EMU for regional cohesion on economies and markets, AMU can plan to protect currencies of members during crisis and competitive devaluation of currencies and stability of exchange rates.

17

INTERNATIONAL MARKETING RESEARCH

What is International Marketing Research?*

International marketing research is the systematic gathering, recording, analysis and interpretation of data on international marketing problems. It consists of specific studies required to develop, implement and evaluate export marketing strategies. Answers are sought to such questions as:

(*i*) What is the potential market for a product overseas?

(*ii*) Who are the present and potential customers across the boundaries of a nation?

(*iii*) How can the international marketer best appeal to this market?

(*iv*) How successful is the international marketing programme; and

(*v*) What are the weak areas in the international marketing programmes.

International market research is essential before real exporting is undertaken. Information must be collected and intelligently interpreted from all the reliable sources. Exporters should pool their resources, or approach such agencies as the STC, the IIFT, the EPCS, etc. Market research has much to contribute to export marketing management; but the different cultures in different socities have somewhat limited its scope. The buyer abroad and the seller at home are separated by a long distance. To some extent, this gap can be filled by international market research.

* International Marketing Research and International Market Research in this chapter have been used synonymously.

International market research is essential because:

(*i*) It helps to explain change in the status of a company engaged in international marketing;

(*ii*) It helps to examine the international market for a new product: and

(*iii*) It enables us to determine whether a new company is justified to go in for the international market.

Main Parts of International Market Research

International market research may be divided into the following four main parts:

(A) Elements which Influence the Market

(*i*) Resources and Production;

(*ii*) Transportation;

(*iii*) Location;

(*iv*) Climate;

(*v*) Population;

(*vi*) Standard of living;

(*vii*) Government;

(*viii*) Foreign trade; and

(*ix*) Per capita income.

(B) General Market Elements Related to International Product

(*i*) Foreign trade policy; and

(*ii*) Foreign exchange policy.

(C) Specific Market Factors Concerned with International Product

(*i*) Domestic production;

(*ii*) Imports; and

(*iii*) Alternate sources.

(D) Particular Factors Affecting International Markets

(*i*) The policy of the company;

(*ii*) Adaptability of the product to the export market;

(*iii*) The price of the product;

(*iv*) Channels of distribution; and

(*v*) Terms of sale.

Having collected the infomation on these points, an international market research report must conclude with a summary of findings and recommendations.

International Market Analysis

There is no one correct and inviolable method of export market analysis. The method which should be used in analysing an export market should be adapted first to the product and then to the market.

There have been literally dozens of plans to market analysis proposed and published, and almost every one of them has special merits of its own, as well as some special demerits. One cardinal point should be kept uppermost in the mind of the exporter making the analysis. The area under consideration should be analysed as a market for a given product. Unless all of the facts necessary to determine whether a market can be found for that specific product are included in the market analysis, the study would become defective to that extent, and extraneous material, which is not essential in determining whether a market exists for the product, should be discarded.

Any market analysis falls naturally into two essential divisions:

(i) General information; and

(ii) Information pertaining to a particular business or particular products under consideration.

Information on the following subjects is of value for it would have a bearing on international marketing.

(1) Product Analysis

(a) Do my production facilities and domestic distribution justify my entry into the export market?

(b) Is my product of the type that will be in demand abroad?

(c) What changes, if any, should be made in my product to meet foreign preferences?

(d) What volume of production can I allocate regularly to international marketing?

(2) International Marketing Facilities

(a) In India

(i) What are the international marketing facilities in India available to me?

(ii) Should I set up my own international marketing organisation, or should I use such middleman as an internatinal marketing commission house or export merchant or manufacturers' export agent?

(b) **In Foreign Countries**

(i) What channel of distribution should I use in foreign countries?

(ii) How can I select a satisfactory agent or distributor?

(3) Foreign Area Analysis

The international marketer will need such detailed data on each country in which he sells as:

(a) **Geography**

(i) Area, topography, climate and seasons.

(ii) Natural divisions or sales regions of the country.

(b) **Resources**

(i) Character of resources and extent of development.

(ii) Minerals, agriculture, chief crops, forests, water power and potential and developed electrification areas.

(c) **Industries**

(i) Kinds, location, amount and quality of output, labour conditions and unemployment record.

(ii) Degree of competition with my export products.

(iii) Growth of industries during the last decade or so.

(d) **Population**

(i) Amount, density, rural and urban, location and size of important cities.

(ii) Historical background, religions, nationality distribution, social classes, progressiveness, customs, bias in favour of or against, India or other nations.

(iii) Literacy, educational development, language groups.

(iv) Purchasing power, wages, per capita figures in savings, bank deposits, cars, telephones, radios, TVs, etc.

(e) **Transportation and Shipping**

(i) What transportation facilities to the country are available—steamship, air services, railways, frequency and rates, harbour facilities, free ports?

(ii) What are the transportation conditions within the country—railways, highways, air, river ports, carriage?

(f) **Business Customs**

(i) Business methods as compared with those in India, ethical standards.

(ii) Business hours, buying and selling seasons.

(iii) Importance of formality in correspondence and selling tactics.

(iv) Trade association, chambers of commerce.

(v) Organisation of trade, channels of distribution of particular products.

(vi) Advertising development, media available, character and circulation of newspapers and magazines, radio advertising, outdoor advertising, availability of local advertising agencies.

(4) Analysis of Competition

***(a)* Local Competition**

(i) How efficient are these local industries?

(ii) To what extent are they protected by tariffs?

***(b)* Indian Competition**

(i) Can I meet the competition of other Indian exporters to market?

(ii) How are they selling there—through branches, subsidiaries, distributors, sales agents or directly to consumers?

***(c)* Foreign Competition**

(i) What competition will I meet from manufacturers in other countries?

(ii) Do these manufacturers enjoy tariff preferences?

***(d)* Trade Statistics**

(i) Domestic—value, principal articles, quality.

(ii) Foreign—imports, value, competitive articles, chief sources of supply.

(iii) Balance of payments with India and with the world.

(5) Government and Laws

(a) Type of government, stability, progressiveness, financial position, foreign loan record, bias against India or other countries.

(b) Attitude towards investment in India and other countries.

(c) Commercial treaties with India and other countries.

(d) Tariffs in general and for particular products, types of duties levied, stability of duties.

(e) Customs regulations regarding packing of shipments, marking of goods and cases, documentation, commercial samples, catalogues.

(f) Laws covering taxes on foreign business enterprises, salesmen's licences, patents and trade marks protection.

(g) Systems of weights and measures.

(h) Government of India's regulations governing the export of my product.

(6) Financial Factors

(a) Currency, stability, foreign exchange control regulation.

(b) Domestic credit conditions, customary credit terms.

(c) Availability of capital, interest rates.

(d) Current economic conditions, employment, volume of trade, crop conditions, price situation.

(7) International Marketing Cost Analysis

The cost of international marketing which affects export prices and profits must be estimated with care:

(a) Customary quotations, F.O.B. or C.I.F., port of destination;

(b) Packing, transportation, documentation fees, marine insurance; and

(c) Selling cost, registration fees, and selling licences, discounts, commission, advertising cost, credit financing, etc.

Options Available to Internatinal Marketer who Wishes to Conduct Market Research

1. Sending home country personnel overseas or travel himself.
2. Asking the foreign subsidiary or office to either do it or lease with a local supplier overseas.
3. Hiring and dealing directly with a foreign research supplier.
4. Asking its domestic research supplier to conduct the research and then the domestic research supplier may contract the work to a foreign research supplier.
5. Asking a multinational marketing research firm to conduct the study.

Indian companies could entrust the job to multinational research firms to minimize the problems and risks inherent in overseas marketing research projects, to standardize and centralize the research process, and to provide closer-to-home co-ordination. But finding the right group to carry out work of overseas research is just the first part of the process.

International Market Research Problems

There are a number of problems that affect the quality and way international marketing research is designed and conducted abroad. These include:

1. Population, socio-economic, and other market statistics are non-existent, unavailable, or inaccurate in many LDCs, and even in some developed countries.
2. Religious and cultural customs make research difficult in some nations. Interviewing women in the Middle East, for example, is a problem because of the laws of *purdah*.
3. Levels of industrialisation and the general rules of business vary from region to region.
4. All or some marketing activities are closely regulated in some countries. In Europe, for instance, some data laws affect the research industry.

In conducting actual studies, differences in marketing environment, economic levels, culture, and nationality influence results. Market environment factors include legal constraints; physical distribution facilities; and traditions in such areas as selling policies and practices, pricing, discounts, customer service, and technical aid. In many LDCs, the economic level creates selective market segments. The market for many packaged goods, for example, is limited to the upper social strata. Cultural and national differences may also necessitate sharp variations in research design.

Common questions to all types of international marketing research include:

1. Does the international marketing research represent value for the money?
2. How does the client communicate overseas?
3. Will the client get the quality control, data analysis and interpretation required?
4. In what currency will the client pay for the services?
5. Will the costs of the international marketing research be greater than the profits resulting from the level of expected sale.

International Market Research and Secondary Data Sources

The marketing distance between exporter and final customer is generally wider than that between domestic manufacturer and customer. Marketing distance is the distance created by intermediaries, at least one of whom is foreign, standing between the exporter and the final consumer and the cultural distance arising out of the fact that these consumers are members of another culture and society. Together, these distances produce an information gap that must be overcome for rational planning of export sales.

A large part of the information gap can be met by data collected from secondary sources and interpreted. Overall, the Government of India, Ministry of Commerce publications, EPCS, RBI are probably the best secondary sources. Foreign countries can then be classified by the volume of imports of the exporter's product or product group. It may be necessary to examine trade restrictions that may have constrained imports and analyze whether these restrictions are likely to be lifted. Apart from the UN and IMF, trade data can also be obtained from government sources. Trade data can be misleading at times.

The UN, IMF, and national sources also give data on items such as population, education, size of national income, and foreign exchange position. Further, country yearbooks and some international publications have data on political and governmental factors. At a more detailed level of analysis, national government publications sketch out import regulations, customs duties, and other laws and regulations that affect export marketing.

Secondary data is becoming more plentiful in quantity and better in quality. Some of the major governmental and paragovernmental sources are listed in Table 15.1.

Table 15.1
Selected International Marketing Secondary Data Sources

UN	Statistical Yearbook Monthly Bulletin of Statistics FAO Yearbook (Food and Agriculture Organisation) *Yearbook of National Accounts* *International Trade Yearbooks*
OECD	General Statistics and a number of other relevant publications and special studies
GATT	Special studies
IMF	International Financial Statistics and IMF Survey
National Governments	Statistics and market information through a number of publications
Chambers of Commerce	Various publications
Trade, Business, and Service Organisations	Business International Predieasts The Conference Board Large Commercial banks Large Accounting firms
Commercial Publications	
Economist Intelligence Unit	

Besides these sources there are a number of other specific to industry sectors and/or parts of the export marketing mix. Each major industry has a plethora of data sources: governmental, from the industry itself, from trade journals, and from other commentators. For instance, the automobile industry is commented upon frequently in the financial newspapers and magazines as well as in trade magazines. Another example of data sources can be gotten from advertising. For this sector of the international marketing mix, there exists the *Media Guide International,* which contains a directory of advertising rates and data with over 6,000 entries concerning business, professional, and trade publications in over 100 countries. The newspapers and magazines section have special pages on the international news media and market data on each country. Further, it lists rates and other data on leading newspapers and news magazines. There are also good indexes and computer search programmes that will track down a sufficient number of references in a very short time.

Much international marketing research consists of studies of industry and market sectors across the world or at least in a number of relevant countries. The sector study, done basically by using secondary data, is relatively inexpensive. It usually provides enough information for decision making, especially regarding overall multicountry marketing strategy. Despite this, it is extremely difficult to determine the type of degree of competition in the foreign market unless the export marketer pays an on site visit. During the visit the marketer has the opportunity for face-to-face discussions with knowledgeable bankers, distributors, and business executives of noncompeting firms resident in that country. Moreover, the vist would be most helpful for forming perceptions of prevailing business practice, consumption patterns and habits, and from these, the required product, packaging and marketing mix modifications. Besides, the personal visit enables a rapid collection of information and an element of flexibility to interpret the information meaningfully.

Besides above, various domestically published sources may be used by international markets to their advantage. Internatinal Marketers are advised to consult the *Indian Trade Journal, Journal of Industry and Trade, Udyog Vyapar Patrika, Foreign Trade Review,* and various specific publications brought out by the IIFT, New Delhi. Registered international marketers may make use of the periodical publications of the respective export promotion councils and commodity boards. For every specific information, the MMTC, the STC, and ISI, banks, and commercial representatives abroad may be approached. Done systematically and thoroughly export market research can help in identifying markets and develop fairly accurate projections.

Gathering the Data. Eventually a personal computer and telephone line will be the main tools for accessing international market data. But until enough databases are available, one will have to do the initial tedious job of digging up statistics and shaping them into a format that makes sense.

The best source of international trade statistics is the government. Government export figures are the basis of all statistical market analysis. Product categories, however, are frequently large, and one may have to do a bit of additional digging on his own to come up with more precise figures.

Official statistics usually give only a partial picture. To make government statistics more meaningful to their members, some trade associations hire consultants to do detailed overseas market studies and to develop statistics for more narrowly defined product categories.

One should know that some countries have done away with product descriptions and switched to international trade codes. If one deals in two or three products, this is no problem. If one has to look up twenty or thirty items, one may have to constantly shift back and forth from a reference list.

There are three international codes: the Standard International Classification (SIC), the Standard International Trade Classification (SITC), and the Brussels Tariff Nomenclature (BTN). The United States uses a fourth system, Tariff Schedules of the United States, to report its own import-export figures.

A "harmonised system" has been developed internationally among industrialised countries which came into effect in 1987, clearing up much of the current confusion and making indentification of product categories much easier and quicker.

Early in research one should get into the habit of using product codes. Eventually they will come in handy when one is entering research data into computerised databases and spreadsheet projections. By computerising data, one makes it easier to standardise research, reporting, and forecasting procedures, particularly as new data are culled from reports submitted by regional managers, overseas agents, support staff, and consultants.

Statistics from the major industrialised countries, particularly the United States, Canada, Australia, Japan, the United Kingdom, Germany, Italy, and France, are usually broken down into narrow product classifications. Figures are fairly recent, seldom more than six to nine months old.

Reports from smaller countries are of limited value because figures are for broad, and therefore meaningless, product classifications. However, these reports could give at least two important items of information: size of the country's exports or imports, and their destination or source.

Some countries' statistics may be two or three years old, and of no use.

The minimum data needed before one starts putting together a list of tentative target countries include:

1. Exports and imports of your particular product for the last three or four years, with breakdown by country of destination.
2. Country's share of leading markets.

3. Exports and imports by other leading manufacturing countries (with breakdown by country of destination).
4. Total imports of leading importing countries.

Factors to be Considered

(1) The priority markets for the initial phase of export operations to focus at, must be decided first.

(2) Developing sales in a small country can take just as much time and effort as going after a large one with 100 times the potential.

(3) Never select a country as a first-priority market purely on the strength of internationally financed development projects.

(4) Export-import data from all countries are readily available from government sources, including embassies. Becoming familiar with the many services and publications offered by these sources is a must. Most of it is free or available at nominal cost.

(5) Find out plans there may be for official, government sponsored events and exhibitions abroad in your product category during course of your visit to embassies. These promotions are usually preceded by a fair amount of research by consultants hired by government, and will give a very good clue as to which countries are seen as having a good potential for your product. Take advantage of this free research.

(6) Visits to foreign embassies can also be useful; they may reveal information and opportunities one might have overlooked. Most embassies maintain commercial references libraries which are open to business people regardless of nationality or of whether one wants to buy from or sell to the particular country.

(7) During the visit to embassy of a country which might be also an exporter of your type of product, find out also about any special international promotions the country may have sponsored around the world or has in mind in the next year or two. This will give an idea of where the country's industry is concentrating its efforts.

Methodology Considerations

Special issues of concern in methodology arise when economic levels, culture, and language are dissimilar. These include functional equivalence of the phenomena being studied across nations, cross-national equivalence of the concepts and research instruments being employed, translation of the research instruments into different languages, and the comparability of the samples in each nation. Difficulties arise in countries such as Singapore, where up to six languages are spoken, or Switzerland, which has three main languages.

Obviously, if similar activities have different functions in different societies, their parameters cannot be used for comparative purposes. For instance, bicycles provide basic transportation in some countries but are essentially recreational in others. Differences in responses cannot automatically be attributed to national differences on the variables being measured, since it is equally plausible that the differences are functional or related to the buying situation.

Conceptual equivalence recognizes that some concepts are culture bound and are inappropriate for use on a cross-national basis. Similarly, there can be an issue in the selection of terms that are employed to measure certain items. Once functional and conceptual equivalence has been established, the problem becomes one of devising a research instrument that adequately measures the phenomena under study in each of the nations being surveyed.

A five-point buy scale, for instance, would have to be translated into French for use in a country such as the Ivory Coast and also, according to one study, be reduced to three points, because local consumers have difficulty appreciating the subtleties of intention to purchase. Moreover, in countries where illiteracy is prevalent, it may be necessary to use a pictorial scale with faces showing a variety of expressions. In one study done in Nigeria, for example, it was found in pilot testing that beer consumers had difficulty in responding to the semantic differential scale with the polar adjectives bitter-sweet. Some consumers perceived the midpoint of the scale as not bitter, others took it as not sweet, but both groups saw a difference between not bitter and not sweet. Therefore, two new scales were devised: one running from bitter to not bitter, and the other from sweet to not sweet.

In most cases, research instruments have to be altered to some extent from nation to nation. Long questionnaires do not seem to be much of a problem in the U.S. if handled intelligently. But it is reported that they do not work in Hong Kong where everyone seems to rush breathlessly about. At the very least, certain classification items have to be different in each nation, since educational systems and income levels vary so.

Research instruments need to consider such differences as might exist in the availability of products used in the study and their substitutes, in the media employed in each nation, and in the literacy of the respondents. The results of studies can provide valuable insights into cross-national behaviour, but it is important that the limitations of this approach be clearly understood and reported with the results.

Questionnaire Translation

The development of the research instrument is generally followed by its translation into the languages of the nations in which it is to be administered. Thus, the achievement of instrument equivalence depends upon proper translation. One problem frequently encountered is that terms cannot be translated directly into another language and still retain their full meaning. The English word *tough*, for instance, has a variety of meanings, which makes perfect translation of it difficult to achieve. Further, an equivalent for a term may not exist in another language; the Spanish word *machismo* is impossible to translate into an equivalent English term. Moreover, idiomatic expressions may be outside the range of experience of the sample. The term *supermarket* is capable of being translated into several languages, but it is probably that many people in some countries have not been exposed to a supermarket in the North American sense of the term.

A good translation for a US MNC-commissioned study is so important that the original instrument should be written in easily translatable English. To overcome many of the problems of direct translation from one language to another, a process called *back translation* is often employed. In this process the instrument is first translated into the other language by a second translator. Back translation permits the identification of discrepancies between the original and retranslated instrument. Another way to overcome translation problems is to incorporate items and adjectives from each nation into the instrument. This process is called *decentering* and usually results in a much longer instrument. However, it is a highly regarded technique for the development of a cross-national research instrument.

Sample Selection

The researcher should select samples in each nation that are as closely comparable as possible in order to insure against sample deviation as an explanation for differences in results. When pertinent to the investigation, one can try to draw a truly representative sample from each nation. While this, if achievable, has the virtue of sample comparability, the representative samples themselves may exhibit extreme variation which could make cross-national comparisons difficult.

A commonly employed sampling technique in cross-national studies involves drawing the samples from an identifiable subgroup of the national populations; for instance, samples of middle-class housewives may be drawn. For two or more countries, it is virtually impossible to select samples that share all the same traits. Middle-class housewives in the US and Mexico will differ in terms of their absolute levels of income and perhaps, education. It has been suggested that cross-national researchers should attempt to hold age, sex, social class, and rural-urban residence constant across samples. Then, differential results may be confined to other noticed causes, such as unreliability, in the measures being used.

Women in the workforce who are among the samples pose problems. In the U.S., for instance nearly 55 percent of working-age females are in the workforce. But in the Netherlands and Brazil the figure is 28 percent and in Pakistan only 8 percent. Further, women interviewed in Kuwait could be Egyptian. Kuwait nationals in fact are in the minority in their own country. More than half the population is expatriate Arab, Pakistani, and Indian — good test for the question, "Who is your real market?" Moreover, it is relatively easy to get groups of working-class women to attend focused group interviews in England and West Germany. But in Southern Italy or Spain a researcher would be regarded with suspicion.

The raw material for area probability samples varies considerably from country to country. In very few countries are there reliable electoral registers, local maps for selecting blocks and planning interviewer routes, and automobile registration lists available. Moreover, even if there are lists, locating them is not always easy. In Italy, voter lists are kept in each commune, of which there are over 9,000.

It goes without saying that any lack of comparability in samples should be reported as a limitation and incorporated into the interpretation of the data.

Limitations of International Market Research

(*i*) Trained investigators are not available.

(*ii*) Different educational systems available in different societies.

(*iii*) Information on customers abroad is difficult because of:

- (*a*) Suspicion of strangers; and
- (*b*) Structural conditions in societies interfere with data collection.

(*iv*) In less developed countries very little data are available.

Organizing the Data. What to do with import-export statistics and how to make sure they are put to good use — in other words, how to convert them into a practical tool of international marketing — has always been a problem. Invariably this type of information is so boring that it is filed away and seldom used.

If one is able to put his statistics into simple computer spreadsheets, his task will be enormously simplified and he will end up with a format which allows him quick updating and retrieval at any time, as well as a simple formula from which to work out projections.

Total Exports and Imports. To analyze export and import markets it should be enough to identify the top six to ten exporting and importing countries in one's product group. Look up, for instance, total exports of

India, United States, Canada, Japan, West Germany, the United Kingdom, and France. From this one can get an idea of the world market shares.

If one compares figures for the last three or four years, one will be able to establish trends. If one carries, this step further and works out growth or shrinkage ratios, one can also create rough projections for the next three or four years.

In India, information on the top exporters can be obtained from secondary government sources or the countries' embassies in New Delhi.

Once entered on a computer spreadsheet, this sort of data can be easily updated every three months, whenever new official statistics are made available by the top exporting and importing countries.

Destination of Exports and Imports. For each exporting and importing country draw up a list of the countries of destination. Figure out what percentage of the exporting country's product went to each country of destination. A quick study of these lists will reveal the best and worst markets for each exporting country. If one wants to make the analysis more elaborate, one can take the trouble of figuring out how each country of destination performed over the last three of four years.

This information can also be handled quickly and effectively if one enters into a computer spreadsheet format. However, a word of caution: These lists will become too cumbersome if you include too many countries. The number of exporting and importing countries can usually be kept down to five or six — and this list will probably take care of the bulk of world exports and imports in the product line.

Country-by-Country Imports. One can also organize import-export data in the form of a more detailed analysis of a particular country's imports. That is, one can look at imports from the viewpoint of the importing and not the exporting country. This is a good way to see how a particular country has shaped up over the years and where it has done most of its buying.

To be useful this information should cover a period of at least three or four years. If the importing country is also a manufacturer of the same product, one should add to his tabulation some data on local production and determine what share of the total market it covers.

Gathering and evaluating this information requires considerable work and initiative when countries report import-export figures in broad categories or when reports are delayed for a year or more. The best sources of information will be the exporting countries rather than the countries of destination. For instance, if one is trying to compile total Saudi A abian imports for the product, it may be wiser to find out what Saudi Arabia imported from the major exporting countries and create a Saudi Arabian trade profile from these data.

End User Population. One may want to back-up his trade statistics with an evaluation of the size of specific overseas markets. Government and embassy sources will be helpful, as will trade associations and chambers of commerce. Specialized government agencies will also have significant data.

Criteria for Target Countries. Having gathered the basic statistics, one must now decide what basic requirements a country must meet in order to qualify as a specific target for a particular product. In addition to special criteria related to the type of product, consider the following general ones.

(*i*) *Volume Potential.* One's object is to seek the highest sales with the least investment, promotion, and personnel. Other factors being favourable, it therefore makes sense to go after those countries which have been importing the largest quantities of particular type of product one intends to sell.

(*ii*) *High Market Share:* If India's exports have a significant share of a particular country's market for a particular type of product, Indian exporters should have a reasonable advantage there.

(*iii*) *Location.* One will save travel time and expenses if one can concentrate on initial-priority markets that are in the same general region.

(*iv*) *Language.* For Indian, Canadian, Australian, and British manufacturers there is definitely an advantage in choosing countries where English is an official or widely understood language.

(*v*) *Steady Import History.* Be wary of countries with erratic import histories. One cannot rely on them year to year. A sudden burst of imports may have resulted from a massive international loan for one or several projects, creating a distorted picture of a country's import volume. A great year could easily be followed by a long dry spell.

Also question any country showing a decline in imports from a particular country even though the overall total still keeps its among the top importers on your list. This decline may be caused by increasing competition from other exporting countries or from local manufacturing, or by a steady depletion of foreign exchange reserves and tighter import restrictions.

(*vi*) *Stability.* One should be particularly careful of those countries which may have gone through major economic or political upheavals in the last few months. This will not yet be reflected in official trade statistics.

Completing Export Marketing Research. When one lists down twelve to fifteen countries, try to talk to people who can give information about local conditions and outlook based on their own experience.

Trade association is a good place to start. Some of its officers may have personal knowledge of these countries. They may also refer you to manufacturers of noncompeting products who may be happy to lend a hand. This sort of advice is by far the best. In the course of an informal chat one may pick up priceless information on competition and hints on potential agents. One may even decide to restore to his list, one or two countries one had already discarded, and cross out some which are not as promising as statistics may have indicated.

Major banks with foreign departments are a good source of information on economic and political conditions, payment procedures, and shipping problems.

For an Indian businessperson a two- or three-day visit to New Delhi is a good investment at this point. Call on the various Government of India, Ministry of Commerce Offices and call at foreign embassies. But don't allow yourself to be carried away by enthusiastic commerce ministry officials. Some of them view export promotion as an idealistic crusade to "sell India", and may ignore the truth about conditions and opportunities in certain countries. At the other extreme are those extra-cautious officials who go strictly by the book.

Either viewpoint is quite different from that of the businessperson, who must look at markets outside India in terms of cold, hard profits.

At the embassies you visit, the person you want to see may go by the title of commercial attache, commercial officer, economic secretary, or one of several other variations. Some embassies have excellent reference libraries.

In addition to verifying or refining one's statistics, on an embassy visit one has a chance to look up trade publications, newspapers, and directories. *including classified phone books, among the most valuable sources of information anywhere in the world.*

Allow enough time to browse around an embassy's reference library. One will come out with a great deal of practical, useful information including names and addresses of possible agents and major lines they currently handle (easily obtained from a classified phone book).

There is one more important step one can take before one settles on a list of target countries: *Attend a major trade fair.*

Find out which is the biggest and most important international fair for your product, then go and browse around. It will probably be somewhere in Europe, most likely Germany. See who is exhibiting. Note how much effort and money your competitor is investing in the event. Get a feel for the types and numbers of buyers attending the event from all over the world.

Don't rush the visit. Stay the entire time. Stop for a chat with competitors. Introduce yourself to exhibitors and to the officials responsible for the fair. Pick up catalogues and reports. Attend meetings, get yourself invited to a cocktail party or two, mix with foreign visitors in your hotel's bar and restaurant. Be nosy!

You will come home with a wealth of information and may even have been lucky enough to meet important visiting agents from other countries.

You will have not been the first or the last businessperson to become excited about international markets as a result of attending a major fair.

Information on important trade fairs is readily available through trade associations and through embassy and other government sources.

Your research need not take more than a month. This should give you ample time to identify your priority markets.

If the research is done in-house, it will need one full-time person. Find a meticulous (within reason!) person who can do all the preliminary data gathering and tabulation. If you have an idea of whom you would eventually choose to run your export department, you may want to give this person responsibility for the research. It will give him a good opportunity to start learning about foreign markets and conditions.

Another possibility is to give the job to an outside consultant—someone who is familiar with government and embassy sources and who has personal overseas experience. A consultant will charge you a fee but may be able to give you a list of the ten best markets fairly quickly, without tying up any of your staff of executives.

A reliable consultant could also be useful later on in helping you take your first steps in your own export operation. Or, if you are already into exports, in helping you redirect your efforts where they will produce the greatest benefits.

One may even be lucky enough to have the research done for himself free of charge. If an MBA could do research project as a part of his curricula offered by the university where the unit is located. This would be free of cost.

The export marketing research is still in a developmental stage. It is in the interest of every organisation involved in export marketing to build such a system. This is essential for export marketing managers to be able to plan ahead and to make more effective judgements with speedier decision making with lowered risk. The difficulties of obtaining accurate data for the system should not be minimised. The preferred approach would be to build a system and then improve it as experience dictated.

International marketing research studies are important in themselves, forming a useful subset of the overall information system. The export marketing manager should be aware of the problems of marketing research. The informed marketer can purpose proper procedures and carefully interpret the findings. The problems exist both on the technical side and in selecting the agency best suited to conducting the research.

There are many sectors in which export marketing research is necessary and can be quite beneficial. Cross-national research is increasingly done in order that strategists and planners can decide to what extent to alter a standardised marketing programme or mix. Discerning international attitude differences is a by-product of cross-national research. But the by-product is specific to countries in which economic levels tend to be relatively similar.

The other vital field for research is in international marketing linked with international market potential assessment. There are many methods of trying to assess such potential. Where good statistics are available, as in a number of the industrialised countries, the methods range from the relatively simple to the complexities of advanced statistical techniques. Where statistics are not so accurate, the international marketing manager has to fall back on an entrepreneurial flair. Estimation by analogy is a method that can work well if a suitable product with a proven market is selected. The ability of the international marketer is tested by his choice of a suitable product. In general, to estimate market potential the export marketing manager must have an excellent knowledge of which secondary information sources are available and what each one can provide. Studies based on good sources can often give more than adequate information for decision making. The number of these sources and their publications are increasingly rapidly. However, the user must always be extremely careful about whether the classifications are, in fact, similar.

The Feasibility of Market Entry

The decision to market products and services internationally generally requires that the firm make a major commitment of resources to such activity. Before making such a commitment, careful analysis is needed to reduce entry risks and to improve profit possibilities. Resources applied to the international markets will not be available for other opportunities arising in domestic markets. Furthermore, competitive pressures, government regulations, and market development needs work against short-term commitments. Although some companies may limit their international activity to filling occasional orders from foreign customers or use foreign markets to dispose of temporary surpluses, many firms have committed themselves to establishing and maintaining market share through substantial investment in plants, organisation and promotion. In order to successfully export and produce abroad, continuous marketing effort is essential.

Fig. 15.1, graphically portrays the major environmental influences that need to be considered in making the entry decision. If executives are to make this important decision on the basis of fact rather than hunch, they need to establish procedures for selecting the most profitable markets to enter and for determining the operating conditions once entry occurs. Information is needed on all the environmental forces bearing on effective marketing, but a major problem is the development of a database. Information sources which provide insight for evaluating the political, economic, social and marketing environment must be identified in order to determine market potential, forecast sales, and project profits. Somehow, the facts and opinions that form the basis for intelligent judgment must be obtained. That is the objective of market analysis.

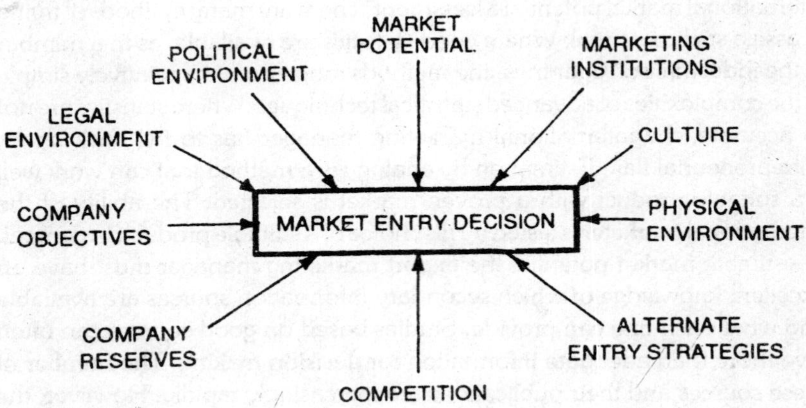

Fig. 15.1
Environment and Policy Forces Affecting the Marketing Entry Decision

The specific information inputs for analysis are established by the executive decision process. They include all of the normal inputs for analysis of a comparable domestic decision plus environmental and company data to judge factors specific to the foreign market. Since the data requirements differ among executives and market situations, this chapter concentrates on basic concepts, sources, and approaches. These can be adapted to fit specific models appropriate for specific products, markets, and available information. Companies that market a small volume through independent intermediaries take fewer risks and may require far less information and less elaborate analysis than those contemplating overseas operations through direct investment. The decision to licence, enter a joint venture, or establish production abroad entails more risk; therefore, a more complete understanding of the market situation is needed.

This chapter introduces the concept of market analysis, review the process for screening countries to determine whether a marketing opportunity exists, sets forth the information base for developing a marketing strategy, presents sources of information on foreign markets, and relates the marketing information system to the requirements for comparative analysis.

Market Analysis — A Two-Phase Approach

Market analysis begins with the initial decision to investigate foreign market opportunities. This decision, grounded in the firm's objectives and goals, sets in motion a series of investigations and choices that culminate in a decision to commit resources to the foreign market or to withhold these resources. A broad outline of this process appears in Fig. 15.2.

The analysis may be viewed in two phases. *First*, the countries of the world are subjected to a selection process for determing those countries which show promise for successful marketing. This is called "determining foreign market opportunities." *Second*, a very few countries with the greatest potential are analysed in detail to determine the feasibility of alternate entry strategies and the marketing programme needed. This second phase is the "development of the marketing programme." This process involves desk research using published secondary sources of information as well as surveys, interviews, and personal contacts. Much of the information needed for initial screening is available through government sources, libraries, and other local sources.

As Fig. 15.3 indicates, the analyst first needs to know the company's objectives in considering the foreign market. Does the company contemplate further expansion, foreign manufacturing, or extended use of domestic manufacturing facilities? The company objectives, together with a knowledge of the information that is relevant to the decision process, leads to a search of available information sources. The resulting data are then used to rank the marketing opportunities based on potential return. These countries that show promise are evaluated against feasible entry strategies and company resources that will be available. A marketing plan is developed and its feasibility is assessed. When the company is interested in only one market, the entire analysis may be focused on it. However, such concentration may overlook profitable alternative strategies in reaching regional

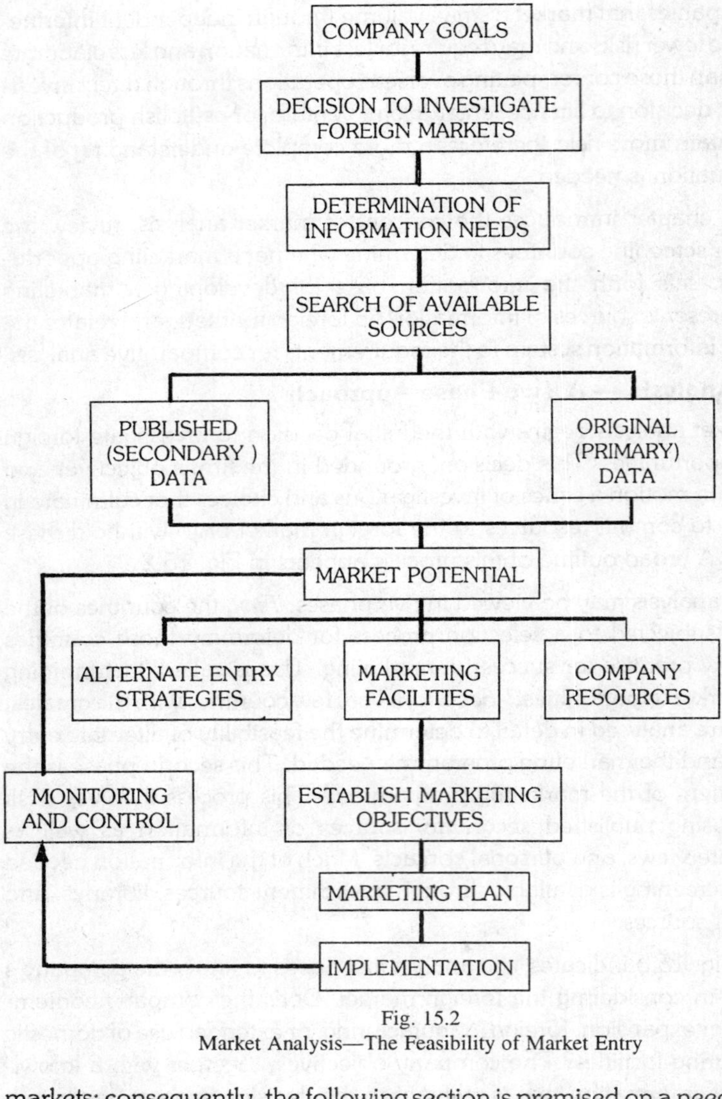

Fig. 15.2
Market Analysis—The Feasibility of Market Entry

markets; consequently, the following section is premised on a need to screen several markets.

The Screening Process

When initially screening potential foreign markets, executives are interested in thorough coverage without a great deal of depth. The objective is to isolate the best potential markets for further study. In this screening, the analyst is interested primarily in market size, market trends, competitors and their policies, pricing, and restrictions on market entry. Essentially, the determination of marketing opportunity entails a series of steps.

Step 1. Determine the basic needs served by the product and the characteristics of the potential customer. Often the needs are similar to those served in the home market. For example, Campa Cola and other soft drinks are representative of this group. But sometimes a product may serve different functions abroad such as the refrigerator without a freezer that serves only as temporary storage between frequent shopping trips or that becomes a status symbol in lesser developed countries. At this stage the analyst must also be aware that the basic use system may differ in the foreign market so that, for example, highly automatic washing machines may not be necessary when the buyer has servants within the household to perform such tasks. For industrial goods, the needs and use conditions may be quite similar around the world, yet even here differing wage rates, physical conditions, and maintenance programmes affect the buyer's needs. Under conditions of rising incomes or industrial development, the needs of potential buyers may be changing rapidly.

Potential consumers may be identified by age, income, tastes, style and quality preferences, and life-styles. Industrial customers are characterised by the type of product produced, the production processes, technology levels, and cost structures. Thus, producers facing a cost squeeze as a result of high wage rates are a better market for automated machinery than those where labour is abundant and cheap.

Step 2. Establish the manner in which these needs are currently being met. The analyst can consult published government and trade data to determine whether the basic product is available in the market from local sources or as imports from India or other countries. The published data, discussions with informed people, and primary research can also establish the degree to which present products meet the market's requirements. An essential concept is to find out whether the company's own products and/or marketing strategies have advantages from the customer's viewpoint over existing products. Without some superiority in product or marketing, it is increasingly difficult to establish the product overseas in the face of both local and import competition.

Step 3. Select market indicators to reflect the market potential for the product. For consumer goods these might include population, market growth, income per capita, or others that have been earlier established as being correlated with purchases of the product. Industrial goods indicators include the sales of industries using a process, number of companies, employment in an industry, transporation costs, planned government projects, etc. It is essential that these indicators be: (*a*) correlated with market potential; and (*b*) readily available.

General economic indicators are widely available from Indian and foreign governments and from international sources such as the United Nations or the International Monetary Fund. Trade data may be gleaned from trade associations and trade journals. Published sources may provide composite indicators. For example, Business International publishes a series of indicators including one of market size which measures the relative size of each national market as a percentage of a regional market (*e.g.,* European). It is based on an average of nine underlying indicators. A market intensity composite measure the degree of concentrated purchasing power on various per capita and ownership levels.

Step 4. Estimate market potential from the chosen indicators. Single factor indices (based on one indicator) or multiple factor indices may be used for this purpose. Multiple regression or other analytic techniques may help establish the relationship between the indicator and the market potential.

Step 5. Eliminate countries which do not meet the country's minimum requirements for market potential, economic growth, political risk, and available labour or natural resources.

Step 6. Rank the remaining countries by potential.

Step 7. Check for geographical clusters that would facilitate expansion. In this part of the analysis, the company is interested in determining the best base for regional market penetration. Hungary or Finland might provide access to Eastern European markets. Similarly, England or West Germany could be the base of penetration of the European Economic Community, or Brazil could be a compatible environment for marketing to the other Latin American Integration Association (LAIA) countries.

Step 8. Eliminate countries where trade or investment barriers prohibit profitable market entry. These barriers would include tariffs, quotas, currency regulations, investment restrictions, or other laws establishing operating conditions that are not acceptable to the firm.

Step 9. Select the most suitable countries for further analysis, the development of entry strategy, and the formulation of marketing plan. Generally the firm will want to select relatively few countries for initial entry. A successful penetration of these will facilitate expansion later.

APPENDIX A

LOCATING THE BUYER ABROAD

The exporter who squarely confronts the problem of seeking an export market for his products finds himself facing two distinct but related problems. These are:

(*i*) Can my products be sold in the export market? and

(*ii*) Where can they be sold?

As background for export market analysis, four sets of facts are necessary:

(*i*) The course of exports from India over a period for the last 10 years.

(*ii*) The overall direction of exports from India — the principal areas of the world to which exports have been made;

(*iii*) The best customers of India; and

(*iv*) Principal commodities exported from India during the last decade.

Anything which has been properly made can find an export market somewhere in the world. The size of potential export sales will depend upon the utility of the item, the way in which it is presented, its relative quality, and its price. The utility of the item is not only its usefulness but also its appeal to the eventual customers. Thc product may have no practical use but may have an appeal which induces people to buy it. Presentation is the most important of all the requirements in opening up export markets. The products must be packed properly and neatly. It is the packaging which attracts attention. If the article looks good from the outside, its initial sales are at any rate assured.

The manufacturer-exporter's potential customer is likely to be a merchant or an importing agent abroad, but before an attempt is made to find him, the manufacturer-exporter must be well prepared and able to show that he is going to sell. This implies two things:

(*a*) A good and well-designed letterheading on good quality thin rice paper. Letter heading is the exporter's ambassador for the product and the first letter will either win the confidence of the buyer abroad or lose it. A lousy or shabby letterhead will give the impression of a lousy and shabby product; and

(*b*) Good printed leaflet with illustration of the merchandisé in coloured printing with a brief description of the merchandise highlighting the salient points. Many buyers do not read, but, in the leaflet, if good blocks of the merchandise have been reproduced they would at least convey a fair idea to the buyer about what the product looks like. The sending of samples to every prospective buyer is neither feasible nor economical.

The quality of merchandise is as important as presentation. Good presentation sells the goods initially; but only the quality of products ensures repeat sales. Quality must be commensurate with price and goods should be supplied only of the quality claimed for them. Indian exporters in general have earned a bad name on this score, they are universally known for sending a sample of one quality and then shipping goods of an entirely different quality when the order is placed with them.

The prices of export products should be reasonable — neither too high nor too low. If they are too low, they would give rise to the suspicion that the products for exports are of an inferior quality. Quick shipment is another requirement. Buyers abroad do not wait for a long time even if the goods are cheap and of a good quality. Besides, the buyer abroad is not interested in tying up his money in letter of credits for longer durations for the convenience of the exporter.

The following would be great help in finding customers abroad:

(*A*) Circular letters asking for the names and addresses of potential buyers with copies of leaflets may be sent to the following institutions:

(*i*) Foreign Trade Commissions and Commercial Secretaries of Indian Embassies;

(*ii*) Chambers of Commerce, Trade Associations and Federations in the main cities of foreign countries;

(*iii*) Indian High Commissions, Embassies and Consulates abroad;

(*iv*) Regional offices of banks in India which have foreign branches of correspondents;

(*v*) Various Export Promotion Councils and Commodity Boards;

(*vi*) S.T.C., I.I.F.T., etc.; and

(*vii*) Letters to importers or agents abroad who deal in similar products.

(*B*) Small advertisements may be inserted in international journals.

(*C*) Sending salesmen abroad to find out customers would be a relatively costly proposition.

APPENDIX B

HOW TO ASSESS SALES PROSPECTS

In investigating sales prospects for a product in a particular market, you should gather and assess the following information:

Basic Factors

(*i*) Area of the country, terrain, climate, distances between main centres, and other geographical factors that may influence the demand for the product.

(*ii*) Size, age distribution, and concentration of population.

(*iii*) Level of income, distribution of income. What sectors of the population might use the product.

(*iv*) Natural resources (limited, potentially rich); importance of staple agricultural or other products in earning income.

(*v*) Extent and stage of industrial development; plans for further development; amount of foreign investment coming in.

(*vi*) Present economic situation, trade balance, credit standing and availability of foreign exchange.

Access to Market

(*i*) Import restrictions, such as licensing or quotas.

(*ii*) Rates of customs duties; whether goods from your country receive preferential or MFN (most favoured nation) treatment.

(*iii*) Method of calculating the value of goods for duty purposes.

(*iv*) Marking and labelling regulations; need for health certificates for animal, plant and fisheries products; testing procedures for pharmaceuticals, etc.

(*v*) Convertibility of currency and currency controls; controls on remittances.

(*vi*) Added value or other internal taxes.

(*vii*) Bilateral trade or barter agreements that favour imports from particular sources.

Market Potential

(*i*) Current and potential demand for products.

(*ii*) Domestic production of product or one closely related to it. Major producers and location, investment plans, etc.

(*iii*) Statistics of imports of products by volume, value and country of origin. Are these increasing or decreasing?

(*iv*) Indicate the price and quality ranges of imported and domestic product; range with the largest current and potential sales.

(*v*) Prices at the importer, wholesale and retail levels.

(*vi*) Control of market by traditional suppliers; acceptability of new products.

Market Requirements

(*i*) System of measurement used; imperial, metric, etc.

(*ii*) Preferred price quotations: ex-works, CIF, FOB, C&F, etc.

(*iii*) Terms of credit considered normal; letter of credit, sight draft, etc. If credit is necessary, what are the standard terms?

(*iv*) Preferences in styling, quality, etc., because of national characteristics of interests that differ widely from those in the exporter's country.

(*v*) Need to conform to certain standards, such as electrical standards, and the procedure for approval; also grading system, if any.

(*vi*) Need for special packaging because of climate, shipping conditions, government regulations, or local tastes and prejudices.

Distribution

(*i*) The normal importer of the product, whether manufacturer, commission agent, merchant, stocking distributors, or others; mark-ups and commissions expected in each instance.

(*ii*) Normal distribution patterns.

(*iii*) Should one firm have an exclusive agency for the whole market or should a number of representatives in various locations be preferable?

(*iv*) Do importers normally carry large stocks to supply the trade or are frequent small shipments common?

(*v*) Will the representative expect advertising support?

Sales Promotion

(*i*) What media are available for advertising the product: newspapers, trade magazines, radio, television, cinema, etc.?

(*ii*) What is the cost of advertising space or time in the media not suited for advertising this product?

(*iii*) Are there any suitable trade fairs or exhibitions in the area and what is the cost of participating in them?

(*iv*) Is there a large reading public or would radio or cinema advertising be preferable?

EIGHT KEYS TO SELECTING MARKETS

In general, when selecting markets, keep these points in mind:

(*i*) Concentration on one or two markets to start with; don't spread yourself too thin;

(*ii*) Don't overlook the smaller, less obvious, and perhaps less competitive markets;

(*iii*) Plan to spend some time and money visiting foreign markets. These visits, says one export veteran, "break down exporting difficulties into practical problems you can deal with;"

(*iv*) Keep within your capacity to service customers in accepting orders; don't go after foreign business that you can't handle efficiently;

(*v*) Make certain at the start that your export business is going to be profitable;

(*vi*) Find a need and fill it; this will ensure success;

(*vii*) Stay away from markets in which import restrictions or exchange controls will restrict your scope; and

(*viii*) Be sure that your export organisation is in good shape to handle business promptly before you accept your first orders.

APPENDIX C

CHECKLIST FOR RESEARCH AND TARGET MARKETS

I. Collection of Marketing Data

(*a*) *Product of Your Own Types and Sizes*

Quality
Packages
Design
Manufacturing costs
Suitability for different areas and climatic conditions
Trade mark
Patent
Technical details
Delivery capacity
After sales service

(*b*) *Country*
Population
Standard of living
Social and economic background
Major industrial branches of importance
Banks and other financial institutions
Geographical characteristics
Climate
Political conditions
Language
Religion
Education
Currency
Communications

(*c*) *Import Conditions*
Customs duties
Fees
Price Control
Quotas
Licences
Package regulations
Standard trade marking

(*d*) *Distribution Channels*
Available ports and terminals
Warehousing capacity
Inland transport
Delivery periods
Agents, wholesale dealers

(*e*) *Market Potential*
Present consumption of similar and competing products
Potential consumption categories
Number, size, position, development possibilities
Estimated volume of sales

(*f*) *Present Market*
Import and Export
Country of origin
Value and quantity
Local competitors
Names, numbers, size
Manufacturing units' capacity
Foreign competitors
Names, numbers, size
Exports to the country
Competing products
Names, types, sizes, quality
Design
Technical data

Sales arrangements
Annual consumption
Seasonal fluctuations
Types of consumers who decide and influence purchases
How often do the purchases take place
Distribution channels
Major distributors of importance
Position, capacity
Business methods
Terms of payment
Credit terms
Discounts
Treatment of claims
Delivery and installation conditions
Service and spareparts
Branch organisations

(g) *Advertising and Sales Promotion*
Effectiveness and costs of different media
Fairs and exhibitions

II. Profitability Judgement

(a) Calculated total costs for introduction to the foreign market.

(b) Calculated sales price for different customers and market areas during the coming years.

(c) Estimated possible volume of sales.

(d) Estimated profitability at the estimated sales volume.

III. Final Examination—Choice of Market

Decision about possible introduction to the market, considering profitability, resources and risks.

IV. Elaboration of Marketing Plan

(a) *Marketing Methods*
Product strategy
Price policy
Packaging policy
Distribution strategy
Sales strategy
Service strategy

(b) *Plan for advertising and information*

(c) *Costs and Revenues*
Revenues
Costs
Coverage contribution
Marketing costs
Capital demand

(d) *Summary for a total plan with alternative development lines*

APPENDIX D

RESEARCH FOR OVERSEAS MARKET EXPLORATION

Select Sources of Information (Indian)

Indian Institute of Packaging, Plot No. E 2, Marol Industrial Estate, Andheri, Bombay-400093

1. Packaging India (Quarterly).

Manager of Publications, Civil Lines, Delhi/Kitab Mahal, Janpath, New Delhi

2. Handbook of Export Promotion (Green Book) (Irregular).
3. Economic and Commercial Reports (Annual Reports on Various Countries).

Director-General of Commercial Intelligence and Statistics, 1, Council House St., Calcutta-2

4. Monthly Statistics of the Foreign Trade of India, Vol. I.: Exports and Reexports, Vol. II: Imports.
5. Handbook of Commercial Information (3 Volumes).

Cardamom Board, Ernakulam - Cochin, Kerala

6. Cardamom News (Monthly).

Basic Chemicals, Pharmaceuticals and Cosmetics, Export-Promoton Councils (Chemexcil), Bombay.

Cashew Export Promotion Council, Ernakulam, Kochi

7. Directory of Cashew Importers.
8. India Cashew Journal (Quarterly).

The Gems & Jewellery Export Promotion, Council, (GJEPC), Bombay.

9. Things an Exporter should Know.
10. Export Statistics-Statement showing the commodity-wise and country-wise export of enginnering goods in retrospect during the period from 1956-57 to 1968-69.
11. Indian Engineering Exporter (Monthly).
12. Home Bulletin (Weekly).

Export Promotion Council for Handicrafts, New Delhi.

Council for Leather Exports (CLE), Madras.

13. Leathers (Monthly).

Plastics & Linoleums Export Promotion Council, Nyloc House, 254-D-2, Annie Besant Road, Prabhadevi, Bombay-25.

14. Plexconcil Bulletin (Bi-monthly).
15. Uniplexil (Quarterly).

Handloom Export Promotion Council (HEPC), Madras.

Synthetic and Rayon Textile Export Promotion Council, Resham Bhavan, Veer Nariman Road, Bombay - 1

16. Directory of Importers.
17. Indian Silk of Rayons (Overseas Quarterly).
18. Export Statistics of Rayon (Annual).
19. Markets At A Glance Series (Uganda, Muscat & Oman; Trucial States, Kuwait and other countries).

Sports Goods Export Promotion Council, 1E/6, Jhandewalan Extension, New Delhi. (SGEPC)

20. Sporticil (Quarterly).

Cotton Textile Export Promotion Council, Engineering Centre, 9, Mathew Road, Bombay-4. (TEXPROCIL)

21. Texprocil Bulletin (Quarterly).
22. Texprocil (inland edition-fortnightly).

Wool and Woollens Exports Promotion Council, Churchgate Chambers, 5, New Marine Lines, Bombay-20.

23. Newsletter monthly

Carpet Export Promotion Council, New Delhi.
Engineering Export Promotion Council (EEPC) Calcutta.
Overseas Construction Council of India (OCCI), Bombay.
Electronics and Computer Software Export Promotion Council, New Delhi.
Chemicals and Allied Products Export Promotion Council (CAPEXCIL), Calcutta.
Shellac Export Promotion Council, Calcutta.
Apparel Export Promotion Council (AEPEC), New Delhi.
Indian Silk Export Promotion Council, Bombay.

18

PRODUCT DEVELOPMENT FOR OVERSEAS MARKETS

Among the early and critical decisions to be made by the firm interested in international marketing is the choice of products to be offered. What products can the firm profitably market in the chosen market areas? In what areas is the firm's existing and potential product line of value? How can the firm maximize its impact on the market by offering the most appropriate product service combination? Is the combination currently available to present customers likely to be most productive abroad, or should the firm adapt its mix to the new set of market conditions? These represent but a few of the continuing questions involved in establishing and maintaining an effective product policy.

Each product to be offered must, above all, meet the needs of the potential user; therefore, each must be subjected to extreme scrutiny from the user's viewpoint before committing the company's resources to the development of products. The product decision calls for others involving the provision of production facilities and the development of effective marketing programmes. The physical product itself needs review to determine its appropriateness in the overseas environment. Trademarks, patents, packaging, and promotional activities, all hinges in the product decision. In addition, the decision to manufacture or sell a certain product sets the sources and types of competition that will be encountered and the investments that will be required. To cope with these complex decisions an effective marketing team must evolve that is alert to product marketing opportunities, able to screen the potential offerings, and able to design and implement an effective product introduction. It must also provide for continuous review of the product line and the elimination of products that are no longer profitable.

In this chapter, we have tried to identify the product concept that is most useful for international marketing; determine conditions that permit extension of the present product line into new markets or require adaptation; a look at the packaging, branding, labelling, and service aspects of the total product concept; and determine the role of research and development in international marketing. It is assumed that the company has already chosen the market segments it is to serve. The primary concern, then, is with the development of appropriate products to meet the needs of these segments. However, in some instances a company may seek market segments with needs that can be satisfied by a product already developed for other markets. In either case, the product must match the needs of the market segment to which the company will address its marketing effort.

What is Product?

The definition of a product may be clarified with the following quotations:

If we define a product in its simplest commercial terms, it is this:

"A product is something people will buy—that is, some magnitude that makes it profitable. If people don't buy, it's not a product."

"People spend their money not for goods and services, but to get the value satisfaction they believe are bestowed by what they are buying. They buy quarter-inch holes, not quarter-inch drills..."[1]

The concept of product used in marketing is broader than that of an assembly of physical or chemical components in a certain size, shape, and colour combination. Marketers are more inclined to view the product through the eyes of their potential customers. As the previous quotation suggests, customers are interested in the benefits they expect to receive as a result of the purchase rather than that tangible good itself. What will it do for them — provide transportation, reduce labour costs, add sex appeal? This is epitomized in the statement of a Mideast executive:

"They (foreigners) come wanting to sell us air-conditioners, but what we want is cool air. They sell us the air-conditioner and they leave with our money. Eventually the air-conditioner breaks down. When that happens, we have the air conditioner, but we have no cool air."[2]

1. Theodore Levitt, *Marketing for Business Growth* (NY: McGraw-Hill Book Company Inc., 1974), pp. 8-9.
2. "The Middle East Mirage", *International Management* (April, 1979), p. 21.

Thus, he defined the product in terms of what the customer wanted, not in terms of what the factory made. This concept of defining the product in terms of demand is especially pertinent for international marketers where the temptation has often been strong to offer the same product/service-mix abroad that is available at home without adequate market analysis and ignoring the possibility that the product may be viewed in an entirely different light in the overseas market. It may serve different functions or, at the very least, may be used in very different manner and may be more difficult to service.

It is easy to slip into the view that similar physical products perform exactly the same function for all customers, but consider the cycle that is a basic means of transportation in some underdeveloped countries where it is common to observe whole families riding. As many as four or five members of the family may be travelling on one cycle at a time, or the cycle may be employed as a means of hauling freight, either in its normal form or in a threewheeled version. In contrast, in North America and Europe the cycle appears more frequently as transportation for only one person and cycling may be more of a sport than basic transportation.

The market's concept of the product has been variously described as an "augmented", "extended", or "total" product, to distinguish it from the narrower view. This total product concept is the tangible product plus the services that accompany it as expressed in Figure 16.1. The physical product is the core value, but is extended by the addition of packaging, labelling, and branding, and is accompanied by both pre-sale and post-sale services in order to provide the consumer with a maximum of satisfaction from its use. No doubt many will question the value of the extended product in the belief that the consumer receives value only from the tangible product itself. There is reason to believe, however, that these other elements do add to the benefits or utilities the consumer receives.

The brand gives the consumer assurance that a specified quality is present and can be expected every time the brand is purchased. The brand may further convey appropriate images that enhance the psychological value of the product. Labelling aids by providing information regarding the contents of the package and information as to its use and preparation; thereby providing for proper operation and efficiency in durable goods and avoiding the possibility of spoilage by improper care and preparation. The package can be a plain container that protects the product in transportation and storage, but it may also provide more convenient use through proper size and design.

Services are especially important in the sale of industrial products where suppliers may aid the buyer in determining requirements by surveying needs, providing the assistance needed to make the product effective (software for computers), or assuring that the delivery will occur at the time and place needed to maintain a continuous production flow. Business people may require assurance of readily available repair parts and service personnel in case there is a product failure.

For some companies there is no tangible good in the product they offer. In these firms the total product may be a service. Examples of international industrial firms providing such service would include advertising agencies, marketing research agencies, management consultants, transportation companies, and insurance firms. In the consumer field many similar services exist such as car leasing, communication and broadcasting, travel agencies, and financial services. In these companies there is also a need to consider the total product. For example, advertising agencies operating in other countries have found it necessary to offer clients more than media space purchasing, art and copy ideas, and production facilities. They may differentiate themselves from local and other foreign competitors through services such as marketing research, public relations, and sales promotional aids.

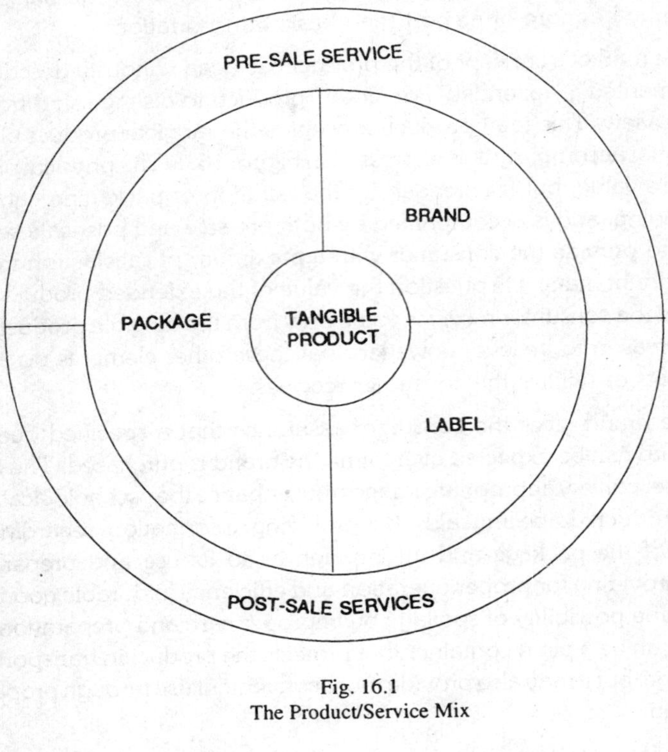

Fig. 16.1
The Product/Service Mix

When contemplating international markets, a company may have a choice of selling either physical goods or services. Thus, the turnkey operations, management contracts, licensing, as alternative strategies for entering the international markets, represent methods whereby companies offer services featuring their specialities without directly selling the product. Franchising is another popular means of capitalizing on the knowledge and reputation of the firm in foreign lands without direct ownership. These alternative views of the "product" often offer advantages to the international firm without substantially increasing the risks associated with inventories and/or facilities abroad. That may be the only way to enter the market. For example, the Middle Eastern countries have imported many items directly from India but expressed a keen interest in manufacturing some of these items over the longer period, despite a present shortage of personnel for building and operating the facilities. Our firms have been able to capitalize on this latter development through management contracts and turnkey projects. The potential scope for such operations is evident in the Saudi Arabian Government's plan for turning one fishing village, Al Jubayl, into an industrial complex including a three million-ton-steel mill, a half-million-barrel oil refinery, a 500,000-ton fertilizer plant, a 21,000-ton aluminium plant, a 375-million dollar port, a desalination plant to provide 52 million gallons of fresh water per day, and an electric plant of 1,000 mega watt generating capacity. This is only one such project in the country. Similarly, railway lines spreading in various parts of Iraq have recently been completed by Indian Railways.

Product Functioning: How should an exporter position a product? An exporter should position his product differently from one country to the next. When Renault introduced the Renault 5, its newest entry in the European small car market, it positioned the car in France as an amusing, fun car suitable for both urban and highway driving. Advertisements took the form of a cartoon strip showing a bouncy, chatty car with eyes and a mouth. In Germany, on the other hand, where purchasing a car is a serious matter, the advertisements stressed the Renault 5's modern engineering and interior comfort. In Finland, the emphasis was on solid construction and reliability, and in Italy, on the automobile's road performance.

The International Product Life Cycle: Many products go through a trade cycle, during which India may be initially an exporter, then it might lose its export markets and may finally become an importer of the product. Tea is a very good example on this score.

India has been the largest exporter of tea but now a stage has come that it might have to import tea due to enormous rise in domestic demand.

The four stages of the international product life cycle include-

(*i*) *Indian Manufacturers/Processors Export Product—Stage I—New Product* - An innovation is launched in India whether it is handicraft or computer software and the country succeeds because of huge market and highly developed infrastructure. Eventually, Indian producers start exporting the product to other countries.

(*ii*) *Foreign Production Starts - Stage II - Mature Product* - As foreign manufacturers become familiar with the product, some of them start producing it for their home market. They do this under licensing or joint-venture arrangement or simply by copying the product. Their government often abets their efforts by imposing tariffs or quotas on imports of the product.

(*iii*) *Foreign Production Becomes Competitive in Export Markets — Stage III- Standardized Product*—By now, foreign manufacturers have gained production experience, and with their lower costs, they start exporting the product to other countries.

(*iv*) *Import Competition Begins-Stage IV — Standardized Product —* The foreign manufacturer's growing volume and lower costs enable them to export the product to India in direct competition with Indian producers.

The implication of international product life cycle is that an Indian manufacturer's sales in the home market will eventually decline as foreign markets start producing the product and ultimately export it to India.

The Indian manufacturer's best defense is to become global marketers. Indian firms should open production and distribution facilities in other countries with large markets and/or lower costs. Global marketers are able to stretch the product-life-cycle of any product form by taking it to the countries that are getting ready to use it.

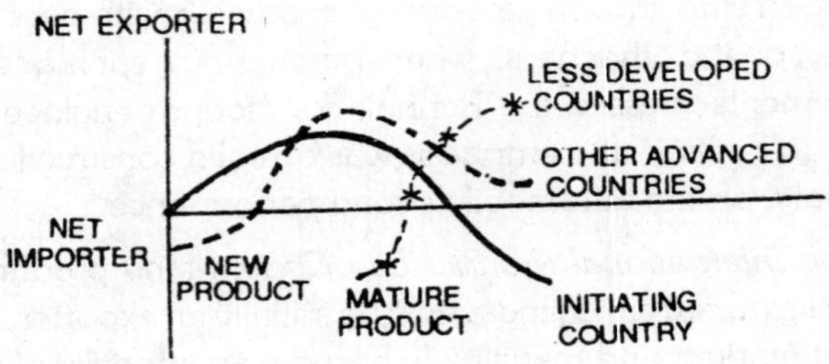

Fig. 16.2
The International Product Life Cycle

PRODUCT POLICY

Export product policy is mainly concerned with issues that arise after the strategic match of products to foreign market segments has been made. The development of export product policy rests on three foundations. One is product positioning abroad. The second is the extent to which products should be adapted or standardized for penetration into foreign markets. The third involves the important accoutrements of the product: brand, label, packaging, warranties, and service requirements.

The key to a successful international product policy is the ability of the product to meet the needs of the foreign market segment. Correct product positioning makes this key work. There are conceptual approaches to positioning but the subject is mastered best by those professional marketers who analyze a variety of examples from the international marketplace. In connection with product policy, two further points should be kept in mind. One is that there are two kinds of products: domestic ones and international ones. The domestic ones are those that require adaptation for each separate foreign market segment; an example is Nestle's famous Nescafe. The export product is standardized; an example is Martell cognac. The second point relates to the better image a foreign product generally has compared to local competition. A French perfume is generally perceived to be superior to a local one. The brand, labels, warranty, service, and packaging decisions have their own facets but essentially they are submerged under the overall product positioning decision.

The export marketing of services requires product policy decisons identical for most part to those for products. Many international marketers are unfamiliar with the marketing of services. Therefore, the successful marketing of services requires a more extensive study of industries and examples, including uncommon fields such as consulting services.

The international marketing of technology to other rich industrialized countries is conducted in much the same way as the marketing of products and services. But when technology is marketed to LDCs the problems are more complex. This is because LDC governments have a number of industrial and social objectives to fulfill through the technology transfer. Moreover the technology absorption capacity of many LDCs is constrained by their relatively limited skill resources. So only certain types of technology can be transferred successfully to LDCs unless the international supplier is willing and permitted to make direct foreign investment. Overall technology transfer to the LDCs deserves great attention. It is a potentially very big market and one through which the economic and social development of the world can be increased.

Product Line Decisions

Once a company has chosen the market segments to which it will cater, it is confronted with the problem of determining whether its present products are the ideal vehicles for such a move.

Should the Domestic Product be Marketed Abroad?

The easiest decision to make is that of taking the established product abroad. By doing so, the firm would capitalize on a proven product and might gain from production, research and development (R and D) and marketing efficiencies as a result of increased scale of operation. Cost savings might be obtained from longer production runs, standardized packaging, and established brand images. This easy approach is deceptive, however, for it depends on the product achieving acceptance in the overseas market before these savings can be accomplished. If the product does not satisfy the basic needs of the market, it won't sell and cost reductions are not possible.

The logic of the dilemma, then, is to pursue a policy of product adaptation to meet the requirements of the new market segments, but such a policy also has its costs. Thus, the marketer is forced into a detailed analysis of the market to determine where and how much standardization is practical and the potential gains and tradeoffs from adapting products and promotion. Often this means research on the individual products and markets to determine the specific characteristics requiring modification of the product and the associated costs. Usually some modification of the basic product, brand policy, packaging, or service is desirable to secure a better fit between the company's offering and the requirements of overseas customers. However, in those instances where the firm exports only to a small number of units, it may not be economically feasible to achieve any substantial adaptation.

The Japanese or Middle Eastern market provides several examples of situations wherein exporting firms should or have adapted to their tastes.

Factors Affecting Standardization of the Product Line

If market analysis is needed for information on which to base a decision regarding standardization, then what are the significant factors to be investigated? Among the factors to be considered, we can isolate several major categories: market demand, economies of operation, governmental restrictions and rules, and compatibility with company resources and policy.

Market Demand

In order to determine the suitability of a product for a given market, it is necessary first to establish the basic function of the product. What is it expected to do? Perhaps the primary function of the product is to provide transportation, shelter from the rain, warmth, cleanliness, or aid in the production of other products and services. In addition, most products incorporate qualities that are not necessary for this primary purpose. These secondary functions can play an important role in the consumer's evaluation of the product. Television sets not only provide entertainment but also are status symbols in some societies. Redesigning the cabinet may have no effect on reception but can dramatically affect sales. For example, Sharp, a Japanese brand, sells in Taiwan in competition with local and other foreign brands; a change in the television cabinet resulted in a substantial sales increase despite a 14 per cent price increase. Another example of secondary function occurred when visitors at the home of the "Muchtar," head of an Arab village in the Judean Hills, were surprised to note a shiny refrigerator which stood in the centre of the spacious guest room. When asked why it was not in the kitchen, the Muchtar replied, "There, in the kitchen, the guests and neighbours won't see it." Apparently the refrigerator served a secondary status function that is no longer present in a country like the United States. In some instances the primary functions may also be different in the foreign market. Outboard motors designed for sports in the United States may be employed on fishing vessels abroad.

Even when the product serves the same functions in various countries, the conditions under which it is used may differ significantly, thus leading to product adaptation. Road conditions and traffic pattern in India account for some of the variations in automobile design between them and the United States. Similarly, variations in water content cause production adaptation not only between countries but some times within countries. More than one brand of detergent may be marketed to meet specific water conditions.

The high mobility of consumers is a factor leading some manufacturers to stress a policy of product standardization. For example, when travellers get upset stomachs in Hong Kong, they would like assurance that the Eno fruit salt purchased there is the same as at home. Likewise, people look for known quality in other products such as film since a picture missed through the use of poor film may not be discovered until the traveller is home, with no chance for a retake. It is no happenstance that the Kodak film and package are readily recognizable in many of the world's cities. Package standardization enhances ready identification and brand similarity lends assurance of performance. Holiday Inns can also attribute some of their popularity to the similarity of service available in different countries.

The image that residents of one country have for products of another country is an important consideration in the marketing of any specific brand. For instance, the image of Danish furniture, German beer, French wines, U.S. computers, Indian spices and tea and cotton textiles, etc., are quite well-formed. In fact, the sales of these products are likely to depend heavily on their maintenance of the "foreign" quality associated with the national image. The little phrase, "made in ——" can have a tremendous influence on success of a product. Manufacturers may wish to capitalize on their foreign image by exporting their product when it has a superior image.

Economics of Plant and Marketing Operations

The economics of operation usually favour standardization of the product offering. Advantages from standardizing are expected to accrue as a result of large scale operations. If the company's plants currently are operating below their most efficient levels, the additional volume from the standardized production enables the firm to spread its costs over a larger volume of output. Standardization permits the firm to import component parts from subsidiaries and to transfer knowledge, equipment, and systems among the production points. Product development costs are minimized and some marketing efficiencies may be possible in training and advertising. The auto maker's attempt to establish a "world car" is an attempt to secure the advantages of standardization.

On the other hand, several factors work against standardization. If there is already an established demand for a product line that has been acquired through purchase or merger, the marketing costs associated with obtaining market acceptance of the home version can be substantial. It might pay to develop the goodwill already present by maintaining the separate product in its market.

When different measurement systems are in use, it may be difficult to achieve standardization. For example, the metric system is used in all the major trading nations except the United States. Theoretically, it should be possible to merely translate metric standards while selling to USA, but this often results in the need to buy a special part in the foreign market because the standards differ, thus increasing costs. Several Indian industries, including pharmaceuticals and high technology groups, use the metric system but manufacturers have not been especially active in establishing international standards. Although there may have been advantages in the past for insisting on Indian standards, the current level of international competition is rapidly changing this position.

Governmental Effects

Governments affects the product design in numerous ways, each of which has a potential effect on decisions to make product modification. A direct influence is exerted through government purchases for defence, supplies and equipment, and state enterprises. The extension of governmental services in recent years has greatly increased these direct effects. Government programmes for power sources, medical programmes, and energy conservation represent vast markets for goods and services from private enterprise. The purchasing influence on design is exerted through specifications which must be met before a corporation can bid on government projects. The government may further restrict the entrance of firms into industries where governmental monopolies exist.

Indirect influences are exerted through laws that establish minimum standards for safety and health regulations. Government may participate in the consumer movement through information, and acting as consumer advocate. Labelling laws may require specific information and sizes of containers. Building codes lay down specifications. The local content regulations that are designed to speed up economic development can make modifications necessary for continued production. Taxes and tariffs frequently are establishing in a manner that gives competitive advantage to the local firms and works against foreign products, either by making them more expensive or by reducing the profit available.

Compatibility with Company Resources and Policy

Any product offered must present a reasonable compromise between the requirements of the market and the resources available to the firm. The firm seeks reasonable alignment with production and marketing capabilities as well as meeting the company's profit goals. Where production abroad is restricted by limitation on imports of raw materials and component parts, the company may find it necessary to modify the product through the use of substitutes. In some instances company policy no doubt reflects management policy to present a standard product line due to inadequate market analysis or stubborn belief that the market should want what management believes to be a superior product. However, competitive pressures from other Indian firms and foreign companies are likely to make this position less tenable than in the past when Indian products may have been the only ones available. These competitive pressures for change are likely to be strongest in the latter stages of the product's lifecycle.

The adaptation of a product to meet the market's needs is illustrated in designs by Maruti for the underdeveloped country-markets. The Maruti version, the Basic Transportation Vehicle, is a light, short-distance hauler that can be adapted as a pick up or minibus. The car is easy to assemble with no curved body parts. Maruti cars represent a major departure for the automobile firms in adapting to less developed markets.

Brand Policy

Brand policy becomes more important to the multinational firm as competition tightens in the local markets. Local producers and other foreign firms provide a basis for an effective communication strategy. If the producer is to gain the advantage of promotional effort, the consumer must be able to identify the product and to separate it from those of competitors. That is a function performed by the brand. Part of the significance of the brand policy derives from the fact that both the seller and the buyer can benefit from branding. The essential function of the brand is that it identifies a product which stands for some quality connotation — either high or low — so the buyer has the assurance that repeat purchases will result in similar satisfactory experiences in consumption or use.

Before viewing the branding alternatives available to the producer, it is desirable to distinguish among several closely related terms used in reference to brands. The term brand refers to a name, term, sign, symbol, or design used to identify the goods and services of a seller and to differentiate them from those of competitors. This identification may be placed directly on the product or on a label, tag, or package. Also, the brand may identify the product of a single seller (either producer or distributor) or a group of sellers. The brand name refers to that portion of the brand that can be spoken. Well-known examples of brand names in the world market include Taj Tea, HMT Machinery, Reliance Textiles etc. The trademark is that part or all of brand that has been given legal protection. It is a legal term referring to the exclusive rights of the owner of the mark.

Brand Options

The international marketer has several potential alternative brand policies from which to select. No one of these is most advantageous in all situations; therefore, the producer must carefully consider the potential gains and costs of each before making a decision. This is especially pertinent in view of the heavy promotional costs that are associated with establishing the brand in a market. The four branding alternatives may be identified as:

(*i*) A policy of selling unbranded goods, or selling goods to be resold under the brand of a distributor;

(*ii*) Establishing a single worldwide brand to identify the producer's product in all markets;

(*iii*) Establishing local brand names for the separate national markets; and

(*iv*) Establishing several brands in a market to identify individual products or groups of products in the manufacturer's line. These might distinguish different types of product (*e.g.*, food and cosmetics) or different quality or styles.

No Branding

Most marketers of manufactured products probably believe that branding is desirable, but there are a number of instances in which it is costly and difficult to establish a brand sufficiently to make it profitable. Among the conditions usually deemed necessary for effective branding are:

1. The product must have the potential demand and margin to support the additional promotional costs and yet provide a greater profit to the brander;
2. It is imperative that the producer be able to maintain the quality connotation that has proved to be of value to the buyer. That quality may be either high or low and may be based on physical or other characteristics, but whatever the brand stands for, the customer counts in it being consistent;
3. Obviously the product also should be identifiable so the consumer can distinguish among the products in the market place; and
4. If the producer is to gain maximum benefit from branding, the product should be consistently available to the consumer; if it is not, the promotional impact is lost and ill-will may actually result when the repeat purchase is not possible.

For many of the commodities sold in international trade, the above conditions either cannot be met or would be too costly to attempt; consequently, brands are of little significance to these trades. An important segment of Indian exports is composed of agricultural products that are produced by a large number of farmers and are sold by grade. Branding these goods would be difficult and, probably, meaningless to the prospective buyer. In the case of manufactured goods, it is often possible to brand, but may still not be desirable. For instance, some products become components of a final product and are not readily identifiable to the consumer. If these items cannot be shown to provide a special advantage that is important to the final product's performance in the eyes of the consumer, or if they are not important replacement items, the manufacturer may decline to brand them.

A typical Indian company enters the export market with essentially the same product it sells in India. Even when a product is changed expressly for the export market, the modification is ought to be minor — converting an appliance to 110 volt electrical systems or painting and packaging the product to protect it against extreme conditions.

One key to success in product planning is to adapt it to the cultural tastes and economic characteristics of the particular foreign market, rather than try to sell the Indian market products abroad. In Iraq, a jumbo size refrigerator is the most popular size as compared to European demand which is for a 6 cubic feet variety. Many Iraqis go in for large freezers because of a large space for storage for bulk buying at a point of time, for they are not at all sure whether the items they require will be available for the next time. The Iraqi market may be characterised as a scarcity market where items are in short supply. While the cost difference is a factor, the basic reasons for the Europeans' choice lie in the cultural behaviour patterns of the consumers. To many European housewives, a food-shopping trip is a social event. They do so daily, and therefore do not buy large quantities which must be stored for a few days in the refrigerator. Moreover, if they do not have a car, they have to walk to the store and cannot carry large quantities.

Alternative Productive Adaptation Strategies

According to Warren Keegan, there are five alternative strategies for the adaptation of a product and its related market communications to a foreign market.

(i) One Product, One Message — Worldwide (Straight Extension)

Coca-cola has used this alternative successfully; but on balance there probably are more market failures than successes with this approach. When some of the Indian companies tried to market Indian pickles in the USA and Europe, they were not successful because the taste was very bitter and hot. Problems of consumer preferences may occur when one enters a market. In Tanganiyka, consumers prefer a three-hole razor blade rather than a sandwiched razor blade. This strategy is a tempting one because it involves no additional expense for research and development, manufacturing, retooling or set-up inventory control or marketing communication.[3]

(*ii*) Same Product, but Modified Communications (Communication Adaptation)

This is practical when the same product can be used to fill different needs in foreign markets. For example, Indian bicycles are advertised abroad for the pleasure they give rather than for their transportation qualities since bicycles are used more for fun and pleasure in Europe and the USA than for transportation. Logic rather than fancy is used in advertising copy in Scandinavia; big coloured illustrations and terse copy in Spain; sex appeal is avoided in Saudi Arabia; and a hundred other communications adaptations are made. The appeal of a communication adaptation strategy is its relatively low cost of implementation.

(*iii*) Product Adaptation — Communications Extension

In this the exporter uses essentially the same promotional messages abroad as at home, but the product is changed to meet local conditions or preferences. A soap formula is changed to suit local water conditions; chemical fertilisers are altered to fit soil conditions. Voltage requirements

3. The discussion of these strategies is adopted from Warren J. Keegan, "Multinational Product Planning, Strategic Alternatives", *Journal of Marketing*, Chicago (USA), January 1969, pp. 58-62.

result in alteration of electrical appliances, and climatic factors make for packaging changes.

This strategy involves extra engineering and production cost but may be better than introducing an unaltered product possessing less appeal.

(*iv*) Dual Adaptation

It involves changes in both the product and the message-in-effect, a combination of the second and third alternatives. It is done to increase the product's acceptability. For example, the National Cash Register Company took an innovative step backward by developing and advertising a crank-operated cash register that would sell at half the cost of a modern cash register. This unit caught on greatly in the Philippines, the Orient, Latin America and Spain. Dual adaptation is an expensive strategy but is worth-while if the target market are large enough.

Fig 16.3
An Export Product/Promotion Strategy Matrix

PRODUCT

	Do not Change	**Adapt**	**Develop New Products**
Do not change	(1) **Straight Extension** (Same need and use conditions *e.g.* soft drinks)	(2) **Product Adaptation,** (Same need different use conditions *e.g.* voltage requirements, petrol, packaging, soap formula etc.)	
Adapt	(3) **Communicaion Adaption** (Different need, same use conditions *e.g.* Bicycles)	(4) **Dual Adaptation** (Different need and use conditions *e.g.* clothing)	(5) **Product Invention** (Same need, limited ability to buy - *e.g.* Hand powered washing machine with tumbling action of an automatic machine. New theme to be emphasised).

(v) Product Invention

In this strategy, a company develops a new product in response to foreign market demands. For markets with a low purchasing power, a firm developed an inexpensive hand-operated washing machine with the tumbling action of an automatic machine. For example, there is enormous need in less developed countries for low-cost pin-joint wrist-watches on which HMT should do research and develop a mass communication programme to gain product trial and acceptance. Product invention would appear to be the costliest of all strategies, but the pay-offs to the successful firm also appear to be the highest.

Often, in a foreign market product-planning situation, a company is faced with this problem. Can we afford to modify the design, quality, or some other feature of our product? That is, will the demand offset the additional costs of producing and marketing the modified products? Answers to these questions are not easy to come by. Sometimes the management may compromise by making a relatively inexpensive change, such as selling pharmaceuticals by the individual capsule or packaging razor blades singly rather than in multiple units.

Branding is especially important in export marketing. The brand picture may be only part of the product that a consumer can recognize. Foreign consumer preferences for Indian products often overcome their nationalistic feelings; so, in many instances, a company can use the same brand that is used in the domestic market. The legal aspects of brand registration and ownership in foreign countries may create problems. In some countries, a local firm or person may pirate an Indian brand name and thus block its use by the Indian company in that foreign country.

Export management must consider the general types of product adaptation, *i.e.*,

(*a*) Simple changes to conform to specific conditions; and

(*b*) Basic modifications of the basic character of products.

The difficult questions lie in the second type of adaptation — changes that affect the basic character of a product. The chief consideration here is one of production economies. The major deterrent to the production of special products abroad is that some of the advantages of a verified worldwide organisation are lost.

To decide whether a product is suitable for a market and whether it should be modified, one must determine how it fits into the demand requirements of the market. For this purpose, we should start by listing the product characteristics and try to match the main demand requirements with it.

Product Characteristics	*Demand Requirements*
Basic functional purpose	Economic pattern of life
Secondary purposes	Value system, National personality
Durability and quality	Economic level, Education
Maintenance	Education, Value system

The question of basic functional modification in a product arises when a function is performed abroad in a manner not common in India. Most products incorporate some qualities that are not essential to their primary functional purpose. Radios are part of the furniture of a room, bicycles are a status symbol in some societies, and so forth. Because value systems and other attitudes vary widely in many countries, products oriented to the Indian market are less likely to fit foreign markets in this group of characteristics than in performing their primary purpose. But since the qualities are of secondary value to the buyer, it is often more practical than changing primary functional characteristics, because they often involve superficial aspects, such as the cabinet of a radio, where production economies are not so unfavourable. The only area in which systematic analysis is feasible is that of status symbols; status symbols have their origin in the value systems of consumers. There are three major types of value systems:

(*i*) *Pure Economic Ladders:* In low income countries, status is achieved even by the ownership of a sewing machine, a bicycle or a radio. In the middle-income range, ownership of a refrigerator is a status symbol. At the high-income levels, an air-conditioner, a car, etc., are the status symbols.

(*ii*) *Patterns of national aspirations.*

(*iii*) *Values toward Conservation and Tradition*: Material success is often not rated highly in these societies; intellectual, artistic, or other achievements carry greater status.

Attitudes toward durability and quality vary among the value systems but the extra cost of excess durability or quality is not much of a desirable burden to carry into a foreign market. However, it does not mean that Indian exporters should not sell quality products or make items which are not durable. Two aspects of the method of operation of a product have to be considered in relation to market conditions: the power source and the skills required, particularly in the manufacture of durable consumer goods. The question of maintenance is related to the skill required to operate a product to which the exporter should also pay attention.

Nations develop social attitudes and customs which derive from the peculiar patterns of their cultural development. Attitudes towards the family, the social class structure, class mobility and material values, for example, have a basis in the moral and ethical standards of a community. Standards are often rooted in religious beliefs. Some of the effects on the social systems caused by very different religions, *e.g.,* Hinduism and Christianity, will be obvious; other attitudes, *e.g.,* those towards colour, require a close investigation. Significant differences in attitudes and customers are to be found in Christian countries. Attitudes towards certain products and advertising copy are quite different in France from those in Holland. It should be noted that attitudes and beliefs tend to strengthen over time, and that countries are often associated or associate themselves with special abilities or characteristics. The German, for example, considers himself technically superior but is prepared to buy a Ford car combining German technical achievement and American styling. The image associated with a country like India persists long after the basis for the "image" has disappeared.

It is, therefore, more difficult to remove a reputation for poor delivery services than to create it. Changes, however, can be effected.

Standardization of Export Marketing Strategies

When an enterprise enters a new export market, it must determine how it should design its marketing strategy to fit local conditions. The following questions need to be answered. Does the product need to be changed? Are existing sales promotion and advertising campaigns applicable to the new market? Should the type of distribution network used in the firm's other foreign markets be replicated in the new market? There is no easy answer to any of these questions. However, the standardisation of market strategy across national markets is one potentially effective approach.

An assessment of the pros and cons of standardization depends upon a prior assessment of the role of export sales in the firm's overall corporate strategy. If export sales represent a real opportunity for the firm to expand into new, permanent markets abroad, then the firm should consider customising its product line and its marketing strategy to fit the needs of its local markets. In contrast, if export sales are merely an outlet for excess production capacity, then the firm should focus on finding export markets that are receptive to products that have already been developed for the domestic market.

Advantages of Standardization

The advantages of a standardized marketing strategy lie mainly in the areas of cost efficiency, advertising efficiency, and idea utilization.

(1) *Production Cost Efficiencies.* Although it may be possible for the firm to achieve higher total sales if its products are tailored to each individual national market, the firm can also increase its profit margin by taking advantage of cost economies. That is, by offering the same basic product in

all of its national markets and thereby increasing the size of its production runs, the firm can begin to experience the benefits of production cost efficiencies. Moreover, research and development costs can be spread over a greater number of units. The benefit of cost reductions, of course, is that they make the firm's products, whether sold domestically or internationally, more profitable.

(2) *Advertising Efficiencies.* If the firm utilizes the same advertising theme for all of its national markets, total advertising costs can be reduced significantly. Standardized advertising also provides a consistent image of the firm's products across its various markets. Consumers, today, are increasingly mobile, and encountering a common advertising theme from one country to the next tends to reassure them as to the sincerity of the advertiser and the quality and reliability of the product. Standardized advertising can result in both cost efficiencies and customer relations benefits.

(3) *Utilizing Good Ideas.* Marketing ideas that worked in one country may work in another. Certain advertising themes developed for one national market have been shown to have universal appeal. Advertisements for Levi's jeans have a casual, almost rodeo flavour wherever Levi Strauss products are sold; the Coca-Cola company stresses the freshness and sparkle of youth in its advertising around the world.

Disadvantages of Standardization

(1) The most significant disadvantage of standardization is simply that cultural, political, and economic differences among countries may make it all but impossible to a use a single standardized marketing strategy. Unfortunately, many businesses assume that the underlying environmental variables do not affect their marketing strategies either because these variables are the same everywhere or because they are not important.

(2) Advertising is often the key component of the marketing strategy that the firm would like to standardize. Advertising can be broken down into two components: the buying proposal and the creative presentation. The buying proposal consists of the sales points that are the most persuasive and relevant to prospective customers. It is what the advertiser says. In contrast, the creative presentation is how the buying proposal is communicated to the public.

Implications of Standardization

(1) At a minimum, the firm should standardize its procedures for identifying targets markets, establishing price polices, evaluating distribution mechanism and determining which advertisements are the most effective.

(2) An additional benefit of a standardized plan is that sales results from one country to the next are more amenable to comparison. Five factors

influencing the extent to which the marketing plan should be standardized are discussed below:

(*a*) *Type of Product.* Certain products have truly universal sales appeals. Items such as razor blades, electric irons, automobile tires, and ballpoint pens are sold primarily on the basis of their physical characteristics. It is possible for the firm to standardise most, if not all, of its marketing strategy for such products.

(*b*) *Homogeneity of the Markets.* The more alike people are in terms of their income, education, occupation, and similar characteristics, the greater the probability that they will purchase similar products. For this reason, it is relatively easy to standardise marketing strategies for most of the Western European nations. However, if a product is to be sold in Europe and in the Far East, the organization may have to formulate separate market strategies.

(*c*) *Interaction of International Consumers.* The more consumers from various countries interact with the international marketplace, the more suitable is the environment for adopting a standardized marketing strategy. Such interaction could include reading newspapers or magazines from other nations, watching television or listening to radio broadcasts from other countries, or travelling from one nation to another. Thus, as Europe becomes more "internationalised," firms will begin to use European marketing strategies rather than simply Italian strategies or German strategies.

(*d*) *Availability of Marketing Services.* Regarding the country or market in question, how available are advertising agencies, marketing research data, and commercial television and radio time? A market strategy developed for the United States may not be applicable in other countries because US advertising relies heavily upon television. In some countries, the government owns the television stations and does not permit advertising. In others, advertising may be available, but large segments of the population are too poor to own television sets. The greater the differences between nations in terms of the availability of marketing services, the more likely the firm is to adopt a separate strategy for each national market.

(*e*) *Government Restrictions.* All nations have laws regulating their markets. These laws influence how products are promoted, priced, and distributed. Australia, for example, has a law requiring that 85 percent of the component parts of all automobiles sold in that country be manufactured in Australia.

Global Standardization Versus Adaptation

Traditional supporters of the export marketing concept hold that international consumers vary in their needs and, therefore, it would be more effective if product is tailored to each customer target group because in foreign markets economic, political and cultural conditions vary widely.

In contrast advocates of standardization of products globally or at least regionally feel that this would save costs and build-up global brand power, single advertising campaigns. In fact new communication and transportation technologies have created a more homogeneous world market. People around the world want the same basic things — things that make life easier and increase their discretionary time and buying power. This convergence of needs and wants has created global markets for standardized products. It is felt that adaptation results in less efficiency and higher prices to consumers. The global marketers realize substantial economies through standardization of production, distribution, marketing and management. They translate their efficiency into greater value for consumers by offering high quality and more reliable products at lower prices.

Some products are more global and require less adaptation on the whole. Yet even in these cases, some adaptation takes place. Coca-cola is less sweet or less carbonated in certain countries. Indian pickles are mildly hot when sold in Gulf countries but they are not hot at all when sold to USA.

The assumption of global standardization is that it will save a lot of cost, will lead to lower prices, and cause more goods to be snapped up by price sensitive consumers. But these assumptions are debatable. A company needs to think in terms of incremental revenue versus incremental cost.

Standardization might save some costs, competitors are always ready to offer more of what the customers in each country want, and the company might may dearly for replacing long-run marketing thinking with short-run financial thinking. Global marketing is advocated not global standardization.

Product Decisions. Will what sells in India sell in USA, France or Dubai? A moment's reflection suggests that, just as is the case in various parts of India, some products can be sold successfully without adaptation, but others must be adapted to the market. Sometimes new products must be designed.

As product changes are contemplated, so also must packaging and branding changes be considered. Brands may have different, negative, or inappropriate meanings in other countries. The word "sauber" means clean in German, but Procter & Gamble does not call Mr. Clean "Meister Sauber." Instead, P&G has renamed it "Meister Proper," which has a similar meaning and the advantage of conveying that meaning better to Dutch and French consumers.

Packaging is another issue. For export products protective packaging is a great concern. And the promotional roles of a package may be different in countries where grocery buying is not by selfservice or where single unit purchases are common. If products are not on display but are chosen by a salesman, packaging has little influence at the point of purchase. And in a country where many purchases involve a single bottle of soda or a single cigarette, multiple unit packaging can be an inconvenience at best and a detriment to sales at worst.

The principles of product decisions, which are used for home markets, are equally applicable to international markets. Some of the important considerations are briefly described and evaluated:

Decisions on products affect the following:

(*i*) The company's total use of financial and manpower resources;

(*ii*) The kinds of customers or market areas where products are to be sold;

(*iii*) The promotional methods to be used;

(*iv*) The reputation of the company; and

(*v*) The company's position as a leader or follower.

The product mix may be extended in the following ways:

(*a*) By variations in models or styles;

(*b*) By variations in quality offered at different price levels;

(*c*) By the development of associated items, *e.g.,* engines and pumping sets; and

(*d*) By the development of completely different products in terms of customer needs, manufacturing processes, etc., DCM, for example, produces textiles and vegetable oil, etc.

A product policy for exports requires continuing attention since decisions on adding or dropping products will constantly arise. For example, the demand for "bleeding Madras" cloth in the USA suddenly tapered off. As a result, quite a number of workers were thrown out of job. The more volatile the market, the more frequently will decisions have to be made, but the speed of change even in less volatile market areas (*e.g.,* capital goods) is such that policy decisions are equally or more important since more time and more financial manpower resources are usually required to effect a change.

Company profit contribution frequently comes mainly from a small number of items in the product mix. Dropping products which make little or no contribution can frequently make very significant improvements in overall profitability. Weak products are very costly in ways which are not readily seen in accounting returns.

For adding new products, due consideration should be given to demand, resources, competitive and packaging factors.

India's future progress will be determined largely by the Indian exporters' success in the export markets of the world. Export marketing is the number one problem in the 1990s, the number one challenge and the number one opportunity.

Basically, marketing fundamentals are universally applicable, whether a company sells in India or Indiana. Its marketing progress should be built around a good product or services properly priced, promoted and distributed in a market which has been carefully analysed. However, there are considerable differences in the strategic and tactical implementation of marketing programmes for foreign as against domestic markets. These modifications become necessary because of the environmental difference which exist between and within many nations.

A company operates its marketing programme within the economic, political and cultural environment of each of its markets — foreign and domestic; and none of these environments is controllable by the firm. Consequently, an exporter should try to understand this environment and anticipate its effect on his marketing programme.

What complicates this task in export marketing is the fact that the environment — particularly the cultural environment — often consists of elements very unfamiliar to, and perhaps not even recognised by, the exporter. Further complicating the situation is the tendency on the part of a person unconsciously to use his own cultural values as a frame of reference for the solution of problems centered in a foreign environment. Do not mix religion with business. If you send a letter on a letterhead with a picture of Ganeshji, you might frighten away the recipient, for a non-Hindu, he is not a god.

19

MULTINATIONAL MARKETING AND JOINT VENTURES

What is a Multinational Corporation?

A multinational corporation has been defined as "an enterprise which allocates company resources without regard to national frontiers, but is nationally based in terms of ownership and top management." This definition distinguishes the multinational corporation from the *transnational* corporation (which is owned and managed by persons of more than one nationality) and the *supernational* corporation (a transnational corporation that has been legally denationalised by incorporating through an international agency).

Multinationals are multinationals so far as their operation and charging of price in global market. They sell technology as a commodity in the market. It is most necessary for developing country like India to know what is produced or distributed by the multinationals. Whether produced or distributed by the multinationals. Whether they are engaged in manufacturing the commodities and goods or distributing and selling manufactured abroad. As such multinationals have economic, social, political and legal ramifications.

A decade of the nineties provided proliferation of multinationals and dominating in marketing process of both the developed and developing countries. Even a country like China invited technology services from them. Multinationals are UK-based, USA-based, Japan-based, French-based, Germany-based according to their corporate culture in home country.

However, Brandts Commission (1975) and Pearson Commission (1977) provided code of conduct for operation of multinational corporations (MNCs), repatriation of profit in foreign exchange, equity participation, investment, and sharing of gains from the developing countries which have chronic balance of payment situation.

Emergence of MNCs

(1) Multinationals emerged in the 1970s, however, their growth was noteworthy during the first half of the 1980s. FDI inflow in developing countries was contracted sharply after 1981. They played a key role to direct export to the USA. The rise of Japanese corporations to a position of industrial and technological eminence. Their spread was largely due to financial and industrial activities and became international financial centres.

(2) There was a shift in FDI flows in the expansion of multinationals based in Western Europe. Macro-economic factors such as relatively slow growth, anti-inflationary policy and domestic savings surpluses stimulated export surpluses and capital outlays. Both Western European and American multinationals expanded their activities outside their home country in production and distribution of goods and services. Thus, they translated into faster growth due to information technology growth, discoveries of biotechnology and new materials to reactivate growth in the developing world. They took leadership in greenfield investment and the acquisition of existing assets in Europe and USA. Annual income of largest multinationals matches almost with GNP of many developing nations.

(3) Multinationals engaged themselves in internationalisation of their commercial and economic activities. They developed trade between their affiliates and multinationals and between multinationals and their subcontractors and were able to earn competitive advantage in exploiting the opportunity in developing countries, which reflected in the major changes in the world economy.

(4) They have successfully managed developed market economies, financial and securities markets, in syndicated bank lending for internationalisation of financial markets and diversification of financial instruments. Due to integration of financial markets, countries have lost their degree of autonomy in their domestic policies. The sharp fluctuation in exchange rates caused development of their business and created assets in several currencies. Similarly, they benefited by international level interest rate spread and became more profitable. It is a fact that the spread of multinational banking has also created problems for the regulation and supervision financial markets. Therefore, the central banks of several

developed market economics have met time to time since 1975 to reach agreement on co-ordinations of national regulation and common standard and necessitated common international regulatory standard for them.

(5) Deregulation and privatisation of services in international investment, partially liberal FDI policy in developing countries helped them in their expansion through efficiency in services and technology transfer areas. The countries lacking capital and an adequate level of skills or domestic markets are not sufficient of size to supply foreign goods and resources with regard to cost-effective means, multinationals found a way to enter in many nations.

(6) Looking at the present environment of global business, multinationals have gained through Dunkel proposals passed in Uruguay Round, WTO Code of Conduct helps them to develop relations with many nations for global marketing by profit-seeking investment and marketing activities. They have been successful in infrastructure investment by open bid and significantly benefit from emerging market economies in the nineties. It is preferable for the developing countries to contract with multinationals which cannot be managed by the state or local government in an era of privatisation and disinvestment activities of the government in many developing countries. In some cases, they are useful for industrialisation of developing countries where labour cost and new technologies are not as sharp. For this, for long-term sub-contracts for low cost method to generate production surplus and exportable surplus to cope with globalisation of marketing process.

Advantages of Multinational Marketing

Multinational marketing has a number of advantages to recommend it.

(i) It offers a way to make a large sales volume even larger.

(ii) Multinational marketing offers additional economies of scale — that is, reduction of unit costs through producing more units — and ways to spread costs.

(iii) Multinational marketing offers a market for products where none (or only a small one) currently exists.

(iv) Multinational marketing offers an escape to a more favourable political climate. By moving some of their investments and by seeking out new markets in foreign countries, companies may seek to avoid short or long-run problems on the political front at home.

(v) Multinational marketing offers a more favourable economic situation. British businesses, such as the makers of Jaguars and Triumphs, have found that the generally stagnant British economy offers poor growth prospects. Their solution is to export more and more to countries, like the United States, that do offer good growth prospects.

(vi) Multinational marketing offers a way to counteract aggressive competition from foreign competitors at home.

(vii) Beyond these reasons, and certainly of no less importance, is the fact that international operations may provide access to new technologies, cheaper or better labour, and new sources of capital.

Social Responsibilities of MNCs

Social responsibility has become a controversial issue in multinational marketing in recent years. Many nations have few effective legal restraints on advertising, packaging, product quality, credit terms , and after sales service. Critics of multinational corporations charge that many firms take advantage of this opening to manipulate uneducated consumers in developing nations.

In the mid-1970s, several American multinational firms admitted paying large bribes to foreign officials in connection with their marketing activities. These bribes are a common feature of the business practices of a good many nations. But they violate the business sense of ethics, not to mention a few laws. The concern here seems to centre on the immense power (and money) these firms possess as well as the question of as to whom they are accountable. As one observer has maintained, "Our tax laws, labour laws, and disclosure requirements are hopelessly absolute in dealing with a corporate entity which makes its home everywhere and nowhere."

Marketing Commitments Abroad

More and more business firms are operating on a global scale rather than confining their activities to one nation. This change has forced a rethinking of marketing goals, strategy, and organisation.

Common Approaches to International Marketing

There are five common approaches to international marketing. Many firms have changed from one orientation to another over time. Some, however, operate under two or more of these orientations at any one time. Each orientation suggests particular organisational goals and leads to related marketing strategies.

1. *Domestic Only Orientation.* Some firms have no interest in foreign sales. The domestic market satisfies their needs and foreign operations are seen as complicated and risky.

2. *Home Country Orientation.* Some firms view foreign operations as clearly secondary to business activity in the home country — overseas sales are an aid in distributing surplus goods. An organisation with this orientation generally exports its products to foreign nations that are almost like the home country. It will not conduct extensive marketing research or promotional activities in its international markets. Nor will it invest in costly product modifications in order to meet the specific needs of foreign consumers.
3. *Host Country Orientation.* Some firms establish subsidiaries in each overseas market; these subsidiaries are generally managed by local nationals. Marketing activities are planned and administered on a country-by-country basis. The crucial considerations in planning strategy are the legal and environmental conditions in each nation.
4. *Regional Orientation.* Certain firms find that the host-country orientation leads to many problems with co-ordination and control. As a result, they gear operations to a regional orientation. This allows for more economical and systematic planning and administration. It also offers the opportunity to pursue market segments that cross national boundaries.
5. *Global Orientation.* A firm may choose to see the entire world as its "marketing region" and to pursue global market segments. There are severe problems, however, associated with this approach. National differences in laws and currencies make global marketing strategy a difficult undertaking. The worldwide orientation appears more useful for production, research and development than it is for marketing activity.

Worldwide Marketing Opportunities

In evaluating worldwide marketing opportunities, a firm must be flexible and open to new strategies and innovations. Any proposal to begin operations in other countries must be evaluated on the basis of potential returns on investment and risks.

The first crucial question that a firm faces in entering the international market is: "Where can we sell our products?" Local governments and international associations publish valuable population statistics, which assist firms in pinpointing market segments. Unfortunately for most multinational marketers, market share information is relatively difficult to find.

In general, the marketing manager starts off with little first hand knowledge of the marketing opportunities in a foreign country. But the basic tools of marketing analysis are the same for foreign markets as for the domestic market. Table 19.1 summarizes the *five-step process by which managers evaluate multinational marketing opportunities.*

1. *Environmental Analysis.* This includes studying economic, political, and social conditions in the target country. It is most important that marketers understand the rate of cultural change of the host country.

2. *Market Potential.* Here the marketer begins by evaluating the current size and nature of the market. If accurate production and sales figures are not available, the firm will turn to its own marketing research to develop the necessary data. Once marketers understand the dimensions of the current market, they can forecast future market trends (such as industrywide sales) over a five-or ten-year period.

Table 19.1

Stages for Evaluating Multinational Marketing Opportunity

Stage 1	*Stage 2*	*Stage 3*	*Stage 4*	*Stage 5*
Environmental Analysis * Economic * Political * Social-Cultural	Market Potential * Current * Future	Future Company Sales * Total * Market Share	Prospective Profitability * Rate of Return (Profit) on Different Investment Commitments (Assets)	Benefit vs. Risks * Go or No-Go Decision * Time Horizon * Method of Entry * Marketing Mix

Source: Based on David S.R. Leighton, *International Marketing: Test and Cases* (New York: McGraw-Hill, 1966), pp. 22-27.

3. *Future Sales.* What percentage of all industrywide sales can the individual organisation expect to capture? To answer this question, the firm must conduct some kind of market analysis of its industrywide projections. The crucial factors here are competition (the size, market share, facilities, and financial resources of major rivals) and the strengths and weaknesses of the firm (how it measures up to the competition). Careful evaluation should produce a reasonably accurate estimate of the anticipated market share and sales volume.

4. *Prospective Profitability.* When this estimate is completed, the firm must weigh the possible profits of entering the multinational market. Involved in this evaluation is a forecast of the necessary capital, facilities, and personnel. The firm must also analyse the desirability of entering foreign markets through an export approach, a joint venture, or direct operation.

5. *Benefits vs. Risks.* The last stage in the evaluation process is often the most difficult, for there are no simple mathematical tools to guide marketers in weighing the risks of international business. Predicting economic trends is no simple matter, but the political risks of multinational investment can be even more serious than the economic uncertainties. Decisions are also made in this stage as to the time period covered by the entry plan, the organisational method of entry, and the initial marketing mix.

MARKETING ENVIRONMENTS AROUND THE WORLD

In many ways multinational marketers are like all others; one similarity is that to succeed they must understand the environment in which they operate. Of course, marketing environments differ sharply around the world, much more so than within any one country. Still, one can grasp the most important aspects of any environment by focusing on its economic, demographic, cultural, and governmental dimensions.

Environmental information is often understood intuitively by managers and planners in domestic markets. But in multinational marketing, environmental information must be carefully defined, gathered, and absorbed. There may actually be a hidden benefit to unfamiliarity with the local conditions — the outsider may spot a marketing opportunity that the familiar insider overlooked.

(1) Economic Factors

Gross national product is an important consideration.

Another key to economic dimension is the degree of development and competition in a country. In industrialised nations (such as the United States, Canada, West Germany, Japan), a multinational marketer faces competition from local producers and also from other multinationals. These nations are typically contrasted with other countries labelled "underdeveloped," "less developed," "developing," or "third world."

In general, the market places of developing countries are less competitive than those of industrialised nations. Local manufacturers are generally not well established, thus allowing an opportunity for extensive penetration by multinational companies.

Income is also an important economic dimension in multinational marketing. When people have little to spend, marketers must compete feverishly for sales. This problem is most significant for multinational marketing, since in many parts of the world only upper-class citizens can afford to buy more than the bare necessities in goods and services.

The multinational marketer is most interested in two closely related economic factors in any country: income and the level of economic development.

Income. At the individual level incomes differ both on the average and in terms of distribution of income. The United States and several Western European countries, along with the oil-rich nations of the Middle East, enjoy rather high levels of household, or *per capita,* income. In other countries — usually in Latin America, Africa, and Asia — average incomes are less than 10 per cent of those in the "rich" nations. Such relative poverty suggests that many "luxury" items may find small or no markets in the poorer nations. At the same time, the distribution of income also plays a role in determining market potential for products that appeal to a particular income segment. Sweden, for example, with a fairly high average income, is a "middle-class" nation with very few rich or poor and may offer almost no potential for true luxury products. But many Latin American countries, with much lower average incomes, have a different distribution of income — a relatively small middle class — and may have enough high-income households to warrant exporting luxury goods to them.

Level of Economic Development. In the past thirty years we have come to recognize that industrialising countries pass through distinct stages in the process of their economic development. These stages offer differing marketing opportunities. This view suggests that countries progress from primarily subsistence economies, like that of Papua New Guinea, to a stage in which there may be a wholesale and retail trade but in which most economic activity involves the exporting of raw materials under the control of "foreign imperialists" or their domestic counterparts. Except for a very small upper class, which may buy luxury goods, these countries offer relatively little consumer market opportunity. Of course even in less-developed countries there may be opportunities to market industrial products, principally through their national governments. Such countries frequently maintain some kind of military force; and in their efforts to become industrialised their governments often fund the start-up of basic industries.

As countries move through various stages of industrialization, from primary manufacturing (processing of raw materials) to the manufacturing of non-durable consumer goods (textiles, for example) to the manufacturing of durable goods for consumers or industry (appliances and machinery), they become increasingly attractive as markets. Incomes rise and so does education; a middle class develops. Finally, these countries reach a stage where they can manufacture and export goods on a large scale. Trade among such countries — the United States, Germany, Japan — can be quite large because consumers and companies in these nations are relatively affluent and eager to raise their standards of living even further.

(2) Demographic Factors

A firm must gauge the size of potential markets in order to develop needed business projections. Population is therefore a crucial factor. But raw population data are not the only concern of marketers. Population shifts, changes in size of age-groups or families, and changes in the structure of the work force are also crucial.

The most important factor from the multinational point of view is population size and density. Some countries have many people, some have few; they may be crowded, as in Japan, or relatively sparsely settled, as in Australia. Such differences produce differences in market potential and may produce differences in consumption patterns. Another demographic factor involves the birth rate and the distribution of ages. As we pointed out earlier, this factor also affects patterns of consumption. For example, the elderly people account for a substantial part of the population in countries like Sweden and the United States but comprise only a tiny proportion in Mexico. For the marketer of a product targeted at older consumers, the implications are obvious: Sweden and the United States are promising markets, Mexico is not.

(3) Cultural Factors and Social Dimensions

Cultural factors underlie the differences that exist in buying habits and business dealings from country to country. They involve different languages, different customs, and different tastes, and they can cause major difficulties for unwary marketers. Belgium uses two languages. Spain uses many. Translation may turn terrific advertising slogans into vulgar, threatening, confusing, or uninspiring messages. The Japanese try to avoid the fourth floor of buildings just as Americans try to avoid the thirteenth floor. Cream soda is the most popular soft drink in Colombia, lemon-lime has replaced grape as the leading soda flavour in Japan. In India several manufacturers have shown an awareness of cultural factors and capitalised on a return to "traditional thinking." One of them, Ciba-Geigy, introduced a herb-flavoured version of its Cibaca toothpaste, based in part on writing in the *Yajur Veda,* a 4,000-year-old text on the science of life. Helene Curtis introduced an acne cure, Pimponyle, containing camphor and herbs, which was also based on the *Yajur Veda.* It must be mixed with yogurt before being applied to the face.

Religions, family systems, educational systems, and social systems are all part of the social and cultural dimension of multinational marketing. The influence of these factors is as diverse as the many people and nationalities of the world.

National character is a general term used to describe the style of life and thought of a group of people. While the concept is somewhat vague and abstract, it can nevertheless be useful to marketers in understanding the feelings and attitudes of a market segment. Generalisations about national character can be especially helpful in preparing advertising campaigns.

The status of women is an important cultural dimension in multinational marketing. Women still face legal discrimination and subordination to men in most societies in the world. Many cultures maintain a rigid division of labour between women and men. Marketers need to understand the social roles for each sex in a potential host country in order to develop marketing strategy.

Differences in social and cultural traditions lead to significant variations in market behaviour.

For example, 93 per cent of Swedish eat crackers, while only 3 per cent of French people do so. Yogurt can be found in 50 per cent of Dutch homes, but in less than 5 per cent of Portuguese homes.

In studying such national patterns, markets place particular emphasis on how purchases are made by a family, in order to focus their promotion on the person or persons most likely to influence purchase decisions. Does the family shop together and come to a joint decision? Is mass-media influence a critical factor in the decision-making process? Are the views of local opinion leaders (clergy, politicians, influential citizens) important?

(4) Political Dimensions

The attitudes of host countries toward foreign companies varies from place to place. The Belgians have been accepting of multinational investors, the Japanese suspicious, and the French hostile. In any multinational marketing opportunity, the marketer must examine the likely reactions of the citizens and government of each host country. Of particular concern is government policy on the substitution of goods produced by local industries for import goods, incentives for new business development, and taxation.

The flow of business across national boundaries is affected by a number of common control mechanisms. The character and use of each depends on the particular nation and government involved. These controls include tariffs, quotas, licences, and import taxes.

Tariffs may be levied either on the physical quantity of goods being transported or on the total value of the shipment. Many nations maintain tariffs on both imports and exports.

Quotas are imposed when a government wishes to set absolute limits on imports and exports of a product. They are especially popular in regulating the import or export of agricultural goods.

Licences are still another means of regulating international trade. In some cases an exporter may want proof that an importer has the required licences before making a final commitment on a deal. Legal problems often develop in conducting international business.

(5) Governmental Factors

In India the government generally owns public undertakings. It regulates private business — some say far too much — and in particular cases it may also prosecute business, subsidise it, encourage it or thwart it. Governments are major competitors of private firms. They own the manufacturing or marketing operations in various industries. Government control over business is different from one country to another.

Restrictions on Marketing Practices. Advertising and labelling laws may be different in different countries. A magistrate in Italy banned the sale of bottled Coca-Cola because he felt that the ingredients information should be provided on the bottle rather than on the bottle cap. Canada requires that labels be in French and English, but France requires that only the French language be used. In Great Britain, the pharmaceutical industry was required to reduce its advertising-to-sales ratio from 14 per cent to 10 per cent within two years. And many countries either prohibit or severely restrict the timing and context of television advertising. In Costa Rica, for example, ads for products connected with health must be submitted for government approval before they can be aired. In the People's Republic of China advertising is becoming increasingly widespread, but ad agencies are all state-owned.

Trade mark laws can be particularly important. American firms entering a new market may find their brands already used in that market by a foreign competitor. Or they may find no trade mark protection. Until fairly recently China considered trade marks to be tools of monopolies and, therefore, did not allow them to be registered.

Competitive arrangements may be different as well. Few foreign countries share America's distaste for collusion. In fact many countries even encourage cartels or "Orderly marketing agreements."

Finally, civil servants and corporate officials may consider what we call bribes or kickbacks a perfectly normal part of doing business. In Canada, for example, there is nothing illegal about supermarkets demanding kickbacks from suppliers.

That bribery has become so scandalous in this country that it is often a source of amusement in foreign countries, where it is a way of life. It is usually viewed as a payment for services rendered and may be an important part of the income of the executives or officials involved. Firms that operate in foreign countries have had to find ways around Indian legislation banning bribes if they are to continue to operate in those countries.

Inter-governmental Relations. Some countries co-operate to reduce tariffs, taxes on imported goods, and other barriers to international trade, such as import quotas. The best-known co-operative group is the European Economic Community, better known as the Common Market, which involves the United Kingdom, the Benelux countries, West Germany, Italy, Greece, France, Denmark, and Ireland, and a number of associate members. There are many other such groups, but none has so far been as effective as the EEC.

Even when countries do not reach the point of forming a common market, they may still agree to co-operate. The countries subscribing to the GATT — General Agreement on Tariffs and Trade — meet every two years to consider reductions in trade barriers. A very important aspect of their agreements is a provision for most favoured nation status. When such status is granted to a country, it means that a reduction in tariffs for any country means a reduction in tariffs for all.

Countries also take other actions to restrict or encourage trade. The United States complained to Japan about the balance of trade between the two countries — Japan was exporting much more than it was importing. The result? Japan increased its purchases from the United States — planes from Lockheed, for example — dropped some of its resistance to American companies trying to operate in Japan, and "voluntarily" restricted its exports of autos and other products to the United States.

Finally, most countries in the world have at one time or another stopped trading entirely with certain countries or companies. The United States stopped selling to Cuba after the revolution, to Rhodesia before it became Zimbabwe, and to Iraq after its invasion of Kuwait. And Arab nations have often boycotted the products of companies that sell to Israel.

Most of the governments *worried* about operation of multinationals for *following reasons*:

(1) It is a fact that allowing foreign companies can affect sovereignty of the nation. Our nation can be threatened by another. Some of the nations know can threatened by another. Some of the nations have not allowed them in critical areas and critical natural resource exploitation as business expansion can lead to spying activities as happened in the cases of East India Company during British rule in India.

(2) No government would be ready to invite multinationals at the cost of development of home industries. MNCs have abilities to destroy domestic firms and bring political pressure for their expansion activities.

(3) The government is worried about hidden value as they hide profits and tax liabilities. They can move profits from high tax rate country to low tax rate country and follow transfer pricing also. It has been visualised in the USA that they avoid corporate taxes by transferring their profits in subsidiaries of other countries.

(4) MNCs have no social responsibility it they operate elsewhere than their home country. They are engaged in labour-exploitation, chemical explosion, nuclear meltdowns, hazardous waste dumping. Example of Union Carbide and Government of India is very famous.

(5) MNCs are emulated with cost-benefit method in needy areas and opportunity cost to contract them. They have been benefitted by shadow price adjustments in determining revenue benefits, through shadow exchange rate.

(6) Marketing Research "Over There"

Market research is a difficult undertaking in many foreign nations. For example, only 3 per cent of the people of Sri Lanka have telephones. At least fourteen different languages are spoken in India. Census data and area maps are not available in many countries. And many citizens in other parts of the world will not co-operate with a strange interviewer who comes to the door.

We often think of the problems of conducting marketing research in the developing agricultural nations of the world. But even in the industrial countries of Western Europe the job is not easy. For example, telephone sampling, which is popular in the United States, may not be reliable in Great Britain, West Germany, France or Italy, since so few residents have telephones.

As a result of these limitations, there are three principal methods of obtaining information on overseas markets:

1. Collecting and analysing published data;
2. Interviewing knowledgeable individuals within the home country; and
3. Sending representatives to the overseas nations for personal inspection and research.

The importance of reliable marketing research has been underscored in the last decade by the worldwide phenomenon of inflation. This inflation has led to an increase in the risks of international forecasting. In Great Britain, the price of bacon jumped by 80 per cent in less than three years; it is now a luxury item for most English people. The demand for automobiles and air conditioners in India has fallen sharply due to inflation. When prices rise so rapidly, it is more difficult than ever to develop accurate projections about international business prospects.

OPERATING IN FOREIGN COUNTRIES

When a firm decides to market its products internationally, to sell to foreign customers, it faces many significant decisions. Some of the most important are structural decisions regarding how to enter the foreign market and, once there, how to structure the firm's organisation.

Operating in foreign markets presents problems not found in this country. In Latin American countries, for example, import duties inflate the price of Indian made goods to two or three times their price in India. This suggests that perhaps Indian producers should manufacture in Latin America, but to do so requires the permission of the government, and the political climate may make this strategy unattractive in any case. Elsewhere, taxes on profits may be more onerous than those in India. Foreign governments may place restrictions on ownership of operations, for example, by requiring 51 per cent ownership by citizens of the host country.

Monetary exchange rates must be considered. In a few years the value of the US dollars increased considerably. This represented considerable rise in the power of Americans to buy Indian goods and a similar decline in the ease with which Indian customers could buy from USA. While exchange rates fluctuate, inflation around the world advances at varying speeds. In some Latin American countries inflation is so high that hotels raise their rates every three days, while elsewhere prices are almost stable. How can a multinational marketer set prices?

Yet another important consideration is a country's *balance of trade.* When the balance is favourable — that is, when the country is exporting more than it is importing — there will probably be few trade restrictions. But if the balance turns unfavourable, a country may impose import tariffs, taxes, or quotas in an attempt to improve it. The effect on marketers can be considerable.

In short, many factors affect a marketer's entry into a foreign market. As these factors dictate, the marketer can enter the country in one of several ways.

METHODS OF OPERATION

Exporting is undoubtedly the most popular way to operate in foreign markets. This is typically accomplished in one of two ways; by selling to or through foreign middlemen or by selling through the companies' own sales branches in foreign countries. The former strategy involves very little time, risk, or investment by the domestic firm but offers little motivation or control over marketing practices. The latter strategy requires a greater investment, but more aggressive marketing can be expected. Products are still made in this country, so the firm may face major problems with long-range transportation and sales management from afar. And both methods of exporting may require much governmental red tape.

Indirect Export

The normal way to become involved in a foreign market is through export. *Occasional exporting* is a passive level of involvement where the company exports from time to time on its own or in response to unsolicited orders from abroad. *Active exporting* takes place when the company makes a commitment to expand exports to a particular market. In either case, the company produces all of its goods in the home country. It may or may not adapt them to the foreign market. Exporting involves the least change in the company's product lines, organisation, investments, or mission.

Companies typically start with *indirect exporting,* that is, they work through independent middlement. Four types of middlemen are available to the company.

(i) Domestic-based export merchant. This middleman buys the manufacturer's product and sells it abroad on its own account.

(ii) Domestic-based export agent. This agent seeks and negotiates foreign purchases for a commission. Included in the group are trading companies.

(iii) Co-operative organisation. A co-operative organisation carries on exporting activities on behalf of several producers and is partly under their administrative control. This form is often used by producers of primary products — fruits, nuts, and so on.

(iv) Export-management company. This middleman agrees to manage a company's export activities for a fee.

Indirect export has two advantages. First, it involves less investment. The firm does not have to develop an export department, an overseas sales force, or a set of foreign contacts.

Second, it involves less risk. International marketing middlemen bring know-how and services to the relationship, and the seller will normally make fewer mistakes.

Direct Export

Companies eventually undertake handling their own exports. The investment and risk are somewhat greater, but so is the potential return. The company can carry on direct exporting in several ways:

(i) *Domestic-based export department or division.* An export sales manager with some sales assistants carry on the actual selling and draw on market assistance as needed. It might evolve into a self-contained export department performing all the activities involved in export and operating as a profit centre.

(ii) *Overseas sales branch or subsidiary.* An overseas sales branch allows the manufacturer to achieve greater presence and programme control in the foreign market. The sales branch handles sales distribution and may handle warehousing and promotion as well. It often serves as a display centre and customer-service centre.

(iii) *Travelling export sales representatives.* The company can send home-based sales representatives abroad at certain times to find business.

(iv) *Foreign-based distributors or agents.* Foreign-based distributors would buy and own the goods; foreign-based agents would sell the goods on behalf of the company. They may be given exclusive rights to represent the manufacturer in that country or only general rights.

Exporting is only one way to serve markets overseas. All the others, however, involve foreign manufacturing or processing, either through wholly owned subsidiaries, licensing, joint ventures, contract manufacturing, or management contracting.

Licensing and wholly owned subsidiaries are two extremes. With *wholly owned subsidiaries* domestic firms take all responsibility for manufacturing, managing, and marketing their products in the foreign country. With *licensing,* by contrast, domestic firms authorise foreign firms to use their techniques or trade marks in exchange for a fee or royalty. The foreign firms have responsibility for manufacturing, managing, and marketing.

Licensing has potential disadvantages in that the firm has less control over the licensee than if it had set up its own production facilities. Furthermore, if the licensee is very successful, the firm has foregone profits, and if and when the contract ends, it might feel that it has created a competitor. To avoid creating a future competitor, the licensor usually supplies some ingredients or components needed in the product. But the main hope is for the licensor to lead in innovation so that the licensee will continue to depend on this licensor. Weak legal systems may allow many foreign licenses to steal the know-how for making the products and stop making payments to Indian firms at all.

But this change in emphasis may put Indian firms in a dilemma. Licensing is less profitable than wholly owned subsidiaries, while more and more countries are demanding a share — even a majority share — in the ownership of foreign subsidiaries. The threat of nationalisation can also be great, causing Indian firms to lose all their investments in wholly owned subsidiaries.

Joint Ventures

In joint ventures, foreign investors join with local investors to create a local business in which they share joint ownership and control. The foreign investor may buy an interest in a local company, a local company may buy an interest in an existing operation of a foreign company, or the two parties may form a new business venture.

A jointly owned venture may be necessary or desirable for economic or political reasons. The firm may lack the financial, physical, or managerial resources to undertake the venture alone. Or the foreign government may require joint ownership as a condition for entry.

Joint ownership has certain drawbacks. The partners may disagree over investment, marketing, or other policies. Where many American firms like to reinvest earnings for growth, local firms often like to take out these earnings. Where American firms accord a large role to marketing, local investors may rely only on selling. Furthermore, joint ownership can hamper a multinational company from carrying out specific manufacturing and marketing policies on a worldwide basis.

As a result several intermediate approaches are growing in popularity. *Joint ventures* are becoming quite common. These involve partnerships between an Indian firm and a foreign firm, with the shares of ownership being equally or unequally divided. Although such ventures require the Indian firm to give up some control over manufacturing and marketing activities, this may be the only way Indian firms can maintain ownership interests, and the accompanying profits, in a foreign country. Or this may be the only way the firm can operate successfully because the foreign firm brings a knowledge of local conditions that the Indian firm might have trouble duplicating on its own.

Alternatives to joint ventures for some companies are contract manufacturing and management contracting. In *contract manufacturing* the Indian firm retains control over the marketing process but contracts with foreign manufacturers for the goods they wish to sell. In *management contracting* firms sell their management skills rather than their products. Although mining and drilling operations have been nationalized in some countries. Indian companies can make money by advising and training the foreign firms.

Direct Investment

The ultimate form of foreign involvement is investment in foreign-based assembly or manufacturing facilities. As a company gains experience in export, and if the foreign market appears large enough, foreign production facilities offer distinct advantages. First, the firm may secure cost economies in the form of cheaper labour or raw materials, foreign government investment incentives, freight savings, and so on. Second, the firm will gain a better image in the host country because it creates jobs. Third, the firm develops a deeper relationship with government, customers, local suppliers, and distributors, enabling it to adapt its products better to the local marketing environment. Fourth, the firm retains full control over the investment and therefore can develop manufacturing and marketing policies that serve its long-term international objectives.

The main disadvantage is that the firm exposes a large investment to risk, such as blocked or devalued currencies, worsening markets, or expropriation. The firm will find it expensive to reduce or close down its operations, since the host country may require substantial severance pay to the employees. The firm, however, has no choice but to accept these risks if it wants to operate in the host country.

The Internationalisation Process

Many companies show a distinct preference for one mode of entry. One company might prefer exporting because this minimises its risks. Another company might prefer licensing because this is an easy way to make money. Another company might favour direct investment because it wants full control without having to satisfy any partner. Yet insisting on one mode of entry is too limiting. Some countries will not permit imports of certain goods, nor allow direct investment, but will only accept a joint-owned venture with a foreign national. Consequently, companies must learn and master all of these entry methods. Even though a company might have preferences, it needs to optimally adapt to each situation. Most sophisticated multinationals manage several different entry modes simultaneously.

The problem facing most countries is that not enough of their companies participate in any international trade. This keeps the country from earning sufficient foreign exchange to pay for the goods it needs to import. Consequently, governments have turned to aggressive export promotion. Yet export promotion programmes rarely achieve their goals. They are not based on a deep understanding of the process by which companies become internationalised.

Table 19.2 identifies the crucial structural decisions that have been made for each method of operation described above. Each of these methods of operations implies a home, headquarters country to which the corporate hierarchy owes some allegiance and one or more foreign countries that are viewed as subservient to the headquarters. But some companies attempt to conduct their business as though there were no international boundaries and without any real loyalty to a particular country. These companies are truly *multinational corporations.*

Such companies are not necessarily new or Indian. Nestle, Unilever and many oil companies are multinational corporations. They market in many countries, carry out research and manufacturing in many countries, and have owners and managers from many countries. Their decisions about how and where to operate are not based on loyalty or tradition. Instead, decisions are based on where the economic and political advantages are greatest.

TABLE 19.2

Structural Decisions for Various Operating Methods

Method	*What is being sold?*	*Who makes the product? Where?*	*Who has mix responsibility?*
Exporting	Products	Made in home country by firm	International middlemen
Wholly-owned Subsidiaries	Products	Made abroad by firm	Company has complete responsibility
Licensing	Trademark or Process	Made abroad by foreign firm	Foreign manufacturer
Joint ventures	Products	Made abroad jointly	Shared marketing mix responsibility
Contract manufacturing	Products	Made abroad by foreign firm	Firm has complete responsibility
Management contracting	Service ("advice")	Made abroad by foreign firm	Firm influences mix decisions

Standardisation

The basic marketing mix decision is whether to use a standardised marketing mix in all countries or to adapt the marketing mix for each country. Coca-Cola, for example, has used basically the same advertising themes and ads around the world ("I'd like to teach the world to sing"), for instance. But Unilever may use different types of ads in each country in which it markets its household products.

MULTINATIONAL MARKETING STRATEGY

The development of a strategic marketing view for multinational operations is a critical business goal. As one analyst has observed, "The over-riding talent which I would wish on all is the managerial ability to visualise our products overseas in marketing terms. But this quality of marketing mindedness is all too rare around the world."

Adapting the Marketing Mix

When a corporation expands into overseas operations, it must determine if its domestic marketing mix can be adapted to foreign markets. Of course, as John Fayerweather has pointed out, "There is nothing absolute or sacred about a particular marketing mix ... Goods may well be sold by one combination of efforts in one market area and a second combination in another."

Standardisation is a key issue in adapting a marketing mix to foreign operations. Some marketing specialists have stressed the differences between foreign markets and have argued for differentiation in multinational marketing.

Marketers may not have absolute (or even any) freedom to set prices abroad. Some governments in developing countries legislate low retail prices in order to promote a higher standard of living, especially on necessities such as food.

Dumping of products is a common practice in international marketing. A manufacturer of television sets may have an oversupply of last year's models in its warehouses. He dumps these goods by selling them at a lower price than consumers in his domestic market are being charged. This practice has become unpopular in many nations, and import duties may be raised when there is a suspicion of dumping.

Promotion Strategy

The ideal promotion mix for a foreign nation depends on the characteristics of the society. For example, Nigeria has a low literacy level and there are few important print media. Only 14,000 Nigerian homes own television sets. But there are 1.5 million radios in use in the country, and motion picture advertising reaches 5 million Nigerians each year.

As we can see from the Nigerian example, the use of advertising abroad is determined mainly by the importance of various communications media. French people listen to the radio three times as much as West Germans. Twice as many Germans read daily newspapers as Italians.

Occasionally, an advertising theme or slogan can be "translated" for foreign appeal. In 1974 Chevrolet initiated a successful new campaign in the United States around the theme, "Baseball, hotdogs, apple pie, and

Chevrolet." This led General Motors Holden of Australia to introduce the theme, "We love football, meat pies, kangaroos, and Holden cars." But some slogans can lose a lot in the translation process. In Japan, the General Motors slogan "Body by Fisher" becomes "Corpse by Fisher."

In order to be effective, international advertisers should follow three important guidelines:

1. Make the message meaningful to people in terms of their day-to-day lives. Don't centre a theme around automobiles if they are virtually unknown to most citizens in a rural country;
2. Strike a responsive chord. Use images or comparisons that reflect the feelings of the target audience; and
3. Do not offend. Understand the sensitive points and biases of the people of the country, and stay away from dangerous themes.

Marketing management faces several key issues in designing strategy for personal selling in foreign markets. These include design of sales territories, control systems for field salespeople, and type of compensation to be paid.

Displays are a popular means of sales promotion in multinational operations. Wording and layout arrangements are selected with local conditions and cultural norms in mind.

Distribution Strategy

Before making decisions about distribution strategy, a multinational marketer must first gather as much information as possible about the available alternatives. Ultimately, the complexity of the selling job is a key factor in all distribution decisions. If servicing the product is likely to be frequent and difficult, the marketer may find it necessary to perform the distribution task directly rather than relying on a local intermediary.

There are three main channels of distribution for international marketing:

1. Representatives of foreign firms;
2. Resident buyers within India who work for foreign firms or governments; and
3. Intermediaries, such as export commission houses, export merchants, export agents, export brokers, and export managers.

A company may choose different distribution channels for each nation it views as a market. For example, Del Monte relies on distributors to handle its operations in Holland, West Germany, Austria, Sweden, Spain and France. Food brokers are responsible for the sale of Del Monte products in Norway and a number of Mideast states. In Switzerland, Del Monte products are sold exclusively through a powerful supermarket chain known as the Federation of Migros Co-operatives.

Physical distribution systems vary greatly in different nations. Centralised warehousing has become the dominant approach to food distribution in the United States, the Netherlands, Switzerland, West Germany, and the Scandinavian nations. Large central warehouses are run by retail food chains. But, in France, small wholesalers are more important, and in Italy food retailers are licensed by location.

THE MULTINATIONAL'S FUTURE

Although rapid change and shifting conditions in the multinational market place make prediction a risky undertaking, the following trends seem likely:

1. *Economic Environment.* Shortages will persist through the end of the 1990s. Export managers will be competing with domestic divisions for output.
2. *Government Influence.* Multinational marketers will be under increasing political pressures. Decisions about production, expansion, and allocation of profits will be deeply affected by political and social forces. The days of the "free hand" for Indian corporations in many parts of the world are coming to an end.
3. *Third World Development.* The trend towards economic nationalism among Third World nations will continue to grow. This will conflict with the desire of multinational corporations to expand operations in Third World nations in order to obtain raw materials and reach new markets.
4. *Growth of Multinational Corporations.* Multinational corporations have become a fixture in the business world. Despite political opposition and legislative restrictions, it seems inevitable that they will continue to grow and multiply.

MULTINATIONAL FIRMS AND MANUFACTURING OPERATIONS IN DEVELOPING COUNTRIES

Multinational firms' operations in developing countries can be studied under accommodative approach instead of power-balance approach. Most of the developing countries perceive some advantages as well as disadvantages in such operations. The tension between multinational firms and the host country is created whenever the host countries feel that their interests are undermined. To minimise the disadvantages, national governments of the developing countries try to control the entry and operations of the multinational firms.

The motives in encouraging multinational firms to establish foothold in developing countries are: technological, finance, management and marketing superiority enjoyed by multinational firms. Developing countries often discern that they can have easy access to modern technology and can save the expenses on R and D. They can also adopt the superior technology. The disadvantages perceived are that a particular country cannot resort to other sources of technology, because this change would involve heavy costs. The excess in price of licensing and long duration of contract are also perceived as disadvantages to the host country. In the financial field, multinational firms can resort to local or foreign financing for its operations. In the case of joint ventures, the local company has an advantage of being associated with a multinational firm and can have easy access to finance from in the local financial institutions. It is the experience of developing countries that most of the multinational firms try to have majority control in the equity ownership in their establishments. This creates a doubt among the developing countries and they feel that multinational firms are practising neo-colonialism when they want to exploit the host country. Here also there are restrictions for the entry of multinational firms in both equity ownership and local financing. In the field of management, multinational firms are supposed to inculcate the modern managerial techniques and modernise the national management. However, multinational firms try to have their own personnel in top positions in the subsidiaries or joint ventures. They again motivate the developing countries to insist upon recruitment of local personnel in managerial cadre. In the marketing field, the host government perceives that they can get the advantage of brand or sales network and profit by the establishment of multinational firms. They may not be able to export because of restrictive territorial or product agreements entered into.

Once a multinational firm enters a developing country in the field of manufacturing, it has to walk on a tight rope, and minimise competitive disturbances. Behrman views that competitive disturbances can occur in the field of pricing, wage, marketing, finance, employment and exports. The host governments expect multinational firms not to undercut prices so as not to disturb the local manufacturers but at the same time they expect that the prices to consumers should be lower. But in the field of pricing most of the multinational firms try to reduce the cost of production by increasing productivity. Accordingly, the difference in the costs of multinational firms and local firms is utilised for non-price promotion and maintaining the local price level.

Multinational firms are also expected to give wages to the labour, as are prevalent in that particular industry in that country, instead of increased wages. Yet the host governments expect from multinational firms to increase wages through higher productivity. In the marketing field, they are expected not to use their aggressive sales method of the parent company and also to adapt to the society where they are also expected to use the modern marketing methods and train local managers accordingly. In the field of finance, multinational firms use both local and foreign sources and flout the local financial controls. In recent years some of the developing countries are imposing controls on local funds, India has given to the nationalised banks an option of converting their loans to equity in any Indian company.

Multinational firms are expected not to use their hire and fire method in their employment policy but to adopt to the local provisions so far as exports are concerned; developing countries want manufacturing units to be independent of the network of international integrated market system. Multinational firms have to pay attention to some of the complaints of the developing countries and at the same time have to look to their own interests.

The method of entry and operation of multinational firms sometimes leads to uncertainty of its position in the host country. To reduce this uncertainty multinational firms can try to communicate with the host government through the local associations and by maintaining good public relations. This is to create a good image by showing that the multinational firms are taking interest in the development of the country. They can also endeavour for the reduction of the evidence of control such as of ownership, management and identification of the company with the country, perceived by the host country. In ownership they can associate local nationals or the local government. In management they can recruit and train personnel to take over management of the local unit. This helps a multinational firm not only in decentralising its decision-making power but also identifying the company with the host country.

To illustrate the regulations adopted by the governments of developing countries for scrutinising and ascertaining the criteria for approval we can take India as a case (Friedman and Bhandari). The proposals of multinational firms have to get approval of the government. They have to procure the following approvals:

1. Industrial license under Industries (Development and Regulation) Act of 1951;
2. Approval from the Reserve Bank under Foreign Exchange Regulation Act of 1973;
3. Licence to import capital equipment under Imports and Exports Control Act of 1947;

4. Approval under Capital Issues (Continuation of Control) Act of 1947; and
5. A Certificate of Incorporation under the Indian Companies Act of 1956.

The Government of India established a Foreign Investment Board in 1968 so that the proposals of foreign parties can be screened without delay. The Foreign Investment Board draws up lists of areas under different headings:

(a) Foreign investment permitted with or without foreign investment;
(b) Foreign technical collaboration permitted but not foreign investment; and
(c) Foreign collaboration, both financial or technical.

The above action is to give priority to the national interest, as perceived by the Indian government.

The Government of India of late is trying to encourage foreign collaboration. The foreign collaboration which is competitive in nature *vis-a-vis* Indian industries is not much encouraged. The foreign enterprises, which are of commercial and financial nature or involve in packing or assembling of imported components, are also avoided.

The criteria adopted for the selection of the foreign collaboration in India are:

1. The foreign exchange requirements. This is to find out whether the project is import-saving or export-earning because recently the Indian government has given priority to export-oriented industries;
2. The management control involved in the ownership of equity and management personnel. It is the policy of the government that majority ownership should be with the local nationals and as far as possible managerial personnel are Indian nationals;
3. It is also of prime importance to see whether foreign collaboration will encourage indigenous technology and the technological knowhow is given at reasonable royalty rates; and
4. The employment opportunity created for the Indian nationals.

Recently, the Indian government has taken a series of measures to put constraints on the operation of foreign collaboration. They are:

(a) Reduction in patent right protection;
(b) Limited exemption to foreign technicians;

(c) Converting by nationalised banks their loans in private companies into equity;

(d) Fixation of minimum export obligation of 60 per cent in the expansion of new product which has to be exported within a period of three years. In case foreign collaboration takes up the manufacture of such articles which are reserved for small scale sector, the export obligation is 75 per cent; and

(e) Licensing agreements allowed only for a short duration, namely five years.

The Indian case represents the measures adopted by developing countries to bargain with the multinational firms for the advantage of the country. There may be some variations in intensity of curbs or incentives to lure foreign collaboration, depending upon the endeavour of a government for the economic development through diversification and lessening the foreign exchange burden faced by them.

MULTINATIONALISM IN DEVELOPING COUNTRIES

Since the Second World War, most of the developing countries have been putting in hard efforts to industrialise their economies by diversifying investment. Most of these countries experienced difficulties in maintaining

Figure 19.1

Genesis of Multinationalism in Developing Countries

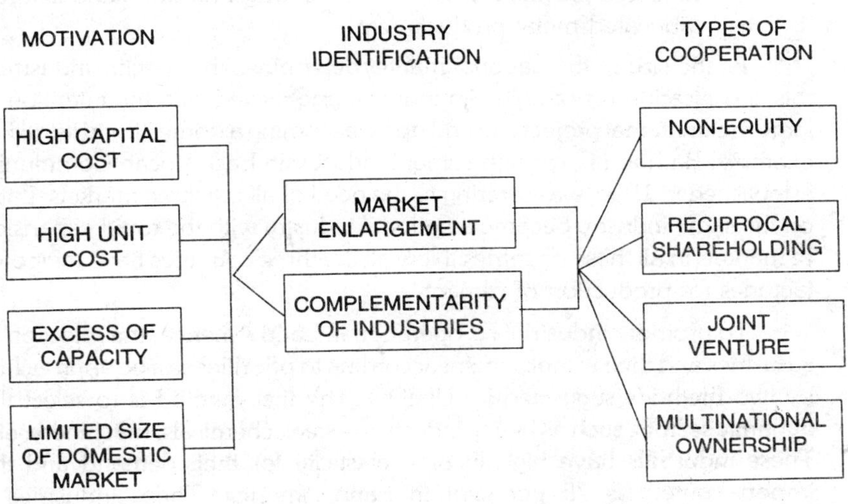

their establishment in viable economic units. This was due to the limited size of domestic market which in turn increased the cost of capital, the unit cost and also created excess capacity. These factors motivated regional grouping of developing countries in order to enter into agreements which will enable them to enlarge the markets for their units and reduce competition by implementing the plan of complementary industries in the region. This, in turn, has helped in the formation of different types of firms, *viz.,* non-equity co-operation, reciprocal share-holding, joint venture and multinational ownership (see Fig 19.1).

Identification of Industries

There are attempts in developing countries to identify heavy industries for multinational co-operation. The East African Team which was organised by ECA (Economic Commission for Africa) and the Centre for Development Planning, Projections and Policies (CDPPP), has tried to identify industries, taking into consideration the minimum technical and economic scale required for such projects. These industries have been classified into three groups, *viz.,*

1. Large multinational projects, *e.g.,* iron and steel industries, manufacturing of machinery, manufacturing of electrical machinery and apparatus.
2. Projects which have heterogeneity of the end projects, *e.g.,* textiles, paper and paper board, etc.
3. Projects though small yet need large markets, *e.g.,* food and hindered products, wood products, drugs, furniture and fixtures, fabricated metal products, etc.

As the size of the national market determines the specific industries, this classification is not rigid. An industry established with the intention of large multinational project can end up by becoming a domestic industry. For example, Bamburi Factory, a cement industry in East African Community established in 1950, was catering to the need of all the three markets. Later on the same industry became a national industry with the rapid expansion of markets in all these countries. Now all the three countries have their own factories for production of cement.

To promote industrial co-operation in Latin America, the selection of industries and their establishment according to priorities can be approached by two methods suggested by UNIDO. The first method is to select the dynamic sectors, such as heavy industry — steel, chemicals, machinery, etc. These industries have high income elasticity for their demand and the import content is 75 per cent in Latin America. These industries if established with the regional co-operation can achieve economies of scale and higher utilisation of capacities. The second approach is to select industries which are essential for industrial development: traditional industries, like textiles, clothing, glass, etc.; industrial complementarity industries, *e.g.*, tractor, rail road, etc; and new sectors for import substitution, *e.g.*, electrical and electronic equipment, chemicals, etc.

Types of Co-operation

Latin America leads the world in an attempt to achieve industrial complementarity through bilateral and multinational agreements. The countries there have entered into a complementarity agreement which in turn is expected to increase trade liberalisation among the participating countries. During 1962-68, Latin American industrialists have selected 55 bilateral and multinational projects and entered into 530 concessions for liberalisation of trade among their countries. This type of co-operation is non-equity co-operation trying to achieve economies of scale by entering markets. For instance, Empresa Colombiana de Petroleos and Empresa Petroleos Fiscal del, Peru, have entered into bilateral agreement for co-operation in production, exchange of goods and exchange of technical experience. Most of the initiative for the co-operation in Latin America has come from industrialists. Another type of cooperation among developing countries is reciprocal shareholding by different enterprises in different countries. This has been envisaged to co-ordinate the activities across the national borders. This is experimented in some textile enterprises in Central American Economic and Customs Union.

The joint ventures between two countries can take different forms, such as:

1. Jointly operated undertakings where one enterprise provides capital goods on long-term credit basis and paid back by the output of the firm.
2. Equal participation in capital between partners in joint establishments.
3. Mixed companies with equal shares of the partners.
4. Joint ownership where one country provides capital and technology and the other provides buildings, raw materials and manpower.

Most of the joint ventures undertaken by developing countries are of the nature of joint ownership, where one country provides capital and technology which are converted into equity shares of the company. This type is mostly followed by India in its joint ventures abroad. In this respect, we can take India as an example which has more joint ventures and collaboration agreements among the developing countries.

Indian government policy towards joint ventures abroad is that Indian industrialists are expected to participate in minority ownership and to collaborate with the host government and other institutions. Most of the equity capital is provided by the export of indigenous machinery, equipment and technical knowhow. Indian industrialists have to train local personnel to take up the management of the projects. Most of the joint ventures are in textiles, aluminium sheets, air-conditioners, scooters, etc. The industrial co-operation of India with Egypt and Yugoslavia is of the nature of a tripartite agreement. Though they have identified 10 projects, the progress of these projects has been very slow.

The East African team and others are of the opinion that most of the multinational co-operation among developing countries can have joint financing whereby all the participating countries will have ownership on an agreed basis and the products will be sold in regional markets.

So, we find in the developing countries many attempts to initiate the formation of multinational firms. The types vary from the nascent formation, *i.e.*, a project in a country serving the markets of several countries, to a wider co-operation, *i.e.*, the ownership, markets and management is multinational. This can be illustrated with the help of a cement factory in Bamburi and milk powder project Prolacsa in Nicaragua. Between these two extremes, one finds various nuances of multinational firm formation in developing countries.

Joint Ventures — An Indian Perspective

Objective

India's objective in encouraging and promoting joint ventures or joint enterprises abroad reflects its overall strategy to participate in the developmental efforts of other countries. India is capable of supplying a wide range of capital goods, equipment and technical knowhow not only to the developing countries but to some of the developed countries as well. This has been achieved due to planned economic development of the country which has resulted in steady growth and diversification of our industrial base. Indian joint ventures have worked in the interest of development of local economics and have generally created large employment. They have also helped in the transfer of technology and knowhow.

For a developing country like India, the problem is two-fold — to propel the economy forward and limit the extent of foreign participation, management and control. This dual purpose may be achieved by encouraging the establishment of joint ventures with local partners. The basic concept in the joint international business venture is that the partnership has two sides — technical and emotional. On the technical side, there is a joining of contributions; on the emotional side there is a feeling of co-operative effort.

What is a Joint Venture?

In the widest sense, any form of association which implies collaboration for more than a very transitory period comprises a joint venture. But pure trading operations are not included in this concept. Such a broad definition encompasses many diverse types of joint overseas operations, sharing of ownership and control in an economic enterprise, licensing agreements, contract manufacturing, and management contracts. In general, a joint venture in an overseas market is created when a foreign company gets together with a local interest in that country, and together they own some type of business operation.

There are three ways in which joint ventures may be initiated:

(a) A new business enterprise may be created;

(b) The foreign concern may invest in an existing local company; or

(c) A local company may acquire an interest in an existing operation of the foreign company.

Regardless of the manner in which it is created, the central feature of a joint venture is that ownership and control are shared.

Reasons for Joint Ventures in Home Country

(i) Utilise the special privileges and influence of the local authorities.

(ii) Make use of production facilities, sales network and indigenous capital offered by the local participants.

(iii) Reduce the risk, if any, involved in the venture caused by the economic and political circumstances of the capital importing country by sharing it with the local partners.

(iv) Enjoy the special tax benefits of the capital-importing country.

Why Joint Ventures Abroad?

People want to have joint ventures abroad in order:

(i) To expand foreign manufacturing and service activities;

(ii) To develop a source of supply of required raw materials;

(iii) To integrate the joint venture activity and the normal activity of the local partners (supplier-customer relationship) for the advantage of both the local company and the foreign company;

(iv) To ensure government participation in joint ventures with a view to increasing the rate of economic development in its country; and

(v) To acquire a means by which an international marketer is able to penetrate an overseas market.

Joint ventures have been created in response to situations in which international marketers are forced to make changes in operating methods because:

(i) Local government policies cut them off from export markets that were formerly profitable;

(ii) Trade marks and patents needed protecting;

(iii) Competitors began manufacturing in these markets and were able to offer buyers a lower price; or

(iv) Political conditions in certain overseas markets were upset by the successful methods of overseas operators.

The reasons why a company may be forced into joint ventures as a means of penetrating an overseas market may be grouped into two broad categories:

A. The Reasons may be Economic

An overseas manufacturing project requires a great amount of relatively scarce resources, and a company may not have the necessary capital and personnel available to make the project a success. A local partner can provide these.

B. Policies and Attitudes of Government

The policies and attitudes of the government of the country in which manufacturing facilities are to be established are important. Behind many joint ventures are national pressures on foreign companies to include some local capital in their manufacturing operations.

Two forces create these pressures:

(a) Local businessmen, who want to profit from industrial growth;

(b) National feelings which may be opposed to the high degree of control which many foreign companies exercise.

Not all joint ventures are established by companies that are forced into them. Some companies may elect to do so voluntarily.

Why Joint Venture is more Profitable?

A joint venture is more profitable than others as it is generally in a field that is different from that of the international marketer, although it may be related to it. For example, Pan American World Airways has gone into hotel building and operate on a joint venture basis. A joint venture promotes integration by combining an existing operation with another and precedes or follows the stage of production. Local partners can contribute more to a joint venture than money, facilities and personnel to help get it started. He may have more experience in dealing with customers, competitors, government officials and labour in his own country than most foreign companies can hope to achieve within a reasonable time.

Advantages of Joint Venture

These advantages are many and varied.

(i) A joint venture approach enables a company with a limited capital and manpower resources to enter more overseas markets than would be possible if it depends only on establishing wholly-owned subsidiaries. Because of the resource saving and the potential ability to enter more markets, business risks are minimised and an element of protection is gained when investments are diversified.

(ii) Risk is minimised because the management skills and experience of a local partner facilitate easier adaptation to the particular changes of an unfamiliar business environment.

Risk is also reduced in that the resulting project is generally less subject to the danger of adverse action by the local government, especially in those ventures where the local partner is some agency of the government.

(iii) There is the potential of a favourable effect which local participation in ownership can have on the morale of labour.

(iv) The sales and profits of the joint venture may be greater than those of a wholly-owned subsidiary because the operation is looked upon with more favour by nationalistic consumers than would be the case if it was considered a foreign operation. A joint venture approach can, therefore, achieve good public relations.

Limitations of Joint Ventures

These limitations are:

(i) The amount of resources needed is reduced; so is the profit potential. All profits that are made must be shared;

(ii) Potential disagreements between partners and those who run the managerial activities;

(iii) Companies that are either multinational in character or tend to become multinational may find that joint ventures can complicate long-run international manufacturing and marketing policies. This is particularly true when the control of a joint venture is in the hands of local partner. For example, a multinational company may have a transfer pricing system which it may not be able to use because the profits of the joint venture would be understated.

(iv) When a party enters into a joint venture, its operations in other markets may be affected. For example, problems can arise in the

international markets if one desires to create a new venture in a third market in which the joint venture has been selling its products. By creating such a new enterprise, the international marketer becomes a competitor while still being a partner. Competing with oneself is a policy that many companies in foreign countries have not yet accepted.

(v) Where a foreign company buys an existing local enterprise, a serious problem may arise. Often, a joint ownership does not work out satisfactorily because, unknowingly, by changing the ownership of the company, a change is made in the combination of attributes that made it successful before the foreign company entered the picture.

Joint ventures are appropriate when:

(i) A company lacks the necessary resources to expand its international operations;

(ii) A company wants to enter an overseas market where wholly-owned activities are prohibited;

(iii) A company can utilise the market position or management skills of a local partner; and

(iv) Complete control is not necessary for the success of the venture.

Factors which make Joint Venture a Success

The real success of every joint venture is dependent upon some other factors as well. For example:

(a) The extent to which such co-operation is forthcoming from each local partner depends upon the characteristics of each partner.

(b) The selection of each local partner is perhaps the single most important activity involved in establishing a joint venture.

(c) Since it is extremely difficult to find compatible partners, the situation can be eased somewhat if the partners attempt to anticipate all possible areas of disagreement and specifically provide for them in the joint venture agreement. In other words, the agreement should assist the partners in becoming, and remaining, compatible.

Use of Joint Ventures for India

Joint ventures for India are particularly useful for the following reasons:

(i) *They overcome the obstacle of freight cost (Discriminating Freight Rates):* For example, freight rates from the UK to New Zealand are lower than those from Calcutta to New Zealand.

(ii) *Adverse cost effect may be neutralised through joint ventures:* The MacDougal Committee found that the differential rates between India and international prices for non-traditional goods was 25 per cent to 30 per cent. If a joint venture is set up in a foreign country near the market and near the raw material sources, it would give a fillip where there is solid domestic demand.

(iii) *Through joint venture arrangement* with the countries desiring rapid industrial development, we can gain their goodwill and co-operation by proving that we are interested not only in exporting goods for consumption but also in furthering their industrialisation programme through pooling resources for joint individual members.

(iv) *The developing countries* welcome long-term investments in the form of capital or knowhow by offering tax concessions, investment guarantees and other benefits. Thus, countries which are less developed offer attractive possibilities for joint ventures. Of course, India, in this regard, will have to meet a stiff competition from industrially advanced countries. But this is a challenge rather than an obstacle. In joint ventures, India can also offer consultancy services and technical and management expertise.

The joint ventures help not only in finding an initial outlet for capital goods, tax benefits, increased sales in the country concerned, but opportunities for re-investment and expansion, repatriation of profits; and they also stimulate the tourist industry. They can be set up by India in a third country along with other countries. There can be co-operation in the field of international tendering and international marketing. A compulsion in the matter of exports must be introduced in new collaboration agreements and at the time of the renewal of old agreements.

Most of the capital importing countries are not aware of India's progress and the help she could render to them in their economic development. As a consequence of this ignorance, our products do not find a sufficient external demand. This has a bearing on joint ventures because the export of goods usually precedes the setting up of joint ventures. To overcome this, a vigorous publicity drive should be launched: we should take part in industrial trade fairs, screen short-length movies by industrial houses, etc.

Exim bank which has been set up 10 years ago is paying great attention to financing exports and joint ventures. It is necessary to enter into double taxation and investment guarantee agreements with those countries where we are likely to set up joint ventures.

The finalisation of inter-government investment guarantee agreements with individual countries takes considerable time. India should, therefore, evolve a scheme for investment guarantee with Indian businessmen. This scheme should cover all the Indian investment in joint ventures abroad against:

(i) Risks of exchange fluctuations;

(ii) Political risks, the threat of nationalisation, war risks, the possibility of threat of cancellation of permission for repatriating profits, etc.

This scheme may well be operated by the ECGC/EXIM Bank.

Indian Enterprises Set Up Joint Ventures Abroad

Indian enterprises have set up 150 joint ventures in 35 countries, where another 43 joint ventures are under various stages of implementation. Three-fourths of these joint ventures are located in just ten countries. Several of these joint ventures are restaurants and hotels, marketing of films, ice-creams, pumps, automobile, rubber products and readymade garments, real estate investment and development, construction and trading, consultancy, financial consultancy, leasing, tea auction, blending and packing of tea, travels and tourism, palm oil processing and refining and jewellery trading. Along with these there is a substantial number of joint ventures where the Indian industrial and technical capability is at work in industrial ventures. Their successful working promises to bring good income and good name to India.

Inter-Ministerial Committee on Joint Ventures

The joint ventures/wholly owned subsidiaries established abroad are given approvals under Section 27 of Foreign Exchange Regulation Act, 1973 (FERA) by an Inter-Ministerial Committee on joint ventures abroad (IMC) headed by an Additional Secretary in the Ministry of Commerce. As on 31st December, 1986, there were 187 joint ventures. Out of these, 150 joint ventures were in operation and 37 were at different stages of implementation.

Pattern of Investment

In the 150 joint ventures which are in operation, the Indian investment by way of equity share capital has been effected mainly through export of capital machinery and equipment technology or capitalisation of income due to the Indian company with cash remittances playing only a supplementary role. The total quantum of Indian equity in the joint ventures in operation was of the order of about Rs. 9.2 crores (including bonus shares). The approved Indian equity with regard to projects under implementation amounted to about Rs. 18 crores.

Size of the Indian Joint Ventures

The size and scale of operation of the majority of the joint ventures abroad has generally been small. In 75% of the operating joint ventures, India's share holding is less than 50% and value of investments being less than Rs. 50 lakhs each. In many cases it is as low as Rs. 5 to 10 lakhs. But it has been noticed that this trend is gradually being reversed, particularly in the units which have been coming on stream during the past few years. This orientation has been, to a large measure, aided by the entry of well established Indian companies both from the private and public sector who have started embarking upon well conceived, carefully planned and economically viable projects capable of yielding not only higher returns but also of projecting abroad a better image of Indian expertise.

Regional Dispersal

The Indian joint ventures which are presently in operation are dispersed over 35 countries. More than 80 per cent of operating joint ventures are concentrated in 11 countries. Malaysia (21), Singapore and Sri Lanka (16 each), Nigeria (12), U.K. and Indonesia (11 each), UAE and Thailand (each) USA and Nepal (7 each) and Kenya (6).

Field of Collaboration

Among the 150 joint ventures that are in operation, 100 joint ventures *i.e.,* 67 per cent are in the manufacturing sector, headed by light engineering sector, followed by textile and allied products and chemicals and pharmaceuticals. These are fields in which Indian entrepreneurs have acquired a certain degree of capability of competence in the international technology market. The other industries chosen by the Indian companies to set up joint ventures are leather and rubber products, oilseeds crushing, palm oil refining, pulp and paper, glass and glass products, food products, commercial vehicles and cement products, etc. In the non-manufacturing sector the largest number is in hotels and restaurants, trading and marketing, followed by engineering contracts and construction, consultancy, etc.

BENEFITS FROM JOINT VENTURES

The benefits accrued to India from the successful joint ventures operating abroad are in the form of dividends and other entitlements of Indian promoters such as technical knowhow, engineering service fee, management fee, consulting and royalty, etc. Some joint ventures have also been declaring bonus shares from time to time and the pro-rata allotment to the Indian companies which are currently in operation, has exceeded Rs. 14 crores. The issue of bonus shares has enlarged Indian investment and also enhanced the capacity of these units to remit larger amounts by way of dividends in future. As per the information received from Indian promoters, the benefits that have accrued to this country from the joint ventures in operation/under implementation in the form of dividends, knowhow other fees, etc., and the additional exports generated are as under:

(Value: Rs. crores)

Dividends	"Other Repatriations"	Additional Exports
11.57	34.79	161.63

Notes: *(a)* "Other Repatriations" includes fee for technical knowhow, engineering services, management fee, royalty, etc.

(b) Additional exports include exports of plant and machinery, spares, components and raw material effected over and above exports towards equity.

(*c*) In addition to the figures given above exports of plant and machinery, etc., for equity contribution have amounted to above Rs. 51.56 crores.

Latest Position of Joint Ventures Set-up in India with Foreign Collaboration

A total of 79 joint ventures abroad were approved by the Government of India during the last three years. The Government, had scrutinized 173 such proposals since the beginning of 1988 and approved only 79 till July 1991.

India stands on the threshold of technological infusion from the advanced countries, with this view Government of India has facilitated the entry of foreign firms by lowering of the customs tariff. This would lower the production cost and is a big incentive for international companies planning to set-up technology bases in India.

By introducing the policy of economic liberalisation one of the primary aim of the government have been to induce multinational corporations to bring latest technology into India.

(1) Motorola has been the first American company to invest in India following the liberalisation policy of 1991. Motorola in collaboration of Blue Star of India has set-up a production unit in India which will make the latest communication technology available. Technology will be used in modernising police wireless systems, wiring operations, Air India reservation counters and the banking set-up within the country.

(2) Phoenix, Germany producing interfacing technology, will supply connecting terminals.

(3) Carl-Zeiss Jena of Germany making precision instruments and opthalmic lenses.

(4) Honeywell (USA) in collaboration with Tata India will make distributed control systems in chemical plants.

In addition Pepsi Foods collaboration with Punjab Agro and Voltas Ltd., and joint venture arrangements of Procter and Gamble are well known.

A number of MNCs that have set-up joint ventures in India hope to up date Indian technology through a tie up between their Indian organisation and their overseas set up. However, MNCs feel the hazard of devaluation and excessive regulations governing repatriation of profits back to their countries is still there.

Some of these joint ventures have been successful. But the central purpose of earning foreign exchange through the setting up of joint ventures in vitiated by the fact that there is great tardiness on the part of the Indian partners in repatriating the returns on investment and other earnings to India. In certain cases repatriation of dues such as technical knowhow, management consultancy charges, engineering fee, etc., are sought to be withheld without any proper justification.

The Indian joint ventures abroad, wherever successful, have been meeting the felt need of the host countries and they are not confronted with any local competition, although they have to cope with competition from the firms of third countries. This is a highly favourable factor. No doubt as the host countries acquire manufacturing capability over time to meet their own demands, the Indian firms would have to meet with greater obstacles than now. But the extent of underdevelopment in the developing countries leaves scope for the simultaneous development of indigenous capacity as well as joint ventures.

However, that does not mean that the Indian parties floating joint ventures abroad can be smug and remain indifferent to the actual policies and conditions of working available in the host countries. In Malaysia, for example, where the failure rate of Indian joint ventures is very high, Indian promoters had not done their homework thoroughly, nor planned their projects properly. There was even failure to assess the viability of projects. Obviously the Indian parties involved in such indifferently conceived joint ventures were not seriously interested in business success and no degree of support of the Government of India can make any difference to the outcome in such case. In the final analysis it is the quality of entrepreneurship that will be the determining factor.

In about 85 per cent of the operating joint ventures overseas, Indians' shareholding is less than 50 per cent and the value of investments is less than

Rs. 50 lakhs each. This leaves the dominant role to the local entrepreneurs. This is in sharp contrast to the attitude of the Western multinational companies coming to invest in India, where they very often seek the majority share of equity holding.

Joint ventures have made their appearance in the developed countries as well. And these joint ventures are not only those promoted by the entrepreneurs of the developing countries. Firms in one developed country now form joint ventures with firms of a second developed country to do business in the second country. These joint ventures appear at all stages of the development and marketing of products and services and in all industrial and commercial sectors. Their growth is giving rise to new competition within the second country as it also is hurting competition so that the governments in the host countries have had to enact laws and adopt administrative measures to control the joint ventures. The Organisation for Economic Co-operation and Development (OECD) has brought out a report made by the OECD Committee of Experts on Restrictive Business Practices on Competition Policy issues related to mergers, acquisitions and concentration, under the title *Competition Policy and Joint Ventures.* Information available suggests that international joint ventures represent a significant proportion of international operations.

CONCLUSION

Multinational marketing works on the same basic principles as domestic marketing, except that the environment itself is different. Overseas marketing involves interaction among the parent company, home country marketing environment, foreign unit, host country market and marketing environment, and international environment.

There are five basic marketing orientations among international marketers. A company may have a domestic orientation, home country orientation, host country orientation, regional orientation, or global orientation. The multinational corporation can be defined as an enterprise that operates internationally yet is nationally based in terms of ownership and executive management.

When a firm decides to "go international", several decisions must be made. It must choose the specific nations that provide solid marketing opportunities. Then it must arrange its entry method. The major entry forms include exporting, licensing, joint ownership, and direct investment. Finally, a marketing mix must be tailored to each foreign market. In many cases, standardised elements of the marketing mix may be used in different countries.

In this chapter, we have analysed the nature of genesis and changing pattern of multinational firms in different environments. In developed market economies, the aggressive strategies of U.S. firms are of the nature of operating in several countries, but ownership is concentrated in the country of origin. Slowly, the tendency of decentralising and integration processes are underway, starting from product-market, finance, management and ownership. There are indications towards this process, for instance, Royal Dutch/Shell and Unilever where the ownership is binational.

After the dismantling of U.S.S.R., there is closer relationship between East and West through the efforts of multinational firms. The specialisation, exchange of technology and economies of scale are taken advantage of irrespective of socio-political set-up of the respective countries. They have been able to penetrate various markets in spite of inhibiting incidence of tariff and non-tariff barriers.

The case of interaction between multinational firms and oil-producing countries is interesting. This is explained through power balance approach. The early decades of this century witnessed politico-economic nature of multinational firms, and now this power has been with the producing countries who are trying to integrate their policies through OPEC.

The case of manufacturing operations of multinational firms in developing countries is quite different from that of oil producing countries. Here, the approach has been more of accommodation than of power balance.

Finally, the experiment in multinationalism among developing countries is worth studying. One will get numerous experiments varying from simple extension of a national firm to many markets, to composite ownership and management style of multinational firm.

Import Substitution and Export Promotion Prospects

The policy of import substitution should be enshrined as a major national objective in a developing economy like India. As far as practicable the process of import substitution is the resultant effect of many national policy instruments aimed at achieving self-reliance as well as a favourable balance of payments position. Import substitution implies substituting what is imported by indigenous items as far as practicable. The detailed policies and programmes of various government departments like the Planning Commission, Department of Science and Technology, DGTD — Directorate General of Technical Development, MMTC — Metals and Minerals Trading Corporation, STC, etc., should be coordinated to achieve this laudable objective. The various policy instruments, enacted by Parliament, such as Industrial Policy Resolution, the Industry's Development and Regulations Act, the Five Year Plans, Guidelines for Industries, Annual

Import Trade Control Policy, etc., are supposed to be focused towards the aforementioned national objective of self-reliance.

The country spends about 300 crores per year on the import of spare parts. This difficulty has been accentuated because of the large scale imports of machineries and thinking only in terms of part number and not the function of components through codification process. This process has resulted in industries carrying Rs. 2,500 crores of obsolete (mostly imported) spares. While importing the capital machinery, adequate precaution should be taken to buy the drawings as well.

It is too well known that the lead time for the clearance of import requirements is very long. Further, the requirements of imported material are to be purchased on an annual or six-monthly consumption quantities. These factors compel all organisations to carry a high inventory of imported materials. Inspite of several procedural changes introduced recently by the DGTD, the senior materials executives attending Administrative Staff College courses, are of the firm view that there is plenty of scope for reduction of lead time in DGTD and DGIT.

These central organisations should also take initiative in setting up "Banks" for critical imported raw materials and the spare parts. Obviously this will reduce not only the imports at the macro level but also investment on the inventory at the micro level.

Role of R & D in Import Substitution

Technological innovation is essential to the birth and growth of industrial enterprises and the economic, social and political health of nations. The stock of technology on which innovation depends can be increased by Research and Development. It is neither necessary nor practical to rely entirely on one's own Research and Development and it would appear that every country must buy technology from abroad. But to make the best of the bought-out technology it needs an internal Research and Development effort to adapt and to absorb. Therefore, the strategy for achieving technological self-reliance must include: (1) Selective buying of technology, (2) Import substitution, (3) Development of threshold technology, and (4) Development of essentially indigenous technology.

CSIR

The agencies in our country that are supposed to look after the development of indigenous technology as well as keep pace with the technical developments in advanced countries are the laboratories of CSIR — Council of Scientific and Industrial Research — and the unit level R & D. The CSIR has a chain of forty laboratories covering almost all the fields of technology. Some of the laboratories have been in existence for more than a quarter of a century. The annual budget is about Rs. 30 crores. And over 10,000 technical and scientific personnel are employed in them. Admittedly, a few of these laboratories have done commendable work; but unfortunately, the measure of the output from CSIR laboratories, according to information from NRDC — National Research Development Corporation — adds an additional 10 crores only to the gross national product (GNP).

Unit Level R & D

Individual organisations, instead of waiting for the government to introduce the above suggested change, should take the initiative to establish their own R & D. Obviously at the unit level, design and development will be more productive. In this context, the concept of research surcharge, which has been floating around for the last four years, is yet to be implemented. However, the industry can emulate the example of BHEL, which has set up a separate corporate R & D unit. Though the National Committee on Science and Technology (NCST) has recommended that one per cent of the Gross National Product (GNP) should be spent on R & D efforts, progressive companies like BHEL, BEL etc., are spending more than three per cent of their sales on R & D efforts. Small units can invest in R & D by also sponsoring projects in universities and IITs in order to properly utilise the talent of over one lakh scientific and technical personnel in the country.

Technology Transfer

The difficulties in the transfer of technology from research institutions to shop floor in the country, are too well known to be enumerated. This obviously arises due to lack of communication and the inability to understand the constraints of a production organisation by the scientists and vice versa. In this context our earlier suggestion of having laboratories that are responsible to industry groups, assumes great significance. Further, we piously hope that the idea of the polytechnology clinic, which is being promoted by CSIR, will be a step in the right direction.

As mentioned earlier, all countries to some extent have to import technology. This has a dynamic role to play in a developing country like ours, but only when dovetailed to and closed-knit with other technologies in our reckoning. Having amassed imported technology over the past two decades, the quickest pay-back to our economy is from adaptive technology or import substitution. Development of essentially indigenous and threshold technology, however, has to be the bulk of our effort not only to achieve self-reliance, but also to build up export potential. However, for better assimilation of imported technology, it should be purchased outright or a dynamic research institution has to be associated with every import of knowhow.

Technology Transfer Centres

In order to achieve the above, the government should set up "technology transfer centres" for conducing techno-economic reviews of the old and new patents filed in India. Such technology transfer centres can pick up some of the promising inventions for commercial exploitation after input of requisite R & D effort. While lapsed patents may be utilised freely, in the case of current patents, provision of compulsory licensing under the patent laws may be availed of to break the foreign monopoly hold on the existing knowhow.

The same centre may also conduct techno-economic review of foreign patents and allied publications of industrially advanced countries, classify promising ideas industry-wise and feed the same to appropriate R & D institutions and industries. This will provide them with the necessary starting point for marginal R & D work needed for an import substitution effort, development of threshold technology, improvements in production methods, as well as diversification of production to stimulate growth of new industries.

Problems in Import Substitution

In the process of import substitution, companies and various central agencies, particularly the DGTD — encounter a series of bottlenecks. Some of these are illustrated below:

1. Authorities in charge of execution of projects — whether in public or private sectors — tend to give very tight specifications and standards. These critical specifications make the task of mobilising the manufacture of such equipment from indigenous resources very difficult. Normally many of the specifications are borrowed and the relevance of such tight specifications for Indian conditions should be reviewed.

2. Project authorities ask for imported capital equipment on the strength of absence of quality assurances or performance guarantees from the indigenous machine building sector.

On the one hand it is difficult in the context of early commissioning of projects to resist such claims, on the other, it is equally necessary that sufficient time, based on advance and coordinated planning, is given to indigenous machinery manufacturers to be able to satisfy the quality and performance aspect. It is DGTD's experience that unless there is a start with development contracts, indigenous manufacturers rarely come up.

3. There is a large communication gap *inter se* between industries in a situation where the output of one industry is the input of another. This gap results in pressures for import.

4. Engineers and users are accustomed to part numbers, usually of imported components, and are reluctant to go into development of drawings and to question the specifications.

5. Sometimes import substitution becomes difficult in view of the high image of foreign brand names amongst the elite consumer in India — Coca Cola is a case in point. Coca-Cola has staged a come back when Pepsi in walked.

6. The foreign collaborators would like to keep the Indian licences and subsidiaries indefinitely dependent upon their raw material, components and know how.

Examples in India

In India several public and private sector undertakings have applied value analysis techniques successfully for cost-reduction and import substitution purposes. Some are discussed below:

1. Substitution of solid aluminium extrusions for hollow rolled steel sections in wind shield frames in cars. This effected a saving of Rs. 80,000 per annum.

2. Use of aluminium in place of copper in the cable manufacture has helped conserve valuable foreign exchange.

The country is now self-sufficient in aluminium and the imports of copper have come down by about Rs. 8 crores. Aluminising in place of galvanising has helped reduce the imports of zinc.

The use of duplex board carton in place of tin containers for milk powder packing.

Conclusion

There is a growing awareness at all levels for self-sufficiency and import substitution. The responsibility of this task is shared by the government and the industry. Industry should take a constructive attitude towards import substitution and shed their inhibition for a change. At the micro level, in the industry the responsibility of initiating import substitution rests on the materials manager who is in charge of source development. However, he has to get the cooperation of his colleagues for technical aspects, quality, quantity, price, etc. Scientific laboratories like CSIR should take an active part in the process and aid the industry with sufficient information and testing facilities.

The facilities and expertise already established in the country have to be availed of to full advantage in making more exports, fuller utilisation of capacities, materials conservation and import substitution, coupled with a curtailment of non-essential imports catering particularly to elite consumption. It is hoped that the country with the available infrastructure will achieve greater import substitution and reduce the trade deficit in the near future. Particularly in view of Government of India's liberal export-import policy which has loosened its belts as far as imports are concerned but it is seen that the items imported definitely give boost to India's export promotion drive.

20

CASE STUDIES ON INTERNATIONAL MARKETING

CASE STUDY NO. 1

(1) A CASE STUDY ON SPICES EXPORT MARKETING

Government of India has made special efforts through macroeconomic reforms in industrial, financial and trade sector to boost export business. Fiscal and financial incentives are provided to our corporate sector engaged in export business. It is a controversy among the economists that there will be growth-led export or export-led growth in India due to economic reform process in India. Inspite of either of the phenomenon, ever increasing domestic market is also considered as one of the significant factors for slow rate of growth of Indian exports. There is one school of thought believing that Indian trade has been essentially inward looking largely due to its size and ever expanding internal market. Economic liberalisation and reforms opened new avenues for export growth in general and specific commodities in particular as policy measures like simplification of excise and custom procedures, deregulation of licensing, formation of special focus group of commodity exports and a host of other incentives directed at the export front.

This case study examines the pattern of export growth in general and export of spices in particular with a view to suggest action plan to boost the exports up to the target of 2000 A.D. An attempt is also made for projection of production and growth of spices exports in Indian case.

The case study is divided into 3 papers: the first one reviews literature that has grown in the recent past in area of exports of spices so as to sort our issues, the second one examines trends and of production and exports of spices among overall export of India, whereas, the third one offers action plan to reach the target of 2000 A.D.

Retrospect

Considerable amount of literature has grown to know export marketing and diversification of export business by Indian economists. These include Pendse[1], Attri[2], PNB[3], Saxena[4], Kameshwar Rao[5], Deolanker[6], Debroy[7], Government of India[8], Singh and Madhavan[9]. All these studies attempt to measure growth rate of exports in general or showing policy measures for diversification of Indian export business. Commodity-wise and country-wise studies also highlight behaviour of world export market and share of Indian exports. However, authors like Siddharthan[10] and Sharma[11] attempted to throw light on implifications of economic reforms and liberalisation policy for possible solution of problems arising in export management. Decontrol and derregulation policy is welcomed by all exporters inclusive of exporters of spices.

In the case of export business of spices, there are studies undertaken by Garg[12], Sandhu[13], UNCTAD,[14] Murlidhar Rao[15] and by others with a view to know strategy of production and diversification of exports of species as well as expansion of multilateral trade of spices. Most of the studies have shown projections of production and export. Commodity wise and country-wide efforts have been made to know expansion of exports of spices. One can draw following issues faced by exporters of spices.

Major Issues

1. Growth-led exports for India in the case of production of spices draw attention of growers, processors and exporters.
2. Problems faced in getting hhgh yielding varieties and their use with technological change in production, processing, packing and forwarding of spices.
3. What kind of role can be played by Kerala Market Federation in order to achieve targets of exports in 2000 A.D.?
4. Role of banks and financial institutions to fund production technology and special export finance as pre-shipment and post-shipment credit of spices.
5. Conservation, protection and storage of spices to stop wastage in export business.

6. Role of Spices Board, state government as well as central government. In India to boost exports with brand and specification of investment spices.
7. Relaxation in formalities of exports for new entrants in export of spices in India apart from budget exercise.
8. What kind of action plan is necessary to achieve targets of production and exports of spices about 300 million dollars in 2000 A.D in Indian case?

This paper is not answering all the above issues but attempts to touch the last one regarding action plan and related policies to boost exports of spices in India.

II

Production and Exports of Spices

It is necessary to know the macro view of production and exports scenario of spices. According to Bureau of Indian Standards, there are 63 spices grown in India. These include black papper, chillies, cardmom, ginger, turmeric, coriander, cummin, garlic and others and leading both in production and exports too. As the level of living of people goes up, consumption of spices tends to increase. Spices are used worldwide to enhance or to vary flavour of the food. They act as appetisers and some of the spicies have anti-oxidant properties. Most of the spices are used in food processing as well as pharmaceuticals and perfumery and cosmetics industry.

Considering popular economic theory of growth-led exports appear to be true in the case of production and export of spices. Therefore, it is necessary to glance through macroeconomic management of spices in India. Spices are grown in all states of India but their production differs from state to state largely due to climatic changes. It is reported by Bureau of Indian Standards that there are 63 spices grown on two million hectares and having production of about 16 lakh tonnes per annum. Exact figures about productions of the spices and state-wise data is not available. However, estimates are available from Ministry of Agriculture, Directorate of Economics and Statistics as well as state departments of trade.

By and large, spices are divided into annual and perennial. Price fluctuation is affecting area under cultivation in different states of India, whereas, in the case of perennial, the area does not change significantly unless, exceptional change in price is found. The weak mechanism of marketing, lack of appropriate price policy has also hindered higher productivity in the case of Indian spices. As corporate sector in India has taken active interest and is playing a major role for production and exports of spices, the production of spices needs to be on professional basis. This is so as uneducated growers do not know about high-yieling varieties in spices, ravages due to pest and diseases, unscientific post-harvest technology of processing and storage of spices reduces actual usable production.

It must be understood by the professionals in corporate sector of India that a country which is committed to globalisation needs to reproduce far more efficiently than it had been doing so far. Atleast, it must be made sure for that the growers get reasonable return on their investment. The support price mechanism has to be worked efficiently in commodities where self-sufficiency is to be achieved.

The share of spices export in total exports in the fiscal year ending 1952, 1960,1970,1980 and 1990 were 4.18, 2.87, 2.45, 2.55 and 2.42 respectively. The compound rates of growth of exports of spices in percent per year were 4.2, 3.0, 2.5, and 2.9 during fifties, sixties, seventies and eighties respectively. In the case of pepper, Indian had been exporting roughly about 79% of production to the world market. There are other competitors like Brazil, Indonesia, Malaysia, Srilanka and Spain. Quantity exported by Indonesia is in big bulk considering her export volume but there are quality differences. In India 95% of the area under cultivation is in Kerala, where 82% of pepper holdings are less than 3 hectares each and average holding is low as 0.73 hectares. As a result productivity of pepper in India is as low as 230 kg per hectare consisting of 580 vines, 925 kg in Indonesia, 417 kg in Malaysia and 3333 kg per hectare in Brazil. However, trend of exports of pepper is not steady but fluctuating from year to year after 1988. Looking to direction of trade of spices USA and European countries were dominating. Nowadays USSR, East European countries, Canada, USA and Italy are major buyers provided that our prices come down to international parity. It is to be noted that export performance of Indian spices remain very high subject to the world level growth of output of spices. Elasticity of Indian exports of spices remained high with respect to world output of spices. In the case of exports of pepper pimento in the world had resulted in increase of per capita consumption in the importing countries.

Earnings from Spices

Trends of export earning both in terms of rupees as well as in dollars is rising. However, export earning in terms of dollars is not as high due to exchange rate policy and other technical reasons. One can safely project as the basis of export earning of Rs. 69,751 crores in 1993-94 to Rs. 2,20,000 crores in 2000 A.D. for India. Similarly, in terms of dollars, it was 22239 million dollars in 1993-94 which is likely to be 66,000 million dollars in 2000 A.D. considering overall growth pattern of Indian export growth.

Similarly, export earning of spices, notably increased during the years of the eighties, it was Rs. 11 crores in 1980-81 to Rs. 278 crores, whereas, in terms of dollars from 14 million to 227 million during the period. During the initial years of the nineties, export earning of spices in rupees increased from Rs. 239 crores in 1990-91 to Rs. 569 crores in 1993-94, while registered 225% growth, whereas, in terms of dollars increased from 133 million to 181 million dollars, it registered only 25% growth. On the basis of such trends as well as liberalisation policy under economic reforms, researchers projected export earnings for India in 2000 A.D. about overall export of Rs. 1500 crores and in terms of dollars about 300 million in the case of spices, and India has already achieved the target.

At the time of independence, our contribution in world export was about 1.52% which declined to 0.6% in 1970 and again 0.4% in 1980, whereas, it improved up to 0.6% in 1992. In order to have about 0.9% share in 2000 A.D., overall Indian export earnings need to be increased above 60,000 million dollars. Similarly, in the case of share of exports of spices, at world level it has notably increased during the years of the eighties, whereas, India's share increased 15%. It is interesting to note that during 1992, the share of India in world exports of spices was 64.1%. However, due to technical reasons value of Indian spices were 110 million dollars against world level export value of 1720 million dollars. One can safely project on this basis that there will be 70% share of India in world exports of spices In terms of dollars, it would be about 3000 million dollars total world exports of spices, whereas, the value of Indian exports of spices would be around 300 million dollars.

It is necessary to know the area and production of different spices in India so as to know decinnial rise in area in hectres and production. It is estimated to project about production of spices in 2000 A.D. considering past trend record of two decades. The projection is made on the basis of 20% annual rate of growth in exports and percent potentiality of each item of spices mentioned in the table. Thus, in order to taken over challenges of 21st century at the export front of spices, importantion item-wise new area and possible requirement of production is necessary.

Action Plan to Boost Indian Exports of Spices

Economists and management experts can offer action plan for both macro and micro management of exports of spices as under:

1. In the case of produce of spices for quality exports and diversification of trade, it is necessary that micro propagation and rapid clonal multiplication of high yielding lies varieties in genotypes to generate adequate good quality and disease free planting materials.

2. Crop improvement devices of farm management on professional base will pave a way for quality and quantity of spices for more exportable surplus. Concentrated R & D efforts for production and marketing is absolutely necessary both at farm level and corporate level.
3. Indian spices need brand and name to cope with competition of global level through standards and specifications in the case of all 63 import spices exported from India.
4. Role of the state would be vital for market intervention and price mechanism in order to save prices from crashing down so as to protect interest of growers as well as small producers in particular in the case of spices and other items.
5. Corporate sector, export and process houses, will have to take over the challenges to face in the process of globalisation of market for spices. The eighth five-year plan of the Government of India aims at a growth rate of 10% in production compared to 4% in the seventh plan. Investment strategy under the central sector scheme is Rs. 150 crores. All potential exporters of spices should take advantage of the scheme.
6. Very recently researchers maintained that in the case of pre-shipment credit by banks, 1% increase in wholesale price, tends to increase the credit required by 0.7% and 1% increase in quantity of exports trends to increase the requirement by 1.7%. As against this in the case of postshipment credit, 1% increase in quantity of exports tends to increase the credit requirement by 1.58% and 1% increase in normal effective exchange rate tends to increase the requirement by 1.06% considering the fact that banking sector will have to play a vital role to boost our export business. After the nationalisation of banks export credit as per concept of total credit has fallen from 9% in 1969 to 5.5% in 1990.
7. The phenomenon gives us a clue that there is a need for 8% of export credit of total credit span, whereas, in 2000 A.D. Banks and financial institutions will have to come forward to finance export growth. And in such a case there will be a demand for export credit in India at about 11.5% of total credit for export business. Financial markets will have to meet with growing need of export finance for globalisation process, which will demand about Rs. 60,000 crore export credit by 2000 A.D.
8. Factoring services to boost exports will play a vital role in Asia-Pacific region. Factors Chain International reported that Asia.

Pacific total factoring volume was 25075 million U.S.$ in 1990 in 33858 $ in 1992. Annual growth rate is found 22% in 1992 over 1991. The contribution of Asia-Pacific region in factoring turnover reported 12.8% growth in total international trade, in 1992. Indian banks need to be involved in factoring service development for potential export units. Through factoring collection and financing of receivers, manufacturers and sellers of goods have been able to improve their cash flow through prepayment facilities by drawing up to 80% of the value of the assigned invoices as and when necessary factoring services by banks increase turnover of exporters, maintain continuity of supplies and economies factoring costs. Factoring facilities need to be enlarged to cover international trade for countries of Asia. Line management of Asian Development Bank, Exim Bank of India, and Indian commercial bank business will provide a vital boost for exports in general and in the case of export units and export houses in particular. Dynamics of international factoring will help to raise competitiveness, reduction in risk and higher purchasing power. Availability of export factoring services will help Indian corporate sector in product diversification, market diversification and overall turnover of export business. Export factoring will benefit the exporters like protection against bad debts, provides flexible form of financing, ensures prompt collection of sales, having provision of multi-currency sales ledger, ledger against foreign exchange fluctuation, healthier customer portfolios and companies using factoring services have a better chance to compete in the increasingly competitive international markets. It is equally attractive for importers offering quality products, prompt delivery system with better credit terms.

9. Reserve Bank of India should permit big exporters having more than Rs. 5 crores of export transaction for currency option contracts other than banks and financial institutions. Financial liberalisation process must allow private corporate sector in foreign exchange markets both in India and abroad against export business. Cross-currency options and rupee based options for Indian exporters will broaden horizon of exports likes over-the-counter (OTC) market, such option exchange will run and manage through internal control system. Risk weighted and Disclosure requirements through bank instruments. The pricing of currency options are driven by: (a) variables like time to maturity, exercise prices and spot price of currency, (b) estimated variables

like future volatility of the currency. Rupee interest rate, foreign exchange rate, (c) Ledge is obtained through purchase of the currency in the spot market or in forward market. RBI and SEBI must allow export corporates to operate such currency option through bank and money markets.

10. 100% export oriented unit has been launched by Government of India since 1980. The policy need to be competitive in international markets, regarding quality of products, in time delivery with better credit terms revised in changing circumstances. The exim policy, RBI rules, industrial policy are liberalised and streamlined but custom and excise is unfortunately not synchronised. The budgets of 1994-95 and 1995-96 have made efforts in this direction. Exporters of all important items inclusive of exporters of spices should take advantage of this liberalised external sector policy of the Government of India.

Conclusion

Researches maintained that Indian export sector happens to be the next important factor after domestic demand in determination of industrial growth but in the case of income elasticity of demand for export of spices is noteworthy. The above stated action plan might be useful not only to boost exports of spices but also percolate to other commodities too. Massive efforts are necessary by the government and non-government agencies to reach the target of production and exports of spices in 2000 A.D. as stated for important 11 spices in Table No.3. For this, polarisation of south-Asian country is necessary for export business considering globalisation process and single market in Europe.

REFERENCES

1. Pendse, D.R.: "Export and Growth : The emerging prospect", *The Economic Times*, 5th Sept. 1992.
2. Attri, V.N.: "Industrialisation in India: An export-oriented approach," *The Indian Economic Journal*, Vol. 38 No. 3 Jan-March 1991.
3. P.N.B.: "Exports and Role of Banks," *Punjab National Bank Monthly Review*, July 1993.
4. Saxena, K.K.: "Emerging export markets: Latin America," *SBI Monthly Review*, Sept. 1993.
5. Kameshwar Rao K.: "Policy, problems and prospects of 100% Export-oriental unit growth" *SBI Monthly Review*, Oct. 1993.
6. Deolanker, G.H.: "Case for starting international factoring in India," *SBI Monthly Review*, October 1993.

7. Debroy, Bibek: "Agro-exports: blue print for Reforms" *The Economic Times*, 6th Sept. 1993.

8. Government of India: "Economic Reforms - Two years after and the task ahead", *SBI Monthly Review*, July 1993.

CASE STUDY NO. 2

A CASE STUDY ON MARKETING OF TEXTILE PRODUCTS

Introduction

Indian textile Industry is facing acute problems of costs, price, normal profit for survival all among private sector units as well as National Textile Corporation of state level textile development corporations' units. There are seven segments of Textile: Cotton Textiles, Woolen Textiles, Silk Textiles, Art Silk and Synthetic Fibres, Jute, Hemp, Mersa Textiles, Hosiery and Readymade Garments Sector.

Growth Pattern

It is very clear that the textile sector recorded a lower rate of growth than the overall industrial growth rate during 7th, 8th and 9th plan period. Productwise growth rate of textile industry indicate that the growth rate of cotton and non-cotton yarn was about 4.48% and that of the blended yarn about 8.47% during the last fifteen years. This period has shifted the market share from mill sector to powerloom sector in India.

Plan	Industrial Growth Rate	Growth Rate of Textile Sector
7th five-year plan	8.5%	4.2%
8th five-year plan	7.3%	5.3%
9th five-year plan	8.2%	7.0%

The above table reveals actual achieved rate of growth and estimates for the ninth plan. China and Soviet Russia are great competitors of India, in production, sales, low cost and export marketing in global markets. There are no major countries at global level engaged in production and marketing of their products these include, China, India, Russia, USA, Japan, Pakistan, Egypt, Turkey, South Korea and Hong Kong and others.

International Scenario

US textile sector is facing competition of Japanese textile exports. India is facing competition from China, Taiwan, South Korea, Hong Kong etc. Cross country scenario of production, distribution and marketing of the industry in major sectors of the industry. The emergence of WTO has opened up new and expanded markets. To encourage free trade of the goods of this sector, removal of tariff barriers is a most and the WTO has sought to reduce and remove import quotas over a period of ten years. WTO is also expected to boost Indian exports particularly of above stated textile sectors. Ceasing of protectionism is to be encouraged, free market forces will play a vital role to increase production to cater to rising global demand. Under Multi Fibre Agreement (MFA) made with USA, Canada, Australia, and countries of European Commission for marketing purpose, under the terms of Agreement 15-1-2004 existing 51% quota will come in open market and remaining 49% quota is to be abolished. There are immense opportunities before Indian textile exports in initial years of the 21st century. To takeover challenges of the market, India will have to update technology, prepare effectively to cope with market competition with China, Taiwan, Hong-kong, Japan etc. Textile sector occupies a very important place for output, employment and income generation apart from generation of exportable surplus for global markets. Corporate sector like Reliance, Century, Bombay Dyeing are dominating in export and marketing practices.

Issues related with International Marketing for Textile Sector

1. Removal of cotton ginning/pressing malpractices like watering of baled cotton for increase weight.
2. Proper selection of cotton for promising products in the markets. These include quality yarns, spinning premium yarn.
3. Choice of technology to cope with global markets, cost minimisation, with competitive products.
4. Machine designs and problem of technological obsolescence, dumping of machinery, mergers and modernisation.
5. Industrial sickness in the industry caused merger process to habilitate employees, The Cotton Textiles Companies Act posted in 1967 for winding up of units, rehabilitation of units, preparation of scheme for reconstruction, the textile modernisation fund scheme of IDBI, export orientation, energing saving, anti-pollution measures are taken for fuller utilisation of capacity.
6. Restructuring textile sector in the post reform period poses challenges. Some of the experts suggested to restructuring through new demand driven policies. By identifying consumer needs and segmenting the market accordingly, scientific studies to assess demands of products, exports, demand considering right market segment to the right type of the product.
7. Recession evaluation, dimensions and proper policies for survival of textile units.

8. Foreign exchange earning needs to increase both in dollar and rupee terms. Except jute products deceleration in foreign exchange earning was sharp in textile processing, synthetic fabrics, and other textiles, investory control; stock of raw material, average stock of finished goods.
9. Problem in export and import of raw cotton, as strong negative co-relation exists between export and import of the sectors.
10. Reports of Cotton Textile Ministry revealed declining trend in Cotton Textiles than with other group of industries. Gross profit to sales declined sharply from average 6.2% in 1951-61 to 5.7% in 1979-88, whereas, the figures in the case of other groups of industry, remained 9.2% and 9.3% during the period respectively.
11. There are financial problems like cash losses, rising trend of salaries and wages to the extent of 20% of the sales turnover, very high interest commitment of over 10% of sales, accumulated losses exceeding the entire networth. Operational problem like labour productivity is half of STTRA standards, production per spindle per shift less than 65.9 for 40% and spindle utilisation below 40%.
13. Diversification of design, ensuring quality output and technological growth at micro level become core issues.
14. Price policy on fabrics and cotton is not linked with the inflation indices and large amount of financial resources of bank, financial institutions and government are blocked in non-viable sick units.
15. Excessive government controls and heavy excise duties both by the state and the central governments.

Export projection for IXth five-year Plan:

Planning Commission has estimated export growth of textiles as given in the table.

Textile Sector	*1996-97 DGCI & S*	*(Rs. in million) RBI*	*2001-02*
1. Cotton Textiles	110365	113980	212194
2. Woolen Textiles	3553	3669	7254
3. Silk Textiles	4296	4436	4403
4. Art, Silk, Synthetic Fibres	25250	26076	59467
5. Jute, Hemp, Mersa Textiles	4582	4732	6364
6. Readymade Garments	132748	137095	249770

Source: Ninth Five-Year Plan 1997-2002 Vol. I April 1999

It can be seen from the table that export marketing of textiles will required special efforts to cope with global situation and environment of competition with other countries. Estimates of DGCI & S and the RBI for 1996-97 about growth of exports per capita availability of cotton cloth was 13.8 metre in 1960-61 which increased to 15.1 metre in 1990-91 and climbed up to 16.2 metre in 1996-97. At the end of Ninth five-year plan, it will reach to 18.6 metre. As again this, per capita availability of man made fabrics was 1.2 metre in 1960-61 which picked up to 11.7 metre in 1995-96 and 16.8 metre in 1999-2000. Level of living and expenditure pattern of people substantially affect rise in demand for total availability in India. Corporate sector plants can plan for marketable surplus and exportable surplus for overseas marketing. Fashion, design, technology and quality upgradation notably affect the local demand and export markets. Post-liberalisation from 1991-92 to 1998-99 proved a boom for Indian textiles sector as it achieved 24% rate of growth in total export earnings. However, export growth declined to 4.7% in 1997-98. For progressive global marketing product quality and cost efficiency appear absolutely necessary. The government of India launched Technology Mission and Technology Upgradation Fund to improve quality and possible reduction in cost of production.

A Case for Restructuring Textile Industry

1. For efficient marketing practices adequate and cheap concessional finance should be available to large, medium or small scale units in all segments of textiles.
2. 1985 textile policy aimd to encourage employement providing sectors like handlooms and powerlooms.
3. Number of closed textile units in Bombay Ahmedabad and in other cities are located in heart of cities where price of land rose very sharply. Land Ceiling Act should be lifted and land should be used for commercial complexes or residential purposes.
4. It is most necessary to reopen, restart economically viable sick and closed units.
5. All efforts should be made to organised the unorganised industry, centralise the decentralised sector. Formation of industry association must be encouraged to share infrastructure and modernisation expenses.
6. A number of computer aided deisgn centres have been opened all over India and scope for powerloom fabrics to compete in the international markets is rising.

7. Under the active leadership of Reliance, Garden Silk, Century and Bombay Dyeing marketing practices and marketing management need thorough changes not only for survival of a particular segment but also to market exportable surplus to be generated in the initial years of the 21st century.
8. Readymade garment exports need to be increased through export promotion houses.
9. Emphasis needs to made on man-made fibre products than that of traditional cotton items, as there is a large demand for synthetic fabrics, particularly polyster stapel fibre in world markets.

10. Macro-level and micro-level production, productivity and efficiency needs to be increase to cope with global market with viable survival of units moving towards sickness or are already sick.

Table No. 1

Exports of Raw Cotton, Textiles and RMG

(Rs. in crore)

Year	*Raw Cotton*	*%*	*Textiles*	*%*	*RMG*	*%*	*Total Exports*
1991-92	3.6	0.69	6148	14	5421	12	44041
1992-93	182	0.33	7509	14	6931	13	53688
1993-94	653	0.93	9013	13	8112	12	69749
1994-95	134	0.16	11963	14	10305	12	82673
1995-96	203	0.19	14500	14	12294	12	106353
1996-97	1574	1.32	17266	14	13324	11	11817
1997-98	840	0.66	18472	15	14.33	11	126285

Source: Centre for Monitoring Indian Economy As per 1998

Exports of Textile Yarn Fabrics and Man-Made Fabrics

(Rs. in crore)

Year	*Cotton*	*%*	*Man made*	*%*	*Total*
1991-92	3203	80	821	20	4024
1992-93	3911	78	1079	22	4990
1993-94	4821	78	1335	22	6156
1994-95	7014	78	1927	22	8941
1995-96	8619	77	2511	23	11130
1996-97	11082	82	2494	18	13576
1997-98	12093	81	2854	19	14947

Source: As per Table No. 1

Decision

Looking to both the tables, it appears that:

(1) There is a need for foreign direct investment to increase production as a strategy to encourage textile production and exportable surplus.

(2) Actual export figures and projected figures for ninth five-year plan reveals a vital scope for further export marketing in global markets.
(3) There are both the sides to export and import of textile yarn products in the textile sector, strategy is necessary to cut down imports in order to save foreign exchange.
(4) Export promotion councils related with textiles and handlooms are strengthened to meet future need of external sector.
(5) Modernisation of funding of machinery scheme (soft loan scheme) needs to be continued to fund textile sector.
(6) Phasing out of central and state excise burden on textile sector.
(7) Hunting for new overseas market for competitive global trading of textiles.

CAST STUDY NO. 3

A STUDY OF SOFTWARE BUSINESS DEVELOPMENT AND E-COMMERCE MARKETING

E-commerce or e-marketing all form of transactions executed over the electronic media. Business transactions are going through internet and fax-E-commerce contains e-marketing by the delivery of information on website for product and service marketing through the use of internet and World Wide Web. E-commerce is a tool to cut service costs and improve the quality of services. Thus, the form of e-commerce denotes commerce through a variety of electronic media. E-commerce wave has given birth to globalisation of trade by personal computers with a modem and a browser installed with connectivity to one of the internet service providers.

Computer technology affects a common, corporation of e-agent for marketing avenues commodity-wise, country-wise, region-wise at global level. There are three types of market place viz., those controlled by sellers, those controlled by buyers and those controlled by neutral third parties. The basic objective of market place is to create or retain value and market power in any transaction. The web being intrinsically interactive aids by Cisco system in providing value added services. E-commerce is changing a way of business is done one a global operation. E-commerce makes it possible to shop in Hong Kong, Sydney, New York, Paris in a matter of the seconds. The British Government realised it and the task force for I/T came into force in April 1999. The same is the case with European countries. As the internet market has suddenly come alive because of government's progressive steps which are finally unsnackled the dominant potential of this powerful technology to desired marketing strategy.

Selling on the net is also e-selling of goods and services on the internet Web servers provided shops for the visitors of web. Such shop environment,

Skill development in the industry depends upon thousands of software engineers and technically skilled people active in software, internet and web related services. They took leadership in overseas marketing of software products. Exports of the industries increased from Rs. 560 crore or $ 400 million in 1988-89 to Rs. 25,000 crores or $ 6 billion in 1998-99. As per NASSCom estimates, software business can be developed more than ten times looking at global shortage of software skilled people not only in USA but also in European countries.

The Government of India has implemental a task force for information technology. An important aspect like interference in marketing or facilitating information. National Internet is the backbone for accelerating the drive for setting up a world class info infrastructure with fibre optic network, wireless networks, to ensure a fast nation wide onset of Internet, Intranets and extranet. For this high speed telecom system need to be developed. PC penetration will play a vital role in software development business. The use of expected from 3 persons out of 1000 to one per 50 people along with universal access to Internet by the year 2008 in India with a flood of internet is application.

Table No.1 provides domestic activity and exports of software in 1998-99. Projects on hand were 36.5% in export sector than that of 28.55% domestic projects of Indian corporates for software companies. It is interesting to note that product and packages activity is highest for domestic sector whereas, export share is about 8% of total. National Association of Software Services Companies revealed that 203 out of the Fortune 1000 corporations, that is nearly two in five outsourced their software requirements from India, U.S. customers bought 61% of total software exported from India. India exported $ 2.6 billion or Rs. 10,940 crore of I/T software and services to 91 countries around the world. The marketing professional can developed this business globally. Graph No.1 given indicates that software domestic market increased from Rs. 200 crore in 1995-96 to about Rs. 70,000 crore in 1999-2000 with a steady rise and compound rate of growth. Similarly the second graph also indicates software exports increased from $ 300 million in 1995-96 to about $ 18,500 million in 1999-2000. E-governance include intelligent, smart, morally accountable responsive and efficient governance through transparent and positive policy of Government of India to boost e-business, e-marketing to cope with globalisation challenges.

Indian market parted ways with global trends and totally setting with ISDN and ADSL which are costly technology and telecom did little to promote faster growth of technology. The demand for modems necessarily for Internet connection and a growth 88.4% in 1999-2000. In 1998-99 turnover in value term Rs. 125.60 crore inspite of falling of modem prices in the market. 25,000 persons are employed in the sector in India and generated more than Rs. 1130 crore in revenue during 1998-99 in different activities of information technology.

Table 1
Trends in Software Activity (1998-99)

	Domestic		*Exports*	
	Rs. Million	*% of total*	*Rs. Million*	*% of total*
Projects	14,100	28.5	39,950	36.5
Professional service	2,500	5.0	48,300	44.1
Products and Packages	23,900	48.5	8,650	7.9
Training	2,300	4.5	1,880	1.7
Support and maintenance	2,000	4.0	4,650	4.3
IT enabled	4,700	9.5	5,970	5.5
Total	48,500	100.00	1,09,400	100.00

Source: The Hindu Survey of Indian Industry, 1999.

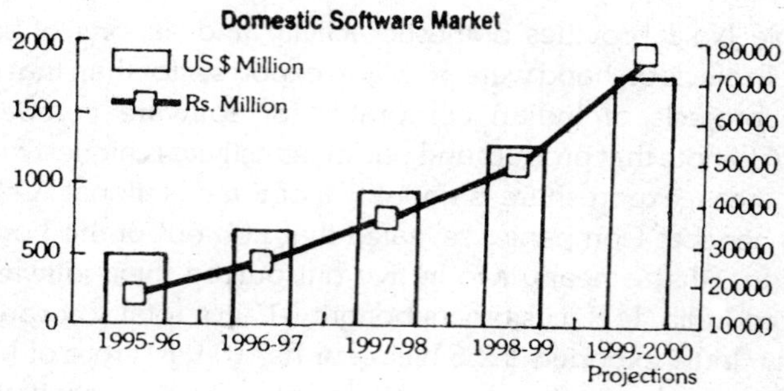

Fig. 1

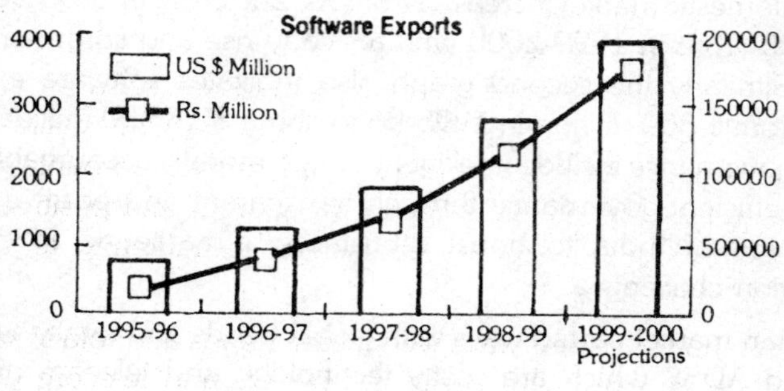

Fig. 2

Source: The Hindu Survey of Indian Industry, 1999.

Decisions for Marketing Practices:

1. Liberal and cheap internet and PC holding policy by the government by revolutionising the telecom system.
2. Fiscal incentives are necessary for the growth of software business which may lead to market capturing in western countries.
3. Venture capital to encourage young students, scientists, professionals with innovative ideas need to be promoted by angel capital, seed capital and venture capital culture to promote private sector business.
4. For promotion of localisation of software in local language for wider cross-section of Indian economy to make use of I/T technology.
5. Information Technology parks must be developed in all states of India or as per requirement of growth of the industry. For this cities like, Bangalore, Hyderabad, Pune made special efforts. There are cities like Vishakapatnam, Mysore, Ahmedabad, Gandhinagar, Baroda, Indore, Bombay, Burdwan, Jamshedpur, Lucknow having vast potentiality to develop the cities as information technology parks to cope with global marketing of software.
6. There is need for a policy for software-led growth and growth-led software development of the industry. Indian planners must follow the said both the strategy to cope with global demand, market and service expansion. This is the only industry which can make India as a debt free country through software and dotcom driven infotech industry in India.
7. The marketing for internet access burgeoned in unexpected by service providers which are increasing very fast. Internet via TV video cable.
8. Withdrawal of VSNL monopoly on internet access, Friendly telecom regime regulated by TRAI, and permission to cable TV operators to carry Internet traffic.
9. Development of e-business is most necessary in India than just building a website. Comprehensive strategy for e-business, customers services, dealer connectivity, sales force automation, purchasing or direct selling to customers.
10. There is a need to modify labour laws to support 24 hours work a day and constant 7 days a week for the operators.
11. Reduction by 50% of current prices charged for international leased circuits.

12. A vast infrastructure of training institutions both in public and private sectors for needy professionals to develop software to match with rapid growth of the industry.
13. Setting up of single window clearance system by Department of Telecom for entrepreneurs applying for telecom facilities with privatisation of internet connection.

CASE STUDY NO. 4

MARKETING OF ENGINEERING GOODS IN GLOBAL MARKET

Engineering goods and equipment play an important role to boost export market from India as they contributed 13% of total exports earnings during 1991-92 which increased to Rs.14,800 crore in 1996-97 recorded with 17% growth rate than previous year's performance. Then in 1998-99, the sector contributed 40% of total share in total export earnings during last liberalisation period. The share of western region for export increased from 3.6% in total exports of engineering goods in India in 1994-95 to 40% in 1998-99. This means engineering goods need rigorous efforts to capture western market through improved marketing practices. Engineering goods are treated as capital goods involve industrial plant and machineries for different group of industries. These include, machineries for textile, jute, knitting, sugar and chemical machineries, cement mill machines, food processing machinery, water treatment plants, construction machinery, crane, lifts and winches, earth moving equipments. Agricultural equipment, other industrial machineries, aircraft equipment, coastal vessels and machine tools. Moreover industrial fasteners, nut bolts, screw, railway track material, steel wire and wire products, ferrous holloware, steel pipes and tubes etc. are included in marketing of goods under the engineering industry.

Export marketing of engineering goods skyrocketed largely due to economic liberalisation, free import of technology, dynamic marketing strategy, international specifications to delivery schedules. Engineering sector contributed less than 10% in total export of the country in 1989-90 which climbed to 12.7% growth in 1996-97. The share of South-East Asian countries constitute 56% of total exports of engineering sector. USA tops the list of individual country markets. In 1996-97 engineering sector recorded an impressive growth of 11% in dollar terms over 1995-96, whereas overall growth rate of exports by the country was 4% Among the export marketing of engineering goods during past liberalisation period, capital goods had 34% share, then iron and steel products 35%, 8% non-ferrous metals and product thereof, consumer durables 22.5%, management consultancy services 45 to total export earning of the industry.

Engineering Export Lessons from Australia

During 1989-90, Australia received our export in engineering industry which formed 2% of total share of the industry in India. There was a cry about inappropriate marketing approach, poor finishing, packaging, uncompetitive pricing, delayed reponses and shipment problems gave a bad name to our engineering exports. There are three reason why Australia accepted our engineering exports in 1990.

(1) Both the governments decided to give a push to Indian exports; as to ignore an Australian $ 13 billion engineering goods market will be an exercise in self-delusion.

(2) Inspite of the presence of South-East Asian tigers and even China have established a large presence to boost their foreign exchange earnings.

(3) Australia is a very high quality conscious and competitive market that have marred our export performance highly relevant to our efforts to America and European countries. India can correct through proper action to increase its exports at least 10 fold in Australia. It is necessary to improve our show in OECD markets.

Australians can be made by a good chunk of auto-parts, pipes, tubes, diesel pumps, electric motors, aircraft components, consumer durables, electronic components, heavy earth moving equipment etc. It is unfortunate event that Indian exporters failed miserably in packaging and finishing. China offers machine tools superior to ours in finish that makes all the difference. In automobiles and heavy engineering products, the paints are of poor quality and drip over sealants and weldings that add to use comfort are absent. It is most necessary to pay attention by the exporters to 'cosmetise' for wider acceptability of our products which may ultimately lead to a decisive impact on the marketability of a product. Indian exporters are notoriously behind their competitors in terms of prices, packaging and quality of goods.

We had engineering industry exports only of Rs. 12 crore in 1961-62 to Rs. 408 in 1975-76 which recorded annual growth rate of 29.1%. Both capital heavy engineering goods and consumer durables increased their share to about 38% during the period. As against this, post liberalisation period also higher rating growth of Indian engineering exports which recorded 17.3% during 1991-92 to 1997-98. In amount, it increased to Rs. 14,800 in 1997-98.

According to data available during 1996-97, it is reported that there are Indian firms which have 36 collaboration with German firms, 39 with U.K. firms, 58 with Japanese firms, 28 with US firms and 7 collaboration with Italian firms in automotive components in automobile sector. India's market share in ELU autoparts and accessories market was 0.29% in 1992 which increased to 0.45% for items like brake drum, break shoes, mechanical hydraulic and pneumetic brass, brake assemblies, water pumps, starter of motors, alternators, distribution of caps, exhaust system of radiator, lighting system like head lamps, rear lamps, flasher lamps, cranckshaft, gear boxes etc. For three reasons such exports have not developed:

(1) Indian manufacturer or exporter cannot supply directly in large quantities they require.

(2) It is very difficult for any Indian firm to maintain a huge stock in the market to stick to "just-in-time." Indian manufacturer must convince European car or truck manufacturers about the quality standards and reliability of their products through the channel of prestigious export house or the main suppliers.

(3) Indian firms will have to deal professionally with multi-colour produce leaftlets distributed by Korea, Taiwan, Japan and Europe. Packaging of auto components and accessories with requirement if global standard appear necessary.

(4) Bigger companies in the field satisfy both the local and export markets in the product.

Industrial castings from India enjoy readymade market in Indonesia to their quality and reliability in performance in cement mills, agriculture machinery low and medium capacity tractors, power tillers, hand-operated implement besides our diesel engine and pumpsets.

Looking to globalisation of engineering goods and product markets, one gets an impression that the present level of exports is *much lower* than desired from the sector. Contribution of the large and medium-sized engineering units in the organised sector is rather small. Liberalisation has meant greater interaction with the global forces, competition and access to foreign technology, know-how and investment also. For this infrastructure for skilled and unskilled manpower appear necessary.

Decision for Marketing:

(1) India should glance through experiments and experiences of marketing of engineering products in global market.

(2) For diversification of engineering goods, it is most necessary to have diversification among segment of production of engineering goods and geographical area.

(3) A new manufacturer or marketer will have to check export price in relation with prevailing international prices of engineering goods and consumer durables.

(4) Attractive packaging, forwarding is necessary with due care in order to reach the goods to the ultimate consumers/users.

(5) Engineering export promotion council needs to encourage R & D in engineering goods for further promotion of exports of different segments of engineering goods.

(6) Entrepreneurs in Western Region of India contributed more than 40% of exports of engineering goods. They must be encouraged for exports of turnkey projects, high-tech products, managerial and consultancy services.

(7) Engineering goods and accessories should make use of services of big export house like Gazebo Industries Ltd. which received pretigious award for engineering goods industry.

(8) Indian engineering manufactures must receive big shot like ISO-9000 and similar other certification for sustainable growth of engineering manufactured goods, switch gear items, electrical land automobile accessories.

(9) Indian manufactures should have technical collaboration with Europe and Japanese companies to achieve competitive cost, quality and liaison for exports in global market.

CAST STUDY NO. 5

A CASE STUDY ON ETHICS AND RESPONSIBILITIES IN INTERNATIONAL MARKETING

This case study aims to know professional ethics and human responsibilities in international marketing, keeping in mind operation of multinationals in a developing country like India for this, an attempt is made here to know responsibilities and ethics of Union Carbide Corporation created in capital city of Bhopal in M.P. state of India. Most of the multinationals sell technology as a commodity for different industries and for different countries also. Chemicals and petro-chemical industries caused environment problems with regard to waste water pollution, solid waste and air pollution considering the gas leakage in Bhopal.

Bhopal plant of Union Carbide Corporation designated to produce hazardous chemicals and pesticides like Sevin and Termik. It is also producing methyl isocynate and alpha-napthan which may be very useful to chemical industry but most hazardous to human life in the case of an accident. The initial investment of the company was us $ 1 million which increased to $ 25 million in 1984. Urbanisation process and flow of migrated population increased in the city which gave a birth to three times higher rate of growth of population in Bhopal than rest of the country during 1971-81. Population increased from 3,85,000 in 1981 to 9,00,000 in 1984 which resulted in slums and squatter development with inflow of migrated labourers.

License was granted to the foreign company to manufacture, rather than mixing and packaging, up to 5000 tonnes per year of Sevin and Termik. The area where factory is located, the land was permitted for Sant Kanwer Ram housing colony near the place. The commissioner and director of country and town planning of that time objected the location of the plant but was ignored by company and local political leadership. Before occurrence of the accident NGOs also objected about environment created by the industry but was totally ignored by M.P. and central government as well as by the company. Employees and people who died on the spot and after some years were not fully covered under insurance as per international standards. As against this, rival companies like Dupont in Texas and Mitsubishi Chemicals took due weightage where they located their plants.

Regarding managerial aspect of the plant, in most of the cases technical staff trained in USA or Japan. Union Carbide plant was expected to train with Indian employees. Such a large company used services of American technicians and managers for a very short period of time. Before the year of accident, staff was reduced to 642 from 880 as a cost cutting device to cope with loss generated in previous year. It was difficult for management in removing excess staff except for serious infractions.

Considering growth of industries and environmental regulation, there were only 15 factory inspectors to inspect 8,000 plants in M.P. State. Each of them had to visit a quota of 400 factories within a year by public transport. No inspector suggested technical defect of operation of plant about gas leakage or otherwise MP Pollution Control Board had not taken any preventive measure or any notice pertaining to environment violation. At that time main activity of the board concentrated to deforestation and social forestry than that of active supervision of factories like Union Carbide. It was reported that safety devices which had become faulty several weeks earlier due to shortage of staff. It appears a case of total negligency not only on the part of the company but also to the government organisations engaged in environment, health and safety measures prior to the accident.

On 3rd December 1984, gas escaped from the safety valve of the plant. People saw presence of the toxic cloud and burning sensation in eyes, throat before being defected by the operator after two hours. Hundreds of villagers died in their make shift houses unable to leave their place immediately. Railway Station Master Harish Dhuney closed railway track and stopped railway traffic passing through the city inspite of incredible vision and burning of eyes and saved the life of travellers. The next day newspapers reported estimated death of 410 people due to gas leakage accident, 1,60,000 people admitted in hospitals. However, within a week, it was reported a death toll between 2000 to 5000 and hundreds of injured, blinded, aches in legs, lungs, hands and chests. It was reported about permanently disabled were about 60,000. A lot of pregnant women abortel prematurely and there were many cases of still born or malformed babies reported.

Death in Bhopal Gas Accident

Source of estimate	Estimate of death & injuries
1. Indian Government lawsuit filled in New York.	1754 dead, 200,000 injured
2. Public Relation Review 1991	more than 3,000 dead, 200,000 injured
3. Chemical Week Feb. 22,1989	3,300 dead 50,000 injured
4. Delhi Science Forum	5,000 dead, 2,50,000 injured
5. Voluntary organisations	3,000 to 10,000 dead, 3,00,000 injured
6. Number of shrous sold	10,000 death

Source: Various Newspapers and Magazines

Legal Actions

Chief Minister Arjun Singh arrested the Chairman of Union Carbide as he was visiting site of accident. Bhopal Airport Authority arrested him for corporate and criminal liability but released him after a few hours.

There was a debate among lawyers to file claim/criminal changes against the company whether in India or in America $ 15 billion suit of damages was filed in San Francisco in West Virginia court. The charges were about negligency of the company in its design and construction of the plant as a wishful default affecting safety of Bhopal residents. US court allowed victims to come forward and sue separately but there was no mandate from people of Bhopal as well as Government of India over 45 different federal law suits were filed and hundreds more in Indian courts against the company. Indian Government appointed its own lawyers to file a suit in Supreme Court for about $ 1 billion on behalf of all victims.

Here the question arises about international code of conduct of multinationals in the prevention of accident not only to pay claims in Indian rupees but post accident period caused many affected people's death or permanent disability to work. What is the kind of moral and ethical grounds of the company in underdeveloped country like India? The following issues emerging in this case study:

(1) Moral responsibility of business for production, moral responsibility of government employees those engaged in issuing of license, inspection, checking of environment, health and safety of the people.

(2) Need for pesticide production growth for agriculture sector was necessary at that time, but it is a fact that a country like America has established such hazardous chemicals plants on the level of underdeveloped countries on an intelligent device to export pollution and risk of life of people. What would have happened if the Bhopal plant of Union Carbide was established in Washington DC, New York or in any leading city of USA?

(3) Managerial actions have always protected interest of shareholders and a company as a whole than that of social responsibility of business — development of hazardous chemical business in third world country like India.

(4) Whether claim settlement would be in favour of such innocent uneducated people of Bhopal affected by the accident? We do not have insurance sector reforms along with industrial and financial sector reforms.

In the case of multinationals, it is necessary to have international level standard for insurance claim settlement. Death or disability of people should be treated equally by insurance companies both in the case of America or India for equal compensation by accident caused by multinational company.

It is the duty of business manager to produce manufacturing item within certain environment safety standards as demanded by the society. Here social values of business, social values of customers and social values of affected parties by the accident of the company are to be taken into consideration.

Keeping the issue in mind and other activities of multinationals, the Government of India has decided to keep a watch on marketing and manufacturing activities of the corporation. Large number of non-resident Indians abroad are asked to work in a new company set-up in India for direct sales. These companies include, Amway, Maykay, Avon, Tupprware developing their network in India. China has recently banned some of the activities of direct sales companies. A market insider says they are interested only in trading and lobbying than that of manufacturing commodities. Multinationals in India produced prohibited chemicals and pharmaceuticals which is banned in developed countries are considering their environment norms, which are comparatively strict in execution. Otherwise, they cannot enjoy low cost profit there.

Operation of Multinationals in India

The Economic Times Bureau revealed that Indian companies have performed poorly as they lost investors' confidences. Multinationals have not only succeeded in raising their stock prices but also have added to their investors base. It is interesting to note that, Indian companies and multinationals are working in the same Indian environment and similar economic and political conditions. Despite recession in India some of the multinationals maintained their profits. Indian companies are dealing with infrastructure, whereas, multinationals dealt with consumer goods and pharmaceuticals. They have better management control and prudent working capital. There are 30 Indian companies and 30 MNCs whose return on shareholders' fund measured as percentage of net profit to net worth which was 24.6% in the case of MNCs and 15% in the case of Indian companies. Some of the multinationals have succeeded in maintaining their profit growth even when the economy in general has faltered. They have a definite advantage compared with Indian companies.

Table given on the next page provides aggregate return on shareholders fund. MNCs distributed nearly 55% of their net profit to the shareholders in terms of dividend in 1997-98 which increased from 40% in the previous year. Multinationals distributed fair dividends to their 51% shareholders who are foreign equity holders. Multinationals companies like Proctor & Gramble, Reckitt and Colman, Smith Beechams registered macro growth in net worth and rate of equity dividend in percentage.

Return on net worth (profit after tax as percentage of net worth remained higher in the cases of Carrier Aircon, Castrol, Hind Lever, Colgate Palmolive, Park Davis, whereas in the case of Bata, Madura Coats, SKF Bearings, BASF remained considerably low.

Share capital as percentage of dividend in the profit was higher in the cases of Hind Lever, Castrol, ICI, Colgate Palmolive, Recktitf and Colman Avery India.

It appears that better financial performance or higher dividend yield apart, the sudden change in the policy of foreign institutional investors helped multinational scrips to out perform the market. Information system of multinationals is superior to local corporates in India to gain advantage of the market situation.

Decision for Marketing

(1) To identify areas and commodities for multinational corporations in India.

(2) India can develop trade through multinationals provided there is code of conduct for equity participation, repatriation of profit, take back profit in home country in foreign exchange, reinvestment of profit guidelines etc.

(3) Globalisation will bring uneven growth, strong multinationals will become stronger and can develop regime for trade.

(4) Emerging market economy like India will have to depend upon multinationals where specific time should be decided for operation.

(5) For fair competition in Indian insurance market, there is a need for joint ventures for insurance sector reform in India.

(6) Commodities like preventive medicine, drugs and pharmaceuticals are areas where they can manufacture or develop a skill for manufacturing in India.

(7) For consumers goods which can be produced and distributed by even small scale units of India we need a vital policy to protect infant industries.

(8) They are charging for technology transfer discriminately from country to country, commodity to commodity. For this, they should follow recommendations of Brandt Commission (1976) and Pearson Commission (1977) for a third world country like India.

(9) They should be stopped in activities like exploitation of labourers, creation of adverse environment for manufacturing of drugs, pesticides and other hazardous chemicals.

(10) Need-based approach should be followed for items, commodities and area of operation for them.

21

DOCUMENTS USED IN SHIPMENT OF GOODS

Introduction

At the outset it must be mentioned that improved system of documentation for exports announced by the Government of India on 31 March, 1991 is fine and should be adopted by the exporters as far as possible. However, a word of caution would be in order. To date we have arrangements with only 80 countries around the world where UN Key Layout (Master Documents) are followed. With these countries Indian exporter could jolly well use the improved version of documents announced by the Government of India as per the New Exim policy 1992-97.

For the remaining countries (other than 80 countries where UN Key Layout (Master Documents) is not in use, the Indian exporter has to ascertain from the importer of his requirements and must comply to his dictates for documentation. The basic dictum for the exporter is "comply 100% the Letter of Credit requirements for Documentation", otherwise exporter could be in problem and his payment may be stopped. Moreover, exporter prepares export documents not for his own convenience but largely to meet the requirements of the overseas importer who largely conveys it through Letter of Credit. Treatment in this chapter is, therefore, slightly exhaustive of documents where the old requirements have also been kept in view while introducing master documents.

Export documentation work constitutes a heavy charge on our export activity. It is complex, cumbersome and costly. This is partly due to the nature of export trade itself involving, as it does, a number of intermediary organisations and authorities at different stages of export activity between the seller and the buyer. All these, in turn, generate a lot of paperwork and procedural formalities. The documents material to an export sales contract are not many in number. However, the problem is complicated due to the heavy paperwork and the procedural formalities which are required to be complied with before the essential documents can be procured.

The procedural and documentary formalities associated with exports have been evolved and practised over the years by different authorities/organisations to suit their own convenience without much regard to the repercussions they might have on the total export activity. The resultant mass of paperwork caused much inconvenience and inordinately long delay in the movement of goods. There was a need for a total approach to the problem. This meant evolving not only simpler export documents and procedures in each of the individual areas of export activity but also ensuring their compatibility and harmony in the totality of export operation.

Notwithstanding the need for such an approach to the procedure-generated problems, it has been appreciated that the task of procedural simplification is a continuing and long-term one requiring, in some cases, prior amendment of the statutes, policies and regulations they stem from. One of the ways in which this has been done is through the use of standardized documents in our export trade.

The documents used differed in size and layout, despite the fact that most of the information requirements are common to a number of them. Because of the difference in their sizes and designs, these documents had to be completed individually. This method of preparation of documents was susceptible to errors and discrepancies which, even though minor, caused delays at different stages in the processing of documents, costly hold up of consignments at checkpoints and terminals, and ultimately in the realization of export proceeds.

Master Documents

All these problems of late have been avoided by following a system which provides an alternative to the repetitive, unproductive and time consuming work necessitated by the exporters' compulsion to prepare separately a number of documents, all containing practically the same information. This system is known as the 'Aligned Documentation System'. Already in use in a number of countries, this system is reported to have made for simplicity, convenience, speed, accuracy and economy in documentation work.

United Nations key Layout has made it possible to many countries to reproduce in 'one run' the repetitive information on all the export documents from just one document called the 'Master Document'. As a result, exporters in these countries have been able to reduce the documentation costs by 50 to 70%.

The introduction of simplified export documents has reduced the burden of the exporters and has given a push to the country's ongoing export drive. The exporters now can save atleast 50% of the time and cost on documentation. It will thus help in expediting decision-making process, virtually eliminate the chances of errors and facilitate electronic transmission of export documentation and data. Therefore simplification of export documentation and procedures are key measures to promote exports.

Earlier Indian exporters were required to submit 25 documents to various agencies and authorities merely to ship the goods. Each document had to be individually prepared. The new system standardised these documents and aligned them to each other on the basis of the United Nations Key Layout which has already been adopted by most of India's trading partners. Thus now instead of typing out 25 documents, exporters prepares only two master documents.

The new system also includes simplification and relaxation of related procedures, which will further reduce the delays and time component currently involved in export effort. It is expected that as a fallout of the introduction of the new system, a self-propelling process towards further rationalisation of documentation and procedural requirements would get in motion in all the conceived organisations. And at the end of it, the exporter should be able to spend his resources and energy more on export production and marketing than on meeting the demands of archaic export procedures.

In the new set-up, attempts have been made, first to standardise and simplify each document and secondly to align them to each other using as far as possible the UN Key Layout. These aligned documents are in tune with the proforma used by countries with whom more than 80% of India's foreign trade is transacted.

The two master documents — one for commercial use and the other for regulatory documents meant for customs, RBI and port trust — have maximum advantage of alignment and minimum cost and time for preparing individual documents.

The two-master documents contain all the information that was common to individual documents. Earlier, there were a plethora of commercial documents, which include among others, invoice, packing list, intimation for inspection, insurance declaration form, shipment advice and the exchange control declaration form.

The system has provided for change in some of the earlier procedures for submission and preparation of documents by various agencies. The system envisages that the export inspection agencies, insurance companies, export promotion councils, chambers of commerce, federation of Indian export organizations, shipping companies, freight forwarders and banks would provide the exporters blank forms of their respective documents to facilitate their preparation at one stage. As a result, now the certificates for various purposes can be issued virtually across the counter, without the exporter having to pay repeated visits and waste time.

Considerable simplification of RBI and customs procedures have taken place. Under the new procedure, numerous port trust documents have been replaced by one form. It also stipulates adoption of uniform practices by all respective port trust authorities, including a procedure for collection of all port charges at one point instead of at multiple points as used to be earlier.

Simplification of pre-shipment documentation is only the first step. The post-shipment documentation and numerous procedures connected with clearance of import and export goods, inspection, warehousing in bound operations, road haulage of import/export goods, operations at ICS's and CF's are also important areas which call for rationalisation and simplification in keeping with the recognised international practices. Coordinated efforts towards this broader objective will be pursued by the Commerce Ministry in the coming months.

It is proposed to conduct training and orientation programmes at all export centres to familiarise the exporting community with the new system.

The Government of India, therefore, identified some export documents for standardization with the help of the concerned official and commercial interests in the country. The documents taken up for standardization include: Invoice, Certificate of Origin, Packing List, Bill of Lading, Mate's Receipt, Shipping Order, Shipping Bill, Port Trust Document, Insurance Declaration Form and Certificate of Insurance. Different forms in respect of each of these documents used in the country were examined from the point of view of standardization and putting them into an aligned system. In preparing these standard documents, the UN Key Layout has been followed. The common items of information appearing in each of these documents were recorded to develop a common denominator — a master document — from which the repetitive information could be reproduced in one run on all the documents, leaving only the information specific to individual documents to be filled in separately. Any information on the master document which is not required on a particular document can be omitted by different masking techniques at the reproduction stage.

The System

Thus, the one-run method of preparation of documents involves the use of standardized and aligned documents. A standard document means that different forms in respect of a document presently used by different exporters, agencies and bodies are printed on the same size of paper with identical layout and design. Alignment means that all the documents included in a series are prepared on a standard size of paper and so designed in relation to one another that the common items of information occupy the same relative position on each of these documents. This makes it possible to derive a master document recording the information common to all the documents included in the aligned series, and to reproduce the necessary information on each of the documents from the same master document by employing suitable reproduction techniques.

Documents which are of immediate interest to exporters have been included in this chapter. Once a basic aligned set of this nature has been established, individual users might find it convenient to add other documents to their own series. Other documents which can conveniently be brought within the fold of this system include the Shipping Instruction Form for forwarding agents, Export Order Forms, Acknowledgement Forms, Instructions to Suppliers, etc.

Advantages

The one-run method of reproduction of documents from a common master has a number of advantages. These can be summed up in one word: efficiency. The whole set of documents included in the aligned series can be reproduced with economy, speed, accuracy and convenience. Since the documents included in the series are the offspring of one master document, only one document, *i.e.,* the master, has to be the typed, checked and corrected. Accuracy of all other documents derived from it is automatically ensured. Besides, checking and processing of documents at different stages are also facilitated because the documents are prepared on the same size of paper with common items of information occupying the same relative position on the respective documents. Additional savings can also be obtained if exporters and others can align and produce their internal documents in the same way.

Typing the Master Document

Most typewriters can be used to complete the master document satisfactorily. Ten to twelve characters per inch is common to most manual typewriters available in the country. For better results, the electric/electronic typewriter may be used, as it offers the benefit of clearer print and speed.

On the master document, each item of information must be typed clearly and very concisely within the confines of its own box. Otherwise, the reproduction of any typed information overflowing its own box will be cut off at the masking stage.

Duplicating Methods

After the master document has been typed, the other documents can be reproduced conveniently by using different reproduction techniques. As these vary considerably in cost and benefits, the choice of the technique by an individual firm will obviously depend on the volume and the frequency of export business.

Standardized Documents

The standard documents included in the aligned series which this chapter presents are the Invoice, Packing List, Certificate of Origin, Bill of Lading, Shipping Order, Mate's Receipt, Shipping Bill, Port Trust Document, Marine Insurance Declaration Form and Marine Insurance Certificate. Each of these documents can be reproduced from the same master by using the relevant mask. Reproduced signatures on individual documents may indeed present some problem. Until an agreement is reached among all concerned as to their acceptability, it would be necessary to mask the signature column also on the master and to sign the individual documents manually. Besides, as all the copies of the reproduced documents, particularly where the spirit duplicator is used, will have the same impression, it will be difficult to distinguish the original from the copies of the document. This is, however, not a serious problem and can be solved by a universal understanding that unless 'COPY' is marked, the document will be treated as original. It is no doubt convenient to give the dates on the documents in the numeric way. In doing so, however, the exporter should ensure that such dates will be interpreted abroad in the same way as they are interpreted by them. To avoid ambiguity, it would be better to express the date of the month in two figures, followed by the name of the month in three letters and the year in four figures.

A. PRINCIPAL DOCUMENTS

Export Invoice

Invoice is a document of contents. It is the exporter's bill for goods and sets forth the terms of sale. The invoice is a basic document. As a document of contents it must fully identify the overseas shipment and serve as a basis for the preparation of all other documents which in greater or lesser detail reproduce information from it. The exporter should strictly follow the requirements of the importer in regard to invoicing. The standard document in respect of the invoice is based on the United Nations Key Layout which has been accepted as the basis of this document in many countries. The information requirements of the document have been determined after examining a number of forms of invoices used by leading export organizations and after a series of discussions with the representatives of the Department of Customs and Central Excise and the Federation of Custom House Agents' Associations in India. Invoices based on the suggested design will be acceptable not only in many countries but will also help facilitate processing of documents at various stages. The 'Declaration' given at the bottom (left hand) of the Invoice follows the UN recommendation. The Standard Invoice can be reproduced from the master by masking only three columns, *i.e.* Notify Party, Insured Value and No. of Original Bs/L. Sometimes, exporters may be required to give some information like the name of the shipping line, expected time of departure of the ship from the port of shipment, expected time of arrival of the ship at the destination port and B/L No. and Date on the invoices. But, under the present procedure for customs clearance and shipment of export cargo, this information, particularly in respect of the B/L No. and Date, will be available to exporters only after shipment has been effected. Where required under letters of credit, such information will need to be included in the invoices at the time of submission of documents to the banks for negotiation. But for this, the rest of the information can be reproduced from the master. The information referred to in the preceding lines can be given above the columns for Country of Origin and Final Destination in the order of name of shipping line, ETD (port of shipment), ETA (destination port) and B/L No. and Date. Unused space, in the Buyer's column and below the Consignee's column, can be utilised for incorporation of any other information which may be special to a transaction. Value and Origin Clauses can be printed on the back side of the Standard Invoice.

There may be cases when exporters are required to give detailed descriptions or specifications of the various items forming part of the consignment exported in one lot. In such cases, exporters are advised to use 'Continuation Sheets' to the Invoice.

Consular Invoice

This is also known as Certified Invoice. The importer might require the invoice to be certified by the consulate of his country stationed in the exporter's country. Consular Invoice facilitates clearing of the goods through the customs at their destination and also serves as authentification of the particulars it sets out. Charges of certification may vary from country to country. Some of the country have prescribed the form *e.g.,* Philippines.

Packing List

This may be shown on invoice, or separately, and should contain item by item, the contents of cases or containers or of a shipment with its weight and description set forth in such a manner as to permit checks of the contents by the customs on arrival at the port of destination as well as by the recipient.

The Packing List is a relatively simpler document and the whole of the information can be reproduced from the master by masking information not desired on the Packing List. Special information, if any, can be given in the blank space in the lower third portion of the document.

Certificate of Origin

This certificate certifies the place of origin of the merchandise. Besides the Federation of Indian Chambers of Commerce and Industry, EPCs and various other trade associations have been authorised by Government of India to issue certificates of origin. These certificates are important in the case of shipments to countries which have preferential rates of tariff for Indian goods.

Certificates of Origin are issued by chambers of commerce on their own printed forms differing in sizes and layout. The standard document in respect of the Certificate of Origin included in the series of aligned documents in this chapter has been prepared after taking into consideration the requirements of the different certificates of origin issued by the different chambers of commerce in the country. It is suggested that all chambers of commerce should follow this pattern and make available printed forms of their respective certificates of origin to exporters so that the necessary information could be reproduced from the master at the reproduction stage. The exporter will complete the 'Declaration' after shipment as given at the bottom (right hand) of the document and present it for certification at the office of the chamber of commerce.

Bills of Lading

A bill of lading is a document issued and signed by a shipping company or its agents acknowledging that the goods mentioned in the bill of lading have been duly received for shipment, or shipped on board a vessel, and undertaking to deliver the goods in the like order and condition as received, to the consignee, or his order or assignee, provided that freight and other charges specified in the bill of lading have been duly paid.

Bill of lading serves the following purposes:

(i) It is receipt for goods received by the shipment company;

(ii) *A Contract With the Carrier.* It contains the terms of the contract between the shipper and the shipping company, between stated points at a specific charge; and

(iii) *Evidence of Title.* It is a certificate of ownership or title to the goods.

For the bill of lading to be negotiable, in fact, three requirements must be fulfilled:

(*a*) It must be made out to the order to the shipper.

(*b*) It must be signed by the steamship company.

(*c*) It must be endorsed in blank by the shipper.

Endorsement on Bill of Lading

By practice and custom the bill of lading has been transferable. If, however, the bill requires the goods to be delivered to a particular named person and does not include a reference to his assignees, the bill of lading is not transferable. It is only rarely that a bill of lading would be drawn this way.

The consignee or consignor, as the case may be, can transfer the B/L either by a special endorsement, *i.e.,* an endorsement which names the transferee to whom delivery is to be made or by an endorsement in blank (*i.e.,* not naming an endorsee). In the latter case, the goods are deliverable to the bearer. The holder may, however, convert the blank endorsement into a special endorsement by inserting the name of a person to whom delivery is to be made. It is then called the "endorsement in full".

Sending of Bill of Lading to Importer

B/L are made out in sets and any number of copies may constitute the set according to the requirements of the particular transaction and the importer. The number of copies to be made out will be indicated by the importer before the shipment takes place. In case there is no such indication, normally two copies of the B/L are prepared together with a number of the non-negotiable copies. One set of documents is sent by the first class air-mail and the second by the following mail, so that if one is lost, delivery of the goods can be taken by the importer on the basis of the second set.

TYPES OF BILLS OF LADING

(1) Stale B/L

A B/L that has been held too long before it is passed on to banks or consignees, is termed as "Stale B/L". Therefore a B/L should be presented to the negotiating or collecting bank soon after it is issued by the shipping company, so that it is made available to the overseas importer before the ship carrying the goods arrives, to avoid fines and other inconveniences. If this cannot be done, the banks will consider the bill of lading as stale.

(2) Clean Vs Claused B/L

As an acceptable receipt, the B/L must be a clean one. This means no adverse notation of any kind must appear on the B/L in regard to apparent order and conditions of goods or packing, etc.

When cases or packages of a shipment are not received in first class condition, the steamship agent, in order to avoid possible claims against the shipping company, notes this fact on the B/L. B/L bearing such notations are referred to as "Claused B/L". The terms of "foul bills", "unclean" and "dirty" bills of lading are sometimes, though not generally, used. Because the exporters are responsible to the importer for shipping goods in first class condition and in tight case of package, they make every effort to avoid receiving "Claused B/L". A clean B/L is always insisted upon by the importer. If damage claims arise when "claused B/L" have been issued, the consignor is practically bound to make good the damage. B/L must bear the requisite stamps. The shipping company calculates freight on the basis of the measurement or weight whichever is higher.

The design for the bill of lading is based on the Standard Bill of Lading recommended by the International Chamber of Shipping. A number of shipping lines in India's overseas trade are already issuing bills of lading on the ISO A4 size paper. However, in some cases, these bills of lading are based on the old pattern. The Standard Bill of Lading included in the aligned series can be reproduced from the master by using the relevant mask. Blank forms of bills of lading are supplied by shipping companies to shippers who prepare these documents and present them for signature at the shipping company's office. This document is exchanged for the mate's receipt which is issued to the shipper by the Chief Officer of the ship through the port trust. While preparing "To Order Bills of Lading', care should be taken to mask the Consignee box also. The words 'Unto Order' may be typed in the Consignee box and the name and address of the Consignee given in the box for the Notify Party. The other details on the bill of lading will be completed by the office of the shipping company before the document is signed and handed over to the shipper in exchange for the mate's receipt.

Shipping Order and Mate's Receipt: When the cargo is loaded on the ship, the commanding officer of the ship will issue a receipt called the "mate receipt" for goods. The mate receipt is first handed over to the port trust authorities that all port dues are paid by the exporter to the port trust. After making payment of all port dues, the merchant or the agent will collect the mate receipt from the port trust. The bill of lading is prepared by the shipping agent only after the mate receipt has been obtained.

The aligned Shipping Order and the Mate's Receipt have been prepared after examining the forms of the two documents issued by different shipping companies. The information required in these documents can be reproduced with great ease from the master. The issuance of these documents in the standard form will also facilitate the processing of documents at various stages, particularly at ports where exporters are required to submit shipping orders along with other documents to the port trust's office, as also the customs certification on various other documents on the basis of the mate's receipt. In order, however, that the shipping order and the mate's receipt can be reproduced from the master, blank forms of these documents will need to be made available to exporters by the shipping lines.

Under the present commercial practice with regard to the issuance of the mate's receipt, this document was prepared by the ship's staff and signed by the chief officer of the ship after goods are loaded on board. This document was required to be exchanged immediately for the shipping company's bill of lading duly signed by an authorised officer of the company. With the inclusion of the mate's receipt in the aligned series of documents, it would be possible to roll it off the master at the reproduction stage and keep it ready for signature by the ship's chief officer after the consignment is shipped. This will considerably reduce the time and money involved in the preparation of this document, but will require the blank standard forms of the document to be made available to the shippers. If for some reasons it is not possible to do so, it is suggested that the shipping lines operating in India's overseas trade should issue the mate's receipt in the standard form for this document.

Shipping Bill

Shipping bill is required by the customs. It is only after the shipping bill is stamped by the customs that cargo is allowed to be carted to the docks. The aligned shipping bill has been prepared after taking into consideration the requirement of the Custom's Public Notice No. 39 which suggests a uniform shipping bill for different categories of exports, viz. Free Goods, Dutiable Goods and Goods under Claim for Drawback. As the standard A4 size paper defies accommodation of all the information requirements as per this Public Notice, some columns for duty/cess and drawback particulars have been printed on the back of the standard shipping bill. It is also not possible to accommodate all the declarations as per the Public Notice. Care has, however, been taken to incorporate those declarations which are material to exporting goods and claiming duty drawback. Other declarations which have not been included in the standard shipping bill can be taken as implied. In fact, these have never formed part of the declarations on the shipping bills currently in use. The name and address of the Custom House Agent as also the CHA Code No. can be printed in the boxes provided for the purpose. To facilitate identification and processing of different categories of shipping bills, it will be desirable to introduce a uniform colour scheme at all ports. Identification will be easier and quicker if the different categories of shipping bills can be distinguished by the colour of the forms rather than by the colour of the letter print on the shipping bills.

Bill of Entry

The importer fills up Bill of Entry with reference to relevant documents in his possession. It is on the basis of value of imported goods as mentioned by the importer in the Bill of Entry and as appraised by the customs official that amount of import duty, if any, payable by the importer is calculated. Besides other particulars the Bill of Entry contains Line Number and Rotation Number. The Customs Official after comparing the particulars of goods as mentioned in the Bill of Entry with those in the Import Manifest passes the same to the Appraiser. The Appraiser is an officer whose duty is to calculate the rate at which duty is payable by the importer. To verify the correctness of the particulars of goods mentioned by the importer in the Bill of Entry, packages of goods imported are physically checked by an officer. Thereafter the importer shall pay the import duty and the cash counter. Thereafter a Gate Pass is to be procured and it now becomes easy for the importer to obtain delivery of imported article. It may so happen that the importer is either not in a position to pay the customs duty immediately or does not like to lock up his capital that way. With a view to extending facilities to these importers, bonded warehouses are established and managed under the supervision of the Customs. The importer may warehouse his goods in bonded warehouses and obtain piecemeal delivery by paying proportionate amount of duty.

Bill of entry is drawn in triplicate. It attests the fact that goods of specified quantity, value and description are entering the bounds of the country. Separate forms of the Bill of Entry are used for each one of the three classes of goods: (*i*) free goods which are exempted from customs duty, (*ii*) goods for home consumption, and (*iii*) bonded goods.

Port Trust Documents

Dock Challan/Export Application/ Port Trust Copy of Shipping Bill

Port trusts in India have prescribed their own documents for payment of port charges and handling shipments through their respective ports. Differing widely in sizes and layout, these documents are known differently at different ports, *e.g.,* Dock Challan at Calcutta, Export Application in Madras and Cochin and Port Trust Copy of Shipping Bill at Bombay. As all these documents essentially serve the same purpose, the introduction of a standard and uniform document for all ports, preferably with the same name (say 'Shipping Note'), will go a long way towards facilitating trade and reducing the cost involved in printing different sizes of documents for different ports. The aligned Port Trust Document has been prepared after taking into consideration the information requirements of the port trust documents of some of the major ports in the country. Information regarding receipt and shipment of cargo and also payment of port charges can be recorded on the reverse of the document.

Marine Insurance Declaration Form and Marine Insurance Certificate/Policy

The Standard Marine Insurance Declaration and the Marine Insurance Certificate included in this chapter are based on the format approved by Lloyd's and The Institute of London Underwriters. It is suggested that open cover/policy holders may be supplied with blank forms of these documents. These can be reproduced from the master and then sent to the appropriate office of the General Insurance Corporation. The Insurance Certificates policy can be issued after completion of necessary entries and certification by the Corporation.

BILL OF EXCHANGE (B/E)

One of the common methods of payment in international trade involves the use of bill of exchange ((B/E), also known as drafts, provide documentary evidence of obligation and the financial risk of the transaction is more widely spread.

Foreign B/E are drawn by the exporter, calling upon the importer to pay or to accept a designated sum of money at a determinable future time. Acceptance consists of an acknowledgement to this effect written across the face of the B/E and signed by the drawee (importer), obligating the importer to provide payment of the amount stated within the period of time designated. When accepted, a draft becomes a trade acceptance. The method of payment provides the documentary evidence of obligation that is readily transferable.

A draft drawn without collateral documents attached is known as a clean draft, while one with certain stipulated documents of shipment, insurance, etc., is known as a documentary bill. In export marketing, it is the documentary bill that is employed most commonly.

There are three parties to B/E (See figure below)

(*a*) *The Drawer (Exporter).* The person who executes the B/E, therefore, the person to whom payment is due (Exporter B.S. Rathor).

(*b*) *The Drawee (Importer).* The person on whom the B/E is drawn and who is required to meet the terms of the document (Importer, John Marshall).

(*c*) *The Payee (Exporter or Exporter's Bank).* The party to receive the payment (State Bank of India).

Figure

FOREIGN BILL OF EXCHANGE

$

1,00,000 June 22, 1992

Ninety days after sight pay to the order of State Bank of India one hundred thousand dollars value received and charge to account of

To

John Marshall
Marshall Field & Co., B. S. Rathor.
3140, Down Town, Partner
Chicago (USA) Kay Sons

When trade bills or drafts are drawn in international trade, the exporter may dispose of them by discounting, by borrowing, or by placing them for collection. The accepted draft can be discounted or sold to a bank, or an advance or loan may be obtained from a bank, using the accepted draft and collateral documents as security. If the exporter is not seeking to discount or to borrow on a draft, the draft and all documents attached are sent to the bank with instructions to send them abroad for collection.

The draft method of payment, as has been pointed out, places the final responsibility upon the exporter, as the exporter is subject to recourse until the drawee has paid. Therefore, the necessity for securing adequate credit data on the drawee is apparent. In addition, the exporter runs the risk that the importer may reject the merchandise. In this case the importer will not accept the draft and the exporter is faced with the problem of disposing of the merchandise by forced sale abroad, storage, shipment to another country, or bringing the merchandise back to the home country.

Annexures Needed Under FERA

(*a*) *GR-I Form.* In pursuance of the provisions of FERA and the rules framed thereunder, every exporter has to satisfy the Reserve Bank of India about receipt of the foreign exchange in respect of exports. The Act makes it obligatory on every exporter to complete GR-I in respect of the shipment and submit its copies at the port of shipment and to the authorised dealers in foreign exchanges through whom the bills or documents covering the shipment are negotiated.

GR-I has to be prepared in triplicate. The exporter should submit the original copy to the customs authorities at the port of shipment and the authorised dealers in foreign exchanges through whom the bills or documents covering the shipment are negotiated.

GR-I has to be prepared in triplicate. The exporter should submit the original copy to the customs authorities at the port of shipment. The duplicate and triplicate copies should be lodged with the authorised dealer through whom the proceeds of exports will be realised.

(*b*) *GR-3 Form.* These are used when exporters have obtained permission from the RBI to retain the proceeds of their exports with agents abroad and to utilise those proceeds for financing their imports into India.

(*c*) *PP Form.* Exports to all countries by parcel post, except when made on "value payable" or "cash on delivery" basis should be declared on PP Forms.

(*d*) *EP Form.* Shipments to Afghanistan and Pakistan other than by post should be declared on EP forms.

(*e*) *EP-I Form.* Exporters who have been permitted to retain the proceeds of their exports to Afghanistan with their agents or branches in that country and to utilise those funds to finance their import from that country or to make other approved types of payments, may declare their exports to Afghanistan, otherwise than by post, on EP-I forms.

(*f*) *VO/COD Form.* Exports to all countries by parcel post under arrangements to realise the proceeds through postal channels on "Value payable" or "Cash on delivery" is required to be completed on VO/COD Form and it should be submitted to the postal authorities along with the parcel at the time of despatch thereof.

B. AUXILIARY DOCUMENTS

(1) Letter of Credit

It is a written instrument issued by the buyer's bank, authorising the seller to draw in accordance with certain terms and stipulating in a legal form that all such bills (drafts) will be honoured.

The letter of credit is a means of payment that provides the exporter with more security than open accounts or bills of exchange. A commercial letter of credit is issued by a bank at the request of a buyer of merchandise whereby the bank itself undertakes to honour drafts drawn upon it by the seller of the merchandise concerned. Thus, the letter of credit substitutes the bank's promise to pay for that of the importer. Before the seller can receive payment, however, all the requirements specified in the letter of credit must be met, including the furnishing of documents, delivery dates, product specification, etc.

There are three essential parties to a commercial letter of credit:

1. The opener or importer — the buyer who opens the credit.
2. The issuer — the bank that issues the letter of credit.

3. The beneficiary — the seller in whose favour the credit is opened.

In practice, however, there may be additional parties introduced in order to perform certain necessary functions. The confirming bank is a bank in the beneficiary's country which, at the request of the beneficiary, guarantees the payment and/or acceptance of the seller's draft. The advising bank, located in the beneficiary's country, notifies the seller of the opening of the credit. The advising and confirming banks may be the same. The paying or accepting banks is the one on which the drafts are to be drawn.

Types of Letters of Credit

Letters of credit are of various types to fit differing conditions. Therefore, the exporter should carefully scrutinize them to determine the responsibilities of the parties.

(*a*) Letters of credit may be either *revocable or irrevocable.* The privilege of revocability refers to the right of the issuing bank to revoke its promise to honour drafts drawn upon it. When the letter is revocable, the issuer can cancel or change an obligation at any time prior to payment. Revocable payments are not legally binding undertakings between banks and beneficiaries. When the letter is irrevocable, the issuer agrees not to cancel or modify the credit without the permission of the beneficiary.

(*b*) In addition, the letter of credit may be either *confirmed or unconfirmed.* If the letter of credit is confirmed, the irrevocable obligation of the issuer is guaranteed by a confirming bank in the beneficiary's country. Thus, in a confirmed letter of credit, payment is guaranteed by both the issuing and the confirming bank. An exporter may seek confirmation because of dissatisfaction with the security offered by the issuing foreign bank.

(*c*) *With Recourse and Without Recourse.* In the case of the recourse letter of credit, if the buyer fails to pay the bank after a specified period, the bank can have recourse on the exporter. There is no such provision in the letter of credit without recourse.

It is perhaps obvious that letters of credit might take various combinations of the above. Thus, they may be revocable and unconfirmed, irrevocable and unconfirmed, or irrevocable and confirmed. While an irrevocable and confirmed letter of credit is a virtual guarantee of payment from the standpoint of the responsible banks, it is no guarantee that the conditions of the credit will or can be met. For example, accidents, strikes, or government allocations of material may delay the production of the order so that the expiration date cannot be met. The best thing for the exporter is to insist for confirmed, irrevocable and without recourse L/C.

Checking Export Letters of Credit and Documents

Exporters are encouraged to check letters of credit carefully to be sure so that there is no later misunderstanding. The beneficiary should check for the following:

1. Has the correct title been used in addressing you as beneficiary?
2. Has the correct title of the buyer been used?
3. Is the amount sufficient? Take into consideration the terms of the sale and possible addition of any charges.
4. Is the tenor of the drafts the same as your quotation to the buyer?
5. Is the credit available at the banking institution or in the locality requested by you?
6. Are the documents required in the credit in accordance with your arrangements with the buyer, and can such documents be furnished?
7. Is the description of the merchandise correct? (Check unit price, trade definition, point of shipment, and destination).
8. Do you agree with any special instructions which may appear in the credit?
9. Is the expiration date and place of expiration satisfactory.
10. Is the credit confirmed by a domestic bank, or is an unconfirmed credit satisfactory?
11. Does the letter of credit permit partial shipments or transhipments?

Since the terms of a commercial letter of credit are so exacting and payment under the credit depends upon meeting all of the letter's requirements, the beneficiary cannot be too careful in checking every step of the transaction.

Advantages of Letters of Credit to Buyers

Although the burden of financing is placed upon the buyer under a credit transaction, this method of payment also provides certain advantages:

1. Perhaps the greatest practical benefit derived by the buyer is the protection of setting a definite date by which the seller is required to ship the order. The buyer, accordingly, may figure on prompt delivery, as the credit will expire on the date set unless an extension is granted.
2. The buyer can receive low prices when a letter of credit is submitted. Since contingencies are fully guarded against that, exporter finds it unnecessary to cover them in the price.

Advance Allotment of Indigenous Raw Materials

While the allotment of indigenous raw materials as indicated above will ordinarily be made after the export has been made, advance allotment may also be made in cases where such advance allotment is considered necessary in order to enable production against firm export orders. Application for such allotment should be made in the separate form direct to the Director of Export Promotion, Ministry of Commerce.

4. Drawback of Import and Excise Duties

The scheme of drawback of import and excise duties has been formulated by Government with the object of relieving the Indian exporter of the burden of import and excise duties on the products exported, so as to put him on par, in the matter of competitive position, with foreign competitors.

5. General Security/General Surety for Executing Bond (Form B-I)

The excisable goods can be exported outside India either under claim for rebate of excise duty or under bond. The difference between these two procedures is that in the case of former the duty is first paid and its refund claimed after exportation, and in the latter case the goods are allowed to be exported without payment of duty provided a bond in executed in Form B-I (General Security).

6. AR-4 Form

Before excisable goods are removed from the factory for export, each consignment is required to be presented to the Central Excise Officer having jurisdiction over the factory together with an application in form AR-4 for claiming rebate of excise duty. When the goods have been removed from the factory, a copy of this application together with the goods is then presented by the exporter to the Customs Collector or other duly authorised officer at the port who will certify that the goods have been actually exported. On the basis of this endorsement the exporter will claim the rebate of excise duty if he has already paid, or discharged his obligation to that extent in case he has executed the bond.

Manufacture of Goods under Bond

Provision exists under Section 65 of the Sea Customs Act and under Rule 191-A of the Central Excise Rules for the manufacture of goods under bond. This facility would enable the manufacturer to take into bonded warehouse, imported material without payment of customs duties and indigenous excisable material, without payment of central excise duty, for use in the manufacture of a finished product.

Application for Fixation of Drawback Rates

If a manufacturer is interested in having drawback of import or excise duty authorised for any item not already covered by the existing rules, he should apply to either the Ministry of Commerce or the Ministry of Finance, Department of Revenue, New Delhi. On receipt of the application, the government will examine the question of making a provision for drawback for the commodity for which the manufacturer will be asked to furnish information.

7. Drawback Shipping Bill

In order to take advantage of the drawback of import duty on the products exported, shippers are required to give the details of the goods intended to be exported under claim of drawback in a shipping bill which should clearly be marked "Under claim for drawback." Normally four copies of the drawback shipping bill are prepared. Exporters should furnish the information under the various columns in the drawback shipping bill so that the drawback is allowed expeditiously.

8. Drawback Bill

When the goods have been exported "Under claim for drawback," a drawback bill is prepared in order to claim the amount. This bill is in addition to the shipping bill and requires information about the date of presentation of original bill of entry, number and date of the drawback shipping bill, marks and number on the packages, description of goods, weight and quantity of the goods, amount of drawback, etc. It has to be certified by the Collector of Customs that the amount of the bill does not exceed the amount of import duty paid on the goods specified therein and drawback has not been allowed on the same article in any previous bill.

APPENDIX-A
MASTER DOCUMENT

Exporter	Invoice No & Date	Exporter's Ref.
	Buyer's Order No & Date	Export Licence No.
	RBI Code No.	GR-I No.

Consignee	Buyer (if other than consignee)
Notify Party	Country of Origin of Goods / Country of Final Destination
	Terms of Delivery and Payment

Pre-Carriage by	Place of Receipt by Pre-Carrier
Vessel	Port of Loading
Port of Discharge	Final Destination (if -On-Carriage)

Insured Value Rs.

Marks & Numbers	No. & Kind of Packages; Description of Goods	Net Weight (kg)	Gross Weight (kg)	Cube (m³)
		Quantity	Value Rate (Rupees)	Amount

Amount Chargeable

F.O.B. Value Rs
Freight Rs.
Insurance Rs.
Commission Rs.
Discount Rs.
(Specify Nature)

(Amount in Words Rupees____________________

Exchange Rate

Amount in Rupees

Freight Payable at	
No. of Original Bs/L	Name of the Authorized Signatory
	Place & Date of Issue Signature

Mask for Invoice

APPENDIX - B

INVOICE

<table>
<tr><td colspan="3" rowspan="3">Exporter</td><td colspan="2">Invoice No. & Date</td><td>Exporter's Ref.</td></tr>
<tr><td colspan="3">Buyer's Order No. & Date</td></tr>
<tr><td colspan="3">Other Reference(s)</td></tr>
<tr><td colspan="3" rowspan="2">Consignee</td><td colspan="3">Buyer (if other than consignee)</td></tr>
<tr><td colspan="2">Country of Origin of Goods</td><td>Country of Final Destination</td></tr>
<tr><td>Pre-Carriage by</td><td colspan="2">Place of Receipt by Pre-Carrier</td><td colspan="3" rowspan="3">Terms of Delivery and Payment</td></tr>
<tr><td>Vessel/Flight No.</td><td colspan="2">Port of Loading</td></tr>
<tr><td>Port of Discharge</td><td colspan="2">Final Destination</td></tr>
<tr><td>Marks & Nos./ Container No.</td><td>No. & Kind of Pkgs.</td><td>Description of Goods</td><td>Quantity</td><td>Rate</td><td>Amount</td></tr>
<tr><td></td><td></td><td></td><td></td><td></td><td></td></tr>
<tr><td colspan="5">Amount Chargeable
(In words)</td><td>Total</td></tr>
<tr><td colspan="4">Declaration:
We declare that this Invoice shows the actual price of the goods described and that all particulars are true and correct.</td><td colspan="2">Signature & Date</td></tr>
</table>

APPENDIX - C

PACKING LIST

<table>
<tr><td colspan="2">Exporter</td><td colspan="3">Invoice No. & Date</td></tr>
<tr><td colspan="2"></td><td colspan="3">Buyer's Order No. & Date</td></tr>
<tr><td colspan="2"></td><td colspan="3">Other Reference(s)</td></tr>
<tr><td colspan="2">Consignee</td><td colspan="3">Buyer (If other than consignee)</td></tr>
<tr><td colspan="2"></td><td colspan="2">Country of Origin of Goods</td><td>Country of Final Destination</td></tr>
<tr><td>Pre-Carriage by</td><td>Place of Receipt by Pre-carrier</td><td colspan="3"></td></tr>
<tr><td>Vessel/Flight No.</td><td>Port of Loading</td><td colspan="3"></td></tr>
<tr><td>Port of Discharge</td><td>Place of Delivery</td><td colspan="3"></td></tr>
<tr><td>Marks & Nos./ Container No.</td><td>No. & Kind of Pkgs.</td><td>Description of Goods</td><td>Quantity</td><td>Remarks</td></tr>
<tr><td></td><td></td><td></td><td></td><td></td></tr>
<tr><td colspan="4"></td><td>Signature & Date</td></tr>
</table>

APPENDIX - D

SHIPPING BILL FOR EXPORT OF DUTY FREE GOODS

ORIGINAL

Exporter	Invoice No. & Date AR4/AR4A No. & Date Q/Cert. No. & Date	SB No. & Date Import-Export Code No. RBI Code No.
Consignee	Export Trade Control	If export under: Deferred Credit [ ] Joint Ventures [ ] Rupee Credit [ ] Others [ ] RBI's Approval/Cir. No. & Date
Custom House Agent LIC No.		
Pre-Carriage by / Place of Receipt by Pre-Carrier		Type of shipment: Outright Sale [ ] Consignment Export [ ] Others [ ] (Specify)
Vessel/Flight No. / Rotation No.		
Port of Loading	Nature of Contract: CIF [ ] / CFR [ ] / FOB [ ] Others (Specify) [ ]	
Port of Discharge / Country of Destination	Exchange Rate U/S 14 of CA	Currency of Invoice

S.No.	Marks & Nos.	No. & Kind of Pkgs. Container Nos.	Statistical Code & Description of Goods	Quantity	Value FOB

Net Weight

Gross Weight

Total FOB Value in words

Analysis of Export Value	Currency	Amount
FOB Value		
Freight		
Insurance	Rate	
Commission		
Discount		
Other Deductions		

Full export value OR where not ascertainable, the value which exporter expects to receive on the sale of goods

Currency ________

Amount ________

Declaration:
I/We declare that all particulars given herein are true and correct.
I/We also attach the declaration(s) under clause No.(s) . . . .
Public Notice No.. . . . . dated . . . . Signature of Exporter/CHA & Date

SHIPPING BILL FOR EXPORT OF DUTY FREE GOODS

ORIGINAL

DOCUMENTS SUBMITTED

1. Invoice [ ]
2. Packing List [ ]
3. GR Form [ ]
4. AR-4/AR-4A Form [ ]
5. ETC Licence [ ]
6. Indent [ ]
7. Acceptance of Contract [ ]
8. Letter of Credit [ ]
9. QC Certificate [ ]
10. Port Trust Document [ ]
11. Any other (Specify) [ ]

SHIPPING BILL FOR EXPORT OF DUTY FREE GOODS

DUPLICATE

Exporter	Invoice No. & Date AR4/AR4A No. & Date	SB No. & Date
	Q/Cert/No. & Date	Import-Export Code No. RBI Code No.
Consignee	Export Trade Control	If export under: Deferred Credit [ ] Joint Ventures [ ] Rupee Credit [ ] Others [ ] RBI's Approval/Cir. No. & Date
Custom House Agent LIC No.		
Pre-Carriage by / Place of Receipt by Pre-Carrier		Type of shipment: Outright Sale [ ] Consignment Export [ ] Others [ ] (Specify)
Vessel/Flight No. / Rotation No.		
Port of Loading	Nature of Contract: CIF [ ] / CFR [ ] / FOB [ ] Others (Specify) [ ]	
Port of Discharge / Country of Destination	Exchange Rate U/S 14 of CA	Currency of Invoice

S.No. Marks	Marks & Nos.	No. & Kind of Pkgs. Container Nos.	Statistical Code & Description of Goods	Quantity	Value FOB

Net Weight

Gross Weight

Total FOB Value in words

Analysis of Export Value	Currency	Amount
FOB Value		
Freight		
Insurance	Rate	
Commission		
Discount		
Other Deductions		

Full export value OR where not ascertainable, the value which exporter expects to receive on the sale of goods.

Currency

Amount

Declaration:
I/We declare that all particulars given herein are true and correct.
I/We also attach the declaration(s) under clause No.(s) . . . .
Public Notice No.. . . . . dated . . . . Signature of Exporter/CHA & Date

SHIPPING BILL FOR EXPORT OF DUTY FREE GOODS

DUPLICATE

DOCUMENTS SUBMITTED

1. Invoice [ ]
2. Packing List [ ]
3. GR Form [ ]
4. AR-4/AR-4A Form [ ]
5. ETC Licence [ ]
6. Indent [ ]
7. Acceptance of Contract [ ]
8. Letter of Credit [ ]
9. QC Certificate [ ]
10. Port Trust Document [ ]
11. Any other (Specify) [ ]

'LET EXPORT'	**'ALLOWED FOR SHIPMENT'**
Signature of Officer of Customs	Signature of Officer of Customs

Vessel's name may be altered after check with original Entry for
Fresh one may be granted to ....
for the portion shutout or not shipped

Fee Rs.

Received

Handed over to C.H.A./Party Signature of Asstt. Collector of Customs Cashier

Contents Received on Board	Date of Shipment
Date Signature of Master of Vessel	Signature of Officer of Customs

Examination Order and Report

EXPORT PROMOTION COPY

TRIPLICATE

Exporter	Invoice No. & Date AR4/AR4A No. & Date	SB No. & Date
	Q/Cert.No. & Date	Import-Export Code No.
Consignee		RBI Code No.
	Export Trade Control	If export under: Deferred Credit [ ] Joint Ventures [ ] Rupee Credit [ ] Others [ ]
Custom House Agent LIC No.		RBI's Approval/Cir. No. & Date

Pre-Carriage by	Place of Receipt by Pre-Carrier		Type of shipment: Outright Sale [ ] Consignment Export [ ] Others [ ] (Specify)
Vessel/Flight No.	Rotation No.		
	Port of Loading	Nature of Contract: CIF [ ] / CFR [ ] / FOB [ ] Others (Specify) [ ]	
Port of Discharge	Country of Destination	Exchange Rate U/S 14 of CA	Currency of Invoice

S.No. Marks	Marks & Nos.	No. & Kind of Pkgs. Container Nos.	Statistical Code & Description of Goods	Quantity	Value FOB

Net Weight

Gross Weight

Total FOB Value in words

Analysis of Export Value		Currency	Amount	Full export value OR where not ascertainable, the value which exporter expects to receive on the sale of goods
FOB Value				Currency
Freight				Amount
Insurance		Rate		
Commission				
Discount				
Other Deductions				

Declaration:
I/We declare that all particulars given herein are true and correct.
I/We also attach the declaration(s) under clause No.(s) . . . .
Public Notice No.. . . . . dated . . . . Signature of Exporter/CHA & Date

SHIPPING BILL FOR EXPORT OF DUTY FREE GOODS

EXPORT PROMOTION COPY **TRIPLICATE**

Verified Mate's Receipt No. ____________________

of ____________________

Issued by ____________________

For ____________ Cases/Bales/Packages/Containers ____________

Shipped per ____________________

Which sailed on ____________________

From ____________________

Under Preventive Supervision

Signature of Officer of Customs

OR

Shipment declared on this Shipping Bill has been air freighted on

Flight No. ____________ Dated ____________

AWB No. ____________ EGM No. ____________

Under Preventive Supervision in full/party (Specify quantity airfreighted).

Signature of Officer of Customs

APPENDIX - E

CERTIFICATE OF ORIGIN

<table>
<tr><td colspan="2">Exporter</td><td colspan="2" rowspan="5">No.

NAME OF THE
CHAMBER OF COMMERCE</td></tr>
<tr><td colspan="2">Consignee</td></tr>
<tr><td>Per-Carriage by</td><td>Place of Receipt by Pre-Carrier</td></tr>
<tr><td>Vessel</td><td>Port of Loading</td></tr>
<tr><td>Port of Discharge
Rostock</td><td>Final Destination (if On-Carriage)</td></tr>
<tr><td>Marks & Numbers</td><td>No. & Kind of Packages:
Description of Goods</td><td>Gross Weight (kg)</td><td>Measurement</td></tr>
<tr><td colspan="2">Certification
It is hereby certified that this declaration was made before me and that to the best of my knowledge and belief the above mentioned goods are of Indian origin.</td><td colspan="2">Declaration by Exporter
We hereby declare that the above mentioned goods were produced in the Indian Union and are shipped to ....
from the port of ....
....
per .... sailing
on or about ....</td></tr>
<tr><td colspan="2">
Place & Date of Issue</td><td colspan="2">Name of the Authorised Signatory
Place and Date of Issue</td></tr>
<tr><td colspan="2">Signature
Secretary</td><td colspan="2">Signature</td></tr>
</table>

APPENDIX - F

SPECIMEN OF BILL OF LADING

Shipper		B/L No.	
Consignee (If 'order' state Notify Party & Address)		NAME AND LOGO OF SHIPPING LINE	
Notify Party (leave blank if stated above)			
*Local Vessel	*From		
Ocean Vessel	Port of Loading		
Port of Discharge	*Final Destination (if On-Carriage)		
Marks & Numbers	No. & Kind of Packages; Description of Goods	Gross Weight (kg)	Measurement

Particulars of goods are those declared by shippers but not admitted by the Shipowner who makes no admission as to the kind of description of the goods.

Freight details, charges, etc.

Shipped on board in apparent good order . . . .

Freight Payable at	Place & Date of Issue
No. of Original Bs/L	Signature

*Applicable only when document used as a Thorough Bill of Lading

APPENDIX - G
SPECIMEN OF MARINE INSURANCE DECLARATION FORM

Name & Address of the Insurance Company

LOGO

Please issue a Marine Policy/Certificate of Insurance in duplicate/triplicate/ quadruplicate. in accordance with the following particulars

Issuing Office

Insured

FOR OFFICIAL USE

	Rate	Premium
Marine		
War & S.R.C.C.		
Stamp Duty		

Vessel	Port of Loading
Port of Discharge	Final Destination

Insured Value Rs.

Marks & Numbers | No. & Kind of Packages; Description of Goods

IMPORTANT

Terms of Insurance

Special Instructions, if any:

Declaration

(a) *We hereby certify that the Insurance charges on the above shipment will be borne by us and that we are not making the payment on behalf of any one outside India.

OR

(b) *Although we are defraying the Insurance charges on the above shipment, which should be borne by the overseas buyer of the goods, we undertake to recover the payment so made from the buyer in an approved manner.

Agent ____________________

A/C. Code No ________ ACCEPTED

For The

Name & Address of Proposer

Signature

*Delete (a) or (b) as appropriate

APPENDIX - H
SPECIMEN OF MARINE INSURANCE CERTIFICATE

Name & Address of the Insurance Company

LOGO

Survey: In the event of loss or damage which may involve claim under this certificate notice of loss or damage should be given to: Claim Payable by:			Issuing Office
Insured	Open Policy/Cover No. Date of Issue		Certificate No.
	Marine War &/or S.R.C.C. Stamp Duty	Rate Premium	Date of Issue
Vessel	Port of Loading		
Port of Discharge	Final Destination	Insured Value Rs.	
Marks & Numbers	No. & Kind of Packages; Description of Goods		IMPORTANT

Terms of Insurance

This is to certify that insurance of the above mentioned goods has been effected with this Company as per details specified in the Schedule herein above, subject to the terms and conditions of the relative Open Policy/Cover.

For The

Authorized Signatory

APPENDIX-I

EXCHANGE CONTROL DECLARATION (GR) FORM

Is Export Under L/C arrangements Yes ( ) No ( ) If yes name of advising Bank in India	FOR CUSTOMS Customs Assessable Value Rs. (Rupees ....
Bank through which payment is to be received	Export Value Verified Custom appraiser
	Cargo shipped in Full/Part Quantity Value
Whether Payment is to be received through the ACU Yes/No	Date of Shipment Customs Official

Declaration under Foreign Exchange Regulation Act: I/We hereby declare that I/We am/are the SELLER/ CONSIGNOR of the goods in respect of which this declaration is made and that the particulars given above are true and that (a) *the value as contracted with the buyer is the same as the full export value declared overleaf (b) *the full export value of the goods is not ascertainable at the time of export and that the value declared in that which I/We, having regard to the prevailing market conditions, expect to receive on the sale of goods in the overseas market.

I/We* undertake that I/We will deliver to the bank named herein the foreign exchange representing the full export value of the goods on or before @ ....in the manner prescribed in Rule 9 of the Foreign Exchange Regulation Rules, 1974. I/We further declare that I/We am/are resident in India and I/We have a place of business in India.

I/We* am/are OR am/are not in Caution List of the Reserve Bank of India.

Date: ——————   ——————— (Signatue of Exporter)

@ State appropriate date of delivery which must be within six months of the date of shipment but for exports to warehouses established outside India with the permission of the Reserve Bank the date of delivery must be within fifteen months.

* Strike out whichever is not applicable.

FOR AUTHORISED DEALER'S USE

* Indicate ( ) in the box applicable

Uniform Code Number: ....
Date of* (i) negotiation/ (ii) receipt for collection ....
Bill No. .... Type of Bill* (i) DA ( )/ (ii) DP ( )/ (iii) Others ( ) ....(Specify) Type of shipment: (i) Firm Sale Contract ( )/ (ii) Consignment Basis ( )/ (iii) Others ( ) ....(Specify) The GR form was included in the Statement send to the Reserve Bank with the R-returns for the fortnight ending...........sent on .... We certify/ and confirm that we have received the total amount of .... as under being the proceeds of exports declared on this form.
(Currency Amount)

Date Receipt	Currency	Credit in Nostro Account in .... (Country)		Debit to NR Rupee Acccount of a Bank in ....(Country)		Period of R-Return with which the realisation has been reported to RBI
		In our name	In the name of *	Held with us	Held with*	
(1)	(2)	(3)	(4)	(5)	(6)	(7)

(* Write the name of the concerned Indian Authorised Dealer/Branch. Any other manner of receipt (Specify)
....
....

(Stamp & Signature of authorised dealer)

Date : ....

Address : ....

....

....

SPACE FOR USE BY RESERVE BANK OF INDIA

DOCUMENTS USED IN SHIPMENT OF GOODS

EXCHANGE CONTROL DECLARATION (GR) FORM

Is Export Under L/C arrangements Yes ( ) No ( ) If yes name of advising Bank in India	FOR CUSTOMS Customs Assessable Value Rs. (Rupees ....)
Bank through which payment is to be received	Export Value Verified Customs Appraiser
Whether Payment is to be received through the ACU Yes/No	Date of Shipment Customs Appraiser

Declaration under Foreign Exchange Regulation Act: I/We hereby declare that I/We am/are the *SELLER/CONSIGNOR of the goods in respect of which this declaration is made and that the particulars given above are true and that (a) *the value as contracted with the buyer is the same as the full export value declared overleaf (b) *the full export value of the goods is not ascertainable at the time of export and that the value declared in that which I/We, having regard to the prevailing market conditions, expect to receive on the sale of goods in the overseas market.

I/We undertake that I/We will deliver to the bank named herein the foreign exchange representing the full export value of the goods on or before @ ....in the manner prescribed in Rule 9 of the Foreign Exchange Regulation Rules, 1974. I/We further declare that I/We am/are resident in India and I/We have a place of business in India.

I/We* am/are OR am/are not in Caution List of the Reserve Bank of India.

Date: ______________ ______________________ (Signatue of Exporter)

@ State appropriate date of delivery which must be within six months of the date of shipment but for exports to warehouses established outside India with the permission of the Reserve Bank the date of delivery must be within fifteen months.

* Strike out whichever is not applicable.

SPACE FOR USE BY RESERVE BANK OF INDIA

APPENDIX - J

SPECIMEN OF SHIPMENT ADVICE

Exporter	Invoice No. & Date	Exporter's Ref.
	Buyer's Order No. & Date	
Consignee	Document being negotiated/sent:	
	Commercial Invoice	[ ]
	Packing List	[ ]
	Consular/Custom Invoice	[ ]
	Bill of Lading/Air Way Bill	[ ]
Name of Party	Insurance Certificate/Policy	[ ]
	Bill of Exchange	[ ]
	Certificate of Origin	[ ]
	GSP Certificate of Origin	[ ]
	Export Certificate	[ ]
	Inspection Certificate	[ ]
	Any Other Document	[ ]
Pre-Carriage by / Place of Receipt by Pre-carrier	(Specify)	[ ]
Vessel/Flight No. / Port of Loading		
Port of Discharge / Final Destination		

Marks & Nos./ Container No.	No. & Kind of Pkgs.	Description of Goods	Quantity	Rate	Amount
				Total	

We have shipped the goods as per details given herein and are negotiating the above listed documents under Documentary Credit of ....

(Name & Address of Bank)

OR

We are sending the above listed documents for collection through .
....

(Name & Address of Bank)

* We have also despatched the following documents through .....
.... Fr. No. .... Date ...
....

(Carrier)

[ ] Certificate of Origin/GSP Certificate of Origin
[ ] Export Certificate
[ ] Invoice
[ ] Packing List

Signature & Date

* May be included if necessary.

APPENDIX – K
SPECIMEN OF SHIPPING ORDER

Shipper

No.

NAME AND LOGO OF SHIPPING LINE

To
The Commanding Officer,
Please receive on board from
M/s. . . . .
who have contracted to ship the goods mentioned hereunder.

Signature

Vessel	Port of Loading
Port of Discharge	Final Destination (if On-Carriage)

Marks & Numbers	No. & Kind of Packages;	Description of Goods	Gross Weight (kg)	Measurement

The Shipping Order is issued and the goods to be received and carried subject to all the clauses and conditions and endorsements on the Company's Bill of Lading current at the time of shipment as well as the conditions overleaf.

Carting Date . . . .

Freight Payable at — Place & Date of Issue

Freight Broker

Signature

APPENDIX – L
SPECIMEN OF MATE'S RECEIPT

Shipper

M/R No

NAME AND LOGO
OF
SHIPPING LINE

Vessel	Port of Loading		
Port of Discharge	*Final Destination (if On-Carriage)		
Marks & Numbers	No. & Kind of Packages; Description of Goods	Gross Weight (kg)	Measurement

Received from . . . .
on board the above mentioned goods in apparent good order and condition subject to all the terms and conditions of the Company's Bill of Lading.

Freight Payable at

Place & Date of Issue

Signature of Chief Officer

• *Applicable only when document used as a Thorough Bill of Lading

NB: This receipt must be exchanged immediately for the Company's B/L duly signed.

APPENDIX - M

SPECIMEN OF DUTY/CESS PARTICULARS

S. No. of Item Overleaf	Tariff Export Head No.	Value under Sec. 14 of C.A.	DUTY		CESS		TOTAL DUTY & CESS Rs.
			Rate Rs.	Amount Rs.	Rate Rs.	Amount Rs.	

DRAWBACK PARTICULARS

Sr. No. of Item Overleaf	Sr. No. & Sub. Sr. No. of Drawback Schedule PN No. & Date (for Brand Rates)	Quantity/ Value on which Draw-back is Claimed	DRAWBACK		Market Value Rs.
			Rate Rs.	Amount Rs.	

FOR DEPARTMENTAL USE

The above claim has been checked by me and passed for Rs. (Rupees .... only). The amount may/may not be deducted from the duty/cess payable and assessed in the Shipping Bill.

Signature
(With Designation and Date)

Vessel's Name may be altered
Fee One Rupee

Assistant collector
Cashier

Fee Received
Handed over to CHA/Party

After check with the original
Entry for
Fresh one may be granted to
for the portion shutout or not shipped
Fee One Rupee

Assistant Collector

APPENDIX - N

SPECIMEN OF PROFORMA INVOICE

Proforma Invoice No. . . . . (place and date) New Delhi 27-5-1992

Invoice of Sim-Sim Padlock
By M/s. Orient Industrial Corpn.

C/O "EAST" Scheme, State Trading Corpn. of India Ltd.,
Post Box No. 79,
New Delhi (India).

To M/s. Souther Traders

of 15, Jalan Ali Ditchar,
P.B. No. 335,
IRCH-(MALAYA)

to be shipped per . . . .
Order Number as noted below
IND/ST/3 dated 18-5-1992

Marks & Numbers	Description of Goods/Quantity	Selling Price to Purchaser: At per doz.	Selling Price to Purchaser: Amount £-sh-d
ASI-ORIENT (S.T.) PENANG 1/50 to 0/50	SIM-SIM Tumbler Padlocks, solid die-cast non-ferrous, silver enamelled finish, with toughened chroming plated hasps and complete with 2 keys	Sh.	
	1 3/4" (45 mm) size 450 dozens	21/9	489-7-6
	1 $\frac{1}{2}$" (38 mm) size 450 dozens	17/6	393-15-0
	1 $\frac{1}{4}$" (32 mm) size 480 dozens	15/2	364-0-0
	1" (25 mm) size 720 dozens	12/4	444-0-0

1691-2-6

Commission @ 5% 84-11-2

1606-11-4

Qty. Discount @ 3¼% 52-4-3

1554-7-1

Publicity Allowances @ 2½% 38-17-2

1515-9-11

Early payment Discount @ 1 % (Only valid for payment through L/C) 15.3.1

1500-6-10

Nett CIF Penang plus L/C negotiation charges.

Packing

Each padlock complete with two keys in a sealed polythene bag and then in a glossy varnished) individual carton. Six tumbler padlocks per display outer and then in waterproof paper lined seaworthy wooden export case as under

A. 1 ¾" 30 dozens per case Total	15 cases
B. 1 ½" 30 dozens per case Total	15 cases
C. 1 ¼" 48 dozens per case Total	10 cases
D. 1" 72 dozens per case Total	10 cases
	50 cases

Size of each case

	Gross wt. (each case)	Nett wt. (each case)
A. Approx. 21" x 18" x 14"	104 kg	85 kg
B. Approx. 21" x 16" x 12"	78 kg	58 kg
C. Approx. 22½" x 15" x 12½"	79 kg	61 kg
D. Approx. 19 ½ x 16" x 14½"	79 kg	60 kg
Total cubic measurement (approx.)	163.00 c. ft.	
Total Gross weight (approx.)	5249.00 kgs.	
Total Nett weight (approx.)	4165 kgs.	

Shipment

4/6 weeks from receipt of confirmed order and establishment in India of letter of credit, subject to availability of shipping space.

Payment Terms

Strict nett cash through letter of credit as under:

(a) Established at a reputable bank in Bombay in favour of the State Trading Corporation of India Ltd., 'EAST'
Scheme, Industry House, Churchgate Reclamation, Bombay-1;

(b) Confirmed and irrevocable;

(c) Valid for shipments up to six weeks from the date of establishment in Bombay;

(d) Part shipment permitted;

(e) Transhipments permitted;

(f) Valid for presentation of documents up to eight weeks from the date of establishment in Bombay; and

(g) In the amount of £ 1500-6-10 sterling.

This proforma is issued on the following conditions:

(i) Subject to withdrawal or fluctuation without notice at any time before receipt of acceptance by us and without engagement at this stage;

(ii) Subject to circumstances beyond our control; and

(iii) Not valid for acceptance beyond 22-6-1992 unless with our written concurrence.

Accepted
Signature . . . . . .
Witness
Signature . . . . .

Sd/-
Signature . . . .

APPENDIX-O

Specimen Of Letter Of Credit

Punjab National Bank

(*Head Office:* Parliament Street, New Delhi)

(Not Negotiable)

Branch ________________

Dated ________________

OPENED BY AIRMAIL CABLE

THROUGH . . . .

If this credit has already been advised by cable, it is available only for such amount as has not already been availed of under the cable advice and is not available for utilisation at all unless attached to our correspondent's notification of such cable advice.

OUR IRREVOCABLE CREDIT NO . . . .

Dear Sirs,

At the request and for account of . . . . , we have opened in your favour an irrevocable letter of credit for . . . .
(say . . . .) available
available by your draft without recourse at . . . . sight
on . . . . for . . . . % of invoice cost of . . . .
From . . . . To . . . .

Drafts are to be accompanied by the following documents:

1. Your signed invoice in .... quoting import licence No. .... dated .... certifying goods to be of .... origin (in accordance with Indian Import Trade Control Regulations, shipment must not be made prior to the date of licence).

2. Full set of clean "On Board" Ocean Shipping Company's bills of lading to order blank endorsed or to order of Punjab National Bank marked "Freight Paid" and "Notify Punjab National Bank, ... Branch" and the consignee dated not later than. ....

Or

Parcel Post Receipt	Evidencing despatch to Punjab National Bank ....
or	Marked "Under L/C ....
Air Consignment Note	Dated not later than ....

3. For Sea Shipments: Insurance policies or certificates endorsed in blank, in the currency of this credit, for the Invoice value plus .... % covering marine risks WPA as per institute Cargo Clauses (all risks) dated 1-1-1963, institute strikes, riots and civil commotion clauses dated 1-1-1963, institute war clauses, including theft, pilferage, non-delivery and customary institute warehouse to warehouse clauses up to delivery at .... claims payable at ....

For Post Sendings (Sea or Air): As for sea shipments above with institute war clauses (post sendings) ....

For Air Sendings: As for sea shipments above but with institute war clauses (Air Sendings)

Or

Insurance covered by buyers in ....

Your certificate required that a copy of your advice to the openers giving particulars of shipments for insurance purposes has been forwarded by airmail to Punjab National Bank ....

4. Other documents and/or conditions.

Partial Shipment Permitted/Not Permitted   Transhipment Permitted/Not Permitted

(*Cont. on next page*)

This credit is irrevocably valid for negotiations at .... until ....

Drafts must state "Drawn under irrevocable Letter of Credit No. .... of Punjab National Bank, dated .... " and must bear the clause "Payable at the Bank's current selling rate of exchange on .... with charges and interest at the current rate from the date of this draft until the date of payment."

We hereby engage with the Drawers, Endorsers and Bonafide Holders of Drafts drawn under and in compliance with the terms of this credit that such drafts shall be duly honoured on presentation and delivery of documents as specified above.

Negotiations under this credit are restricted to ....

All charges are for your account/our account.

The Negotiating Bank should forward to us the drafts and original documents by Air mail and duplicate documents by the following Airmail.

Except as otherwise expressly stated, this credit is subject to the uniform customs and practice for documentary credits (1962 Revision) International Chamber of Commerce Brochure No. 222.

Yours faithfully

Signatures

APPENDIX – P

SPECIMEN BILL OF EXCHANGE

No. . . . . New Delhi . . . .

At sight pay this First of Exchange (Second and Third of the same tenor and date unpaid) to the orders of . . . . the sum of . . . . for value received.

Drawn under . . . .

. . . .

For the State Trading Corporation of India Ltd.

To

. . . .

. . . .

. . . .

. . . .

No. . . . . New Delhi . . . .

At sight pay this Second of Exchange (First and Third of the same tenor and date unpaid) to the order of . . . . the sum of . . . . .for value received.

Drawn under . . . .

. . . .

For The State Trading Corporation of India Ltd.

(*Cont. on next page*)

To

. . . .

. . . .

. . . .

. . . .

New Delhi . . . .

No. . . . .

At sight pay this Third of Exchange (First and Second of the same tenor and date unpaid) to the order of . . . . the sum of . . . . for value received.

Drawn under . . . .

. . . .

For the State Trading Corporation of India Ltd.

To

. . . .

. . . .

. . . .

APPENDIX I

SELECT BIBLIOGRAPHY

A. BOOKS

1. Miracle, B. Gordon & Album, Gerald S. — International Marketing Management.
2. Leighton, David, S.R. — International Marketing Text and Cases.
3. Livingston, James M. — International Marketing Management.
4. Krammer, R.L. — "International Marketing", Prentice Hall, Inc., N.J., 1965.
5. Fayer-Weather, J. — "International Marketing", 2nd ed., Cincinnati, South Western Publication Co.
6. Thorelli, H.B. — International Marketing Strategy, Penguin Books Ltd., Harmonds-Sworth, Middlesex, England, 1973.
7. Rayans, Jr. John Baker, James C. — World Marketing — A Multinational Approach, John Wiley & Sons, Inc., 1967.
8. Martyn. H. — "International Business: Principles and Problems". The Free Press of Glencoe, New York, 1964.
9. Root, F.R. — "Strategic Planning for Export Marketing," S. Cranton, Pennsylvania, International Text Book Co., 1966.
10. Blough, Roy — "International Business: Environment and Adaptation," McGraw Hill Book Company, New York, 1966.
11. Farmer, R.N. & Richman, B.M. — "International Business: And Operational Theory," R.D. Irwin Inc., 1966, Homewood, Illinois.
12. Hess, J.M. & Cateora, P.R. — "International Marketing", R.D. Irwin Inc., Illinois, 1966.
13. Domke, Martin — "Commercial Arbitration", Prentice Hall-Englewood Cliffs, N.J., 1965.
14. Dowd, L.P. — "Principles of World Business", Allyn and Bacon Inc., Boston, 1965.
15. Fleming, J.M. — "The International Marketing Fund: IIS Form and Functions", IMF, Washington, D.C., 1964.
16. Baker, J.C. — "The International Finance Corporation: Origin, Operations and Evaluation", Frederick A. Praeger Inc., 1968.
17. Morgan Guaranty Trust Company — "Export and Import Procedures", M.G.T. Co., New York, 1962.
18. Fayer-Weather, J. — "Management of International Operations," McGraw Hill, N.Y., 1960.
19. Dwschampsneufs, H. — "Selling Overseas: The Principles of Export Marketing", Business Publications, London, 1960.

20. Fayer-Weather, John — "Facts and Fallacies of International Business", Holt, Rinehart and Winston, N.Y., 1962.
21. Bartels, R. — "Comparative Marketing: Wholesaling in Fifteen Countries", R.D. Irwin Inc., Illinois, 1963.
22. Carson, David — "International Marketing; A Comparative Systems Approach", John Wiley & Sons Inc., N.Y., 1967.
23. Yamey, B.S. — "Resale Price Maintenance", Aldine Publishing Company, 1966, pp. 1-12.
24. Bala Gopal, T.A.S. — "Export Management", Himalaya Publishing House, Bombay, Latest Edition.
25. Varshney, R.L., Bhattacharya, B. — "International Marketing Management — An Indian Perspective", Sultan Chand & Sons, New Delhi, Latest edition.
26. Irudyam, Y. — "Export Marketing", Asia Publishing House, Bombay.
27. Getting Started in Export Trade — International Trade Centre, Geneva.
28. Ico-Term, 1953 — International Chamber of Commerce, Paris.
29. Uniform Customs & Practice for Documentary Credit — International Chamber of Commerce, Paris.
30. Export Handbook — British Overseas Trade Board, London.
31. Yarker, K.A. — International Marketing, Business Books, London.
32. Andrew Duguid and Elliot Jaques — Case Studies in Export Organisation, Department of Trade and Industry, London.
33. Cases in International Marketing — IIFT, New Delhi, 1979.
34. Tookey, G.D.(Ed.) — Export Marketing Decisions, Penguin, 1975.
35. Concentration on Key Markets — A Development Plan for Exports, Royal Society of Arts (London), 1976.
36. Thorelli (Ed.) — International Marketing Strategy, Penguin, 1973.
37. Handbook for Exporters — Basic Chemicals, Pharmaceuticals and Cosmetics Export Promotion Council.
38. Exporting in Practice — Hardy Heating, BBC.
39. Kahler, R. — International Marketing, 5th edition, S.W. Publishing Company, Cincinnati, USA, Latest edition.
40. Terpestra, V. — The Cultural Environment of International Business, 1978.
41. Erik, W. — International Marketing, Making Exports Pay off, McGraw Hill Book Co., 1986.
42. Doz — Strategic Mgt. in Multinational, *e.g.,* Perman Press, 1986.
43. Kriplani, V.H. — "International Marketing", Prentice Hall, N. Delhi. Latest edition.

B. PERIODICALS

1. *International Trade Forum,* Quarterly.
2. *Foreign Trade Review* (Quarterly), Indian Institute of Foreign Trade.
3. *Finance and Development,* Quarterly.
4. *IMF Survey,* Fortnightly.
5. *The Economist,* Weekly.
6. *Economic and Political* Weekly.
7. *Eastern Economist,* Weekly.
8. *Commerce,* Weekly.
9. *Economic Times,* Daily.
10. *Business Standard,* Daily.
11. Financial Express, Daily.

C. PAPERS

1. Keegan, W.J. — "Multinational Product Planning: Strategic Alternatives,"'Journal of Marketing' (AMA), January, 1969, pp. 58-62.
2. O.E.C.D. — "Basic Considerations in Connection with the Establishment of Export Marketing Groups", in 'Export Marketing Groups for Small and Medium Size of Firms', OECD, 1964, pp. 13-19.
3. Cateora, P.R. & Hess, J.M. — "Pricing in International Markets", R.D. Irwin, 1971, pp. 667-710.
4. Thorelli — "International Marketing: An Ecological View", 'International Marketing Strategy', Penguin Books Ltd., 1973, pp. 23-40.
5. Stoutjesdiz, K. — "LDC Regional Marketing: Do They Work?" — 'Economic Integration Among Developing Countries', Columbia Journal of World Business, September/October, 1970, pp. 53-60.
6. Massel, J.S. — "Non-Tariff Barriers as an Obstacle to World Trade," 'The Expansion of World Trade: Legal Problems and Techniques', The British Institute of International and Comparative Law, 1965.
7. Business International — "Antidumping Rules in the European Communities Today and Tomorrow: New Rules for the Seventies", 'Business International', 1969, pp. 75-78.
8. Sassen, E.M.J.A. — "Ensuring Fair Competition in the European Community", 'Community Topics', No. 35, European Community Press and Information Service, Washington, DC, 1970, pp. 3-8.
9. Preston, L.E. — "Market Control in Developing Economies", Journal of Development Studies, Vol. 4, No. 4, 1968, pp. 481-486.

10. Katona, G., Strumpel, Zahn E. "Socio-cultural Environment: Aspirations and Affluence". McGraw Hill, 1971, pp. 27-28.
11. Lipson, H.A. & Lamont, D.F. "Marketing Opportunities and Marketing Infrastructure in Less Developed Countries", 'Journal of Marketing', Vol. 33, 1969, pp. 24-31.
12. Moyer, R. "International Market Analysis, Journal of Marketing Research", Vol. 5, 1968, pp. 353-360.
13. Wells (Jr.), L.T. "A Product Life Cycle for International Trade", 'Journal of Marketing', Vol. 32, 1968, pp. 1-6.
14. Keegan, W.J. "Five Strategies for Multinational Marketing", 'European Business', January, 1970, pp. 35-40.
15. Stone, P. "The Massive Market for Simplicity", 'Business Industry Week', April 11, 1969.
16. Hamilton, C.A. "Opportunities for International Market Development", 'Business Horizons', Vol. VII (Summer 1965), pp. 23-30.
17. Yoshino, M.Y. "Marketing Orientation in International Business", 'Business Topics', Vol. 13 (Summer 1965), pp. 58-64.
18. Wadia, M.S. "The Concept of Culture", 'Journal of Retailing', Vol. XLI, Spring, 1965, pp. 21-29, 55.
19. Lee, J.A. "Cultural Analysis in Overseas Operations", HBR, Vol. XLIV, March-April, 1966.
20. Nichols, J.D. "Organizing for Export: Tips on Planning and Budgeting a Sound International Division", 'Export Trade' (October 22, 1962), pp. 7-9, 2-24.
21. Wadilnambia, Ratchi G. "Channels of Distribution in Developing Economies", 'Business Quarterly' Vol. 30, Winter 1965, pp. 74-82.
22. Morgan, F. 'Little Guys and Trade: Export Managing Firms Help Business Gain Markets Abroad", "The Wall Street Journal", September 8, 1965, pp. 1-10.
23. Woff, A.H. 'Independent Export Management", 'Export Trade', December 17, 1962, pp. 10-11, December 31, 1962, pp. 6-8.
24. Hickey, L.C. "The Case for an Exporting Program", 'Management Report', No. 67, AMA Publication, 1962.
25. Nielsen, A.C. Jr. "Do's and Don'ts in Selling Abroad", 'Journal of Marketing', Vol. 23, No. 4, April 1959.
26. Leonticades, J. "Is a Common Market a Single Market?" 'Columbia Journal of World Business', Vol. II, No. 4 (July-August 1967).
27. Kerschull, Dietrich "Worldwide Export Promotion Requires New Concepts", 'Intereconomics', July, 1966.

28. De Vries, B.A. — "The Export Performance of Developing Countries", 'Finance and Development', Vol. 5, No. 1, March, 1968.

29. Waterman, M.H. — "Financial Management in Multinational Corporations", 'Michigan Business Review', January, 1968.

30. Lall, Sanjaya — "The Foreign Exchange Market", 'Finance and Development', Vol. IV, No. 3, September 1967.

31. Hagler, J.J. — "How are Marketers Meeting the Import Challenge?" HBR, September/October 1960.

32. Phelps, D.M. — "International Competition — Is it Desirable?" HBR, May, 1964.

33. Dichter, E. — "The World Customer", HBR, July-August, 1962.

34. Buell, V.P. — "How to Study Foreign Markets", 'Journal of Marketing', Vol. 3, July 5.

35. Boyd, H.W. Frank, R.E. Massy, W.F. Zohier, M. — "On the Use of Marketing Research in the Emerging Economies", 'Journal of Marketing Research', November, 1964.

36. Stvart, R.D. — "Penetrating the International Market", 'AMA Management Report', No. 84, AMA, N.Y., 1965.

37. Parameswaren, K. & Watson, D.L. — "The Challenge of the Underdeveloped National Market", 'Journal of Marketing', October 1961.

39. Miracle, G.E. — "Product Characteristics and Marketing Strategy", 'Journal of Marketing', January 1965.

40. Lightman, J.M. — "Trade Marks as Silent Salesmen", 'International Commerce', October 28, 1963.

41. Linneman, R.E. — "A Case for Minimum Marketing Efforts in International Markets", 'Mississippi Valley Journal of Business and Economics', Vol. 1, Fall, 1965.

42. *Business Abroad* — "A New Approach to Export Management", March 22, 1965.

43. *Business Management* — "Co-operative Exporting: An Easy Way to Sell Overseas". January, 1966.

44. Myers, J.G. — "Foreign Licensing — An Export Alternative", 'Marketing Canadian', 1964.

45. Fayer-Weather, J. — 'LRP for International Operations', CMR, Vol. III, No. I, Fall 1960.

46. Dunn, S. Watson — "The Case Study Approach in Cross Cultural Research", 'Journal of Marketing Research', Vol. III, No.I, Fall 1960.

47. McGarth, R.E. — "Logistics for International Manufacturing," HBR, Vol. 44, No. 2, March-April, 1966.

48. Miracle, G. — "Management of International Advertising", 'Michigan International Business Series', Number 5, 1966, pp. 6-12.

49. Elinder, Eric — "International Advertisers Must Devise Universal Ads, Dump Separate National Ones. Swedish, Adman Adverts", 'Advertising Age', November 27, 1961, p. 91.

50. — Directory of International Advertising Media, "Business Abroad', January 24, 1965, pp. 77-78.

51. Hickman, J.H. — "Leasing: New Global Tool for Business", 'Business Abroad', July 26, 1965, p. 29.

52. Foote, Peter C. — "How to Meet Price Competition in Selling in Overseas Markets", 'Export Trade', March 26. 1962, p. 23.

53. Shulman, J.S. — "Transfer Pricing in Multinational Business" (Unpublished D.B.A. Dissertation at Graduate School of Business Administration, Harvard University, 1966).

54. Deardon, John — "International Pricing", 'Harvard Business Review', Vol. 38, No. 1, January-February 1960, pp. 117-125.

55. IIFT — "Role of Small Industries in Export Promotion in India, USA and Japan — A Comparative Study", December, 1980.

56. Mehrotra, K.N. — "Export Import Bank — The Emerging Contours", 'Foreign Trade Review', New Delhi, January-March, 1981.

57. Teff, T.S. — 'Consumers in India Slowly Coming of Age', 57 (March 24, 1986), pp. 91.

58. Tinsley E. Parry, J, — "The Soviet Promise of Expanded Markets/How to Penetrate USSR Market", 'Advertising Age' 57 Jan. 6, 1986, pp. 1938-39.

59. Bertrand, K. — "New Export Trading Companies Turn to Services - They Know Best", 'Business Marketing', 7 March 1986, pp. 21, 32.

60. Czinkota, M.R. — "Distribution in Japan: Problems and Changes", 'Columbia Journal of Business', 20 (Fall 1985), pp. 65-71.

61. Hoke, P. — "Wunderman's View of Global Direct Marketing," 'Direct Marketing', 48 (March 1986), pp. 76-88. 153 [Interview].

SELECT BIBLIOGRAPHY — JOURNALS

62. Neale, C.W. & Shipley, — "An International Comparative Study of Credit Strategy," 'European Journal of Marketing' (UK), 19 (No. 6, 1985), pp. 24-38.

63. Hallen, L. & Johnson, J. — "Industrial Marketing Strategies and Different National Environments", 'Journal of Business Research', 13 Dec. 1985, pp. 495-509.

64. Amine, L.S. & Cavusgil, S.T. — "Demand Estimation in a Developing Country Environment: Difficuities, Techniques and Examples", 'Journal of the Market Research Society' (UK), 28 Jan., 1986, pp. 43-65.

65. Darling, J.R., Postnikoff, J.F. — "Strategic Export Information for Small Business", 'Journal of Small Business Management', 23 (October 1985), pp. 28-37.

66. Dawson, L.M. — "Marketing to Less Developed Countries", 'Journal of Small Business Marketing', 23 (Oct. 1985) pp. 13-19.

67. Lester, Tom. — "Japanese Marketing", Scrutable Orientals (Part I). Tom Lester Marketing (U.K.), 24 (March 20, 1986), pp. 27-34.

68. Parkinson, J.M. — "Marketing in Lesser Developed Countries", 'Quarterly Review of Marketing' (UK) Autumn 1985, pp. 12-15.

69. Beasish, P.W. — "The Characteristics of Joint Ventures in Developed and Developing Countries", 'The Columbia Journal of World Business', Fall, 1985, p. 13.

70. Chakravorthy, B.S. — "Strategic Planning for a Global Business", CJWB, Summer, 1985, p. 3.

71. Kotter, P. — "Strategic Global Marketing: Lessons from Japan", CJWB, Spring, 1985, p. 65.

72. Kriesberg, M. — "More Jobs and Earnings, for Caribbean Basin Countries by Export", CJWB, Winter, 1985, p. 65.

73. Perlumutter, H.W. — "Strategic Planning for a Global Business", CJWB, Summer, 1985.

74. Stoever, W.A. — "The Stages of Developing Country: Policy Toward Foreign Investment", CJWB, Fall 1985, p. 3.

75. Tapan, David S, Jr. — "Project Management of the Future", CJWB, Winter 1985, p. 27.

76. Hendryx, S.R. — "Implementation of a Technology Transfer Joint Venture in the People's Republic of China: A Management Perspective", 'The Columbia Journal of World Business', N.Y., Spring 1986, Vol. XXI, No. I, pp. 57-66.

APPENDIX II

(A) REVIEW QUESTIONS (THEORETICAL)

1. Define international marketing. How does it differ from domestic marketing? What are the important determinants of international marketing policies?
2. Explain briefly why international trade takes place. What are the gains from international trade? Illustrate your answer with Indian examples.
3. Distinguish clearly between the operation of tariffs and import quotas. Which would you prefer — tariffs or import quotas — for a developing country like India?
4. What are the functions of the IMF? How do they differ from those of the IBRD? To what extent has the IMF helped India?
5. State the objectives of UNCTAD.
6. Analyse the recent trends in India's exports. What would be your suggestions to restore the growth in India's exports?
7. What do you understand by Overseas Market Research? Explain in this context the role played by the Trade Commissioners and the Export Promotion Councils.
8. Critically examine the contribution of the following agencies in the export promotion effort of India:
   (*i*) Commercial Banks; and
   (*ii*) Export Credit Guarantee Corporation.
9. What are the functions of Export Promotion Councils? To what extent have they been able to achieve their objectives?
10. Discuss the salient features of the latest EXIM Policy.
11. Describe briefly the various measures taken by the Government of India to help Indian exporters increase their exports.
12. What are the various incentives offered by the Government to the Indian exporters to improve their export performance?
13. How would you analyse foreign markets to identify a few possible markets for your product? From which sources would you get the necessary information?
14. Discuss the protectional and promotional aspects of packaging for international markets. What are the problems faced by Indian exporters in this connection?
15. How would you determine the suitability of a particular product for a particular market?
16. Write a note on product packaging and presentation for an export market.
17. "Differentiation in pricing for exports and for the domestic market is unavoidable". Comment.
18. What should be the basis for export pricing in a developing country like India?
19. Discuss the relative importance of price and non-price factors in international marketing. What, in your view, should be the strategy for export pricing to be adopted by Indian manufactures?

20. Write a note on differential export pricing.
21. What is the type of information needed by an export executive for pricing purposes?
22. Differentiate between *cost-oriented* export pricing and *market-oriented* export pricing. Examine the relevance of *market-oriented* pricing in exporting.
23. What are the factors that influence the pricing strategy for exportable products of a firm? What is the rationale of differential pricing in exports? To what extent has it been used?
24. What criteria would you adopt in the selection of overseas agents? How can agents be involved in market planning?
25. Describe briefly the main channels of distribution used in export markets. Which one would you recommend for the product of a small manufacturer, and why?
26. What are the points that you would keep in mind while selecting an agent in a foreign country?
27. What are the advantages of direct exporting? Why are more and more Indian manufactures taking recourse to direct exporting? Do they always have a separate export department for this purpose?
28. What are the functions performed by an export house in India? Discuss the reasons for the recent growth of export houses?
29. Identify some of the underlying factors affecting the channel of distribution pattern. Explain the role of each.
30. (*a*) What are the criteria for determining the suitability of a particular channel for export marketing?
    (*b*) Discuss briefly the advantages and limitations of foreign sales branches.
31. (*a*) What are the advantages and limitations of indirect exporting?
    (*b*) Explain why more and more Indian manufacturers are resorting to direct exporting.
32. Discuss the salient features of export organisations which would suit exporters with a limited turnover.
33. What is the importance of physical distribution decision to management? What are the areas of decision in this regard?
34. Why and how does advertising for foreign markets differ from that for domestic market?
35. Discuss the part industrial trade fairs and trade centres play in international marketing of industrial goods.
36. Enumerate the steps involved in preparing an export marketing plan. What are the principal elements of such a plan?
37. How are India's exports financed? How far has the Export Credit Guarantee Corporation helped the exporters in obtaining finance?
38. What are the various types of credits available to Indian exporters to finance their exports? Do you think that these credits are adequate to take care of the current situation?
39. How has the ECGC helped the exporters in obtaining finance?

40. Explain:
    (*i*) Confirmed irrevocable letters of credit; and
    (*ii*) Packing credit.
41. (*a*) What do you understand by
    (*i*) Unconfirmed revocable credit.
    (*ii*) Unconfirmed irrevocable credit.
    (*b*) What are the various type of credits available to Indian exporters to facilitate their exports?
42. Make a critical appraisal of the working of the Export Credit Guarantee Corporation.
43. What is a Letter of Credit? How does it help in financing foreign trade? Explain the operation of a Letter of Credit.
44. Explain the various stages involved in the processing of an export order.
45. State the particulars and explain the significance of any five documents used in the export trade.
46. What documents must accompany an export shipment? Describe them briefly.
47. Critically evaluate the role of state trading in India.
48. Briefly analyse the economies of state trading. In what ways is the State Trading Corporation of India helping to promote India's exports?
49. Describe the problems of and practices in Export Marketing. Comment briefly on the regulations governing export marketing.
50. Write short notes on:
    (*i*) Consular Invoice.
    (*ii*) Mate's Receipt.
    (*iii*) Bill of Lading.
    (*iv*) D.A. and D.P. Bills of Exchange.

(B) APPLIED TYPE OF QUESTIONS

1. Develop a list of Indian products that might have a good acceptance in Saudi Arabia. Select one of these and discuss the major problems you anticipate.
2. Thums-up has used the advertising theme "Happy days are here again." quite successfully in India. Do you think the same theme would make sense in Singapore, Dubai and the U.S.A.?
3. An Indian heavy machines manufacturer operating in Eastern Europe has been using Indians as salesmen. The company feels that it could reduce its costs by hiring and training the natives for salesmen. What are the advantages and disadvantages of using Indian *versus* natives of that country for selling abroad?
4. A large shoe manufacturing company decided to enter the Russian market some years ago. The company produced shoes to meet the Russian demand. Its subsequent experience was bad; many of its shoes wore out very soon. The company acquired a poor image; and so did the Indian Government in Russia as a result. What went wrong?
5. Select one of the following nations — Iraq, Japan and the USA — and describe its marketing institutions and practices.

(C) OBJECTIVE TYPE OF QUESTIONS

(CORRECT ANSWERS HAVE BEEN TICKED ✓)

1. Which of the following generalisations can be made about export markets:
   ✓ (*a*) Nations can be distinguished into four groups on the basis of their industrial structure.
   (*b*) A high correlation between population and per capita demand for most goods.
   (*c*) Very high and very low incomes in industrializing and advanced nations respectively.
   (*d*) Widespread, uniform need for basic products, such as laundry detergent.
2. Export marketing should be studied in addition to marketing fundamentals because:
   (*a*) It involves new principles not normally discussed in general marketing.
   (*b*) Export markets are areas of higher opportunity than home markets.
   ✓ (*c*) Inter-nation differences in market behaviour and institutions are typically more pronounced and it would be useful for the market to be sensitized to these differences.
   (*d*) Every Indian business firm does some export marketing.
   (*e*) The multinational firm will soon be a challenge to every firm.
3. Which of the following strategies should an Indian producer of cotton textiles concentrate on when trying to introduce his products to Kuwaiti Arabs:
   (*a*) Straight extension.
   (*b*) Communication adaptation.
   (*c*) Product adaptation.
   (*d*) Dual adaptation.
   ✓ (*e*) Product invention.
4. The most accurate generalization about marketing research in underdeveloped nations is that:
   (*a*) It is based unavoidably on a different set of concepts and techniques.
   (*b*) It is limited to household buyers because industrial buyers will not cooperate in surveys.
   ✓ (*c*) Data is scarce and data collection is more difficult.
   (*d*) It is non-existent.
   (*e*) It is of less value than marketing research findings in India.
5. The export market selection decision should be based on:
   (*a*) Sales potentials in different countries.
   ✓ (*b*) The rate of return analysis.
   (*c*) Risk differences.
   (*d*) Break even analysis.
   (*e*) Payout period analysis.

6. Most business firms proceed through the following stages in their penetration of an export market:
   (*a*) Direct investment, joint venturing, exporting.
   (*b*) Exporting, direct investment, joint venturing.
   ✓ (*c*) Exporting, joint venturing, direct investment.
   (*d*) Joint venturing, exporting, direct investment.
7. A company can enter another market through joint venturing in any one of four ways:
   (Management contracting, joint ownership venture, licensing, and:)
   (*a*) Indirect export.
   (*b*) Assembly.
   (*c*) Foreign subsidiary.
   ✓ (*d*) Contract manufacturing.
8. Which of the following is the strongest reason for Indian firms to expand their export marketing effort?
   (*a*) The Government of India urges Indian firms to invest abroad.
   (*b*) A company has surplus productive capacity.
   ✓ (*c*) A company discerns an export market with a high profit potential for its products.
   (*d*) A company expects export markets will eventually buy more of its product than will be sold in the domestic market.
   (*e*) A company expects foreign governments will eventually raise their tariffs against Indian goods.
9. Which one of the following statements is true of socialist economies:
   (*a*) Marketing has no role to play.
   (*b*) Marketing plays same role as in the USA.
   (*c*) Marketing plays an even larger role than in the USA.
   ✓ (*d*) Marketing is less developed but most of its content finds actual or potential application.
   (*e*) Marketing is the salvation of these economies.
10. Which one of following is a fair generalization:
   (*a*) Although culture varies from country to country, businessmen are pretty much the same world-wide.
   (*b*) Spanish and German wholesalers are pretty much alike in the way they run their business.
   (*c*) Although business practices vary from country to country, they are pretty much the same within any country.
   (*d*) It may be said that businessmen around the world are profit maximisers, whatever other differences they might have.
   (*e*) None of the above.

[Circle T if the statement is true and circle F if it is false]

11. Multinational marketing is a way to improve the efficiency of domestic production, but it is rarely profitable in itself. T F
12. In selecting foreign markets, the most important economic considerations are income and the level of economic development. T F
13. Both average income and the pattern of income distribution are important in determining the type of products demanded by a nation's population. T F
14. Although countries at the subsistance level may offer few consumer goods opportunities, they may be market for industrial products. T F
15. Cartels are approved as "orderly marketing arrangements" in many countries. T F
16. An unfavourable balance of trade usually prompts a country to loosen its trade restrictions. T F
17. The most popular means of entering foreign trade is through joint ventures. T F
18. A joint venture is a partnership arrangement between domestic and foreign firms. T F
19. Nationalisation usually involves the purchase of a controlling interest in a foreign firm's operations by agreement with parent country. T F
20. Straight extension is a low-cost standardization strategy. T F

Select the one best answer and circle the letter to the left:

21. Multinational marketing allows a firm to:
    (*a*) avoid taxation.
    (*b*) reduce domestic employment.
    (*c*) create new domestic market for existing products.
    (*d*) counteract aggressive foreign competition in its domestic market.
    (*e*) increase its marketing costs.
22. Many foreign companies have been opening plants in India. Which of the following is the most likely reason for such actions?
    (*a*) accessibility to cheap labour.
    (*b*) accessibility to a vast potential market.
    (*c*) reduced distribution costs to sell in India.
    (*d*) accessibility to the new technology.
    (*e*) accessibility to new sources of capital.
23. Multinational marketing:
    (*a*) is a defensive strategy to help maintain domestic sales volume.
    (*b*) benefits the firm by making lower production costs possible.
    (*c*) is capable of creating demand for unwanted products.
    (*d*) encourages a strong spirit of nationalism.
    (*e*) is under the regulation of the United Nations.

24. Indian automakers have had plants in India for sometime. Recently, several joint ventures involving Indian and foreign firms have been announced. Indian firms are trying to:
    (*a*) gain access to foreign markets with greater growth potential than India.
    (*b*) counter the impact of foreign competition in the domestic market.
    (*c*) take advantage of a more favourable political climate
    (*d*) escape taxation.
    (*e*) escape the ravages of inflation.
25. All of the following factors are considered to be vital to the understanding of a foreign environment *except*.
    (*a*) economic characteristics.
    (*b*) demographic characteristics.
    (*c*) psychographic characteristics.
    (*d*) cultural characteristics.
    (*e*) governmental characteristics.
26. Generally, it is thought that lesser-developed nations which must rely on the export of raw materials are in a very weak position in international trade. Which of the following has proven most recently that such is not always the case?
    (*a*) Japan.
    (*b*) OPEC.
    (*c*) the business factors.
    (*d*) China.
    (*e*) Poland.
27. Of all the factors affecting success in international business, which is *most* likely to present the greatest difficulty to the Indian marketer?
    (*a*) economic factors.
    (*b*) demographic factors.
    (*c*) cultural factors.
    (*d*) governmental factors.
    (*e*) business factors.
28. Which of the following factors would give HHEC the *greatest* difficulty in any effort to establish operations in USA?
    (*a*) governmental factors.
    (*b*) economic factors
    (*c*) business factors.
    (*d*) demographic factors.
    (*e*) cultural factors.
29. The opposition of the Indian Government to cartels and other forms of collusion is rooted in:
    (*a*) economic factors.
    (*b*) business factors

(c) demographic factors.
(d) cultural factors.
(e) governmental tradition.

30. The effective price of foreign goods is increased by:
(a) tariffs.
(b) quotas.
(c) boycotts.
(d) balance of payments regulation.
(e) joint ventures.

31. Which of the following places a rupee or volume limitation on the importation of foreign goods?
(a) tariffs.
(b) quotas.
(c) boycotts.
(d) joint ventures.
(e) import duties.

32. Japanese steel can be imported and sold in this country for less than comparable domestic steel. The steel industry might seek governmental aid in overcoming this price advantage by the imposition of:
(a) quotas.
(b) boycotts.
(c) tariffs
(d) joint venture regulations.
(e) balance of trade indexing.

33. Pricing in foreign countries is made difficult by:
(a) import duties.
(b) complicated tariff systems.
(c) fluctuating exchange rates and inflation.
(d) unintelligible quota systems.
(e) unreasonable and unannounced boycotts.

34. India has experienced an unfavourable balance of trade in recent years. In an attempt to remedy this situation, India may:
(a) reduce tariffs.
(b) reduce import quotas.
(c) reduce taxes.
(d) increase tariffs.
(e) refuse to sell abroad.

35. Which of the following places the greatest responsibility for successful foreign operations upon a domestic firm?
(a) exporting
(b) wholly-owned subsidiaries.
(c) joint ventures.

(*d*) licensing.
(*e*) contract manufacturing.

36. The Action Corporation desires an ownership interest and some degree of control in foreign production operations. In view of the fact that its chosen foreign markets insist on some degree of domestic ownership, Action is *most* likely to employ:
(*a*) exporting.
(*b*) wholly-owned subsidiaries.
(*c*) joint ventures.
(*d*) contract manufacturing.
(*e*) management contracting.

37. Indian firms "sell" their management expertise as the principal products under:
(*a*) exporting.
(*b*) management contracting.
(*c*) contract manufacturing.
(*d*) joint ventures.
(*e*) wholly-owned subsidiaries.

38. The Hershey Corporation has received increasing competition in the chocolate and candy bar industry from the Swiss-owned Nestle Corporation's American plants. Nestles is a(n):
(*a*) exporter.
(*b*) contract manufacturer.
(*c*) management contractor.
(*d*) multinational corporation
(*e*) joint venturer.

39. An Indian firm operating in foreign markets is *least* likely to be able to draw on foreign governments or businesses for aid in which of the following areas:
(*a*) pricing.
(*b*) advertising.
(*c*) distribution.
(*d*) branding.
(*e*) marketing research.

40. The Zenon Corporation desires to market soft drinks in Russia. The firm is convinced that a non-alcoholic drink with appearance and taste of vodka would be welcomed by the government and popular with Russian youth. Zenon would employ:
(*a*) product invention.
(*b*) dual adaptation.
(*c*) communication adaptation.
(*d*) product adaptation.
(*e*) straight extension.